Design and planning of swimming pools

JOHN DAWES

Editorial assistant
Pam Dawes

The Architectural Press . London
9 Queen Anne's Gate, London SW1H 9BY
CBI Publishing Company, Inc.
51 Sleeper Street, Boston,
Massachusetts 02210

Frontispiece *Doric temple pool pavilion and peristylum in*
Dorchester
Chilstone Garden Ornaments, Kent
Architect: Charles Worthington
Photo: John Dawes

First published in 1979 by The Architectural Press Ltd: London
Published in the United States by
CBI Publishing Company, Inc.
51 Sleeper Street,
Boston, Massachusetts 02210

© John Dawes 1979

Illustrations were prepared by P. J. Small: Pool designs and systems;
Bryan Williams: Plant diagrams; Robert J. Chitham: Thermae Caracalla

© Illustrations John Dawes 1979

British Library Cataloguing in Publication Data

Dawes, John
    Design and planning of swimming pools.
    1. Swimming pools – Design and construction
    I. Title
    690'.5'74   TH4763   79–40059

    ISBN 0–85139–143–5 (*British edition*)
    ISBN 0–8436–0169–8 (*United States edition*)

Printed litho in Great Britain
by W & J Mackay Ltd, Chatham

Contents

**PART II POOL TECHNIQUES
STRUCTURAL**

Foreword

More and more people throughout the world are using, owning or getting involved with swimming pools, and the modern swimming pool is developing into a highly sophisticated and controlled environment.

As new and advanced technology and methods help reduce costs and increase scope, so the worldwide demand for swimming pools is increasing. Paralleling the increase is an expanding international industry catering for this demand. In such a climate of rapid growth, it is essential that a certain order be maintained to safeguard the public from misguidance, and to avoid unsightly and impractical pools, or inadequate sports and leisure centres. Bad workmanship soon spoils even the best scheme or, on the other hand, 'poor design and planning cannot be salvaged by superb craftsmanship'.

In the UK, for example, leading organisations involved with swimming and leisure have produced, from long experience in pools and baths, regulations and criteria providing invaluable guidance. On the commercial front, SPATA (the Swimming Pool and Allied Trades Association) lay down comprehensive standards for pools and their equipment to which all members are ethically bound. However, it is not sufficient only to lay down minimum standards of quality and design, but also to ensure exciting creativity and imaginative planning in harmony with the practical needs of today's recreational and competitive swimming. A depth of knowledge and experience in this field is vital before new ideas and new skills can be freely and fully used.

There are varied technical books and papers already available, some of which are excellent, but too often not always so easy in their application. This is where I feel that John Dawes' book *Design and planning of swimming pools* is likely to become a familiar and much consulted publication for today's professional people involved with the swimming pool and leisure industry. This book is just what is needed – the work of a talented writer, well versed in the subject without being fully immersed or biased in any one direction, who can also see it all from an outsider's point of view. I have been impressed by its comprehensiveness, pleased to find it full of useful and well-researched data, and delighted to see the subject treated with originality and freshness.

John Dawes travelled widely and delved deeply in researching for his book and is not unfamiliar to many readers as the author of other works on the subject; having been working in the pool industry for a number of years, he is able to combine down-to-earth experience with an exciting, imaginative approach that should give enjoyment and long-term reference to the reader.

Graham Rutherford
President, Swimming Pool & Allied Trades Association
London
1978

Preface

Swimming pools are for people who want to enjoy themselves or take exercise, or simply remain spectators; they may even be used for therapy. All modern places for bathing have their own specialised needs, with sophisticated systems and constructions involving many branches of science, with constant management and maintenance demanding that extra attention. Whenever problems are not clearly understood, designing can be complex, only to increase the normal hazard inherent in every swimming pool. And pools must always be made safe places for people.

This two-part book offers a comprehensive review in straightforward terms for professional people involved in pool making and the decision taking. The first part, *Pool schemes*, concerns evolution, arrangement and layout of all different kinds of swimming pool in use today; the second part, *Pool techniques*, details leading structures and equipment and explains their role and activity in the modern pool system. The diagrams and information sheets mainly summarise vital basic information or specification, and illustrations give topical examples. The text sets out to provoke deeper thought on designing better swimming pools. The whole book brings together criteria of continuing value that planners and designers will need in offering swimming pool schemes for any country, now and in the future.

Some references relate to changing regulations and standards published over recent years by different official bodies and organisations concerned with swimming; where precise reference is necessary or detailed interpretation of national and international specification is wanted, the reader should refer to the original publications of the appropriate authority shown in appendixes II-V.

Acknowledgements The pool building experience of the Rutherford Group of Battle is reflected by much of the book's practical material. The drawings were mainly produced with the help of P. J. Small of the Rutherford design office, from his years of pool planning background for many schemes around the world: there can be very few technical illustrators who have also carried out almost every task involved in successfully designing, selling and building the modern swimming pool. Bryan Williams provided valuable assistance by preparing many of the plant and equipment diagrams.

Many other individuals and organisations (see appendix I) from many countries provided useful information which is sincerely appreciated; especial thanks also must be offered to David Butler, Technical Unit for Sport, London; H. S. Davis, New Zealand Association of Swimming Pool Managers Inc, Bulls; H. et H. Dieken, Fresco Artists, St Paul-de-Vence; Dr H. T. Friermood, United States Olympic Committee, New York, and Council for National Co-operation in Aquatics, New York; Basil Gillinson, Gillinson Barnett & Partners, Leeds; Michael P. King, Electricity Council, London; William P. Markert, National Swimming Pool Institute, Washington; John Morton, Landscape Architect, Christchurch; Frank L. Strand, Stranco, Illinois.

Although I have endeavoured to ensure all information given in this book is clear and accurate, no liability can be accepted for mistakes nor misunderstandings which may occur.

John Dawes
Hawkhurst, February 1979

Children screaming, laughing, playing, splashing
In the cool blue water.
Just forget them, forget the heat,
Jump into the pool and dive beneath.

Suddenly silence, nothing moves or speaks,
You're cut off from the outside world,
And free to swim wherever you please.

How you wish you could stay forever
In the silent worlds of the water
Gliding like a fish in a carefree manner.

But then you feel that deepdown feeling
Crunching up your lungs and then you have to surface.
Leaving your adventures before they've begun.

FROM A SCHOOLCHILD'S NOTEBOOK

Reproduced by permission from
The Schools Council's
Swimming Pools for Primary Schools
Evans/Methuen Educational, 1972

PART I Pool Schemes

1 Balneology: the science of swimming pools

1.1 The bathing place

Bathing began as religious ritual. Previously it had been a straightforward matter of keeping clean. But gradually purification rites developed into training routines, and finally into popular bathing. The original bathing place slowly changed from the sacred temple lake into the incredibly vast thermae; later, the new competitive swimming pool became today's leisure centre complex.

Evolution of the bathing place took over 3000 years to complete its first cycle: but then it reached its climax from which it declined along with the Roman Empire nearly 2000 years ago.

How much has been accomplished over all this time? In spite of all our striding advances, we have yet to build a modern complex more magnificent than the Roman thermae of the 3rd or 4th century AD. Our Olympic complexes do compare, but cater only for a small and privileged minority – the superathletes, rather than the citizens.

1.2 Historical review

Pure balneology – the treatment of people with water – began in the holy streams of the Ganges and the Nile. Temples stationed along the rivers provided convenient bathing spaces for ceremonial purification. The locals washed in the open, the nobility and priests were rather more selective. Their symbolic cleansing took place in bathing rooms and sacred lakes; afterwards, pleasant unguents and scented oils were carefully applied. All manner of comforts and conveniences were dispensed in those early baths. There were extremely vivid murals painted on the walls of the rooms, and very practical in-situ steps leading down into the water of the lakes, for levels varied according to the time of the year.

Although the more fortunate ancient Egyptians revered their artificial pools, they never provided facilities for the masses. The ancient Greeks, emerging from the Bronze Age, swam well and loved athletics, but they never organised mass bathing either. They did, however, include cold water baths as part of their palaestrae, and maintained warm water baths within their cities from public funds. Hippocrates founded water therapy, or balneotherapy, while Plato considered any man who did not swim uneducated.

The Romans Just as in modern times, an army that can swim has a strategic advantage. Where the Greeks had baths in their gymnasia, the Romans had gymnasia in their

1.1 *Frigidarium at Thermae Caracalla in Rome AD 215*
Drawing reconstruction prepared by Robert Chitham

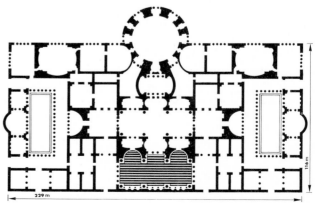

1.2 *Plan of Caracalla Baths complex. The shaded area shows the Frigidarium*
Drawing by Robert Chitham

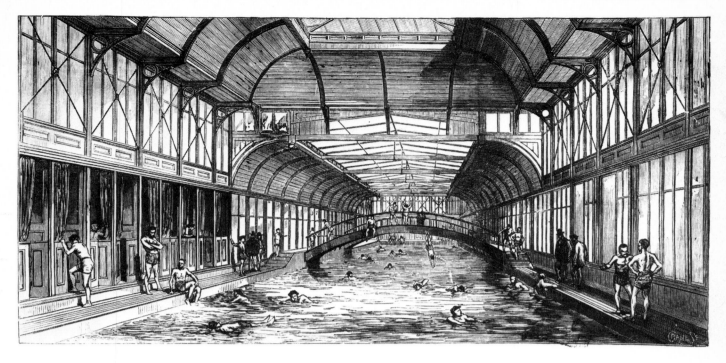

baths. Initially, the military junta ruled that legionaries must be taught to swim, in full armour, carrying weapons. And most soldiers soon found they enjoyed their training. Emperors who rose from the ranks took with them the knowledge that 'water released inhibitions and reduced insurgencies', and so being sensitive about keeping the peace, they built more baths than before.

Thermae The Baths in Rome flourished with all kinds of facility – thermae, Turkish and sauna; every size of swimming pool – basin, plunge and piscina; whole ranges of additament – tavernae, library and theatre; even a vast congregational centre set in open gardens between interlinking courtyards. No wonder they became *the* fashionable meeting place.

Roman bathlife meant citizens could spend most of the day there several times a week. They would rest, acclimatise, gossip and gamble in the great hall, before taking sweating sessions in the progressively hotter sudorific rooms. Or they could choose strenuous exercise in different athletic halls and ball-game courts. There were various cosmetic treatments, massages and oilings, applied before the almost obligatory skin scraping performance with strigils, followed by warm soaks, cold immersions, plus perhaps a calm closing swim in the main bath. Possibilities afterwards might mean attending an oration or reading and a gentle stroll along colonnaded walks through decorated gardens, before eventually a full evening of eating, drinking, dicing and bedding.

The Fall Although the very largest concourses, such as the town-like thirty-three acre Baths of Caracalla, the overall 18,000 bather establishment at Thermae Diocletian, and the final Great Constantine complex, were to be built in the closing few hundred years of dominance, the initial vigour of Rome was already spent.

After the Romans The dark ages of bathing followed, and the baths remained suppressed as much by ignorance as by theocratic policy. Mostly baths degenerated and became places for the spread of infection and vice. Henry VIII closed down more than the monasteries – he included the

1.3 *The Floating Swimming-Bath in the Thames at Charing Cross*
Illustrated London News, 1875

'stews' or bath brothels, which were sources of infection and plague. Similar problems were seen and solved throughout Europe.

In 1750, the 'detergent action' of seawater was discovered by Dr Richard Russell at Brighton, and publicised widely through his book *Dissertation of the Use of Seawater in Diseases of the Glands* which, surprisingly, became a bestseller. It earned him a profitable reputation as 'l'inventeur de la mer'. Inland spa waters were already producing expensive cures, but his far wider seaside cure introduced cheap bathing once again to the masses. People in those days soon benefited by plain washing, for many diseases were simply due to dirt. Until then, most were bathed only three times – at birth, on marriage, after death.

The Victorians With travel and reform, newly built places to bathe started to appear again in many different ways and forms. A floating bath barque named *Waterloo* was moored on the Thames in 1819. The first public municipal bath was opened in Liverpool in 1828, and was looked upon in similar standing to the workhouse. There were six baths in London by 1837, and an Act of Parliament in 1846 granted local authorities official leadership for public baths and wash houses; but the underlying social reason was fear rather than philanthropy. With the spreading of industrial revolution slum conditions, epidemic plague was very real indeed. Cholera claimed many thousands, speeding the hygiene boom in public bath and waterworks building.

In the 1880s, floating bagnios might have been made popular on the Seine, but an attempt to reintroduce one commercially on the Thames failed dismally. Probably the established London public baths, now getting so well organised for amateur swimming, offered much more competition than credited. In the USA increasing river pollution had a strong hand in stifling the floating bath when the 'people's baths' on the New York waterfront declined around 1900.

Roman revival Most countries rapidly developed public baths, Italy being well placed in Romanesque design. With European emigration, hydro enthusiasts spread bathing much further afield. Christchurch in New Zealand installed their tepid pool in 1880; Brooklyn, Massachusetts completed theirs in 1887. Unexpectedly, such a broad new interest in bathing had been further stimulated in Britain with the 1871 rediscovery of the monumental Roman bath at Bath in Somerset. Archeological finds had been uncovered several times before, but until then, public interest was never strong enough to bring about the clearing away of the mediaeval baths to expose the original unique 1st century thermae of Aquae Sulis.

Most Victorian architects of baths drew heavily for inspiration upon the considerable classical reservoir of Roman design, even if they embellished with Gothic ornamentation. Many of their enduring buildings are still in everyday use. In fact, over half the public pools in Britain were designed in Victorian times or built before the First World War.

1.3 American progress
Until 1920, the pattern of American baths closely followed the European, with two-thirds of all the establishments public and the remainder commercial. A steady growth in numbers reflected the similarity to Europe's institutional provisioning. And then matters changed dramatically.

A phenomenal acceleration in swimming pool installa-

1.4 *The Roman Great Bath at Bath . . . and Victorian reconstruction*
Bath Spa Council

tion began to build up. The 1930s showed the first small but steady increase in residential pools in America; the lull of the 1940s was totally deceptive, for twelve million American servicemen were taught to swim; then in the 1950s, sales literally took off at 2000 per cent increase in swimming pool numbers with greater pressure for even more pools. Rapid expansion in population, leisure time and income created a residential swimming pool industry almost overnight which, by the 1960s had eclipsed the 18th century English sea spa boom and the 19th century European swimming sports scene many times over.

By the 1970s, one family in ten in America had some kind of pool in their own backyard, or immediate neighbourhood. A recreational resources investigation begun during President Eisenhower's term of office had forecast a rapid rise of swimming to first place, and this became a reality in 1970.

1.4 National characteristics
Every country has its own flavour, every designer has his own taste. The way of life, climate, habitat and particularly wealth, all affect design perspective. Pool designers often introduce an association of ideas relating to the surroundings or the period. Also settings look better when reflecting certain characteristics of the locality. Often a national pre-

1.5 *A swimming pool of the 70s with 'straight-line random shaping, Kooldeck and High Rate permanent media filter'. This 150 m³ residential pool 1 to 2·5 m deep in Tucson, Arizona, is a 1975 NSPI award winner*
Whitaker Aquatech Pools, Arizona

ference can be recognised. Pools in North America are highly stylised, involve innumerable gadgets and cater for a tremendous variety of leisure activities. In South America, they are much more concerned with emphatic striking shapes; which in the Caribbean become exhuberant. Pools in South Africa are as varied as there are designs for living rooms outdoors; similarly in Australia, where the great outdoors is synonomous with sport and swimming. New Zealand, though, follows an individualistic line using natural plant forms, rather like the Japanese preference for exacting water gardens or Sawara – their concept of borrowed scenery. The exceptionally hot, dry climate of the Middle East inspires cool architecture, smooth and round shapes for reflective pools, to which Mediterranean areas usually add the bleached colour of their local stone.

Strongest traditions, however, are found in European countries where trends follow well-established patterns. Germany, for example, specifies very high pool standards which present a feeling of cleanliness and strict symmetry. They prefer straight up and down swims with no frills – except matching footbath and co-ordinated shower. The Scandinavians also like geometrical shapes, but perhaps a little rounder at the corners, like their furniture. UK pools in private pool gardens usually include level lawns and an all-year interest in colour: shapes tend to be conservative and classical, similar to the Italian pool designers' care and attention to architectural order and statuary. But for pools with natural flair and flamboyance, casual style with

1.5 *A swimming pool of the 70s with 'straight-line random shaping, Kooldeck and High Rate permanent media filter'. This 150 m³ residential pool 1 to 2·5 m deep in Tucson, Arizona, is a 1975 NSPI award winner*
Whitaker Aquatech Pools, Arizona

impeccable appointment, there is no need to look further than France.

1.5 National specifiers
Most national swimming pool associations publish their own standards and technical information for the designer and owner. Regulations are stringent for diving depths (absolute minimum 2·3m), wading areas (maximum 1·1m), hopper slopes (45° limit), electrical standards (no unprotected circuit connection), general safety requirements (non-toxic materials), etc. Standards clauses also specify no sand floors beneath in-ground liners, walls to be vertical until at least 0·8m below water level, no protrusions or obstructions, and even arrange classification of diving boards to suit different pool profiles, and so on. Associations particularly encourage codes of ethics, organise trade exhibitions, arrange design competitions and maintain membership lists all helping promote confidence in the industry (see appendixes II, III and IV). Safeguards on training, workmanship and quality are vital in an expanding industry, where newcomers have reliable reputations to establish.

1.6

1.7

1.6 *Leisure pool surround designed with competitive swimming in mind at Swindon Oasis Leisure Centre*
Architect: Gillinson Barnett & Partners
Photo: O. F. Clarke

1.7 *The unmistakable shape of an Olympic interior – Schwimmhalle in Munich, 1972*
Architect: Behnish & Partner

1.6 World development

As a comparison for future trends in pool construction, a maximum of 5000 pools per annum in the 1970s have been installed in the UK, France and Canada; 10,000 per annum in Germany, Australia and South Africa, and a soaring 100,000 per annum in the USA. And these figures can be increased two or three fold when including free standing above-ground pools. Construction methods and conservancy systems exploited by American industry have crossed over to Europe and back again. The marketing opportunities available in the EEC for the final quarter of this century are possibly as colossal as were those in the early American pool boom. Following America's experience, explosive growth of low priced pools in the world was clearly a foregone conclusion. With a small open space outside in the garden, a favourable climate or supplementary heating, simple system controls and the desire to swim, the home pool economy package has become worthwhile to millions.

Many pool-developing countries, although already self-sufficient in pool hardware, have now attracted American endeavour and investment. Britain and continental Europe, and particularly South Africa and Australia also have well established industries with fast increasing exports. And, of course, there is the untapped enterprise and immense manufacturing potential of Japan, whenever pools become small enough to be an integral part of the home.

Most countries can now produce pools well within the pocket of any car-owning family. Above-ground pools are strongly competitive with the smallest motor car, pre-fabricated in-ground pools compare favourably with the family saloon, or, if you like, luxury garden pools can be as expensive as the dearest automobile. Almost 90 per cent of the total pools built every year are installed for private ownership, and the rising potential in Europe might one day equal North America, South Africa and Australia combined. At the same time, the public sector is fast gathering momentum, especially where development programmes involve government sponsorship as in Germany, Holland, Sweden and France.

Another strong factor compelling a push-pull economy for a future grand total of swimming pools follows from modern, well-equipped educational systems that try to satisfy an expanding population earning increasing wealth and leisure. Inevitably, the greater the number of children who can swim, the greater the demand for swimming when they grow up. Public and private desire for pools of all kinds soon brings relative costs down, as the scale of manufacturing rapidly goes up.

Pool technology has taken us a long way, but in fully enjoying bathing life we still have a long way to go. Our swimming pools today are cleaner and better, but they offer no more entertainment than the Roman baths of two thousand years ago. The future hydrospace is vast.

INFORMATION SHEET 1.1

Leading baths of the ancients

Century	Baths and thermae
BC 30th	Indus Valley, earliest baths for purification and lustral immersion
25th	Great bath at Mohenjodara in the Indus Valley, was made from burnt brick backed by a layer of bitumen, surrounded by a paved walk and eight small baths, all probably served by the same well
	Egyptian swimming bas reliefs of Nagada
15th	Minoan bronze age bath systems in Crete at Palaces of Knossos and Phaistos
14th	Tel-el-Amarna sacred bathing lakes and Egyptian Palaces of Medinet Habu and Malkata
9th	Assyrian martial swimming bas reliefs from the reign of Ashurnasirpal II
5th	Greek luxury baths houses and gymnasia included provision for the poor
4th	Baths of Heracles, attributed as first Greek baths to use heated water
3rd	Piscina publica, the earliest Roman bath following the construction of Appius Claudius aqueduct
1st	Stabian and forum, the earliest bathing complexes installed in Pompeii
AD 1st	Palladio's Baths of Nero
	Central baths were under construction when Pompeii was overwhelmed. Titus Baths, introduced great statues into bath houses
	Aquae Sulis, unique Romano-British bathing establishment at Bath
2nd	Trajan Baths, new aqueducts and public buildings commemorating the height of the Empire
	Great Baths of Lepcis Magna
	Hadrian's Baths including a private villa bath at Tivoli
3rd	Caracalla thermae occupied 33 acres; the main bath 1100 × 1100ft catered for 2000 bathers plus seating for 1600. (Inspiration for main waiting room of Pennsylvania, NY railway station and St George's Hall, Liverpool)
4th	Diocletian bath, the largest thermae in the world catered for 18,000 at a time. The main bath held 3200 and was twice as large as anything similar: it was built in AD 305 by an army of workmen including 40,000 Christian slaves. The Vestibule was eventually converted by Michelangelo into the Church of Santa Maria del Angeli, 1563.
	Constantine baths, the last of the great thermae in Rome before the capital was transferred to New Rome (Constantinople)
5th	Baths in Rome now equalled one establishment for every 1000 citizens. At this time there were in the city 11 public baths, 856 private baths, and 1352 fountains and cisterns, at the culmination of thirteen aqueducts
6th	Luxury Roman bath design continued in the Eastern Roman Empire for over one thousand years.

INFORMATION SHEET 1.2

Balneographical glossary

A widely expressive vocabulary often reflects a progressive branch of activity, and building ancient thermae was no exception; suprisingly, many of the original words are still in use today throughout the world

aedile	baths superintendent
alipterium	oiling room
alveus	hot bath surrounded by stepped seating
ambulatorius	cloister or arcade for walking

apodyterium	cloakroom or clothing room
apses	recesses for bathing tubs
aquae	water areas
atrium	courtyard garden room and cistern
bagnio	bathing-house, stew-bath, brothel
balneae	warm baths
balneal	pertaining to bathing
balneary	bathing place
balneation	bathing
balneatores	bathguards or bathkeepers
balneography	descriptive science of baths
balneology	scientific study of bathing and medicinal springs
balneum	small bathing room gave name to great public baths
baptistery	baptismal bathing tank
caldarium	hot bath room
calida lavatio	hot water bath
capsarium	clothes room
castellum	reservoir
clepsydra	water flow, measuring device
condominium	American joint-owned neighbourhood pool
conisterium	powdering room
coreicum	corn cutting, shaving and depilation room
crypto-porticus	covered way for exercise
cupola	spherical roof or dome developed for thermae
daubfest	ice-hole bath
elaeothesium	oiling room
emollient baths	tissue softening solutions
exedrae	sanctuary alcoves for philosophers
forum	public assembly place
frigida lavatio	cold water bath
frigidarium	cold plunge bath room
hamman	oriental bathing establishment, Turkish hot-air bath
heliocaminus	open-roofed sunbathing pavilion
heliotherapy	air or sun bathing first prescribed by Hippocrates
Hippocrates	Greek founder of balneology
hydropathy	treatment of disease with water
hydrotherapy	therapy of water
Hygeia	goddess of health
hypocaustum	underfloor furnace for heating in baths
impluvium	water basin or pool within atrium
inhalatorium	inhalation room
labrum	warm water bath or shower
laconicon	alcove for brief immersion bath
laconicum	hot, dry room (sauna)
latrinarium	latrine
lavarium	massage or shampoo room
lavatorium	wash-room
natatio	swimming bath
natatorium	American swimming-bath house
necessarium	'necessary house' or toilet
olfactarium	fragrant room
palaestra	gymnasium, wrestling school
pensiles balneae	hammock bath
pergola	covered walkway
peristylum	columns surrounding courtyard or temple
pilae	tile stacks supporting hypocaust floor
piscinae	bathing ponds
propignea	hypocaust furnaces heating air or water
shampoo	massage after hot bath
solarium	sunbathing parlour
spa	mineral spring named after Spaw, Belgium
sphaeristerium	ball game court – tennis, etc
stew	bath room, hot-house, brothel
strigil	skin scraper used in baths
sudatorium	hot air steam bath room, sweat chamber (Turkish)
tabernae	stalls or sales booths
tepidarium	warm reception room
tesserae	mosaic paving pieces
thalassotherapy	medical seawater pool treatment
thermae	bathing establishment involving heated baths
unctuarium	anointing room
vestiarium	undressing room
xystus	garden walk or terrace

See technical glossary of swimming pool terms: information sheet 2.2

INFORMATION SHEET 1.3

Baths Acts of the 19th century which helped revive public bathing

1846	Encouragement to establish public baths and wash-houses	UK
1850	Law giving Ministry of Commerce power to build baths	France
1854	Similar laws followed in Austria, Belgium, Germany, Italy, Switzerland	Europe
1878	To incorporate 'covered swimming baths' within public facilities	UK
1895	Mandatory for 'people's baths' to remain open all year for towns over 50,000 population	NY State
1896	To allow 'music and dancing by licence' when baths closed	UK

A selection of modern Codes, Specifications and Standards controlling today's swimming pools are listed in appendix IV.

INFORMATION SHEET 1.4

North American growth of swimming pools

Year	Canada	USA
1950	5,000	15,000
1960	10,000	255,000
1965	20,000	565,000
1970	35,000	985,000
1975	50,000	1,455,000

Breakdown of 1975 USA figures to compare with UK estimated figures for same year

	UK estimated	USA
Camp	1,000	40,000
Club	1,000	50,000
Hotel	3,500	190,000
Municipal	1,500	45,000
School	8,000	30,000
Residential	35,000	1,100,000
Total	50,000	1,455,000

(Based upon *Swimming Pool Weekly* market report figures)
See also Swimming pool sources of statistics and surveys: appendix VI.

INFORMATION SHEET 1.5

Some national plans

Germany	Golden Plan to reach 7,500 public pools completed by mid 1970s
Holland	Programme to install 500 public pools by mid 1970s
Sweden	Scheme to provide 250 public pools by mid 1970s
France	Concours des Mille Piscines (1130 in practice) with the design winning schemes adopted nationally and built by late 1970s
USA	Teaching every child swimming in formal education by the 1980s
UK	Sports Council requirements to make up a potential deficit of nearly 500 public indoor pools by the 1980s plus the ideal of at least 200 new leisure complexes before 2000
Germany	Every 5 year old child to swim before starting school by 2000 and this programme is already well under way in DDR with most schools having pools and schemes already working

INFORMATION SHEET 1.6

Possible pool park 1980

	Estimated private pool/ share %	Estimated total pools per continent
Africa		
South Africa	110,000	90	150,000
Americas		
Canada	80,000	75	
USA	2,000,000	80	2,200,000
Asia		
USSR	10,000		
Japan	30,000	50	
Middle East	10,000	90	100,000
Australasia		
Australia	210,000	90	250,000
Europe		
Balkans and Mediterranean islands	15,000		
Benelux	25,000		
DFR	160,000		
France	90,000		
Iberian Peninsula	35,000		
Italy	45,000		
Others	45,000		
Scandinavia	15,000		
UK	80,000	80/90	500,000

In-ground pools	**Total**		3,200,000
Above-ground pools	**Total**		6,800,000
1980 World pool park			10,000,000

Note Although very few countries maintain full swimming pool statistics, the comprehensive US market report figures published annually by *Swimming Pool Weekly,* plus figures from other main swimming countries, in particular *CASPA* statistics on Australian numbers, enable these projections to be suggested. By 1976 the number of new pools installed per year in Europe exceeded half the American rate (approx 80,000) and was still increasing or holding rather than contracting as in the USA.
See also Swimming pool sources of statistics and surveys: appendix VI.

INFORMATION SHEET 1.7

UK growth of indoor public authority swimming pools

(Based upon CCPR reports and Sports Council Index)

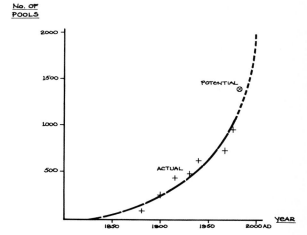

⊗ A SPORTS COUNCIL SURVEY FORECASTS A POTENTIAL DEFICIT OF ALMOST 500 POOLS BY 1981 ; 95% OF NEW OR REFURBISHED POOLS SHOULD BE 25m TYPE AND BUILT 50/50 URBAN/RURAL AREAS

INFORMATION SHEET 1.8

Guide to swimming pool sizes

Public Town pools	Shared dual-use Community pools	Private Residential pools
20m for 25,000 population	10m for 20 bathers	8m for family of 4 and friends
25m for 50,000 population (25m per 25,000 better)	15m for 40 bathers	10m for family of 6 and friends
33m for 100,000 population (25m with children's pool is better arrangement)	20m for 80 bathers	12m for family of 9 and friends

See also information sheet 2.14.

2 Designing and planning

A swimming pool is no longer a special architectural case. It safely involves people in a well-ordered environment; it often requires a multi-discipline approach to the complete design; and it not unnaturally introduces a highly specialised language, most new terms being borrowed from other industries and sciences.

2.1 Outlining the scheme

There are many ways of setting about designing swimming pools, and the pool industry can offer many schemes to meet most situations for the investor's benefit. Swimming pool operators and contractors generally have preferences or prejudices for one system or another.

Some manufacturers offer their pre-planned, brand-named pool system, just like a new vehicle from an automobile showroom; the model size, style and shape being adjusted to suit the budget available. Additional specification changes, or new instructions, usually increase costs, so it falls upon the owner to agree or to adjust, or perhaps to consider another manufacturer.

The well-thought-out 'package-pool' is perfectly satisfactory for almost every circumstance, and would lend itself to mechanised building, similar to the successful CLASP school building schemes in the UK. Such an industrial approach has been successfully adopted in France in the construction of over 1000 community pools (see chapter 4.3 on community pools). Most of the standardised designs are now well developed and offer very effectively costed private or public pools indeed.

First look around Looking at other people's pools is profitable design education. But classic mistakes are still being repeated through insufficient understanding, or care for what went wrong previously. Some problems actually date back to the Romans, who evidently overcame most troubles with water and humidity in their baths complexes by adopting basic environmental rules, and bather flow routines, that still work today. See chapter 10.9 for 'wet and dry' areas, chapter 11.4 on facilities.

The puzzle is how to make the right decisions without stacks of inside knowledge, and this situation applies just as much to the pool 'out the back' as to the vast, multi-million international contract. An expert might seem to know his way, but it may be only one way, or a very narrow route indeed.

2.1 *Cutaway – typical 10 × 5 m swimming pool*

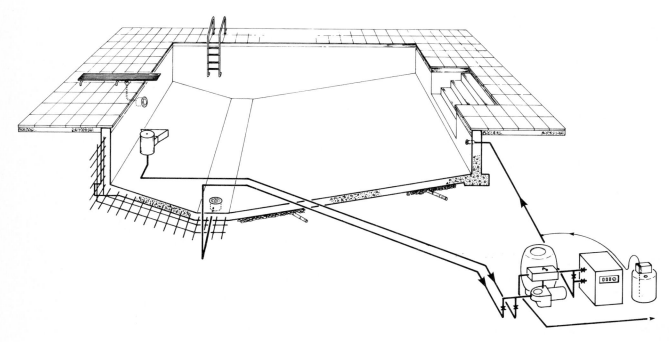

2.2 *The trouble with condensation: avoid ponding with a fall of 1 in 24 recommended for indoor pool surround areas*
Architects' Journal
Photo: Henk Snoek

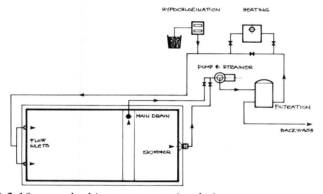

2.3 *10 m pool: skimmer water circulation system*

The very first premise to consider, particularly in designing public pools, is that every bather leaves his sanity outside! Providing for exaggerated behaviour is the essence of good pool design, and the function of its hard wearing components, the most dominating factors for any grouping of which are in fact safety and hygiene. They are put to extreme test with peak attendances at weekends and holidays – the perfect time for planners to visit other people's pools to find out the joys and frustrations for themselves.

Only 10 per cent of the public actually go to swim: the remainder go to enjoy themselves, to play about, and, the younger or more active they are, to let off steam. There is strong argument to direct anti-social behaviour into a well-prepared environment, and swimming pools must cope with this viewpoint, whether the opinion is acceptable or not (see also chapter 16.4 and information sheet 16.6 on vandalproofing).

By relating pools to other social services and activities, such as sports centres, libraries, schools, police stations, old people's community centres and even hairdressing salons, there is excellent chance to rationalise and optimise facilities while offering wider ranging and more exciting joint provisioning – a very real factor in the success of original thermae, or recreation parks, or leisure centres.

2.2 Programming

All pools start with a preliminary survey. A client first surveys his hopes, his funds, and his plot before calling in the architect or contractor.

Simplicity is difficult Knowledge of the whole interwoven environmental subject and a clear understanding of basic circulation systems is invaluable to the designer, but it is more important and less expensive to concentrate upon taking the right decisions clearly, and early on.

Collect ample and accurate information to help appreciate the subtleties of the various systems in relation to local data. The objective – the feasibility study – is to select all relevant information for the best possible pool within the available resources, and always to create originality,

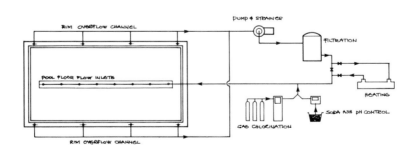

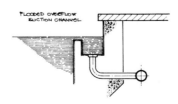

2.4 *25 m pool: rimflow water circulation system*

empathy or ambiance. It is interesting how many swimming pools are being built based purely upon a picture in a brochure, or from someone else's plans, or as a constantly repeated formula for convenience.

In planning pools, there are several useful techniques that help make sensible management of the masses of different criteria. The discipline of having to test and organise ideas and data produces a necessary clarity. And most early problems are more of organisation than anything else. By working through a well-organised schedule, the planning routine becomes straightforward.

Flow techniques Although modern pools can be complex affairs situated somewhere between building and engineering, once a design is planned, a flow chart, or network analysis plan, or basic bar chart, greatly simplifies construction matters. Work sequences help illustrate efficiency, or otherwise, and the best sequences will allow for last minute adjustments to the schedules without wrecking progress.

Thinking a structure through from beginning to end tests the components and puts the facilities in their place: in planning layout, clear through-routes design (or flow) must lead the bather into the pool and back again, defining and separating wet from dry areas. Conveniently related side-routes to refreshment and leisure areas, toilets and washing facilities are also needed. In public pools especially, entry to the pool should be from the shallow end, learners must be separated from swimmers and divers, and spectators are best sat apart from bathers.

Scheduling – the shortest routes Distinguish jobs from materials and prepare a work schedule of jobs through every construction stage, with completion time allocated to each job. List all materials and equipment, noting delivery time against every item.

Recording the material requirements against the sequence of work, with both delivery and completion times plotted alongside, presents a clear progressive picture of each job routine: the critical path shows the earliest possible completion date for each stage, and ultimately for the whole scheme. Critical path analysis (CPA) draws attention to potential weaknesses in order to make adjustments at an early date, and helps make it simple to juggle with items as changes occur.

These programmed evaluation review techniques (PERT) have been adopted and developed successfully by the motor industry to ensure each new model comes out in proper working order, and on time. A new pool should also come out right, and well on time.

Scheduling – the optimum situation Another useful and seemingly obvious preplanning technique brings together all pool operations and facilities into a comprehensive total design for long-term conservation.

Integrated environmental design (IED) means designing a structure that relates functions and integrates both capital and running cost to achieve maximum use and efficiency of resources throughout the whole life of the building. The architect (as managing director of the project) co-ordinates operations from the outset with the specialist team of advisers, consultants, contractors and manufacturers, *plus* the pool management, their service and maintenance enterprises.

In effect, this concept and process, applied to a building's performance and to the complex mechanical services it requires, draws experts together to find a practical working solution in optimising quality with cost. Success is measured by counting the total costs of energy and resources for a building throughout its lifespan, while providing the most efficient operating conditions for the occupants. Conclusions tend to raise capital expenditure, but in return offer considerable improvement in operating and use efficiencies over the whole working period. In other words, quality pays in the long run.

As obvious examples, the introduction of more effective insulation, heat recovery systems, or double glazing to the pool hall cost more at first sight, but should be looked at in the light of the *total bill* over all the years of operation.

2.3 Budgeting

Counting the cost As more pools are built and systems simplified, so the unit cost to the contractor is improved. But, as already explained it is the long-term total cost to the client that is more important in the end.

Costs are first saved by reducing water and air volumes not materials specifications. A 10 per cent saving in *cubic* capacity can reduce initial prices without even affecting the water surface *square* area: moreover operating costs will be less every year thereafter. Contrary to general belief, the overall cost of most complexes is proportional to poolwater and airspace volumes, *not* to water surface areas. In fact, the standard 10×5m garden pool, with volume saving design in its tank, can reasonably reduce a $75m^3$ water capacity to $45m^3$ with little loss of surface area. The shallower the swimming pool, the less the expenditure. The public pool also, with controlled sloping roof design can equally reduce air volume without difficulty – and since ventilation and space heating might count for at least 50 per cent of energy consumption, the saving on running cost alone is worthwhile (see chapter 14.7).

The smallest pool is not always the most economical per bather. There can be as much as 25 per cent saving per m^2 in installing a larger and more favourably sized pool (see also information sheet 2.8).

A swimming pool is *the* most efficient athletic facility available in terms of total users per area, whether active or recreational. Where else can you allocate only a few m^2 per person for exercise? (see also information sheet 2.15, Water area allocations).

Managing the cost Every well-managed pool investment budget tries to control as cost effectively as possible:
- physical environment: in cleanliness, sound and safety
- thermal environment: with temperature, humidity and transmittance
- water environment: with treatment, chemicals and controls
- visual environment: for light, colour and shape.

This means 'the engineering problems of swimming pools are related to providing large clear spans in the hall while allowing access to lighting and ventilation; ensuring that the structure is protected from the corrosive effects of chlorine; limiting condensation and preventing its occurrence on glazing; lighting the pool evenly with sufficient penetration to the pool bottom; providing economical water filtration plant that can be easily and safely operated and maintained; locating plant rooms to improve economy of pipe and duct runs, and inhibiting noise from swimmers'.[1]

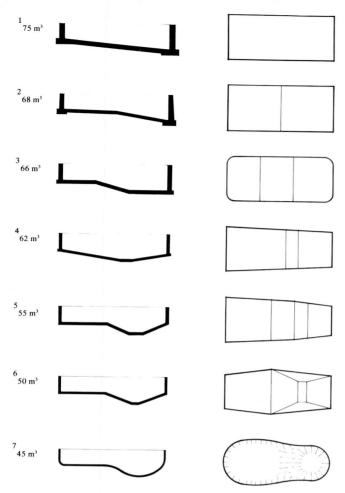

2.5 *Development of profiles: the evolution of volume-saving techniques for a 10 × 5 m pool tank*

There is one other factor that is particularly relevant today and that is inflation. In the UK, when we are comparing the 60 years from 1915 to 1975, we can note that over half of all building cost increases came about between 1972 and 1975.

Planning the cost Private owners might think carefully about funding their new pool, but how much deep thought is given to its setting or maintenance?

Management of funds starts with an outline plan and should not finish until the pool is demolished. The surveyor starts the whole chain of events by measuring intentions with reality. The architect then turns the range of ideas into reality. He must meet the budget, and often still make savings if inflation bites harder than expected.

It is practically impossible to say how much should be allocated to building a pool. In public finance, it depends upon the social need, which perversely increases as districts get poorer. Almost the opposite is true of the private pool; here a better guideline is one of property values. The choice of design and structure, siting and construction of a normal pool may range in cost up to about 10 per cent of the property value, with the setting and landscaping possibly as much again. Any extraordinary pool . . . and the sky is the limit.

2.4 The site survey

This part of the whole procedure might take only a few hours, but the information properly gathered will save time and money over and over again. It is 'the most neglected

2.6 *'21st century' superstructural Hallenbad styling, Landeshauptstadt Hanover*
Architect: F. Grünberger, Ing
Photo: Hans Jurgen Fratzer

discipline in the planning and development of building projects'.[2]

First, the surveyor should question whether the allocated site is the most suitable, even if the feasibility study, or an insistent client demands that it is. Prejudice does exist with reviewing committees, and wishful thinking with hopeful clients.

Next, examine carefully the proposed access. The site owner or neighbours want little or no disruption. Sometimes possible fuss has to be weighed against increased costs; then perhaps the long run-in the back way over soggy ground is allowed to double up rates for excavation and materials handling. Then take levels and measurements; map existing features and services; if necessary dig a borehole to determine soil structure and watertable: finally, consider pool requirements (see information sheet 2.11, swimming pool survey report) against fieldwork plotting; the basic tools being pencil and paper, tape and rods, surveying instrument and wellington boots.

The ultimate placing of the pool, orientation, shaping, datum level, drainage, type of tank, provision of ancillary facilities, and, of course, the sheltered setting preferably using spare spoil, all form the detail of the careful report and its sketch. From this information, will be prepared an outline scheme for critical examination of practicalities, for vetting local authorities records, and eventually for gaining building approval. A good survey anticipates problems beforehand and takes advantage of the lay of the land in preparing the final level and the setting of the pool. In the private sector, often the really attractive and well-presented plan for a pool will sell the scheme and the landscaping to the client.

It is interesting to note how many preliminary studies and reports persuasively argue the case for an international sized pool in the public sector, and how few international pools are really necessary. How many of the 25 per cent UK local authorities who operate pools would like an Olympic scheme? Is the competition pool really what the bathers and the taxpayers want?

2.5 Problem places

For a price, a pool can be built almost anywhere. Among the range of tanks and techniques now available, there is probably a solution for even the most daunting of structural problems. There are swimming pools erected in Arctic tundra like 'cargo container' modules on pods. There are schemes safely built in earthquake regions using flexible membranes. Others are built on massive sub-rafts or installed in skyscraper penthouses or luxury hotel cellars; and still more are inset in tidal basins or desert sands, into hillsides or acid soils (see chapter 9.5).

Once the problem is recognised and the appropriate watertight structure selected, a newly built tank can be filled with water that is easily kept clean for years at a time. Too much effort is spent worrying over providing the right type of monolithic structure, for in practice it is exactly how and where to put it that is more important.

Conditions of extreme Where the oil boom has attracted pool construction for extreme exposed locations well above the Arctic Circle and modular structural design is necessary, detailed knowledge of local conditions is still critical. Permafrost ground conditions must not be thawed by warmer foundations (or even by water storage tanks) otherwise structures sink into unstabilised ground or distort and crack.

Large, prefabricated but easily transported and assembled units are needed to withstand high winds and very low temperatures (down to $-50°C$), and aluminium structures best fit this specification. Aluminium plate also allows faster construction with minimal maintenance needs over maximum periods of time.

To build a large pool, steel piles need to be sunk at least 10m deep on which to stand the pool container projecting at least 2m *above* the ground. Heat can no longer be transferred to the permafrost and snowdrifts will no longer pile up so easily.

Small, private unit-panel pools can be located wherever the Arctic summer allows open-air swimming. Flexible liners may be set into unfrozen or semi-permafrost ground conditions, providing there is suitably insulated backfill to stop the warmth of the poolwater reaching nearby frozen soil. The flexible structure must be capable of absorbing ice expansion for winter conditions when the pool will freeze 1m or 2m deep, but a covering blanket of thick snow usually prevents it from totally freezing solid.

Dead airspace insulation principles are adopted also for many aluminium tanks set into the ground in normal conditions. Then a washed gravel backfill of 0·5m to 0·75m wide insulates, to inhibit the heat transfer that will always occur through packed sand/earth in-fills (see chapter 9.4).

Another common form of dead airspace practice requires a concrete substructure to be raised to rest upon the ground allowing the tank to be further insulated along all sides by the services galleries containing piping, ducting and plant (see also chapters 13.7 and 14.4).

A direct illustration of controlled environmental habitation is the Arctic Recreation Centre and Pool set above the tundra that not only prevents melting of permafrost, but conveniently doubles as an unfrozen emergency firefighting reservoir. Inside, different levels offer opportunities for indoor gardens, cladding is made bright and colourful, walls are given unusual texture and decor. The tedium of the long winter conditions within this container are relieved by versatile materials made to work across the whole spectrum of design – suitable living structures for Space 2001.

Below-ground The standard basic rule is first 'find firm ground': otherwise make the ground firm. But with solid rock, build on top if possible, to save soaring excavation costs. Foundation costs must seem exorbitant and disturbing to the eventual owner, since none of the expensive work will ever be seen again.

Civil engineering solutions can be found only when the full extent of a problem is known. Often it is the actual excavation that causes surprises. When an excavator strikes an unexpected porous layer of saturated sand, emergency dewatering costs can work out more than the total value of the garden pool. And the builder can run into unforeseen snags even in deep city centre foundations if archeological finds are unearthed. He wants to cover the exposed and susceptible site rapidly; the archeologist wishes to freeze contracting programmes for the longest possible time.

There must be no surcharge from nearby buildings or extra weight bearing upon pool walls. Neither should the tank form the foundation nor be a basic part of the superstructure. This independence means building settlement can no longer affect a pool. But in mining areas, a pool tank may need to rest upon support points with jacks to lift it back into position again if settlement should occur.

It is rare for properly constructed pools to move, but doubly dramatic when they do. They might twist and break their backs, slide down and out of slopes, or rise up and float in the ground. They rarely settle back into the same position. Such troubles typify insufficient consolidation, ineffective foundation or inadequate drainage (see also chapter 9.2 and 9.3 on digging and drainage).

Excess water Most troubles during construction stem from water filling the hole too soon. A sudden downpour can turn a peaceful, profitable site into a money-losing morass. Flood water for the unprepared can gum up excavation or silt up reinforcement.

Subsequent cave-ins, contaminated or washed-out concrete and similar problems inflate costs so much that contractors often specify underground or unknown hazards as 'extra-over'.

The one-way hydrostatic relief valve allows external water pressure to flow into an empty pool; a dewatering sump set beside the pool helps drain a site; or, if necessary, an extra thick anti-flotation sub-raft anchors down an empty tank even in very high watertables. A well-point system guarantees keeping water at bay in gravel pit places,

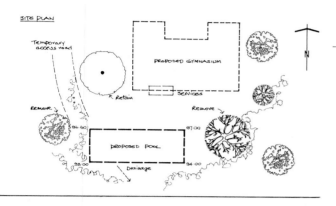

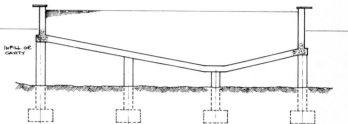

2.9 *Raised pool shell above high water table or over unsatisfactory ground conditions*

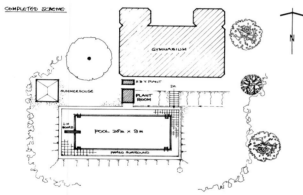

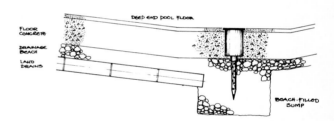

2.10 *Hydrostatic relief valve, incorporating non-return valve*

2.7 *25 m pool: site plan and completed scheme*

2.11 *Example of water tables: 10 × 5 m pool and subraft*

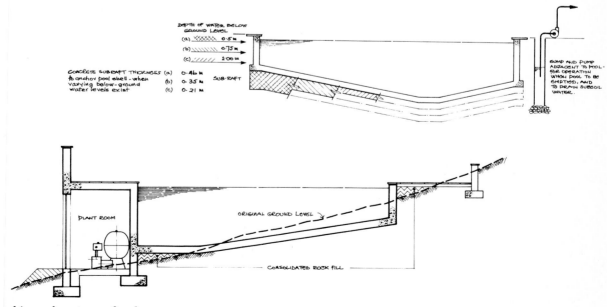

2.8 *Pool shell taking advantage of a slope*

but might cost as much again as the pool itself (see chapter 9.3 for more detail on the control or relief of subsoil water conditions).

It is always the unexpected that brings the greatest trouble. An experienced pool builder keeps a wary eye open while the excavation is at risk, for that is where he can make or break his profit. Once the floor is down and the walls are up, the remaining work is generally a straightforward calculable risk.

2.6 Regulations and standards

There are no universal common regulations and standards, except for international competition pools.

In New South Wales there are twice as many inground pools as in the UK, and in California at least eight times as many. If only because of the numbers involved, certain local regulations are imperative in these States. Current laws specify minimum pool distances from boundaries, and that pools must be built away and uphill from septic tanks; ordinances control backwash discharging to sewers, pool emptying, and wasteful heating. The increasing numbers of people drowned in private pools has alerted county authorities to insist upon a perimeter safety fence at least 1·25m high and to include a childproof gate lock (see also chapter 16.1 on safety).

Some regulations are clear in Australia, South Africa and the United States, but vary from place to place. They might involve direct bans on natural gas supplies or even 'first-fill' water to pools in California; all pools over 1500 gallons need planning consent in Australia which concerns filtration, chlorination, heating, lighting, soundproofing, amplification, and so on; also for safety reasons, direct access from home to pool in South Africa is not permitted.

Things are more confused in Europe, where old laws control new structures: Austrian authorities can prohibit the use of wood, since public pools can be considered within the emergency regulations designed for theatres; conversely 80 per cent of all pools in Sweden are built in timber; British rating authorities can levy local taxes on home pools, yet admit no responsibility for maintaining standards. Private pools in England do not require planning permission for construction, unless there is a building over the pool: often the swimming pool may only need local byelaw approval. Pools charging entrance fees, however, are subject to the 1936 Public Health Act, which concerns water purification, hygiene and conduct in public places; furthermore the involved pool environment is also affected by the 1976 Local Government Miscellaneous Provisions Act.

There is no doubt that safety and building services requirements for pools, private and public, need rationalising and updating in many countries. Far too many problems and dangers do arise from inadequate attention to the simplest basic standards – and the hazards will obviously continue to grow with an expanding pool population (see appendix IV for codes).

Swimming pool and operators associations National associations offer their non-mandatory requirements and publish their standards for safety, codes for construction, specifications for equipment, and even ethics for businessmen. One of the main reasons for the formation of national associations is mutual protection for members *and* public. But

every expanding industry attracts its shady charlatans who stay outside of confederations; also one should not rely too much upon the integrity of all advertising blurb.

Even with strict regulations, it is one thing to get some contractors to agree to do business one particular way, but it is quite another to make sure it is carried out that way. Similarly, the quality of management for pool operators relies upon effective and continuous training for all staff and people involved in service industries. Pools, just like highways, are dangerous places, unless sensible controls are reasonably enforced.

Internationality Fédération Internationale de Natation Amateur (FINA) publish their full competition International Standards for *Olympic type* diving and swimming with amendments every four years, but such 'super' pools comprise less than 0·01 per cent of all those existing (see chapter 3.5 and national standards listed in appendix IV for more details).

Although the main clauses of approved contracts can be itemised carefully, and the important items such as diving dimensions for different pools can be fixed almost precisely, the basic principles of sufficient water areas for each bather can only be debated. At this early planning stage, the best minimum area guide is to allow $2m^2$ per public bather, and $4m^2$ per private bather (see information sheet 2.14).

National Association Standards do provide especially useful starting foundations to consider collective opinions for minimum water depths. Some contractors have become so proficient at reducing the quantity of materials used,

2.12 *Compelling ceramic decor for a decklevel pool in Daun, GFR*
Villeroy & Boch, Saar

without loss of pool water area, that modern space saving shapes require sophisticated rules, eg curved spoon-shaped *hopper* deep-end profiles cut down water volume, but as a result, require three-dimensional standards, variable radii for adjustable springboards, perimeter wall criteria, transition break slopes, etc for safe recreation diving alone. Most people float at around 1·5 to 1·8m depth – the transition point. The NSPI, ASA and TUS have tackled diving depths in detail, and their recommendations have been adopted in many other countries, hence the growing internationality of the swimming pool with its need for common safety specifications.

Specifications The corrosive environment of the swimming pool means an impeccable specification. If the budget is insufficient, reduce the size or the facilities, cut the next phase or the trimmings, but *do not* lower the standards. Most pool problems arise from inadequate standards, and poor specifications. Troubles can be as simple as staining by rusting screws, or as tragic as collapsing roofs. Materials should be selected for their resistance to corrosion, their fire-retarding properties and sound absorption, and finally their appeal (see chapter 16.3 and 16.4 on wear and tear).

There is great diversity of equipment, but more and more consortia or group organisations now collate their designs to offer a cost saving project scheme for the complete pool tanking, water treatment, enclosure, heating and ventila-

tion sections, and so on. But it is surprising how few modifications need be added into a design in the first place to bring in more groups of swimmers such as the elderly or the disabled, or to cater for schools or families.

References
[1] Oscar, Faber & Partners, *Baths Service,* March 1977
[2] Site Work, *Specification 1976/7*

INFORMATION SHEET 2.1

Pools: a definition of positions

Above-ground   or on-ground: exposed swimming tanks mainly erected as garden, or school teaching pools, using a liner to hold water within a freestanding metal, timber or GRP structure.

Semi in-ground   or parapet: protected structures partially raised out of the ground and built for home schemes and training pools using concrete or reinforced plastic materials.

In-ground   or level grade: sunken schemes primarily for private, commercial and public design made of concrete, vinyl liner, GRP, metal and suitable for covering with a pool enclosure.

Underground   or concealed: totally sunken, pool hall for private or commercial application, built below ground of GRP and concrete for environmental conservation.

INFORMATION SHEET 2.2

Technical glossary of swimming pool terms

Backwash   reverse flow of water through a filter for the cleansing cycle
Body feed   continual addition of chemical or media for precoating the filter
Breakpoint   level at which poolwater pollution is entirely broken down into harmless substances
Chemical feed   injection of chemicals into poolwater circulation for pollution control
Circulation system   entire flow arrangement of fittings, pipework and equipment
Chlorine   major chemical used in disinfection
Coarse strainer   basket within pipeline to trap large debris before the pump
Coping   perimeter edging around a pool
Decking   surfaced surround area to a pool
Deck level pool   water surface level with deck
Disinfection   sterilising means of pool pollution
Diving-board   non-rigid board for recreational diving, as opposed to a firm stand
Diving platform   rigid stand for diving
Facework   pipe valves and manifold fittings connecting the filter to the circulation lines
Filtration   removal of suspended solids from water
Filter aid   coating material to improve filtration
Filter bed or cake   effective water filtration material within tank
Filter element or septum   porous internal structure trapping suspended materials from poolwater
Filter media   material used to collect solids
Flocculating agent   compound that coalesces finely suspended particles
Freeboard   distance between poolwater surface level and deck level
Freeform   freely adapted poolshape
Galvanic action   electro-chemical corrosion or deposition of materials, with water the electrolyte
Hopper   deep water basin with all four sides sloping for diving
Hydrostatic relief valve   one-way valve into pool to relieve external water pressure outside of shell

Inlet or pool return   fitting through which filtered water flows into pool
Liner pool   waterproof membrane for pool – usually flexible vinyl
Linerless pool   prefabricated component pool that retains water without additional waterproofing when assembled
Main drain or sump pot   deepest point outlet for main suction of poolwater to filter
Manifold   pipes and valves connection assembly
Marblite   'plaster' lining of marble granules with white cement to finish concrete pools
Monolithic tank   one-piece shell structure
Multiport valve   filter control valve changing direction of water flow
Overflow system   surface water collection or draw-off arrangement
pH   measure of the acidity or alkalinity of poolwater – its hydrogen-ion concentration
Pool   a body of water; or bath, hydro, hot tub, lido, pond, spa, splasher and thermae, or covered balneum, bath house, leisure centre, natatorium, poolarium, pool enclosure, pool hall and pool house
ppm   part per million measurement of minute substances in poolwater
Plantroom   operational pool equipment location
Pressure differential   pressure difference across hydraulic system
Rate of flow   volume flow per unit of time
Residual   free acting disinfectant remaining in poolwater after treating and breaking down pollution
Return lines   pipework returning filtered water to the pool
Scum channel   perimeter overflow inset into pool wall as surface water collection for filtration
Shell or tank   pool floor and walling structure
Skimmer weir   overflow device set into wall to collect surface water pollution
Spreader   distribution of poolwater inside filter
Spring-board   flexible board for competition diving
Suction lines   pipework supplying the main circulating pump
Test set   equipment used to check standards of water condition
Total dynamic head   sum of resistance within the complete circulation system
Transition point   point at which floor slope changes from shallow to deep area
Turbidity   clarity level of poolwater
Turnover   rate time taken to circulate a poolful of water
Underdrain   collection system beneath filter returning water to pool
Vacuum sweeper   an underwater sweeper using pump suction water for cleaning
Wet niche   underwater light with a water cooled sealed beam unit

INFORMATION SHEET 2.3

Six pool layouts

These are selected from Technical Study 3 of AJ Information Library *Sports Building Design* section 2, *Swimming Pools* Part 2, 24.8.1977.
The layouts below show the arrangement of facilities area to pools
(**a**) Tournesol Pool
by Durafour Tournesol International
(**b**) Richmond Regional Pool
by Leslie Gooday
(**c**) Northfleet Local Pool
by Vincent Gorbing
(**d**) Austrian Sport and Conference Centre
by Seefeld/Tirol
(**e**) Rushcliffe Leisure Centre
by Nottingham County Council
(**f**) Whitley Bay
by Gillinson Barnett & Partners

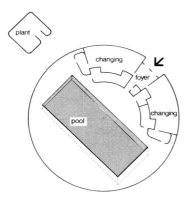

(**a**) *Tournesol Pool*

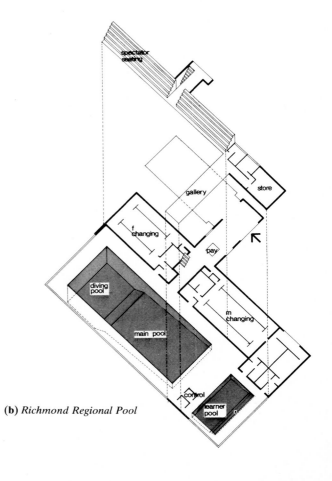

(**b**) *Richmond Regional Pool*

(c) *Northfleet Local Pool*

(e) *Rushcliffe Leisure Centre*

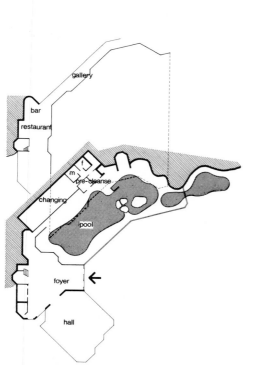

(d) *Austrian Sport and Conference Centre*

(f) *Whitley Bay*

INFORMATION SHEET 2.4

Construction sequence: A list of activities for private or public schemes carried out after preparation of the survey, planning and budget, working drawing, quotations, contract and setting out on site

	1	2	3	4	5	6	7	8	9	10
Substructure	Tank excavation	Subsoil drainage	Sub-floor	Base	Reinforced walling	Lining	Coping	Poolside accessories	Safety and sports equipment	Finishes
Plumbing	Trenching	Hydrostatic drainage	Gravity outlet	Main outlet	Inlets and overflow	Pipeline layout	Plant-room layout	Water treatment equipment	Water heating equipment	Make good
Services	Trenching	Drains and sewers	Conduits and infilling	Plant-room base	Underwater lighting	Storage facilities	Electrics	Controls and tests	Lighting equipment	Provisioning
Superstructure	Foundation excavation	Surface drainage	Footings	Floor raft	Load bearing walls	Roofing and ceiling	Plastering and flooring	Fittings and insulation	Heating and ventilation equipment	Decor and painting
Landscaping	Site clearance	Subsoil disposal	Contouring	Service surfaces	Backfilling tank	Oversite foundations	Paving decking	Screen-walling and features	Site clearance	Planting and turfing

Routine maintenance

Commissioning → Annual repairs

Refurbishing

INFORMATION SHEET 2.5

Critical path analysis—Example: filter installation programme

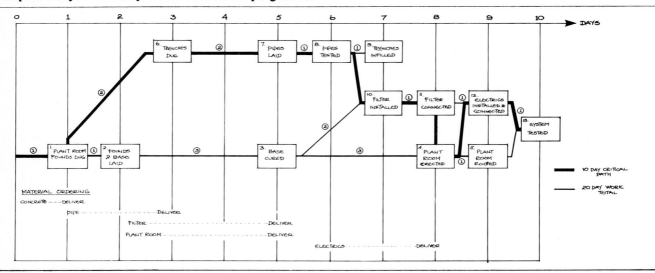

INFORMATION SHEET 2.6

Capacity calculation for freeform pools

SECTIONS	MEAN OF WIDTHS	AREA		MEAN OF DEPTHS	VOLUME
a	2·6 × 1·0 =	2·6	×	1·05	2·73
b	4·7 × 1·0 =	4·7	×	1·15	5·40
c	5·4 × 1·0 =	5·4	×	1·25	6·75
d	5·5 × 1·0 =	5·5	×	1·325	7·28
e_1	5·3 × 0·5 =	2·65	×	1·375	3·64
e_2	5·0 × 0·5 =	2·5	×	1·45	3·62
f	4·7 × 1·0 =	4·7	×	1·7	7·99
g	4·6 × 1·0 =	4·6	×	1·95	8·97
h	4·5 × 1·0 =	4·5	×	1·95	8·77
i	4·0 × 1·0 =	4·0	×	1·65	6·60
j	2·3 × 1·0 =	2·3	×	1·20	2·76
	TOTAL =	43·45		TOTAL =	64·51

i.e. POOL OF 10m LENGTH AND SECTION AS SHOWN HAS A SURFACE/FLOOR AREA OF APPROXIMATELY 43·5m² AND A CAPACITY OF APPROXIMATELY 64·5m³

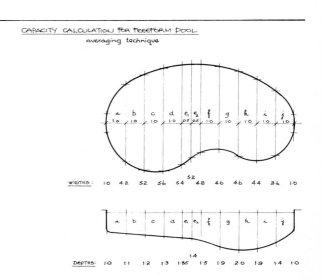

CAPACITY CALCULATION FOR FREEFORM POOL
averaging technique

WIDTHS: 1·0 4·2 5·2 5·6 5·4 4·8 4·6 4·6 4·4 3·6 1·0

DEPTHS: 1·0 1·1 1·2 1·3 1·35 1·5 1·9 2·0 1·9 1·4 1·0

INFORMATION SHEET 2.7

Grouping of components
The relationship between facilities for a multi-sports complex

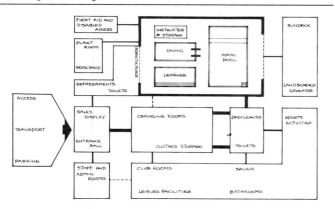

INFORMATION SHEET 2.8

Cost comparisons for pools

Rate per square metre of poolwater area

Private garden pools
***Base: UK 10 × 4m pool = 100**

Cost effectiveness	10 × 4m	11 × 5m	12 × 6m	Remarks
UK	*100	95	125	} Double these rates
USA	85	80	110	} for indoor pools
Market share by size				
USA	20%	70%	10%	} The proportion of
UK	35%	60%	5%	} smaller pools is fast increasing

Public (+ learner) indoor pools

	25 × 8·5m	25 × 12·5m	25 × 12·5m (+12·5 × 7·5m)	33 × 12·5m (+12·5 × 7·5m)
Cost effectiveness				
UK	1200	950	900	1100
Europe	1350	1200	850	—

(Rates increase by 50% with high diving facilities)

Market needs by size (forecast)

	25 × 8·5m	25 × 12·5m	25 × 12·5m	33 × 12·5m
UK suggested	30%	37%	27%	6% or similar size

Cost comparisons of construction

	Poured concrete	Gunite	Liner	Others
Cost of pool structures				
Base: US Others = 100				
USA private	60	75	50	100
UK private	80	95	70	110

Popularity of pool structures by type

	Poured concrete	Gunite	Liner	Others
USA	8%	45%	45%	2%
UK approx	50%	10%	35%	5%

	Prelims and foundations	Pool structure	Finishes and fittings	Services and equipment
Cost allocations				
UK public	15%	35%	20%	30%
UK private	20%	40%	15%	25%

Sources: AJ Technical studies/Council of Europe study/Sports Council reports/ *Swimming Pool Weekly* market reports
See also Sources of statistics and surveys concerning swimming pools: appendix VI.

INFORMATION SHEET 2.9

An ideal garden pool location – the bather's view

	Near to the house	Away from the house
Accessibility:	Most convenient, but house can become just a changing room	Can be irksome getting to and from the pool, but wet and dry areas are well separated
Amenity:	The house doubles as a pool house: sunlight reflecting off the water can be a nuisance indoors	The bathers can 'get away from it all' providing a pool house has been thought of
Privacy:	It is sheltered *and* noisy	There is peace at home but the pool is often overlooked
Safety:	Easy to supervise the children	The pool can be a hazard unless some security arrangement is provided
Viewpoint:	Ideal family focal point but can dominate the whole garden	The pool will not rule life: and bathers cannot hear callers
Facility:	Services are already provided: possible leaks can undermine house foundations	Service runs are long: the pool garden is usually self-contained
Setting:	The house and pool patio can be combined: a neglected pool in winter is mucky and murky	Extra paving is needed but the whole pool area often introduces an attractive garden feature
Economy:	It is less expensive to build close at hand and often the pool is smaller	There is usually more activity space available which costs more to landscape and look after

INFORMATION SHEET 2.10

How new pools are equipped — USA
Private and public built pools nowadays install the following equipment

	Item	% of pools having the equipment
1	Fencing	10%
2	Automatic cleaners	20%
3	Pool covers	30%
4	Chemical feeders	40%
5	Heaters	50%
6	Underwater lights	60%
7	Diving boards and suction sweepers	70%
8	Ladders	80%
9	Skimmer weirs	90%
10	Filters	100%

This trend is indicated by *Swimming Pool Weekly* annual market reports

INFORMATION SHEET 2.11

Swimming pool survey report

Initial details for the outline scheme

	Planning	Tank	Oversite
Determine:	type of pool	type of tank	type of decking
Consider:	allocation of budget and contingency	gradients, steps and datum level	preliminary works and site clearance
	feasibility and facility	protection from weather	pool enclosure
	pool uses and users	disposal of soil	new and existing landscaping
Check:	water	water table	reinstatement
	electricity	below ground situation	potential neighbourhood development
	gas	subsoil drainage	additional amenities
	local regulations	extra reinforcement	

	Planning	Tank	Oversite
Select or locate:	orientation 's' list – site, sketch, setting, size, shape, style, sun, shade, shelter, soil, spoil, surcharge, safety, services, access	method of excavation working and storage areas drains and sumps lining freeboard or deck level	levels and contouring features and walling planting terraces and wetseating surfaces decor and finishes
	Treatment plant	Environment plant	Pool equipment
Specify:	type of filter filter rating – max bathing load turnover period circulation system pipework category control valves location of plantroom and datum inlets outlets – drain – overflow backwash cistern or soakaway	type of heaters: water/air heater rating – max temperature build up flow/turnover energy recovery system insulation standards absorbent arrangements lighting and reflection sound disinfection system pH system chemical controls testing controls	optional extras – ladders or grabrails diving boards chutes handrailing autosweepers underwater lights underwater sound cleaning sports safety specials commissioning

INFORMATION SHEET 2.12

Problem places

Note Build only upon firm, consolidated subsoil

Nature of problem	Some solutions
Temporary watertable with seasonal variations	Provide a porous layer beneath floor, land drain network, gravity outlet to gulleys and soakaways; sometimes include extra thick or heavier flooring; never empty pool in wet conditions.
Flood watertable tidal, river and waterlogged conditions	Drain site and provide sub floor drainage, sometimes sub raft; dewater site and install artesian sump beside pool to inspect water level and to pump level lower if pool needs emptying during flood conditions; also include one-way hydrostatic relief valves in floor to release external build-up of pressure. Or build tank partially above ground to reduce excavation depths.
Permanent watertable and highly porous soils	Design to resist hydrostatic pressure; provide anti-flotation sub rafting; anchor lightweight shells, tie to piling or suspend as bridging; never empty. Or build tank above watertable. **Best to** install shell with both internal and external water retaining faces.
Unstable ground mining subsidence and earthquake	Consider raft designs to 'float' pools; for ground liable to settlement, engineer deep free-standing walls and caisson supports for pool floor resting on loose fill; provide flexible joints to pipework and fittings to allow for differential settlement or varying stratas and degrees of compaction. **Best to** use a flexible membrane type liner pool.
Shearing ground shale, slate, gravel, clay strata, cliff	Engineer special reinforced barriers and structures. **Best to** build elsewhere.
Sloping ground hillside or mountain	Cut and fill: consider projecting peninsula, cantilever construction and piers; shoring-up, piling or buttress; terrace the pool surrounds. **Best to** construct lightweight free-standing 'Alpine' type framework.
Troublesome soils: hard rock	Avoid excavation, blast or bury boulders, locate and shape pool to suit rocky outcrops, use the 'quarried' material within structure or landscaping.
loose sand	Prevent low angle of repose in excavation with temporary retaining framework, trenched rubble infill surround, or by applying light gunite crust to hold edges; provide a consolidated hardcore sub floor.
running sand sulphates and salts	Dewater, or retain with sheet piling, or excavate elsewhere. Counteract corrosion in marshy conditions, use sulphate resisting cement; trench and refill with neutral soil or infill with sacrificial lime/chalk for acid soils; in severe cases use an isolating coat of bituminous material or similar compound.

permafrost	Overdig and replace with classified material to totally insulate from 'hot' pool: install ground refrigeration around or suspend one-piece tank on piles with a 2m air gap over frozen ground. In freeze-thaw soils increase concrete density and reinforcement to resist expansion and contraction.
adobe or expansive clays	Increase reinforcement and use slab foundations for paving surround: replace top 1m of soil with non-expanding material or dig expansion trench. **Best to** build above ground pool structures.
Hazard situations: Sewers, septic tanks and surcharge	Tank foundations must be kept clear and separate from all other sub-site structures or their surcharge bearing. **Best to** bridge over, reinforce or relocate.
Cellars and roofs	Isolate within the building. **Best to** install extra waterproof membrane for security.

See also Substructures: chapter 9.5-8.

INFORMATION SHEET 2.13

Does the contract include .. ?

Plans and specifications
Full description and precise pool location
Costs in detail
Validity period for quotation
Guarantee provisions

Performance
List of work to be done, materials to be used, equipment to be installed and optional extras to be considered
Starting and completion arrangements
Maintenance – when is the owner responsible?
Reinstatement – who is responsible?
Notice for termination or suspension of contract and arbitration arrangements

Excavation
Costs of access and unknown underground hazards – see information sheet 2.12 for problems man-made or natural
Who pays for excavation 'cave-ins' or re-location of services?

Payment
Financial terms and arrangements
Ownership when the question of possession arises – such as in bankruptcy

Legal conditions
Permits and planning compliance arrangements
Compensation or damages involvement

Refer to national pool (or construction) associations for their recommended standard contract clauses: see appendixes II and IV.

INFORMATION SHEET 2.14

Water area allocations

Public baths: 2m² of water surface per bather
                  1m² maximum load
Private baths: 4m² of water surface per bather

The above guide allocations are based upon various suggested maximum usage areas adopted since the 1960s.

Notes

1 For information, the original figures as published are given in square feet below:

	Shallow water learners	Deep water swimmers	Average bathers	Sources
Public ft² allocation per person				
UK	10	36	23	MHLG 1962
			18	CCPR 1971
			30	Sports Council 1972

	Shallow water learners	Deep water swimmers	Average bathers	Sources
USA			27	First precept
	10	24		APHA 1964
	15	25	20	CNCA 1975 outdoor
		20 indoor		

Private ft² allocation per person

UK	18	54	36	General guides
	15-20			SPATA 1976
USA	27	54	40	General rule

2 Public pools:
On average for every three bathers in the water, another two are in changing rooms or surrounding areas. Hence if deck area is increased shallow/wading area bathing loads can be made greater, eg up to 8ft² allocation per person. Anticipated total annual attendance: local population × 3.
Alternative water area allocation to serve local population:
50ft² for every 1000 people   CCPR 1971
55/65ft² for every 1000 people   Sports Council 1972
5m² for 500/1000 people   EEC 1970
Diving: allocate 300ft² for each board   APHA 1964
        allocate 200ft² for each board   CNCA 1975

3 Private pools:
On average only 10% pool time is spent swimming.

INFORMATION SHEET 2.15

Pool design dimensions for minimum areas and volumes (metric)

Type			Pool			Hall				
				Surface area	Volume			Surface area		Volume
	Size (m)	Depths (m)	Shell (m²)	Water (m²)	Water (m³)	Size (m)	Height (m)	Walls (m²)	Deck (m²)	Air (m³)
Residential deck diving	10 × 5	0·8 to 2·3	100	50	75	13 × 7	4·5	180	41	410
Learner	12·5 × 7·5	0·6 to 0·8	125	94	65	16·5 × 11·5	3·5	196	96	664
Training	16·6 × 7·5	0·7 to 1·0	165	125	105	22 × 11·5	3·5	234	128	885
Swimming local	25 × 8·5	0·8 to 1·8	300	213	275	31 × 12·5	4·0	348	175	1550
Swimming district	25 × 12·5	0·9 to 2·0	425	313	440	31 × 16·5	4·0	380	199	2046
Competitive (25m preferable)	33·3 × 12·5	1·0 to 2·0	555	417	625	39·3 × 16·5	5·0	558	232	3242
International	50 × 21	1·8 to 5·0	1500	1050	3050	65 × 35	15·0	3000	1225 with seating	30,000
Diving: Springboards 1m–3m Fixed-board 5m	12 × 11	3·8 even	320	132	500	18 × 15	8·0	528	138	2160

INFORMATION SHEET 2.16

Recreational diving dimensions (metric)
Guide meeting recreational requirements
(Refer national standards for detailed minimum dimensions or diving board manufacturers specifications for board performances)

Diving board		Water depth				Surface clearance			Overhead clearance
Height above water	Overall length	Deepest floor		Forward to		Forward length	Width over deepest point	Overhang of board	Height above board
		Point	Width	Deep point	1·5m Transition point				
A	B	C	D	E	F	G	H	I	J
up to 0·50	up to 2·5	2·3	2·5	3·0	5·0	8·0	4·5	0·5	4·0
0·66	3·0	2·5	2·5	3·0	5·5	8·0	4·5	0·6	4·0
0·75	3·5	2·7	3·0	3·5	6·5	8·5	5·0	0·8	4·0
1·00	3·5	3·0	4·0	4·5	7·5	9·0	5·0	0·9	4·5

Measurements from deep end poolside

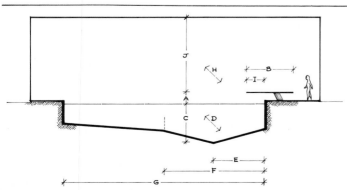

Sources: NSPI/SPATA minimum dimensions.
Spring-board/high-board arrangements: Competitive diving dimensions: information sheet 3.6.
Profiles and gradients: see pool profiles: Guide to gradients and critical dimensions: information sheet 2.17.
Slides: see Slide dimensions guide: information sheet 4.5.
Poolside diving: see Diving levels: information sheet 7.2.

INFORMATION SHEET 2.17

Pool profiles
Guide to gradients and critical dimensions

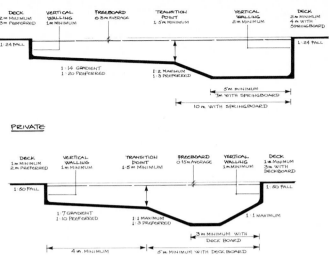

Public pools		Private pools	
Summary guide depths			
Types of pools		**Minimum for diving**	
Paddling	0·2–0·4m	Deckside	2·0m
Wading	0·4–0·6m	Deck level board	2·3m
Learner	0·6–0·8m	1m spring-board	3·0m
Training/teaching	0·7–1·0m	3m spring-board	3·5m
Swimming	0·8–1·8m	5m fixed-board	3·8m
Sporting	0·9–2·0m	7·5m fixed-board	4·1m
International	1·8–1·8m	10m fixed-board	4·5m

Minimum transition point 1·5m: preferred 1·8m
Minimum for life saving practice 2m

See also Recreational diving dimensions: information sheet 2.16.
See also Competitive diving dimensions: information sheet 3.6.
See also Water depths for age-groups: information sheet 6.6.

INFORMATION SHEET 2.18

Ten basic lists of pool equipment and materials
(to consider at the planning review)

Substructure	Water circulation	Plantroom	Superstructure	Hygiene
Tank structure	Hydrostatic valve	Filtration	Ventilation	Footwear dirt grid
Waterproofing/	Pipework system	Pumps/strainers	Air conditioning	Toilets
sealants	Flow inlets	Disinfection system	Humidity control	Wash basins
Liner	Overflow system	Water monitoring	Heat recovery	Showers
Pool paint	Drain outlet	Heating	Insulation and	Footbaths
Tiling and mosaics	Gravity outlet	Electrics	acoustics	Litter bins
Coping and decking	Cover grilles	Control panel	Internal facilities	Towelling
Underwater windows	Hair trap	Water gauges	Sauna bath	Hair dryers
Wave machinery	Backwash drain	Valves/manifolds	Diving platform	Drinking fountain
Adjustable floor	Water level control	Sewage treatment	Seating	Floorwash equipment
Moving boom			Audio system	

Safety	Accessory	Sport	Maintenance	Materials (non-toxic and non-corrosive)
Fencing	Ladders	Starting platforms	Underwater suction	Copper
Handrailing	Diving board	Lines and lanes	sweeper	Brass
Lifebuoy and line	Water chute	Line floats	Robot cleaner	Bronze
Rescue hook	Warm bench	Swimming aids	Water hose	Gunmetal
Lifeguard stand	Deckside furniture	Sports gear	Cleaning equipment	Stainless steel
Safety net	Wall anchors	Touch pads	Surface debris cover	Cement
Floodlighting	Underwater lights	Time clock	Water test set	Plastics
First aid equipment	Underwater sound	Recording controls	Chemical dispenser	Vinyl
Gas mask/respirator	Therapy equipment	Display board	Fire alarm	Glass fibre (GRP)
Resuscitator	Hydrojet	Play equipment	Earth trip device	uPVC
			Emergency lighting	

See also Swimming pool survey report: information sheet 2.11.

INFORMATION SHEET 2.19

General brief – indoor public pools

	Considering the bather	Considering the disabled
Access	Present a clear, pleasant and imposing entrance	Reserve at least 3·5m wide parking space near entrance
	Include multiple doors for emergencies	Use double swing entrance doors
	Add motifs to all-glass doors	Provide bypass gate for direct entry if turnstiles installed
	On slopes, keep steps outside	Avoid obstructions and infilled steps
	If possible, a level, easy approach is best	Ramps: short runs of 1:10 possible with 1m level at top
	Enter pool hall at shallow end	average slopes 1:15 and 1m paths
	Make pool easy to get to, and pay special attention to	preferred gradients 1:20 and 1·3m wide at 90° corners
	road safety	Stairs: maximum risers 150mm height, minimum treads 250mm depth
	Paving must remain non-slip and is best butt-jointed	Consider 1 × 1·5m minimum size short rise service lift

Consider the needs and kind of local bathers for catchment area

Changing areas

Cater for heavy use and abuse	Provide disabled persons toilet
Design a simple and obvious flow routine	Double up (with a direct access) first aid room as disabled
Establish clear precleanse procedures plus hygienic conditions	persons changing area to include a 2m bench
Arrange versatile facilities to cope with variable users	Install corridor and dry area handrailing at 1m height
Allow enough room to move freely and allocate ample	Place fixtures and fittings within reach – 1·5m height
clothes storage space	Preferred door widths 0·9m minimum

Keep all amenities on one level

Tank

Use non-toxic materials	Include safe handgrip coping/handrailing
Allow no protrusions	Inset wall safety ledges
Allocate 75% area to shallows	Consider the deck level circulation system first for easiest
Install locked gratings with unpokeable grilles	entry into water

CP2007 (UK water retaining specification) now replaced by BS5337 requires that no less than 12mm water drop occurs in seven days for water retaining structures

Indoor pools must be absolutely impermeable

Poolside

Offer non-slip flooring with 1:24 minimum fall	Cushioned flooring/walling preferred
Fit ladders on depths over 1·5m equivalent depth at 1 every	Wide in-situ steps preferred or sometimes a portable chute
20m max total perimeter	Never accept narrow tread ladders
Use toughened glass only beside pool	Clearly distinguish pool/step edges and depths for poorly
Introduce 0·5m high warmed seats, helping also to	sighted bathers
protect low windows	Endeavour to arrange reserved sessions for handicapped clubs
Outdoor pools:	keeping in stock a skeleton-wheelchair or wheeled trolley
Fix frost resistant tiles	
Allow for paving surround	See also chapters 5, 11 and 16
Erect security fence	

Environment

	Specify exacting standards to withstand the corrosive atmosphere, the abrasive cleansing solutions and a high content of excited juveniles
Water:	Do not stint on filtration, disinfection or heating plant
	Save on air space/water space volumes for more efficient operations
Heat:	Carefully review transmittance values and fire resistance
Light:	Reduce fenestration and solar glare
Sound:	Limit reverberation and high reflective surfaces
	Consider energy recovery, increased insulation and absorption materials
	Employ high quality finishes requiring no redecoration
	Baths should be sociable, entertaining, healthy and a place to 'let off steam'

Part II Pool techniques of this book develops environmental data in depth.

3 The competition swimming pool

Built with increasing complexity at successive competitive locations in the world every four years, the modern architectural equivalent to a mediaeval cathedral is the Olympic swimming pool hall. There is no doubt whatsoever the expert ingenuity and diversity in structures for these stadia well matches the skills of the super-athletes. But how many cathedrals to how many churches do we need? Is the swimming pool a place for sport, for leisure, or both?

3.1 Local pools

A profile of the existing and potential population within the catchment area of a public pool is useful for sizing and provisioning facilities. In the UK about half the pool users travel to their swimming baths by car, with half the remainder using public transport, and the rest go by bicycle or on foot. The number of young people visiting a pool drops off dramatically if they have to travel more than 5km.

Although the typical user indicated by surveys and reports is in his teens, travels for less than 15 minutes, and attends regularly with his pals, the general public swimming pool must cater for every taste, from beginners to sportsmen, paddlers to lifesavers.

The better the facilities and the warmer the water, the greater will be the number of people interested in swimming. Then, the keen swimmer who needs constant practice and attention to training has to travel to a less busy pool, swim very early or very late, and belong to a strong swimming club.

Commercially, the best site for most public pools is considered to be centrally placed, well served by transport, convenient for schools and safely accessible to children, who often represent almost 90 per cent of regular users. Such highly sought after land space should be clear of mining subsidence, be good load bearing, free from subsoil water pressure and, of course, reasonably priced. Excellent topography and access, convenient services and sewers, a sunny aspect and freedom from pollution all contribute to the making of a perfect pool. Siting an attractive municipal pool to serve the public well has always required clear orientation towards the sun. Years ago, Vitruvius summed up the situation by saying: 'Firstly a site must be chosen as warm as possible, that is, turned away from the north and east. Now the hot and tepid baths are to be lighted from the winter west; but if the nature of the site prevents, at any rate from the south'. In those days, the opposite southern hemisphere did not figure in the Roman engineer's orientation (refer to chapter 2.4 for site surveying).

3.2 Sports pools

More boys probably took up active swimming after Mark Spitz's seven gold medal wins in 1972, and more girls started gymnastics following Olga Korbut's dazzling performance at the Munich Olympics than at any previous time. Champions are vital for inspiration in any successful sport. They are as important as proper facilities. The competition swimming pool must offer equal chances to all-comers in sporting swimming, consequently the rectangular shapes have proved to be the most practical for sportsmen and sportswomen so far.

In the minds of many, only the rectangular sports pool enables competitive swimmers to improve style, stamina and ability through determined coaching and dedicated training. Speed in swimming and skill in diving can only be achieved with considerable practice and concentration. A shallow pool, an irregular shape, or a crowded play area does little to encourage the development of swimming, it is argued.

The sportsman holds a relativistic point of view: 'Success in international sport has great value for the community in raising morale and inspiring young people', and to support this the 'rectangular tank is still the cheapest swimming pool to build'.[1] Swimming associations still firmly have an 'institutional grip on bathing'[2] which can stultify pool design and dull the ordinary pleasure of swimming, while the leisure pool enthusiast emphatically opposes 'a clinical rectangle where future world-beaters can be soullessly manufactured'.[3]

However, for the sportsman there can be no compromise in maintaining training schedules. Hence FINA regulations for international pools categorically specify dimensions and standards in language that eradicates any possibility of an international error of judgement.

3.3 National pools

Swimmers training to national standard need at least one two-hourly swimming session each day; an international swimmer might need five hours or more at the peak of his programme. Usually they have to practise very early morning or late evening, sometimes even collecting the key from a helpful manager. Australian teams have swum 10 miles every day for three months as part of the build-up for their Olympics in the past. No small wonder well-organised sportsmen have made the rules following such constant demand for routine and better facilities. In order to succeed

in world class championships, athletes have to be selfish in devotion of time and life. Mark Spitz said, 'at my level, swimming is a lot more mental than physical'.

National competitive pools and sports centres are vital for the perfection essential for champions. But as competitiveness increases, so the rules become more definitive, and most changes of the FINA regulations affecting swimming pools are made immediately after each Olympics. Unfortunately, as these rules multiply, so the phenomenal costs inflate. Already, many countries cannot afford the staggering expenditure of holding the Games, in which the whole set-up of water events is no small item. Separate sport international championships are already being mooted as more suitable to the athletes than the conglomerate Olympic Games.

Such arrangements already exist for the largest Olympic host nations. In USSR 1980, two 50m main racing pools are located in central Moscow with water polo in Luzhniki district. The diving pool is in a recreation park Sokoliniki-Ismailove; and there are also practice pools situated nearby in the Olympic training camp on the outskirts of Moscow. Other ideas have been put forward for Olympic sized pool schemes to be specially constructed in suitable existing stadia, and then to be taken down and removed after the event for re-use again later, or for the Games to be shared between co-operating nations and so spread costs and facilities.

3.1 *The city pool for Melbourne built in 1934 conforming to standard Olympic specifications of that time*
Australia House
Photo: Jack Gallagher

3.4 Guide to sports pool basics

The competitive pool depends upon well-regularised standards, precise dimensions and a good measure of uniformity. In general:

● Training/teaching pools require less head room, less depth, but warmer water and air, plus a great deal more thought towards limiting noise.

● Diving/synchronised swimming pools have far higher ceilings, stricter depths and greater lighting controls; warmer air with warmer water has to compensate for the divers' continual heat losses.

● Racing/main pools – involve overall 2m swimming depths, 8 or 10 training lanes and 50m proportional lengths; there are conflicting problems of light and dazzle, with bright illumination and no windows preferred; pool temperature can be kept lower since swimmers generate their own warmth with exercise.

3.5 Championship dimensions

Modern swimming races are based upon 100m multiples. The most convenient competitive pool lengths keep start and finish at the same end. Hence, the popularity of local 25m, over 33⅓m sizes.

3.2

3.3

All national and international events are now specified around the full 50m pool and world records are only recognised when swum in this size of pool. However, in America the many existing 25yd short course pools are still recognised for national championships, but for future constructions wherever possible and when funds permit, the 50m pool is preferred; the 25m length is not yet recognised for US national competitive swimming. One solution to the metric/imperial dilemma is demonstrated by the 50m Swimming Pool Hall of Fame at Fort Lauderdale, where the length can be reduced to 50yds with a boom, or the pool can be made into two 25yd square training sections with a barrier. But be careful of dissatisfying everybody by putting in an all purpose pool that meets metric rules missing current needs, or offers ample shallows slowing racing times, and brings popularity to crowd out serious swimmers.

In the UK, where ASA swimming pool requirements for competition are now entirely based upon metric measurement, the existing proportioned pools of 110yds are easily adapted to metric dimensions by reducing the length several inches (see information sheet 3.2 on new and traditional dimensions). In Europe, mechanically moving bulkheads and floors make rapid transition from sport to leisure or general swimming (see chapter 11.5 on options and chapter 3.8 on dual roles).

Lane and Depth Although international regulations stipulate 2·5m (8ft 3in) for lane width, the American 7ft and 6ft (2·1m and 1·8m) lanes are far more satisfactory for regional and local competitions. Similarly for depth, although 1·8m is the metric minimum for international events, a tumble-turn can be carried out in 3ft (0·9m) of water, though 3ft 3in (1m) is preferred (4ft in USA). And water polo with its specified depth of 1·8m can be played satisfactorily at 1·2m. Deep water canoe practice in a 25m pool will, however, require a shallow area 0·6 to 1·0m deep where an instructor stands to direct capsizing practice. Unfortunately, shallow pools are slow for racing. Therefore, the pool used for NCAA Championships at Cleveland State University is 12 to 16ft deep to ensure even less drag upon the swimmers – but the water is also perfectly clear, inspiring better swimming times.

Depth gradients An international championship pool requires uniform depth of a minimum 1·8m throughout the complete 50m racing lane length, though 2m water or deeper allows for faster swimming times by reducing drag from the floor.

A regional competition pool also has to be suitable for the general public with standard 1 to 2m depths over the 25m minimum length. But the question now arises, at which point will the shallow end become deep end – where along the length does the walking bather have to start

3.2 *25 m racing course with separate diving and children's sections at the Grosse Pointe Yacht Club, Michigan, and built from prefabricated aluminium panels*
Chester Products Inc, Ohio
Photo: Lens-Art Photo

3.3 *The grouping of commentary/console positions above the finish line for the Montreal Olympic Pool – one month to go!*
Architect: Roger Taillibert
Montreal Olympic Organising Committee

swimming? Demarcation or the position of change from shallow profile to steeper depth gradient, is termed the transition point.

Since local and regional pools have to cater for those who can as well as those who cannot swim, the point of change of slope from standing to swimming is highly pertinent. Swimming will almost take place when the shoulders are immersed, and the average adult shoulder height for 95 per cent of Western world population just exceeds 1·4m. Therefore, a transition point, where shallow gradients can safely turn to steeper gradients, justifiably starts at 1·5m of water (UK standards specify 1·7 to 1·8m) when almost every adult will be swimming, or getting out of depth even on tiptoe.

But when providing mainly for children, the transition point can be set shallower at 1·3m or less (see chapter 2 and information sheet 2.17 and chapter 6 and information sheet 6.6).

An alternative and wasteful method of bringing racing depths up to satisfactory recreational standards is to lower the water level, but unfortunately the increased freeboard can be hazardous, surface skimming systems become unsatisfactory, and a costly holding tank for the extract water is necessary. Raising the pool floor hydraulically is worth considering for dual use training and swimming if budgets allow (see chapter 11.5).

Accuracy Championship dimensions are so critical in modern swimming that it is essential to refer to the controlling body for precise data at the preliminary design stage, and then to check once again at the final approval stage, since it is quite possible for regulations to have been amended in between.

The installers of the Munich Olympic pool introduced sonic surveying for the strict construction measurement accuracy needed. When a race is measured to 2/1000 of a second (equal to 4mm in racing length terms) every millimetre of the 30mm overall tolerance permitted is critical to the swimmer. In one international long distance race held in Federal Germany, an American won a split second in front of a Swedish swimmer. If the Swede's lane which was later proved to be a few millimetres longer, amounting to several centimetres over the whole distance, had been accurately measured at the time, then the result could have been reversed. Such is the state of modern competition.

Capacity International competitive dimensions concern more than the pool alone, for the hall should provide seating for at least 1500 plus perhaps another 3500 temporary positions installed when the few major events take place. In the UK, although there are excellent 50m pools, none fully meet the latest FINA regulations which include seating requirements.

Seating for local competition is sufficient at 200 or 400 permanent places with two or three times the number for temporary tiers. Even at these numbers, permanent seating spectator galleries remain excessive until there is a major event in the swimming calendar. Interest in swimming or water shows is reviving the art of seating where every spectator can see everything. But pools are still being built with insufficient height to back rows even when people stand on their seats, and frequently the front rows are also too low to see over the decking and into the first lane (see information sheet 3.9, and chapter 11.4).

3.4a *The diving tank at the Royal Commonwealth Swimming Pool, Edinburgh designed to save water with shallow depth main pool, and air volume with a roof well above the diving pool*
Architect: Matthew Johnson-Marshall
Photo: P. Barstow

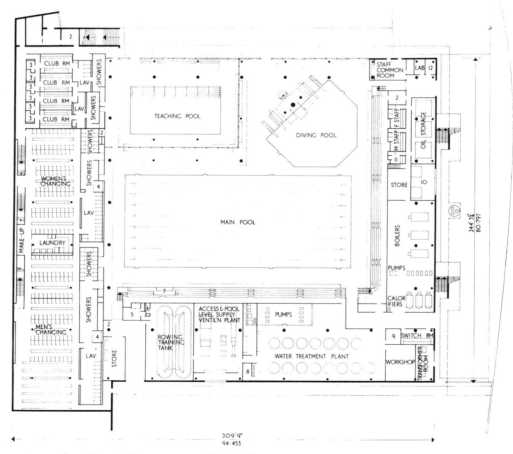

3.4b *Family sports pool – Royal Commonwealth Pool, Edinburgh: plan*

The Munich Olympic Hallenbad allowed for over 9000 spectators, Mexico 10,000, Tokyo 11,000 and Moscow 12,000. Most modern Olympic halls cater for between 5000 and 10,000 spectators at the Games only and inspire spectacular roofing design to cover such cavernous spaces. *'Piscina monstera'* Greatness is relative: seating accommodation for the competition pool in Osaka, Japan, provides for 25,000 spectators; in terms of water volume, the huge inland pond that was the Fleishacker swimming pool in San Francisco holds 7½ million US gallons (28,400m³) – in comparison a standard Olympic 50 × 21m pool holds only 2000m³; but even this Californian Olympian is dwarfed by the Orthlieb pool in Casablanca, Morocco, measuring 480 × 75m and holding an ocean-full of seawater (see information sheet 4.3, Hyperpools).

3.6 Diving

Over the past 100 years, the Americans and the Swedes between them have changed the 3ft straight plunge dive into complex gymnastics from 10m high-boards and the waterspace needed now for each diver averages from 25 to 50m². Accordingly, to calculate the total bathing load for public swimming pools with a diving section, the 2m² guide rule per swimmer (chapter 2) has to be adjusted. For example, a 25 × 10m swimming tank with 1 to 2m depths that caters for 125 to 200 bathers can only accommodate 75 swimmers when a 1m spring-board is provided, which requires 9m forward length and 5m clearance width with 3m depth (see information sheet 3.6, Competition diving dimensions).

It is always better and safer to provide separate facilities for diving. Safety is the most critical concern for diving pools, and national associations for swimming, pool construction or public pools all publish details of critical dimensions. The diving dimension charts in this chapter (and chapter 2 for residential pools) give information for convenient reference, but specific regulations of the competitive ruling body must still be consulted for there are differences of standard between various official organisations. FINA standards are the most stringent of all.

Extra or combined facilities Opinions differ for and against separate diving pools. Nine tenths of diving training techniques can be satisfactorily coached from a 1m springboard alone, but 5m and 10m high diving requires fully separated or specially shaped pools. I, L, T and Z shapes for pools offer useful designs for keeping two pools together, providing there is clear demarcation from diving. The most common of all pool accidents involve divers hitting the water incorrectly, or colliding with a swimmer or some part of the pool floor, walls or equipment.

When planning a separate diving pool, the design extras should be carefully evaluated. For only 1m spring-board diving, they will be:

Increased
- total construction costs, by 50 per cent at least
- interior building heights, up to 6m at least
- water depth, down to 3m at least
- water volume – by 50m³ at least.

Additional
- filtration plant
- ventilation plant

3.5 *Waterwheel diving tower in ferro-cement at Ostia, near Rome: 10m and 5m fixed-boards, 3m and 1m spring-boards plus seawater cascade for dramatic effect*
Cement & Concrete Association, London

- heating plant
- chlorination plant.

Greater
- pipelines
- surface areas
- excavation
- plantroom capacity.

Diving tanks should stand at least 5m, preferably 6m, from the main pool, well clear of the shallow end, and completely separated from children's play areas.

Heights and sizes Basic diving facilities include:
- Practice fixed low-boards: ½m, 1m, 2m, 3m – general training and recreation
- Diving-boards: decklevel – recreational and residential use (see chapters 2 and 7)
½m – semi-athletic activity
- Spring-boards: 1m – ideal for teaching and training: the

first recognised competition level (2 × 1m boards are more popular than 1 × 1m plus a 3m level)
3m – all classes of competition
● Platform fixed high-boards: 5m, 10m – all classes of competition
7½m – practice only.

Diving is rapidly increasing in popularity and queues quickly form for the low-boards. The very first optional extra should always be a standard ½m diving-board for a private pool, and the more resilient 1m spring-board for a public tank.

High-board diving can be dangerous: visit the topmost board and stand on that leading edge in the balanced way that young divers carefully position themselves before the plunge. The height (twice as tall as a house) is terrifying, and the distant water surface like a postage stamp! In fact, high-board divers can reach 50k/h at the point of impact, so modern methods of softening water, or providing underwater diving cushions are growing in importance. A viewing section through fixed stand-boards enables the diver to see down to the water and lower boards; also dulling the clear water surface with a spray is necessary for him to measure distance safely. Provision should also be made for safety barriers alongside boards of 3m and over, plus guardrails to the water's edge. An underwater window is invaluable for coaching, especially if linked to an audio system (see also chapter 11.5).

Diving pool dimensions (fullest 5m depths) are:
● Championship tanks – 15 × 9m
● National tanks – 15 × 12·5m
● International tanks – 20 × 15m (but usually 21 × 20m is adopted, or up to 25 × 25m × 5m depth).

Water depths There are fixed-boards, diving-boards and flexible spring-boards. The fixed or firm-boards are really rigid wide platforms set on stands or staging structures; diving-boards are non-rigid and their longer, narrower planks will bend to absorb some force from the diver but without very much deflection or reaction; spring-boards are flexible and will reactively help propel the diver to great height and performance. However, the real difference between a diving-board or firm-board and a competition spring-board is not in flexibility alone, but in the need to increase water depth. A 1m flexible spring-board *must* have 3m water depth beneath rather than the common 2·3m depth for a firm deck level diving-board, or normal 2·6m depth for a 1m fixed-board.

In practice, the deepest part of a 1m spring-board diving provision for a competition pool should be at least 3m in front, rather than beneath the board's edge.

Staging Spring-boards especially take gruelling pounding, and the most common problem with diving equipment is failure in rigidity of the frame structure, particularly column supported designs into reinforced concrete. For better stability, tie diving board structures to the building, or if the equipment is to be installed at a later date, provide firm anchor points and proper foundations at the construction stage.

As diving is very much a spectator sport, additional care in creating the best setting at the focal point is important. For example, man-sized dolphins in wall high murals behind the diving tower confuse those watching the diver, but this does not mean decor to an end wall has to be clinically pure or anaemic: it must not catch the eye. Avoid windows behind the diver, or at least ensure any windows are clear of direct sunlight and can be curtained. From the diver's point of view, he wants no distractions; no spectators in front of him, nor bright lights shining into his eyes.

3.7 Sporting fixtures and fittings

The range of fitments and auxiliary equipment is enormous: the diversity of quality and efficient design is equally vast. Non-corrosive, long-suffering equipment is necessary, and durability is not cheap. Nor is it always easy to locate to buy (see appendixes II and III for associations and journals with useful buyers' guides).

The judging standards in competitive swimming, and coaching standards in training, are now so high that second-rate, potentially inaccurate, sporting fixtures and fittings are definitely out. Even the simplest matter of separating lane from lane will affect swimming speeds.

Consider the racing swimmer who at 2m/s can win or lose, perhaps literally by the few millimetres growth of a fingernail! Anti-wave patterns for racing lines and special non-reflective overflow systems along the pool edge were important reasons for so many new world records at Munich in 1972. At Montreal in 1976 lanes 1 and 10 were unused to reduce turbulence and help speeds.

Turbulence is troublesome to swimmers, and reflections or deflections of wake waves mar their close fought competitive millimetres. Thus, race timing is absolutely critical, and systems of recording and display are made sophisticated to the 'millisecond' on the clock, and the 'centisecond' on the TV video tape deck (normal TV pictures operate at only 32 frames per second).

Timing and results Future sporting events will continue to improve on today's racing times since so many youngsters are now being taught to swim powerfully in better facilities. Closer margins in swimming races require diligent poolside officials and computers to supervise events, which for an international meeting can involve:

1 referee	
1 chief timekeeper	
(2 computer console scorekeepers)	
1 starter	5

3 finish judges		
2 style judges	per lane × 10	100
2 turn judges		
3 timekeepers		

Total officials 105

In other words ten officials for every swimmer.

Special timing control designs are often purpose-made. For example, the Electronic Swim Training Apparatus (ESTA), specially developed for the Crystal Palace National Sports Centre in the UK, ensures no interference with the swimmers while providing all the desired data.

The most up-to-date timekeeping electronic computers can provide all information processes for competitive swimming and are capable of simultaneously monitoring up to 10 swimming lanes; yet the nerve centre of the control system can pack into an attaché case, or be built into a central power console (see information sheet 3.9 for more details of competitive equipment list).

3.6 *The most popular accessory of a competition pool: a 1 m spring-board with adjustable fulcrum*
Ambassador College, St. Albans
Architects' Journal
Architect: Denkers & Maddison in association with Daniel, Mann Johnson and Mendenhall
Photo: W. J. Toomey

3.7 *Diving tower at Crystal Palace National Sports Centre: fixed-board positions 10 m, 7·5 m and 5 m; spring-boards 3 m.*
Note: glazed wall behind the diving tower is curtained to make comfortable viewing for spectators; water sprays dull surface to aid the diver
Architect: Designed by the Greater London Council, Department of Architecture & Civic Design, Sir Roger Walters
Photo: GLC Photographic Unit

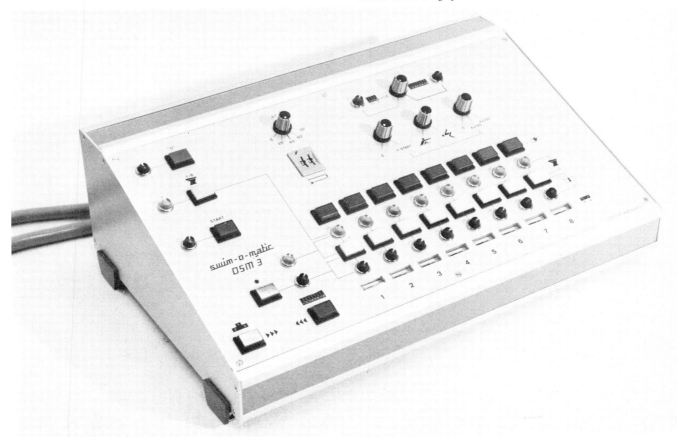

3.8 *8-lane control panel for electronic timing system*
Omega Electronics, SSIH Equipment (UK) Ltd, London

33

3.9

3.9 *'Bubble machine experimentation' for the National Sports Centre, Crystal Palace. Air bubbles released from this test rig on the diving pool floor provide a safety cushion for practising high-board divers. The entire system is operated from oilfree compressors with storage receiver and control valves*
Lacy-Hulbert & Co Ltd, Croydon

3.10 *Diver plunging into high safety cushion of water produced by 'Bubble Machine', Crystal Palace National Sports Centre*
Lacy-Hulbert & Co Ltd, Croydon

At Moscow Olympic Pools the swimming information is fed into a computer from the various regional centres around the city. Automated control systems are devised to bring rapid results to officials and journalists at the internationally linked main press centre and to about 20 terminal sub-centres. Strategic judging services now often depend upon radioelectronic and laser equipment and advanced computer link-up systems in order to display instantaneous information.

3.8 Dual roles

The question for the designer of sports pools, though, is how far should the swimming pool become 'part of the general fabric of the social service'?[4] Is there possible compromise between easy-going leisure and disciplined sport? Olympic planners commission post-Games investigations to overcome white elephant claims and to make better use of highly specialised facilities afterwards. But the pool catering for leisure with sporting specifications does require larger, more durable and more comfortable facilities. Since spectator galleries will be idle most of the time, temporary seating is best (see chapter 6.6 on dual-use pools).

In Edinburgh, the Royal Commonwealth Pool, although meeting the 50m FINA length, does not provide the all-over 1·8m depth specified for full international pools. This Scottish pool has a deliberately larger shallow area that is ideal for family bathing, yet still remains sufficient at the 1·05m deep shallow end for racing swimming and tumble-turns. The National Recreation Centre at Crystal Palace, on the other hand, concentrates upon training racing swimmers, and so provides a greater depth of 2·2m throughout. At Munich, they compromised by installing an

adjustable floor for one third of the length. This reduces the 2·7m shallow end depth to less than 1m for general local use.

When a feasibility study shows there will be full-time support and regular use of a sports pool by racing swimmers alone, there is good reason for the overall stipulated 1·8m depth. But logic, let alone economics, often moderates strict international specifications in order to make optimum use of a pool. As an indication of use densities, the smallest practical competitive proportioned pool for local baths of 25 × 10m will take 14 waterpolo players, maybe 25 racers training for competition, or between 125 and 200 recreational swimmers. Sports pools situated in schools offer the most practical opportunities for dual use. Management and facilities can cater for teaching and recreation using the scope of all the campus buildings as a sports centre or leisure complex – the joint arrangement making full use of pools every day and evening (see chapters 6.5 and 6.6).

Conversion mechanisms In Europe, an appreciation for recreational bathing and sports swimming has promoted the development of special mechanisms to convert sports pools into bathing pools:

● moveable booms convert one pool into two
● submersible bulkheads (eg an 11½in barrier at the Empire Pool, Cardiff reduces the 165ft length to 50m) must be rigid when scuttled, and also when raised by compressed air
● rising hydraulic floors can safely lift the pool floor up to ice-skating rink levels.

But the very high cost of such conversion equipment needs to be carefully measured against that of providing separate facilities elsewhere, especially since a compromise

3.11 *Underwater windows, lighting and inset safety ledge to a diving pool at Hallenbad Fellbach*
Buchtal, GFR

never quite satisfies both sides. Many consider the additional investment better put into additional pools.

Even so, foresight in providing the maximum, or adjustable, shallow area for recreational swimming, and segregating deeper pools with floating booms can be more suitable for most local pools (see also chapter 11.5).

Synchronised swimming There are fashions in sporting activities. Since the heyday of water polo in the 30s, when people queued to see their home team compete, this sport has fallen out of popularity, and the spectator gallery is now almost exclusively used by racing and diving fans. However, a new sport of synchronised swimming, which has been likened to water ballet is coming along to fill the gap. Although this has only minority interest at present, the 'swimming equivalent of figure skating' will attract even greater support when included in the *Games*. Movement with music in water is as compelling as the freestyle gymnastics, which have jumped to international popularity. And displays increasingly encourage water shows for the family to watch.

In USA, where there is a large and growing following, the preferred water area is 2000 to 3000ft² at over 6ft water depth (200 to 300m² at 2m depth approximately); a 40 × 20ft at 10ft depth (12 × 6m at 3m) is an acceptable minimum – a typical small diving pool section, in other words. But shallower water is necessary for learning the early stages of new routines.

Training schemes and events It has been claimed that every German child can swim on leaving school; and now with a new programme of improving and increasing training

3.12

3.13

3.12 *The training pool is an essential adjunct to an international swimming centre. This 6-lane, 25 m tank at Crystal Palace National Sports Centre is bordered by lowered decking areas for easier teaching with underwater observation windows located at end turn*
The Sports Council
Photo: GLC Photographic Unit

3.13 *A sense of the theatre in Olympic pool building for the Tokyo 1964 Games*
Architect: Kenzo Tange
Photo: Retoria O. Murai

facilities to teach every child to swim *before starting* school, there will be even more startling achievements in future competitive swimming.

In the UK, 1700 clubs share public pool facilities, but they still represent only 5 per cent of all swimmers, excluding recreational clubs. In the USA, well-organised age-group swimmers number over the million and mainly use 25yd pools, or natural water courses enclosed as 'bulkhead pools'.

Facilities can be purpose-made to fit the swimmer, or the swimmer can adapt to fit the pool. The local pool offering the best combination of facilities in any neighbourhood is often a recreational pool with provision for several racing lanes. While they are invariably rectangular in shape they do not have to be. Latest style freeform leisure pools can easily include two parallel ends for suitable competition length, though the leisure pool, being so popular with such constant use, forces sports swimmers to wait until the pool is less crowded for satisfactory training purposes.

And it should not be forgotten that competitive swimming is also an ideal sport for disabled swimmers.

References
[1] Ron Pickering, *Leisure in the 70s, Recreational Engineering,* August 1971
[2] Alfred W. S. Cross, *Public Baths and Wash-houses,* London, Batsford, 1906
[3] Swimming Pool Review *Pools and Pools,* December 1975
[4] DOE *Sport and Recreation,* August 1975

INFORMATION SHEET 3.1

The Olympic specification

FINA Rule 63 specifies the **international swimming pool**
50 × 21m of minimum depth 1·8m and to provide 8 × 2·5m racing lanes, and whose overall length offers a maximum tolerance of +30mm excluding any 10mm touch pad: water temperature 24°C ±1°C.

FINA Rules 107–113 specify the **international diving pool**
minimum and preferred standards for 1m to 10m high positions into a pool 5m deep with forward plunge length 15 × 12·5m width at least, according to the number/height of boards involved: water temperature 29°C ±1°C.

FINA Rule 120 specifies an **international water polo area**
to be 30 × 20m at minimum depth 1·8m and to provide 1m clearance behind each goal line; lines and goals to be marked with contrasting colours.

INFORMATION SHEET 3.2

Competitive pools
New and traditional dimensions

Pool length × width	Traditional feet (110yd proportions)	= Metric conversion	New metric (100m proportions)
International or Olympic	165 × 69	50·29 × 21·03	50 × 21*
National – minimum	165 × 42	50·29 × 12·80	50 × 12·5/13·0
Regional or district standard	110 × 42	33·53 × 12·80	33¹⁄₂ × 12·5/13·0
Local or European standard	82¹⁄₂ × 42	25·15 × 12·80	25 × 12·5/13·0
Local or US short course	75 × 30	22·86 × 9·15	25 × 8·5

Pool length × width	Traditional feet	= Metric conversion	New metric
School	55 × 24	16·76 × 7·32	16²⁄₃ × 7·5
Training – practice	41¹⁄₄ × 21	12·58 × 6·40	12·5 × 6·5
Lane widths			
International/national	8²⁄₃	2·64	2·5
Regional/short course	7	2·13	2·0
Local/school	6	1·83	1·9

Pool depths
International	: min depth 1·8m overall
National/public	: min depth 0·9m
US national (Long course 50 × 22·9m)	: min depth 4ft
Freeboard	: 0–12in
Deck width	: 15ft both ends, 10ft sides

See also Pool design dimensions for minimum areas and volumes: information sheet 2.15.
See also Conversions and equivalents: appendix VII.
*50 × 25m preferred so as to leave outer lanes free for reduced wave reflection; alternatively use 2 or 3 strings of wave dampening racing lines in outer 0·5m margins.

INFORMATION SHEET 3.3

Competition pools
Basic sizes

Training 0·9–1·8m depth			Local 1·0–1·8m depth			National 1·8m depth overall		
16²⁄₃m			**25m**			**50m**		
	¹⁄₄m outers				outers			outers
8·5	4 lane		8·5	4 lane	¹⁄₄m	17·0	6/8 lane	¹⁄₂m
10·5	5 lane		10·5	5 lane	¹⁄₄m	21·0	8 lane	¹⁄₂m
12·5	6 lane		13·0	6 lane	¹⁄₂m	25·0	10 lane	¹⁄₂m
			17·0	8 lane	¹⁄₂m	27·0	10 lane	¹⁄₂m
20m			**25yd US short course**			**33¹⁄₃m UK**		
	¹⁄₄ outers				outers			outers
8·5	4 lane		10yd	4 lane	1ft	13·0	6 lane	¹⁄₂m
10·5	5 lane		15yd	6 lane	1¹⁄₂ft	17·0	8 lane	¹⁄₂m
			20yd	8 lane	2ft			

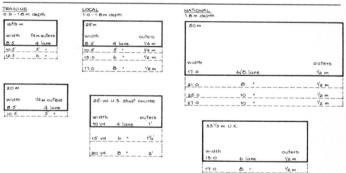

INFORMATION SHEET 3.4

Sports pools
Min/max sizing and rating

		Training pools min/max	Diving pools min/max	Racing pools min/max
Lengths	m	16²⁄₃/25	10/24	25/50
Widths	m	7·5/12·5	9·0/20	8·5/21
Depths	m	0·7/2·0	3·5/5·0	1·8/3·5
Heights	m	3·5/5·0	8·0/15	4·0/15
Filtration turnover	hours	4/6	5/10	2/4
Water temperature	°C	26/28	28/30	23/26
Illumination	lux	250/500	600/1200	500/1200
Seating	No places	50/500	100/10,000	200/12,000

INFORMATION SHEET 3.5

Water polo dimensions
For international/local matches
(Based upon FINA Rule 120, ASA and NCAA requirements)

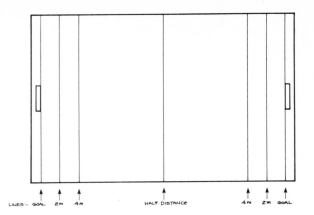

Playing area:
international events:	30 × 20m min depth 1·8m	
local events:	20 × 8m min depth 1·2m	
women's matches:	25 × 17m max	

Pool temperature: 24°C but min 18°C and max 27°C

Goals: posts 3m apart with 0·5m margin behind, but 1·00m preferred
crossbar – above water surface 0·9m over 1·5m water depth
– above floor of pool 2·4m under 1·5m water depth

INFORMATION SHEET 3.6

Competitive diving dimensions (metres)
Guide meeting general competitive regulations for separate diving pools
(Refer to current FINA rules and regulations for minimum or preferred Olympic dimensions for high performance diving. These international standards are more stringent than national competitive requirements which vary from country to country.)

Board			Water depth			Surface clearance				Overhead clearance		
Height above water			Beneath board	Maintained		Behind	Forward	Side	Adjacent board	Above	Maintained	
				Forward	To side						Forward	Side and behind
A			B	C	D	E	F	G	H	I	J	K
	Overall length	Board width										
Spring												
1·0	4·8	0·5	3·0	5·3	2·2	1·5	7·5	2·5	2·5	4·6	5·0	2·75
3·0	4·8	0·5	3·5	6·0	2·7	1·5	9·0	3·5	2·5	4·6	5·0	2·75
Fixed												
1·0	1·5	0·6	2·6	4·5	2·0	0·75	7·5	2·5	2·5	3·0	5·0	2·5
3·0	2·0	0·75	3·25	5·0	2·6	1·25	9·0	3·5	2·5	3·0	5·0	2·5
5·0	5·0	2·0	3·8	6·0	3·0	1·25	10·25	3·8	2·5	3·0	5·0	2·75
7·5	6·0	2·0	4·1	8·0	3·0	1·5	11·0	4·5	2·5	3·2	5·0	2·75
10·0	6·0	2·0	4·5	10·5	3·0	1·5	13·5	4·5	2·5	3·4	6·0	2·75

Measurements taken from centre leading edge of board
Maximum slope of profile 30°; but 45° maximum sometimes used
Preferred diving pools: international 21 × 15m to 25 × 20m; UK 15 × 12·5m; US 75 × 45ft
Up to 1m spring-boards only should be permitted within the main pool
Sources: AAU/ASA/NSPI/NCAA/TUS
See also Recreational diving dimensions and profiles: information sheet 2.16.

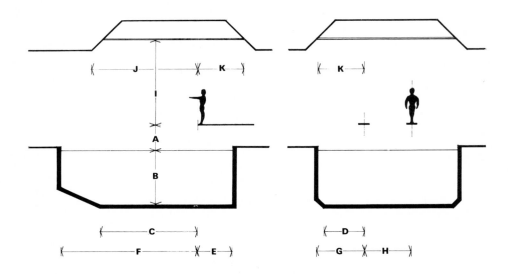

INFORMATION SHEET 3.7

Olympic dimensions for international swimming competitions
(Based upon FINA Rule 63)

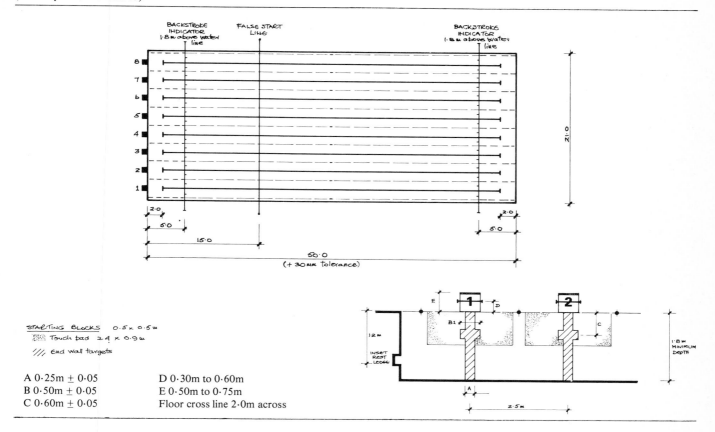

STARTING BLOCKS   0.5 × 0.5 m

Touch pad   2.4 × 0.9 m

End wall targets

A 0·25m ± 0·05   D 0·30m to 0·60m
B 0·50m ± 0·05   E 0·50m to 0·75m
C 0·60m ± 0·05   Floor cross line 2·0m across

INFORMATION SHEET 3.8

Diving: competitive equipment list

Stands and towers: Stages may be appropriately custom designed as a single piece of functional sculpture combining all boards; alternatively, separate pieces or popular standard combinations are made economically by equipment manufacturers.
Firm foundations or anchors are imperative since boards have to take considerable pounding.
Foundation pads or framed beam supports are important for stability and must be compatible with the relatively thin decking surround.

Spring-boards: Competitive – 1 and 3m. Supplementary – $\frac{1}{2}$m.
Typical design – aluminium extrusion with non-slip surface covering entire 5m length by 0·5m width (4·3m for general purpose use and 4·8m for competitive use).
Adjustable fulcrum range 0·75m forward minimum, with level tolerance of 1° above horizontal when dead centre. Overall height tolerance for general practice is +100mm.
Competitive tolerance ±5% for 1m, ±2% for 3m boards.

Fixed-boards: Competitive – 5 and 10m. Practice – $7\frac{1}{2}$m. Supplementary platforms – 1, 2 and 3m.
Maximum thickness of leading edge of board 200mm.
Competitive height tolerance +100mm maximum.
Overlapping top boards must project 0·75 to 1·5m beyond leading edge of lower boards.

Surfaces: Coverings to boards, stages, platforms, landings, stair and ladder treads must be durable, resilient and non-slip, while being hygienic, anti-fungal and easy to clean.

Access: When stairs are not provided, step ladders should not be inclined less than 15° from the vertical: but for high-board diving, especially where championship diving is involved, a hydraulic elevator is invaluable. The waiting area for divers should be screened from draughts with a warm seat provided.

Water agitation: Sprays dull the surface to aid height judgement, while bubblers increase depth perception and produce an opaque surface over the area of the dive. They are mandatory for international diving competition.

Diving cushions: One system aerates the water while another introduces a thick, rubber safety pad (3 × 4m) on the floor to cushion the diver. 'Water softening' by aeration makes water less dense; and the high cushion of air bubbles reduces risk of injury, like an aquatic safety net. Even from the 3m spring-board, speed on hitting the water is 10m/s (22$\frac{1}{2}$mph) with deceleration at 1m/s for first 3m depth of water.

Safety rails: Set 1m high beside boards or used as perimeter guardrail between decking and diving pool: where small children can approach diving pools an extra protection of infill stainless mesh is important. Pools with integral diving areas must have safety separation of a distinct barrier.

Viewing: Sunlight is enjoyed by bathers, but glare is troublesome to divers and spectators. End walls behind diving boards should be opaque and non-reflecting – windows and wall murals can confuse onlookers. No possible distraction for diver – blank wall facing is best: never facing restaurant gallery or unshielded lighting. Carefully angle any diving spotlights.

Sources: AAU/ASA/FINA/NCAA/NSPI/TUS.
See also chapter 11.5.

INFORMATION SHEET 3.9

Racing: competitive equipment list

The competition swimming pool is actually a theatre and benefits by careful selection of the various necessary theatrical props.

Starting blocks: Secure but easily fixed and removed, corrosion free, lightweight racing start platforms are made from reinforced plastic, aluminium or stainless steel – these materials, unlike timber, will not become waterlogged.

Dimensions 0·5 × 0·5m, with non-slip top surface set to 10° maximum slope for international competition at 0·5 to 0·75m above water level.
Backstroke crossbar fixed to block 0·3 to 0·6m above water line.
Lane numbers should appear on all sides of the block.

Timekeeping and judging: World records will only be ratified by FINA when recorded by electronic timing/judging apparatus installed in 50m pools.
To automatically record start, take-off, lap placings and total times to two decimal places of a second for each lane (printouts read to 1000th second).
To sense early starts from top surface and backstroke grip.
To check correct changeovers in relay racing.
To count laps and correct erroneous touches.
To be linked preferably to TV/videotape recording system able to make corrections.

Touch pads should be 10mm narrower than the racing lane, a maximum of 10mm thick, portable, sensitive on top edge and activated by starter and light hand touch; they must not be affected by water turbulence nor offer any sharp edges.
Circuits must be fail-safe with no possible risk of power electricity leaks – a supplementary automatic switchover battery back-up system is advisable.
Systems should be easily dismantled without draining the pool and must not interfere with swimming in any way.
Note Allow adequate floor area behind start for judges *and* timekeepers – absolute minimum 4m decking depth.

Display console results board to be set vertically and show information for each lane.
Over several hundred thousand light points can be involved in the main display to allow for computer data analysis, readout of splits, and video screen with provision for replay presentation.
Diving results to show diver's name, number, dive value, 5 to 7 judges marks with summary for dive and points score taking into consideration degree of difficulty.

Options to include computer summaries, result printouts, 8 or 10 lane control desk, with printers located in soundproof, air conditioned room clearly overseeing the finish line.

Markers Lane and depth notices, board heights and edges of pool, ledges and steps must be clearly distinguishable.
False start posts are located 12m from start where a recall rope is suspended over the water ready for releasing.
Backstroke indicator lines are located 5m from lane ends and 1·8m above water surface.

Pacing clocks: Dial of 1m diameter including clear sweep second hand timing.

Portable pacing system: Used as a swimmer training incentive or pacemaker in the water.

Winners' rostrum: Officials' tables and seating.

Cup anchors: To include securing hooks and tensioners for racing, or safety lines that are easily detachable.

Safety barriers, perimeter fences and splash screens.

Underwater ledges: 100 to 150mm inset ledges 1·2m deep, but none located near any diving position.

Flotation booms, bulkheads and adjustable floors must also provide for markers and touch pads.

Ladders: No obstructions are permitted in the pool and rung ladders or grab rails should be removable or inset into walls or step niches. Recessed in situ steps are better.

Water polo goals: Should be light, portable, white and maximum 75mm section, yet capable of being securely fixed into position. Limp nets are required attached to the whole goal space.

Lifeguard chairs: Observation posts or positions are specified by law in many US areas.

Rescue poles, hooks, life rings with 15m throwing line.

First aid kit, resuscitator and gas mask: Site first aid room with 1·1m doors for stretchers near to diving pool and outside access – consult local health office.

Observation windows: Invaluable for coaching and checking underwater actions in swimming and diving.
Additional interest created for spectators.
Windows range from 40mm acrylic or 25mm polycarbonate sheets to 20mm tempered plate glass which is improved when laminated with acrylic film.
Link to underwater speakers for training instruction.

Floodlighting, spot, night and safety lighting: Illumination 1m above surface of an international pool should be 500 lux.

Underwater lighting: Beams angled down with white light only.

Underwater sound: Permanent or temporary.

Public address system and **visual display boards.**

TV circuitry and tracking for events and/or internal management.

Auxiliary rooms: Judges' control area and computer console, temporary press office, plus TV monitor panels, commentary stands and competitors' warm room.
Dry training area, exercise or class assembly area, to involve diving training, trampolining, canoeing practice, sub aqua preparation and synchronised swimming stunt tuition.

Seating: Clear sighting for permanent and temporary spectator galleries – especially the line of sight for the *whole* pool from back rows or low front rows. Set first row minimum 2m away from poolside and allow at least 0·3m for spectators' knees: consider angle of sight to first lane from height of first row.
Consider rollaway spectator bleachers, removable forms, stackable chairs, splash curtains, etc.
Heated poolside seating for swimmers should be solid construction to deck with good fall away from wall for fast drainage.
US short course minimum 500 seats: long course 3000 seats.

Sources: AAU/ASA/NCAA/TUS
See also chapters 10 and 11.

INFORMATION SHEET 3.10

Lanes and lines

Lanes: Contrasting markers and target dimensions detailed in 'Olympic' dimension chart: lane widths range from 1·8m to 2·6m according to category but 2·5m specified for international competition. See information sheets 3.1 and 3.5.
CNCA colour code recommendations for US national competitions: Lane 1 – blue, 2 – red, 3 – white, 4 – orange, 5 – green, 6 – yellow, 7 – brown, 8 – grey, 9 – pink, 10 – lavender.

Lines: Must be securely anchored and easily visible with rope tensioned sufficiently to prevent swinging: rope diameter 5mm to 10mm: floats of 110mm maximum diameter and 50mm minimum should not show more than 50mm above water level.
Racing line accoutrements when not required for general swimming tend to clutter spare spaces unless properly planned storage is considered in advance: some can be coiled in a chamber behind start wall or moved sideways to stretch along side of the pool.
False start ropes for 25m and 33$^1/_3$m pools are set 12m from start and 1·5m above water surface.

Regional/local competitions: final 2m of racing lines at both lane ends can be left free of floats to allow officials to time and judge swimmers clearly: 2m to 4m at each end marked with red floats either continuously, or at a maximum of 0·6m apart: remainder line markers are white or yellow continuously placed at maximum of 0·9m apart: pool length centre clearly distinguished with 2 or 3 abutted red floats. Line floats present little storage problem with mobile winding racks.

National/international competitions: continuous cylindrical marker float dividers, of equivalent colour coding, significantly reduce turbulence and contribute to better racing times; they also provide clear demarcation, especially for TV viewers; often an expensive system, especially for storage. All wave breaking lane dividers essentially prevent racing wash encroaching upon adjacent lanes.

Sources: AAU/ASA/CNCA/FINA
See also chapter 11.

INFORMATION SHEET 3.11

Synchronised swimming needs

Separated diving pools are particularly suitable for synchronised swimming.

Dimensions:

Ideal minimum 12 × 12m and 3m depth, but 250m² pool area preferred
Depths: 2m for limited routines, 3m allows greater stunts or skills
Deck surrounds: 4m preferred for scene staging
Gradients: 1:24 maximum flooring surround slopes for indoor pools acceptable: 1:50 maximum paving slopes to outdoor pool decking preferred
Gallery level seating is important

Water:

Perfect clarity essential
Temperature: 27°C ideal; 24°C practical

Light:

Preferred deck level 1100 lux
Underwater lights essential and should be individually connected with separate dimmer controls
Underwater windows offer advantage for coaching and spectators
Spotlighting facilities are important: theatrical staging and lighting effects useful
Permanent or portable orientation markers for performers are useful

Sound:

Air speakers and underwater speakers are essential
Public address system bounce amid concrete, steel and title can be incomprehensible, instruction can be impossible: inert acoustic controls or ceiling/wall baffles are most important for coaching and successful events: refer chapters 10 and 11
A crystal microphone housed in plastic will not transmit any potential that may exist at the amplifier; it is highly directional to stop feedback, and should be durable, humidity and heat resistant. Outdoor, marine, or all-weather speakers are best – glass fibre being particularly durable

Competition:

First section stunts and second free routines are approved by FINA but not included in Olympic Games. Competitors select from 77 strokes or stunts, and restrict their routine to 5 minutes including 20 seconds maximum deck sequence

INFORMATION SHEET 3.12

Swimming events list

Freestyle: breast-stroke: butterfly: backstroke: medley: relay.
100m: 200m: 400m: 800m: 1500m

Diving: 1m and 3m spring-board
5m and 10m fixed-board

World records are only recognised when swum in 50m pools.

INFORMATION SHEET 3.13

Munich, Montreal and Moscow
Munich Olympic pool – 1972

(Now a sports complex within modern urban village)
Architect: Prof Behnisch & Partners

Main pool:	50 × 21 × 2·66–3·76m plus adjustable floor for $\frac{1}{3}$ length
Training pool:	50 × 12·5 × 2·9–3·5m plus adjustable floor for $\frac{1}{3}$ length
Diving pool:	21·5 × 20 × 5m
Teaching pool:	16$\frac{2}{3}$ × 8 × 0·3–2·77m
Capacity:	Main pool: 3100m³ water with 4 hour turnover
	All pools: 7240m³ water with 5 hour turnover

Temperatures:	Main pool: 26°C
	Diving pool: 28°C
Diving:	1–10m complete facilities, including high lift elevator
	1–3m hydraulic tower board
Seating:	9400 during games, but 2000 thereafter
Timing:	Triple banked circuits plus 3 TV cameras per lane, able to record at 100fps (turning and stroke judges only necessary)
Overflow:	Deck level overflow drainage with water levels lowered 120mm during training
Deck:	3·6m surround with 40mm lip for sloping coving run off to pool of studded non-slip rubber tiling adjusted to suit colour TV illumination
Underwater lighting:	41 units of 1000 watts each
speakers:	12 amplifiers
windows:	6 at head and 1 along the shallow end length

Montreal Olympic pool – 1976

(A modern 'centre de natation')
Architect: Roger Taillibert

Main pool:	50 × 25 × 2m
Training pool:	25 × 12·5 × 2m (with additional 50m pools for training elsewhere in Montreal)
Diving pool:	25 × 25 × 5m with boards/stages positions at 1, 3, 5, 7·5 and 10m
Sub-aqua pool:	10 × 14·6 × 14m
Seating:	10,000 reduced to 2500 afterwards
	Provision for 800 press
Overflow:	Water drained off by shallow perimeter trough 400mm wide, whose outer lip remains fractionally below surface. To reduce water resistance, waves and bounce-back, only 8 of 10 lanes used in Olympics to achieve faster world speed records: considered better than Munich's 8 lanes and 0·5 outer margins required by FINA
Facilities:	At 3 main levels within triple cupola enclosure of 10,000m², covering:
	Reception area
	1500 places for clothing
	Gymnasia
	Massage rooms
	Sauna bath
	Medical centre
	Cafeteria
	Electronic controls room
	Judges and officials annexes
	Press office and service areas

Moscow Olympic pools – 1980

(Facilities located in widely separated city districts)

Swimming:	Main all-weather 45,000 public stadium in central Moscow includes two 50 × 25m pools with 10,000 seating grandstand
Diving:	Palace of water sports in recreation park Sokoliniki-Ismailove stages the diving separately from swimming contests
Water polo:	Indoor gymnasium sports palace at Luzhniki district caters for water polo and 12,000 seating: main field events central sports arena of 103,000 capacity also located close by
Training:	In the Olympic village just beyond Luzhniki there are a further 2 indoor pools and one outdoor
Recreation:	Even at Baltic resort of Pirota, Olympic yachting events include a swimming pool and international club

There are already 22 other public community pools in Moscow and seven 50m pools reserved for Olympics.

4 The leisure pool complex

Not so very long ago, Roman bathing meant a festive orgy. More recently to possess a private swimming pool, especially if it was heart-shaped or piano-shaped, showed extravagant taste. At the same time, however, all public pools were always built square, and most managements carefully practised segregation by sex. So it is astonishing to discover our municipal authorities now setting the pace with leisure complexes that have more in common with ancient Rome or modern Hollywood than with parochial local baths of more recent time. The result is 'water experience'[1] for a community, one that can compete with the seaside, day trip, or television. Leisure pool structures should 'seek a sense of wonder or enjoyment, an adventure of discovery'.[2]

4.1 A new concept

Pools where the 'contents matter more than the container',[3] can become adventure playgrounds for adults as well as children. Hence, designing the leisure complex is less a science applied to buildings, more a science applied to people.

When considering the activity of people, it becomes apparent they sit in groups of family or friends, wander back and forth to promenades, or cafés, or piers for entertainment; shallow beaches encourage toddlers to the edge of the water; all children enjoy the movement of water and most older bathers rarely swim out of their depth.

A small number of architects have pioneered a new generation of free-style swimming pools. Some have already reached their second and third generation of

4.1 *A community leisure pool. This artificial lake at the holiday village of El Capistrano, Malaga in Spain, is an efficiently filtered swimming pool. Notice the skimmer in the far wall and the pool ladder on the right*
Rutherford Espanola, Madrid

4.1

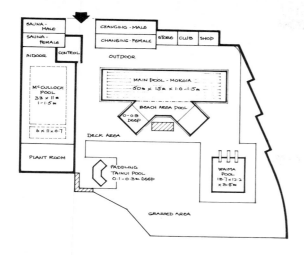

4.2

4.3

designs with resulting leisure palaces that are positively exuberant. This theme introduces pools that are not restricted to up and down swims, but bulge brashly into unusual shapes. As with all good progressive themes, ideas develop better with freedom from the establishment, or in this instance, freedom from the sporting regulation. An exciting environment can be the result, but a hazardous one if careful thought is not given to detailed specification and safety.

One in five British people already swim regularly. The rapidly growing appeal of multi-sports centres has given rise to a forecast that 200 new leisure and sports pool complexes could be operating by the year 2000, and that by then, two in every five people will be swimming regularly either for leisure or for sport. It was the French who said 'the English take their pleasures sadly'; yet it is in England where the local public pool *pleasure centre* has been mainly developed.

Leisure resorts When it is appreciated that *ideal resorts* naturally offering sun, sand, social entertainment and swimming are very few and far between, the need to provide more artificial recreation places is a driving force.

In France, where the government reclaimed the salt

4.2 *Leisure pool, Swim-Arama, Mount Wellington, New Zealand. Indoor/outdoor complex using natural thermal waters; indoor 30°C and outdoor 25°C*

4.3 *Leisure activity areas: the relationship between activities in a leisure complex*

4.4 *Large areas of shallow water, waves, waterfalls, pliable rocks, and tropical plants are some of the essential ingredients for the modern leisure pool. Whitley Bay*
Architects: Gillinson Barnett & Partners
Photo: Tony Whibley

4.4

4.5

4.6

4.5 *An emphatic pyramid for the leisure pool's roof at Bletchley*
Architects: Faulkner-Brown, Hendy, Watkinson, Stonor

4.6 *Inside the Bletchley pyramid freeform leisure pool*
Architect: Faulkner-Brown, Hendy, Watkinson, Stonor
Photo: W. J. Toomey

marsh shores of the Golfe du Lion to create the new regional resort and marina of La Grande Motte, the impressive pyramid architecture, hard and soft landscaping and intimate courtyard dwellings for the Village du Soleil clearly show that 'today there are moments when an extraordinary environment is needed . . . . Certain people find it in travelling, others in a return to nature, others in dreams of the artificial and luxury of a palace . . . the framework must create a sense of wonder . . .'.[4] The leisure centre design should understand this spirit and then supply ways to excite interest.

An ordinary swimming pool offers the most concentrated possible use of space, but a 'pack-em-in' philosophy must never be allowed to develop. The leisure pool is usually more expensive, incurring extra maintenance as a result of the extra use.

Very few public pools recover their annual operating costs, although compared with most other municipal activities they incur least expenditure. There are 'user and economic advantages in linking sport with recreation'[5] and swimming pools can become profitable when part of an overall thriving local complex. A leisure pool creates profitability, especially when economies can be gained from sharing common services, administration, design and construction.

Leisure resources In leisure pools, shallows might range from beaching to 0·5m, play areas from 0·5 to 1·2m, activity areas from 1·2 to 1·5m, with swimming and wave chasing at 1·5m plus. They require at least as much deck area as water area, plus a wide variety of fun and play ideas (see information sheets in chapter 12, Landscaping).

One recurring American layout design for regional park pools introduces interlocking-circular shapes to distinguish play and activity areas, and, at the same time, to provide at least 1:1 pool to deck allocation around the whole pool, 90 per cent of which is shallow water area. Nearby country club-house facilities are also provided to serve the whole pool park area. At Whitley Bay, England, the swimming range is extended further into bathing proper in the popular tonal baths in Hadrian's Suite (Sauna and Aeratone, Turkish and Russian). When comparing leisure pools with existing sports pool stocks, even a fairly casual study soon shows that most people prefer almost everything else *but* swimming!

There are: *water activities* in which people like to paddle, splash, play, swing, climb, slide, jump, dive, bathe and swim, and *poolside activities* that involve sitting, reading, sleeping, sunbathing, relaxing, lounging, onlooking, picnicking, playing and running.

The main users are children, teenagers, families, beginners, and senior citizens, and *the main areas* in use are water, deck, water's edge, shallows, refreshments, solarium, changing, cleansing, back and forth routes.

4.2 The seaside inside
Europe was never noted for enjoying its pools: 'European bathers are patients and even the English are washed'.[6] The idea that baths should be fun and an encouragement to swim developed mainly with the American yard pool and the Californian climate. In large-scale planning, Disneyland was the first to create a huge imaginative aquatic environment.

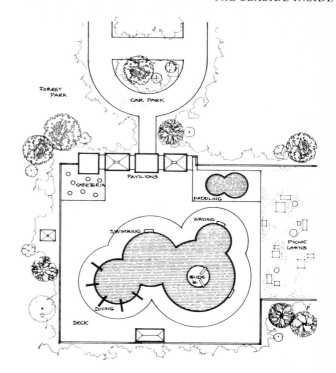

DECK AREA 50% : WATER AREA 50% : 90% SHALLOWS

4.7 *Bull Run Leisure Park, Fairfax, Virginia, USA*

4.8 *A series of deepening pools with over 90 per cent of the water area given to shallows and ample decking at this large east coast pool of Pohick Bay Regional Park, USA*
Hoffman Publications: Swimming Pool Weekly/Age
Photo: Blue Ridge Aerial Surveys

45

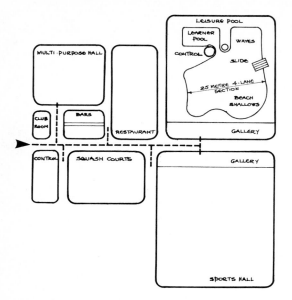

4.9 *Herringthorpe Leisure Centre, Rotherham. The first generation of public leisure pools in the UK*

Then the Japanese created their 'art of holiday entertainment which is more than 50 per cent psychology'.[7] Just an hour's drive from Tokyo, promoters developed a 500-acre Summerland Park (designed by Ishimoto Architectural) that focused upon a 70 × 25m spaceframe covered wave pool, pulling-in well over one million visitors every year. The rectangular pool with rounded shallow end has waves and shallows, and plenty of carpeted and covered areas for hundreds of families to picnic inside as if on ordinary meadows. There are also snack bars and souvenir stands, tropical gardens, wading and boating moats, with Polynesian dancing shows on stage every hour beside the central wave pool. This huge leisure structure draws a weekend peak of 8000 visitors a day and even inveigles people into the park away from the countryside and banks of the local river meandering outside.

Exotic façades The architectural idea of seaside fantasy has long and established traditions in Britain. The first real compact seaside-inside emerged with a modest scheme dubbed 'Costa-del-Rotherham', a leisure centre built near the steel town of Sheffield. In the era of the shopping precinct and boating marina, it was reasonable for the sports centre and leisure pool to combine in one covered complex. By using multi-coloured surfaces, bright and artificial textures, and plenty of side-show attractions, an all-year holiday atmosphere was created.

The glamour of show business, warmth and night life appeals to a far larger catchment area than does the plain sobre public pool. Developing leisure and recreational centres for drama, the arts, crafts, debates, boulevard restaurants, and so on draws communities together, and attracts visitors into exciting sunny domes or transparent paraboloids. Large covered areas might involve huge engineering costs, but the economic persuasions add up to many more people continually using such facilities than any equivalent sized Olympic sports stadium.

A variation on the inside-outside theme is the Scandinavian leisure pools complex. Here, an outdoor lido-type pool makes up the major part of the whole centre, along with several other indoor pools having adjoining sliding glazed walls. There is one snag though. Such dual schemes often need to operate separately, sometimes even with separate changing facilities, for bathers can flood from out to in, and the other way round, according to the changing weather. With careful management, however, such schemes can offer cost benefits in mutual plant and services making them cheaper to construct and maintain than an all-under-the-one-cover complex.

4.3 Community pools

Olympic sports pools can become grossly expensive and giant leisure schemes often get clumsy; there is strong argument to accept the advantages of the versatile community size pool. The overall cost of a 50m Olympic pool complex can be 100 times that of an everyday 25m community pool. And prestige schemes become more a national decision than a local affair.

There is no denying the need for national and regional centres for serious sport, but the thoughtful provision of local satellite pools in and around an urban sprawl is a more useful and economic proposition, giving a far better service to the many different communities. These local pools are an essential community centre just like the shops, or the church, or the school, since most people prefer their own kind of surroundings with scaled-down versions of the best facilities.

National plans for pools A number of different approaches have been used to find the ideal satellite pool and its most favoured size. The Germans introduced their series of Golden Plans and built at least 7500 public pools by the mid-70s. Their consistently high specifications and immaculate operating standards are probably the best in the world. The Dutch and the Swedish have similar, but smaller-scale programmes.

The French conceived the Concours des Mille Piscines which probably amounts to 1200 additional community pools created over a 12-year period. With admirable flair, a national competition was held and three winning designs selected, each scheme featuring an opening roof structure. The prize was the opportunity to mass produce components. The programme has proved very successful – there is even a busy swimming pool training school now in operation – and some attractive ideas have been used in creating that outdoor feeling indoors.

British governments have taken a more pragmatic view. They preferred to allocate funds and to encourage through information and advice the adoption of suitable designs. So they supported the idea of a Sports Council technical unit in sport to gain practical experience and to design their own model for a community. Following the principle 'don't expect ideas if you've none yourself', the special design unit drew together local pool needs into one scheme for the town of Ashton-under-Lyne. They published plans and findings and then helped the town see the ideas through. As a result, realism has been brought into their specification and into the swimming pool advisory service.

There is one common element throughout all National Programmes – the need to combine leisure with sport, and to blend regular proportions with informality. The result has been the popular choice of providing basic 25m unit lengths to allow proper sports swimming practice with sufficient space for recreation.

4.10 *Inside view of the Swindon Leisure Centre showing the control module at the opposite end of the main pool, with the diving pool behind it. Note the observation portholes into the diving pool beneath the control platform*
Architect: Gillinson Barnett & Partners
Photo: JRW Photography

Self-help schemes Some communities cannot wait for official sponsorship and financial support and so set up self-help schemes. With an enthusiastic fund-raising campaign, one town in Yorkshire developed their very own kind of pool into a self-operated centre, and now their *people's pool* regularly makes a continuing profit.

But it is in America that the philosophy of self-help and free enterprise has really developed many neighbourhood pools, with a financing principle that 'people who do not use the pool pay nothing towards its cost and upkeep'. One social club, in order to prove their enthusiasm to set up a community pool, collected $100,000 advance annual fees as down payment from over 1000 local families in less than three weeks. In such circumstances, the pool designer can consider his particular clientèle totally and generously.

A public pool design for the community should involve all ages, all citizens, learners and experienced swimmers, in an all-embracing environment for recreation, competition, teaching, safety training, synchronised swimming displays, events, parties, games or sun lounging. A formidable task! Building individual satellite pools for different needs offers the chance to separate main facilities to satisfy more inhabitants of large population areas.

Financing principles cover government loan, local tax or grant, endowment or company donation, prospective user fees, local subscription and official lotteries.

How many? When planning pool numbers and assuming half the population will want to swim in summer, an American ideal promotes:
- local outdoor 'walk-to' pools (75ft length) for every 10,000 neighbourhood population
- an indoor pool for every 50,000
- a large community complex for every 150,000.

In Europe, satellite pools might well be:
- $16^2/_3$m for 10,000 population, or
- 25m for 25,000;
- with perhaps 33m for 50,000 to 100,000.

Federal Republic of Germany *indoor* pool coefficients suggest water area for population as follows:
- $16^2/_3 \times 8$m for 10,000
- 25×8m for 25,000
- 25×10m for 40,000
- 25×12.5m for 60,000
- 25×12.5m
  plus 12.5×6m for 70,000
- 25×12.5m
  plus $16^2/_3 \times 8$m for 80,000
- $25 \times 16^2/_3$m
  plus $16^2/_3 \times 8$m for 100,000

plus *outdoor* pools totalling 10 times greater water areas for similar populations.

Perhaps the ideal is to aim for a 25m equivalent pool for every 25,000 population (see also information sheet 1.8). It is often better to consider various facilities than standardised provisioning and to try for better coverage by relating local pools with educational programmes. Since there is really no typical bather, there should be no typical pool.

4.4 Hyperpools

Economies of scale can apply with the swimming pool. Not only does the greatest attract more attention, but bigger budgets buy in the 'superstars', such as surf pools and wave

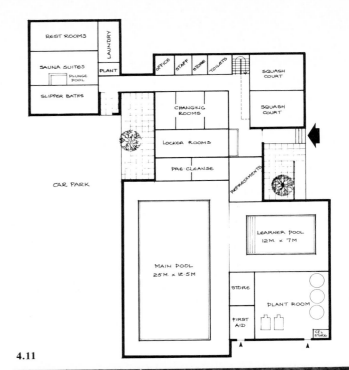

4.11

4.13

4.12

machines, tropical gardens and adventure playgrounds, often all under one roof.

Leisure places depend upon different national characteristics. And social environment plays a large part in what the swimmer expects from his swimming pool. In America, outdoor picnics play leading parts for larger leisure pools set in forest range lands. Space and interchanging open-air activities draw the crowds to these out-of-town parks, while keeping the noise factor at distance.

A cosmopolitan approach has been developed for the German urban recreation park. A wide range of popular interests are situated all within walking distance, giving city people choice and space to roam. As some example of the complete complex, Gruga Park in Essen completed in 1969 includes:

- exhibition hall and rotunda
- concert pavillion and building school
- restaurants and milk bars
- playgrounds and leisure gardens
- aquarium and terrarium
- lake and chine
- cemetery and memorial
- open parkland and hothouse
- tennis courts and roller skating rink
- zoo and model ship pool
- Gruga hall, baths and swimming pool
- as well as road and rail links within the park area.

Similar concepts are rapidly being developed in the Middle East for pool parks or conference centres where relaxation and recreation must be close at hand for tourists and travelling executives.

The Japanese favour the closely concentrated and covered Summerland centre located well out of town, but on a direct transport link, where pools and waves, wading channels and 'half-a-jungle' of tropical gardens entertain the visitors. In Indonesia, a tourist programme encourages the Dreamland concept outside in the sun, where there are different attractions throughout one huge complex, involving cottage-hotel, golf course, motor racing circuit, zoological gardens, drive-in cinema, bowling alley, restaurants, nightclubs, lakes, oceanarium, medical baths, and of course, separate pools for Olympic style racing, waves, playing, diving, sliding, fountains and even flowing moat for strolling in at 1m/s, all circumnavigated by a pleasure boating canal.

An altogether different approach has been taken in Russia where one of the world's largest single outdoor pools,

4.11 *25m swimming pool. Community centre pool for Ashton-under-Lyne by Technical Unit for Sport (TUS)*

4.12 *In some leisure parks wave-making machines are particularly powerful*
Wellenbad Dolder, Zurich
Swiss National Tourist Office

4.13 *It should be remembered that any large recreation complex will attract large numbers of visitors, so all the amenities must be suitable, as for instance this vast car park for the Anthony Wayne Recreation Area, Bear Mountain, NY*
Palisades Interstate Park
Photo: Stockmeyer

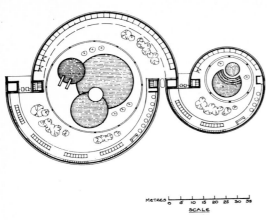

4.14 *Middle East pool park, based upon design for South Kodai Park, Mecca*
Architect: John S. Bonnington Partners

4.15 *Jaya Ancol Dreamland Project, Djakarta. Water park complex: 'A garden of fantasy'*

4.16 *This giant circular open-air public pool in Moscow is used throughout the year. It is cordoned into sections around the international standard competition and 6 m diving pools, and the whole complex can cope with 10,000 bathers*
Novosti Press Agency – A.P.N.

catering all year round for bathing by Moscovites and their families, provides also for racing and diving in the sports pool centre of the huge heated circular pool. A kind of 'steam pillow'[8] heat layer above the warmed water surface protects swimmers in the winter, who seem to prefer outdoor leisure bathing in the waters surrounding the central sports pool (see also chapter 14.2).

4.5 Entertaining architecture
It has taken considerable time for baths to move from strict symmetry into freeform ideas. Classical lines still help curb mad-capped bathers by making it simpler to devise a socially acceptable pool. Breaking tradition in the baths

world means first turning away from the rigid rectangle. The 'boxed-in' pool with ample roof well lights is still considered the best by many, but too often turns out the most boring.

Simply covering a pool to 'keep the weather out and the sunshine in' is usually easier for formal designs. But an all-glazed walling to box-like buildings often means glare on water or total artificial illumination, which is unappealing to sunshine swimmers. Natural top lighting has proved better so far. Most contemporary designers prefer to adopt the all-roof light type structure with limited walling windows. Architects, in returning to elemental enclosure forms, have reintroduced the pyramid and the dome to cover latest pleasure pools. But, the rigid geometry of an all-glazed pyramid can be difficult to relate to other buildings alongside. And the smooth curve of an acrylic dome does not take kindly to squareness inside (see chapter 10.11).

Extra fans and ventilation will be needed within transparent structures to offset the greenhouse effect (see chapter 14.8 and 9, Ventilation and humidity control). In a temperate climate, designers take advantage of the free solar gain to plant tropical trees, or to create solaria, or to send cable cars up into the roof space for fairground fun over and above wave, surf and slide pools. Large beach areas and coloured changing tents all add to the much preferred outdoor illusion (see chapter 12.4, Landscaping).

'*A stately pleasure-dome*'[9] As the Romans discovered, the dome can span large areas, does save space, and is self-supporting. It also combines well with freeform pool shapes . . . which the Romans did not try! A 45m translucent dome at Swindon, England blends on top of a berm – an earth bank that grows out of the landscape – to cover a freeform leisure pool that is an extremely popular centre for the town, especially when at night the whole place glows with light from within (see chapter 10, Superstructures).

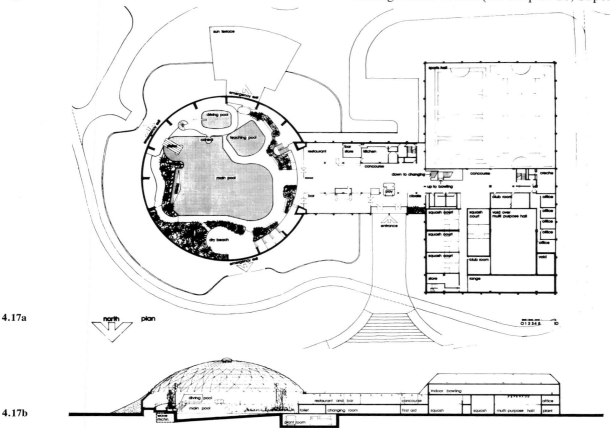

4.17a

4.17b

4.17a and b *Swindon Leisure Centre, Oasis pleasure dome: plan and section*
Architect: Gillinson Barnett & Partners

4.18 *Swindon's Leisure Centre 40m dome blending into the soil berm*

Architect: Gillinson Barnett & Partners
Photo: O. F. Clarke

4.19

4.19 *Safer, non-swimmers' pool water slide at Böblingen near Stuttgart*
Cement & Concrete Association
Architect: Werner Gabriel
Photo: Fred Naleppa

4.20 *As many as 2500 slides per hour can be provided by this 6·5m water lubricated multi-slide. The sliders safely speed into 0·9m of water since the lowest section is just covered by poolwater that acts as a brake on 50kph velocities*
Playsafe Ltd, Sussex
The Aldershot News

4.6 Entertaining extras

There is almost no limit to extras and accessories. They cover an amazing variety of useful ideas and, of course, plenty of gimmicks. Most fit into every kind of pool, and even before people get into the pool, there are places for pin-tables and one-armed bandits to guarantee better profits and divert attention from vandalism (see information sheets 8.3, 11.9 and 12.3).

Slides This item, whether straight plunge, humped, curved or giant-sized, is consistently popular everywhere in all leisure pools. If slides are set over deep water, their use is restricted to swimmers only: if set in shallow water, they are then restricted by safety requirements. Some pool designers maintain, with good reason, that water depths for plunge slides should be equivalent to those for similar height diving-boards: a straight slide down by a swimmer at steep angle into water can be almost as fast as a diver's entry.

There must be no obstacles nor sudden depth variations, and there must be consideration for a safe separation between slide lanes. Slightly splayed ends can help on multi-slides. The overhanging lip end must be set firmly, preferably on a solid deck or underwater plinth, though some on floats rise and fall with main water level changes. A guide to safe pool dimensions or age-group depths is given in information sheets 4.5 and 4.6, but precise specification depends primarily upon different manufacturers' stipulations.

When slides are too fast or too steep, children will be bumped along any intermediate and more level sections. In order to cope with both 'the sedate descent that scarcely ruffles the hair and the frightening velocity that even the wildest teenager cannot criticise',[10] the slide lip over a suitable horizontal length can be set just below surface water level: providing swimmers are made well aware of this underwater obstruction, the layer of water over the chute end acts as an excellent brake, permitting slides into shallow waters where youngsters can safely and quickly regain their feet. Reducing speed this way avoids collisions in the pool water, but supervision must be provided to control overcrowding at the top and to stop the next slider following on too quickly.

Giant slides are so popular and so heavily used that their inspection and maintenance has to be increased accordingly. Often the 7m height level alone is more than satisfactory; those continually traipsing up steps to the 10m level or higher find it tiring – even for youngsters. In Japan one very successful 16-lane high slide has a busy poolside elevator.

In Kentucky enthusiasts are offered a downhill water toboggan, giving swimmers 45 second 'wet and wild rides' on Styrofoam mats: the winding downhill run is constructed from gunite concrete and finished in pool epoxy coating – in all, a permanent summer and more moderate version of the bobsleigh Cresta Run at St Moritz. Or how

4.21 *37m long giant multi-slide is extremely popular with the youngsters. The climb to the full 10m height is somewhat daunting for many adults, but there is a more popular half-way stage. Jaya Ancol Complex Djakarta*
Biwater Ltd, Surrey

about pools at different levels to build exciting cascade waterchutes from pool to pool.

4.7 Conversion to leisure

As leisure pool popularity is accelerating, demand is exceeding supply. Existing facilities are being converted to new uses – admittedly with never quite the same advantage as the all new purpose-designed pool. Each situation needs looking at on its own merits. For instance, there are two particularly interesting and appreciative conversions in England on town sites that fortunately also offered invaluable car parking space.

Following a fall in market activity, an obsolete corn exchange was economically converted into an indoor, semi-circular pool of 300m³ water, yet providing four competition training lanes. The original balcony over one end of the floor of the Exchange is now a glass-fronted cafeteria overlooking the pool. An even more unexpected revamp of an institution building was made with an old gaol, which has now been suitably converted into a sports centre complete with 25 × 10m pool. And at Barnveld, in the Netherlands, a cattle market has now taken on new meaning to become their converted indoor sports centre and swimming pool (see chapter 16.5 for conversions and refurbishing). If anything like a future 50:50 share between sports pools and leisure pools is to come about quickly, some imaginative conversions will have to be developed fast.

References

1 Gillinson Barnett & Partners, 1975
2 Kenneth Lindley, *Seaside Architecture,* London, Hugh Evelyn, 1973
3 Gillinson, Barnett & Partners, 1975
4 Jean Balladur, 1970
5 Sports Council TUS Bulletin 1, *Public Indoor Swimming Pools,* 1973
6 Lawrence Wright, *Clean and Decent,* London, Routledge, 1971
7 Lindley, op. cit.
8 Vera Kondratenko, *Swimming: a mass sport in the USSR,* 1975
9 Samuel Coleridge, *Kubla Khan,* 1797
10 C. R. Clayton, *Slides for Leisure Pools, Swimming Pool,* March 1976

INFORMATION SHEET 4.1

Leisure complex – 'a town within a town'

Modern leisure centres involve:

Swimming	Recreation	Entertainment	Sport	Amusements	Viewing
Main pool	Bowling alley	Conference room	Playing fields	Deck games	Oceanarium
Diving pool	Beauty parlour	Exhibition hall	Ball game courts	Table games	Motor racing circuit
Wave pool	Discotheque	Restaurant and night club	Gymnasium	Solarium	Zoological gardens
Play pool	Picnic lawns/lounges	Gambling casino	Skating	Theatre	Drive-in cinema
Sauna baths	Adventure grounds	Beer garden	Golf driving range	Model boats	Pop concerts
Scuba tank	Nursery	Shopping precinct	Shooting range	Arcades	Gardens
Medical baths	Playground	Airdomes	Combative sports	Water ski tank	Parkland

INFORMATION SHEET 4.2

Community pool specification

Based upon 25m project, sponsored by the Departments of Environment and Education and Science, for Ashton-under-Lyne, UK (TUS Design Note 2).
To cater for casual swimmers and to meet local competitive needs.

Facilities

To anticipate heavy usage; the specification also to emphasise resistance to corrosion, and especially to consider economic control of heat, light, sound needs.

1 Open plan design and to cater for disabled persons singly or in groups.
2 Based upon two/four duty staff for quiet/busy periods: cashier/foyer desk to oversee several control areas.
3 To provide dry access to staffroom/staff toilet, store, office and self-service refreshment facilities.
4 Changing rooms to be adjustable for varying male/female ratios and to provide 12 modesty cubicles.
5 Dressing areas for 58 adults (considering open changing area at 0·5m² per person and bather flow of 300–340 per hour); 315 communal lockers; and combined clothing store.
6 Easy to maintain precleanse area with showers/wash basins/wcs en route to pool from changing area; toilets to provide paraplegic cubicle.
7 First aid room with direct access outside.
8 Refreshments, vending and viewing area.
9 Plantroom and poolside stores.
10 Two squash courts.
11 Sauna suite for 14 bathers, restroom for 35, with 1·35m plunge bath, needle jet shower, and slipper/shower baths.
12 Launderette.
13 Public address system.
14 Warmed window seats.

Tanks

15 Main: 25 × 12·5m (6 lane), 0·9 to 1·8m depths, capacity 450m³, potential bathing load 250 peak.
Note: 1m and 3m spring-boards excluded, reducing airspace, waterspace and costs; water chute preferred.
16 Learner: 12 × 7m, 0·5 to 0·8m depths, capacity 55m³, floor tile markers spaced out as standing points for 70 children.
17 Full width steps for entry and to build up confidence in children's pool.
18 Glazed ceramic tiles (frost-proof vitrified not considered necessary for an indoor pool).
19 Inlets and outlets 'childproofed' to prevent tampering and to include 'unpokeable' orifices.
20 Four pool ladders and pool slide.

Services

21 Main pool water temperature 27°C/air 28°C, learner pool 28°C.
22 Two by 460kW automatic gas-fired, low pressure hot water boilers, each capable of 60 per cent design load – 82°C flow and 71°C return.
23 Heat exchangers for main pool 275kW and learner pool 36kW.
24 Ventilation: input 6m³/s, extracted 6·65m³/s, to provide 0·015m³/s of air per m² water/wet surface area, separate system to provide eight air changes per hour in changing room; ducted plenum system, no opening windows, nor recirculation. Negative pressure (−10 per cent) in hall to ensure air flow from other rooms and to minimise spread of chlorine corrosive air.
25 Air distribution at low velocity to minimise draughts with added background warmed seating; no cooling, heat recovery system via heat wheel.
26 Lighting at water surface 250 lux, changing rooms 100 lux, emergency lighting system.
27 Gas chlorination system offering 1 to 2ppm free residual chlorination.
28 Pressure sand air scoured filters rated at 12·5m³/m²/hr with dolomitic pH control layer. Turnovers: main – 3½h, learner – 1h.

Deck

29 Asbestos-cement, hollow cavity decking with stainless steel fixings.
30 Profiled and textured floor tiles, non-slip and easy to clean.
31 Flutes and open channels to gravity drainage.
32 Side widths: 2m; 2·4m to traffic areas; 3·25 to shallow end; falls 1:24.
33 Washdown hose points.
34 150 stackable chairs.

Structure

35 Lightweight, value for money building with external walls of loadbearing cavity brickwork.
36 Internal walls fairfaced with smooth dense red brick of low water absorption, flush pointing in pool hall, and cavity insulation.
37 Roof-steel castellated beam structure exposed to interior but protected by zinc-rich epoxy primer, micaceous iron oxide undercoat and four chlorinated rubber based topcoats.
38 Suspended ceiling not specified. A vapour barrier may not remain inviolate indefinitely – even with a pressurised roof zone and expensive sealing.
39 Main pool ceiling height 4·4m; learner at 2·75m to improve acoustics and confidence for children.
40 Sound absorption to achieve maximum reverberation times – main pool 1·8 seconds; learner 1·5 seconds at 500 to 2000Hz.
41 U value: 0·85W/m²/°C: bituminous roof felt finish with insulation and roof lights; windows double glazed to pool hall and limited in number to save expense, limit maintenance and reduce glare: glazing below 0·9m height in toughened glass.

Costing allocations

Preliminaries and foundations (additions for soil stabilisation work included)	18 per cent
Pool structure and superstructure	37 per cent
Finishes and fittings	17 per cent
Services and equipment	28 per cent
18 month work schedule	

Source: TUS.

INFORMATION SHEET 4.3

Hyperpools – local, regional and national

Location		No of pools	Pool shape	Bathing load	Pools area	Pool depths	Water capacity	Water temperature	Filter turnover average
					m²	m	m³	°C	Hours
Local projects									
1974	Project 25m Ashton-under-Lyne	2	Rectangular	250	400	0·5–1·8	500	27	3½
1974	Leisure centre Herringthorpe, Rotherham	4 in 1	Freeform	300	550	0·15–1·7	450	28	3
Regional and national									
1972	Bull Run Park Virginia	4 in 2	Interlocking circles	700	1800	90% @ 1·2	2500	28	4–6
1967	Summerland Tokyo	1 + 1	Main – rounded rectangular	1500	2000	1·0 av (0·7m perimeter wading)	2000	26	2–4
1974	Jaya Ancol Djakarta	7	Main – fanshape	3000	6000	1·2 av	7000	26	4½
1960	Moskva pool Moscow	1–4	Round – 7 sections	6000	13,000	1·6 av (6m diving centre)	23,000	28	8

Notes

1 Filtration turnovers range from ½ hour for paddling pools with high disinfection rates; to 3 or 4 hour main pools, to 10 hour diving pools.
See chapter 13 for details of recommended pool turnovers.

2 See chapters 3 and 4 for illustrations and plans.

INFORMATION SHEET 4.4

Extra leisure pool features

Waters
Waves – various patterns
Waterfall and cascade
Fountains and spouts
Sloping shallows
Turbulent baths
Jetstreams
Flaming waters
Play stream
Canal ride
River pool
Play pool
Poolwater bar and seats
Scuba pool

Equipment
Giant slide
Underwater lights and sound
Observation windows
Control bubble
Water treadmill
Water see-saw
Trapeze
Surf rafts
Floating bandstand
Cable cars
Waterski tank
Needlejet showers
Pneumatic rocks

Environment
Solarium and artificial suns
Tropical jungle
Beaches
Picnic lawns
Games area
Poolside alcoves
Underwater exploration
Caves and shelves
Rock platforms
Rubber rocks

Environment
Panoramic balconies
Acoustic spheres
Aerial walkways

See also Checklist of suitable landscape features for pools: information sheet 12.3.

Multi-slide at Jaya Ancol Complex Djakarta

INFORMATION SHEET 4.5

Slide dimensions guide meeting recreational requirements
(Refer National Associations for approved standards and manufacturers for slide performances)

Metric

Slide			Water depth		Surface clearance	
Height above deck	Width	Overall length	Beneath slide lip	Maintained forward (1·5 × A)	Forward length (2 × A)	Deck width min.
A	B	C	D	E	F	G
1 Straight 1·5	0·5	2·5	0·9	2·25	3·0	2·0
2 Straight 2·0	0·6	3·0	0·9	3·00	4·0	2·5
3 Straight 2·5	0·6	4·0	1·0	3·75	5·0	3·0
4 Straight 3·0	0·7	4·5	1·3	4·50	6·0	3·5
5 Straight 3·5	0·7	5·5	1·5	5·25	7·0	4·5
6 Curved 2·0	0·6	3·5	0·9	3·00	4·0	1·0
7 Curved 3·0	0·7	5·0	1·3	4·50	6·0	2·0

Notes

1 Manufacturers must be consulted for their own recommended depths and clearances in consideration of their slide speeds and angle of descent into the water. Speeds up to 30mph are achieved.

2 A slide must not project a swimmer into a diver's path; nor should the slide centre line intersect a diving board centre line within 3m (also refer to F).

3 There must be at least 1m clearance all round from pool edges or other equipment at a point 1m along the centre line from the slide lip.

4 The slide lip should overhang the water's edge at least 0·5m.

5 The slide lip should not exceed 0·5m above the water.

6 **Alternative Age guide to water depths when slide lip flattens out for 1m and is covered by 100mm of pool water H:**

Age of user	Slide lanes	Water depth at slide lip submerged for 1m at 10° slope to 100mm under-water	Safety area no depth variations, nor protrusions, no obstacles nor water currents	User capacity
Year	No	m	m²	per minute
up to 5	1	0·25	10	3
5 to 10	2	0·5 to 0·75	15	10
teenagers and	2 × 4m high 1·00		20	15
adults	4 × 7m high 1·0		25	50
swimmers	4 × 7m high 1·50		30	40

Note

Peak capacity approx 20 slides per minute, which equals 80 per minute on a 4 lane slide. However, these short-term peaks depend upon proper supervision on the platform and in the water (see photograph **4.20**).

Sources: NSPI/SPATA/Aquaslide/Playsafe.
See also chapters 2, 3 and 7 for Diving dimensions; and information sheet 11.9.

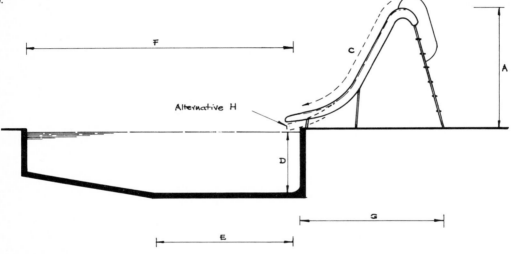

Slide dimensions guide: recreational requirements

Slide dimensions guide: heights

INFORMATION SHEET 4.6

Slide and deck level board installation – plan

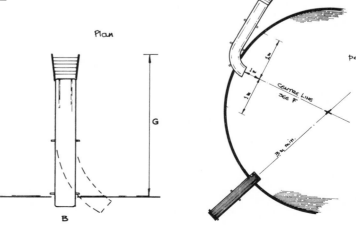

5 The special bathing place

5.1 Bathing therapies

There are innumerable *specials* in bathing all of which, in one way or another, offer comfort and therapy. What might seem unusual to many people of the world is often quite ordinary to the few. Spa bathing, for instance, is now neglected, though English-speaking countries are reviving, and promoting a need for more building, or better maintenance of existing special pools and baths. For example, even though the famous medical spa treatment centre at Bath in England was eventually closed down in 1976 (at its peak it provided 50,000 treatments per year) it was estimated in the 1977 *Proposals for the Redevelopment of Bath as a Spa* that with group therapy for patients, and by developing spa pools, probably 200,000 treatments per year at a conservative estimate would be possible.

The natural hot spa waters gush away and are soon forgotten if facilities are not kept up to date; or if the water-doctors who prescribe the treatments are discouraged or untrained in spa treatment methods, then the 'cure' is neglected or becomes unfashionable.

Contemporary therapies The opposite of this situation exists throughout Europe where there is great experience in constant spa hydrotherapeutic practice. The development of thermen hospitals in spa towns, of old and new facilities and varied mineral waters and bathing treatments, is now a vital part of the private and state social health services. Yet Britain, now in Europe, looks curiously at Continental hydropathic clinics where such extensive 'Social Thermalism' flourishes.

Britain's widespread 19th-century water treatments have long been replaced by a National Health Service that is almost totally non-bathing orientated, except for physiotherapy in water. Water itself, in official eyes, has no real curative effect; yet the Continentals actually seem to enjoy their next-to-nature basic cures getting real relief from traditional waters. The British (and Americans) argue modern medicine is better, and drugs and pills are simpler to administer (if becoming more expensive). Continental Europeans do not disagree, but now take both systems for their own health.

The main medical pools used today can be considered to provide:
- Spa-therapy: medical treatment in mineral waters
- Hydrotherapy: recuperative treatment in fresh waters
- Thalassotherapy: medical treatment in sea waters
- Heliotherapy: use of sun-baths or solaria in treating disease
- Hydropathy: medical treatment by internal and external application of waters.

5.2 Health spas

The soothing effects of both hot and cold mineral waters have been venerated for centuries and ancient Romans provided both sauna baths and spa baths in their thermae. The natural waters of the classical thermalism now used at balneotherapeutic centres all over Europe except the UK allow patients, or rather physicians, to select a health spa and climate to suit the particular ailment (although artificially doctored bathing waters are considered by some equally effective). There was and still is medical support for chalybeate, sulphurous and saline waters for prevention, treatment and convalescence. It is generally agreed that the lavish style and ornate architecture of the bathing places and seaside add a psychological tinge to the physical fillip given by water treatment. Enjoying the treatment is more than half its success.

West Germany publicises over 250 *Bad* towns for water and climatic cures; Italy has at least 100 thermal resorts; France another 100 spas with 1200 mineral springs and 30 thermal hospitals; Eastern Europe is almost equally well served with many state-run centres.

True balneology In Germany, Institutes of Balneology scientifically examine and investigate their health resorts and centres of rehabilitation, not only for medical suitability and better treatment, but also for benefits in the bioclimate. For the climate and the area (and local entertainments) around a resort are just as important as the mineral waters it offers. Usually, a geological fault provides the thermal waters and moderates the climate where, for example, in places like Ulm City, the commercial benefits were recognised as far back as the 15th century by their flourishing 200 public baths.

Today the majority who adopt the 'Fitness-Bad' consider spa-water the vital asset, more valuable than primeval or even potable stocks. Balneologists explain the best natural warm mineral springs are formed from nascent hydrogen distilled out of granite rocks at great depths, which combines with the oxygen of metallic oxides to produce original water and pure mineral ions.

German, Swiss and Japanese epidermists have shown

5.1

5.2

5.3

that active agents in the natural spring waters are passed through skin, similar to dissolved substances assimilated within the body, to form antibodies which induce beneficial clinical reactions in the blood. Consequently the blood test is a vital indicator in diagnosis to prescribe appropriate but wide-ranging forms of balneological therapy.

Spa tubs Not very long ago, the spa bath in America was a mere curiosity – the swimming pool was the thing! An energy crisis encouraged the pool industry to look wider afield, and the spa pool or sparkling water alcove was reborn and actively redeveloped more as a bathroom fitting providing hot, aerated spring-like bathing tubs for tonal relaxation, similar to the Japanese family hot evening bath, or the early American practice of hot-tubbing in wooden vats outdoors.

The advantages of taking spas at home have now been explored in these small volume, refreshing foams and health giving waters. And extra, practical benefits have been found since an existing swimming pool's filter and heater can be switched over to maintain the smaller spa water capacity of around $10m^3$ for hot tonal baths in winter, and then back again for warm swimming in summer.

Prefabricated one-piece or easily assembled unit designs for spa baths with extra resilient interiors (from reinforced plastic surfaces to close fitting timber staves) are widely marketed. They all require fast turnover, rugged filtration (2 to 5 hours preferred) to cope with all the extra grease and grime and hard wear at high temperature. There are rapid rise heaters, patented aerator and blower systems, directional inlets, massage jets, and integral interior tub lighting.

High temperature and unbalanced water soon corrodes inadequate equipment; heavy use soon seeks out a hollow shell or fractured gel coat lining. Excavation and backfilling must be precisely carried out and all services supply lines securely fitted. Thermoplastic fittings and pipes must be able to withstand the higher temperatures.

Whether indoor or part of the pool outside, the unit gets extremely hard wear. Scaled-down equipment will never cope. If anything, mechanical equipment is needed that is even more durable than for normal pools, eg extra powerful pumps to deal with high flow rates, non-corrosive materials for special waters, purification chemicals without troublesome side effects at higher temperature, etc.

This compact individual treatment, or toning spa pool, offers, like the Sauna or Turkish or earlier Roman bath before, invigorating and comforting sessions which hotels and hospitals, private homes and sports clubs now install as singles or suites within their premises. Even the Moscow

5.1 *The classical entrance to an Italian thermae today: Salsomaggiore Terme, Le Terme Berzieri*
Italian State Tourist Office
Photo: Tosi

5.2 *One of the 19th-century thermal baths still in use and very popular in Wiesbaden, Germany*
Kurbetriebe der Landeshauptstadt Wiesbaden
Photo: Hilde Laskawy

5.3 *Ground floor spa halle, where you can choose your own blend of mineral water; reception area of the Augustabad, Baden-Baden's new 8-storey health complex*
Bäder-und Kurverwaltung, Baden-Baden
Photo: Photo-Tschira

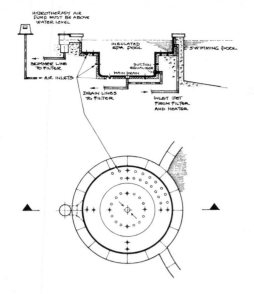

5.4

5.5

5.6

Olympic complex has health spa waters to include massage, paraffin and dry-steam baths.

5.3 Hydrotherapy pools

Nearly one person in every twenty is handicapped in some way. The treatment of disease or debility with water is complementary to physiotherapy or kinésitherapy. While spa mineral water therapy is widely accepted in Europe and the Far East, only hydrotherapy as a facet of physiotherapy or rehabilitation is practised in the UK and USA. The specialised hydrotherapy pool or bath is now an essential aid to recovery and normality. Schools, hospitals and church authorities provide treatment pools for the crippled, the blind, or mentally retarded, and rehabilitation baths for convalescent, paraplegic or disabled patients.

In France, there is a revival of thalassotherapy-treatment within a medical pool where the natural extra support from seawater allows movements otherwise impossible to patients. A new 3000m² seawater and physiotherapy centre at Saint-Trojan, Ile d'Oléron caters for chronically ill and disabled persons, as well as health buffs and seabathing addicts.

Pools for medical treatment Pool designs may vary according to their particular requirements for the patients, but they all require rapid water treatment services, highly effective circulation and above average water temperatures, from 30 to 35°C. These pools are basically ordinary tanks adjusted for disabled people. They might have raised side walls to suit wheelchairs, water access ramps and chutes, safety handrailing, underwater kinésthesic equipment, treatment bays, as well as mechanical hoists operated by electric motor, lever or waterclock type weights for special needs of totally disabled bathers (see information sheets 2.19 and 16.9). The true hydrotherapeutic pool clinic is controlled and operated by a medical doctor for his patients, rather than a baths manager for his customers. In Europe, the hydrotherapy pool centre also includes mineral remedial baths, the basis of balneology and treatment by doctors trained and practising water cures and prophylactic medicine.

Pools for the disabled Confusion can arise when designers think disabled people only want *treatment*. They can enjoy water too, and more often than not accessibility into a *normal* pool means everything. No swimming pool should discriminate between levels of capability by providing solely for the physically able. No architectural barrier must exist within a building since even a thoughtless step or narrow doorway can restrict a disabled person (see chapters 2 and 16). In the UK, the Chronically Sick and Disabled Persons Act 1970 requires public buildings to provide unhampered access and extra facilities for handicapped people.

When planning a multi-use pool, think out the approach, access, and mobility within the building (no unnecessary changes of level, restrictions to toilets, cramped changing

5.4 *Spa tub alcove and swimming pool: an increasingly popular health accessory sharing the treatment plant of a residential swimming pool*
5.5 *Moulded GRP spa bath*
Hydro-Spa Inc, California
5.6 *American outdoor spa pool setting*
Baja Industries, Arizona

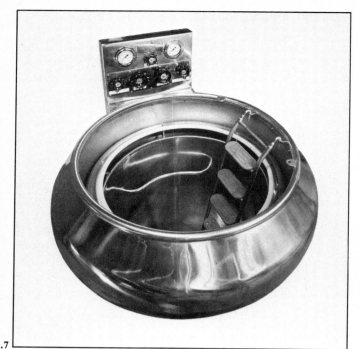

5.7

5.10

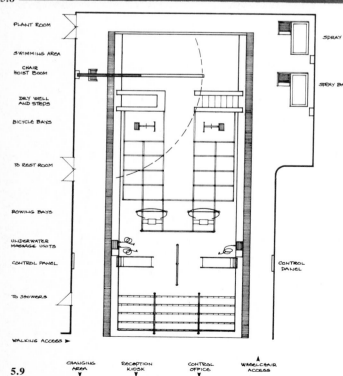

5.8

5.11

Plan labels (5.9):
PLANT ROOM
SWIMMING AREA
CHAIR HOIST BOOM
DRY WELL AND STEPS
BICYCLE BAYS
TO REST ROOM
ROWING BAYS
UNDERWATER MASSAGE UNITS
CONTROL PANEL
TO SHOWERS
WALKING ACCESS ►
SPRAY BATH
SPRAY BATH
CONTROL PANEL

CHANGING AREA ▽   RECEPTION KIOSK ▽   CONTROL OFFICE ▽   WHEELCHAIR ACCESS ▽

5.9

5.7 *A wide range of specialised treatments can be provided by jets and foaming massage of thermal waters in this stainless steel aerotone bath, fitted half into the decking of a public hydrotherapy unit or colliery pithead baths*
Aeratone – SSV Ltd, Cheshire
Photo: P. A. Studios

5.8 *A one-piece complete therapy pool made in aluminium for a hospital for the physically handicapped in Nebraska*
Chester Products, Ohio

5.9 *Hydrotherapy thermal mineral waters bath: deck level multi-purpose treatment bath*
Astrid Centre, Spa, Belgium

5.10 *The mineral waters of Spa in Belgium are used in this specialised hydrotherapy unit to treat arthritic and cardiac conditions, as well as locomotive and recuperative disorders: Heures Claires Clinic, Astrid Centre*
La Prévoyance Sociale, Brussels

5.11 *A deceptively simple and inexpensive poolside hydrotherapeutic, hand operated, mechanical hoist for paralysed patients*
Mecanaids Ltd, Glos

accommodation, or awkward precleanse facilities, etc) *before* looking at the pool itself. Normal swimming depths are suitable, for the steeper flotation angle of disabled swimmers often prevents them swimming in a shallower pool. And the usual leisure temperature of 27°C is admirable.

Deck level pools are obviously advantageous for disabled bathers who can then roll into the water easily, but for the majority in wheelchairs, a 0.5m high parapet pool section is better. In-situ, shallow steps and dual handrailing are helpful to people who have to lower themselves down into the water on their bottoms; easy steps are also encouraging to the everyday non-swimmer. A 6m long ramp with a 1:6 slope or a low incline deck level slide is especially useful besides being fun for children. Only rarely will a hoist be required. If temporary changes in pool depth are likely to be necessary, it is better to provide for raising the floor hydraulically, rather than lowering the water level.

The family type of cabins offer better facilities for those who need help with changing and a few extra large lockers will be needed to store limb supports. Taking a sauna bath is an excellent pre-cleanse system that needs no special equipment, nor special routine for disabled or physically handicapped people. It tones the disabled body just as well as the physically fit one (more information about all equipment and facilities for pools, special or standard is detailed throughout Part II, Pool techniques).

5.4 Pools for animals
At present there is very little legislation concerning the dangers of poor water conditions for animals. Their environment is left to the relative standards of each zoological establishment. Fortunately for the animals and animal lovers, clean and pure water conditions are becoming the rule as awareness grows that untreated ponds are unhealthy and unappealing, not only to the animals, but to the visitors. When animals are more in water than out, it is often impossible to see them at all. Mainly through the need for its continual water clarity, development of the dolphinarium has shown up inadequate conditioning of the commonplace green pool in which penguins and seals, otters and polar bears live.

Some zoos have installed full water treatment plant or at least circulating pumps. Mammals appreciate healthy conditions and are not disturbed at all by controlled chlorine residuals or equivalent disinfection methods in well-balanced water. A filtration turnover of 1 to 2 hours is the best with efficient breakpoint chlorination of reasonable free residual (no different from normal pool hygiene where all oxidisable material is destroyed). It is also especially important that 7·5 pH at least and stable salinity levels are carefully maintained to avoid skin or eye irritations (see chapter 15).

Within the next decade, it is quite on the cards that many people will want to keep water animals as pets outside zoos. Some families already have grey seals and freshwater otters in their own swimming pools, and there is even a successful trout 'fishery' in one self-sufficient enthusiast's converted back-garden swimming pool.

Dolphinaria The most popular swimming pool built for sea animals is the dolphinarium. The pool should be shaped to

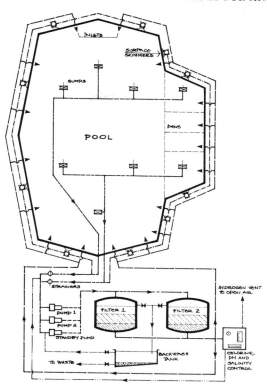

5.12 *Dolphin pool: schematic layout based on Brighton dolphinarium*

allow these mammals to swim easily and safely around at speed, and should include ample observation windows to watch them below water. Adult dolphins vary from 2 to 3m long, weigh 200 or 300kg, and can easily reach 60k/h within a few metres: they surface every half minute to breathe, although they can stay underwater for six or seven minutes; they like to show off and to play; they navigate by sound, their sonar system adding information to sight.

After a day of four or five performances and feeding upon fish, unfiltered water becomes turbid with up to ten litres of highly nitrogenous waste matter per dolphin, uneaten fish scales and even the odd lollypop stick or two. There is great need for rapid surface water draw-off to stop 'oil slicking', with large main drains to collect heavy debris which the dolphins themselves, by activity and agitation, help sweep along the floor. Extra large pre-strainers to the filter pumps are particularly important (as for all animal pools) and should be cleaned regularly to reduce the load on large-capacity filter beds and total oxidation disinfection system. Combination disinfection systems are ideal with their low residuals for safety (see chapters 15.3 and 4).

Just like humans, dolphins suffer water-borne diseases such as conjunctivitis, fungal skin conditions, enteric infections and worm infestations. Where the public sit close beside a pool, especially indoor dolphinaria, the safety glass partition barrier around the pool perimeter not only stops most splashing, but also helps reduce the spread of contagious coughs and sneezes to the dolphins. Healthy dolphins enjoy their shows and germs must be neutralised immediately by residual disinfection which gives better water clarification too. The filtration must keep the water clear all day long in order to see the dolphins, especially at the last performance.

If extra water polishing is necessary, carefully applied

alum coagulents, or better still DE coatings, can be used on the filter bed, with perhaps a percolation of charcoal for organic absorption. Most pools though use medium rate pressure sand or vacuum precoat filtration – not high rate units with small tank capacities (see chapter 13.3).

Operators (and dolphins) prefer seawater to converted fresh water, and try to maintain 2 to 5 per cent daily dilution rate as replacement water. A fall-off in total dissolved salts in artificial seawater necessitates an alarm system to signal correction before the health of the animals is affected. Accurate pH control is vital with equipment constantly registering the acid/alkaline state of the water.

Liquid chlorination is expensive and alkaline, so gas systems, properly neutralised, or electrochemical cells are often more practical. Iodine as an alternative to chlorine, although uncommon, can be equally effective and less troublesome to sensitive animals (see chapter 15.3). An electrolytic cell unit producing pure chlorine gas in the water is efficient, and the secondary ozone byproduct reaction comes as a bonus with these automated systems. The huge Hong Kong Oceanarium relies upon total oxidation of pollutant organic matter by ultraviolet radiation – hence introducing no possible chemical byproduct side effects in maintaining seawater's purity (see chapter 15.5).

As a basic guide, a minimum standard indicated by the US Department of Natural Resources sets a maximum average Coliform Density of 1000 MPN/100ml and the following levels:

Salinity   15,000 to 36,000 ppm
Chlorine   a maximum of 0·3 ppm as free chlorine
Copper   a maximum of 1·0 ppm as copper sulphate
pH   7·8 to 8·3
Temperature   5° to 35°C

These levels offer very wide parameters, which higher level disinfection of standard breakpoint chlorination technique clearly supersedes. Operational practice has indicated that above 2ppm free chlorine, dolphins tend to scale. But it is the chemical compounds partially destroyed or reduced that give the greatest residual problems – hence total rather than marginal disinfection methods are best.

Water without purification will turn septic and foul. Rapid development in marine biology and seafarming is already bringing new ideas into the husbandry of sea animals and their training techniques, and into further oceanic exploration. Provisioning with purpose-built water tanks for animals and the balancing of their environment on a large scale is just beginning.

Not only aquatic animals enjoy water. 'Many zoos fail to realise how essential a bathing pool is to a tiger's enjoyment of life . . . . In very hot weather, tigers often lie in shallow streams or pools, or go for a swim to cool themselves.'[1] One notable big cat lover swims daily *with* his tigers. The special animal pool is fast becoming commonplace.

Equine pools One way of speeding return to normal training for a lame racehorse is swimming. Pool therapy is particularly good for certain injuries, especially back and shoulder troubles, keeping muscles in trim without strain. There is also the development of horse hydrotherapy pools – in reality, a trotting ring with only 1m deep water for muscular development and toning, for strengthening legs and ligaments.

Many healthy horses welcome a swim after a hard day's repetitive training routines. But some never take to it, and are terrified of the water. It needs skill to lead a horse into poolwater, and two leading reins are necessary, one on either side of the head to guide the animal round the course. Extra care has to be taken on the first occasion to prevent panic. A long, slow slope with padded corridor type walls will stop the few really frightened animals from further injury. Most horse pools are circular with a central trainer's island. This island might also require padding if it is very close to the access ramp, for some horses can lunge right across the pool in one or two strides, or strokes. Generally most horses become relaxed when used to the pool and then require only one handler in charge.

The provision of equine swimming pools has recently developed from an idea in the USA which other leading horse racing nations have been quick to apply. In France at Chantilly, for example, there is a circuit for a double ring pool with 40m straight length between; in England at Newmarket, the smaller, more practical single ring pool is preferred, and by early 1978 a dozen or so such pools were operating at stables throughout the UK, and many more in America such as the famous circuits in California and Florida, including Chula Vista and Ocala Stud. One pool can easily cope with several hundred horses every week.

Practice usually involves giving each horse two or three swims, for three or four minutes each week, with a 10 to 15 minute session occasionally. Although this may only involve several circuits of the pool, the variation in the programme also helps the training schedules and keeping the horse in good condition. An animal can be swimming only 10 days after an injury, shortening the normal recovery training by several months.

Pools require rapid surface circulation, extra and larger coarse pre-strainers, two to four hour turnovers with large capacity filters. There is still debate about heating equine pools. Some stables prefer 18°C minimum water temperature; the commercial pool operator argues horses do not mind cold and ice out in pasture, so a few minutes in a cool pool causes no ill effect: in fact, the too warm pool will only promote chills from the cold air afterwards!

The pool must not be too shallow, otherwise some horses will never swim, preferring to walk through the water on their hind legs instead. Water depths should be between 25 and 30 hands (3m) at least to overcome this situation.

5.5 Unusual baths

Pools attract even greater attention when they are unique or unusual or eccentric, like King Solomon's tree-lined pool near Bethlehem; King Nezaualcoyotl's fountains, ponds and canals in the vast gardens and park of Aztec city Tetzcotzinco; King Herod's hilltop palace fortress at Masada on the shore of the Dead Sea, offering bathing suites in which the court often discussed problems of state in the waters and in the nude; or reflecting pools set before princely Arabian and Indian architecture. But however

5.13 *Therapeutic swimming pool for horses helps maintain a training programme even when convalescing: Winsor House Stables, Lambourn*
Photo: Gerry Cranham

5.14a and b *Horse therapy pools: long course and short course*

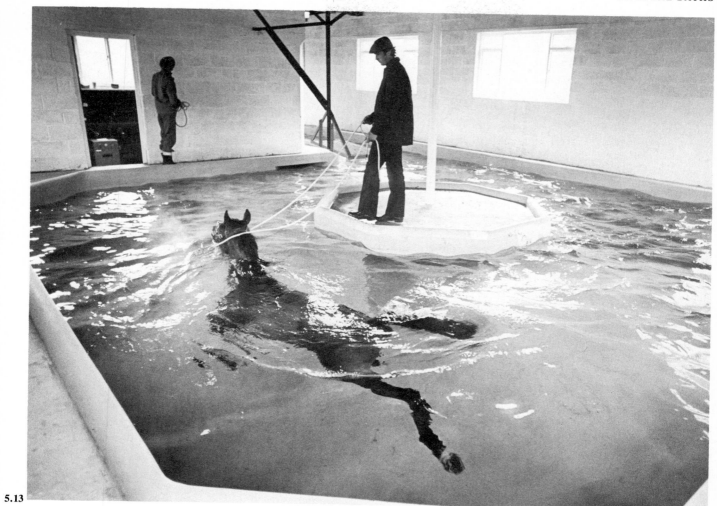

5.13

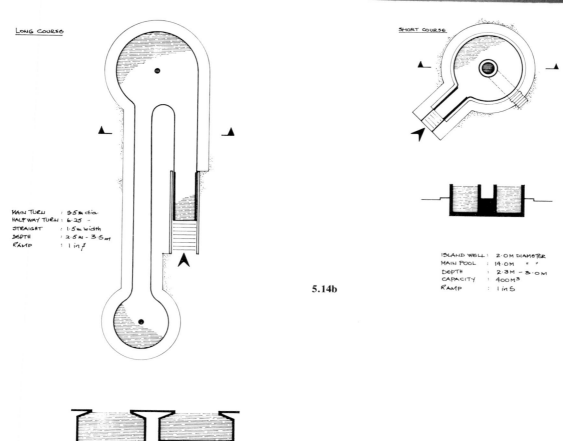

LONG COURSE

SHORT COURSE

MAIN TURN : 3·5m dia
HALF WAY TURN : 6·25 "
STRAIGHT : 1·5m width
DEPTH : 2·5m – 3·5m
RAMP : 1 in 7

ISLAND WELL : 2·0M DIAMETER
MAIN POOL : 14·0M " "
DEPTH : 2·3M – 3·0M
CAPACITY : 400M³
RAMP : 1 in 5

5.14b

5.14a

imaginative the designs, pure fresh water was essential, and still is. Without polishing by filtration, all waters rapidly deteriorate in any water-retaining structure, no matter how elaborate.

Floating pools In the 19th century, it seemed a sensible idea to float a swimming bath in a river where there were continuous supplies of fresh clean water! The earliest illustrated floating baths off London's Somerset House Gardens, introduced a 'bagnio and tavern' on the River Thames which was aptly named 'Folly'. Other pool boats came and went (in many countries) but the cold, murky and increasingly polluted replenishing water eventually defeated all the engineers competing against the hygienic and more permanent shore establishments. The Seine river barques were the most successful and stayed longest with their 'Odoriferous plants' and two-horse hydraulic machinery to empty and refill the bath within the hour (see chapter 1.2).

A recent American revival of this *floating* idea creates an inviting pool moored safely in surrounding water in the very bathing places most people prefer, such as the lakeshore or along the riverside. Easily assembled light-weight components allow for rapid and economic vinyl membrane construction and dismantling.

Swimming pools are still popular on board ship, and every remaining cruise liner needs at least one. The QE II has two between decks and two on deck. Bright finishes and interesting designs (such as circular booths for the circular motion of changing, as well as tan simulating screens of sepia glass, etc) are standard. Liners usually offer luxurious pools, but unfortunately still very few offer totally clear water that can compare with a shore-based swimming pool. Ships' engineers find it too easy to refill rather than regenerate the pool water, which, whether fresh or salt, takes several days to bring round to that sparkling polish most people now come to expect. Moreover, shipboard pools need deep freeboards to cope with any possible roll.

Flowing pools The *whole body of water* held in a canal or special tank is moved around by pumps, paddles and turbines. Poolwater speeds range from promenading pace in meandering perimeter pools (such as around the Jaya Ancol Dreamland complex in Djakarta, see chapter 4.4), up to frenetic rapids chasing around an Olympic canoe course, such as at Munich. An unusual German invention simulates rolling ocean breakers inland for enthusiasts training in surfboard riding or water ski-ing. The action and water are contained within a 10m tank that varies the water flow according to the angle of tilt at which it is set. A small volume of fast-revolving water is easy to heat and clean, and to maintain even in frenzied momentum.

Freezing pools Some swimming pools are built specially to take up ice expansion and convert into an ice rink in winter that can cope with crashing skates. When permanent brine pipes are not installed, special freezing equipment, looking rather like floating mattresses, can be laid into the water to rapid-freeze top surfaces (see chapter 11.5 and information sheet 11.9; chapter 14.5 and information sheet 14.16).

A reverse of this idea, collects heat discharged in the freezing of an ice rink, and stores it in the warm water of a swimming pool nearby (see chapter 14.5).

Flourishing conversions A few redundant railway stations have inspired enthusiastic owners to install long, narrow

5.15 *Modern swimming pool on the deck of* Stella Solaris *of the Oceanic Sun Line. Coloured mats are laid on the gratings beside the pools for extra sunbathing facilities*
Holland America Cruises, London

pools between platforms (see chapter 16.5 for more on conversions); but more pessimistically, there are some who plan an alternative future by incorporating in their pool design possible conversion into a private bomb shelter.

5.6 Sub-aqua pools

Scuba diving or underwater swimming is one of the fastest growing sports in the world today. Natural outdoor water facilities predominate, but most clubs also make use of conventional swimming pools for initial training. Existing pools allow opportunity to practise with underwater equipment, but not the experience of club expeditions. This sport is dangerous for untrained divers and there is a need for specialised facilities where wider experience can be gained within a controlled environment.

Off-shore mining and sea-rig engineering now inspire wider undersea water programmes. But there is nevertheless almost a total lack of suitable training facilities apart from one or two places as far apart as Montreal and Paris. In the latter city, there is now a 14m deep sub-aqua tank which does include 5m deep shelves for beginners.

Some mine rescue stations are equipped with swimming pools to train men with underwater apparatus, but these are insufficient for the full range of sub-aqua activity. Only naval submariner escape pools, complete with observation windows and underwater sound, offer reasonable deep-water facilities at present. But depth alone is inadequate. Experience with unexpected hazards and exploration in difficult places is also needed.

Diving adventure in underwater photography or archaeology, sport or research, needs new skills and practice within specially suitable and controllable facilities. A *scuba-dolphinarium* – one idea put forward by enthusiasts – shows perhaps just the tip of the possibilities.

5.7 Cold baths

If at all, people prefer only to leap in and out of a cold water bath. Admittedly, some make a habit of winter swimming after breaking the ice of the Volga or the Serpentine; others, such as Cecil B. de Mille, used to suitably chill their pool waters to swim briskly every day, but generally these enthusiasts are rare. Probably it is the abrasive towelling afterwards that is more invigorating than the icy swim.

Cold, clear springwaters have always appealed, but the charm is very limited and the bathing place invariably small. The old Roman Spring Bath off Fleet Street in London, for example, like all the best sauna plunges, is barely 4m long – but Charles Dickens made David Copperfield take 'many a cold plunge' in it. It is difficult to enjoy cold water for long, and the bleakness of nearly every cold bathroom reflects this viewpoint.

Water below 10°C cannot be stood by the body for very

5.16a and b *Plan and sections AA and BB. A pool for stimulation and enjoyment: a BSAC design for sub-aqua enthusiasts*
F. C. Goodall, British Sub-Aqua Club
Designer: Ian Graham of the John S. Bonnington Partnership, prepared on behalf of the British Sub-Aqua Club for the publication *Pools for Sub Aqua Use*

long: cold water contracts blood vessels, hot water dilates them. A repeated contradiction of cold water plunging and hot room luxuriating relaxes body and mind in the sauna bath routine. Another variable version is created by the impulse shower of alternating hot and cold needle jets of water, often used at health hydros and beauty clinics. In practice, cold baths form only a small part of a suite, and never the whole establishment for 'one must be very fit to take the cure there'.[2] Cold bathing is still really a ritual, like the Laplanders' Daubfest ceremony, when the yearly bath means cutting a hole in the ice in winter and ducking under three times.

5.8 Hot baths

Warm water has always been enjoyed by the majority – even more so in warmer climates. Most pool people today would prefer 30°C water temperature, but can only afford 25°C. Somewhere in between lies the optimum. This narrow band of 5° in temperature change is only a fraction of the full bathing temperature range, but almost every country has developed its own kind of bathing ideal (see information sheet 14.1).

Sun warmth We now practise sun bathing to a fine degree. Climatologists in Europe try to recognise and exploit healthy and stimulating bioclimates. But where necessary, the artificial sun courses prosper instead. A range of equipment from the mini-sun ray lamp right up to the giant solarium treats sciatica, lumbago, and rheumatic pains, colds and catarrh, strains and sprains, through the three main kinds of ultraviolet wavelength – A, B and C – plus warming infra-red.

UVC rays are filtered off by the atmosphere (or by glass surrounding lamps); the very small percentage dose of

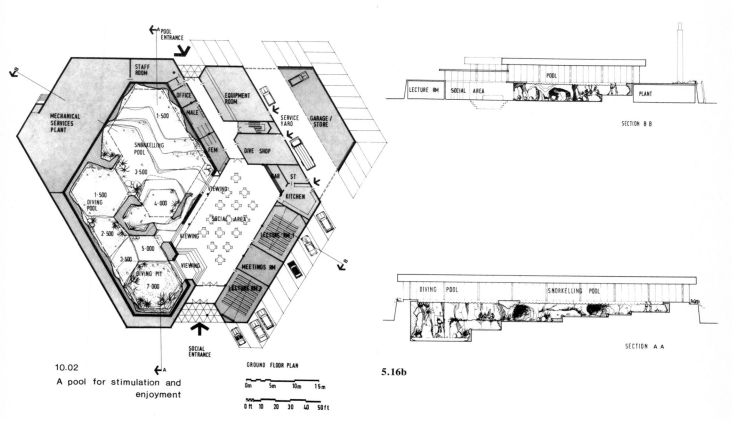

10.02
A pool for stimulation and enjoyment

GROUND FLOOR PLAN
0m   5m   10m   15m
0ft 10 20 30 40 50ft

5.16a

5.16b

UVB irradiation over too long a period produces that painful sunburn; whereas safe and satisfactory systems concentrate upon the advantageous UVA – light for healthy exposure and rapid browning. With sun lamp solaria, the choice will vary from a few minutes' intense exposure for busy hospital health programmes to 40-minute sessions of sunbathing on each side for individual relaxation (see chapter 14.2, Temperature).

The healing effects of sunlight – heliotherapy – is one of the oldest schools of medicine. The Assyrians and Egyptians set their sick in the sand under the sun; the Greek athletes sunbathed to improve their performance at the Olympics; Hippocrates prescribed it; and today many private pools have a sun patio or solarium couch to soak in it.

The public pool outside requires as much sun decking as the pool area at least; or for indoor facilities, it can include sun rooms or alcoves, where most people seek a golden tan, with the few to treat their acne. The modern solarium unit in at least two or three places will be needed by most club pools, sauna baths and health hotels for about a quarter of their pool patrons (see chapter 12.3–5).

Dry and moist heat Even if Pliny 'used to indulge in baths of sunshine' outdoors, most of his contemporaries still preferred the artificial equivalent of increasingly hotter and drier rooms in their Roman bathing suites. Ultimately, the Persian bath and pool developed out of the Roman bathing suite, but now caters more for toiletry, cosmetics and hairdressing than simple bathing.

Dry heat rooms and their related comforts are still more popular in Eastern countries than in Europe. One traveller in the past was so enthusiastic that he wrote: 'the Roman Bath should be an appendage of every Hospital and Dispensary, of every Gaol and Reformatory, of every Nobleman's mansion, and be established in every town in the kingdom as one of the most useful Institutions of the country'.[3]

Dry and löyly damp The Finnish *sauna bath* is a building not an activity. It is a place to perspire and cleanse, to relieve aches and pains, to calm and soothe, to share and enjoy. There exist in Finland alone over one million of this kind of bath that depend upon hot and cold air, plus hot and cold water. In the process, the skin is stimulated, waste products removed or oxidised by better circulation of the blood; muscles, joints and tissues envigorated, and a comfortable feeling of relaxation achieved without exercise. Very hot dry air (up to 120°C) can be spiced with steam by ladling a little water onto heated volcanic stones in the stove. The resulting löyly – a steam which rises from the stones – envelops the bather making the air seem hotter. Dry heat can be withstood, when a steam bath temperature would just take away the breath or sear the lungs. It is dangerous to go into a sauna with a weak heart condition or 'when suffering from too much alcohol'.

Purists maintain there is 'no sauna without smoke',[4] but log burning stoves are really far fewer than the more conventional electric stove. Bathers sit or lie on wooden benches; they raise humidity by adding water to the stones, and increase sweating by sitting at higher and hotter levels, or nearer the stove. Even after 2000 years, the swimming pool and the sauna bath still make the most appealing of all bathing partners.

Steam heat Turkish or Russian steam baths involve a pre-

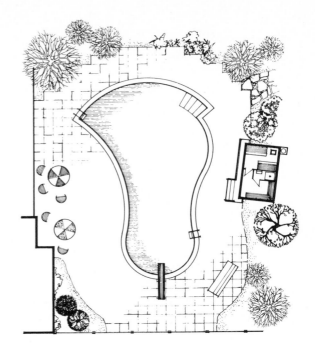

5.17 *Sauna bath and poolgarden*

cleansing shower, ten minutes in a steam vapour room to induce sweating, then staged progress through three increasingly hotter rooms followed by a massage, a cold plunge, and finally a cooling-down period in a rest room. The smallest room is the hottest at approximately 95°C, the warm room at 75°C is half as big again, the coolest room at 55°C twice as big.

Frequent sweat and steam baths are believed to keep ailments under control and certainly offer complete mental and physical relaxation. Their popularity in the West and Far East has waned considerably since the 1950s: in the Middle East, Islam does not accept the tub bath and the 'Moorish' is still a communal affair. The Russian vapour bath is more a private cubicle as opposed to the log hut Russian and Scandinavian style sauna.

The massage or shampoo is an essential part of the Turkish, where 'having been pinched and poked and pressed sufficiently, this genius of the bath lathered me from head to foot'[5] before the relaxation in what seemed the air of an ice-house, and endured 'ecstatic enjoyment, it was elysium'.[6] People suffering from a heart condition or with abnormally low or high blood pressure require a doctor's approval to take a Turkish bath.

The small plunge pool in the frigidarium is best kept down to 15°C, and although traditional cleaning practice has usually meant a 'fill and empty' process, simple filtration and purification plant guarantees the water will always be safe and of good appearance. Essentially, the humid environment of the Turkish steam bath requires careful waterproofing membranes to walls and ceilings, plus surfaces that are easily and regularly cleaned.

Warm water English social bathing at popular watering places eventually became hygienic washing at public bath houses. Christopher Anstey's *New Bath Guide* explained that,

> today many persons of Rank and Condition
> Were boil'd by command of an able physician.

Fun is still not part of the Englishman's slipper bath with

5.18 *Log cabin sauna to complement the swimming pool*
Rutherford Swimming Pools, Sussex

'hot water being a preservative against vice'.[7] Interestingly enough, the 19th-century American way of life proclaimed baths at home repugnant; even President Fillmore in 1851 found himself widely opposed when first introducing a bathroom into the White House.

Hot water The hottest baths and the cleanest bathers are in Japan; for the Japanese are addicted to taking hot baths every day. They use water so hot (over 50°C) that any Westerner would find it a torture. Their soaping and scrubbing before entering the tub is merely a prelude to enjoying a soak in clean, barely tolerable, scalding water. And at Japanese natural hot springs: 'the bathers stay in the water for a month on end, with a stone on their lap to prevent them floating in their sleep'.[8] It seems there is nothing more unusual than the bathing habits of others.

References
[1] John Aspinall, *The Best of Friends*, 1976
[2] J. Buckley, *Recollections of the Late John Smedley*, 1888
[3] Dr R. Wollaston, *Thermae Romano-Britannicae,* London, Robert Hardwicke, 1864
[4] Allan Konya and Alewyn Burger, *The International Handbook of Finnish Sauna,* London, Architectural Press, 1973
[5] *Illustrated London News,* 24 April 1858
[6] ibid.
[7] Geoffrey Ashe, *The Tale of the Tub*, London, Newman Neame, 1950
[8] Geo. Ripley Scott, *The Story of Baths and Bathing,* London, Werner Laurie, 1939

INFORMATION SHEET 5.1

40 famous spa towns
(Their waters and hydropathic centres with medical pools, to enable comparisons in this reviving form of treatment and prophylactic medicine)

Resort	Spa waters	'Cure' treatment for
Aachen, FDR	thermal springs	rheumatic fevers, nervous disorders and exhaustion
Abano Terme, Italy	volcanic muds and waters	locomotiove and spinal disorders, post-operative convalescence
Aix en Provence, France	spa waters	circulatory and gynaecological disorders
Aix-les-Bains, France	sulphur and alum springs	rheumatics, gout and respiratory problems
Baden, Switzerland	20 hot springs and thermal baths	rheumatics from Roman times
Baden-Baden, FDR	radioactive salts thermen	arthritis and myalgias; rheumatic and psychosomatic disorders
Baden bei Wien, Austria	thermal pools and spa centre	rheumatic and spinal disorders, slimming
Badgastein, Austria	radioactive thermal springs	circulatory and geriatric disorders and convalescence
Bad Kissingen, FDR	Rakoczy springwater; carbonic acid and brine	gastric, dietry and circulatory problems
Bad Nauheim, FDR	thermal waters and research centres	arthritic, heart and respiratory complaints
Bagnères, France	38 mineral springs	nervous system maladies and rheumatics
Bath Spa, England	hot, radioactive springs and treatment centre	originally famed for 'leprosy, gout, gynaecological disorders and gunshot wounds'
Berkeley Springs, USA	mineral springs	health resort charted 1776 in name of Bath
Brighton, England	seawater and chalybeate	now seaside resort, but originally used to aid 'hydrophobia, barreness and overeating'
Caldas da Rainha, Portugal	warm sulphur springs	'the Queen's hot springs' general treatments since 1485
Caldas de Reyes, Spain	warm mineral springs	general health cures since Roman times
Carlsbad, Czechoslovakia	hot mineral springs	digestive and metabolic 'diseases of civilisation'
Castellammare, Italy	saline and ferruginous	dietetic and gastric conditions
Chaudfontaine, Belgium	hot, carbo-gas springs	chronic rheumatism, cramp and weight control
Droitwich, England	brine spa	originally cholera treatment and strengthening the skin
Harrogate, England	varied sulphurous and ferrous	now a conference town, but originally treated 'scrofula and gout' and skin troubles
Heviz, Hungary	thermal lake	stiffening joints, sciatica, slipped discs, neuritis
Hot Springs, USA	47 mineral hot springs	all cures and originally used by American Indians
Llandrindod Wells, Wales	chalybeate, sulphurous and saline	rheumatic and skin complaints
Lourdes, France	spring 'contains no active ingredients'	'miracle cures of healing'
Matlock Bath, England	thermal springs	'colic, consumption and cutaneous cases' in the past
Montecatini, Italy	radioactive sulphates, bromines and iodines	digestive, hepatic and toxic effects
Piestany, Czechoslovakia	gypsum and sulphur thermal springs	rheumatic and locomotive disorders
Radenska, Yugoslavia	minerals and carbonic acid	cardio-vascular and 'manager's disease'
Sakhalin Island, USSR	hot springs	general cures and relaxation
Saratoga Springs, USA	mineral springs	varied curative baths
Scarborough, England	ferrous and seawater	now a seaside resort, but used to treat 'scurvy and preternatural thirst'
Spa, Belgium	carbon dioxide and chalybeate	cardiac, hypertension and recuperative tonics
Tamagawa, Japan	thermal sulphur water	eczema and skin disorders
Taupo, New Zealand	hot springs	general health and a recuperative resort
Trentschin Teplitz, Czechoslovakia	thermal gypsum and sulphur springs	rheumatism and osteo-arthritis
Tunbridge Wells, England	chalybeate	originally used to 'strengthen the brain and help childbearing'
Vichy, France	alkaline and thermal	liver, digestive and nutritional disorders
White Sulphur Springs, USA	mineral springs	general ailments and skin disorders since 1800
Wiesbaden, FDR	ferrous thermen	rheumatic, respiratory and locomotive problems

INFORMATION SHEET 5.2

Some remedial baths for balneotherapy

Aerotone bath: A stainless steel bath cylinder holding 2m³ at 35°C in which the bather sits upright; after soaking for 15 to 20 minutes in the warm water, compressed air is bubbled through to give a hydraulic massage to the whole body. Ideal for blood pressure, circulatory and rheumatic complaints. Various aromatic extracts can be dissolved in the water; a hot shower precedes the tonal bath, a cold shower follows it.

Brine bath: Bathing in warm salt water is a stimulant and a tonic and toughens the skin; the salinity ranges from 1 to 10kg of common salt per 100 litres of water at 30 to 40°C.

Jet massage: A powerful underwater jet played onto the body and limbs: the hose sprays hot, warm or cold water according to the treatment. Bays are often allocated within the hydrotherapy pool for underwater jet massages. A variation of this device has been developed into a fixed jet-stream that bathers can swim against for practice and recreation.

Lassar bath: Cold, warm or hot showers from overhead and side, original-ly described by Dr Lassar as a 'rain bath'.

Needle-jet shower: or electronic impulse shower, where myriads of small water jets ovehead and all round direct warm water interspersed with flashes of cold water onto the body; alternating hot and cold jets can be spaced from ¹/s to 10 second intervals to tone and to massage.

Pine bath: A tonal bath of special solution taken for 15 minutes to aid bronchial subjects; or provided as 'pined' steam inhalatorium.

Soda bath: Bathing in natural or artificial alkaline waters at 35 to 38°C is followed by oiling of the skin to improve its condition.

Vichy douche: The patient lying on a towel-covered bench, through which warm water is percolated at body temperature, is given a massage while water at 40°C is sprayed onto the skin; the process is often finished off with a needle-jet shower that aids circulation or relieves fibrositis.

Wet sheet bath: The patient is wrapped in wet cloths for the pack to work as a cold poultice and refresh the whole body; it has somewhat lost popu-larity in the 20th century.

INFORMATION SHEET 5.3

Spa pools

The public spa water treatment bath has been modernised in America to provide a new facility, ideal for the private and commercial market . . . the spa pool or hot tub or whirl bath, etc.

Spa pool systems that are designed primarily for home family use utilise existing swimming pool plant to maintain the necessarily warmer water (40°C) within the separate 'bathing' section, or they are installed complete with their own special air injection and circulation fittings. A typical 'hot tub' kit comprises:

- GRP pool or sectional redwood vat including steps and seating plus insulating cover
- Circulation lines, by-pass manifold suction grating, and plumbing services with filtration and disinfection plant, heater and/or solar system plus necessary pumps and motors, leaf trap and drain cock
- Hydro-massage jet inlets and bubbler system or air blower infuser, anti-syphon and pressure relief valves
- Time clock, thermostat, thermometer, and skimmer and underwater and lighting.

The very small water volume is relatively inexpensive to raise 5°C temperature overnight, but still requires a surface insulation blanket to conserve heat and reduce evaporation. With the high filter turnover and fast water flow required, using heavy duty equipment and minimal bends to plumbing the potential pressure loss will be reduced. Effective installation and extra durable finishes, fittings and sealants, are essential to withstand the concentrated use, hard wear and higher temperature. Filtration media must cope with greater pollution per m³ of water than for most other kinds of pool (see chapter 13.3 and 4).

Sizing indications

Requirement	Persons	Pool diameter at 1·25m depth m	Heating provision kW
Couples	2–4	1·2	6
Families	4–8	1·5	9
Condominiums	8–12	1·8	12
Community clubs	12–16	2·2	12

Pools are also available at 1·2 to 3m depth for 3 to 10m diameter, with additional insulation, equivalent fittings but lower temperature operation. Suppliers also provide suitable solar systems that are unglazed for low temperature pools, and glazed for warm temperature spas.

Fast heating by supplementary heaters requires water diverted to return to the spa through the floor to save 25 per cent on fuel; note that soaking in temperature above 40°C can be injurious to health.

Provide:
fast spa water turnovers for filtration (1 to 2 hour heavy loads)
7·5 pH level
chlorine residual 1·5ppm minimum
total alkalinity 150ppm
air blower rating 300 to 400W per spa inlet jet.

INFORMATION SHEET 5.4

Hydrotherapeutic equipment and facilities

Examples of the specialised needs for curists or handicapped people:

Aids	Apparatus	Diagnostics
Handrails	Water parallel bars	Thermen baths
Safety railings	Bicycle machines	Directional douches
Wallbars	Ergotherapy devices	Electrotherapy
Splash racks	Subaqual jet massage	Physiotherapy
Wheelchairs	Vibro-massage	Pulmonary
Stretcher trolley	Inhalatory dispensers	Cardiac
Low angle steps	Gymnast respirators	Blood testing
Access slide	Spa water fountains	Radio-isotopes
Bather hoist	Treading baths	Electrocardiograms
Changing couches	Resting cabins	Oxygenators

Purpose-built pools for specialised hydrotherapy exist at:
Aix-les-Bains and Paris

Bad Ragaz and Heidelberg
Basle and Geneva
Baltimore, New York, Palo Alto
Edinburgh
Helsinki
London and Stoke Mandeville
Oslo and Stockholm
Spa
Vichy and St Trojan

See also chapter 11.5.

INFORMATION SHEET 5.5

Dolphin pools
Data for schematic drawing

Specification based upon Brighton Dolphinarium

Pool: 30 × 10m – 3m deep, with holding pens 13 × 4m.

Capacity: 800m³ seawater for 10 dolphins.

Tank: shuttered reinforced concrete, above ground structure, lined with glass fibre epoxy resin finish; including rest pens with one suited for veterinary purposes.

Facilities: observation windows from surrounding refreshment area beneath auditorium; souvenir shop; indoor auditorium seating 1000, and allied aquarium.

Filtration: 2 × 2·3m diameter medium rate vertical sand units using 2 × 17½ HP stainless steel centrifugal pump/motors (plus one for standby) to produce a throughput of 350m³/hr and a 2¼ hr turnover, or the equivalent of 10 complete turns of water every 24 hr. Backwash daily to holding tank for partial recovery. Average top-up: 5m³ seawater per day via weed trap, when sea is calm. uPVC pipework services.

Water balance: pH 7·5 to 7·8.
Salinity 28,000ppm.
Temperature 22 to 27°C.
Heating not required after initial build-up since space-heating, lighting and sunlight maintains water temperature.
Breakpoint chlorination and pH controller by electrolytic cell producing 0·5kg chlorine gas per hour for

free chlorine residual	1·5ppm
combined chlorine residual	0·5ppm
total chlorine residual	2·0ppm

Superchlorinated once every two or three months.
Sodium carbonate is used occasionally to raise pH affected by alum and dolphin excretions.

INFORMATION SHEET 5.6

Horse pools
Typical specification

Design range from 300m³ capacity, 12m diameter pools with 2 to 3 hour filtration turnover, to 600m³ capacity, double ended courses, with 4 to 5 hour filtration turnover.

Dimensions: 6 to 16m diameter with perhaps 20 to 40m straight lengths between turns if required.

Depths: 2·5m minimum; 3m preferred; 3·5m where practical.

Access ramps: 1·5 to 2m wide at 1:5 maximum slope; 1:7 preferred; 1:10 where practical. Non-slip ridges helpful and padding to sides necessary. Slope must be easily cleaned of mud and straw.

Trainers' island: 2 to 4m diameter with drawbridge type access: additionally 1m walkway required around the outside perimeter of the pool for the second handler on the other side of the bridle.

Freeboard: Endeavour to arrange deeper (250mm) freeboard for skimmer draw-off surface circulation, with 1 to 1·5m at the entry ramp if possible. A parapet type pool might be practical when animals are controlled by one handler.

Filtration: Standard and medium rate filtration preferable for large capacity storage. Pre-filtering and large coarse strainers essential to deal with foam and froth, mud and coat shed into the pool, with some stable straw brought in as well. Filter is required to cope with large amounts of foamed oil and grease sometimes in an overloaded situation.

Turnover: 4hr rating minimum, 2hr rating preferable, with extra surface skimming, eg 1 unit per 20m³ of filter rating at 4hr turnover, or 1 skimmer per 10m perimeter, to provide extra deep basket traps.

Purification: Standard disinfection and pH control. Heavy duty cleaning equipment.

Temperature: Minimum 18°C preferred, but colder water not a problem: too high temperatures and animals with their higher body temperature at 38°C shed their coat and also become more vulnerable afterwards to chills.

INFORMATION SHEET 5.7

Sub aqua pools for scuba diving

Provision: A 25m unimpended length is practical with the whole pool best formed into sections and bays, some with underwater ledges and hollows, rocks and caves for snorkelling, training and diving. 27°C minimum water temperature preferred. Skin diving, scuba or aqualung depths to range from 1·5 to 7·0m.

Dimensions: Primarily to provide training and experience in underwater activities within spaces allocated for groups of an instructor plus four trainees:

Activity	Minimum depth	Minimum area for groups of five (standard pools)
Kneeling	1·5m	5 × 4m nearly level area before transition point depth
Standing	2·0m	6 × 4m deep end level area
Diving	3·0m	6·8 × 4·4m pool floor of a 1m spring-board pit
Pressure changes	5·0m	12 × 6m pool floor of a 10m high-board diving well

Maximum floor gradient 1:10 otherwise underwater equipment slides down slope: stepped pool floors preferable where safety and circulation arrangements can be provided.

Access: A 1:7 ramped gradient with handrails is best for entry, and ideal for non-swimmers or handicapped bathers also using the pool. Ladders at least 0·6m wide should be set 0·3m minimum away from wall with broad treads; rungs 0·3m apart and rails taken down to the pool floor wherever practical. Steps inset into pool walls are unsuitable for flippered feet. Deck level pools are preferred, rather than high freeboards that can be problematical to other bathers as well.

Equipment: Expedition support gear: a couple of inflatable dinghies, outboard motors and stands, fuel tanks, a portable compressor and an underwater tug plus stores.

Divers' gear: fins, masks, snorkels, camera housing, flash lights, etc. (Only toughened glass for face masks and flashlights is permitted, but care is still required.)

Club stores: at least 20 air cylinders, valves, harnesses, weight belts and life jackets; tool kit, spares, emergency kits, markers, floats, anchors, and an air compressor.

Protective arrangements: rubber buffers to cover air cylinders/valves, preventing tiling damage, plus covers to stop lead weights marking walls and floors; heavy duty finishes and tiles should be specified for pools used for scuba diving.

Mats at least 2 × 1m on which to lay out five sets of diving gear, to protect decking.

Facilities: Underwater windows are important for training, preferably linked with underwater speakers; and they add interest for spectators; observation windows should be suitable also for television camera operation.

Club room (for approx 50 people) and refreshment lounge.

Include some larger lockers for extra gear.

Compressor room: with separate access from outside preferred; area at least 5 × 4m, and to house a high-pressure output compressor in a separate compartment to dampen noise and vibration; silencers for exhausts and clear vents, are also important.

Wash-tanks are required to recharge cylinders underwater and dissipate heat and increase safety should a cylinder fail. Secure supply air lines firmly to walls at frequent intervals to overcome any whiplash in case of pipe failure.

The external intake must collect uncontaminated air; any impurities can become toxic under pressure, therefore ensure intakes are well clear of any chlorine fumes, air conditioning exhausts, drainage vents, etc.

Equipment rooms are inspected several times every year; extra fire risks must be taken into account.

Set storage racks 0·3m apart and only up to 1·5m high for heavy club equipment.

Cater for a small engineering bench and tools.

Potential: Hydrospace should offer some of the excitement of underwater exploration within lagoons to simulate seascapes, tropical corals, seabed canyons, seaweed curtains and sunken wrecks: provide depth-diving into 15m and 5m basins, as well as shallow water free-dive exploration in a marineland aquaria environment.

See fig **5.16**.
Source: BSAC.

INFORMATION SHEET 5.8

Sunlight baths
(The electromagnetic spectrum existing between longer waves of radio and television, and very short penetrating rays of radiology)

Wavelength in nanometers: 1nm = 10⁻⁹m or 1 millionth of a mm

			Approx % of sun
Ultraviolet:	UVC	200–280nm	minute
	UVB	280–315nm	0·04
	UVA	315–400nm	4·9
Visible light:	violet, blue, green yellow, red		
		380–760nm	39
Infra red:	IRA	760–1500nm	37
	IRB	1500–3000nm	16
	IRC	3000 + nm	3

Solar radiation is filtered by clouds (50 per cent) and air pollution (20 per cent), and the intensity increases with altitude. With low UVB and nil UVC radiation, sun browning mainly by the UVA rays will be noticeable within an hour. At modest current absorption of about 1000 watt per person, ideal 'sun-bathing' solaria will artificially induce deep browning and healing without side effects on the second exposure, the sunburn factor of the radiation having been filtered out by the sun lamp design. Units operate instantly, offering a service life of around 2000 hours without noticeable output loss.

A 10mW/cm² radiation intensity is achieved in the UVA range, using low pressure mercury vapour lamps. Most bathers only require about half an hour each side, and most public pools only require 4 or 5 couches for average artificial sunbathing needs, but outdoor sundecks are essential for outdoor pools and increasingly for indoor/outdoor terraces too.

See chapters 11.4 and 12.4.

INFORMATION SHEET 5.9

Sauna baths
Specification guide

Arrangement:

Private – 3 rooms: hot, washing and dressing.

Public – 4 rooms: hot, washing, dressing and resting.

Minimum plunge pool: 3 × 2m – 1m deep at 10°C.

Minimum swimming pool: 4 × 2·5m – 1·5m deep at 15°C.

Ideal turnover for water filtration: 4hr though fill and empty can sometimes be practical.

Outdoor cabins facing afternoon sun are best located by a lakeside for the final cold plunge; alternatively, provide cold/hot shower for indoor panel saunas.

A 'saunapala' relaxing room completes the environmental conditions of a sauna bath.

Routine:

Undress, shower, dry heat sweat for ten minutes and introduce water vapour to add a sting, plunge, rest, return to dry heat room and 'löyly', shower, eat, drink and relax. Do not mix wet and dry areas, especially with soiled traffic areas.

Dimensions:

Allocate between 2 to 4m² area per person, but minimum dimensions for the hot room may be:

    1 person 1 × 1m
    2   „   1 × 1·5m
    3   „   1·5 × 2·0m
    4–6 „   2 × 2m

Average family size: 2·5 × 2·5m preferred. (Too large a room and the 'löyly' is lost.)

Height: family sauna – 2m; public – 2·8m.

Proportions:

● changing and precleanse area to equal half the sauna bath hot room, unless massage area required;

● wet area twice the sauna bath hot room;

● rest area four times the sauna bath hot room.

Benches: allow 600mm width per person with 400mm risers, and placed at least 1m above floor for family saunas, or 1·5m for public, *and* always above the top of the stone pile.

Extra facilities: exercise room, massage area and solarium; reception, storage, staff and refreshments area.

Heating:

Temperatures:

● restroom 20°C

● dry heat room 50°C minimum; 75 to 100°C ideal; 120°C maximum preferred.

● floor approaches 30°C maximum.

Humidity: 40 to 70gm water per kg air.

Stove: wood fuel kindled with dry heather preferred by purists, but usually only installed in country cabins, also oil and gas-fired systems, but electric units (5 to 25kW) most popular of all.

It is better to allow 1½ hours 'to ripen', rather than a faster heat up, as all round re-radiated heat from the wood is required.

Locate stove near door on outer wall.

Electric elements work at 800°C and a small humidifier helps reduce that dusty smell of too dry air.

Stones: must be heavy and compact, igneous type rocks tolerable to the 400°C operating temperature necessary for smooth löyly.

Insulation:

Guide U values 0·35 W/m²/°C indoor panel and introduce vapour barrier.
        0·5 W/m²/°C log cabin and caulk timbers.
        0·85 W/m²/°C 100mm western red cedar.

Vapour barrier installed nearest to interior surface to resist condensation from löyly, damp-proof membrane to exterior, turf roof adds charm not insulation (see chapter 14.4 for insulation). Allow approx 5 per cent of floor equivalent for window area (double glazed). Small doorway – public width minimum 0·8m; 1·0m better for disabled bathers.

Ventilation:

Do not reduce interior air space by infilling between benches to save on heating as this spoils circulation.

External air is introduced at *low* level and vented at *low* level for best löyly sweep.

Timber:

Seasoned softwood – use widely available timbers such as western red cedar from America, Australia, Europe.

Structure to offer weathertight joints with outdoor cabins supported on piers. Smooth and round all fittings and fixtures.

Dark timber is best rather than smooth, pale boards, since it will absorb and reradiate heat more efficiently.

Timber should be durable, stable, non-splintering, smell pleasant, and be free of knots; it is scorched rather than stained, but if chemical stain is necessary, treat with a non-toxic solution such as pyrogallic acid.

Source: *Finnish Sauna Society International Handbook.*

INFORMATION SHEET 5.10

Turkish baths
Specification guide

A 3-hour process of hot rooms and steam room, massage and douche, cold plunge and cooling rest area for relaxation from stress.

Room	Type	Temperature range °C	Area approx m²
Lavatorium	Washroom and showers, Scotch douche or needle jet massage	30–35	20
Sudatorium	Steam or Russian vapour room, with teak benches or towelled marble slabs	45–50	15
Interconnected rooms with hot dry air			
Tepidarium ⎫	Warm room	50–60	40
Calidarium ⎬	Hot room	70–80	30
Laconicum ⎭	Hottest room, with hot air flow to cooler rooms at maximum 0·75m/s to avoid any discomfort	80–105	20
Lavarium	Massage/shampooing room	20–25	40
Frigidarium	Cold plunge pool and cooling rest room	15–20 / 20	10 / 200
'Liquidium'	Essentially non-alcoholic provisioning only	20	10

Provide sufficient toilet and lavatory facilities (see chapter 11.4), obvious fire escape exits, and clear sighting for supervision.

Safety is vital with non-slip surfaces, rounded corners and good lighting: ensure electrical gear, sockets and lamps are placed beyond bathers' reach, and are suitable to withstand long periods of moist heat; provide no exposed metals to cause burns; make all surfaces easily cleaned; double or triple glaze, carefully insulate and include waterproofing membranes to inside and outside leaf of rooms (see chapter 14.4).

Maximum steam supply to the vapour room (40 to 50°C wet temperature) at 0·4 kg/cm² is adequate. Sufficient ventilation must be provided to clear waste steam. Continuous filtration will ensure pool water retains an attractive appearance; chilling apparatus may be required.

Decor to be restful, fittings to be durable and good quality, all glass to be toughened, armour plate or clear Georgian wired.

Sources: DGFdB/IBM.

Dolphin pool theatre at Brighton
Brighton Dolphinarium, Sussex

6 Swimming in school!

We learn to walk at a very young age, but not to swim. Someone once estimated that if it were necessary to swim 50ft, one quarter of all Americans would drown!

6.1 Objectives

Once learned, swimming is never forgotten. Instructors have shown it only needs a dozen lessons within one month to ensure every schoolchild 7 years old can swim. Immediately a beginner can stay afloat and swim a few strokes, confidence leaps forward, in every way. Schoolteachers tell of some children having trouble keeping up with their classmates mentally and physically: then overnight, these youngsters can suddenly shine in their school work simply following their own achievement in learning to swim.

It was Plato who said, 'Any man who does not swim is uneducated'. But the opportunity to learn must also be available in the first place. The waterspace at school plays as much a part towards the full education of a child as proper playing space.

School swimming pool schemes Nowadays most children learn to swim in special classes run by schools at local pools, or at nearby lakes and lidos. As swimming develops, additional lessons need to include more complex training techniques and to develop such sophisticated skills as high-board diving and synchronised swimming routines.

In reality, a pool is a busy classroom, taking about 25 per cent of the PE timetable; but this 'room' is often considered a luxury to a school's complement, and only a 'privileged minority' of schools have their own swimming pool. Some schools, however, *do* build their own.

A few philanthropists bequeath pools to their old schools. Some leading educationalists raise funds for pools at local schools, but it is mainly central and local government investment that has created one of the largest existing single market groups of swimming facilities.

Heavy-duty specification Economy package deals might subsequently mean more costly operating expenses, but worse still, flimsy pool equipment is soon explored and taken apart by inquisitive children. Unfiltered pools and marginally chlorinated waters are totally inadequate for busy schools, and sometimes it seems that hordes of children wash rather than swim in the pool, soon creating a bacterial haze in the water. Maintenance staff are invariably part-time poolkeepers and often unpractised in controlling health standards or handling dangerous chemicals. Pool routines must be simple and straightforward and car-

ried out *daily* without fail. It is the small and insignificant items such as footbaths without outlets, or stale, weak liquid chlorines, that encourage the most stagnant water. But, regardless, children are expert at avoiding most hygiene routines anyway.

The clear answer lies at the specification stage when robust construction, rugged equipment, unavoidable pre-cleanse routines and the well-planned purification system will pay dividends by extending the active life of the pool. When funds are limited, it is more prudent to separate pool provisioning into two or three building stages. Do not cut back on standards at all. And all pool extras can easily be planned for in advance, and added afterwards.

6.2 Pools for young children

These can be 'splasher' pools for nursery schools where a fill-and-empty system works best; *port-a-pools,* in pool-less areas that are transported into cities for hot summer days by local authorities on road trailer or water barge; or combination type pools in junior schools for paddlers and beginner swimmers, where an L-shape layout can offer two pools in one. The real questions to consider are: how much use can shallow waters give and how safe really are they?

Very small children are often put off by large pool areas

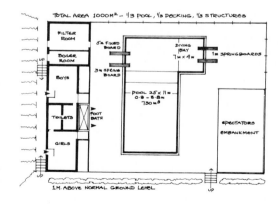

6.1 *'Self-help' school pool: St Christopher School, Letchworth, Herts involved a labour force of 450, ages 5 to 72, a series of holiday workcamps over several years, and an investment of approximately one tenth of the comparable cost for a fully contracted pool. This scheme, probably the largest do-it-yourself pool in the UK, was designed and built to UK Code of Practice for water retaining structures and in accordance with ASA diving standards*

6.2

6.3

6.2 *A truly travelling tank complete with purification plant and rubber tyre inner tube lifebuoy. Ideal for schoolchildren in learn-to-swim programmes*
Game Time Inc, Michigan

6.3 *Care and attention to detail with cushioned surfaces*
Royal Blind School, Edinburgh

with the uncertainty of what is, for them, deep water, and frightened by the noise in echoing indoor pools. Even a 12 × 6m shallow learner pool no more than 600mm deep can be intimidating if the hall in which it stands is cavernous and booming. Lowered ceilings over the pool with higher, light wells over the decking are best for all children's pools. Extra sound absorption may be necessary involving acoustic baffles, plus appropriate wall and ceiling tiles, and cushioned flooring that will be invaluable to parents as well as youngsters. Such floors are also softer to the inevitable toppling toddler (see chapters 10.12, 11.3 and 12.4). Wading pools are easier for cautious children if broad steps are set all along one side.

A temperature near 30°C is best for young children – sometimes to the detriment of a nearby main swimming pool, since older children (and adults) are drawn to the warmer water. Sudden surges of excessive bathing loads can make normal chlorination obnoxious and even dangerous. Proper controls are needed with properly cared-for and balanced pool water (see chapter 15.7).

Wherever the children's pool is sited, there should be an area alongside or a separate gallery for parents to keep an eye on events, and still to be easily accessible to clear up tears when their child gets pushed over or under.

Paddling pools Very shallow pools are preferable for under-fives. Depths may shelve from nothing to 400mm,

6.4 *Ideally, safe shallow steps for children's pools should take up the whole of one side of the bath*
St John's Baths, Tunbridge Wells
Photo: W. H. R. Godwin

where the mere act of being able to sit or lie in the water safely eases many minds. Average 400 to 600mm depth offers wading and playing where young children will acclimatise and enjoy water before learning to swim. If possible, provide interestingly shaped pools with islands and places for inquisitive youngsters to explore.

The shallower the water, the greater its pollution. Some outdoor paddling pools are so badly designed that dirt from the surroundings is carried into the water every time a child runs in, and that is every few seconds.

Children will drink the water, whatever its colour; and to believe that because it is only finger deep children will not drown is avoiding the expense of installing proper water treatment plant to keep the water clean and the pool floor in sight. Very fast water circulation from one half-hour to two hour turnover (or even a quarter of an hour for beach areas) is essential for all shallow pools, plus special anti-vortex safety grilles to cover all sump outlets, and non-finger trapping grilles for the inlets. Powerful filter suction should be shared between two or more large safety drains to cater for possible blockages by children sitting on them (see chapter 13.6). Always put fast turnover pools on

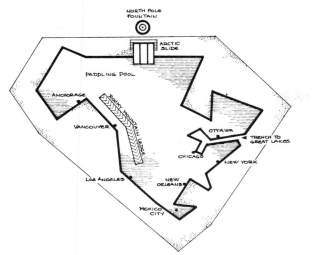

6.5 *Fun pool – for children to paddle in Alaska, Canada, United States and Mexico*

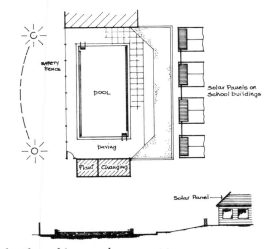

6.6a *School teaching pool: parapet type*

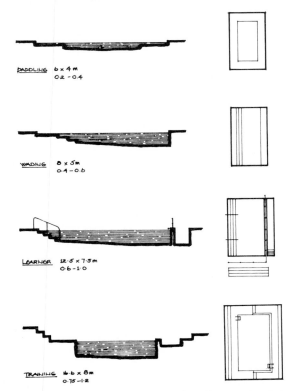

6.6b *Teaching pools: paddling/wading/learner/training*

separate filtration and purification circuits to the main pool (see chapter 13.4).

Hygiene is supremely important in densely used water; the surrounding deck should be extra large, for all the busy toing and froing that goes on, and especially easy to clean.

6.3 Teaching pools

Deeper tanks (0·6 to 1m) are necessary for teaching swimming. Long-term investment in more durable facilities may not necessarily increase overall basic costs. To provide a reliable teaching pool is mainly an exercise in good buying, since manufacturers, with the help of education authorities, have now planned and produced hard wearing but cost effective schemes, often available *off-the-shelf*. For classes of 20 to 40 children, simple, functional pool rectangles built on, in, or half-in the ground are the most practical of all.

Package-deal schemes, large or small, involve system-build techniques coming complete with total unit filtration/disinfection/skimming module to standardise the whole circulation services. A single permanent classroom costs two or three times as much per square metre to provide than a basic teaching pool, even including its circulation system. The nearest comparison is the mobile or portable unit-build classroom temporarily stored on the playground during population bulge years. The price paid to teach that extra class is the same as to teach the beginners and swimmers in the equivalent freestanding pool classroom.

Economy pool schemes designed for the light use of home owners will *never* suit the heavy duty needs of schools. Circular shapes, and variations on circles in light engineered structures, are usually for lightweight residential use only.

Portable pools – freestanding type (usual capacity range 10 to 50m^3) Heavy-duty, reinforced, rectangular pools of wood, plastic, aluminium, steel or even concrete, usually with a heavy gauge flexible liner, are termed portable in the sense that they can be dismantled and moved elsewhere. Some designs suit rapid construction, and dismantle for winter storage, while others will stand up to winter ice and frost. There are also truly *port-a-pool* tanks and portable purification units transported by trailer from district to district, when temporary facilities for a week or two only are wanted.

Besides being cheaper, the advantage with all above-ground pools is that a priority programme, such as to supply schools with pools, can start immediately. One hot summer, New Brunswick town council, USA, involved their community in providing four above-ground swimming pools for local schools. From conception to completion, the rush programme took only one month to fund, provide and install.

Some authorities consider portable pools to be bad risks in view of higher maintenance costs than for fully in-ground schemes; others still prefer their portable pool after 20 years of careful use.

Modular constructions in plywood based upon box beam reinforcements and A-frame buttresses are popular. Pressure impregnated timber preservative that will not attack vinyl or PVC is used to guarantee at least 30 to 40 years' life. All above-ground pools, especially the metal walled

6.7

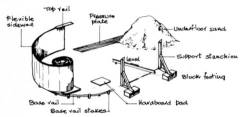

6.9

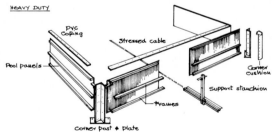

6.8

6.7 *A shelter and screen surrounding an above-ground school learner pool will extend the swimming season, help keep the water warmer and cleaner and encourage beginners to learn faster*
ICI Translucent Panels, Kent

6.8 *Above-ground structures: lightweight/heavy duty*

6.9 *The 0·5 m parapet for this junior school pool enables the instructor to stand, rather than crouch, to teach his class of beginners. The pool keeps cleaner since most windblown debris is prevented from entering the water*
Photo: John Dawes

6.10 *25 m competition pool sheltered by gymnasium and mature trees*
Rutherford Group, Sussex
Bedgebury Park School, Kent
Photo: John Dawes

6.10

type, are quickly warmed by the sun during the day. They are just as quick to shed their heat at night unless insulation is wrapped around the sides and laid over the water surface. Almost any size of even-depth teaching pool can be built with modular sections, sometimes adjusted to be partially or completely inset into the ground (see chapter 7.3, Portable pools).

Permanent pools – parapet type (usual capacity range 20 to 150m³) Semi-in-ground tanks are preferred for their economy in excavation and reinforcement. The walls project approximately 0·5m out of the ground and prevent much of the dust, dirt and leaves blowing into the poolwater. Flow return inlets are set proportionally lower in the walls. Piers have to be built around skimmer weir suction units. Double-sided bull-nosed coping is used to cap the walls.

Some swimming coaches claim the lower angle of view into the water is a safety hazard, while most others maintain that closer contact to teach swimmers in the water is much more important.

The parapet pool is not so obtrusive as a fully above-ground structure, and its half walls can be fair faced in matching materials to suit existing school building finishes.

Permanent pools – in-ground type (usual capacity range 100 to 300m³) These are expensive, but most schools still prefer the *permanent* ground level type reinforced concrete, concrete block, fibreglass, or all-metal structure since the capital investment can be spread over a long term. Ready-made 'linerless' pools of pre-determined dimensions are the most economical, but the versatility of in-situ

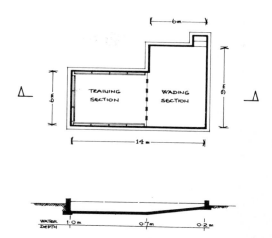

6.11 *Two-in-one pool: wading and swimming pool for toddlers and juniors*

6.12 *Precast reinforced concrete building framework erected over a 75 × 25 ft school parapet teaching swimming pool. Parents and teachers provided nearly all the skills needed to turn the bare frame into an operational and useful natatorium. Such structures with lightweight cladding can be added as 2nd or 3rd stage work years after the original pool has been built*
Tyler Mouldings Ltd, Kent

.12

6.13 *A lightweight cover for a junior school parapet training tank to introduce all-year-round swimming classes*

Clear Span Ltd, Lancs
Photo: Mack of Manchester Ltd

6.14 *Fully equipped deck-level racing pool for the eighties: the 50m length 8-lane provision meets international standards, and the 25 yard width of 7 + 8 + 6 lane facility* satisfies *US short course competition requirements*
University of New Mexico, Albuquerque
Chester Products Inc, Ohio

concrete enables almost any size and shape to be built. New Zealand two-in-one L-shaped, junior school pools have already proved their value for beginners and swimmers alike and are built in concrete to any suitable size. With potential large-scale production, L-shaped fitted liner structures or fair-faced pool panels are becoming attractive teaching pool systems for lower cost.

Whatever structure at whatever datum level, all teaching pool schemes need careful screening from weather by existing buildings, surrounding shelters, or permanent enclosures to extend the use of the school pool.

Surrounds and dimensions The primary purpose of the learner pool is teaching swimming. Maintaining water temperatures near 30°C for beginners makes all the difference to early progress, for youngsters who are warm in the water, and not combating the cold, will learn to swim far more quickly. They can swim comfortably in 0·6m depth and carry out tumble turns in 0·75m of water. Deeper water should be selected according to the teaching stages and to the pupils ages. Large area deep ends are unnecessary in teaching pools, but they are essential when training for diving, life-saving, or synchronised swimming routines.

Water should be kept as shallow as possible in order to save on heating, chemicals and filtration; likewise, enclosure ceilings should be kept down (2·5m minimum in smallest pools) to help cut space heating and ventilation costs (see chapter 10.1). Most teaching pools range in length from 12 to 16⅔m, with larger training pools at least 20 or 25m. Handrailing along the sides of teaching pools is invaluable for swimming stroke lessons and should always be insisted upon. Safety fencing, with gate locks beyond the reach of 8-year olds, is mandatory in many parts of USA and Australia.

6.4 Shallow water filtration

The American code for minimum filtration standard in school swimming pools is 6 hours turnover. Generally, learner or teaching pool filtration turnovers range from 2 to 4 hours. School pool filters are extremely hard pressed and must be simple to operate (see information sheets 13.11 and 13.12).

The shallower the pool the greater the need for a faster filtration turnround, for even if the bathing density remains the same (and it usually increases), there is far less water to dilute the dirt. All shallow depth teaching pools can save consistently on filtration and purification operating costs by insisting that every child takes a shower first.

Since most permanent pools are expected to last up to 50 years, the essential supporting systems will need to be maintained economically, or replaced reasonably over that time.

When a large number of pools are operated by one administration, it is good business sense to standardise on equipment and save on servicing and spares.

6.5 Inter-college pools

Senior school pools cater for swimmers with more varied needs.

Pool lengths of 20m will allow for swimming, life-saving, 1m spring-board diving and racing training, although 25m is far better. The total complement of students tends to predetermine the size of the pool, with the popular activities of water polo for boys and synchronised swimming for girls further influencing basic dimensions (see chapters 2 and 3). The popular American college pool is 75 × 45ft (though an adjustable 25 × 13m is better) and often financed from students' fees alone. The 25yd short course pool is officially recognised and still preferred in USA.

Two or even three side by side, low level diving boards will be more useful, since one only will always be overcrowded. Any built-in or built-on steps must be set to one side and clear of racing lanes.

Where possible, build a senior school pool alongside the gymnasium to share changing rooms, showers, toilets, lockers, etc. It is sufficient to allocate drying and changing areas to suit wet and dry routines: the drying area leads to the dressing area/locker room where carpeting can increase overall comfort: multi-sports use is more economic when even the same showers can be used for 'before and after' sporting activities (see chapter 11.4 on facilities).

When under cover, the main pool should be physically and acoustically separated (at least by heavy, sound absorbing sliding partitions) from any other sports areas within the same building.

Wide deck space for benches and spectators means that galas and water shows can be well supported.

Some colleges and universities specialise in swimming as a main subject or offer swimming scholarships within their physical education syllabus. Consequently, they set impeccable standards that even prestige public pools find difficult to match.

6.6 Dual-use pools

Pools in schools are often left idle out of lesson time, and more so out of term time. The idea of shared facilities with the local community is growing fast.

Dual-use, multi-use or extra-curricular schemes justify additional expenditure for the swimming pool when the local community also has access, but there will be more need for better facilities, or even a bigger pool to be planned in the first place. Extra use means 24-hour filtration and increased standard of purification, stronger fixtures and fittings, more changing accommodation with provision for both sexes, some spectator facilities, increased lighting for evening sessions, and probably some vending machines (see chapter 4.3, Leisure pools).

Even the village teaching pool can continue to operate throughout summer holidays, providing proper supervision and control is arranged. Often, though, it is this extra care, or the supervisory problem, that forces educational authorities to avoid opening their pools to the public. Club-type organisations, or pupil-parent-teacher schemes can help dual-use pools to develop by introducing supervision and subscriptions for contribution towards the higher operating costs.

One fact is assured, that students throughout the day and adults in the evenings and weekends, will use a swimming pool to a far greater extent than any other single school facility.

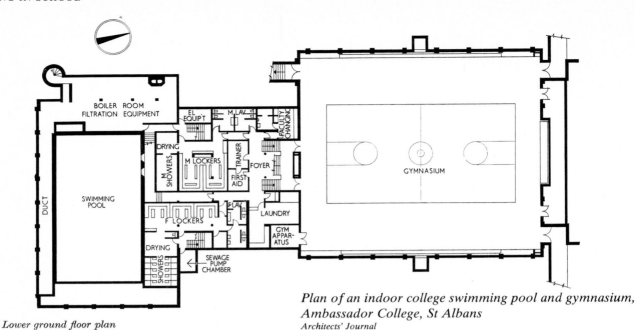

Lower ground floor plan

Plan of an indoor college swimming pool and gymnasium,
Ambassador College, St Albans
Architects' Journal

INFORMATION SHEET 6.1

School water space

Swimming pools		Paddling pools
Outdoor recreational bathing	– 1m² per bather	– public use
Indoor learning in water	– 2m² per bather	– private use
Teaching swimming	– 3m² per bather	– wading and playing
Beginners' requirement	– 4m² per bather	– initial learning

See information sheet 2.14.

INFORMATION SHEET 6.2

School pool specification

Consider:
the kind of pupil
the depths according to children's ages
the anticipated daily use
all levels of activity (learning, teaching, diving, competitive, swimming,
water sports, life saving, synchronised swimming, canoeing, etc)
physically and acoustically separating the pool from other activities

Cater for:
learners *and* swimmers where possible
classes averaging 30 every half hour (preferred number is 20, but 40
is manageable)
unattended times over weekends, evenings, holidays, meal periods, etc
proper poolcare training and maintenance
especial emphasis on personal hygiene – pre-cleansing saves filtration,
water treatment and school epidemics
sufficient temporary seating for gala events: allow approx 10 seats
per metre of pool length (or at least 30 on bench type seats for teaching
pools)

Provide:
a safe, sunny, sheltered and easily supervised site
extra tough construction materials
heavy duty fittings and equipment
adequate decking space for one class in (eg boys) and one class out
(eg girls)
durable filtration, preferably with long cycles between backwashing, and
a simple operating system.

Guide to water turnover for school pools:
diving   – 8hrs
swimming – 6hrs
training   – 4hrs
teaching   – 2hrs

See also information sheet 13.11.

INFORMATION SHEET 6.3

A school pool by stages
(Site and plantroom must be chosen from start to permit additions and expansion)

When funds are limited and a pool budget has to spread over several years, the following stages in an overall plan might be adopted:

	Stage I: budget for basic pool to include:	Stage II: budget for embellishment to add:	Stage III: budget for pool enclosure to further add:
	outdoor pool: 10 to 25m	windscreen and surface water insulation cover	double insulated clearspan enclosure
	filtration: 6 hour turnover	additional filtration: 4 hour turnover, and water heater	space heating and ventilation
	hand chemical application	chemical dispenser treatment	chemical control units
	paving surround – sand bedded	concreted decking surround	deck surfacing and seating
	footbath tray	poolside shower	precleanse shower and toilet block
	classroom changing	timber changing cabin	inclusive changing rooms
Probable use:	1 term	2 terms	whole year
Cost allocation:	2/5 budget	1/5 budget	2/5 plus inflation

See chapter 2 for programmes; chapter 10 for enclosures; chapter 13 for filtration; chapter 14 for heating; chapter 15 for water treatment;
chapter 16 for conversions.

INFORMATION SHEET 6.4

School pool extras

Teaching	Safety	Sporting
Floats and armbands	Safety line/net	Benches and seats
Swim floatsuits	Handrailing	Water sports equipment
Towing harness and rope	Life ring and rope	Starting blocks and lines
Blackboard	Rescue pole	Spring-board
Flippers	Lifeguard chair	Trampoline
Masks and goggles	First aid kit	Scoreboard
Snorkels	Portable resuscitator	Racing clock
Scuba gear	Safety fencing	Kayaks

Refer also to chapters 11 and 16.

INFORMATION SHEET 6.5

Teaching pools
(Popular dimensions and use numbers for swimming only)

Type of pool/tank	Imperial ft	Metric m	Sloping depths m	Even depths m	Preferred size m	Practical maximum bathers nos guide
Beginners – paddling: unreinforced one-piece liner membrane	15 × 10	5 × 3	0·2/0·4	0·4	6 × 4	20
Beginners – wading: portable	24 × 16	7 × 5	0·4/0·6	0·7	8 × 5	30
Teaching – learner: heavy duty sectional above-ground or semi in-ground parapet	40 × 20	12 × 6	0·6/1·0	0·9	12·5 × 7·5	40
Teaching – training: outdoor in-ground liner or concrete	55 × 24	16⅔ × 7·5	0·5/1·2	1·0	16⅔ × 8·5	60
Training – swimming: concrete block/liner, etc with cover	66 × 28	20 × 8·0	0·8/1·8	1·2	20 × 10	800 pupil school
Competition – racing: reinforced concrete/aluminium etc enclosed	75 × 30	25 × 8·5	0·9/2·0	1·8	25 × 13	1200 pupil school

See also Pool design dimensions for minimum areas and volumes: information sheet 2.15.
See also Pool profiles: information sheet 2.17.

INFORMATION SHEET 6.6

Water depths for age-groups

The depth at which a bather's shoulders are covered by pool water is termed the transition point, and indicates the position in the pool at which the bather must be a swimmer. If a school intends to provide a *swimming* pool exclusively for one age group, then the swimming depth, or transition point from standing to swimming, can be taken as the average shoulder height plus a 10 per cent allowance, eg the adult transition point of 1·5m is calculated from:

50th percentile shoulder heights of adult population –

Male	1·40m
Female	1·30m
Average	1·35m
110 per cent	1·485m

Transition point 1·50m (Note: 95th percentile TP = 1·65m).

A safer TP 1·80m is often used for public pools, where the shallow end may shelve more steeply to the deep point. Such sudden depth changes must be clearly marked or well out of reach of most people.

Estimated 50th percentile shoulder heights of children
(Western world countries)

Age 3	0·65m
Age 6	0·85m
Age 9	1·00m
Age 12	1·15m
Age 15	1·30m
Age 18	1·35m

Source: based upon *AJ Metric Handbook* data.
See Pool profiles: information sheet 2.17.

7 Swimming at home

Many thousands of ordinary people now have their own swimming pool, and the trend to private ownership is still rapidly increasing. The sector of the swimming pool industry catering for pools at home is the largest and most vigorous of all, and the most varied in its methods and designs.

7.1 Client relations and site conditions

Introducing a pool in the garden is an expensive decision for the client to make, and the structure, the builder and the setting need to be chosen carefully.

For the pool builder, the diplomatic necessity of keeping a client happy with potential disruption all around is a major consideration. Pre-planned routines for tracking over soft ground, lifting garden paving, shielding precious bushes, protecting plantroom machinery during construction, or pumping concrete across the lawn, speak effectively of professionalism and competence. Sometimes pool components are manhandled down into cellars, mono-

railed through garage windows, hoisted forty floors up, or trucked, floated and airlifted into position. Inevitably, there will be points of negotiation over everyday working difficulties, and even when the pool is fully operational, unexpected repair items can re-involve the builder.

7.2 Basic specification

In most countries there are various (and sometimes conflicting) building regulations and permits, or byelaws and planning permissions applicable to ordinary backyard pool construction. Many authorities are primarily concerned with proper water supplies, conservation and hygiene, drainage, pollution and safety. In front gardens, however, open-air pools are more often subject to far greater control and restriction. Covered pools everywhere involve close reference to building regulations and always incur higher valuation assessment for local taxation.

In Europe, the typical family pool is sized for seven or eight people at 8 × 4m to 10 × 5m average dimensions: in

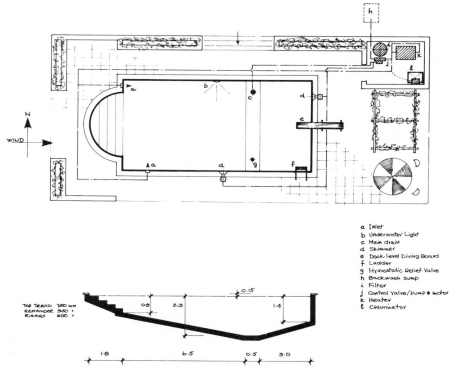

a Inlet
b Underwater Light
c Main drain
d Skimmer
e Deck-level Diving Board
f Ladder
g Hydrostatic Relief Valve
h Backwash sump
i Filter
j Control Valve/pump & motor
k Heater
l Chlorinator

7.1 *Layout and circulation, and depths/slope for deck-level diving*

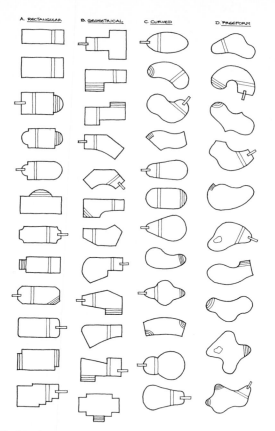

7.2 *All kinds of pools (a) rectangular (b) geometrical (c) curved (d) freeform*

7.3 *Pool designs and porticos, California. NSPI Award winning pool 1975. The bedroom balcony staircase leads to the spa alcove of the pool*
Ken Nelson Aquatech Pools, California
Photo: Baird Photo Service

America, the preferred size is more 10 × 5m to 12 × 6m. Another way of resolving the sufficient sizing dilemma is to allow at least 6m³ of water per bather (or 4m² surface area – see chapter 2), unless planning for an all-shallow leisure pool when half this capacity allowance will do (but keeping the same surface area). If there are any doubts, tape out the perimeter and spread paper or polythene over the area. It is amazing how big that small expanse of water grows in a garden setting.

When it comes to considering diving depths, at least 2m is required for poolside dives with care. As a deck level diving-board is frequently specified for residential back-garden pools, a diving trough, small plunge basin, or pan-profile hopper to 2.3m is the absolute minimum (see chapters 2 and 3 on diving depths).

Basic siting Private pools should be sited safely, conveniently and enjoyably. They are at their best facing the sun and sheltered from the wind, yet protected from glare and the neighbours, clear of trees, and with a good view from the house, in such a way that services from the house do not have to be relocated by the pool. At least three-quarters of a swimming pool should be shallow end and there should be as much room around as there is surface water area, for 'swimming' is the wrong description – 90 per cent of bathers in a home pool spend 90 per cent of their 'swimming' time standing, walking or playing in the water, and then more of the remaining time sunbathing. Indoor pools should also provide solaria or opening roofs and patio windows for sunbathing – a major activity beside most pools.

7.3 Basic classification

At the risk of oversimplification, there are three main types of garden pool or yard pool, termed, within the industry, *portable* pools, *liner* pools and *concrete* pools.

Portable pools Taken straight from the swimshop shelf or mail-order catalogue, these can be erected on the ground by a family within a day or two. They are easily the best ready-made buy, giving by far the largest swimming area for the least expenditure. There is no excavation nor special reinforcement to worry about. And it is the only type of pool that can actually be moved or packed up for winter – a necessary practice for extreme climates or mobile families. If not packed up in winter, they are kept filled (and covered if possible) to protect susceptible materials from weathering, but all equipment must be suitably winterised (see chapter 16.3).

The raised walls of all above-ground pools are a valuable safety feature since young children cannot fall in when outside ladders have already been removed.

'Free-standing' models of about 50m³ capacity with at least 1m even depth throughout are designed as circles, or oval rectangles, for an even distribution of forces. A few pools are 'hoppered' to a 2m deep end; more permanent type rigid panelled structures may reach even 25 × 12·5m dimensions. Usually, a poolside up-and-over filtration system is provided with each kit. Saving money by cutting out the filter is like laying a lawn and then economising by not buying a lawnmower.

Package pool assembly on the ground is very simple. The site is cleared of stones and weeds and levelled and surface drainage is provided. Sloping sites are cut into, and any fill to the slope is well consolidated to stop possible sinkage when the pool holds water: a sinking tilting pool will throw intolerable pressure onto one side. Flexible pool walls are uncoiled, or rigid panels mounted, about a levelled sand base over a protective underliner or strong groundsheet.

7.4 *A straightened oval above-ground pool set in a country garden*
Cranleigh-Clark Pools Ltd, Reading
Photo: Percy Butler

This 50mm sand layer provides a soft, absorbing surface for the liner that is set firm by the weight of water alone. Care must be taken on sloping gardens that underflooring sand cannot be sluiced away by rainwash. When wall retaining stanchion posts and buttresses have been fixed to base rails, it only remains for the vinyl liner to be draped inside the tank, flow and return positions cut in the vinyl and the pool filled with water. A top perimeter coping rail clips the liner tight and adds strength to the structure. Raised decking framework also contributes to strengthening the above-ground pool. Usually the whole assembly process can be reversed to dismantle these pools (see chapter 6 on above-ground structures).

A wooden sundeck provides the patio, sometimes to make the pool seem set below ground. The whole structure, together with supporting framework and sun decking set around on piles or posts, is sometimes used for pools installed by professionals onto steep hillsides or over unstable ground, other forms of structure being too costly to build in such situations.

Probably the greatest problem for a garden conscious pool owner, though, is screening the exposed sides of the tank. But a little imaginative landscaping soon works wonders.

The dilemma whether to build above-ground or below-ground is resolved by using a heavier duty portable type structure that resists soil corrosion and settlement, and then banking some soil all around, or even sinking the tank

7.5 *Classic pool and pavilion*
Aquatech Pools, US

partially into the ground. But such schemes move beyond the average family weekend job, and into the hands of a well-practised do-it-yourselfer (see chapter 6.3, *Portable pools*).
Liner pools These are tougher instant pools taking up to two weeks to install, but fitted into the ground. Some heavier reinforcement is involved, and there can be problems getting diggers in and out, estimating for underground snags, forecasting weather conditions, managing the excavation, etc. Quality of teamwork makes or mars an in-ground pool (see chapter 2.5, Problem places, and chapter 9, section I).

Liner pool structures have been designed to overcome most of the normal problems met during installation, though deviation from design tolerances can spell trouble, making reinforced concrete necessary for such problem soils, or those extra deep pools or load bearing sloping sites. The average liner pool put into a slope without any protective reinforcement in safe dry conditions, can soon bow or fail spectacularly when the wet comes later. Some designs of liner pools must never be emptied unless special protection to the shell is arranged, while others can remain stable even when the internal balancing weight of water is removed, though after 24 hours, the stretched liner may have shrunk unevenly back to initial size. In fact, *any* in-ground pool that is emptied under high watertable conditions and without special measures provided in the structural design is liable to float, or to rupture (see chapter 9.3, Water and drainage).

Prefabricated tank walls employ standardised components and effective bracing systems for fast and simple assembly. A hard, compacted, in-situ vermiculite/concrete type floor slopes to a hopper deep end for diving. Modern parachute slung flexible liners up to 1 or 2mm thick give a two-way stretch ensuring perfect fit, providing installers smooth the liner, extract air trapped behind, and accurately set the particular frame in the first place. Backfilling is compacted behind liner pool walls to bear or equalise pressures as water fills the pool (see chapter 9, Substructures, section II).

The range of standard structures, shapes and sizes is considerable, and vinyl linings (or butyl rubber, PVC, etc) come ready-made to size, or can be heat or solvent welded in place on site to suit (see chapter 11.2 to 4, Finishes and facilities).

Liners, or waterproofing membranes, are by no means a new invention; the early Romans fitted a 50mm thick lead lining in the Great Bath at Bath – and it still holds water! In more modern terms, the give and take of the well-designed liner pool is excellent for temperature extremes. Even up in the Arctic, where they have to contend with winters of 50°C below freezing, vinyl pool liners prove themselves invaluable. Or, in unstable regions, the water retaining flexible membrane remains intact even after an earthquake (see chapter 9.5, Tanking and lining).
Concrete pools These are purpose-built for durability and design. They can take two months to construct, though guniting a shell is often finished in a day, so the whole pool garden takes only a week or two to complete (see chapter 9.4, Materials and methods).

Concrete is such a versatile material that almost any pool shape, size or style can be created and the reinforced concrete base slab can be placed reasonably quickly. The strength of reinforced concrete is especially important where subsoil problems exist or when water-tables are troublesome (see chapter 9.4 on cement and concrete reinforcement and steel distribution, blockwalling and reinforcement and information sheets 9.4 and 9.5).

There are many different kinds of suitable concrete pool structures involving, for example:
- panels, solid bricks, hollow-core blocks
- mass reinforced, pre- or post-stressed
- pargetted, pressure sprayed and compressed

all designed to answer a variety of demands and needs for:
- high dry sites or low marshy grounds
- corrosive or compressive soils
- hillsides or tidal river banks, and so on.

Whether the tank is monolithic (one piece) or assembled from factory-tested panels, cost-effectiveness of concrete is excellent over the long term (see chapter 9.6 to 9.8 for different forms of substructures; and chapter 2.5, Problem places).

Most garden pools are built in concrete and should last the lifetime of the house. The economic advantage of lightweight tanking structures now means that more than half today's pools are built from modern concretes and other materials. Many people prefer the solid feeling provided by a concrete pool. To their way of thinking, the expense of bricks and mortar appreciates with their home and should eventually outweigh the immediate *savings* of plastic and tin.

Since ground movement or corrosion disposes of the weak and the badly built, poorly designed pools soon deteriorate. The too large structure exposes huge running costs. It is particularly difficult to hide an unwanted concrete pool. It cannot be dismantled like a modern liner pool and it is often too costly, but it is possible and fairly common practice, to build a smaller tank inside the larger one (see chapter 16.5, Conversions).

Finishes The in-ground pool market is split 50:50 liner versus concrete, with distinct rivalries in contractor competitiveness.

Since a pool structure is never seen again (if the construction work is properly carried out) it is the finish that home pool owners measure foremost in their preferences. That means comparing paints and liners with renders and tiles. The former are less expensive and warmer to the touch, though contra arguments say they are less durable and can feel uncomfortable. The latter offer a wider selection of styles and are easier to clean, which the opposition refute by producing printed liners and descriptions of expensive render or tiling refurbishing work.

A concrete pool structure can accept any modern or traditional finish available, and so scores in the sheer range of variety. But for simpler and quicker techniques, the plastic liner, coloured or tile printed, one-piece or tailor-made, reinforced or laminated, sprayed or sheet lined, has become vitally important to the pool industry. And now also the in-situ impervious *linerless* structures, invariably using *plastics* to bind materials within the shell, are rapidly entering the field (see chapters 9 and 11).

Datum point It was pool prefabrication in the USA that helped the vast increase in pool numbers all within a 10-year period. The original type of above-ground structure was strengthened and sent below ground.

7.6 *Classic-Mediterranean parapet design in textured gunite concrete, 17·5m × 6m and 100m³ capacity. NSPI Award winning pool 1975*
Patio Pools, Arizona

Similar ideas and expansions occurred in Australia and South Africa, and later in Europe, where the variety of inexpensive manufactured structures make active use out of traditional small back garden plots, and vacant indoor cellars.

Glass reinforced plastic pools are particularly popular in Germany, and England, where manufacturers have concentrated upon modular and one-piece constructions, ideal for densely packed housing estates in towns. Austria has taken to the above-ground pool with surrounding wooden decking, in harmony with timbered architecture and mountainous slopes, while the long hot summers of Italy means a huge market for their manufactured above-ground structures. Scandinavian countries also build economical unit schemes on or in ground, mostly from wood, metal or plastic to suit their short, but hot summers.

In all parts of the world, the fully above-ground pool claims around a 3:1 majority over all other kinds of pool datum level. The more expensive sunken pool has to be levelled to the ground in traditional natural style. But the in-between parapet pool, even if only projecting 0·25m from the ground is cheaper to build, keeps cleaner and is claimed by some to be safer for small children and animals. Parapet pools built in a sequence of terraced levels certainly look more practical and appealing than a flat, level sheet of water plus paving plane.

In Austria and Germany, the datum level goes far lower down to become the 'under-garden-pool' that is delivered and buried in one prefabricated glass-fibre, fully insulated,

7.7 *Bright interior from two roof well lights for this pool built underground*
Maderna America Corp, Baltimore

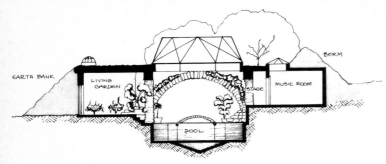

7.8 *Under-hill pool*
Architect: Arthur Quarmby

container-like load. A hole is dug, the 'unterflorschwimm-hallen' or pool-room is craned in, connected to the house cellar, and topsoil packed back on top to recreate a garden or lawn over the buried pool. The high insulation capability of this building system means only a third of the energy of standard enclosed pools is needed; and for total safety, it can be totally locked away.

A variation is the heat dump scheme built right into a bank or berm to form an integral part of the home (see chapters 12 and 14).

7.4 Cost saving principles
Starting with the budget, plan always for both the construction *and* the setting. They are complementary and represent the two main pool components (see chapter 12). It is usual to think in terms of allocating a percentage of the property value for the pool structure, and possibly as much again for the setting – either as landscaping or as pool building.

• Portable pools cost up to 10 per cent of the house value, and cater for more than one half of the whole pool market.

• Liner pools can cost around 15 per cent of the house value and take equal share of the remaining market with other in-ground structures.

• Concrete pools might cost almost 20 per cent of the house value even with faster, more economical methods such as guniting, and generally only cater for one quarter of the in-ground market.

This rough guide allocation obviously varies to some extent since values and economics change from town to country, type of property and style of owner, and so on (see chapter 2.3, Budgeting).

To sell the benefits, some pool company advertisements spell out the fringe savings of less money spent on holidays or hotel bills, and the plusses of more time spent in keeping fit and enjoying the sun. A pool project is not expensive measured against the amount of use it gets, and when compared with other rooms of a house. In practice, a pool is extra investment in living, since outdoor activities in summer will centre around the pool, meaning the children prefer to stay at home, and the family social circle widens – greatly so during heat waves.

Large pools are dramatically effective and dramatically expensive. Invariably, the smaller the pool, the greater the care devoted to its design.

Pool garden design is still an unexplored area for self-expression in architecture. Traditional Romanised rectangles and formal shapes make the most elegant pools; modern freeform ideas better suit the natural scene for gardens, but need skill in setting alongside house architecture. The usual basic choice is between hard architecture with classic formalism, and soft architecture with informal planting.

The quantity and the cost What is the cost to society of private pools? Public pools serve the community, while private pools satisfy only the individual. Yet the explosion of pool building in the private sector since the 1950s has just not been matched in the public sector, even though authorities have built more pools than ever before and more people swim communally than ever before. As an example, in the USA over a 10-year period, the total *pool-park* has developed three times faster in the private sector than in the public – with manufacturing economy of scale affecting private pool costs accordingly. Generally, a public pool costs at least 10 times more per square metre than a private pool, and private ownership with the investment benefits involved will continue to grow, and to seem less extravagant as more advantages are realised (see information sheet 2.8).

However, there is still such a wide range of prices it is often difficult for a buyer to choose. The public sector plays safe with establishment structures, while the private sector takes the chances with cost saving schemes. The public sector cannot afford mistakes – the private sector too often has to bear them.

Pool communes As leisure time increases, the benefits of having a pool close by become even more important. Family-shared pools help distribute high capital costs, and spread operating responsibilities to a more acceptable level. In the USA 2, 3, 4, 5 and multi-family estate pools, or condominiums are extremely popular. Advantage is taken of mutually shared garden boundaries, or a spare plot on which to put a private neighbourhood pool.

Groups of people form non-profit corporations involving directors and shareholders with assets and liabilities. There are even associations of several hundred families owning joint pool stock, and paying annual operating costs of a small percentage of their holding for the privilege of having their own 'private-public' pool. Apartment owners seeking their pool often elect to combine community needs and install a club style pool that is available only to those holding private keys.

Community pools are popular and usually profitable whenever private ownership is involved. But in all multi-owner schemes, automation is better than volunteers in taking care of the cleaning, and special rules sometimes have to be made to limit the number of guests.

The savings of self-build schemes Another way of installing a quality pool with cost saving principles, is the self-organised pool building scheme offered by some specialist companies. These are not totally DIY construction kits, since most equipment schemes include plans for a 'do-it-

7.9 *Rectangular indoor pool in Germany with crisp ceramic decor*
Villeroy & Boch, Mettlach

7.10 *An American condominium: this privately owned swimming pool is shared by a group of families to save expense and bring about community atmosphere. The pool is the major social focus in the grounds of these apartments.* *Landmark Tampa Apartments*
Lang Aquatech Pools, Florida

7.9

.10

yourself-with-the-aid-of-the-local-builder' system and construction is simplified to straightforward concreting.

'Self-build' means a self-managed contract with the owner-builder taking the risks of excavation and the responsibility for quality control; the owner becomes more a resident site agent. Very many successful private pools have been built this way, especially in England, from self-build plans, resulting in a fair number of local builders being able to install a reasonable swimming pool. The calibre of workmanship and attention to detail is usually exceptional.

Approximately one-third cost savings can be made. Some experienced self-help owner-builders carry out the job themselves, and gain the satisfaction of knowing how solidly their pool is built. Some allow several months for the work – others have taken several years with their project, splitting the budget into scheduled chunks for the dig, tanking, finishing, filtration, heating and finally, landscaping. Nearly all owners increase their allocation of capital expenditure as they discover the great amount of use the swimming pool gets. Whatever the timetable, it is still better to sub-contract out skilled tasks.

All good schemes cater for weekend working, provide approved plans and should indicate stages in the construction when the building inspector is involved: above all, the company selling the self-build pool package has to be prepared and capable of giving occasional expert advice.

7.5 Ambiance

One of the best scene setters is the pavilion beside the pool, and whether it is a fully equipped guest house or simply a sun shelter does not alter the effect such a dominant structure will have upon the atmosphere around.

Since most people, encouraged by profit-conscious pool builders, settle for simply getting in their pool as fast as possible, the character building opportunities that exist in arranging surroundings are too often overlooked. By striving to create a balanced composition from the outset, one that suits the locality, character can develop across the whole setting.

Problematical sites, awkward shapes and controversial ideas often combine to produce far better results than the plainness of the usual straightforward plot. Whether planning for simplicity or sophistication, the relationship of pool, patio and people should reflect the owner's lifestyle – ambiance grows from things around adding to a pool's personality. It is usually fairly simple to recognise an architect's or builder's pool, a gardener's or landscaper's pool – and sometimes even an owner's pool.

Calm and peace created by a walled, secluded pool garden, can be shattered by children (and adults) who never seem to talk moderately in water. Open-house swimming sessions by new pool owners ease back to swimming-by-invitation only, well before the second season starts. Din is dissipated in an open plan site, but only to be shared between the neighbours. By planting leafy shrubberies strategically around as a barrier, sound will be absorbed. If the pool surround is large enough, a 'room' each can sometimes be allocated to suit both the sunbathers and the splashers.

A pool is many things to many people: in US law, its appeal can become 'an attractive nuisance'[1] to lure small

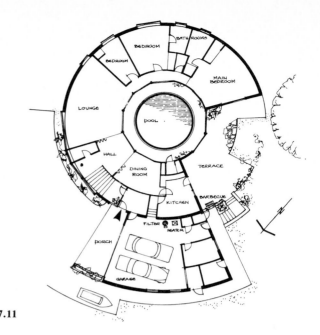

7.11

7.12

7.11 *Circular house around a swimming pool*
Architect: Norman J. Williams

7.12 *Observation style domed enclosure for a round pool in London town*
Architect and Photo: James Gowan

7.13 *All rooms lead into the inner pool in this cleverly designed bungalow: a kind of ancient Roman atrium but in 1975 Woking, Surrey. The marble-lined walls are plastic laminate*
Formica Ltd, London
Architect: Norman J. Williams
Photo: Felix Fonteyn

7.14 *Oast house changing room for a freeform pool in Kent. The brick paving complements the brick and tile building*
The Swimming Pool & the Garden
Cement & Concrete Association, London

7.13

7.14

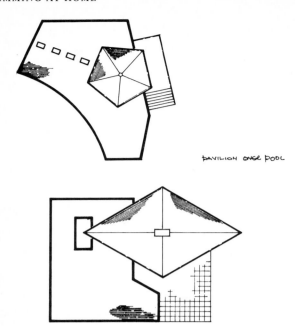

PAVILION OVER POOL

ROOF OVER POOL

HINGED BARRIER

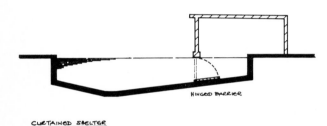

HINGED BARRIER

CURTAINED SHELTER

CANTILEVER ROOF

SUSPENDED CURTAIN

7.15 *Some indoor-outdoor pool arrangement plans: pavilion and roof over pool; hinged barrier and curtained shelter*

7.16 *Atrium garden. Natural sunlight and an open aspect are always preferred by the swimmer in an enclosed swimming pool*
Architect: Macintosh Haines & Kennedy
Unit Swimming Pools, Wolverhampton

boys who might climb in from outside and put themselves, as well as the pool, at risk. Safety fences might restrict, but do not stop youngsters determined to swim illicitly. An all-risks third party insurance offers security against claims or damages when total security cannot be achieved reasonably.

7.6 Inside-outside pool
Private pools used to be tucked far away out of sight. Today's ideas develop the room in the garden theme and make the swimming pool an integral part of the living area (see chapter 12).

Modern ideas place an all-year pool partially indoors to project under sliding glass patio-like partitions into the garden outside. Sometimes the pool portion inside is separ-

7.16

ated by folding doors across a barnside entrance; or a translucent curtain screen is hung to one side wall; or a portcullis type roller blind is pulled down to the water level (see chapter 10.7, Convertibles).

Indoor winter swimming means increased heating, so a hinged insulating barrier gate lifting from the pool floor can shut out the colder water. The indoor pool section need only provide 30 per cent of the total surface water area for 15 per cent of the total water volume.

An indoor alcove for all-year use could be a thermal spa pool or modern hot tub set as an adjunct to the main pool alongside (see chapter 5.2, Health spas).

The indoor pool section should be as appealing as the garden view looked at from within the house. Two-part pools can be *decorated and furnished* as an extension to the

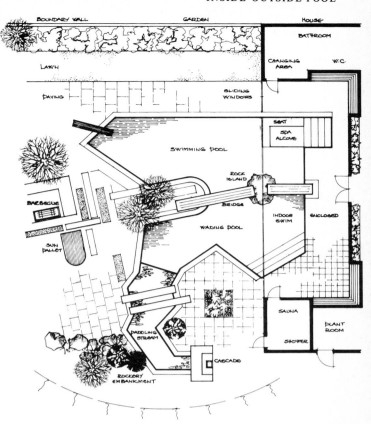

7.17 Indoor-outdoor pool: 'Balneum 2000 AD' plan

home using plants for soft fabrics and decor, with landscaping and architectural devices as furniture and fittings.

Still pool waters taken indoors should use reflection to advantage by perhaps making the ceiling or roofing into a mirrored architectural feature. A roof spanning the two environments and supported by pillars or stylobate actually standing within the pool can be unusual, as are various other intriguing arrangements of connecting underwater corridors and tunnels, overflowing stepped cascades and waterchutes.

To conserve heat and reduce condensation, indoor areas may have wooden floor sections set over and around the pool well (see chapter 14.11, Self-sufficiency for the home pool used as a thermal store). Some of these cover decks are built drawbridge-like. Some are manoeuvred with a ceiling slung jib.

Other ideas might introduce a small Swedish indoor planted garden with imitation pond to include steps as swimming access under and through the house wall to the main pool beyond.

The Romans came closest to solving the inside/outside problem for perfect lifestyle by turning their backs on the streets, setting their villas to face inwards from all four sides, and looking into their own sheltered courtyards – the garden atrium. Nowadays, our pool-garden outside is an intriguing theme for landscape architects. An extension to this scene is the modern balneum, which wholly combines house and pool-garden, linking the poolroom inside to outside.

References
[1] James F. Stern and Earl R. Hendry, *Swimming Pools and the Law*, Milwaukee, S & H Books, 1977

INFORMATION SHEET 7.1

Typical family 10 × 5m pool specification

(Pool to be viewed from the livingroom as a garden design)

Oversite: Availability or provision of satisfactory access
Some on-site soil disposal for landscaping
Terracing or retaining walls to sloping areas
Surface drainage gulleys and sumps or ring drainage

Substructure: Land drains or beachstone underfloor drainage
Hydrostatic relief valve or relief sump
Free draining aggregate or lean mix backfill

Tank: Pool size: 10 × 5m
Water depths: 0·9 to 2·3m
Free-board: 0·2m
Deep point: 3m from end wall
Transition point: slope change at 1·5m depth
Capacity: 75m³
Reinforced concrete floor/footings
Reinforced pool wall structure to withstand hydrostatic forces
In-situ steps at shallow end preferred

Decking: Coping to walls
Bonding ring beam/reinforced concrete floor foundations
Slab or paved decking 0·5 to 1·0m wide along length and 1·0 to 2·0m at ends: 3m for diving board
Gradient 1:50 (indoor 1:25) away from pool

Lining: Vinyl liner (almost 1mm thick) or 2 coat waterproofed cement render with terrazzo, or painted finish and perimeter tile band at water line

Fittings: Main drain at deepest point
Gravity outlet to waste
Inlet flow return
Surface skimmer weir
Circulation pipelines, involving few bends

Accessories: Deep end ladder
Diving board and/or slide
Underwater lighting
Automatic sweeping equipment
Heat retaining/winter covers

Plantroom: 3 × 2m housing
Filtration down to 10 micron and 8 hour turnover period
Heating to achieve 30°C peak in swimming season
Mechanical dosing equipment to maintain marginal chlorination standards
Storage of chemicals, brushes, scoops, test set, underwater sweeper, first aid kit and poolside extras
Waterproof electrical connections to control panel

Landscaping: Screenwalling, safety fencing, planting, stonework and pool garden design

Enclosure: Ranging from chalet to integral pool house with poolside living facilities

INFORMATION SHEET 7.2

Diving levels – residential pools

| Fixed platform/position above water level | Minimum depth | | Surface clearance | |
	Water m	Forward m	Min width m	Min length m
Poolside 0–0·3m	2·0	3·0	3·0	7·0
½m fixed platform	2·1	3·0	4·0	7·0
Deck level diving board	2·3	3·0	4·5	8·0
1m fixed platform*	2·6	4·5	5·0	8·5

Measurements taken from deep end pool wall.
*Official swimming associations consider the 1m spring-board minimum

depth dimensions should also be applied to diving from the pool deck level. See also Recreational diving dimensions: information sheet 2.16; Competitive diving dimensions: information sheet 3.6 and Slide dimensions guide: information sheet 4.5.

INFORMATION SHEET 7.3

Types of garden pool

Portable	Liner	Concrete
General		
70% of total installed and mainly above-ground liner structures	15% of total installed and over three-quarters of these in-ground	15% of total installed and nearly all built into the ground
Freestanding tank set up in 1 or 2 days	Water retaining panels/membrane erected in 1 or 2 weeks	Reinforced in-ground/semi in-ground structure built in 1 week to 2 months
Shells		
Rigid wall	Rigid panel	Shuttered/formwork
Flexible walling	Flexible walling	Blockwork/masonry
Floating membrane	One piece unit	Precast sections
Pneumatic tank	Sprayed reinforced plastic	Dry pack/ferroconcrete Gunite

Finishes
Painted – most early pools were painted; modern coatings strive for long life durability.
Rendered – most concrete pools are finished with waterproofing render.
Liner – almost half today's in-ground schemes and practically all above-ground pools, employ a water retaining liner of flexible vinyl or durable reinforced plastic coating to totally seal the substructure.
Tiled – mainly used for exclusive pool tanks.

See chapter 9, section II and chapter 11.2.

INFORMATION SHEET 7.4

Poolshapes and poolscapes

Shapes	Scapes
Rectangular and geometrical	Plain or natural
Symmetrical and asymmetrical	Landscaped or architectural
Classical and contemporary	Level or raised
Formal and informal	Town or country
Round and oval	Atrium or courtyard
Curved and freeform	Orthodox or eccentric

INFORMATION SHEET 7.5

Useful extras

Pool	Surround	Ancillary
In situ or built-in steps	Poolside chalet/pavilion	Safety equipment
Heat retaining cover	Security fencing	Automatic disinfection
Winter cover	Sheltered patio	Automatic electrical switchgear
Automatic pool cleaner	Diving board	Water top-up system
Underwater lighting	Pool slide	Pool thermometer
Pool alarm	Wet seating	Pool magnet for iron debris
Handrailing	Floodlighting	Pool insurance cover

INFORMATION SHEET 7.6

Comparison costs – private pools

Approximate cost per m² of pool area

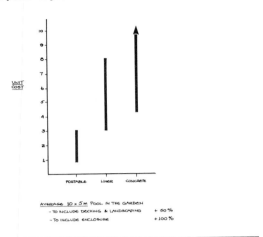

AVERAGE 10 × 5m POOL IN THE GARDEN
- TO INCLUDE DECKING & LANDSCAPING   + 50%
- TO INCLUDE ENCLOSURE   + 100%

INFORMATION SHEET 7.7

Quantities list for a 10 × 5m pool

(Designed as a self-build scheme)

Excavation	– add for bulkage	130m³
Wall area	– internal	55m²
Floor area	– internal	50m²
	– external	60m²
Pool water	– volume	75m³

Pool equipment

Quantities	Item
1	Construction dossier and installation plans.
	Plantroom
1	Housing provision to 3 × 2m at 10m maximum distance and set at water level.
1	Filter unit and self-priming pump of 10m³/h to achieve at least 8 hour turnround at clean running pressure: fresh water supplies.
1	Heater unit of 45Kw to achieve 1°C rise per hour in swimming season: on bypass from pool return line.
1	Disinfection/pH control system to achieve equivalent to 1·0ppm marginal chlorination, and 7·5 pH.
1	Electrical control panel including starter switching, thermal overload and failsafe earth leakage device.
	Circulation
set	Pipelines (50mm diameter), fittings, valves and manifolds – non-corrosive and to pressure rating 9 bar equivalent at 20°C.
1	Flow return inlet (50mm) and adjustable grille – 1·0m/s maximum flow.
1	Automatic surface water skimmer weir including suction sweeping point, leaf basket, equalisation line, and possibly provision for water top-up and disinfection compartment – capable of handling 80 per cent water flow at 8m³/h.
1	Main drain (200mm grille/35mm outlet) and anti-vortex grille – 0·5m/s maximum flow.
1	Gravity outlet (35mm) to waste.
1	Backwash line (35mm) or poolside sump (200mm) provision.
1	Hydrostatic relief valve.
	Options
set	Pool cleansing items including underwater suction sweeper unit, brushes, scoops, etc.
set	Water treatment chemicals, water test set, etc.
selection	Safety equipment such as first aid kit, life ring, etc.
selection	Accessories such as deck level diving board, 4 tread ladder, 300W/12v underwater light with double wound transformer, etc.
selection	Covers for heat retention, winter debris, etc.

Building materials

	Drainage
100	Land drain pipes – 300 × 100mm diameter.
5m³	Subfloor drainage – 100mm of 40mm beach stone.
50m²	Waterproof building paper – 0·2mm thickness.

	Reinforced concrete shell floor (or vermiculite concrete floor)
1·25m³	Subraft screed – 25mm of concrete mix 4:2:1.
10m³	Pool floor and wall founds – 150mm floor/250mm founds of concrete mix 4:2:1.
1500mm	Mild steel reinforcement – 10mm diameter rod including 200 floor to wall starter bars: framework to provide steel at 225mm centres shallow end with double vertical reinforcement to deep end walling (alternative flooring 200mm (3·5kg/m²) tensile steel matting).
2000	Wire ties for reinforcement rod.

	Reinforced concrete block shell walls (or panel walling structure)
550	Concrete blocks – 450 × 225 × 225mm hollow core 150mm² (or equivalent double wall blocking).
5m³	Building sand – building mix concrete 4:1.
4m³	Block infill stone – 10mm aggregate.
3 tonne	Grey cement – building and rendering.

	Finishes (or paint or liner)
3m³	Sharp rendering sand – render mix concrete 5:1.
20kg	Waterproofer to render – non-staining.
1 tonne	White marble chips – 3mm granules.
¹/₂ tonne	White marble dust – fine grain.
¹/₂ tonne	White cement – 6mm (white marblite render mix 2:1:1).

	Surrounds (or decking materials)
30m	Bullnose handgrip coping – 300mm wide.
25kg	Coping stone matching joint mix.
30m	Water line tiling band frost proof – 200mm deep.
2m³	Reinforced concrete surround founds for paving slabs – 50mm concrete mix 4:2:1.
40m²	Non-slip paving – 50mm slabs.
	Screen walling, patio, landscaping materials, etc.

Commissioning of pool and equipment.
Source: Rutherford Group.

INFORMATION SHEET 7.8

Building character into the pool

In a successful pool environment, there is an intangible aura which can often be focused onto one particularly distinctive feature in the setting.
The theme might be:
recreational . . . a games deck
relaxing . . . a sun pallet or sun deck
restful . . . a water cascade
entertaining . . . a barbecue grille
extravagant . . . lighting and sound
invigorating . . . a spa pool

to involve:
shape and form
symmetry and setting
shelter and shade
planting and stonework
colour and texture
finishes and patterns

and create:
modern line through striking architecture
classical style through statues and stone seats
a social focus by means of a bar in or by the pool
a natural surrounding by means of planting
an interesting aspect with different patio levels
an unusual impact with stepping stones to a pool island.

See chapter 12, Landscaping.

8 Swimming on holiday

A hotel pool is a water-retaining structure the same as any other pool, but it has a totally different ambiance: rather like eating out instead of doing your own cooking. Too often pool places are added on afterwards or fitted in somewhere, with too little thought or plan. Imagination is everything. The art of holiday entertainment is '50 per cent psychology'[1] and 50 per cent theatre.

Judging by the large number of travel brochures with poolside pictures, swimming pools also make powerful publicity for a hotel, though some brochures unwittingly seem to illustrate *how to* and *how not to* design hotel swimming pools! A first-class hotel naturally offers personal service, good food and a friendly bar. But the hotel with a superb swimming pool still has the edge over its rivals.

If water alone is compelling, what makes a pool so remarkable? Why do people really go there? Do they want to relax? Or exercise? How many bathers actually swim, in the middle, or in the deep end? How many people just sunbathe? Is the terrace suitable for the pool, or the hotel, or both? And is this all there is to it?

8.1 Surround the pool

The importance of the pool area cannot be overstressed. For a hotel, this is a permanent showplace, the surround being more important than the pool itself. It is a social place, a forum, an inviting place. Guests will use it throughout the day, and often throughout the evening as well.

Such *'places,* are the nodes where movement comes to a stop. They are the parks, squares, courtyards, gardens and sitting areas where we can work, play, rest, or chat with friends'.[2] They are best kept small scale and human, with clear route and movement patterns as 'people tend to take the most direct and effortless path'.[3] The whole pool area should be planned for all comers like any other public hotel room. It is absolutely impractical and most unpopular to park the pool clear away from general activities and all hotel services. On the other hand, when too closely situated to the peaceful areas of a hotel, it causes much annoyance to guests. A busy open-air pool needs sound barriers in the shape of walls, screens, plants and trees; an enclosed pool doesn't project the same pervading sound problem, but will need absorbents and baffles to deal with booming reverberation (see chapter 10.12, *Sound*).

Formula for success There are a number of basic questions to be considered first:

- Is the pool to be a focal point? If it is just one of the facilities, it is likely to be rather plain and simple (see chapter 12 for landscaping and chapter 11 for decor).
- Is the pool to be enclosed? An open-air scheme will suit summer visitors, but not so the winter tourist or business executive (see chapter 10.4 and 7 for covers and convertibles).
- Is the pool to be reserved for swimming (ie large deep end) or developed into a complex of different depth pools? Most guests *bathe* rather than *swim,* and since bather ages range from young children to grandparents, needs also vary greatly (see chapter 4 for leisure schemes).
- Is the pool meant for health or sport? Other than specialist hotels where all facilities are purpose designed, very few guests come to train for competitive swimming (see chapter 3), though some may come to convalesce (see chapter 5).
- Is the pool comfortable or clinical? Concrete decks, plain walls and efficient finishes are most practical and easy to clean, but usually thoroughly unappealing (see chapter 11 for finishes and settings).

To cater for the wide range of needs and tastes, and for the different users and watchers, there are endless variations of pools and surroundings. Landscaping, for example, soft or hard forms, allows different precincts to be grouped around the whole pool scene – for eating, for games, for resting, for children, and so on. Landscape barriers and garden boundaries are far more practical than ordinarily appreciated, for example: *the bridge* really does provide distinctive access to the other poolside; *stepping stones* can separate shallow from deep end; well-placed *planters and borders* do keep bystanders safely clear of deep water diving areas; *sunbathing slabs and sheltered alcoves* will help keep peace and allow relaxation; *soil banks* with walls or shrubs on top will provide seclusion; *rocky outcrops* can become diving platforms; and so on. Sometimes, those blisteringly hot sunny surrounds need cool, leafy shaded spots, or airy lattice shelters, or thoughtfully slung awnings, just so that the bathers can stay beside the swimming pool. The provision of fountains and sprays will do much to cool the immediate environment, with cold refreshments to cool the customer.

8.1 *Islamic influence in a modern East African hotel*
Serena Lodges & Hotels, Kenya

8.2 *A variety of pool facilities for today's tourist: pools flowing to pools as fun water slides*
Corinthia Palace Hotel, Malta

8.1

8.2

8.3

8.4

8.3 *A bridge is a useful device to separate a children's pool from the main pool*
Tamarind Cove Hotel, Barbados
Photo: Alleyne & Carrington

8.4 *The beginning of a winter tourist season for a Queens-land's Gold Coast hotel in Australia: both the pools are raised out of the ground adding interest to the layout, saving on excavation and cleaning costs*
Australian News & Information Bureau

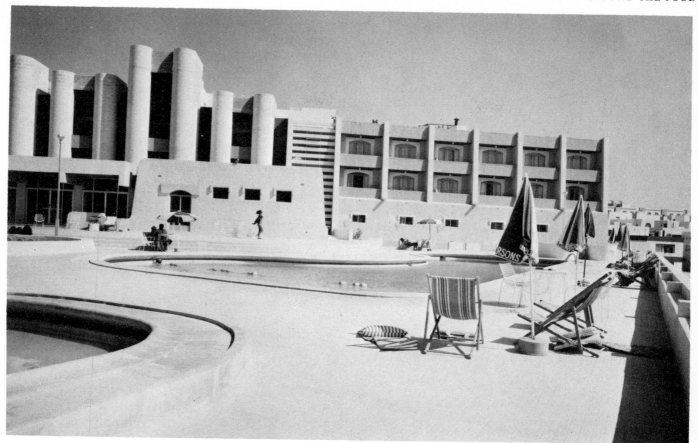

8.5 *A blend of East and West*
Dolmen Hotel, Malta

The deck area Clear space around the pool allows clear view of activities in the water – always a popular hotel pastime – as well as a splashfree place for sunbathers. Watersplash will rarely exceed 3m of wet paving.

At the very least, provide a 1:1 proportion of hard surround to waterspace outdoors, though a larger 2:1 minimum proportion is better, but so much depends upon total landscaping provisions. And allocate for a control area or lifeguard base, beside the pool wherever possible – a mandatory requirement in some states. Try to avoid deserts of paving creating bare, windswept open spaces (see chapter 12.4).

The deck needs areas of shade from the sun and shelter from breezes, space for general movement, playing, eating and drinking, and, of course, the all-essential spaces for sunbathing (see chapter 5.8). A practical plan allows for three-quarters of patrons being spectators, with three-quarters of those bathing, staying in the shallow area (see chapter 12, Pool surrounds).

Where enclosures combine various pool facilities under one roof, the hard deck surround is primarily meant for safe access, but a separate solarium, sun patio or open-to-the-air arrangement will still be preferable (see chapter 10.7, Convertibles).

All paving must be non-slip, non-fade and level; with varied textures or surface materials for greater interest. Providing they are safely positioned, clearly marked, and there is an alternative route for the handicapped, split levels and steps help break up expanses of paving. *Never* float smooth concrete decking, for water on concrete is an excellent lubricant!

Decking must always be easy to clean and with few crevices. Modern fabrics, materials and synthetic carpets will soften decks, but can offer too many crevices and crannies that will harbour bacteria and fungi. Unless proper drain-through, drain-off and deep cleaning arrangements are provided, organisms are easily picked up on passing bare feet (see chapters 12.4, 15.2 and 16.2).

The water area Making the deep end smaller gives more playing space in the shallow end and mid-way depths, which then saves on heating, filtering and chlorinating costs, in turn meaning far less water capacity being involved in the conditioning process. An imaginative presentation of the pool should provide for all three bathing essentials of paddling, playing, and sometimes swimming. If possible, segregate the paddling area for toddlers: create another play pool or wading section for older children. Both kinds of pool will be busy with children, and popular too with their parents. The main swimming pool will also be better for broad comfortable steps for easy access.

Surrounding facilities If the pool is well placed with clear, free movement between its surround and the hotel, consider next the basic needs of bathers.

Adequate provision of toilets and washrooms close by the pool with convenient changing space must not be overlooked. Wet bathers dripping through the lobby, or across a public room are never very appealing. Several all dry routes to the pool area should be provided plus, perhaps, a special entrance for day visitors, or 'swim-and-dine' paying customers from the outside public. Wet routes to and from the water to bather facilities should be obvious and unavoidable, passing through pre-cleanse areas, pool perimeter footbaths, etc.

The now semi-public pool requires very similar facilities to the municipal pool changing block and arrangements (see chapter 11.4) with stricter attention to safety, especially in offering first-aid facilities and maintenance and cleansing routines, which are more rigorous than for the usual freedom-of-the-pool facility generally extended to private guests (see chapter 16.2).

Landscaped wet seating around the pool is extremely useful, but the dry deckchair/sunshade seating and table arrangement will be needed just like any other general sunroom where food and drink are consumed. But do keep food and breakable glasses well clear of the water, and the deck well swept – and not into the pool! A parapet design might be preferable (See chapter 6.3 and 9).

Catering will vary enormously from early morning swimmers to late afternoon rush-hour bathers. Provide ample flexibility of facilities, with storeable furniture for between 25 to 50 per cent of the hotel complement, depending whether business hotel or tourist pension, indoor or outdoor pool, winter or summer season, cold or hot day, and so on. Alternatively, allow for a minimum of 3 to 4 seats for every person in the pool (see chapter 2 for bathing loads).

All-over facilities The original all-enveloping dome is returning to favour as a very efficient cover for large-span areas, since it still keeps the feeling of outdoors by means of its top and all-round lighting. In most parts of the world, too many days are plainly unsuitable for bathing, and a daylight dome over a warm water pool helps create a successful all-year facility.

Bright and durable surfaces The best pool and hall lining is the permanent, easily cleaned ceramic tile or mosaic. In Germany, some of the best flowline ceramics, painted motifs and washable murals in the world are used for pool deck surrounds and facing walls, and in the pools themselves. And the classical painting 'art within an art' of trompe-l'oeil, popular in ancient times, is now returning strongly in pool designing since plain walls and protruding fittings can easily be masked within the frescoed gardens.

The advantages claimed for versatile ceramics amount to chip-proof, scratchproof, crackproof, shockproof – resistant to frost, heat, light and acid all in one material. Ceramics come with textured, patterned and reliefed surfaces, and are available even as acoustically absorbent tiles.

The more temporary the community, the more permanent should be the facings, fittings and the fixtures. Good quality interiors wear well and last longer, borne out by those Roman bath mosaics still in excellent condition after 2000 years (see chapter 11.2).

8.2 Latest ideas

Roman baths provided for almost everything. At Pompeii, their Baths were even 'surrounded with tavernae'.[4] Some

8.6 *A domed 'Pierhead' pool beside a hotel complex in Bermuda ensures a warmer swim than in the sea*
Sonesta Beach, Bermuda

8.6

8.7 *Hygienic ceramic surfaces protect the interior of this*   Villeroy & Boch, Saar
hotel pool and poolhouse

8.8 *Architectural and landscaping form for the modern*   Haden International Ltd, London
traveller beside the Abu Dhabi Hilton pool   Photo: Henk Snoek

20th-century hotel leisure pool centres now also include groups of shops or bazaars. Other schemes set restaurants and bars to overlook the pool, or to be convenient to the bathers, so much so that one swimming pool in Jamaica has a soft drink bar in its centre. (A word of warning – never allow real glass tumblers to be used: it is almost impossible to find broken glass in pool water, except with bare feet.)

The pool area should be profitable, and not a loss-leader enterprise tucked to one side. By drawing together similar entertainments (similar to the successful formula for leisure/sports centres, or Summerland complexes) the swimming pool area can become a focal point to which people flock. Holidaymakers want something more than their normal domestic environment, especially the children. But consider also the ideal of the proprietor, and his concern for a decent return on investment. Look again at some of the pools intended for entertainment. How many are oblong and plainly irrelevant to their surroundings, peculiarly bizarre, badly looked after, or simply gross with more deep end than anyone ever needs?

Classic shaped pools suit grand hotels, while freeform designs with 'Capability' grounds make better community pools. A natural pool lake with islands, palms, rocky outcrops and shelving beaches will add enchantment to the holiday village or motel scene. Such an idea was tackled with verve and charm at Capistrano in Spain, where clear pool water winds through the village along to a broad, cascading weir and a rustic bridge by shallow end grassy banks. Another and more active man-made oasis exists, this time in the Nevada desert, where a wedge-shaped pool has been engineered to provide the real beach strand complete with 1·5m perfect breaker surfing rollers arriving at one minute intervals. In one oil-rich Arabian desert area there is an equally unexpected scheme that includes an animal habitat on an artificial mountain, with underwater grotto beneath, entirely surrounded by a pool flowing round and down a broad cascade to return via tributary inlets.

The widening draw of tourism now means coastal waters are no longer sufficient entertainment alone, hence versatile water park complexes for newly established holiday centres are rapidly proving a key attraction (see chapter 4).

Water parks In developing places such as Dubai and Djakarta, new holiday complexes are springing up to give a leading theme of 'water in action' for new tourist centres (see chapter 4, figs 4.4 to 4.12). One particular pleasure park in Germany, with three open-air pools, demonstrates positive proof that kinetic entertainment in a swimming pool is enthusiastically appreciated. At ten minutes to the hour, every hour throughout the day, a whistle blows to announce mass migration into the middle pool. Its wave-making machinery has proved so compelling that if the mechanism were to work all day long, the two flanking pools would stay practically empty.

However, creating a real holiday scene is not necessarily a question of being able to offer a hyperpool centre. Often it is more practical and better to create a small, intimate design of pleasing style with a 25m size pool, though 33m at least is considered better for wave-making. Such holiday pools can be beach shelved and lagooned to suit children and bobbing swimmers, and are now being financed collectively by business combines or tourist hotel groups. If wave machinery seems too expensive to install or operate, the smaller, individual water-jet mechanisms and fast flowing water currents are equally popular for only a fraction of the cost (see chapter 11 for wave-making and turbo-jet options in pools).

Unique investment Creative ideas transform places. Consider the eccentric imagination in the architectural ideas for the seaside village of Portmerion near Portmadoc, sometimes called the Welsh Xanadu; or compare the original thinking in creating the seaside experiment of La Grande Motte in the south of France (see chapter 4.5, Leisure pools).

Be flamboyant in hotel pool design. Try linking the hotel to the garden with a chain of interconnecting pools. Join an elegant watergarden in the foyer to a paddling pool in the kids' parlour, on through a water stream to various play places, and finally ending in the swimming pool by the beach. Add enjoyable extras such as aerated cascades, waterfall overflows, spa-pool alcoves, higher floor to lower floor chutes, waterslides, as well as straightforward diving-boards (see chapters 2 and 4). It is the sense of fun with water that appeals all round and to all ages.

Never build that stolid deep water swimming bath suitable only for cross-Channel swimmers. Try entertaining everyone.

Anachronistically, it seems the grand style clearly surviving in Germany, where Kurhaus Hotels dispense mineral waters, is still very popular; in England, the grand hydro hotel has fallen totally from favour – and those original hydropathic waters such as Smedley's galvanic and electro-chemical remedial baths that diverted many Victorians are no longer novel, nor even believed in. Quaffing mineral water is not many people's idea of pleasure, and sitting in the stuff can be pretty boring. Today's Continental spa hotels include all manner of different entertainments from mud-packs to jet drenches, saunas to bierkellers, casinos to promenades, recreational parks to . . . the formula does seem similar. And there is now a growing following for health farms, those exclusive places appearing in most Anglo-Saxon countries . . .

Competitive investment Not one hotel along Miami Beach lacks a swimming pool, even though built right beside the sea. It has been said the more unnecessary a swimming pool is, the more successful it becomes. But the first objective for any hotelier wanting a swimming pool must be to improve return on investment. A good host tries to anticipate the needs of his guests so 'creating a holiday mood' and atmosphere. He sets out to entertain in style.

This ideal is no different at busy executive hotels or conference centres, where relaxation by the pool is even more business-like and more earnest with plug-in telephone jacks and portable TV units standard. The play accessories may be more sophisticated but are needed for the pool just the same. Today's boardroom jet-set bring with them their own appreciation and expertness in swimming pools, based upon world-wide travel and probably their private swimming pool at home. It is not unknown for healthy and experienced businessmen to carry their own pool water test set to check hygiene before swimming – a practical precaution in a world of tight schedules and 24-hour tummy bugs. The hotelier should keep in mind that over half today's air travellers are on business and look for

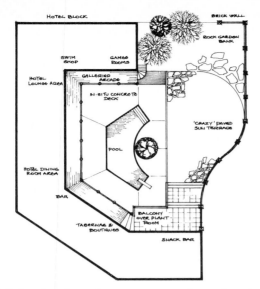

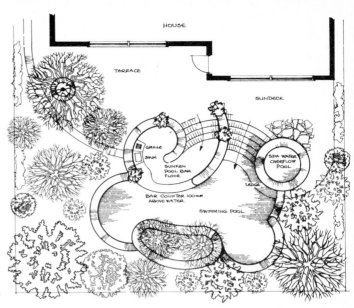

8.9 *Holiday hotel environs: courtyard pool and market arcade*

8.10 *Pool bar will appeal to guests young and old: but no glassware should be allowed, only unbreakable cups*
Courtland Paul/Arthur Beggs & Association, Ca

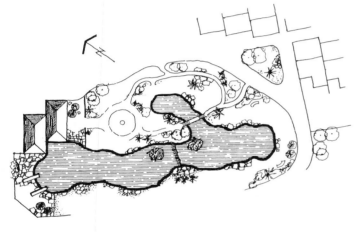

8.11 *Holiday village pool complex, El Capistrano, Malaga, Spain*
Rutherford Espanola, Madrid

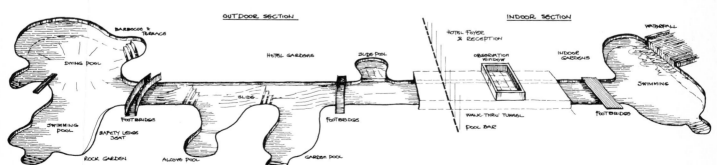

8.12 *Outdoor/indoor hotel pool, East Africa. Based upon sketch by Graham Hill of a pool stream for fun and leisure from hotel reception out into the garden*

103

8.13 *A curvaceous swimming pool of the Windward Islands*
Turtle Beach Hotel, Tobago

hotels offering an opportunity to recover from travel fatigue . . . and providing congenial places to meet people, socially or officially.

8.3 What does the customer really want?

Hotels exist to provide food, drink, shelter and entertainment. Make sure the swimming pool does too.

The 'inner man' There is nothing like bathing to improve the appetite. Taking advantage of this should be routine arrangement for hoteliers who automatically provide snacks, drinks and evening barbecues by the poolside. The smaller pool can easily use a trolley-bar for poolside drinks and snacks. But larger, more involved pools might require a poolside parlour, or waiter-service for drinks with cold buffets brought from hotel kitchens. Hot food may need to be carried in warming-wagons, or perhaps produced in a poolside taverna suitably provisioned with instant cooking units of micro-wave grill and sandwich toasters, deep freezer and cold cabinets. Delivery and service routes should be short, level and separate from public routes; organised so that kitchen sounds, sights, and smells do not filter to poolside guests.

Keep diner facilities well clear of the pool; 5m deck width will stop any possible threat of splashes, or the chance of food getting into the pool to play havoc with disinfection residuals. Clear screens or panels will help. A practical arrangement is the two-way counter permitting indoor serving and outdoor eating. In some leading Continental restaurant concessions, the separately run *haute*

cuisine is a great attraction by itself, with continual live entertainment laid on from all the pool activities and people.

Even in mediaeval times, the privately owned 'shallow water butt bath provisioner'[5] always catered particularly for the better tastes. Wayside house bathtubs, perhaps draped with canopies or even padded inside with linen, were usually suitable for two people, plus tray between them for a meal. Medically speaking, eating in the bath is not advisable, and swimming after a heavy meal is positively dangerous.

But other less catholic, more excessive entertainments were greatly preferred by certain 18th-century travellers, such as Casanova, who wrote in 1765: 'I also visited the bagnios where a rich man can sup, bathe and sleep with a fashionable courtesan, of which species there are many in London. It makes a magnificent debauch and only costs six guineas'.[6]

The spice of intrigue has always made travelling to foreign places that much more fascinating.

References
[1] Kenneth Lindley, *Seaside Architecture,* London, Hugh Evelyn, 1973
[2] Michael Gage and Maritz Vandenberg, *Hard Landscape in Concrete,* London, Architectural Press, 1975
[3] ibid.
[4] George Ripley Scott, *The Story of Baths and Bathing,* London, Werner Laurie, 1939
[5] Lawrence Wright, *Clean and Decent,* London, Routledge, 1971
[6] Giovanni Giacomo Casanova, *Mémoires écrits par lui-même,* 1826-38

INFORMATION SHEET 8.1

Pointers to successful pleasure pools

Surrounds

Make a pool with a view.
An entrance by the shallow end is safer.
Wide access steps everywhere are best.
Never lay bare deserts of pressed paving, nor set a pool indecently alone in the middle.
Introduce mixed texture materials or pattern a large terrace.
Create individual courtyards rather than one vast terrace.
Pool coping distinguishes edges, whereas overhanging paving naturalises them.
Build raised pool levels around and use the surfaces for mosaics, murals and frescoes.
Build plenty of in situ wet-seating niches and sunbathing plinths.
Does the pool blend? Classic shapes need classic surrounds.

Features

Moving water enthralls and reflecting water calms.
Introduce a waterfall or cascade, wallmask spout or fountain, shower waterwheel or inlet sprays.
Poolside catering is popular, so make a feature of the charcoal grille outside.
A stepping stone crossover, or a bridge to an island or pavilion is inviting.
Emphasise cool arbours, alcoves, arches and arcades.
Take the garden into the pool with an inset pond, planters or protruding rocks.
Plant tree islands for shade and stature; shrubs and conifers for shape and form; climbers for screens and cladding; tropical plants for luxury and colour.
Build-in underwater seats and ledges, caves and tunnels, lights and sound.
Run a gallery or treewalk overhead.
Consider out of season uses (from fishing to fashion shows).

See information sheets 11.9 and 12.3.

INFORMATION SHEET 8.2

Relative prices — main equipment

(approximate guide only)
All equipment is costed as a factor of 100, based upon wet niche underwater light unit transformer and deckbox complete = 100

Cost factor of 100		Cost factor of 100	
0·5	Pool painting per m²	2–4	Pool liner per m²
2	Sun cover per m²	3–4	Debris cover per m²
3	Lawn/carpeting per m²	4	Paving per m²
4	Coping per m	15	Stainless steel handrail per m
5	Marblite per m²	15/25	Mosaic-tiling per m²
10–20	Airdomes per m²	100–150	Lightweight enclosures per m²
15–25	Channelling per m²	25–40	Skimmer weirs each
65	Ladders	400	Built-in steps 2m radius
80	Underwater sound/niche	500+	Underwater window
100	Underwater wet niche light complete	600	Underwater dry ducting light complete
100–500	Underwater vacuum sweeper unit	500–1000	Auto-mechanical sweeper system
100	Diving-board 0·5m	900–1500	Spring-board 1m
300	Slide 3m	2000–3000	Spring-board 3m
1200	Turbo-jet device	3000+	Staging-tower 10m
3000+	Multi-slide 10m × 8 channel	12000+	Wave generator system

See information sheets 2.8, 7.6, 13.10 and 14.19.

INFORMATION SHEET 8.3

Accessories

These may be:

Practical	or	Novel
Bleachers, tables and chairs		Bar-in-pool
Sunthatches, brollies and canopies		Jetstreams and wavemakers
Windscreens and radiant heaters		Observation windows fascinate
Solarium		Child-size chessmen on a chequerboard patio
Changing cabanas		Games area and playground equipment
Attractive safety fencing and beginners handrailing		Diving practice trampoline
Diving-boards *not* spring-boards		Hillside waterchute
Deep end ladders		Fitness equipment
Shallow end steps		Carpeted surround
Essential ash-trays and litter-bins		Flaming waters fountain

Residential freeform pool in Sussex: stepping stones make unusual sundais seats
Photo: John Dawes

PART II
Pool Techniques

Preview

The success of a modern swimming pool depends mainly upon modern technology. Since the 1950s, a flood of new ideas has reduced both the size and relative cost of pools and their equipment. The design and control of this complex modern environment has become the responsibility of highly specialised, professional building services engineers, whose job it is to concentrate upon improving environmental engineering using a varied and widening arsenal of supporting hardware. In the long run they are aiming to produce a Henry Ford model T type swimming pool.

It is the equipment and systems having most bearing upon environmental engineering that form the basis of material appearing in Part II of this book. And some of the most challenging and interesting projects unexpectedly play wider roles in other fields of activity involving conservation and energy storage, water reclamation and seaspace exploration, and even in limiting abuse of the environment.

9 Substructures

SECTION I

9.1 Location and distribution

The weather and the time of year generally influence pool construction. Much of the work is below ground and exposed where sudden rainfall can wash-out clean workings, or sharp frost can break up curing concrete. Dry warm seasons are the best pool building periods, but the practice of controlling working conditions with temporary enclosures and rapid building techniques on the site is rapidly spreading.

All the better methods of manufacture and production aim to speed construction, thereby reducing business risks and raising profit margins. *Pre*-fabricating the substructure shortens the time an excavation remains at risk on an open site. Selecting only the best pool location, ensuring an uncluttered access, keeping service runs short, avoiding long hauls over soft ground and watching for overhead obstacles will leave bigger budgets against unsuspected troubles, which inevitably arise among the variety of construction hazards.

Using patent systems of substructure, the franchised pool builder network is now a valuable part of the pool production process. Every site and scheme differs, so installation arrangements really must be versatile. Local distributors make economic sense just by being on the spot to interpret site conditions and adapt structures to suit each situation. The swimming pool manufacturer's task is complete only after he produces *and* delivers the goods.

9.2 Digging and foundation

Digging can be space and time consuming, and hazardous. Before starting, search out *all* the unknowns. Ask probing questions about flood waters and soil conditions, and if necessary take an augured bore hole test (hand operated to 5m maximum, powered to 30m plus) for confirmation about the water-table, or take a series of bores towards the subsoil survey (see chapter 2 for typical problem places).

There might be water. Or worse still, running sand when deep holes widen out, as waterlogged sand runs in. Dewatering (see chapter 9.3, Water and drainage) or a stiffening skin of gunite can save the day. For small-scale emergencies, chemical hardening of the ground or freezing the soil can help.

Subsoil might be corrosive (see chapter 9.4, *Corrosion of concrete*), unstable, or solid rock. Especially beware of instability or uneven expansions presented by adobe type soils. These clays do not readily take up moisture, but when they do, they heave and expand just like freezing soils, exerting considerable pressure to break up paving or pool walling.

Dig wider and backfill with granular classified material, or gravel and crushed rock, as for permafrost. All backfilling should be free-draining and carefully consolidated.

There might be sewers, service lines or road drains. Carelessly cut roots might kill a mature tree, or alternatively, roots could probe the pool. Divert the services or re-assess the location. Protect the pool from the tree or replant if possible (see chapter 12.5).

Ancient ground could unearth archaeological finds. Dig carefully! The larger the contract, the greater the consequences of all these risks.

Mechanical diggers Clearing and digging for an average 10 × 5m pool site will take two men at least two weeks by hand, or one man one day with a mechanical excavator. The men tackling the hand dig will also require extra protection with timber props and struts in the longer exposed excavation.

The world of mechanisation aims at speed for economy, and involves equipment such as bulldozers, dumpers and trackers; mixers, pumpers and vibrators; tippers, trenchers and tampers, but the poolman's favourite machine is a back-hoe excavator with front-end loader. The bucket is best for diggers working in the hole, the backactor beside the hole, and a dumper for spoil removal over 30m. There are special small mechanical diggers which, with all the

9.1 Liner pool assembly – *GRP structure*
Waterways Leisure Industries Ltd, Cheshire
Photo: Walbrook Photo Ltd

(a) The bare excavation: mud and water to face

(b) The wall outline of a 12 × 6m double Roman end tank

(c) Complete pool in GRP panels before backfilling showing clearly the screeded hopper floor

(d) Setting the vinyl liner as the pool fills with water: a lean mix backfill adds support to the braced structure

9.2 *A compact, longreach, versatile excavator is required by a swimming pool contractor: especially a machine like this one that can be squeezed through narrow passages*
Smalley Excavators, Lincs
Photo: Tony Bentley

1a

9.1b

9.1c

9.1d

9.2

trimmings removed, can squeeze through a 1·3m passage and under a 2·2m headway (almost the same space needed by a man and his barrow). Some will strip down to 0·8m in the dismantled form. Standard excavators need at least 2·5m access all round and reasonable room to manoeuvre or swing around the site.

Machine digging from above the work reduces protective strutting necessary compared with hand-dug excavations, though piling or underpinning is still vital within 2 or 3m of a building or crossing a line of surcharge. Handtrimming is still necessary for accurate finishing.

Foundations Pool foundations must rest in firm consolidated subsoil. There are far too many pools that settle, sink, break their backs or slide slowly downhill. Prevent soft spots that can create dangerous hollows beneath tanks and foundations, if necessary by building upon solid piers set 1m apart across filled ground, or infilling sinking hollows with compacted hardcore and dry lean mix. Or perhaps dig deeper still to pour a satisfactory subraft.

The importance of building every swimming pool upon firm foundations cannot be overstressed. The 1970 Royal Commonwealth Pool at Edinburgh is solidly built upon six 65 tonne anchor rocks. At the Roman Bath in Somerset of Aquae Sulis (circa AD 70) 'the welling-up of hot springs below the Great Bath revealed the waterlogged sub-soil upon which the whole building was founded; there must, in fact, have existed a great raft of rubble and timber below the masonry, visible and unexposed alike, with heavy piling at points of stress'.[1]

Consolidation or spreading load Except in gravel or well drained rocky strata, normal sub-foundation work for most well-built pools, of any shape or size, means laying a 100mm bed of rubble or rejects and covering this with a waterproof membrane or slip layer. Then it is good practice to spread a 50 to 75mm oversite concrete layer on which the appropriate reinforced base slab is poured. An innovative method for improving the stability and bearing capacity of low load-bearing ground introduces a semi-permeable, woven, synthetic fabric to carpet weak or boggy areas and save on infill materials and oversite concrete. The matting blanket helps evenly spread load and separates mud from aggregate, yet still allows natural seepage of water to prevent dangerous build-up of hydrostatic pressure. This synthetic substratum material is also excellent for firming-up surrounds, drainage, access areas and temporary roads.

Where substrata rocks are water saturated and liable to slide, additionally reinforced, protective retaining walls need calculating. A simple gravity retaining wall depends for stability upon its own weight. Sheet pile walling requires resistance from the soil in front and behind, and is to some extent flexible. For steep slopes, holding structures of sheet piling, shoring, buttresses or soil anchors are usually sufficient.

9.3 Water and drainage

In ground work, you could say the whole pool substructure is a total foundation to keep the water out as much as in. Water is as much part of the soil as the solid particle: and it is the greatest single cause of variation for engineering design properties.

Highly permeable soils are best fully drained, since even

an immersed subraft foundation is susceptible to differential settlement. Techniques for improving soil properties, or the stability of slopes under pools can involve:
- surface stabilisation, compaction or consolidation
- piling, rafting or injection grouting
- chemical ground hardening or soil freezing with low temperature brine or liquid nitrogen.

However, the different forms of providing local area drainage are usually the most practical of all.

Digging perimeter drainage before cutting into a slope can prevent rainwashed slumps. Protection by covering exposed soil walls after excavation can avoid rain-eroded cave-ins. But dealing with water already present in the ground is the more important.

Main control techniques generally involve dewatering by:
- fitting hydrostatic relief valves into the pool floor (the most popular method, but mechanical devices can corrode open or shut)
- installing land drains beneath and around the pool (ideal for the sloping site)
- pouring an extra thick anti-flotation concrete subraft to anchor down the pool tank (a positive but expensive method often necessary for permanent water-tables)
- lowering an underground water-table with a pumping line from a poolside borehole or hardcore sump (the safest compromise being to make the pool into a kind of caisson with artesian wellhead). (See chapter 2.5.)

The empty pool The argument that modern pools never need emptying would only be true in a perfect world. Unfortunately, water is allowed to go off so badly sometimes that the pool has to be emptied to scrub clean the lining. Or perhaps main drain valves are carelessly left wide open.

In high water-table conditions, an empty tank, even one made of concrete, obeys Archimedean principles, and floats out of the ground. If the pool does not crack in the process, it rarely settles back into the same position after the flooding water-table subsides. And pools with a soft screeded, unreinforced base can be disrupted with the floor shifting or the waterproofing flexible liner stretching (see chapter 9.5, Tanking and lining).

Even when dewatering controls are considered adequate, a liner pool should never remain empty for more than one day, otherwise vinyl shrinkage can result. If Marblite terrazzo render or tiling of a concrete pool is left exposed too long in the sun, unprotected, it can lift with external water pressure, or suffer hairline cracks following thermal expansion (see chapter 11.2, Finishes and facilities).

Flooding Below ground plantrooms may have to cope with local floods or escaping water from the filter. Therefore *always* keep electrics well clear at high level and protected from possible contact with water (see chapter 13.8, Electrics and controls). Pools built in flood plains will benefit with raised poolwalling parapets against periodic flood water and contamination. When underground waters offer too great a hazard, install an above-ground pool, or build on pillars and piers, or go and build elsewhere.

The backwash While laying foundations, prepare also drainage facilities for the filter plant. A 1m³ capacity drainage sump for purged or waste filter water is sufficient to

9.3a

9.3b

9.3c

9.3 *Rutherford Group, Sussex*

(a) Piles of rubble too close to an excavation edge can cause cave-ins requiring clearing out of every vestige of debris between the reinforcement prior to concreting. In the foreground is the 10 mm mild steel reinforcement rod for a kidney shape pool designed by pool specialists for construction by a local builder

(b) A delivery rig and reinforced hosing to carry pre-mixed concrete quickly and cleanly over soft gardens

(c) Delivering the concrete floor
Photo: Arby Davis

deal with backwash water from residential pools. To prevent silt and soil leaching through, cover the drainage base rubble with a 100mm layer of gravel, ballast, or synthetic fabric matting.

Where filters discharge their media (such as diatomaceous earth) along with the dirty water, the backwash sump can soon become blocked or filled, so installing a holding or settlement tank in the outlet line is useful. This temporary holding tank is usually essential for public pools, where ten or twenty times the amount of waste water can be discharged per filter. The settlement/surge storage tanks for public pools can be equal in volume to an average private swimming pool, and can be as costly. But wherever possible, balancing or surge waters to be stored are best included within surface water draw-off systems (see chapter 13.7). Settlement tanks also form part of recovery systems (see chapter 14.10).

9.4 Materials and methods

Cement and concrete There is always concrete somewhere around a swimming pool. Properly mixed, well-placed, dense concrete is impervious to water *without* real need for any admixture. But no ordinary concrete is safe from corrosion.

Corrosion of concrete Peaty, marshland soils with their humic and sulphuric acid solutions attack concrete; sulphate soils produce equally aggressive waters, but alkaline concrete can resist moderate sulphate corrosion, providing soils are well drained. In saturated ground of more than 0·2 per cent sulphate content, supersulphated cement is preferable: over 0·5 per cent this special cement is essential. Of the corrosive salts in soils, calcium sulphate is the more common and moderately soluble: sodium and magnesium sulphate salts are less common, but more dangerous and more corrosive as a result of their greater solubility. In mildly acid soil conditions, a simple backfill around the pool of neutralising chalk or limestone will be sacrificed in corrosion instead of the alkaline pool concrete (see 16.4, Corrosion).

Special cements It is interesting to note that Roman concrete depended for its remarkable hardness and durability on the famous pozzolana of Latium and Camparia. This original volcanic material (slow setting in colder climates) sets hard even underwater. Pozzolanic cement has continually proved to be magnificent and workable material, ideal for building impermeable structures. In using pozzolanic cement rather than Portland for thicker concrete sections, stresses in curing can be lessened because of the small amount of heat generated.

Other than grey or white Portland, cements of particular interest to pool contractors are the rapid hardening, sulphate resisting and masonry types. Special cements such as high alumina (hac) for high early strength should only be used under strictly controlled conditions, ie as in concrete manufacturing processes. But even then, in a pool's hot, wet environment, there are possible subsequent problems with precast products unpredictably losing strength, and suddenly failing (see chapter 10.3 and 14.9).

Standard mix and control In making the finest Roman concrete, Vitruvius recommended pitsand that 'crackles when rubbed in the hand'. Clean, washed, sharp sand is still just as vital for a good concrete mixture. Sound mix design (weigh batched rather than volume) with a low water to cement ratio and 50mm slump offers best workability.

Large concrete areas are cast in alternative bays, or with 0·5m gaps between to allow for substantial shrinkage before infilling seven days later. The minimum compressive strength for comparatively thick sections of concrete in water retaining structures is low at 25N/mm² 28 days cube test.

Careful placing – no dropping from a great height – makes for compact concrete that is watertight. Disregarding any weepy joints, it is segregation, honeycombing or cracking of concrete that mainly cause leaks. Uneven load, water pressure, settlement and shrinkage can induce cracking with weak mixes.

Careful curing and ensuring minimal thermal stress from heat of hydration will control fine hairline cracking. But frost must be kept clear at all cost: curing should take place at above 5°C.

Admixtures and cement There is no substitute for good concrete practice and it is often recommended to avoid admixtures, especially calcium chloride-based accelerators which attack steel reinforcement and increase shrinkage of concrete. Most pool contractors, however, use one sort of additive or another to improve workability, increase density, make non-shrinking concrete, and generally to save time, effort and cost (see information sheet 9.2).

Reinforcement The pool builder, with his reinforced structural design, takes civil engineering into the back-garden. Most reinforced concrete pools are built in skeletal form; most flexible vinyl liner pools are installed with external casings (exoskeletal). But there are pools coming on to the market in expanded cellular or inflated plastic that have no additional reinforcement at all!

The expanded cellular structure of inflated plastic foam gains a stiffness similar to metals and grp, is similarly tough, lightweight, easily worked and, moreover, a good heat insulator. Some overall pool structures designed in this material even exclude the usual bracing every 1m or so, and might even omit an internal waterproofing liner (see below 9.7 and 9.8).

Most pool shell designs strive for a monolithic structure in which reinforcement is the framework, whether galvanised chicken wire or 20mm mild steel rod, chopped polyester strand or laminated glass-fibre matting.

Steel distribution Traditional steel reinforcement must be clean of loose mill scale and rust, oil and grease. It should be distributed in walling at least to 0·5 per cent and covered by concrete to a minimum of 40mm (20mm for denser gunite). Rod ends should overlap at equal to 15 times their own diameter, be tied securely to starter bars or footing/floor mesh, and set with distribution steel fixed outside main upright bar reinforcement. In general practice, most reinforced concrete (RC) tank designs employ either 10 to 20mm diameter mild steel rod, or 2 to 6kg/m² high tensile steel mesh (see information sheet 9.5).

Galvanically dissimilar metals must not come in contact with each other within the structure, or through the electrolytic medium of water, otherwise corrosion by galvanic action will take place as if the pool were some huge low voltage battery (see chapter 16).

GRC – an alternative The main in-situ construction materials at present are concrete and steel, with polyester concretes and poly aggregates coming up fast. Resin laminated and glass reinforced cements (GRC) that harden in or out of water are very similar in weight to aluminium and have a most viable future in pools. They can be laid with great advantage to include an all-in finish coating.

There has been much research into 'fibrous reinforcement of cements' since the 1950s, notably by the USSR, with dispersed mixes of steel, nylon or polypropylene (USA), carbon or glass (UK). Normal extruded glass is badly corroded by the alkalis in ordinary Portland cement, hence glass fibres have had to be developed that are resistant to alkali attack – but they cost half as much again to make either as continuous reel strand rovings, or more practically, as chopped short lengths. Fortunately, in pre-mixed reinforced cements, the weight ratio of the chopped fibre is only about 5 per cent, compared to GRP of up to 50 per cent, for a successful lightweight, plaster-like consistency, basic mix. Such workable material can be used suitably as a *structural render* – a single application skin inside and out to *dry laid* blockwork walls – that is waterproof and decorative yet still makes the walling stronger than if mortar alone were used. GRC is also an ideal material for pool channelling and gratings, covers and surrounds (see below 9.8).

Insulation Until the fuel crisis, it had not been considered generally necessary to insulate swimming pool tanks, except in frozen ground conditions, or where flowing subsoil waters conducted heat away, or over and around deep sunken underground pool hall/tanks (see below 9.7). Dry soils and an insulating backfill generally proved sufficiently satisfactory on the assumption that heat losses into the ground amounted to only 10 per cent of the total.

However, heat dissipated by poolwater from an in-ground concrete tank is measurable in the soil as far as 5m away: consequently, effective tank insulation, especially over the sunny fringes of early summer when the ground is cool, can limit these energy flows, and therefore reduce the initial heat build-up time. Low grade ambient energy systems, particularly, need extra insulation to help maintain their small temperature increases from everyday slow solar gain (see chapter 14.4 for a discussion on insulation).

A good example of a common concrete heat reservoir is the in-ground fuel tank, plus heater intended to maintain storage oil temperature at 25°C. A 100m³ RC oil tank structure, lined and insulated, and sunk 2m deep in dry ground, can maintain a 25°C isothermal around 1m from the tank, and a 17°C isothermal around 4m away. A tank refilled with relatively warm fuel every two or three weeks maintains constant isothermals, even throughout a winter with ambient a few degrees below zero, and therefore usually requires no additional heating service at all.

Since pool walls are being designed progressively thinner, and water temperatures are being raised higher, with heating costs constantly spiralling, better pool insulation becomes more and more valuable.

There are both rigid polystyrene foams and traditional insulating materials suitable for the large subterranean surface areas of tanks. The Munich Olympic pools used an expanded cellular glass insulation which is manufactured in lightweight slabs and easily cut. Before placing a concrete base, the lean mix site concrete is sealed with a cold bituminous primer and insulating slabs set at staggered

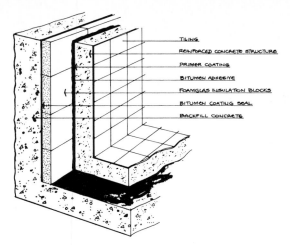

9.4 *Pool wall insulation*
Pittsburgh Corning Europe SA

(a) GRP LINING/SEALANT

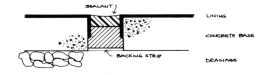

(a) SEALING JOINTS

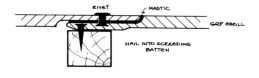

(b) COMPRESSION FILLET/SEALANT

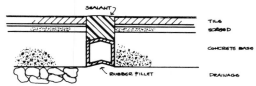

(b) GRP FLOOR/WALL JOINT

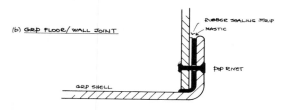

9.5 *Expansion joints and sealing joints*

joints into a flood coat of hot bitumen (or cold adhesive) and then covered by roofing felt or similar lining material. Insulating slabs can also be fixed like tiles into a bitumen coating on pool wall exteriors. This insulation allows the mass of the pool structure as well as the pool water to serve fully as the heat sink or store.

Joints and sealants In practice, design movement joints intended for stress relief in concrete are the main source of leaks in swimming pools. It is now unusual for full movement joints, expansion or contraction, to be included in the floor or walls of a swimming pool, though sliding joints are often required behind the perimeter coping to separate the tank from the deck, or from the adjacent superstructure.

Nevertheless, experts disagree and a British code of practice for water-retaining structures still requires expansion or partial movement joints in reinforced concrete spaced no more than 7m apart (subject to the allocation of distribution steel to control cracking), since 'contraction joints are essential to permit movement caused by heat loss and drying shrinkage'.[2] Yet, many pools – public and private – are built successfully without any joints whatsoever, other than well-prepared normal daywork construction joints (monolithic joints not intended for movement). 'Full movement joints should be provided only where special circumstances exist',[3] (eg where differential settlement may occur between the bulk of a pool which is at 1 to 2m depth, and the combined diving pit to 5m depth, creating a marked higher dead load per unit area of floor).

Where partial or full (when reinforcement is curtailed or reduced) stress relief joints are considered absolutely necessary in construction, 'they must be sealed on the water face and a water bar provided'.[4] A good bond joint is essential with hot or cold bituminous sealing compound filling a thoroughly clean and dry 20mm wide and deep gap. Unfortunately, even two-part polysulphide fillers are picked out by children in the shallows. To prevent this, use a compression strip such as a preformed hollow square resilient fillet, inserted into the joint to absorb expansion, and caulk over with a 'pick resistant' silicon rubber compound. A neoprene strip coated with an epoxy adhesive can be inserted into an epoxide mortar filling for the most effective jointing of all. Polyurethane and polysulphides can be used, but may be affected by chlorine.

Joints and temperature Water is a great moderator by keeping temperature stable and obviating the need to relieve stress, particularly with indoor pools where there is additional protection from extremes of environment.

Although in theory a 50m pool length offers about 20mm contraction over a 30°C maximum drop, at least 75 per cent of the stress is accommodated within the reinforced concrete structure. Full movement joints are not needed for stress relief in *normal* operating conditions: stress being accommodated within the concrete. Thinner walls of gunite generate less heat in curing, thereby reducing stress, shrinkage and hairline cracks. In gunite shells 'there is no need for jointing apart from wide, stepped day work joints'.[5]

The temperature of a structure can drop dramatically in winter when a pool is emptied or left out of use. It is the *rate of temperature change that is critical*. Tests on public pools in constant use over three or four years have shown small shrinkage and creep movement to around 0·05mm in total.

But at shut-down, thermal movements of 1·5mm have been recorded after several days – in fact, this is only a small proportion of the potential movement due to the temperature change. At refill in winter, mains water of 15°C can rapidly increase the interior shell temperature within one day, perhaps increasing hazard to tiling.

Joints and ceramics When tiles or mosaics are laid, a compromise movement joint is taken through the tiling bedding, and preferably in some specifications through the screed/render to the pool shell surface. Construction or expansion joints in the shell should always coincide with tile movement joints at internal corners, floor and wall perimeters, transition points, pit bases and across the whole shell at 5m intervals. Never tile over joints in the shell structure (see chapter 11.2).

Generally, deck tiling and especially above-ground shells are subject to greater movement as greater temperature changes are often involved. Durable sealants and appropriate expansion joints are also important around the pool to stop possible seepage between coping, ring beam and deck.

SECTION II

9.5 Tanking and lining

Techniques There are pool tanks built under, in, half in, on and above ground. They can be divided roughly into concrete pools, vinyl liner pools, and linerless pools, all using many different forms of basic material for the framework structure.

Some pools *are* successfully built with a paintbrush by stippling resin into glass-fibre matting. Some baths *are* attractively made of papier-maché plus coats of varnish. As long as there is a serviceable waterproofing system, the lightest structural shell or tank often can prove entirely satisfactory.

By work studying the job out in the field, American production engineers were first to evolve varied new methods for rapidly building watertight structures. Production line pools are not necessarily stereotyped, since only the shell and the equipment are standardised or modularised, and none of this is normally put on view.

There is no single best method for the most attractive and most durable structure. Like the automobile industry, different manufacturers produce their own design package. Most builders adopt and develop their favourite installation techniques for water retaining tanking, and use tends to vary according to distribution franchises of the manufacturer.

To save complex calculations and problems, designers prefer to keep pool floors and walls (the tank in other words) as a monolithic unit independent of any main building structure or covering enclosure.

Floors Most floor slabs are uniformly supported, though some are still built on piers along the lines of the early 1900 pools with 'subterranean galleries all around the pond'.[6]

There is still no satisfactory replacement for a concrete

9.6a *Infill two-core hollow concrete blocks one course at a time*
Rutherford Group, Sussex
Photo: John Dawes

9.6b *Building with patented two-leaf concrete blocks in a freeform pool in Italy: setting the ring beam steelwork*
Penguin Swimming Pools, Essex
Photo: Cris Sirmione

9.6a

9.6b

type base which might be anything from 100 to 300mm thick. It can be densely tamped or vibrated to compact the concrete into a solid mass, expelling air bubbles and improving water tightness. It is best laid in one day with stepped wall foundations; set in 4m widths, the most practical maximum size for beam tamping. It is especially important to consolidate around the main drain, wall water bars, or floor fittings, since normal concrete shrinks 1 in 3000.

Although tamped down, sand floors kept firm by the weight of water alone are still used for some vinyl liner type pools, they are not recommended by national pool associations since sand floors do get disrupted, causing the water-retaining membrane to stretch and distort. It is better to use smooth concretes that are not abrasive to the vinyl lining, a vermiculite mix being popular for its cushioning as well as its insulating properties.

Hopper bottoms These have all four side walls sloping to a base ridge or deep point in the floor. This configuration introduces valuable economies in construction and reduction of reinforcement and reduces overall water capacity for less costly filtration, purification and heating. The floor acts partly as sloping walling running down from an even perimeter footing ledge upon which average 1·2m high walls are set. Safe hopper slopes and profile dimensions are clearly specified by pool associations (see also chapter 2 and information sheet 2.17).

Always position the hopper basin carefully: excavation can be awkward and shaping of flooring material can be troublesome in the wet. Laying 1:3 slopes (beyond the transition point) requires a concrete mix or similar composition with vermiculite for example, dry enough to hold and to compact with accuracy for subsequent placing of a pre-formed vinyl liner.

Walls Transfer the datum position from floor to walls and regularly check levels as walling progresses, particularly at the corners – for the eventual water level will quickly show up a sloping pool!

The top 200mm of walling is always the most vulnerable part of any tank. There, the internal lining should be protected by hard-wearing finishes (see chapter 11.2), and the perimeter walling sometimes strengthened with an external (or integral) reinforced ring beam (edge beam) tied to walls or deck (see information sheet 9.3).

Steps, ramps and ledges require reinforcement design changes within the tank's structure to compensate for the reductions in wall thickness they bring, especially at ice pressure levels, such as channelling surrounds.

All competition pools must have 'variations' set completely clear of swimmers' lanes (for example, it is better to inset steps in the wall with grab rails on deck rather than protruding ladders overhanging). But most bathers prefer simpler ways to get into and out of the water, and not merely an athletic entry and exit. Built-in steps look good, but are more costly. Built-on steps as a stairway to the floor can save on cost, but interrupt clean design. An excellent compromise is steps set into an alcove in the pool perimeter to create a sloping shallows area as well. Liner pools sometimes have a prefabricated step alcove, or an overlaid matched standing stairway securely fixed against the wall and on the floor.

Risers and treads of even depth with clearly marked leading edges are essential. For young bathers, steps should

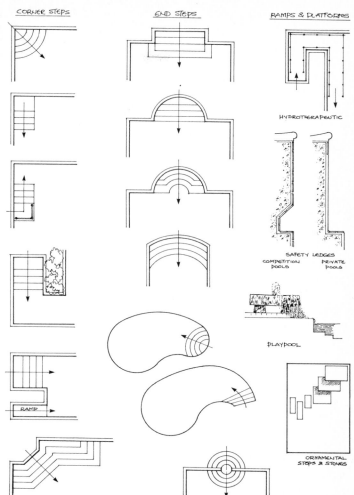

9.7 *Some steps, ramps, ledges and platforms*

span the whole width of a pool, and for the disabled, wide, shallow steps, or slow, inclined ramps with handrails are better (see chapters 2, 4 and 16 for disabled and safety data; also chapter 12 for landscaping steps).

Underwater windows Observation windows are important for training, diving and competition pools (see chapters 3 and 11.5).

Windows are of tough, reinforced, laminated acrylic/glass, or at least 25mm armourplated glass, and any weakness usually shows up in the surrounding seal, unless, as annoyingly seems to happen, they get cracked during installation in the mêlée of construction. Spot lights can be positioned behind windows, but generally, separate underwater wet niche type lighting is more efficient, but not so safely protected from the public (see chapter 11.5).

Waterproofing Many swimming pools rely for water retention upon linings set over the structure. Properly laid concrete tank structures are impermeable, but usually require internal renders, with or without waterproofing admixtures. Often monolithic structures, such as reinforced concrete or gunite, or GRP shells, rely upon their own soundness to hold water. But sectional tanks made up from multi-units such as hollow-core blocks, or reinforced concrete panels, or perhaps dry stacked bricks, subsequently rely upon a suitable, durable lining. When total impermeability is more than vital, on a roof pool, for example, the fully waterproofed one-piece, ready-made tank is the safest answer.

Prefabricated structures may use flexible liners, either tailormade or standard sized for the job, or prefabricated components which can be sealed during assembly on the site, avoiding the cost of an additional lining or membrane. A flexible liner will give and take should a structure shift, but in wet ground conditions, subsoil water trapped behind and beneath a liner can cause it to lift and stretch.

Rigid plastics and lightweight glass-fibre reinforced cements can also be troubled by in-ground water and corrosive soils. No shell will remain waterproof and troublefree, unless installed properly and thoroughly protected.

When external waterproof lining to a concrete tank is required, continuous asphalt (three coats) is most practical. It is easier to back-render walls in sodden ground and a brushed waterproofed cement slurry or waterproof latex will seal surfaces on porous hollow-core blockwork. More modern epoxy coatings or polyvinyl applications are even simpler to seal or waterproof, but are usually more expensive and often incompatible with bitumen.

Internal linings – renders Concrete surfaces are not considered ideal finishes. They are susceptible to algae growing in crevices, are rough on the skin, and look unattractive. They might even need preparing with acid etching, bush hammering or mechanical keying according to age and the kind of final coating required.

The most common coating, cement renders and screeds, involve a two or three layer lining system to approximately 20 to 25mm overall depth. A first truing, scratch coat render is applied to dub out the internal walls. This is then covered with a fine grained render plus corner coving over the thicker bed screeding of the impervious concrete floor. The wall render and floor screed is now ready for almost any decorative finish required. Thicker renders (up to 75mm) possibly used to make-up extra bed depth will need pressurised applications and supporting internal mesh for strength.

Although renders applied by force alone should be impervious, a water repellent, non-staining 'waterproofer' or latex is usually included in the mix. Final finishes such as three coat paints, polyurethane sprays or marblite terrazzo then create the second sealing lining over the rendering.

Internal linings – flexible liners Liner pools, as they are called, are merely pools with a flexible water retaining skin. The skins are fitted in all kinds of structure, sometimes first covered with absorbent material to stop liner chafe.

Most flexible liners are clamped beneath the perimeter coping for easy fit or removal. For better handling, they should be warm (20°C), with the thinner liners (500 micron) proving the more pliable. For a 10 × 5m pool, at least four men and a runner may be needed to lay a preshaped liner. Flexible parachute vinyl lining is suspended over the pool tank and as the water fills, wrinkles and creases in the membrane are brushed and smoothed out to the edges before infilling water pressure makes this impossible, ie at about 200mm above any crease. A rapid fill is best with necessary cuts made in the material when the water level is about 50mm below a fitting. At the same time, air trapped behind a liner can be sucked out by a vacuum unit, whose extraction hose is well sealed with tape between liner and support walling.

Liners come plain or patterned, sanitised and satin finished for hygienic and non-slip properties. They must resist UV light, especially at the water line where most attack and abrasion occurs. (Acid or alkaline poolwater can affect PVC properties, and dry chlorine can bleach and rot the membrane.)

A vinyl pool liner can also wrinkle with the effect of low pH (acid water condition), from too warm water (35°C and above), or by slipping out from perimeter holding clips. Heavy bathing loads can cause a liner to stretch or move putting pressure to breaking point upon weak welded seams. But for the vast majority of liner pools in existence, public or private, sound manufacture and proper installation guarantees at least a 10-year life.

An alternative to the glove-like factory-made liner is the synthetic, flexible sheet material that is cut, laid and welded all within the required pool. This on-site system of waterproofing is ideal for large public pools, and where unusual shapes are involved. Thicknesses can be varied (from 0·5 to 2 or even 3mm) at wearing spots, textures can be coarsened for the shallow end, creases can be cut out entirely and a perfect fit guaranteed (see chapter 11.2).

Testing waterproofing Whichever lining system is selected, water tightness testing is advisable, and definitely required prior to tiling public pools.

If time allows, the pool should be filled slowly – 1m per day – and left to soak thoroughly for seven days, over which period the water level should drop no more than 12mm, compared with a freestanding temporary static water tank and depending upon evaporation rates. Such time-consuming delays are avoided by the majority of pool builders today, who prefer to provide three to seven-year guarantees of water retention by good workmanship and if necessary repair at no charge.

The static water test is also used to help prove leaks when the pool is in use, since the water level will eventually fall to the same level as that of the leak – usually an inlet, or badly set fitting (see chapter 16.4).

Leaks tend to occur in the pipeline circulation system, and they can be traced by isolating various sections at a time, and applying air or water pressure tests (see chapter 13.6).

In liner pools, a poorly installed sealing ring around a wall fitting is the most probable cause of a leak, rather than a split seam in the membrane, or a rent in the material.

The simple process of placing a dye bag (vegetable-based rather than synthetic) close by a suspected leak and watching the traces of dye trickle or stream towards the escape point is usually sufficient. However, slow and difficult leaks can be tracked down by adding a radioactive tracer in the water, and taking a radiation count around the pool to find concentrations of leaked, radioactive material.

It is not unknown for pool companies to hire an aqualung diver to inspect and carry out more obvious repairs underwater (see chapters 16.4 and 16.5).

9.6 Substructures – hand laid

Adaptable and traditional practices Modern pool shell-system substructures have not totally replaced traditional pool building methods, though they now account for most schemes that are built today. A small team of men using basic bricks and concrete can still compete favourably. The argument for traditional methods is that they are known and reliable, the designs are adaptable to meet most circumstances, the materials are relatively easy and

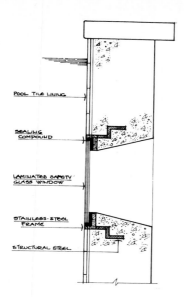

POOL TILE LINING

SEALING COMPOUND

LAMINATED SAFETY GLASS WINDOW

STAINLESS-STEEL FRAME

STRUCTURAL STEEL

9.8 *Underwater window*

9.9 *Blockwork structures must be absolutely stable and sound for eventual concrete rendering to remain satisfactorily waterproof. A concrete slurry wash over a blockwork pool helps for the final render adhesion and improves waterproofing properties*
Rutherford Group, Sussex
Photo: Arby Davis

9.10 *Applying a second render lining and bottle coving over the original 'truing' scratch coat. Final Marblite coatings will finish flush to the underwater lighting niche*
Penguin Swimming Pools Ltd, Essex
Photo: Malcolm L. Keep

9.8

9.9

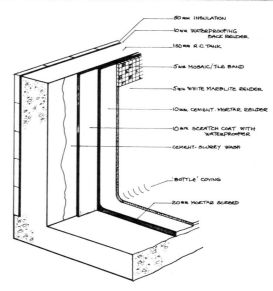

50 MM INSULATION

10 MM WATERPROOFING BACK RENDER

150 MM R.C. TANK

5 MM MOSAIC/TILE BAND

5 MM WHITE MARBLITE RENDER

10 MM CEMENT MORTAR RENDER

10 MM SCRATCH COAT WITH WATERPROOFER

CEMENT-SLURRY WASH

'BOTTLE' COVING

20 MM MORTAR SCREED

9.10

9.11 *Linings indicating thicknesses*

117

9.12 *Patented two-leaf concrete walling block for compact RC infill, dense and waterproof*
Penguin Swimming Pools Ltd, Essex

economical to obtain, and the skilled labour lives locally. No extra special training, nor special equipment, nor special delivery is required.

1 NATURAL STONE   A pool built into solid rock is generally expensive to excavate and usually needs a compact cushion of drainage material beneath. Sometimes re-use of excavated or quarried stone is feasible in tank construction, but the spoil is better used for the landscaping. Unreinforced walling is bulky, time-consuming to lay, and needs constant waterproofing. Such pools are prone to leaks, with renders filling the crevices rather than making smooth, safely waterproofed linings.

2 BRICK   Stone masonry, so favoured by the Romans, often proved leaky. But far more reliable brick walling formers with infill were still popular in the 19th century, as were glazed bricks for the interior lining. Such methods are usually too costly and labour intensive nowadays.

3 SHUTTERED CONCRETE   Early 1900 public pools set on clay had 300mm deep floor slabs with 400mm mass concrete walls. Nowadays, it is more usual for the

• 2m deep reinforced concrete tank to have 150mm thick walls using 10mm mild steel spaced between, 100 and 200mm apart

• 4m deep reinforced concrete tank to have 400mm thick walls using 20mm mild steel spaced between 50 and 150mm apart.

The reinforced concrete floor is poured first, the RC walls between shuttered formwork, next. Concrete is carefully poker vibrated for compaction, and properly protected throughout curing. Timber formwork is kept in position twice as long as metal and, though more expensive, offers better insulation during curing. There is no reasonable limit to size or shape, but usually standard formwork imposes design limitations and a rectangular tank. Flexible metal shuttering, which can be struck in only a few days, enables pool builders with an experienced team to produce very satisfactory curved shapes.

4 CONCRETE BLOCK   The development from bricks into concrete blocks as permanent formers for infilled cavity walling seems obvious. And in fact an ideal DIY block pool system can be built to a 1·2m water depth without any reinforcement in most ground conditions.

Starting from the corners, the first inner and outer row of blocks are laid before the floor footings set off, and ensuring the cavity between the walls is kept clear. Pool walling more than 2·5m deep is better supported by temporary shuttering and stepped in thickness according to the depth involved and surrounding soil conditions (see information sheet 9.4 and fig **9.14**). A few of the first course blocks are omitted in order to rake clear dropped mortar before the RC infill is vibrated: the infill is best poured at several stage levels rather than all in one go. With two render coats, plus paint or marblite or tiled lining, this complete sandwich substructure is equal in strength and durability and water retention to any normal in-situ reinforced concrete. But the permanent shuttering of concrete blocks should not be included in any wall design strength calculations.

Simple 2m in-ground, unreinforced garden pools are sometimes built with concrete blocks laid on their side, or even with mortarless interlocking blocks; a flexible waterproofing liner and firm supporting ground is essential.

5 CONCRETE DOUBLE BLOCK   The progression in multi-unit design (from 150, 225, 300 to 400mm thicknesses) has made twin block walling simpler to lay than two separate permanent block shutters, though in the case of hollow-core blocks, it is difficult to calculate structural effectiveness. But patent blocks (eg two concrete slabs held parallel and apart with steel tie rods) offer a double walling structure with a reinforced concrete interior to full water retaining standards. Such simple, but effective, blocks are laid without difficulty to formal and freeform shapes for small or large pools.

The hollow-core block structure (two cavities per block or two-plus-two rabbets to equal 2½ cavities in special swimming pool blocks) is particularly economical since contractors require no specialised capital equipment. But, being porous, this blockwork system relies totally upon a waterproof lining inside the tank, and outside as well in high water-tables. Core filling of the blocks is carried out every two or three courses with a 100mm recess left in the latest course ready to key into the next. Backfilling is left for several days until the concrete is no longer green. Calculations can only be based upon the RC core pillars within the permanent block shuttering.

Many substructures have been built in blockwork forms with 100 per cent efficiency in normal ground conditions. Hollow-core blocks are best limited to 2·5m in-ground depths and maximum 20m pool lengths. They are most adaptable for diverse pool shapes, but not for problem soils where known wall strengths will be required.

A reinforced ringbeam for additional perimeter strength can be cast between blockwork walling and decking to withstand water, ice or soil pressures.

6 DRY PACK CONCRETE OR PARGETING   Hand-packed concrete is similar to poured concrete, except the highly plastic mix is dumped into the pool and stacked by hand shovel to shape floor and walls. Little, or no formwork is used. The pool is first caged with steel and the mix tossed against the sides of the excavation. It is possible to create vertical walls to 3m with a shovel, but the whole operation for garden pools alone is very hard work for at least five to eight men and requires strength and ability to rehandle and compact the material swiftly. While every kind of shape is possible, slightly sloping walls do present a disadvantage and are

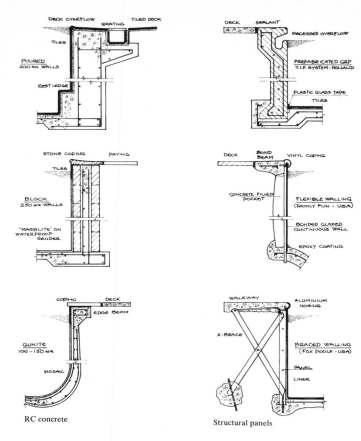

9.13 *Six constructional methods involving reinforced concrete techniques and structural panel systems*

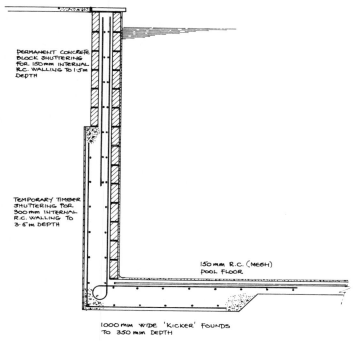

9.14 *Example of reinforcement: stepped concrete block walling shuttering*

unsuitable to competitive swimming. Walling and flooring from 150 to 200mm thick is shaped and smoothed to a finish suitable for paint, Marblite or mosaic.

Pargeting is now little used in building complete pool shells, but the principle has been adapted by liner pool companies for shaping basic hopper floor slabs, upon which prefabricated walling systems stand.

9.7 Substructures – custom made

Versatile and effective production As enthusiasm for swimming pools built up rapidly mid-century in America, the pace quickened for production-model substructures that were as effective as those built traditionally on site. Market demand widened the range of methods and materials, and encouraged, in contradiction to normal manufacturing repetitiveness, mass production of a unique pool shape every time and the freeform pool was created.

Some companies found the best solution was to build a wide range of standard pools under factory conditions, then to transport the components or the complete product to the site. Others developed a kind of peripatetic production line and took their factory technique right into the garden. The result meant pool shells were built stronger, faster, more efficiently and cheaper than ever before.

1 TIMBER   One of the earliest systems used light and convenient plywood panels as the pool walling. These panels treated with preservative (not with creosote which attacks vinyl liners) for a 30-year life can be used as in-ground (depths 0·5 to 2·5m) or above-ground pools. Of all custom-made substructures, they have proved the most suitable and lasting in popularity, especially for the average handyman. In fact about 80 per cent of pools in Sweden are made of wood.

Built really as a former for the flexible liner, wooden units are so adaptable they also sometimes function as liquid or grain stores, research tanks or fish farms, or even storage units for effluent or sprinkler systems.

2 STEEL   The resilience and great strength of steel vessels makes this material ideal for problem sites where relatively light structures might have to stand up to deep freezing, or within loose fill, or perhaps sit securely upon a hillside. Steel plate tanks, bolted or welded in sections, can come complete with built-in service inlets and outlets, but they are more likely to be fabricated on site, or on shipboard. Installation times are faster than for concrete, but overall costs are still higher.

Following the principle of like with like, the steel pool is best built within a steel building. Effective protection and insulation is doubly important to resist rust and retain heat. A steel tank should be capable of inspection all round and underneath. Galvanised finish may be painted, or steel can be bake-enamelled, plasticised or even tiled.

Flexible panelling systems employ thinner, corrugated, coated steel, uncoiled to the required shape and reinforced with suitable ties. Stainless steel is more expensive, easy to clean and unaffected by normal pool waters, which look steely grey on dull days and steely blue in the sun.

3 ALUMINIUM   Like steel, this light but more expensive material flexes and absorbs loads – it deforms rather than ruptures. Up to 10m long one-piece pools can be set into the ground without foundations: larger tanks usually require strip foundations. Aluminium is frost resistant with

119

low heat absorption – ideal for fast pool heating . . . and loss. Manufacturers claim less heat is lost generally by an aluminium tank than concrete, since readily conducted heat hits a 0·5m dead air space behind the walls where washed loose gravel has been used as backfill.

Corrosive soil soon pits unprotected aluminium: chlorinated water dulls and attacks the metal surface. Two bituminous coatings outside, three epoxy-resin coatings inside, or a vinyl lining, increase durability. Maintenance costs are then very low over long periods of time – an ideal material for extremes (see chapter 2 on arctic pools).

Prefabricated double skin sections, with the outer wall corrugated for extra strength, can easily be welded or bolted together on site. Extra care, though, in making and sealing all joints is particularly important for segmented metal pools.

4 GLASS REINFORCED PLASTIC   GRP is another modern material that offers high tensile strength and flexibility, and is excellent in severe conditions. Reinforced resin compounds are as versatile as concrete and they introduce the further advantage of surfaces with a built-in finish. They can be laid directly onto the excavation, set up in prefabricated sections or delivered in one whole piece.

Generally known as fibre-glass pools, the complete structures can be lowered into garden excavations in one day, or easily assembled panel components for large hotel requirements can be fully installed within one week. In comparison, materials for a 10 × 5m pool might involve fifteen 20kg panels, against six hundred 20kg blocks for a concrete pool.

A GRP substructure can be manufactured that does not rot, rust, or corrode; that will hold water, resist algae, and reduce pool maintenance. But badly mixed compounds can flake or delaminate, poor gel coats will harbour algae, inadequately reinforced layers under pressure sometimes stretch and creep, adverse soils do chemically react, thin colours might fade patchily, whilst subsoil hydrostatic water easily lifts a lightweight empty tank.

Complete shells are usually set onto a sand base or lean mix, and as the pool fills with water, a lean mix backfill is packed down to equalise pressures.

Similarly, polyester duo-modules of pool and hall are packed down into position, but in a gunite skin, as an underground natatorium 'like a giant thermos on its side and out of the 21st century'. Such structures are brightly coloured, fully serviced and include stormproof skylights; sealed and insulated pool systems ideal for poor all year round weather areas give total privacy (see chapter 7.6).

On-site fabrication techniques involve brushing resin into layers of glass-fibre matting or spraying polyester and chopped fibre up to 5mm thick and which can continue as the decking, benches, plant containers, etc (see chapter 12).

GRP pools emptied in waterlogged conditions need timber beams set across the tank to hold out the sides unless reinforcement and dewatering systems are already installed outside. Obviously, one-piece tanks are limited in shape and size and manoeuvrability, but their very lightness makes for easier handling.

5 PRE-STRESSED CONCRETE   The ideal shaped pool for this material is round, though from both a swimmer's and constructor's point of view, circular pools are inefficient.

In-situ, pre-stressed, rectangular, concrete substructures are successfully installed in Germany, Scandinavia and Switzerland, but have gained very little support elsewhere in the western world. They have the 'advantage over ordinary reinforced concrete that the whole pool structure is under compression and no contraction or movement joints are therefore required'.[7] The risk of leakage is minimised.

6 PRE-CAST CONCRETE   Another popular technique in Europe, mainly for larger pools, involves assembling on-site factory-made separate concrete units, sometimes each as large as 5 × 4m and complete with fitted tiling, lighting, chanelling, coping, windows, etc. Factory-cast concrete allows stricter quality control, but the joints and seals in matching to the next unit alongside have to allow for minor variations. Generally, the floor slab is formed on-site, but with private pools floor sections are commonly pre-manufactured as well. Delivery, access and lifting can be a problem even with the newest lighterweight dense mixes, but the overall time saved and quality gained is valuable.

7 GUNITE OR SHOTCRETE   Really rapid on-site production arrived with the widespread use of pressure sprayed concrete. The equipment requires a mixing hopper and compressor, with a skilled nozzleman feeding water (5 per cent by weight) to a 1:4½ dry, loose, 8mm fine aggregate to sharp washed sand mix blasted through high pressure delivery hose at 3·5kg/cm². Walls and coving are gunned in sections, followed by the floor in bays. Excessive rebounds (over 15 per cent) must be avoided, as well as weak porous pockets within the concrete. The skill of the nozzleman and the proportion of water in the mix is important. Standard practice of dry pumping sand, aggregate and cement to mix with water at the nozzle is fast and efficient, but can be noisy and dusty. New ideas being introduced, involve wet concrete delivered to the site in bulk to lessen mix variability, which helps arrange quieter operation, and avoids materials handling and storage altogether.

Gunite is most practical for awkward access and cramped sites. In public and private pools, no movement joints are required other than day work butt joints. In garden pools, steel reinforcement is covered by 20 to 25mm of gunite concrete; walls are gunned 100 to 150mm thick with floor varying from 100 to 200mm centre to edge. Curing achieves 60 per cent strength seven days, 28 days strength to 50N/mm² cube test: no additives are required for watertightness – impermeability is ensured by high equal density and compressive strength.

An average 10 × 5m pool of 40 tonnes, can be gunned over 10mm steel and mesh reinforcement against hessian walling or single side shuttering or direct onto the excavation within one morning. The resulting surface is coarse and requires rendering, and finally a Marblite or mosaic finish. The particularly wide floor coving tends to keep non-swimmers away from the sides; this coving radius increasingly widens (1·3m for 4·5m depth) as the pool deepens, making most gunite shells unsuitable for ceramic tiling and competitive swimming events. But overall shell costs are improved by gunning rather than pouring a pool – the time factor contributes greatly in public schemes.

This monolithic lightweight concrete shell is more prone to flotation than thicker, heavier poured concrete, but the increased density gives greater impermeability. Thin walls eliminate thermal stress during curing.

9.15

9.16a

9.16b

9.16c

Complete freedom of shape and very fast construction has made this system widely adopted in USA and very popular elsewhere, offering varied and sophisticated shapes for heavily populated urban market areas.

8 POLYCONCRETE AND FERROCONCRETE   The continuing process in scaling down of material and manufacture introduces new competition. Synthetic fibre reinforced concrete and resinated cement renders point to the future for even thinner, fairfaced walling in one pour. The initial corrosion problems with glass fibrous reinforced concrete are being resolved, and unheard-of sculptured forms are being made from ferro-cements. In the future pool industry, this will mean stronger, more flexible, lightweight, in-situ shells with built-in durable surfaces and even more intriguing shapes at prices lower than ever before.

One New Zealand system borrowed from the boat building industry sets chicken wire for wall, and normal steel mesh for floor, with a ferrocement mix forced into the reinforcement fabric to 40mm overall using a hand vibrator plaster gun, finally finishing with steam curing to produce 28 day strength overnight. There are no bond beams,

9.15 *Assembling a prefabricated pool shell. An increasingly practical form of factory-pool construction in Europe with concrete modules coming completely tiled and finished ready to fit together*
IBACO, DFR

9.16
(a) Formwork assembled, sub floor beach laid ready for steelwork to be set before guniting this 25 m pool tank
(b) Gunning concrete over the steelwork of the middle bay deep end slope of a 25 m pool shell for a 3 m deep end
(c) Gunned shell of a 25 m pool ready for finish and fittings
Gunite Swimpools Ltd, Middlesex

formwork, panels, joints, liners, nor expensive equipment, in building this low priced water retaining structure on the spot.

9.8 Substructures – system built
Economical and practical units Rigid or flexible panelling with the internal membrane suspended from a unit built

121

9.17

9.18

framework, literally halved the cost of in-ground pools in the 1960s. Polyvinyl chlorides and similar materials used as pool liners have excellent stretch factors, are non-rot, UV resistant, durable and easy to repair with solvent or high frequency welding. Later development in the 1970s embedded panelled walling into an impervious concrete base for the linerless type pool.

Most system-built structures make use of poolwater outwards pressure to help retain soil walls. The pool walls in effect are supported by soil and water pressure with the flooring often made firm by weight of water alone. A sloping site bearing upon one side can bow or cave-in unprepared or unreinforced walling. Panel walling standing at least 1m high on hoppered excavations really serves as shuttering, but is better reinforced with extra stanchions, A-frames, X-braces or RC-bolsters, according to design and site, and in order to support decking surrounds.

Manufacturers now produce a greaty variety of shapes, sizes and depths in the rigid panel liner pool, and infinite freeform shapes with the flexible continuous walling linerless pool, equally suitable as private or public schemes. Such designs evolved from the original above-ground structure with its exposed walling and supporting stanchions. When continuous sheet sidewalls were developed for freestanding pools, they were also made more and more rugged and weatherproof, and in consequence were eventually sunk into the ground for the most practical and economical in-ground swimming pool yet. One versatile composite system has cut-your-own flexible urethane foam walling in 200m lengths, with in-built wall pockets outside in which to pour concrete as freestanding, reinforced in-situ supports, to suit any size or shape.

Prefabricated of flexible panels A combination of modern techniques and new materials have led to the vast assortment of formwork wallings for system built pools. In Europe, South Africa and Australia reinforced concrete pool structures still dominate, but in the USA, prefabricated panels and vinyl liner in-ground pools challenge gunite for supremacy. But soon even framework panel type pools will be superseded. Already, reinforced pneumatic membranes, expanded structural moulded polyfoams and inexpensive floating vinyl pools are being developed in various prototypes for public baths and private pools.

One unusual American scheme involves a 100m diameter floating vinyl pool by the lakeshore with a central island for recreation and refreshment. This 'soft form of vinyl shell' will safely yield to bathers who dive too steeply: alternatively, by deepening the profile of the poolskin, a deeper pool can be arranged for very little extra cost or effort. The era of the instant, fully-fashioned, flexible-liner-type, system-built, prefabricated pleasure-pool has only just begun.

At present, a 10 × 5m or 60m³ family liner pool requires 100 man/machine hours to install. Large public pools traditionally involve 3 to 6 months of time and effort.

9.17 *Liner pool assembly: hanging the pattern printed vinyl liner to a hoppered pool structure*
Fox Pools International, Berks
Photo: PBCI

9.18 *GRP factory-made floor and wall panel modules that overlap and fit together on site*
British Industrial Plastics Ltd, West Midlands/A. G. Anitt, Ltd, Woking

9.19 *Lightweight structural foam moulded panels designed to provide rapidly assembled swimming pool shells*
Pacific Pools, NY

The merits and demerits of impermanent vinyls and permanent concretes or synthetics are still hotly disputed between biased experts. But when a full-scale pool can be installed with a 30-year life on a substructure at one-third the cost of traditional shells, there is ample reason to investigate more fully and more urgently the newer methods. The linerless pool design carries on the race of rapid improvements with the newest materials 'to create a self-skinning glass reinforced thermoset foam',[8] equivalent to performance plastic moulded products offering a high density gel-coat, glass-like finish.

The latest patented 'miracle material with many applications for the pool industry'[9] is a synthetic compound as tough as concrete and based upon inorganic silica, as flexible as steel but using glass fibre, as inert as plastic involving a polyurethane, and finally setting with bone-like cellular structural strength. A veritable future swimming pool champion worth watching and supporting.

References
[1] Barry Cunliffe, *Roman Bath Discovered*, London, Routledge, 1971
[2] Anthony Collins, Swimming Pools, *RIBA Journal*, August 1972
[3] Philip H. Perkins, *Swimming Pools*, 1971
[4] Collins, op.cit.
[5] Collins, op.cit.
[6] Alfred W. S. Cross, *Public Baths and Wash-Houses*, London, Batsford, 1906
[7] Collins, op.cit.
[8] Fay Coupe, *Pool News*, June 1977.
[9] ibid.

INFORMATION SHEET 9.1

Nominal mixes – concrete and mortar

Concretes:

Mixes	Cement	Sharp sand – medium course	Fine sand – soft	Vermiculite	Graded shingle 20mm–5mm	Graded shingle 10mm–5mm	All-in ballast 20mm down	All-in ballast 10mm down
Lean mix – make-up	1						18	
Oversite blinding	1	3				4	5	
Footings and foundations	1	2			4		5	
Floor slab	1	2				3	4	
Underliner soft floor	1		2	2				
Underliner sand floor	1		8					
Wall infill, steps and decking base, paving slabs, path screeds	1	2				3	4	
Floor slab screed	1	4						
Floor slab insulation	1			6				

Mortars:

Mixes	Cement	Fine sand – soft	Lime
Walls:			
below-ground	1	3	
	1	5	1
above-ground (landscape) severe exposure	1	6	1
above-ground (landscape) sheltered areas	1	8	2
Coping	1	5	

Mixes	Cement	Sharp sand – medium course	Fine sand – soft	Vermiculite	Graded shingle 20mm–5mm	Graded shingle 10mm–5mm	All-in ballast 20mm down	All-in ballast 10mm down
Lean mix – backfill	1	10						
	1	8	2					
Slurry render	1		1					
Render	1	6						
Render – landscape walls	1	9						
Tile bedding	1	4						
Tile grout	1	2						
Paving bedding	1	6				1		
Paving jointing	1	4						
White marblite render	1 (white)	1 (dust) marble				2 (3mm chips marble)		

INFORMATION SHEET 9.2

Admixtures with cement

The main ones are:
accelerators – to increase early strength
retarders – to allow more placing time
plasticisers – to improve flow
waterproofers – to reduce permeability
air retaining agents – to increase frost resistance

INFORMATION SHEET 9.3

Shell substructure systems

Type	Advantages	Disadvantages
Hand-laid to traditional techniques		
1 Natural stone	Economical when local materials abundant	Labour intensive structure with waterproofing problems
2 Brick	Simple and convenient using local materials	Costly; weak and leaky structure
3 Shuttered concrete	Solid, versatile, water retaining material to known strength	Limited shapes and time consuming formwork; a more expensive method requiring continuous supervision
4 Concrete block	Effective and simple, permanent formwork with RC infilled walling suitable for both rectangular and curved shapes	Relatively slow construction requiring several lifts and temporary shuttering in order to build deep pools
5 Concrete double block	Easy to handle and lay with no special equipment required; well known economical building method	Specialised blocks are costly to transport for what is still a labour intensive structure; hollow-core walling blocks are porous and also unsuitable below 2·5m depths, or for uncertain ground conditions
6 Dry pack concrete	Dense packed concrete for a monolithic freeform water retaining structure, or base, needing no formwork nor special equipment	Hard work; particularly labour intensive, requiring great attention to detail and to mix; sloping walls a disadvantage
Custom-made on site or production type shells		
1 Timber	Convenient, workable material, easily assembled; attractive for patio log pools or hot tubs	Subject to deterioration in undrained soils; limited shapes and styles above or below ground
2 Steel	Strong, flexible material; adaptable, quickly assembled and installed for difficult sites	Expensive shell suffers differential expansion within buildings; needs continual check against corrosion; welded joins are weakest points

Type	Advantages	Disadvantages
3 Aluminium	Very light but very strong components or shells; ideal for slopes, problem sites and extreme conditions	In certain soils, can be prone to corrosion; joints must be thoroughly sealed; will not hold heat without suitable insulation
4 Glass reinforced plastic	Flexible, versatile, rapid installation, long-life; modern finishes inclusive	Unpleasant material to lay up; intensive quality control is essential; one-piece designs limit shapes and extensive distribution
5 Pre-stressed concrete	Strong structures under compression that easily achieve impermeability	Limited shapes and time consuming construction techniques
6 Pre-cast concrete	Quality controlled manufacture of concrete components complete with finishes and fittings; rapid installation especially for large pools	Handling and transportation is troublesome; limited range of designs
7 Gunite	Rapid construction of watertight shells to any shape; ideal for difficult access and most economic for large scale production	Requires skilled application with special equipment that is expensive for small, occasional or dispersed pools; the side wall to floor coving is unsuitable for tiling, and awkward for non-swimmers
8 Polyconcrete	Very fast construction with strong lightweight materials for a fairfaced in situ, low priced, freeform shell	Poor mixes leave reinforcing materials open to corrosion; lightweight empty shell floats easily in wet ground conditions; uv and temperature can affect structure of polymer type materials

INFORMATION SHEET 9.4

Typical examples of blockwork walling widths
(With indication of foundation/reinforcement requirements for normal subsoil conditions)

Concrete block walls width on	Foundations for	Maximum pool water depth require	Mild steel reinforcement to	Inner and outer framework of at least:
150mm hollow core	150 × 300mm wide	1·5m	6mm rod (for single framework only)	300mm centres
225mm hollow core	225 × 400mm wide	2·3m	10mm rod	250mm centres
300mm double wall	300 × 500mm wide	2·8m	13mm rod	200mm centres
400mm double wall	400 × 600mm wide	3·2m	15mm rod	150mm centres
150–300mm stepped wall (excluding blockwork)	1000mm kicker	3·5m	15mm rod	300mm centres for top 1·5m blocked section
			and 20mm rod	150mm centres for bottom 2·0m shuttered section

Examples:

10 × 5m pool   Vertical and distribution reinforcement for a 150mm concrete wall inside blockwork could require:
      10mm rod framework set at 250mm spaces apart to 1·5m depth
      twin 10mm rod framework set at 100mm spaces apart to 2·5m depth

25 × 10m pool   Vertical and distribution reinforcement for a 150 to 300mm stepped concrete wall inside blockwork shuttering could require:
      twin 15mm rod framework set at 300mm spaces apart to 1·5m depth
      twin 20mm rod framework set at 150mm spaces apart to 3·5m depth

See also figs 9.13a and 9.14.

INFORMATION SHEET 9.5

Reinforcement: metric rod

Diameter mm	Area mm²	Weight kg/m	Imp conversion approx in
6	28	0·22	1/4
8	50	0·40	5/16
10	79	0·62	3/8
12	113	0·89	1/2
16	201	1·58	5/8
20	314	2·47	3/4

10 Superstructures

Nowadays, many large pool buildings, while developing an important architectural theme, still tend to neglect atmosphere and the basic social needs of people. Not only the waterspace, but the envelope that modifies the environment should meet the new ideas of leisure requirements.

10.1 Natatoria

Perhaps the perfect swimming pool enclosure has yet to be built, but the great superstructures of clear-span cladding come closest so far, by trying to control the inner environment as well as keeping a visual contact with the outside.

In perfecting control of all the elements of a swimming pool's environment, a wide range of possibilities has already been tested. For example, a major area of top lighting is necessary to control glare and avoid hazard (see chapter 10.11, Light). The early 19th-century search for good lighting encouraged bath designers to favour top open-space daylighting. Later problems of overhead glazing in bath houses shifted design emphasis in the mid-20th-century pool hall to side daylighting. And now, following reaction against specular reflection (or glare) on the water, some designers have turned right away from natural lighting altogether. However, the all-round transparent dome is bringing back daylighting.

A great deal of research has gone into the ideal natatorium (the purpose-made pool hall), especially in the USA, where the name was coined, as well as in Europe. Lightweight metals, reinforced plastics, laminated timbers, and some traditional building materials have been woven together into rugged yet attractive superstructural fabrics, priced within the reach of most owners, that can be erected with the minimum of fuss. In the long run, the real test is whether a natatorium does its job well without looking like a typical airship hangar to the more discerning pool user.
Special case The swimming pool enclosing case needs to be special, as too often the corrosive powers of the atmosphere inside are badly underestimated, or apparently ignored. Pool attendances fall off in almost direct proportion to the deterioration of the fabric.

Designers should therefore consider the effect on the inside of the enclosure, before looking at the facade outside. Durable, good quality, impervious finishes should be specified to resist effects of high relative humidity, atmospheric pollution, chemical and mechanical erosion, clean-

ing acids, corrosive nitrogen trichloride gas, abrasive scourers, as well as boisterous bathers.
What is wanted Clearly define the environmental range. Although there may be major differences between sport and leisure pools, public and private needs, lightweight and heavy duty enclosures, every bather wants warmth and light in an open-air atmosphere. So the design concept should be to create and contain the freedom and pleasure of a warm, sunny day, 24 hours a day, no matter what the outside elements may be.

The efficiency of the superstructure or cover or enclosure or natatorium or whatever is only relative to its intended use. It is no good, for example, building a hydrotherapy pool with water attaining 35°C, inside a bath house structure of poor thermal U value at 2 or 3W/m²/°C; or prescribing rapid rate air changes which might offer 10 to 20m/s velocities that can quickly dry and cool bodies of children playing around in a paddling pool.

Early covered baths encouraged a straight through-flow of air to flush away humid atmosphere, and many modern

10.1 *Low profile of the Royal Commonwealth pool, Edinburgh. A pool hall designed for sporting, recreation and family swimming*
Architects' Journal
Architect: Matthew/Johnson-Marshall
Photo: Henk Snoek

10.2 *Inter-relating roof spans of the Hanover Hallenbad*
Landeshauptstadt, Hanover
Architect: Prof. Friedrich F. Grünberger
Photo: Hans Wagner

10.3 *The Hanover Stadionbad roof. Deceptive simplicity*
Landeshauptstadt, Hanover
Architect: Prof. Friedrich F. Grünberger
Photo: Rainer Franz

10.4 *Sports/leisure pool of Zentralbad, Düsseldorf. The hanging concave pool roof shows the space saving potential of tensile cable constructions*
Stadtwerke Düsseldorf AG
Architect: Prof. Friedrick F. Grünberger

10.5 *'Will you come into my parlour?' – Swindon Leisure Centre dome*
Architect: Gillinson Barnett & Partners
Photo: O. F. Clarke

0.1

10.2

10.3

10.4

10.5

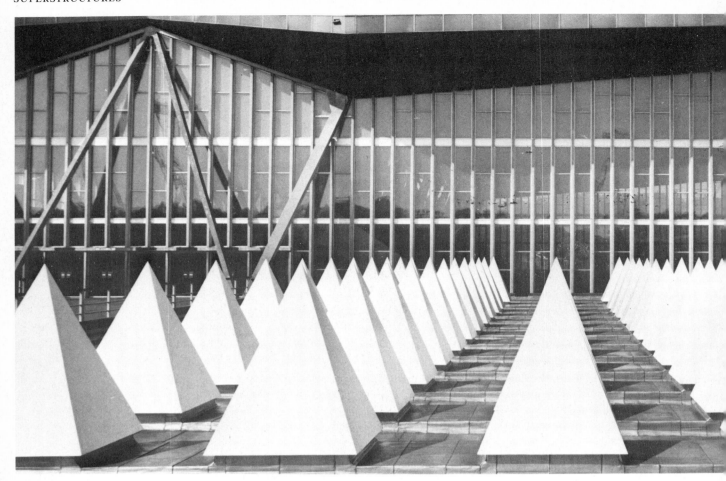

10.6 *The north faces of the 2 m pyramid rooflights are translucent and open up for access to the light fittings suspended inside at Crystal Palace Training Pool*
The Sports Council (GLC Photo, Dept of Architecture and Civic Design)

enclosures still rely upon such through draught ventilation systems. At best, clean, cold air replaces stale, steamy air so delaying condensation and corrosion, but since the real objective of a cover is to modify the immediate environment, this fill-and-empty draught process is of little real use.

Popular pool hall superstructures might involve membraneous roofs, concrete shells, barrel vaults, translucent domes, polyagonal spheroids, hyperbolic paraboloids, spaceframes and pyramids, all striving to create large, effective and uninterrupted spans. They optimise cost and comfort, heat and humidity, light and sound, ventilation and condensation, but do have to cover rooms for changing and ablutions, storage and equipment, recreation and refreshments, each possessing different environmental needs to the water space itself (see chapter 14 and information sheet 10.1).

Foundations for most superstructures involve column bases or strip footings in poor ground, which may need to be taken well below the pool floor level to avoid surcharge pressures bearing upon the walls of the tank, which should not take any additional load unless special reinforcement and differential expansion arrangements are provided (see chapter 9.5).

An economic enclosed space Greatest economies can be achieved when loads are brought down to the lowest level by the shortest route.

The total cost of a swimming pool tends to be directly proportional to the *volume* enclosed, rather than the ground area covered; in other words, increasing the water area need not be more expensive (see chapter 2). Greater savings can be made by cutting down the expensively enclosed airspace.

Doing away with high diving-boards and the extra height needed above the water helps particularly (skylight ceiling wells at the deep end provide an economy roof version for this popular sport). Sloping or tapering the roof to the shallow end effectively reduces unnecessary space, though with some risk of exaggerated perspective. Saving of materials and building costs may be important initially, but the continuing lower operating cost of smaller environmental control systems is far greater in the long run.

Conventional pool building design can also be expensive with 4:1 labour costs in comparing hall with pool: prefabrication encourages a more practical 1:1 proportion, but all too often seems to inspire an ugly building at the same time.

Principles of integrated environmental design lead planners towards the more perfect envelope for their pools by relating management and mechanical services with structure and building in a practical scheme to suit all (see chapter 2).

Increased insulation particularly pays long-term dividends, for example:
• reduce an accepted U value of $1 \cdot 7 \, W/m^2/°C$ for standard cavity walling to under $0 \cdot 4$ U value with an infilled insulation

- increase 50mm insulation to 75mm improves walling U value from 0·5 to around 0·3
- install double glazing to reduce window area U value from over 5·0 to around 2·5
- maintain air temperature at 1° above water temperature to inhibit evaporation and condensation
- protect roofs from moisture laden air with effective vapour barriers and prevent interstitial condensation.

See chapter 14.

10.2 Materials

Concretes, ceramics and chlorinated rubber-based paints are traditional pool materials. They are relatively inexpensive, easily maintained and durable (see chapter 11.2 and 11.3 for more details on finishes). Pools work hard for the whole of their planned 50-year life, and quite possibly have to last twice that time. Long-term costs are important. Concrete will endure. Over half of the public pools in Britain are already more than 60 years old.

Timber is another traditional material, used increasingly in swimming pool superstructures for its hard-wearing qualities and attractive appearance. It is easily shaped and assembled in portal frames for large-span roofs of single-storey buildings, and is better exposed for maintenance. Great attention to corrosion-proof timber fittings, fixtures and adhesives is vital. Properly treated timber can withstand high humidity, survive corrosive atmospheres, and even resist the attentions of insects, fungus and fire. A fully developed fire burns through wood not impregnated with fire retardent at about 50mm per minute, bringing gradual collapse, but no thermal movement. By comparison, steel expansion in a fire causes severe cracking to a superstructure, and at 400°C fails in ten minutes (see chapter 16.1).

The moisture content in pool superstructural timber must not exceed 20 per cent and it should be treated regularly with preservative to stay dry, to ward off possible fungus attack and to maintain its attractive appearance. Highly absorbent woodfibre boards are not suitable for use in swimming pools, though, along with the timber beams, specially treated soft fibre acoustic panels suspended from the ceiling help to baffle noise. Conversely, four coats of varnish over any timber increase surface reflection of sound.

Hardwoods are expensive but best. Softwoods – Redwood, Western Red Cedar and Douglas Fir – are favoured today for the laminated plywood and box beam forms. Timber must never come into direct contact with wet floor areas. And upright beams should not obtrude into the poolside to create hazards.

Low weight timber structures are ideal for difficult ground conditions of poor load-bearing capacity.

Steel and aluminium are frequently used now in swimming pools, but require careful separation from the atmosphere by a suitable barrier, or protection with appropriate coatings (paints, heavy galvanising or anodising, etc). Traces of chlorine in high humidity encourage electrolytic action between dissimilar metals bringing failure in unexpected places, eg the steel locking pins of aluminium door handles. Since durable aluminium roofing panel structures are $^1/_7$ the weight of steel, they are invaluable for portability and prefabrication. (Compare weight/volume ratios of 500kg/m³ for timber, 2400kg/m³ for concrete, 2800kg/m³

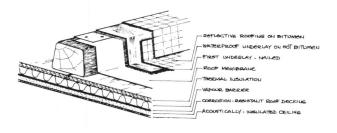

a) SOLID FLAT ROOF

REFLECTIVE ROOFING ON BITUMEN
WATERPROOF UNDERLAY ON HOT BITUMEN
FIRST UNDERLAY - NAILED
ROOF MEMBRANE
THERMAL INSULATION
VAPOUR BARRIER
CORROSION - RESISTANT ROOF DECKING
ACOUSTICALLY - INSULATED CEILING

NOTE: THERMAL INSULATION/VAPOUR BARRIER IS PLACED IMMEDIATELY ABOVE THE VOID WHEN THERE IS A SUSPENDED CEILING AND NO ROOF VENTILATION.

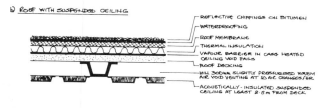

b) ROOF WITH SUSPENDED CEILING

REFLECTIVE CHIPPINGS ON BITUMEN
WATERPROOFING
ROOF MEMBRANE
THERMAL INSULATION
VAPOUR BARRIER IN CASE HEATED CEILING VOID FAILS
ROOF DECKING
FILL 300mm SLIGHTLY PRESSURISED WARM AIR VOID VENTING AT 10 AIR CHANGES/HR
ACOUSTICALLY - INSULATED SUSPENDED CEILING AT LEAST 2·5m FROM DECK

NOTE: IF AIR VOID IS VENTILATED ONLY, AN IMPENETRABLE VAPOUR BARRIER IS STILL REQUIRED ABOVE THE SUSPENDED CEILING TO PREVENT THE PASSAGE OF INTERSTITIAL CONDENSATION.

10.7 *Roof construction techniques: (a) solid flat roof; (b) roof with suspended ceiling*

for aluminium, and 9100kg/m³ for mild steel claddings).

The use of plastic as translucent weathertight superstructural skin has proved highly successful, but very careful questioning over selection of materials is essential to establish long-term durability against ultra-violet radiation and surface erosion; to consider cleaning, repair and replacement; and moreover, to avoid hazards from fire (see chapter 16). Plastic spheres can fill space and absorb sound, looking colourful and attractive inside an enclosure.

Glass reinforced plastics, concretes and artificial aggregates all include useful insulation properties with their high strength for weight ratios.

Stainless steels One of the most important pool materials is stainless steel. There are many forms which can be made hard for engineering but not remain stainless for pools; or can be designed for casting rather than appearance, and so on.

It is the austenitic class of stainless steels of the Type 300 series that suit swimming pool specification. These steel alloys are grouped in chromium/nickel compositions known by their percentages such as 18/8 (18 per cent Cr and 8 per cent Ni) for non-magnetic, ductile and amenable, highly corrosion resistant materials. The martensitic and ferritic steels of the Type 400 series with, usually, plain chromium to 12 per cent and over, are magnetic, less amenable to cold-working and forming, and susceptible to highly localised breakdowns of pitting corrosion from chloride and other halide ions in pool waters and pool atmospheres.

Stainless steel derives its outstanding resistance from a thin protective and tenacious chromium oxide surface film over the iron base; the type of alloy is chosen according to the nature of exposure.

Types 302 and 304 suit most pool environments; 430 is used only for the mildest situation entirely *outside* of the pool's influence. When components must maintain their initial appearance, or have to meet severe conditions such as high TDS or seawater (see chapter 15.9), then type 316 with molybdenum content has exceptional durability in the most aggressive atmospheres. This type is ideal for pools, besides having pleasing appearance, being easy to clean and offering long-term survival; it also has excellent mechanical and physical properties with ease of welding. Although about one-third more expensive, the molybdenum/high nickel 18/10/3 type steels (some with traces of carbon, silicon and manganese) are generally completely resistant to pitting and crevice corrosion in fresh water pools, soon justifying their additional cost over Types 302 and 304.

Type 316 is also ideal for cladding, inside or out, where bright appearance and maintenance is preserved by cleaning. In marine exposure conditions, coatings such as neoprene stop any possibility of bi-metallic corrosion. Recent developments have introduced aluminium sections clad with a thin skin of stainless steel, or encouraged new colouring processes for rigid-type wall panels.

10.3 Roof failure

No matter how well specified and designed in the first place, danger of collapse of the roof into a pool is real, warranting regular inspection of fabric and structure. Pools are not always operated as the designer envisaged. Air

ventilation is switched off at night in the mistaken belief of saving cost. Ventilation fans fail and are not repaired. Space heating is often lowered to below that of water temperature (in over 50 per cent of UK public pools) and resulting humidity soon seeks out the weakest points. Collapse occurs without warning. Or at least, deterioration is encouraged.

Metallic corrosion through accumulated condensation was responsible for a suspended ceiling falling into a Californian swimming club pool in 1976, killing one woman and injuring five other people. In London in 1974, pool roof failures occurred in two entirely separate schools. One pool hall had concrete roof beams and the other plywood box beams.

In the first school, chemical attack on the high alumina cement concrete beams rapidly resulted in disruption of the concrete and total loss of strength. Although the degree of conversion on examination had suggested that critically higher temperatures must have arisen during the first day after casting the beams at the factory, it was the high humidity and condensation within the pool hall that was directly responsible for the failure. Chemical attack had been promoted by the corrosive action of sulphate derived

certain (see chapter 14.7 and 9 on humidity control and ventilation; also chapter 16 on safety and maintenance).

'Condensation occurs on surfaces that are below the dewpoint of the surrounding air'.[1] Sometimes, thermal insulation of an acoustic ceiling can be high enough to reduce temperature within the structure to below dewpoint of the pool hall air, and so we arrive back at moist and soggy materials. Vapour barriers at ceiling level are unlikely to cocoon a roof completely, and the ideal, a good ventilation and humidity control system, can fail or be switched off.

Cavity walling, vapour barriers, thermal insulation and pressurised roof spaces all help control condensation, but if moisture is to be totally avoided, the correct air temperature and relative humidity must be maintained *at all times* (see chapter 14.9 and information sheets 10.2 and 14.22 to 24 for further information on all the control factors).

10.4 Covers

One of the simplest forms of protection, yet still the most successful for both indoor and outdoor pools, is a surface water cover. Most covers are designed for a particular task; few are successful all-rounders. Removing and replacing a cover is often more troublesome than appreciated, and can even deter a private owner from swimming. Nevertheless, a swimming pool without a cover is like a bed without a blanket.

Debris or winter covers These keep a pool clean throughout the winter close-down period. They are definitely *not* safety covers, unless special 'indestructible' threads are interwoven or underlaid. Even with extra tough safety lines included, the cover can sometimes still sag below the water surface beneath a person's weight. Also many covers might remain reliable for years, but a rent unnoticed, or a rotten patch unrepaired, can allow a child to fall through suddenly into the water beneath.

By means of reinforced straps, winter or debris covers are fixed securely to anchors fitted into the deck surround and set between 1 and 3m apart according to the shape and size of the pool. Or waterfilled bags are laid as convenient weights along the pool perimeter on the edge of a sheet cover to hold it taught. Depending upon materials employed, a syphonic device might be needed occasionally to stop sagging by pumping away ponding water. A suspended mesh cover will allow rainwater to drain through; or a large inflated ball floating in the middle of the pool beneath an unperforated cover will cause rainwater to run off.

When a pool cover needs to be made for an existing pool whose precise outline measurements are no longer known, the simplest method to reproduce the pool shape, especially a freeform outline, on paper, is to set pegs and run string lines to make a box around the outside of the pool perimeter. This box must either be staked with right angled corners, or the unequal diagonals carefully measured and noted, along with the sides, to get an accurate representation of the actual box arrangement. Now the shape of the pool can be drawn simply by measuring into the pool perimeter at right angles from the box sides at metre or less intervals, and joining all the scaled perpendicular lines for a good facsimile on paper. The alternative expedient of covering a freeform pool with an overlapping rectangular cover will be more costly, and burdensome to handle for the pool owner (see diagram **10.9**).

10.8 *Fungal attack promoted by humidity and temperature on plywood box beams resulted in collapse of the Ilford County High School pool roof*
Crown copyright photograph reproduced from Building Research Establishment Current Paper CP 44/75

from gypsum plaster in contact with the moist beams, when only one of three fans had been working. Badly damaged hac beams turn brown, are very friable, and crumble easily when wet.

While the use of hac concrete is discouraged for operating temperatures over 27°C, there is no such limitation in the case of timber. And humidity affecting timber was the vital factor in the second school case. Once again, intermittent condensation and rising moisture content beyond safe limits put the structure at risk. An ineffective vapour barrier, inadequate ventilation, high humidity and high temperature conspired with condensation to corrode nails, deteriorate glues, decay wood with fungal attack, cause creep deflections, and thoroughly weaken the basic roof beam structure. And when an increased dead loading occurs through snow or ice, rainwater ponding, or perhaps additional proofing materials, collapse will be sudden and

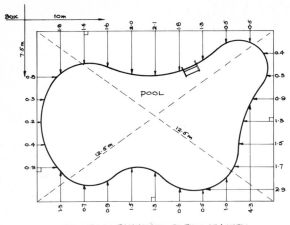

BOX OUTLINE WITH MEASUREMENTS TAKEN AT 1 METRE
INTERVALS: OUTER BOX LINES NEED NOT BE PARALLEL
TO EACH OTHER IF DIAGONAL MEASUREMENTS ARE
TAKEN ALSO. ALLOW COVER TO OVERLAP COPING/DECK
BY ½ METRE APPROX.
(BASED ON AQUAMAT/MEYCO METHOD).

10.9 *Measuring a pool cover*

A cleaned pool with its winter dose of disinfectant can be kept covered for several months, then re-opened in the spring just as clean, so making the effort of the autumn treatment well worth while (see chapter 16.3).

Heat retaining covers They conserve heat, and as a result reduce heating costs by 30 to 80 per cent. They are particularly effective for indoor pools. For example, a floating cover used on a private indoor pool kept to 27°C can cut water heating costs by as much as 75 per cent, *and* air heating/ventilation costs by at least 35 per cent, while also reducing condensation, and as a result the size of the conditioning plant. A hydrotherapy pool, operating at a higher water temperature still, can offer even better savings when closed after hours and put under covers.

Floating quilted-type covers longer than 10m are difficult to manhandle, so several sections, or a roller built into or onto the pool surround can be possible answers. Unfortunately, poolwide rollers can be cumbersome, and do get in the way.

One ingenious alternative to the all-over quilted fabric insulating cover is ping-pong type balls floating in the pool: they do not even need to be removed for swimming. This plastic bubble carpet across the water is effective for both indoor and outdoor pools, also to some extent against frost and ice damage. Lightweight bubble balls should be packed tightly and evenly on the surface of outdoor pools to stop gale winds blowing them about, and show an attractive covering carpet of blue, undulating and moving as if in flight. Shrimping type rakes or wide boom nets easily scoop them to one side for cleaning the pool floor. *But* any person in the water beneath these floating balls cannot be seen.

A cover of snow with entrapped air gives good insulation to the ground underneath. Similarly, foamed floating quilts keep in water heat but can stop solar radiant heating getting through too. These covers mainly score by reducing evaporation, saving re-radiation losses and preventing the wind whipping away the latent heat of liquid into vapour. A cool, cloudless night increases re-radiated heat from the earth's surface, causing the open pool temperature to fall several degrees. But a quilt, like snow, will hold in the energy. The expense of a lightweight heat retaining cover is usually recovered from subsequent savings invariably

made over the following one or two season's heating bills.

Another lightweight heat retaining quilt of UV protected translucent plastic film, retaining air bubbles within the sheet, allows most of the sun's radiation to pass through to warm the top water and trap heat in the pool. Solar trap covers in theory act like a greenhouse to capture energy in the pool, holding back longer-wave radiation energy reflections in the water. A large proportion of the heat of an open-air pool can be gained directly across the water surface from the sun, providing the cover material is not opaque to short-wave energy (see chapter 14.4 and 11 on insulation and self-sufficiency).

Sometimes, instead of an insulating blanket covering the pool surface, an alcohol type chemical cosmetic is added to the water to strengthen surface tension, so reducing the evaporation, the loss of heat and the volatile disinfectants (see chapter 15.10 on special treatments).

Safety covers These covers combine the advantages of the previous two, with the added bonus of overcoming some of their disadvantages – usually at a price. There are 'roll-top desk' floating blinds about 15mm thick, or folding canopies supported just 100mm above the water surface. Both strive for safety, debris protection and heat retention with the easiest possible removal. The simplest form is hand drawn across the pool; the most elaborate automatically covers the pool as easily as flicking a lever to close the blinds. In Sweden, this cover is considered robust enough even to replace a perimeter safety fence.

The surface blind type protection is either coiled into a recess at one end of the pool for storage, or into a bench-seat box that is built in or on the deep end decking. Such covers insulate most efficiently, but on removal collected dust and debris on them can be dropped into the poolwater. The sliding, folding type cover sandwiches an air pocket above the surface of the pool, and under the canopy, to form a 100mm gap of saturated water vapour for a doubly effective barrier against water evaporation and heat loss. Both covers rest upon rails set along the pool side walls, and can be power drawn across the pool within a minute or two, sometimes using only the water pressure motive potential from the filter pump.

To provide a fully automatic safety cover might add 50 per cent to the whole pool bill for a private garden scheme. Rectangular type pools are generally required for automatic safety covers, and any protruberance into the pool such as ladders or slides must be easily removable. The question of safety requires continual investigation, for materials can rot or tear with time, and total reliance upon a cover courts disaster.

Some safety covers give a winter bonus by introducing a series of 25mm shallow trays across the pool surface, beneath which brine pipes remove the latent heat of water to freeze the surface for ice skating. Providing exposed perimeter pool tiles are protected from ice expansion and skate damage with temporary absorbent skirting board buffers, a frozen open-air swimming pool can be fun and profitable in winter (see chapters 11.5 and 16.5).

10.5 Canopies

A flat, suspended, rigid cover of clear cladding over the water surface will allow sunlight through, radically save on pool maintenance for almost no dirt can get in, and almost

10.10 *Heat saving potential of a 15mm floating heat-retaining lamina on the water surface, or a cover set 100mm over the surface of a 50m³ sheltered open-air garden pool*

10.11 *Surface insulation of floating ping-pong type balls which remain in position for general swimming*
Euro-Matic, Copenhagen and Brentford
Keystone Press Agency Ltd

10.12 *A conservation cover automatically shutting in a sports pool to help retain heat, chemicals, and cleanliness, also creating a useful safety barrier*
Grando Schwimmbad – Abdeckungen
Robert Granderath, FGR

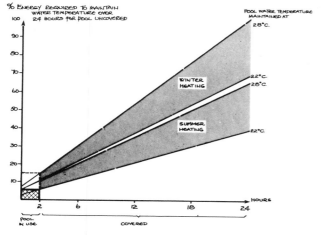

10.10

10.11

0.12

133

eliminate chemical dissipation; some designs even provide extra space on which to sunbathe! When these panels are hydraulically lifted away from the surface for swimming, they can be positioned as awnings to provide shelter from sun or wind. When closed down, usual filtration for the garden type of swimming pool can be reduced to run only two or three hours a day. They are ideal for dusty, sandy and windy districts.

The same protection idea interpreted differently lifts the whole pool deck to ceiling height above the water for shade, and another version has the solid, safe deck on the water surface, sunk to become the pool floor.

In Russia, a fixed, cantilevered canopy with side panelled windshields set all round a pool is sometimes used to encourage swimming in open-air public and school pools throughout the year. Screens stop icy winds, radiant heaters directly warm bystanders, canopies keep the pool cleaner.

However, partial cantilevered roofing set too close to a poolside effectively blocks much of the solar radiation from reaching the water, and some pools with too confining Russian shelters can be colder in the sun than nearby unsheltered tanks. In France, a particular design has only one side screen, and a sliding curtain is run along the outer edge of the overhanging canopy to cordon off a small, enclosed section of the pool for cold weather swimming.

For about a quarter of the normal cost, open-air shelters mean many schools can provide other covered facilities such as outhouse changing cabin arrangements, washrooms, showers and equipment stores. And the complete Russian shelter is a far more practical deterrent than any ugly mesh or chain link barrier for safety fencing, since vertical cladding gives no foothold for toddlers to climb over into the pool area.

An even safer surrounded pool which offers best insulation of all is the 'swimhall' buried in the ground with its own opening skylight canopy set at level grade, and it can be totally isolated and insulated: pool water heat losses at 25 to 30°C in mid-winter may only amount to a few degrees a month.

Air-inflated canopies A new kind of canopy – the air-supported structure – has proved an ideal low-cost covering for swimming pools, and the new science of 'bubbleology' (originating from developments of balloon and airship design) has now been adopted by the pool industry. Inflated canopies have the usual advantage of surface covers, plus the ability to modify the airspace as well.

Airtight membranes might have relatively short lives (10 years plus), allow high heat loss and solar gain, and suffer with acoustic and humidity problems, but they are cheap. *Real* cost is the total of the initial cost plus operating costs throughout its structural life, plus replacement cost – and a well-designed, cable-reinforced, or frame-ribbed airdome can be competitive up to at least a 4000 to 6000m² covered area. It can be made safe even in high winds. If the airdome is left deflated and unsecured in high winds, the fabric can soon rip to shreds. There must be sufficient airlock entrances and emergency exits for safe escape. It is surprisingly slow to collapse if torn, or if emergency doors are left open; it does shed snow, and can pay for itself over four or five years, when compared with maintaining a heated pool in open-air conditions. Sufficient air pressure fans work 24

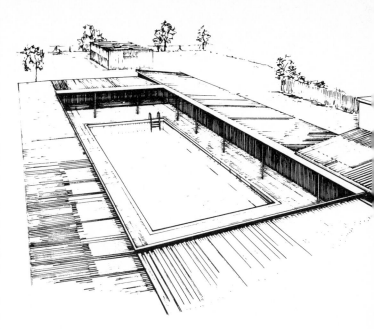

10.13 SURROUND BUILDING ACCOMMODATES PLANT AND CHANGING ROOMS – HAS SOLAR PANEL ROOF

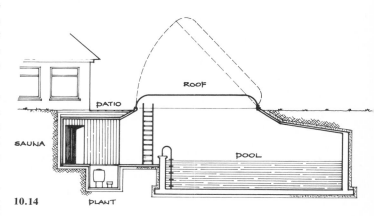

10.14

10.13 *Russian shelter*

10.14 *Unterflorschwimmhalle*
Courtesy: Maderna Pools, Vienna

10.15 *Temporarily enclosing 50m outdoor pool of the Berlin-Mariendorf with an inflatable cover in winter – exterior*
J. B. Sanders & Söhne, Hamburg
Photo: Farbwerke Hoechst AG

10.16 *Inflatable pool hall at Berlin-Mariendorf: 58 × 27 × 11 m high – interior*
J. B. Sanders & Söhne, Hamburg
Photo: Farbwerke Hoechst AG

10.15

10.16

hours out of 24, but consume relatively little electricity for the space covered. Artificial lighting can be arranged as direct or indirect, inside or floodlit from outside. Daylighting penetrates naturally all round, but the larger windowless opaque structures will require supplementary lighting for safety reasons. Increased air pressure inside the dome raises the pitch of voices, but causing no real inconvenience to bathers.

Many people consider the air-inflated structure purely a temporary affair, but with building costs spiralling, the simplicity and convenience of this novel cover does appeal economically and even aesthetically. Savings on superstructure can range from 80 per cent for full airdomes, to 30 or 50 per cent for pillow dome systems on cable supports requiring only upper and inner linings to be pressurised.

Further ideas now sponsor development of high-pressurised polyurethane rafters, supporting environmentally inert roofing of long-term materials; or permanent air supported pool covers of Teflon-coated fibre-glass or vinyl-coated polyester on structural walling; or barrel vaulted, double clad, air pressurised sheathing and pillow roofs spanning low walling surrounds.

New lines in pneumatic architecture are aptly practical for all styles of pool, since overall costs can be more than halved compared with those of the traditional lightweight pool enclosures: the air supported superstructure is here to stay. However, planning authorities can be puzzled by some innovative inflatables and their appropriate classification: consequently, there may be difficulty in translating existing safety requirements and building regulations to embrace flexible or plastic pool 'dirigible' superstructures (see chapter 16.1 on safety and fire).

10.6 Enclosures

Specially designed buildings for swimming pools are costly; but too many cheaper ready-made lightweight pool enclosures, both private and public, are crude and rudimentary, giving the sole impression of function for its own sake. Low standard structures seem almost to encourage corrosive attack which, together with unappealing decor, also invites further attack from unimpressed vandals (see chapter 16.4 on wear and tear, and information sheet 16.6).

Some manufacturers have carefully investigated and adopted the many attractive and durable materials available nowadays for abrasive environments. Satinised aluminium, varnished timber, coloured polyester, moulded GRP, etc, requiring little maintenance, have all paid off with exciting and functional ideas in pool superstructures. Industrialised construction relies upon lightweight frames and modules that are easily handled and assembled. But mass production is important to produce economically, and to recover long-considered design costs. The cheapest form might involve expendable polythene sheeting draped and clipped over low profile hooping; the dearest being moulded acrylic with cladding infilling the prefabricated framework. Pool enclosure-system manufacturers provide optionally extra items such as double opening sliding roofs to create in effect a simple Russian shelter, or revolving skydome pallisading for an American all-purpose style of superstructure.

Geodesy The geodetic dome structure demonstrates, for the material used, the strongest and most efficient way to enclose space. It can cover the maximum volume with minimum surface area, the sphere-like structure taking less energy to heat or cool than the rectilinear box of traditional architecture. But the space frame is still the most used and misused lightweight enclosure for rectangular pools, though with future energy inhibitions in mind, any overlarge cavernous hangar of a pool hall may soon become redundant.

As regards structural materials, concrete is still one of the best. Hence the pneumatic concrete dome, inflated within a week, now shows an ideal potential for pool designers investing in the future. For example, thermal insulation coefficient standards show:

	$W/m^2/°C$		$W/m^2/°C$
Glazing μ *single*	5·7	*double*	2·8
Cavity brick walling μ 300mm	1·7	+75mm insulation	0·3
Concrete roofing with asphalt μ 150mm	3·6	+75mm insulation	0·4

The all-overall preferred figure for pools of $0·5 W/m^2/°C$ is economically possible in concrete, and becoming more and more necessary (see chapter 14.4 on insulation).

Prefab pools An efficiently developed industrialised natatorium helps maintain the pool even in harsh or extreme conditions. It has to lift water from a few degrees to 30°C, to balance relative humidity, provide palatable fresh air mixtures, all with variable turnround in order to make a useable pool place *all year*. As one example only, an aluminium modular pool dependent upon its prefabricated superstructure installed in the extreme climate of Anchorage, Alaska, highlights the popularity of the controlled environment in unexpected swimming places. During the first year of operation, the attendance at this community pool close to the Arctic Circle was 100,000 out of a captive population of 100,000.

10.7 Convertibles

Enclosures or superstructures which can open up, swivel, or pull aside could be defined as convertibles, allowing any pool with such cover arrangements to come closest to the objective of all-year swimming in warmth and comfort, with sunshine and fresh air wherever possible. Some designers argue that two pools (a small one inside for winter, and a large one outside for summer) are really better than the one which is a total compromise (see chapters 4.2 on seaside inside; 7.6 on the inside-outside pool and 14.11 on self-sufficiency).

Sunshine is almost as important as the swimming and an indoor pool is transformed, as far as the swimmer is concerned, when it is bathed in sunlight. Hence, architectural experiments in building curtain walls of glass and the resulting problems of glare (see chapter 10.11). Even the simp-

10.17 *Home built geodesic dome over the garden pool*
British Industrial Plastics, West Midlands

10.18 *Lightweight aluminium structure with translucent acrylic cladding and sliding roof for a garden pool*
Robinson Sun-Fun, Winchester
Photo: B. J. Studios

10.17

10.18

lest sliding patio windows allow stimulating fresh air, if not direct sunlight.

The very special needs for protecting the pool's environment, and the bathers' conflicting preference for open-air swimming, have promoted many useful ideas such as the sliding roof, telescopic hall, tracked sliding cover, as well as the circular cupola opening like a huge iris. However, the underside of a roof can collect moisture, which continually attacks movement gear; frequently there is insufficient space for tracked covers to run in separation; and the engineering of a retractable dome is both complex and expensive.

Generally, the total available market has been too small to encourage specialised industrial design and production of convertible pool covers in the public sector. So to inspire design in France, a national competition was launched in the 1970s to develop convertibles for public community pools with ultimate production runs of several hundred in mind. Architects, engineers and manufacturers formed consortia to present their ideas of 'architecture novatrice', and now several award winning schemes in the Concours des mille piscines has put French pool architecture for people well in the lead (see chapter 4.3). And adaptions of original ideas figure even in the super covers sphere – one of the convertibles award winning architects, Roger Taillibert, took a fixed extension of the design to Montreal (see chapter 3).

Dutch and German engineers have also energetically tackled the convertible problem producing pivoted canopies across hoops, and big top canvas shapes suspended from pylons. And another adaption to Olympic places with fixed, but flexible roofing figured at Munich.

The private sector in all countries is somewhat different: there the considerable number of home pools built, or being built, has attracted inumerable new and not-so-new designs for package-type convertible enclosures, since a larger market seems more commercially rewarding. But the successful formula for an attractive, economic, durable convertible that seals in a comfortable environment without wasting a hospitable climate still seems elusive, for as yet there is no one dominant design.

10.8 Complexes

The great thermae of Rome and the modern swimming pool complexes have had to face the common problem of safely covering large areas. Natural evolution in roofs enabled Roman engineers to stretch 35m barrel and domed spans across the caldarium and laconicum within their vast social complexes (as at the 3rd-century AD Baths of Caracalla). Modern lightweight developments now cover

10.19 *A tracked sliding cover needs space at both ends of the pool*
Rutherford Swimming Pools Ltd, Sussex

10.20a *Overlaying a big top type convertible cover*

10.20b *The toplighting qualities for a canvas convertible*
Roger Taillibert, Carnot
Photo: Ch. Baer

10.19

20a

).20b

larger spans and soar over pool and sports centres in the rediscovery of the dome. Seen from outside, the raised dome architecturally highlights the centre: from inside, natural toplight avoids trouble with glare (see chapter 4.5 on entertaining architecture).

The most recent techniques for covering large pool areas adopt the space-saving flexibility of tensile construction. A concave slung form means less air space to be managed. In Germany, the hanging roof of lightweight concrete slabs tied to cables has been developed to an advanced stage of deep dished shaping. Lighter still, translucent sheeting of suspended tensile cable roofing (as at Munich Olympic Park) illustrates how very large areas can be effectively covered; and the Olympic Swimming Pool buildings in Tokyo demonstrate the architects' aesthetic and structural conviction that 'tension is heir to the future'.[2]

As an alternative for a span of up to 40m, the economic, monolithic, reinforced concrete dome can be pneumatically 'pumped-up' and set-off in only one week, with cutting of doors and windows, and installing the finishes and fittings following later (see chapter 10.6 on geodesy). Or there are large, laminated timber or RC beams which will satisfactorily span 50m, besides creating a very attractive interior. And castellated steel frames or glass reinforced concrete or versatile polymers to offer even greater opportunities for future poolrooms, poolhouses and 'poolaria'.

SECTION II

10.9 Access and exit

Road safety at the entrance to a pool building is as important as the pre-cleanse at the pool access area. User/traffic

10.21 *Detail of cladding construction and access ladder onto dome of Swindon Leisure Centre*
Architect: Gillinson Barnett & Partners
Photo: O. F. Clarke

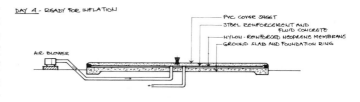

10.22 *Domes in reinforced concrete formed by inflation: Parashell method to 40m diameter*

circulation patterns need to be considered in the planning stage, but the main points that also have bearing upon the superstructure are summarised here (see also chapter 2 for different layouts and chapter 11.4 for facilities involved).

In 1930 it was considered 'the principal entrances to the Public Baths Establishment should be placed in the centre of the main façade, and provision made for men and women to enter the building by separate doorways'.[3] Nowadays, we prefer main double door access (for either sex), suitable for wheelchairs, with generous grid wells and adherent matting to trap dirt. From the foyer, separate entrance/exit arrangements into enclosed spectator areas will restrict spread of dirt or infection.

Provision is always made to separate the dry (and dirty) service areas from the wet (and clean) poolside areas. Barefoot bathers enter the pool properly cleansed by passing through graded wetter rooms for changing, clothes storage and pre-cleanse hygiene.

Planning the best circulation route requires careful thought and study, especially when traffic flow between outdoor patios and indoor decking is encouraged. One safe solution adopted by some outdoor hotel schemes introduces a hygiene moat around, or a footbath at the point of access, through which all bathers must pass on entering and leaving the pool.

Persuasion to pre-cleanse can *halve* cleaning schedules, water filtering and purifying processes. Continental European standards of pre-cleanse hygiene are extremely high resulting in valuable operating dividends (see chapter 16.2, Cleaning systems). For the less heavily used modern private pool, absorbent indoor carpeting, or outdoor artificial grassing is now becoming successful for wet and dry distinctive covering (see chapter 12.4 and information sheet 16.4 for ideal cleaning requirements in public pools).

Ample decking around a pool reduces collisions when bathers run. And no matter how well rules are made, people still run. Consequently, wall cladding with resilient impact materials or glazing at low level with safety glass or thick polyester film overlay is important. At one hard-pressed senior school, a newly erected pool enclosure left such small space around that visiting parents could only watch their children's races on sports day by closed-circuit television from outside the pool enclosure!

Other major points concern sufficient and safe, clearly marked exits, particularly near shallow or training sections, plus the use of safe, non-slip materials only, for all pool surrounds, ramps and stair treads. There should be fire-check doors between a poolhall and the rest of the building with provision of suitable hydrants and fire warning system. Incidentally, some modern materials might not burn very easily, but all too often they produce dense and dangerous fumes (see chapter 16.1, Safety).

10.10 Outside structures

Extra facilities sometimes can be catered for better by special outside structures. There is no imperative need to integrate changing accommodation, plant room and equipment store always within the same pool building, when convenient chalets and cabins, sun rooms and sheds can do the job equally well at far lower cost. Summer houses, pool marquees and changing cabanas are in fact preferable for many private pools, and when the log cabin

sauna can also double up for extra changing and drying space, additional enjoyable facilities will be the result (see chapter 11).

At busy public pools, a nearby car park is an essential outside facility with disabled driver parking nearest to the main entrance (see chapter 4, fig **4.11**, chapter 11.4, Facilities). In Sweden, their parking lot experience has shown the need for spaces to accommodate 10 per cent maximum bathing load in winter, with summer peaks averaging five times the winter numbers. Also, consider the large proportion of children who are the predominating bathing public for most town pools, and who travel by public transport from within a 5km area, or require adequate cycle shed provision. (For further information on outside paving areas, see chapter 12.4, Hard landscaping.)

10.11 Light

Sunlight adds sparkle to a pool water surface – but it can cause glare too. Any pool in bad light – too much contrast or too little illuminance – is dangerous. A white interior lined pool tank with good even reflection is a strong safety factor. But since the amount of sunlight constantly varies, it is incompatible to seek visually bright, completely naturally lighted indoor pools. Controlled lighting is important, and requirements for international competitions and displays are critical.

Overhead Sufficient, balanced, diffuse and directional lighting, powerful and wide ranging is mandatory in international pools, whereas one third of the amount of illumination plus maintenance for fitments is more important in local pools. Good calibre lighting also depends upon the amount of absorption and reflectivity of decorative finishes. Championships and television demand at least 1000 lux available illumination; local baths can be satisfactorily operated at 250 lux, with residential pools as low as 100 lux. It was not too long ago that just over 100 lux was considered sufficient for many municipal baths in Britain!

Underwater Underwater lighting is sometimes thought a luxury for the swimming pool. But beside being attractive, public pool underwater lighting, from sealed beam or fluorescent strip, increases safety, reduces glare and adds necessary lux for TV coverage (see chapters 7, 8 and 11). It is not expensive compared with the cost and heat dissipation of airspace lighting, though if service tunnels have to be provided for access to 'dry' lighting behind safety glazed tank windows, capital cost can be high (see information sheet 8.2). The wet type, water cooled, light unit is far less expensive and also serviceable from the deck (see chapter 11.5).

Emergency The system should be in operation instantly, or at worst within five seconds of the failure of the normal lighting installation. Illumination should never fall below $1/5$ lux in corridors and escape routes, measured at floor level: the ratio of minimum illuminance to the maximum, along any route, should remain within the ratio 1:50, with no abrupt changes from dark to light areas. While it is possible to see by such absolute minimum lighting levels when out on moonlight walks, it is far safer to provide at least 1.0 lux minimum value, or better still as much as $1/100$ of normal lighting values for pool emergency routes.

Fenestration Swimming is too often considered an inward looking activity needing little or no window area, and benefiting greatly from balanced artificial lighting. Nobody looks outwards, it is argued . . . but ask a pool attendant whether a job with a view is important, or a swimmer if sunlight is better than fluorescent light. And if a poolside lifeguard constantly faces any glare, the intensity of light from the water surface can be painful (see chapter 14.4). No more than 5 per cent of top light is really necessary compared with surface water area, for suitable daylight illuminance in deep plan building: also narrow vertical windows of less than 25 per cent glazing/wall area will reasonably cater for the view and pleasant side lighting, with artificial support when necessary.

Glare is caused by the reflection of the sun, bright sky or strong lighting, seen on the surface of the water. If can be avoided simply by placing attendants at points where they see no sky directly or by reflection, or stopping solar glare by reducing window size or introducing external shade. Controlling glare in pool halls is made more difficult because poolwater is always moving, reflecting light over a fairly wide angle (as much as 45° total variation). Moreover, the problem is exaggerated by greater light being needed for the pool than elsewhere, plus the bright, white reflective surfaces so often involved.

Glare is the product of excessive contrast between light and shade at the surface. It is strongest where the water surface is brighter than the pool floor, or where the glazed tile brilliantly reflects.

Large areas of glazing sometimes cause uncomfortable solar gain. This can be controlled with tinted heat-absorbing glass or overlaid reflective film. Never use materials that induce a greenish hue; colour rendering of light is vitally important, especially for poolwater, which should be clear and faintly blue. Cool (not cold) colours for pool hall walls and ceilings help with reflected light, but include some warm and vibrant decor colours for atmosphere (see chapter 11.3).

Dark glazing or solar control film reduce brightness, but not the contrast. Contrast is avoided if light falls vertically to prevent angular reflection, or when underwater lighting adds its illumination to reduce some of the extremes of light and shade: consequently extra top lighting and balancing of the side light reflection will stop glare.

Curtain glazed walling facing the sun, although appealing for bathers, gives rise to glare as well as potentially hazardous breakage. By preventing low angle incident light, increasing top light, adding reflective light, screening side light and balancing all illumination, glare is controllable right from an early stage. When the problem already exists, however, screens, drapes and blinds can diffuse low angle light, shutters will reduce direct intense sun, increased top lighting/underwater lighting levels help prevent extremes of light and shade on surfaces, corrugated glass walling also deflects direct light; and setting up raised observation platforms (preferably with backs to the light) often overcomes problems of attendants being unable to see beneath the water surface at normal poolside levels (see chapter 11.4, 11.5 and information sheet 11.9).

Saving glass Modern energy policies now make previously expensive double, or perhaps triple, glazing economically essential for the fuel-efficient superstructure. Window condensation will still occur in extreme circumstances, and all fittings and fixtures must resist accordingly with

adequate, easily unblocked, drainage channelling always provided (see chapter 14.9 and information sheet 14.10).

One small, but important point to remember: large or small glass areas will need cleaning regularly! And the view might not be important, but the breakages, danger, heat losses and gains, specular reflection and maintenance *are* when large areas of glass are involved.

10.12 Transmission

Sound The most 'piercing feature of the popular indoor pool is the noise'.[4] Pool halls have always been noisy places, especially when young children use them. This is because 'sound is reflected from one hard, easily cleaned surface to another'.[5] Large surface areas and high ceilings prolong reverberation, and the reverberation times (a measure of the extent of noise) should be kept to below two seconds (one second, in teaching areas or private pools). This specification can be difficult to achieve when so many impervious surfaces are involved. Higher sound frequencies always give most trouble: a good reason to remove teaching pools to another room. Noise levels must not reach a point where an instructor cannot make himself heard easily. The average swimming pool hall built without consideration to sound insulation, or rather absorption, can achieve persistent shrieks of 100 decibels. It is established that a noisy factory, with machinery making 95dB of sound, will cause damage to the hearing of operators exposed over long periods of time.

Acoustic pollution requires as much consideration as the rest of the environment. Quite simple arrangements will help. Lowered and suspended ceilings subdue sound (and hide ventilation). Indoor plants, drapes and baffle boards are almost as useful as patent sound absorbing systems. It is the reflection of sound that requires absorption within a space, whereas the passage of sound energy through a barrier from one space to another is the concern of sound insulation: the pool hall that is poorly insulated transmits its sounds easily to be heard by others outside, or next door. The factors of mass, discontinuity, stiffness and uniformity affect the airborne insulation of a construction. But it is mainly mass, or density, that concerns the designer trying to cut down sound with appropriate materials. The most suitable (and usually soft) surfaces deaden reflection, and invariably thermally insulate too. Being hygroscopic, the materials must either stop moisture from getting in or be so arranged for it to be drained away and dried. One hard material that is designed to soften sound that has proved successful is the perforated ceramic block.

Since soft materials and acoustic absorbers will always be poked and pushed, dug into and damaged, they must be set well out of reach. Far worse than probing fingers are water polo balls and leaning ladders, against which provision must be made. Double glazing does not absorb sound, but insulates against transmission; better so when glass and frames are perfectly sealed, and when panes are separated between 100 and 200mm – never less than 50mm – with the sheets of glass of different thickness for even better sound insulation.

Omit tile perpends above 2·5m height, and carefully position and increase medium/high level absorption facings to where water-reflected and water-accelerated sounds can be soaked up.

10.23a *Specular reflection at Coventry swimming pool showing the problem of pool duty and surface water glare*

Architects' Journal
Photo: W. J. Toomey

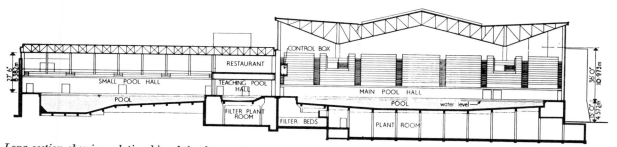

Long section showing relationship of the three pools ($\frac{1}{64}$ in = 1ft). Metric equivalents are indicated with dimensions

10.23b *Coventry City swimming pool*

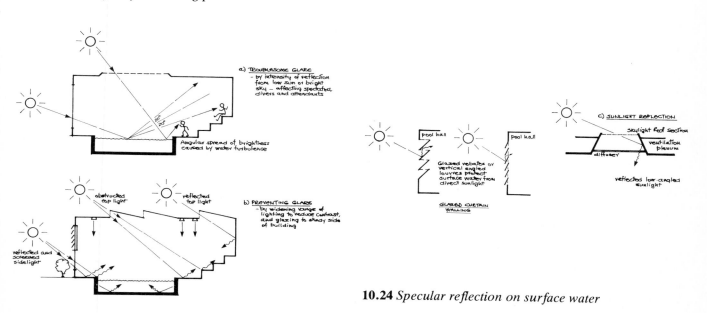

10.24 *Specular reflection on surface water*

The coincidence of occupation is good for controlling sound, dampening with the presence of people, clothing, furnishings, curtains, carpets, etc, the greater the medley the better. Even outdoor pools are troubled with excess sound, for the din of bathing travels some distance in the open, and neighbours will be disturbed until furnishing, screening and planting is provided (see chapter 11.3 and 4). *Vision* Management efficiency throughout the building can be improved with closed-circuit TV located at the cash-desk, helping operate other areas and keeping an eye on vandal spots at the same time (see chapter 16.4).

Visual information from all around the building fed to the ticket or control office is a paying feature in some new Dutch swimming pools. Perhaps more important, though, for all public pools than inward visual information is that comprehensible outward sound information provided by a clear definition public address system – with background music only sometimes a bonus. Occasionally, both sound and vision become high priority, when a day of champion-ships requires TV broadcasting. Most existing well-designed pools will require few special adaptations, while current and future international superstructures are designed with worldwide communications much in mind.

References

[1] J. A. Godfrey, N. O. Milbank and D. K. Woodhouse, *Local Authority Covered Swimming Pools*, Garston, BRE Publications, 1970
[2] Robin Boyd, Olympic Buildings in Tokyo, *The Architectural Review*, April 1966
[3] A. W. S. and K. M. B. Cross, *Modern Public Baths and Wash-Houses*, London, Simpkin Marshall, 1938
[4] H. T. Hitchin, IBM Conference, 1968
[5] ibid.

INFORMATION SHEET 10.1

The special case – enclosing a swimming pool

Swimming pool enclosures
have to cope with:
high air temperatures
high humidity
poolwater acids and alkalis
highly corrosive gases
algae
heavy-handed bathers
determined vandals

need proofing against:
excessive heat loss
solar gain
glare
long reverberation
ravages of insects, fungus and fire

should be:
visually attractive yet still benefit from production design techniques for economic construction

particularly require:
ample light
air
insulation

Services
must control condensation and ventilation and take into account wide variations between internal and external environments which can induce high vapour pressure differentials as great as 100lb/ft^2

Warning:
Do not underestimate the corrosive severity of a pool's humid environment

See chapter 14.7 to 9.

INFORMATION SHEET 10.2

Preferred environmental range – swim halls

		Remarks
Swimming pool water temperature	25–29°C	Hydrotherapy to 35°C
Air temperature: Pool hall	26–30°C	At least 1°C above poolwater
Service rooms:		
alongside pool	to 5°C below hall temperature	To avoid abrupt temperature changes
perimeter hall	to 10°C below hall temperature	
Relative humidity	40–60%	70% in summer. Spectators' range: 30–70%
Maximum air velocity	0·10m/s	High relative humidity with high temperature must be avoided or approx 1m³/min of air supply per bather
Minimum air supply rate per surface water area of pool water	50m³/h/m²	or 1m³/min/m² guideline standard preferable
Pool air changes area	4–6 per hour	Kept low for economical reasons
	10–12 per hour	Recycled if all chemical traces removed
Ceiling void air changes	12–14 per hour	If ventilation never fails, a vapour barrier is unnecessary: circulate heated air with slight pressurisation (+10%)
Changing room air changes	4–8 per hour	
Clothing store air changes	8–12 per hour	To provide ozonation
Reverberation @ 500 to 2000Hz	1·5s	Sound recorded when empty
	1·0s	Maximum for teaching pools
Thermal insulation U value:		
for constant use	0·5W/m²/°C	Roof max 0·5/Wall max 1·5 is reduced to 0·4 with cavity infill
for intermittent use	1·0 to 2·0W/m²/°C	
lightweight single skin enclosures	3·0 to 5·0W/m²/°C	

Sources: AJ/ASA/IBM/NCAA/NRC/NSPI/SPATA/TUS.

INFORMATION SHEET 10.3

Stainless steels

400 series
ferritic and magnetic

Type	Alloy content Percentages		
410	Cr	12	Do not use in swimming pool conditions: only in mildest 'non-corrosive' ancillary rooms
430	Cr	17	

300 series
austenitic and non-magnetic
minimum 1mm, optimum 1·5,
maximum 2mm thickness

Type	Alloy content Percentages		
302	Cr/Ni	18/8	Minimum desirable alloy selection suitable for pool situations
304	Cr/Ni	18/10	
316	Cr/Ni/Mo	17/11/2½ 18/10/3 18/12/2½	Ideal for high chlorine levels and seawaters

Sources: NSPI/Specification.

INFORMATION SHEET 10.4

Pool water heat losses

These mainly result from:

Primarily
{ Evaporation – water to air
  Convection – water to wind
  Radiation – heat to environment

Marginally
{ Conduction – heat to earth
  Dilution – rainfall and refilling minus waste water

INFORMATION SHEET 10.5

Lighting checklist

Although eyes can adapt from sunlight to moonlight, for reasons of safety pool lighting must remain constantly bright.

Artificial lighting
Consider: efficiency, length of life, initial and ongoing costs, accessibility, maintenance, non-corrosive diffusers, vapourproof fitments, operational safety, angle of direction, provision for temporary stage lighting.
Specify servicing access – it is easier from below and located over deck, but focused over pool. Air above the ceiling is less corrosive. Lighting behind portholes is easier to maintain for high pool halls. Do not use sliding glass covers on lights over pool in case of accidental breakage.
Install a separate system of emergency lighting for public pools.
Overhead lighting is best for uniformity.
Reduce glare by allowing some upward light to lessen contrast.
Lock-switches for public pools will save energy wastage.
Lighting efficiency is increased with light coloured finishes for walls and ceilings.

Day lighting
High level top daylight is best to prevent contrasting surface reflections at a 4 per cent factor level to surface water area.

Side lighting
Balance is achieved with daylight factor over pool of 2 to 4 per cent, and 1 to 2 per cent over decking.

Outdoor lighting
Often inadequate for competition when artificial lighting essential.

Underwater lighting
Adds spectacle and safety at night. Will reduce surface water glare caused by strong sidelighting. White reflective background to pool interior improves lighting of tank.
Private pools: shine underwater lighting away from house, angled downwards and positioned under diving-board.
Public pools: ensure evenly spread underwater lighting, but no beams facing along racing lanes.
Wet niche type: must be arranged approx 0·5m water depth for easy removal and replacement. This type can be kicked and although toughened lenses protect lamp, they may become damaged.
Dry niche type: readily accessible through service tunnel but cost of system is greater. Besides the facility of varying lamp power and type easily, their main advantage is that they are isolated from the public.
For safe operation, all underwater lighting units must be wired to low voltage separate transformers and switching, and should have ground fault circuit detectors/interruptors.
An amber lens over an outdoor pool lamp cuts down insect attraction and hypnotic influence. Lens colours for underwater lighting are generally unappealing or garish.

Diving-board lighting
Position spots carefully with beams focused nearly vertically to avoid glare to divers and dazzle to spectators. A separate switching system is advised in case individual spots are troublesome for certain dives.

Sources: CNCA/IBM/IES/NSPI/TUS.

INFORMATION SHEET 10.6

Light: range of pool illumination

Lux illuminance or lumens per m²	Illumination lux outdoor	indoor	Equivalent to: other general areas
Emergency lighting public areas	1–5	5–25	night lighting or street lighting
Dressing room – residential pools	—	75	store rooms
Changing rooms/toilets – public pools	100	100–200	stairways and coffee bars
Residential pools and spectator areas	100	100–300	circulation areas
Entrance hall and plantroom	—	200–300	cafeteria
Local baths: training pools and deck surrounds, manager's office	200	250–350	gymnasia and schools
National competitive Leisure pools } ticket office, cashier	400	500–600	supermarkets/offices (spec US Sports Assoc and UK Sports Council)
International competitive: for start-finish, pool deck and 1m above water throughout events and for TV	600 including underwater lighting	1000–1200	hypermarkets (spec FINA)

Wattages
Overhead lighting: approx wattage/m² to achieve 500 lux in pool area, though usually 250 lux general lighting plus intensity lighting over separate deeper water is better – assuming bright decor.
20W/m²: Fluorescent daylight – white diffuse fitting: as indirect lighting does not penetrate water, supplement reflected light with point sources for sparkle. Best combination warm white fluorescent and tungsten/halogen, etc.
25W/m²: High pressure sodium – golden light } Also highlight sparkling
30W/m² Mercury fluorescent – colour corrected } quality of water.
20–50W/m²: Fluorescent – warm white louvred panel, avoid cold lighting.
70W/m²: Tungsten – has long life and is easily replaced.

Economic life:

fluorescent tubes	: 7000 hours	(relamping to coincide with cleaning overhaul)
long life lamps	: 2000 hours	} estimated working
filament lamps	: 1000 hours	} life

Underwater lighting: approx wattage/m² of pool surface area.
10–20W/m² – private pools to provide approx 150–300 lux iluminance. (150W units – residential only. 300W units – recreational type most often used.) 5–10m spacing apart.
20–50W/m² – public pools to provide approx 300–700 lux illuminance. (500W units – leisure pools. 1000W units – competitive type more economical for specification.) 3–5m spacing apart.

Comparison lighting levels

		Approx lux illuminance
US schools before	1910	35
	1920	200
	1930	350
	1950	500–750 up to 1600
		(Note: 1600 lux offers 4% increase in general performance over 750 lux)
UK schools	1960	100–200
	1975	300–500

Lux range indicator	– bright sunlight	50,000 lux
	– overcast bright day	5,000 lux
(100 lux approximates	– 'bad light stops play'	500 lux
to light at 1m	– brightly lighted main	
distance from 100W	road	50 lux
filament lamp)	– car parking lighting	5 lux
	– full moonlight	1/5 lux

Colour temperature
Colour rendering in white light is:

Warm – high pressure sodium	3000°K
Natural – tungsten filament/tungsten halogen	4000°K
Cold-to-cool – high pressure mercury	5000°K
Cool-to-warm – simulated by fluorescent lamps	3000–6000°K

Sources: AAU/AJ/APHA/ASA/CNCA/FINA/IBM/IES/NCAA/ NSPI/SPATA/TUS.

INFORMATION SHEET 10.7

Emergency lighting

An alternative power supply can be provided by either a prime move generator or by batteries. But a generator, even kept in ideal conditions, cannot be guaranteed to start and run-up within five seconds of a power failure.

An automatic changeover device will be needed to detect failure of normal supply; or the system has to be run at all times emergency lighting is likely to be called upon (which is often uneconomic). A bridging battery will be required to cover the run-up period to operating level, or the system can be powered by battery (two at least), when power failure will switch in the circuit – the charger only being connected to the mains supply, which may therefore indirectly maintain emergency lighting working at all times if required. A separate circuit is better to light strategic routes and exits.

At least one hour (three hours preferably) is needed over which emergency lighting should remain working, for people can become lost, first-aid might be needed on the spot, premises have to be searched, etc.

Source: EC.

INFORMATION SHEET 10.8

Glazing checklist

Overglazed pool halls are preferred by bathers, but not by the management.
Glass Less glass saves heat losses and gains, cleaning and breakages, danger and specular reflection, expensive materials, algae growth. Glazed curtain-walling can be hazardous, expensive, often in need of opaque curtaining.

Inadequate window space is claustrophobic.
Strive for maximum glazing equivalent to 25 per cent floor area, preferably as narrow, vertical windows catering for the view.
Low level glazing in the pool area requires toughened glass or armour plate or glass bricks; windows need protection with warm seat barriers or shatter-resistant polyester film. Main hazard is water polo.
High top louvred-lights can help reduce specular reflection.
Roof light glazing structures are exposed to potential condensation and chemical corrosion attack.
Side lighting schemes permit the installation of a suspended ceiling to create a ventilation plenum continually supplied with dry, clean air, and preventing condensation in the roof space.
Glare is caused by contrast. It is developed by scattered light and shade over a water surface which is brighter than the floor. Turbulence widens the angular spread. Reduced light reduces brightness, not contrast.
To reduce glare from specular reflection, avoid creating areas of strong luminance close to the pool: screen or absorb or deflect or even cut out daylight. Underwater lighting helps reduce surface water contrast. Indirect lighting cuts glare on water, but bright ceilings or skies can also be distracting. To reduce sky glare, angle rooflights at 45°, but ensure they are accessible for cleaning.
To some extent, changing architectural style and economic taste for smaller window area is reducing glare.
Windows Normal glass is almost opaque to uv light also stopping the suntan. Large window areas, if required, are best set away from the sun, double glazed, and protected from downdraughts.
Glazing tilted 10° outward from base lessens direct daylight glare, and tinted mirrored double glazing further reduces bright day lighting. Reflective values range from 20 to 50 per cent.
Some shading colourations induce unwholesome greenish hues in poolwater. Blues/greys are best.
Anti-sun glass or overlaid polyester film can stop 75 per cent solar energy (while warming the glass) to cut contrast facing spectators.
Double glazing at 100mm (50mm minimum, but 200mm is better) separation with different glass thicknesses considerably reduces noise (if totally sealed), also condensation, energy transmission, especially convective transmission which can be lowered by 50 per cent.
Fittings and fixures must be protected by attack-resistant materials, polysulphide glazing compounds, or angled beadings and ample run-off channels.
UK example – swimhall:
Single glaze: Condensation-free hours on average day June to August, range from two to six hours.
Double glaze: Condensation-free hours on average day May to October, ten hours plus.

Sources: ASA/CNCA/IES/IBM.
See chapter 14.4, Insulation and insolation.

INFORMATION SHEET 10.9

Sound checklist

Insulation prevents transfer of sound from one place to another.
Absorption limits reverberation (eg echoes) but not transference. 'Coincidence of occupation' provides absorption by people, clothing, furnishings, fitments, carpets, curtains, etc. Add plants to help reduce noise: this applies equally to outdoor pool areas.
Reverberation times should be kept down to at least:
1·5 to 2 seconds for *main pool hall* when empty,
1 to 1·5 seconds for *private/learner pool* when empty,
taken at 500 to 2000 cycles/s.
Note: Sound travels three times faster under water.

Surface areas
Ceilings are often the main area for acoustic treatment, as well as walling areas behind diving stages.
Low ceilings, especially over instruction areas, help baffle sound; suspended ceilings hide ventilation.
High ceilings prolong reverberation. Large diameter barrel vaults can focus sound undesirably so 'breaking-up' surfaces to foil reflections is important. Teak slatted type ceilings backed by acoustic absorbent glass fibre over a cavity, or egg-crate timber mouldings, or cork tiles/baffles, etc will help achieve 1·5 second reverberation times.

Materials

All materials must resist moisture and be hardwearing. Soft sound absorbents failing in humid conditions need a barrier to stop vapour penetration, eg a plastic coating over asbestos finish.

Select acoustical materials for absorption of sound, resistance to moisture, fire, wear, retention of some attractiveness.

Try to include drapes in glazed areas, easily cleanable pool carpeting for deck surrounds, double glazing to 200mm gap for sound insulation, special surfacing panels, finishes or proprietary tiles backed by non-hygroscopic material, perforated bricks, etc.

Acoustic plasters are susceptible to damage and wear, and can drop particles when rubbed.

Foamed wall/ceiling panels have good acoustical properties but can also be soft and friable.

Sprayed cementitious asbestos offers reasonable conditions and low reverberation times. It is excellent for inside ventilation systems reducing noise travel and plantroom 'hum'. To reduce vibration, set machinery on non-rigid mountings with flexible connections for pipe fittings (see chapters 13.2 and 14.6).

Sources: CNCA/IBM/NSPI/TUS.

INFORMATION SHEET 10.10

TV checklist

Supply equipment Parking provision required for coach-size support vehicles close by pool hall. Safe access for supply cables of approx 25mm diameter. Power supply: generally 3-phase, 50 cycle, 200 or 300 amp.

Camera positions Fixed positions behind or above a results board are invariably unsatisfactory. Located in the spectator gallery, difficulties can arise if operating into a dazzle of light reflection from water surfaces.

Scaffold platforms are often preferred but must be isolated from the public and suitable for 150 kg/m² loading.

Decking surrounds should permit tracking: camera dollies are approx 2 × 1m, weighing around 120kg excluding cable drums.

At least 2m height provision required.

Timing: for setting up period average 2 days.

Lighting Minimum illuminance 800 lux ±20 per cent (long focus events require 1400 lux) at minimum 1m above activity area.

The lighting should not fall off beyond 20 per cent over any 4m in the area of activity.

Brightness range should be no greater than 30:1. An opaque acrylic roof such as at the Munich Olympic pool is excellent, but bright sidelighting can be troublesome. Reduce glare with grey-green fabric screens to minimum 3m height at windows especially behind diving area.

Average incident light to spectator areas should be at least equal to a third the level of incident light to activity areas.

Colour tv Lighting levels need to be higher than for black and white transmission only at 1000 lux ±20 per cent.

Daylight colour varies continually and proportion of natural lighting must be reduced to allow different colour temperatures to be matched artificially. Correlated colour temperature of the light source is preferred at between 4000 to 4500°K – tolerance is acceptable in the range 3000 to 5000°K.

To reduce reflections matt surfaces are preferred: strongly coloured decoration absorbs light and reduces technical quality of pictures.

Controls A control room or press room is not necessary, but plenty of telephone jacks are.

TV monitor banks (each 3 × 2m approx) or a glazed commentator's box, are best suited opposite start/finish lines.

An interview room (minimum 4 × 3m) is useful.

Electronic timing circuitry should be TV linked to all commentary positions.

A sweep second hand is vital on display clocks.

Long reverberation times and poor acoustics are more a nuisance than a problem.

Sources: CNCA/TUS.

Above: Tension cover engineering for the Munich Olympic Park and Stadium
Architect: Prof. Behnisch

Below: Retractible cover dome installed over many French pools in the 1970s following the Concours des mille piscines
Tournesol International, Paris

11 Finishes and facilities

The successful finish for a swimming pool is durable, keeps structural components dry *and* is decorative. Many materials break down in swimming pool conditions and only the toughest and most waterproof should ever be used.

11.1 Colour

Public pool hall surface interiors are usually selected first for cleanliness and secondly for ruggedness. Unfortunately, this decor gives total blank whiteness, or drab nothingness: a place where the swimmer is expected only to swim. A gradual change is coming about, with the leisure pool now presenting surroundings that warmly attract, where texture and colour are important and colour permanence is necessary.

Not all colours blend into the swimming pool scene. Great care is needed in selecting from the many splendid but sometimes loud hues, pigmented into modern materials. Strong blues, sometimes used to spice cheap vinyl liners, create harsh unnecessary tones in the pool. Subtle natural blueness of deep water is deepened when pool linings are only faintly blue. Seagreen and turquoise blue linings are popular with garden pool owners – reds and yellows are definitely out. Strong, warm colours should be kept well clear of the water's edge. Beige brickwork can induce a bilious tinge to the water, and peagreen seems to turn water more than a shade or two off colour. The colour revival for pool scenes is bringing back mosaic pictures, mural panels and magnificent trompe l'oeil.

An underwater mural should not depict shapes that look similar to swimmers, but the canvas of the pool bottom really does offer marvellous opportunity in gigantic proportions for ambitious painters. Pool fresco painting, or aqua-art, has caught on in America in a big way, where even a public community pool can sport the full psychedelic flower setting, and a private estate pool a giant eye that winks when the water ripples. It is important to remember underwater objects in this pool pop-art form look nearer than they are, or larger (by a quarter) than they are.

There is no doubt that tiling, with at least some colour and pattern to relieve the plain monotony, is hygienic. Most ceramic manufacturers have experimented with vibrant colours or dazzling designs, strongly patterned or slip-line motifs, textured or burnished surfaces, but few pool designers have yet experimented with these better visual effects.

A private garden pool, that requires less stringent surface specifications than a public pool, will often include colour in a tiled band limited to the water's edge – there the object is to offer an easily cleanable scum line, and to bring out the tinge of blue of healthy water.

Clean water in depth against a white background takes on a blue or turquoise cast. Finely suspended dust particles in the pool water scatter the blue end of the spectrum 16 times more than the red, so there is more blue to be seen than red. Also the bending and slowing of light by particles subtracts the longer, redder wavelength end of the spectrum – the red is absorbed – all contributing to the attractive filtered water-blue result. What is known as 'Rayleigh scattering' produces that blue colour of the sea and the sky, and not in the case of swimming pools, pigmentation to the floor and the walls.

11.2 Pool finish materials

The most favoured pool finishes are those that also add another watertight lining to a tank. The tougher and more expensive tile and terrazzo, epoxy and GRP reduce maintenance costs, are anti-corrosive, vandal-resistant, easily cleaned and withstand pool disinfectants. Heavy duty vinyl liners are almost as durable, and certainly far cheaper to repair, and they have proved economic even for heavily used outdoor public pools.

Paints are the most economical and practical water retaining pool finish and are easy to apply. Proprietary brands should be compared by *cost per year of life in use*. When pools were drained annually for repainting, cheap cement-based blends were often used, but they are unsuited for swimming pool use as they are not waterproof and wear away very quickly.

Nearly all early private garden pools were coated in chlorinated rubber-based paint, and there are still many hundreds of thousands of painted pools operating perfectly well. But unless a long-life paint formula is specified and applied properly, the time spent preparing surfaces, painting and repainting is the main drawback.

PREPARATION Every paint depends upon a good key preparation, with careful priming being vital for effective covering and colouring. A clean, dry, degreased, non-flaking, roughened surface is required for painting. (New smooth concrete of about 0·5 roughness coefficient is not suitable). Never apply pool paints under hot sun, in temperatures of less than 5 °C, in rainy conditions, or when relative humidity exceeds 75 per cent. Very few pool paints will cover other mixes, the general rule being never to

11.1 *Pool pop art for the director of an art museum in Pasadena: getting ready for filming a TV commercial*
Swimming Pool Weekly/Age
Photo: Del Ankers

11.2 *Water rippling the beard of Leonardo da Vinci painted on a pool floor in England*
Dr R. Wood

switch paint types unless previous coats have been sand-blasted clear or completely stripped first. When using paint strippers, or acid etchers (1 litre *added to* 10 litres water per 5m² area), the surfaces must be thoroughly cleansed and neutralised afterwards.

RUBBERISED PAINTS   The most popular pool paints are still the stabilised chlorinated, moderated, natural or synthetic, rubber-based blends, which although applied in several 30 micron thick layers, build up as one increasing coat. Paint cover on concrete is about 1 litre per 4 to 6m² of surface area; but this is better on metals at 8 to 10m²/litre, where at least 5 or 6 coats will be necessary to prevent possible pinprick corrosion. The pool is repainted after the first year, then every 3 or 5 years depending upon wear and use. On concrete, at least two coatings of high-grade chlorinated rubber based paint are necessary for good body, but a new pool requires at least four coats to start with. For the shallow end floor, or on paddling pool floors, the rubbery-like sheen of the finish can be roughened with sand added into the final coat. Chlorinated rubber paint is susceptible to UV light and abrasion, oils and body fats, so a mosaic/tile scum band at the water line is important. Rubberised paints of indeterminable quality do exist and must be avoided for any pool applications.

Fresh cement render needs to be left to cure for 14 to 28 days before painting with enamel. Each coat of paint should be allowed to harden for 1 to 2 days; and 7 to 14 days are required for all the solvent to be given off before filling the pool. Check that movement joint sealants cannot be dissolved by the paint solvent. The vapour in an enclosed space can be overpowering. Flashpoint is around 30°C.

The trouble to both contractor and client is the length of curing and drying times. In the urgency of pool building programmes, and to allow swimming straight away, new concrete tanks are often filled immediately for the first season to allow ample curing time for painting later, out of season.

VINYL MIXTURES give a silky matt sheen and dry quickly in 3 to 6 hours with a day left between coats. Water-based polymer emulsion coats offer low cost, easy to apply coverage of 8 to 10m²/litre; two coats at least usually being necessary for 3 to 5 year life.

Isomerised rubber paints will cover most existing pool-painted surfaces *that are still sound,* or fresh surfaces also at about 8 to 10m²/litre, and can be brushed on, rollered or sprayed to 50 micron thick films for 3 to 4 year life. The paint needs to harden for 2 to 3 days before filling the pool.

Some companies recommend a latex admixture to a cement slurry, or Marblite render mix (at 5 litres or 10 litres per 50kg cement according to exposed use), to give excellent preparation and stain resistance, corrosion and water-proofing qualities: pool painting later on this cement render can be extended to 12m²/litre, with a longer-term operational life. Plasticisers or latex formulations are also used in slurry mixes for restoration and crack repairs to improve waterproofing abilities and adhesion, providing possible external hydrostatic pressure has been eliminated (see chapter 16.5 on refurbishing).

TWO-PART HARDENERS Another range of pool paints includes the acrylics and the epoxies, some of which in special combination with fillers of stone dust or marble chippings can also offer a cold glazing terrazzo type of screed for concrete and steel. Liquid liners are revolutionising the use of paints for private and public pools, since their first applications offer a longer life. A well-mixed and formulated epoxy resin paint, for example, can last ten years at 10m²/litre cover, and longer still when combined with other compounds. If applied properly, a long-lasting tile-like surface can be economically created. Thicknesses range from 10 micron painted coats to 10mm rendered layers. Epoxy resin two-pack materials after mixing generally have a pot-life of up to 24 hours at 20°C, but curing will be delayed to 48 hours if the temperature falls to 10°C. Poorly mixed epoxies can delaminate and spall, or even never cure at all. Before repainting an epoxy, existing work surfaces will need etching or sandblasting for the bonding key.

Research into polyurethane, polyester resin, polysulphide, polyisoprene paints and poly-reinforced coatings is suggesting new and potentially ideal permanent waterproof finishes that seem set to meet all the harsh conditions a pool can offer, their use being particularly suited to factory production of 'componentised' pools (see chapter 9, Substructures, part II).

Renders Generally, renders and screeds provide a firm, clean base for a waterproofing finish. Plain mortar when applied with force will satisfactorily waterproof, and a blockwork pool depends upon waterproofing rendering to hold water. But to ensure cement rendering gives complete protection, a non-staining waterproofer agent should still be added into the mix.

Even when trowelled smooth, mortar renders are never attractive. They are rough to swimmers and perfect for algae. Early in the 1950s the pool industry discovered marble terrazzo. This pool plaster gives a fine, white waterproof finish known in the trade as Marblite. It consists of 1mm+ marble grains to 3mm chippings of dust-free white marble, and white cement with mixes varying from 1:1 to 2½:1 (see chapter 9.1 on nominal mixes – concrete and mortar). A fatty, not sloppy, mix is cleanly prepared, and Marblite rendered and screeded to approximately 5mm deep layers using stainless steel or wooden floats to prevent any possible iron staining to the bright, white finish. Over-trowelling does cause burns: brown ones can be removed with acid washing, but black ones are far more difficult to deal with and can mean applying a skim coat.

Skill is needed to apply Marblite. And it can be very hot working in an open pool in summer, when the glistening render reflects back most of the sun. Marblite must never be allowed to dry out quickly, otherwise crazing can result. Therefore dampening of the surfaces until the pool is filled is critical in hot weather. Surfaces can suffer thermal shock if the sun raises render temperature too fast within just a few hours; and in curing, any drying or shrinkage cracks are not acceptable. A non-staining protective cover can also be used in hot conditions to shade the working and help slow down the cure. Within 24 hours, the new surface is buffed lightly by a silicon carbide disc on a flexible head. It is not a grinding job and care must be taken not to cut, groove or burn the plaster. Walls can be smoothed to highlight the white glistening terrazzo aggregate effect, but floors need only lightly texturing to retain safe grip by swimmers. The finish must not be coarse otherwise algae is given the

11.3

chance to get a grip. After fair finish texturing, all dust is swept clear, and the pool filled immediately, guaranteeing the slowest possible cure.

This plaster finish has generally proved attractive for most concrete leisure pools, giving an expected life of 10 to 20 years; but because Marblite is very easily stained, a 200mm deep tiling band must be set at the water's edge. Metal objects will mark the floor, leaves add dirt and grime, acid conditions or peaty waters etch into the material, minerals precipitate onto it, etc. When normal cleaning to poorly maintained Marblite cannot cope, the paint manufacturers offer their own ultimate solution of acid washing, then suitable refurbishing with a freshening paint or latex mix or epoxy terrazzo.

Liners

FLEXIBLE Pigmented or printed, plastic vinyl liners require no further finishing (see chapter 9.5). The fitted pool liner is:

- flexible, waterproof and attractive
- easily shaped, relatively longlasting and easily cleaned
- will never need sandblasting, abrading or painting
- cannot craze, chip or crack.

But it can be adversely affected by:

- freezing or baking conditions
- concentrated disinfectants and control chemicals
- harsh cleaning and delinquent vandals

The majority of pools built today use a synthetic material liner of some description. Private pools predominate with pre-made liner shapes and sizes to suit standard pool tanks, but public pools now seeking more economical materials suitable for their hard wearing conditions, can use flexible

11.4

11.3 *Care in applying white Marblite lining for a pool in Italy*
Penguin Swimming Pools Ltd, Essex
Photo: Sirmione

11.4 *Texturing Marblite pool walls and coving should be carried out within 24 to 48 hours: a dust raising skim to the surface*
Rutherford Swimming Pools Ltd, Sussex
Photo: John Dawes

heavy-duty liners tailored to fit on site. Installation time is quicker and filling takes place immediately.

RIGID The GRP integral membrane, applied in situ, covers floor and walls, channels and coping, deck and poolside fittings, all in one continuous coat. Water, which inevitably gets spread around, must not be able to seep behind this membrane. Non-slip groovings or textures can be cast in shallow end beach floors or tumble turn ends; inset racing lanes or water depth markers can be imbedded into competitive length portions. The most favoured waterproofings of all for rigid plastic pools are the fluid to hard-setting compounds, or the tanking systems that come to the site fully finished in durable plastic (see chapters 9.7 and 9.8 on substructures and linerless shells).

Inexpert applications will eventually delaminate, or fade, or spot, or retain grease, or react to harsh waters, or attract algae, etc. and some of the hazard application problems have yet to be solved. For example, there is still a tendency for insufficiently reinforced plastic to 'creep' and slowly distort over a long period of time. But the main advantage is that installation time is faster for well-prepared mixes and planned systems.

Other liner finishes that are successful, if less popular,

include stainless metals, butyl sheets, and polyurethane sprays (see information sheet 11.2).

Average liner thicknesses, flexible or rigid, range from 0·5mm (500 micron) to 1·5mm, though some are even 3 or 4mm thick, and can build up to the 12 to 15mm continuous membranes for some rigid GRP formulations. Ozone and UV breakdown plastics, unless vinyl inhibitors or acrylic hard glaze protective finishes are provided. Water temperature over 30°C shortens the life of some plastics.

Tiling

RANGE AND EFFECT If a pool is built to last, there is only one finish, and tiling of some sort will be required. Most building surfaces can be tiled satisfactorily, and for pools, the main concern is to stop water getting behind the tiling.

Ceramics offer a specification for surfaces that is as hard as steel, can resist acids, alkalis, steam and UV radiation. Soluble salts can stain or crack some tiling, but this is relatively rare.

Sometimes the 200mm decorative contrast scum band is extended in depth to 1m for greater effect (this then appears to stretch down to the floor or rather the floor to the tiling as seen from bystanders' levels). On other economic occasions for easier maintenance (generally in private pools) only the floor is laid in textured ceramic.

Complete tiling for public pools can last indefinitely if laid correctly to a careful specification. This means properly bedded fixing with smooth contours to tight corners, such as underwater window ledges, recessed steps, and so on, where the dirt and oils can collect. Smooth glazed tiles, and even those with a stippled texture, can be dangerously slippery underwater, so must never be laid at shallow end

151

11.5a

floorings, to turning points of racing lanes, or on decking surrounds.

Decorated faience porcelain or earthenware can also make striking permanent murals with designs of separated colours or hand-painted individually fired frescoes, or dazzling patterns that are allowed to merge at firing.

APPLICATION   Thin tack adhesive (3 to 5mm) up to thick bed two-part compounds (10 to 12mm) is spread over wood-float finished render ensuring no voids. If preferred, and providing tiles have been well soaked beforehand, one-part cement mix to three or four parts sand can be used. Tiles are laid evenly in small areas of 1m². It is good practice to press the tile into the bed, then to remove it and check all is in contact. *Never* tight join – set to 2mm minimum tile gaps; never tile over 6 to 10mm movement joints.

Always check watertightness *before* level rendering or screeding; use reinforcement mesh for thick renders, and only include a bonding agent, such as a water resistant synthetic polymer that does not react with the tiling adhesive.

EXPANSION AND CONTRACTION   To reduce thermal shock to tiling, some authorities maintain a slow fill, and a 0·5°C maximum rise per hour to poolwater temperature is important: heating experts on the other hand look for 1°C rise per hour, or more for managers who prefer rapid cleaning and refilling of their pools. The faster expansion differentials of steel tanks also require a carefully controlled slow fill.

Thermal expansion of concrete and reinforcement is about twice that of ceramic tiling, but the water of a pool acts as a great moderator to the possibility of sudden change – the disturbing main trouble for tiling. Usually main change occurs between initial construction at, say, 10°C, and the eventual operating temperature of up to 30°C. Thermal movement for tiling is satisfactorily taken

11.5a *Studded non-slip ceramics for children's pool which is also suitable as a training pool*
Villeroy & Boch, GFR

11.5b *Some ceramics need to be frost proof!*
Buchtal-Schnell, GFR

up with sufficient expansion joints at temperature extremes, but it is abrupt and unequal expansion/contraction between the tile and its backing that causes most failures. A pool should never in its working lifetime be allowed to dry out totally.

A fully-fired, wax-filled, frost-proof tile can cope with icy conditions, though icebreakers, or rather ice absorbants, can be floated in outdoor pools to take up the potential expansion rather than over-pressurise linings to the point of fracture. The thin-glaze finish on partially fired biscuits are easily damaged outdoors. It is the freeze-thaw situation of frost and sun, breaking open crevices and weak grouting that does greatest damage.

PROGRAMME   A drying-out programme for pool tiling could be:
● 4 weeks for the concrete tank to cure before rendering/screeding
● 2 weeks for the render/screed to cure before tiling.
The fixing period could be:
● 3 days for fixed tiles to set off before double grouting
● then 3 weeks to harden fully before slowly filling with water
● and a further 2 weeks before any hard wear or energetic cleaning is allowed.
NB   Also allow in the schedule sufficient time for filling, emptying and drying when testing the tank for watertightness (see chapters 9.5 and 16.4).

MOSAIC   There is great scope with ceramic mosaic tiling or Italian glass smalti for decking or walls, or for giving lasting distinction to a pool floor. Modern mosaicists still draw largely upon original Roman themes perfected

1.5b

11.6 A mosaic panel set into the top tread of a classic radius step of a private pool
Kettlewell Studio, Kent
Photo: John Dawes

around 2000 years ago. As artistic craftsmanship increases, so do costs. Thus most mosaic manufacturers offer some cheaper standard patterns and designs to please the majority of poolowners. But the craftsman working on the spot, or with studio paste-up, is always necessary to adapt and create special designs.

Mosaic patterns come either pasted face down on standard sheets of 300 × 300mm brown paper, or cut to appropriate size for commissioned works. They are then ready for setting into a 5mm bedding that is worked into all of the joins. The mosaic facing is exposed several hours later when the paper is wetted and removed ready for the finishing grouting to be carried out. Alternatively, pieces are backed onto a mesh nylon which is laid directly into the bedding mortar – usually a white cement/white sand grout to creamy 1:1 mix. A little later all traces of smeared mortar is cleaned away from the mosaic surfaces with a very mild acid wash, followed by a thorough fresh water sponge down.

Brighter, lustrous coloured mosaics, such as golds and rich reds, are much more expensive than the lighter blends in random blue/green design patterns which seem to give better water shades for pool interiors anyway. A too strong random colour mixture underwater tends to create flickers of movement in the eyes, and looks busy rather than restful. Standard mosaic sizes are 20 × 20mm with larger tesserae being no thicker than 5mm. Original glass smalti is fragmented, irregular and sharp edged. Normal pool mosaics are usually fully frostproof and permanent. Used for a paved surround, they give good grip, but can harbour dirt in the joins, or if unevenly laid can cut bare feet.

Mosaic tiling is appropriate for a gunite pool where coving will not permit larger ceramic tiles to be applied.
MARBLE   Ultimately, the supreme finish is grained quarry marble. It is rare nowadays for selected marble panels, or even marble mosaics, to be used to line a luxury pool, but

when they are, every care is taken to choose and accentuate colouring to match graining, and, particularly, to keep correct the poolwater – for a low pH with its acid etching effect will soon spoil the perfection of any marbled surface (see chapter 15.7). Avoid grey-greens that seem only to turn clean water algae-green in colour.

11.3 Hall interior decor
There is the opinion that early public pools with all their hard and extremely durable surfaces encourage wonderful continuing echoes that are actually preferred by children, if not by their parents or instructors. Those early designs used cast-iron trusses, timber boarding and roofing slates; fair-faced engineering brickwork, Georgian wirecast glass and glazed bricks; marble tiles, hard teaks and granolithic, in fully exposed interiors that are still thoroughly durable right to this day – but delightfully noisy . . . for the children, that is.

Nowadays, we are open to a wider choice of materials since we can limit condensation, or ensure that it is deposited only on durable surfaces to be drained away. But don't be swayed by mechanical engineering reliability, even if it is guaranteed; human error will creep in or mechanisms will fail at some time to maintain the system properly. Therefore, all surfaces must remain durable and attractive.

Wherever soft, sound absorbent tiles, baffles and panels are used, they must be suitably protected, positioned well out of harm's way, and easily replaceable after any condensation problems.

Materials such as cushioned rubber flooring and perforated wall tiles help to absorb piercing sounds (see chapters 10.2, 4 and 12, 14.7, 8 and 9).

153

Sound absorbing sprayed asbestos and vermiculite ceilings, if left untreated against condensation (and fraying), can soon attract mould requiring very careful cleaning. Rust and damp staining contribute to interior deterioration, and brickwork efflorescence or lime blooming also leave their mark.

There has also been the view for a long while that traditional natural materials and natural colours, without fuss or pattern, are more harmonious with blue-green, reflecting, moving water. Nevertheless, new synthetic materials with contrasting colours, snazzy patterns and compelling murals have clearly arrived. And even GRP cladding can be made to meet maximum fire code standards offering contoured, sculptured, multi-coloured and imaginative facings to transform bare, stark structures into ornamented leisure pools – such materials remain resilient too, especially if their fixings do not deteriorate in humid conditions.

11.4 Facilities

A basic component of every swimming pool plan is its changing facilities. In public pools, principal access to the pool is best directed through the changing rooms, with wet and dry areas being separated to reduce contamination and cleaning, the best flow being

parking → entrance → changing → clothing storage → toilet → precleanse/sauna → shallow end of pool.

Clear, sufficient routing and warning signs are especially important.

All dry access and wet surround areas must be easy to clean, hard wearing and non-slip.

Design emphasis must concentrate upon maximum durability for minimum maintenance, to consider flexible arrangements of facilities to be supervised by the fewest number of staff. As peak demand usually occurs only a few times every year, overall facilities should not be sized up to these high numbers. A local 25m community pool can expect '3 bathers to be swimming, whilst 2 are using other facilities'[1] (see also information sheet 2.14). Obviously, this ratio improves when facilities cater for both pool and sports centre, or pool and ice-rink, helping to change losses into profits.

Changing areas should be central and offer, if possible, flexibility of allocation between men and women, boys and girls. Excluding school bookings, most public pools cater for children to adult ratio at approximately 3:1; and more often than not, a male to female ratio of at least 4:1 which can even become 20:1 though, of course, this varies greatly according to circumstances.

The changing area can suffer vandalism requiring constant management and specification vigilance and discipline (clothes stealing was a capital offence in Roman times!). All fixtures and fittings must cater for extremely hard wear, and certain items, such as modern lightweight doors, are most vulnerable (see chapter 16.4).

It is no longer reasonable 'to change behind a bush and leave a stone on the clothes for safety',[2] and about 25 per cent of swimming time is spent within a changing area. There is a great deal of controversial discussion over changing facilities and allied clothes storage systems. Often a staff operated clothing storage room only increases delays at peak times, and still cannot give the convenience and security bathers prefer.

11.7

11.8

11.9

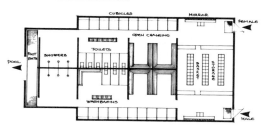

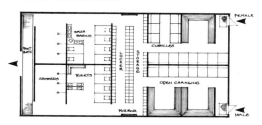

11.10

11.7 *Suspended ceiling tiles also absorb sound and can look as one piece plastering*
Danum Tiles, London

11.8 *Relief mural for plain pool walls and sound absorption.*
David Gillespie Associates, Ltd, Surrey

11.9 *Clearly signed pool entrance pay kiosk: Royal Commonwealth pool, Edinburgh*
Architect: Matthew Johnson-Marshall
Photo: P. Barstow

11.10 *Changing areas: basket system and precleanse; locker system and precleanse*

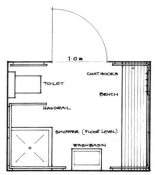

11.11 *Disabled swimmer's cubicle (2·5 × 2·0m) also suitable for first aid room. (2·5 × 2·5m suitable for first aid room and accepting stretcher trolley — 3·0 × 3·0m preferred)*

11.12 *Open area changing room for a community pool*
Architects' Journal
Photo: de Burgh Gallery

11.13 *Dry area lockers and warm floor for quality specification*
Architects' Journal
Photo: W. J. Toomey

11.12

11.13

Without doubt, cubicles and lockers provide the best all-round facilities. Even though open-plan changing areas are far more acceptable today, most people still prefer their own private cubicle and easily accessible clothing depository. Some leisure centres provide large family-size changing cabanas around the poolside, very reminiscent of the seaside beach huts, with extra large lockers nearby.

Designers of private pools too often overlook the dressing and washroom, since it is thought the house close by can provide facilities. But when the swimming party guests, or the neighbours' children, all arrive together on those heatwave days, the inconvenience and difficulties, with wet and dry areas, and clean and untidy rooms, soon become apparent. Some provision for changing should always be made, even if it is only a poolside cabana. But washbasin, toilet and shower facilities are also required wherever possible.

Effective pre-cleansing by bathers considerably reduces chemical treatment of water, and cross infection (see chapters 15 and 16). In Continental Europe, bathers invariably take their soap, flannel and toothbrush along to the public baths, and personal hygiene standards are high. In Japan, where a daily hot tub bath is the rule, standards are even higher.

The range of supporting facilities to any pool should always provide and encourage every 'privacy and security, hygiene and cleanliness'.

11.5 Options

Every pool has its optional extras. Early, simple basins of water included the first option – built-in steps for easy access. From then on, ideas and accessories, in and around water have proliferated.

Nine out of ten pool industry manufacturers today offer standard and special ranges of equipment and accessories with varying degrees of quality or design. Since every single item introduced into the pool area increases hazard in some way, the prime consideration must be, 'is it safe?' The only way to question seriously all the possible variations is to study recommendations and requirements published from time to time by associations concerned with swimming and pool operation. Their standards are the essential criteria, but not necessarily as good as those of some leading manufacturers.

The most difficult consideration is the degree of quality. Corrosion-proofing information is rarely included in sufficient detail, hence national standards for materials and fabrications will help specify the kind of quality required (see chapter 10.2, Materials).

Main equipment options Those items getting the greatest use or growing in importance are:

- diving-board and 1m spring-board
- waterchute and cascade
- in-situ steps and ladders
- handrailing and patio furniture
- underwater lighting and warm bench
- and especially, wave generator and turbojet.

All extras have to withstand very hard use, even in private pools. Ladder fixings work loose, diving-board surfaces ruck, slides and structures flex, handrailing anchorages offer seepage, underwater lighting facias tarnish, furniture rusts and fades, to cite a few. Every pool manager or owner can reel off his list of irksome happenings, stemming from equipment that was not quite good enough, or installation work that did not get carried out absolutely thoroughly. Only well-designed, carefully specified items will be good enough, and then attention to every detail makes much of the difference between early failure and long-term survival. (Refer to individual accessories for general explanation of their merits and performance, and to chapter 16 for operational hazards, wear and tear.)

The recent innovations that are not so well documented in different associations' publications may mean visits to the prototype establishment and to subsequent pools where new items are meant to operate with all the teething problems overcome.

Wave generators One good example is the wave pool which has now become an essential component of every leisure pool – with potential even for private installations. The high capital expense of this equipment and the newer pool design, calls for several visits to earlier installations to draw upon their experience. Different manufacturers have different ideas, such as swing-wing mechanical units to pneumatic chamber principles, or 10-minute operational sessions to all-day working methods. But the system is popular, does draw new custom, and can be self-paying.

Wave pools are not a modern innovation. In America, before even the turn of the century, a long, narrow wave bath was created 'for those who cannot visit the ocean',[3] but it still lacked the 'beneficial tonic effect of ocean air' and could not survive seaside competition of the time. That unique wave facility should not be confused with a small 1908 tub patented in the USA, that looked rather like a baby's enclosed rocking cradle, and which worked by the 'motion of the bather causing the water to impart to the body a feeling similar to that of the waves in the ocean surf'.[4]

Earliest public wave pools in the UK were built in Edinburgh in 1936, and Kilmarnock in 1946. Waves have been a popular pool feature in Europe since 1920, and especially in Germany, where most of the design development from piston to fan pumping has originated. The wave machine *is* the leisure pool and has become a dominant accessory or feature (see information sheet 11.9).

Some items that were out of favour just a few years ago are coming back. For example, modern leisure pools now provide cascade flows and water curtains to create clear impression in sight and sound with clean water. The kinetic-action of water devices in pools today offers air rocks to flowing walking streams, jets to flaming fountains, which young and old enjoy (see chapters 4.6, 5.6, 8.3, 12.3 and information sheet 11.9).

References
[1] J. N. Winter, *Changing Room Accommodation,* IBM 1973
[2] ibid.
[3] W. P. Gerhard, *Modern Baths and Baths Houses,* Boston, Stanhope Press, 1908
[4] ibid.

INFORMATION SHEET 11.1

Colour choice for pool linings

Coloured liners, renders and paints tend to fade in sunlight and chlorinated water

	Choice	Colour	Effect
Best visibility	1st	White	Clean water at depth has a natural tinge of bluish turquoise; bright white reflects blue sky, and a blue tiling band intensifies this hint of colour.
	2nd	Light blue	Enhances natural water colour; helps to camouflage liner blemishes and deposited dirt.
	3rd	Mid-blue	Even more so, but more garish.
	4th	Turquoise	Pleasant sharpening of blue tinge preferred by some people.
	5th	Dark blue	The 'inkwell effect'; or an overwhelming tart blue liable to show mottling and fading.
	6th	Green	Suggests water has 'gone off', or is harbouring algae: takes a bluish or turquoise hue on sunny days, but imitates a duck pond taint on dull days.
Least visibility	7th	Black	Dramatic, deep lake-like appearance; looks dark blue on sunny days, but with cool mirror-like reflections.

Notes

Dark colours absorb heat from sunlight; white reflects. Greys, favoured by landscape architects, have a blue/green tint on bright days.
Avoid: beige and tan with their muddying effect, reds, since they lose intensity and are totally absorbed at 10m depth, orange which is next in range to lose colour, yellows or greens that only kill the blueness of water.

Shielded, subdued lighting complements underwater lighting for the private pool and bar
Seahorse Pools Ltd, Jersey
Photo: John Dawes

INFORMATION SHEET 11.2

Pool shell finishes — functional and decorative

		Advantages	Disadvantages
Paints	Cement-based	Inexpensive; easy to apply on damp surfaces	Short life – 1 year; powders easily and clouds water
	Chlorinated rubber based	An easily applied coat builds up total lining that is resistant to pool chemicals	3–5 year life: cannot apply until concrete cured: can be softened by oils and fats
	Polymer/vinyl	Inexpensive; can be applied and dried rapidly	3–5 year life: susceptible to 'orange peeling', to abrasion and dampness
	Acrylic emulsions	Durable finish: ideal over GRP linings	Specialised application for sound finishes
	Epoxy resin	10 year life, tough finish: especially to GRP pools	Expensive, 2-pack mix causes application difficulties: slow curing (or none) at low temperatures; tends to chaulk and discolour in sunlight
Renders	Cement	Easily applied known material	Unattractive and requires covering
	Cement latex	Natural waterproof finish that bonds well	Tends to be rough unless finally fairfaced coated; flat finish
	Marblite terrazzo	Glinting white finish	Stains easily and requires specialised application and careful curing
	Epoxy terrazzo	Durable white finish	Careful mix required with specialised application
Liners	Vinyl-pvc	Flexible and attractive	Susceptible to damage, to high temperature and UV deterioration
	Butyl rubber/polyisobutylene	Extremely durable	Expensive and invariably coloured black
	Polyurethane	Hard sprayed finish	Careful application for sound coatings
	GRP/acrylic	Superb long-life finish	Can be scratched and delaminated
	Metal/stainless steel	Silver-grey inert finish	Expensive and awkward seaming
Tiling	Mosaics-glass/ceramic	Frostproof, attractive and extremely hard finish	All over mosaic pattern can be visually tiring; tessera can be sharp edged; grouting can retain dirt
	Ceramics-glazed/quarried	Hard as steel; permanent colours; a finish that does not deteriorate	Expensive outlay; must be solidly set; some tiles are not frostproof; large tiles are affected more by thermal expansion/contraction and bedding problems
	Marble panels	Supremely attractive	Acid waters react with marble; economical only in very long term

All pool shell finishes remain better, longer if kept underwater in winter rather than exposed

See also chapter 9.5 to 8 on poolshells and substructures.

INFORMATION SHEET 11.3

Pool hall finishes

Paints	Use only washable, hardwearing coatings such as moderated rubber based, acrylic sheen and epoxy resin types; *never* use easily scratched and stained oil-based paints in exposed places. Trompe l'oeil artistry is very durable in 'poly' type based coatings and can transform plain walls with landscaped scenes.
Renders	Apply only dense, durable, easily cleaned renders; avoid plaster and soft absorbent finishes susceptible to prodding, scuffing and condensation. Useful finish materials: latex cement, resinated concrete; cementitious asbestos and vermiculite reserved for higher surfaces.
Cladding	Inert, easily cleaned, tough claddings, or mural sculptures, are gaining popularity in making pool halls more attractive, sound absorbent and maintenance free. Suitable materials: plastic laminates, plasticised aluminium, vinyl, pvc and GRP bonded textures of concrete, gypsum, metallic oxides, etc; natural materials of fairfaced brick, glazed brick and modular ceilings in perlite, aluminium, teak, etc. Durable and trouble free fixings are particularly important for panels.
Tiling	The decorative tile takes pride of place for durability and glamour: an extensive range of striking styles now take preference as permanent finishes. Murals are created in slip line motifs, textured two-tone vibrant colours, etc. Almost infinite variety is achieved with smaller tesserae of glass or ceramic mosaic. Ribbed or textured wall tiling inhibits graffiti.

See also chapter 10.1 and 2.

INFORMATION SHEET 11.4

Notes on pool facilities (mainly public)

Management – general facilities
Entrance hall (minimum area 20m²)
Must be pleasant and welcoming. Not too large: avoid the drafty and un-appealing lobby in favour of a foyer. A waiting area is always required and particularly a well placed noticeboard: public telephone, vending machines, and general public toilets should be located here. Direct access to changing rooms and to snack bar, restaurant and swimshop is required for all those facilities appealing to the general public as well as the bather. Some auto-ticket machines systems operate very successfully in Germany, but still require supervision. For convenience and cleanliness, separate school entrances can be provided near where children are let off buses.

Ticket/control kiosk (minimum area 10m²)
Avoid turnstiles if possible. The cash counter for tickets, towels and telephone enquiries is prominently located by the entrance area with, if possible, some visual control over locker and vending areas.

Administrative offices (minimum area 10m²)
A central location with direct access to the pool area is required – raised to overlook main pool if possible. Controls for heating, lighting, sound, ventilation, racing systems, etc are best located in the manager's office or a nearby pool controls room. General records and files will be kept by the manager and he will require facilities for meetings of 4 to 5 people.

Staff room (minimum area 10m²)
A lounge-like atmosphere where off-duty staff can relax is important. Planning the room with a view over the pools, aids safety and keeps staff in touch with activities – though some authorities argue the comfortable view might lead to a lax or leisurely duty staff operating from this room. Direct telephone lines to poolside attendants are useful for the baths supervisor. There should be provision for staff lockers and/or changing space and toilet plus a small kitchen area.

Instructors'/Lifeguards' cabin (minimum area 4m²)
A small control area directly overlooking the pool should be set aside for

baths attendants to use as a poolside base, to store personal items temporarily and from which to make public announcements.

Storage/supplies room (from 20 to 30m² minimum area)
A pool complex will need sufficient storage for various items of equipment – racing lines, water polo goals, starting blocks, etc; swimfloats, balls, loungers, etc; speciality items for aqua shows, snorkel diving, canoing, etc. Wide durable doors are best. Stocks of stackable chairs, tables and sunshades will be located here.

Plantroom (minimum area private pools 5m²; up to 10m wide subfloor galleries running the length of a building for a public pool. A 25m pool and learner section requires around 150m² floor area for plant, or 50 per cent water area)
A private pool filter/heater can be located in the corner of a garage. A large complex requires several specialised equipment rooms to be located close by the pool to reduce service ductwork and pipework. Consider deliveries, access and ample drainage. Do not cramp equipment, as space is required for servicing and efficient operation. Additional facilities might include a boiler room, air treatment room, control room, electrical switchgear/emergency battery room, chlorine room, as well as the main water treatment equipment area with space for workshop and spares storage.

Adequate fresh air is essential for boiler combustion, and safe arrangements have to be made for disposal of fumes (see chapter 14.6 and 7). The general public must not be admitted, but a viewing window does increase interest in the pools and helps staff morale. Electrical fittings must be waterproofed; pipework/valves must be clearly identified and easily accessible (see chapters 13.5 to 7).

Chemical store (minimum area 10m² – private pools 2m²)
All chemicals should be stored separately, dangerous materials contained within special facilities. Chlorine gas cylinders should be stored in a ventilated room well clear of pool hall air inlets and not set low into ground where heavier-than-air gas could collect. Gas masks and emergency notices should be located outside the door which has wired glass panels to see clearly into chamber (see chapter 15).

Chemicals must *never* be mixed. Disinfectants, acids and alkalis must be stored separately to prevent accidents that could cause fire, explosion or poison gas hazard, sometimes simply by moisture dissolving dissimilar chemicals.

Maintenance area
This area of 20 to 30m² depends mainly upon the extent of facilities served. Outdoor gardening requires lawn mowers, sweepers and digging tools; indoor cleaning above and below water needs suction sweepers, hoses, handles, brushes, nets etc. Provision must be made for waste disposal and collection and running repairs to plant (see chapter 16).

Public – general facilities
Parking
Too often this facility is underestimated. A capacity equivalent to at least 25 per cent maximum bathing load should be provided (see chapter 10.10).

Swimshop
A small sales counter or exhibition area is useful as a retail outlet.

Spectators' gallery
Every pool requires some provision for seating temporary or permanent: simple, corrosion protected bench tiers will suit casual visitors who should be clearly separated from the wet pool area to maintain deck hygiene. Allow approx 0.75×0.5m (width) space per spectator with maximum 0.4m (0.25 minimum) risers to galleries that start (preferably) 1 to 2m above water level. Upholstered seating helps sound absorbency. Average seating for public pools in the 1950s was often 500, but most large pools today plan for their normal needs for no more than 100 to 200 permanent terraced seats: another 200 being easily arranged with bleachers. Ensure there is some disability provision. Often restaurant areas over the pool are suitable for family and friends spectators. Schools or colleges generally cater for 25 per cent of their student body with temporary seating, but where swimming is emphasised as an educational activity, a seating equivalent to 50 per cent will be required.

It is surprising the number of pools where the rake of the sight lines are poor from terraced top or first rows, when the nearest racing lane masked by the pool edge cannot be seen. Circumstances vary according to pool freeboard, deck width and gallery risers. Specially ventilate, limit humidity and control temperature at 22°C across the gallery as far as possible for gala events, when close packed spectator groups generate their own heat. Consider carefully fire escape routes (risers should be filled in) plus easy cleaning or hosing down routines (drained separately to waste).

First aid room (minimum area 10m² recommended)
An essential facility for every large complex – smaller pools may share the use of disabled/family-sized cubicles. Direct access to pool and street is important. Rooms must be easily cleaned and have good air circulation. Basic fitments include a full length bench or trolley, and telephone, toilet, washbasin with hot water, plus emergency equipment such as resuscitator, first aid cupboard, etc (see chapter 16.1).

Launderette
Last century, baths and wash houses were built primarily for hygiene. Sometimes today, self-service or coin-op laundries are overlooked meaning useful revenue is lost.

Vending location
Dispensers (with hidden water and electricity services) for drinks and snacks are practical and profitable: maintenance contracts will be necessary for machines that are hardworked or bullied. Provide ample litter bins and money change units within sight of supervision, together with storage cabinets for further supplies. A tendency to replace snack bars with vending areas is favoured more by management than users: consider vending plus counter bar extension for peak periods, situated near entrance, but not to cause congestion.

Restaurant/snack bar
Refreshment facilities are a popular social focus if they are not tucked out of the way; they are a necessity for outdoor pools where an ice cream fountain and/or grille bar should be included: a kiosk for the kids (with snacks, savouries, crisps, chocolate, hot and cold drinks) will be preferred to the more comfortable adult lounge. Best location is overlooking the pool, perhaps as bar seating/bar top before a balcony view of the pool. Refreshment areas should be separated from the pools to avoid water/decking contamination. Never allow bottles or glasses into a pool area (see chapter 8.3).

Plan for a summer trade maximum, comfortable furnishing with wet/dry bather segregation throughout. The restaurant, an important social centre, is better self-contained, comfortably furnished and carpeted with pleasant ambiance. In Europe, a main street frontage is important, since the restaurant is often leased to private enterprise and operates even when the pool is closed. In Holland some pool restaurants are leased out for 10 per cent of the gross turnover.

Activity – general facilities
Clubroom
A section of the restaurant can double up to offer club facilities, but when a wide range of swimmer activities is organised, a separate room at least 5 × 5m is better.

Crèche
As swimming families are increasingly visiting the leisure sports centres, crèche facilities and playroom with trained staff in attendance are becoming important. Parents will visit the pool at less busy times of the day when a baby-minding crèche for groups up to 20 are available. Several, secure playpens near the pool can be useful.

Leisure area
Varied activities attract more bathers, eg a trampoline is not only useful for practising divers, but it entertains as well (see chapter 4).

Games deck
When next to a snack bar, these amusements such as bar-billiards, pintables, table-tennis, etc are popular with teenagers.

Sports area
A wide range of indoor/outdoor activities can be successfully based around a leisure pool to share the main block facilities (see chapters 3.4 and 4).

Gymnasium
Sports centres are increasingly orientated for both wet and dry athletic facilities (see chapter 2.1). The compact, self-service fitness room or small exercise equipment room is proving popular for registered members, with modern examples nowadays provided for youngsters in run-down town areas to discourage vandalism.

Entertainment centre
The modern complex sets out to attract a broad cross-section of public and to become profitable. Nearly all public pools lose money, sometimes needing large subsidies to stay open. By widening activities for club-like variety, management becomes more effective with more users bringing more revenue (see chapters 4.6, 5.2 and 8.3).

Casino
Until the 20th century, gaming rooms were always the focal point of leading large 'watering place' establishments. Why not with the leisure pool complex for adult evenings?

Public hall
Even if a theatre is not included in a complex, a central community room for crafts, discussions and social activities can be an asset to the centre.

Bather facilities – other than pools and baths
Changing rooms
Male/female segregation is still required to deal with attendance ratios varying up to 20:1. Separate entrances/exits and separate rooms for changing are preferred; but increasingly practical is one main cubicle area, where both sexes can change separately to leave their clothes in their own locker in the common locker room: supervisory staff can be halved.

Outdoor pools dealing with peak summer month bathing loads, require a clothes storage unit to cubicle ratio of 10:1 (twice that of indoor pools) but open-space changing areas/lockers still offer more efficient and cheaper routines. Although open-plan changing areas reduce vandalism exhibitionism may increase.

Multi-sports changing facilities can work satisfactorily, providing suitable pre-changing showers are directly available to those coming in from outdoor playing fields.

The disabled changing room/toilet is also useful alternatively as family changing since parents often need to help young children get ready (see information sheets 11.5 to 7).

Clothes storage
Choose a system that is the least labour intensive between cubicle, locker or storage unit (see information sheet 11.6). A communal storage unit area equals a total locker area in terms of space required, is cheaper to equip, but is more expensive to run needing extra staff. Lockers reduce cubicle needs by three-quarters; or there can be 4 lockers for each changing place (excluding open area spaces): and the most efficient system has the shortest 'dead time' ie the period through which keys or tokens are handed in and reallocated.

Consequently, self-service coin-op or self-setting combination code lockers can be more efficient. Hangers or boxes must be easily located in clothes stores to reduce long walks by attendants. Double normal air changes will maintain comfortable breathing conditions amongst stored clothing and ozonation is a valuable de-odoriser.

Toilets (see information sheet 11.8 for planning data)
The toilet block is best located within the pre-cleanse area. Secluded places suffer the greatest vandalism, so ensure fittings cannot be removed eg use push-pull washbasin plugs, unscrewable screws for hooks, etc.

Pre-cleanse area
Greater pre-cleanse hygiene saves pool disinfection, especially when hordes of schoolchildren attend baths. The body accumulates dust, scaled skin, bacteria and body fat in the course of the day. It is debatable whether footbaths do stop foot infections – footsprays and foot washing are far more effective. When footbaths are provided a tunnel arrangement will prevent bathers leaping across.

Continuous showers serve to raise humidity spreading steam and wasting energy: spring loaded, time switched controls save. Set showers along bathing route and not tucked away to one side: partitioning between communal showers heads is unnecessary, though private pool users prefer individual showers. Use only rugged and durable fittings throughout. Provide recessed soap ledges for washing showers. For exclusive pools, electronic impulse showers with alternating hot and cold water bathing combines with high powered massage by water for 1/5 level to 10 second cold 'flashes' to attract much interest – especially in saunapalas (see chapter 5.8). Sauna bath routine offers excellent pre-cleanse before swimming. Cleaning disposes and disperses infections, whereas disinfectant only keeps them in check.

Bather Amenities
Bathrooms
Slipper baths or hot tubs alongside the cold plunge for Turkish and sauna still make up a relaxing and favoured bathing suite.

Warm room
Quick drying areas at 50 to 60°C temperature set next to the showers help to keep changing rooms dry: treat these floors, and all heated floors, as part of the wet area. Pre-warming rooms, or competitor waiting rooms, are heated to 30 to 40°C.

Solarium

The indoor version of a sunbathing alcove. UV and IR lamps offer 'mini' suns for 5 to 6 facility room, utilising normal power point circuits: another version for public pools radiates its UVA light from beneath the couch on which you lie. Either version is essential for health clinics and most sauna baths. By reducing UVB to about 0·04 per cent total irradiation there are no concerns at all about 'burns' or 'erythema' or skin inflammation; and there are no creams, or goggles, nor timing needed. It is the UVA spectrum that is required for effective, healthy browning. In hospital treatment systems, it is the UVA @ 10nW/cm², ie long wave ultraviolet light, that is the preventative and curative. With increasing leisure facilities under cover, the artificial sunbathing location is growing in importance (see information sheet 5.8 and chapter 12.4).

Sunbathing terrace

When outdoor debris can be carried into a pool by sunbathers, a wide perimeter footbath helps with cleanliness. A properly sheltered paved or grassed area, well looked after, with nearby snacks and within sight of the children's paddling pool is what many people think swimming pools are all about. Include a stone pallet or altar slab or wheeled wooden bed in the sun for out and out worshippers.

Sources: APHA/ASA/CNCA/IBM/NSPI/TUS.

INFORMATION SHEET 11.5

Changing area specifications

Open plan area Use high density brickwork of low porosity and low efflorescence, and totally non-corrosive materials that can withstand heavy abuse: the need for robust fittings and fixtures placed well out of reach of teenagers is consistently underestimated. The whole area should be easily supervised.

Provide attractive, permanent surfaces that never need redecorating – tiling, terrazzo and polyester resin impregnated compounds. There should be no 'soft' finishes at low levels. Colourful coverings must be impervious and easy to clean, to cope with large deluges of water, resist abrasive cleaning and mild acids, to offer no sharp edges. All corners should present smooth, cleanable covings to walls. Non-slip flooring is essential: orange peel type patterning harbours dirt since it offers no continual channels to drain down water. A non-slip, slotted tile, drain grid that will not trap tiny fingers is also required. Provide well drained flooring sloping away from lockers, cubicles and benches with a 1:25 fall to drains that are large enough for a copious hose down. There should be no changes in level – wet steps are especially slippery – and no kerbs that reduce safety or restrict the disabled.

Ample hose points are necessary for frequent cleaning of floor of dirt from street shoes on incoming bathers. Floors will remain wet unless underfloor heating is provided. However, warm crevices can harbour foot infections. Alternatively, a drying room enables a carpeted locker area to be offered in more exclusive situations.

Ventilate air from changing area to pool hall, maintain temperature at approx 21 to 22°C, do not provide opening windows.

Cubicles Maintenance-free, non-corrosive, very strong, tough and scratchproof partitioning is realistic. All surfaces, scribble resistant and non-staining, should be wipe dry and cleaned. Attractive plastic laminated timbers, GRP mouldings, stainless steels, aluminium alloys, epoxy terrazzos meet these requirements. No painted surfaces will survive.

Adequate ground clearance beneath partitions, no crevices, and no unnecessary fittings, will make for easier cleaning and maintenance.

Stout doors that children cannot swing upon, with heavy duty hinges, short coat hooks, secure catches, etc will be necessary and safer if sprung back when the cubicle is empty. A hinged seat, locking the door, is a good arrangement and should be made self-draining, non-staining, indestructible and cigarette-burn resistant. Extremely tough curtains can replace doors, but rails will inevitably be used to deposit clothes hangers, or for chinning exercises.

Lockers Again, stoutness and quietness in operation is essential. They should be self-draining, corrosion-free, present no sharp edges, employ robust louvred doors closing under their own weight, and be set in accessible blocks raised 100mm above wet floors, and arranged to supervise at a glance. Door lock systems must be robust, straightforward, corrosion-free and unassailable.

Fittings Non-ferrous, corrosive resistant and tamper proof. All supply pipes should be buried. Recessed, encased and durable items for the shower/washroom area are essential.

Pre-cleanse Always arrange that bathers must pass through this section before entering the pool. Avoid unnecessary changes of level throughout. Open plan showers are easier to clean: footbaths require ridged flooring that is also easily cleaned. Footsprays and footrails to be extremely heavy duty and durable. Showers set at 35 to 40°C 10–20 litres/min make it worthwhile to include heat/water recovery systems: use fresh water and enable post-cleanse opportunities by users after swimming.

Sources: APHA/BRE/IBM/NSPI/TUS.

Always provide sufficient space for storage
Photo: Philipson Studios

INFORMATION SHEET 11.6

The changing debate

For cubicles
(Always include a few for privacy at least: between 5 and 10 per 100 swimmers)

Greater privacy with better clothes storage is preferred by most bathers.

Central dressing area with cubicles offers most flexibility in catering for varying male/female attendance ratios.

Central cubicle area can be arranged to separate wet and dry routes easier, keeping allied locker rooms cleaner.

Less stringent environmental control and less supervisory staff required.

Deckside cubicles can save on capital costs, and staff can supervise these facilities while on pool duty.

Bathers can keep an eye on their own cubicle.

Flexible for varying male/female ratios and do provide convenient parent/child changing arrangements.

Extra decking width helps with special events.

No queuing for own cubicle.

Against cubicles

An expensive investment.

$2m^3$ of space used to store $0.2m^3$ of clothing.

Doors or curtains and fittings invariable damaged.

Vandal opportunities increased.

Central cubicle area invites children's races.

Greater opportunity for thefts.

Deckside cubicles make it difficult to stop the spread to the pool of dirt brought in on outdoor shoes.

Facilities limited at peak periods.

Children who cannot swim are forced to walk round pool.

For lockers
(Effective security is expected but can be expensive)

Security is improved and when lockers are grouped together; the whole area is easily supervised.

Clothing can be hung carefully by the owner who does not have to collect and deliver to a central depository.

Less space is consumed to store clothes than for cubicles.

Self-service lockers save time and allow quick, easy access.

Operational savings gained after several years since staffing duties considerably reduced.

Against lockers

A number of 'modesty' cubicles (for privacy) and paraplegic cubicles are still essential.

Some systems corrode quickly, employ inadequate, easily broken fittings with noisy doors, and are too small for bulky or winter clothing.

Staff controlled systems prone to accusation of theft, are slow to operate at peaks and are costly.

Too many keys or tags are lost requiring a master key: coin-op doors prone to attack, or combinations forgotten.

Initial equipment costs are high and 2 or 3 times more than the clothing store.

Difficult to clean and disinfect.

For clothes store
(An additional facility involving extra work)

Least expensive system to equip.

Combined clothes store permits reduced staff, serving both male/female changing areas.

Baskets are easier to carry and occupy less space.

Hangers carry clothing properly and are easily handled by staff with no stooping or stretching to shelving.

Against clothes store

Labour required increases operating costs over locker system.

Bathers dislike queuing for clothes at peak periods, especially at closing times.

Security problems involve innocent staff.

Too much toing and froing collecting clothes and unreturned containers; pick-up point too often coincides with street soiled access area.

Strong smell from clothing requires special ventilation and deodorising arrangements.

Infested clothing cross contaminates.

Baskets must be tough and durable – bulky garments are crumpled, wet clothes and dirty boots cause problems.

Hangers take up more space than baskets, are easily damaged or become damaging weapons in the hands of rowdies.

For clothes storage consider: degree of security achieved, care of clothing, convenience of system and both initial and operating costs.

Sources: CNCA/IBM/TUS.

INFORMATION SHEET 11.7

Cubicle and locker dimensions

Cubicle dimensions (metres)

	Minimum	Optimum	Maximum	Disabled
Width	0.8	1.0	1.2	1.6 (1m door)
Depth	0.9	1.2	1.5	2.0
Height partition	1.5	1.8	2.0	2.0
Seat height	0.30	0.35	0.50	0.50
Seat depth	0.35	0.40	0.50	0.50
Floor partition clearance	0.15	0.25	0.30	0.25

Planning: allocate $2m^2$ per cubicle.

Allocate a changing cubicle for every:

$4m^2$ surface area learner/paddling pools,
$6m^2$ surface area leisure pools,
$8m^2$ surface area competition pools,
$10m^2$ surface area training pools,
$20m^2$ surface area diving pools,

as a proportional basis of minimum number of cubicles *plus* open space changing and lockers/clothes storage units.

Locker dimensions (metres)

Width	0.30	0.40	0.50	0.60
Depth	0.40	0.45	0.50	0.50
Height	0.40	0.85	1.7	1.7
	$1/4$	$1/2$	full size	full size

Planning: allocate $0.2m^3$ per locker and 1m gangways.

Each bather requires at least $1m^2$ open space dressing area.

Install 80 per cent smaller/20 per cent larger sizes.

Benches: 0.4–0.5m per person
0.4–0.5m high
0.3–0.4m deep

Example: 25 × 10m indoor community pool provisioning of:
250 lockers
4   4 × 3m open space changing areas
5   2 × 2m family/disabled changing rooms (10 preferred)
25   1 × 1m cubicles (50 preferred)

Plan to allocate 4 to 6 clothes storage units for every changing cubicle provision.

INFORMATION SHEET 11.8

Toilet facilities
(Based upon peak loading 60 per cent male/40 per cent female)

There should be at least:
- two toilet fixtures for each sex
- one toilet for the disabled
- one drinking fountain in the pool area
- each shower head should be capable of providing 10 to 20 litres of water per minute, at 30 to 35°C
- clean, fast draining floors to the toilet block.

No of bathers per fixture:	Male minimum	optimum	Female minimum	optimum
	Bathers		Bathers	
Water closets	75	40	50	25
Urinals	75	40	–	–
Wash-basins	100	40	50	25
Showers	50	30	50	30
	(communal showers acceptable)		(individual showers preferred)	
No of spectators per fixture:				
Water closets	200	100	75	50
Urinals	100	50	–	–
Wash-basins	200	100	75	50
			(include sanitary disposal bins or incinerators)	

Sources: APHA/CNCA/Depts of Health/DLF/NSPI/TUS

INFORMATION SHEET 11.9

Notes on accessories/options

Deck (See chapters 3, 4 and 5)

Diving-boards All boards require non-slip surfaces that are durable, cleanable and resilient: coconut matting has been replaced by more attractive synthetic textured surfaces or anti-fungal rubber treads. Main materials used are Douglas Fir/fibreglass and aluminium/alloy steel for heavy duty wear: metals are mainly stainless steel, nylon coated or galvanised steel.

Fulcrum spacing affects the life of a standard board, and a single podium requires a dual fulcrum top spaced 300 to 400mm apart. Diving boards as distinct from spring-boards and used for private pools, generally involve:

Board length	Pedestal distance apart	Height above deck
2·5m	1·0m	0·2m
3·0m	1·3m	0·3m
3·5m	1·6m	0·4m

Strict safety standards are recommended by associations with minimum residential pool measurements being:

depth — 2·5m
forward depth — 3·0m
length — 8·5m
headroom — 4·0m

Boards should be coded to suit varying pool dimensions. Most common inadequate dimension is that of forward depth (see information sheet 2.16).

Firm anchor fixings with easily released wedges to allow removal of fixtures when required: escutcheon cover plates conceal fixing points.

All diving-boards are space consumers.

Jump-boards Shorter boards from 1 to 2m long to save space are set from 0·1 to 0·5m heights.

Spring-boards 1 and 3m height competition spring-boards for diving are 5m long and require an adjustable fulcrum with at least 0·5m horizontal movement that should catch no fingers or toes: As 90 per cent diving at public pools involves the 1m spring-board, two boards are preferable. Shorter lengths of 3·7 and 4·3m are also available but they are less springy and less durable. Safety barrier side rails are unnecessary at 1m board height, although they are useful by the pool edge (see information sheet 3.6).

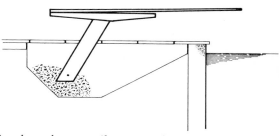

Diving-board on cantilever stand

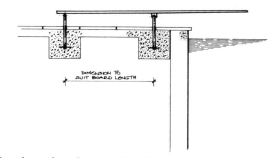

Diving-board and mounting/fulcrum

Diving stage/tower Spring-board positions plus firm board heights at 5, 7·5 and 10m are involved. Designs should be uncluttered so as not to compete with the diver for spectator attention. Absolute rigidity and firmness of fixing is vital. Ladders should be set at least 15° to the vertical. Stairs provide better access. Opaque walling behind the staging should not include distracting murals (see information sheet 3.8).

Diving positions higher than 1m require guard railing to waist height (1m); 50mm diameter steel being ideal for hand and side-railing, 60mm for structural tubing (see information sheet 3.6).

Divers' elevator An essential for 10m competition diving. Fitted behind tower or walling not to disturb competitors preparing to dive.

Steps All pools benefit from in situ non-slip steps: a convenient normal tread to riser measurement being 330 to 110mm. Where practical, wide flights and deeper treads with handrailing help non-swimmers and disabled bathers. Specially manufactured modular designs suit vinyl liner pools with 'walk-in' steps recessed and 'walk-out' steps standing proud.

Wide, broad, safe steps and heavy duty safety railing for the learner pool
The British Bumper Co, London

Ladders Equipment constantly in water must be especially durable. Best material is type 316 stainless steel; next chromed brass or sometimes galvanised steelwork for ladder stringers.

Non-slip, self-draining treads are made in GRP, plastic, nylon, stainless steel, coated metal and hardwoods. All ladders, whether an up-and-over arrangement for freestanding pools, or crossbraced set for competition pools, should be removable from their anchor fixings or wall fixings. On residential and lightly bathed pools, a ladder is anchored to the deck with bottom legs resting on buffers against the wall below water. Generally, ladders need not extend beyond 1·5m deep into the water.

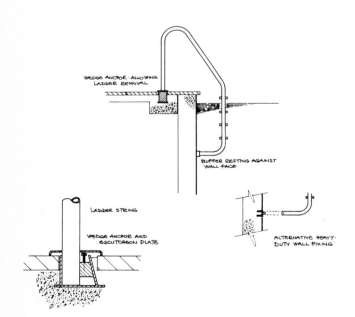

Pool ladder — wall resting and deck mounted

Basic dimensions of pool ladders are:

Side rail diameter:	40 to 50mm
Spacing between positions around deck:	15 to 20m (4 sets per 25m pool)
Height:	to suit 3, 4 and 5 treads (a few 2 and 6 tread ladders are specially made)
Treads: Length	300 to 500mm
Width	75 to 100mm
Riser	200 to 300mm
Clearance from wall	75 to 150mm

Pools over 10m long require ladders or steps, and sets on each side of the length are required when widths exceed 10m.

A set is needed with a diving-board but placed well clear of the diving area.

Pool waterline rests between treads.

Side rails at differing heights will stop ladder acrobatics.

Grab rails An ideal arrangement, where no metal is underwater, allows side rails to be set permanently into decking with separated faience tile, or non-slip plate tread, inset into additionally reinforced pool walling: wall steps may be recessed 100 to 150mm and separated 250 to 350mm.

Skimmer steps Designed for swimming pools without built-in pipework. A skimmer weir is set beneath the top step of a ladder, connected to a filter unit and clean water is returned to the pool through one of the side rails lower down. The 40mm railing pipeline for a skimmer steps unit will cope with pool water filter rate of 10m³/h (see chapter 13.3).

Trapeze An unusual but exhilarating piece of apparatus fixed above some indoor private pools, where dangers of colliding with other bathers can be prevented.

Slides An increasingly popular accessory for all leisure pools (see information sheet 4.5). A steep water lubricated slide can be likened to diving into deep water, but modern designs can also cater for non-swimmers into shallow water with submerged slowing sections. Chute lips must project well beyond the pool edge and into water well clear of equipment, divers, serious swimmers, etc. A curved slide saves space, and perhaps a helter-skelter slide would suit confined spaces (see chapter 4.6).

Low chutes are very practical for the disabled bather and should be set no higher than wheelchair height of about 0·5m: high sides to this low angle ramp help the bather hold back if required.

Hoist Reserved for hydrotherapy units where a hand operated or mechanical hoist at the poolside is necessary to carry incapacitated patients into and out of the water for treatment. These devices are rarely required for public pools where the active disabled prefer to roll in, slide in, or lower themselves into the water (see chapter 5.3).

Safety

(Also refer to chapter 16.1 for safety checks and chapter 3.7 for sporting items.)

Guard railing Safety rails and barriers can hinder life saving, but they are installed around diving areas, as partitions between pools, wherever it is dangerous, and as step guides, etc. Low railings on which children can climb should be avoided, uprights should not exceed 1·2m and perimeter railing should be removable for events in public pools. Rigid mountings, durable materials, and great attention to hardware detailing is essential. OD to rails – 40 to 50mm.

Handrailing There must be no projections in competition pools. Coping or overflow systems all provide some form of handgrip arrangement, but sometimes stainless steel handrailing is still added for sparkle.

Handrailing is required for learner pools, hydrotherapy sections and especially for school pools: railing should not interfere with water circulation nor trap limbs. Extra heavy duty brackets are vital for 30 to 40mm diameter public pool handrailing being set up to 1·2m apart.

Safety net/line Wall anchors are inset at transition points to suspend a float line or weighted net as a barrier to prevent non-swimmers stepping or floating out of depth; suitable mainly for residential pools where steeper deep end profiles are involved.

Pool alarm A useful device to watch over the out-of-sight private pool and audibly warn owners when the water surface is disturbed: the most popular devices employ a mercury floating switch that triggers the alarm with the first ripple. Others include a sonar device on the floor or a sensor tape just above the water line, or an electronic trigger alarm in the water.

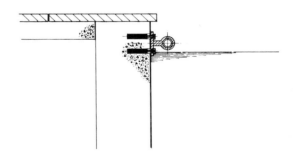

Top left: Recessed sports pool ladders with two-level side-stringers to stop gymnastics
The British Bumper Co, London

Centre: A pool shape and deck should be designed to cope with space consuming slides in private gardens
Aquaslide 'n Dive, California

Left: Poolside barriers safeguard against accidents of collision near diving-boards, but must be removable for competitive events
Architects' Journal
Photo: W. J. Toomey

Top right: Skimmer/ladder: a useful device for water circulation for a pool which has no pipeline services
Penguin Swimming Pools Ltd, Essex
Photo: Malcolm L. Keep

Below right: Handrailing

Alarms are useful secondary arrangements, but no substitute for proper safety fitments, covers, fences, etc.

Rescue hook/line To be located conveniently and obviously. A light alloy type of shepherd's crook for poles from 3 to 6m long to suit smaller pools; a lifeline extending to at least $1\frac{1}{2}$ times the width suits larger pools; a breaking strain to 0·5 tonne is required for 5mm diameter lines.

One hook or line is often specified per 200m^2 of water surface.

Lifebuoy Lightweight, impervious rings from 0·4 to 0·5m diameter. At least 20m of line is required.

Life saving equipment / **First aid equipment** } To include the above items plus a resuscitator, stretcher or trolley and first aid kit.

Lifeguard chair A clear viewing platform and seat set 2m above water level is a distinctive aid to lifeguard duties and rapid rescues: some form of overhead protection to the occupant will be welcomed for outdoor pools. If possible, position with back to the sun, and on both sides of pools over 12m wide. In US pools, lifeguard stations are required by law, or clear warning notices displayed when services are temporarily withdrawn. Plan on the basis of 1 position for every 200m^2 water surface, or 1 per 150m^2 for crowded, shallow water pools (at bathing density 1 per 1m^2).

Safety markers Warning notices such as NO DIVING or NO LIFEGUARD SERVICE etc should be clearly displayed in letters at least 100mm high. Depth indicators at 0·5m intervals down should be marked on pool wall and decking with permanent signs to clearly distinguish safety ledges at alcove floor edges. Too often inadequate information is a hazard incurring heavy legal actions after accidents.

Surface water sprays and diving cushion Sprays, agitators, or compressed air bubblers set flush to the pool floor with maximum 5mm diameter outlets, clearly indicate to a high diver the surface water level or offer safety zones for practising divers; area covered is 1m either side of board and between 2 to 5m forward (see information sheet 3.8 and chapter 3.6).

Leisure
(See also chapter 4)
These items increase the use of a pool and sometimes the risks to bathers. The most fascinating leisure accessories involve moving waters – as waterfalls or water curtains, cascades or fountains and air rocks, water slides and pool-to-pool spillers. They will attract and constantly appeal.

A separate pumping circuit must be provided for moving waters. Do not use the filter equipment as pressures will wane as time for backwashing approaches, besides imposing additional head upon the filter. Ensure rivulet feeds balance with suction pipelines and do not contaminate with other ornamental waters. Remember that attractive, effective bubbling waters dispel heat and soluble chlorine disinfection constantly.

Try to cater for all the basic services around the pool with outlets for power, water, gas, telephone, microphone.

Competitive
(See also chapter 3.4 and 5 for further specification)
Rest ledges Keep clear of diving boards and clearly distinguish positions: a competition pool specification requires any 100mm ledge sloping 1:8 towards the pool and set at 1·2m depth; but the 150mm ledge at 0·75m depth, to 200mm at 1·1m, is equally popular.

Wall anchors Firm, ring or bar type, recessed cup anchors up to 100mm diameter will be required. They must not project into the pool and will have to withstand considerable stress and strain. Where perimeter overflow systems are involved, eyebolts are recessed into the back of scum channelling, set at or near water level.

Lines and floats Spaced out floats are low cost and easy to store, but for competitions where a hundredth of a second counts, a wave quelling racing lane system allows faster racing times. Disc bladed wave absorbent continuous floats of 300mm sections and 100mm diameter require tensioned 3mm monel cables, whereas 225 × 125mm standard life line floats require only three-strand 20mm diameter polyethylene rope lines.

Signal lines Lanes are marked dark blue or black, and stop 2m from end walls: backstroke indicators are set on 1·8m posts, 5m from end walls; the false start rope is set on 1·5m stanchions 12 to 15m from start. All positions are temporary (see information sheet 3.5).

Starting blocks These should be removable, strong and durable. Stand top is 0·75m above water with backstroke rails only 0·5m or lower still for juniors. Leading edge to be flush with pool edge. 25 and 50m pools use one set of blocks, whereas $33\frac{1}{3}$m pools require two (see information sheet 3.9).

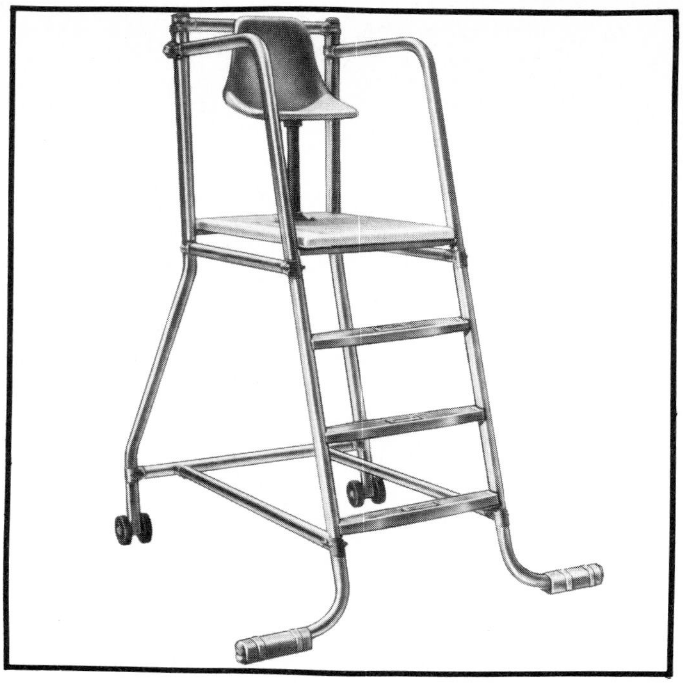

Portable lifeguard chair
KDI Paragon Inc (Neptune-Benson), NY

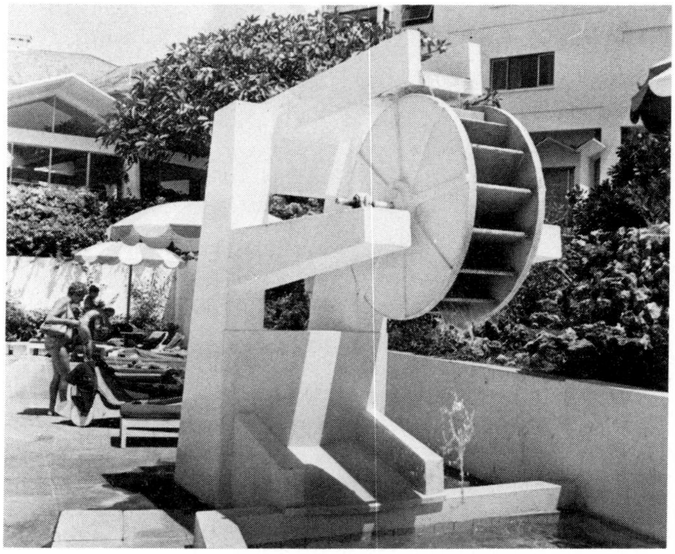

Waterwheel and paddling pool in African hotel
Nyali Beach Hotel, Mombasa

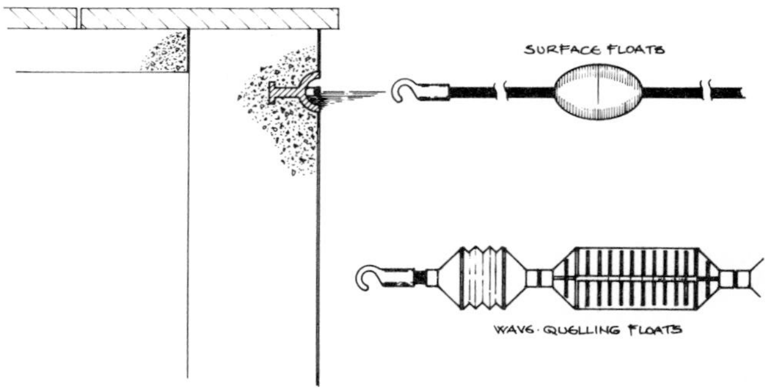

Cup anchors, hooks, lines and floats

Touch pads and results board Must be safe, removable, non-projecting, clearly coloured and linked with starting equipment, recorders and displays. Judging will be to a minimum of three decimal places of a second and timing to two places. Information will be displayed for results and placing, timing and records for competitors and teams: corrections, lap counters, computer summaries will be necessary for this electronic sport (see information sheet 3.9).

Audio/visuals, pacing clocks and pace makers TV link, video playback and audio provision are called for with service conduits: a number of smaller loudspeakers will be understood better than a few larger ones. Pacing in training is important, requiring sweep second hands within sight of the swimmer to auto pace setter systems actually in the pool.

Water polo goals Lightweight and portable, centrally fixed and easily stored: all field of play markings need to be distinctive. Cages should be easily removed (see information sheet 3.6).

Communications concern:
- Signalling for call-out
- Clocks – pacing and timing
- Public Address System – with microphone points at poolside
- Telephones – internal, staff and public
- TV – for closed circuit supervision
- Scoreboards – electronic display and control information
- Controlroom – centralised location or part of manager's office.
See information sheets 3.9 and 11.4.

Other factors Synchronised swimming staging and equipment may also be required. There is even an official brick for diving – weight 5kg.

General
These items should be located so as not to represent hazards. Hose points should only be accessible to attendants and placed high enough to prevent hoses trailing over floors: mirrors, hair dryers, spin dryers must also be safely located. 'Paraphernalia' design needs great care to prevent clutter and out-of-sight vandalism.

A thermometer, in a safety case, is always referred to before bathing in residential pools. A time switch saves energy (providing filter pumps are self-priming and there are fail-safe devices for heaters, chlorinators, etc); a 0·5m sized deck footbath is useful.

In winter, drum floats take up ice expansion to save perimeter finishes; or an underwater pump, thermostatically controlled and safety switched, will bring warmer deep water to the surface and prevent freezing.

Whenever filler spouts are provided, a minimum airgap of 150mm should be allowed according to national standards to stop possible backflow siphon action: the most suitable position is usually beneath a diving-board and covered to reduce the risk of bathers colliding with exposed edges.

Specials
Outdoor lighting Coloured lighting should be reserved for night time landscapes, but not to mar the poolwaters. Use only white light close to the pool. To avoid insects, use subdued, concealed lighting set back from the pool and placed high up. Colours will reduce bright lights and insect attraction. A flybait light or flare is also useful anti-insect planning.

Standard floodlighting of 40 to 50W/m² of water surface and set on 3 to 4m poles around the pool will achieve a somewhat unlovely but well lit concentrated scene. Smaller low voltage lamps well placed on spikes into the ground can be easily moved to advantage of depth and form. Surrounding lighting will not illuminate poolwater and would be subordinate to pool lighting (see chapter 10.11).

Underwater lighting The underwater light is not a touch of mad luxury but a means of safety, extending outdoor swimming or balancing indoor lighting to reduce glare. Always plan to illuminate in volume not area alone. A minimum of 5W/m² in residential pools will give a glow and charm to the water at night; 10W/m² to maximum 20W/m² is preferred by pool associations: public pools have an optimum 30W/m² and maximum 50W/m².

Underwater lighting should shine away from main viewing areas, and beneath diving boards *not* facing them; always angled downwards to increase reflected light. A water cooled wet-niche lamp requires its own deck box and step-down transformer wired in accordance with strict national safety codes, and including an overall ground leakage circuit breaker: note long cable runs will cause voltage drop (see chapter 13.8). Wet niche types for fitting 0·4 to 0·6m deep are easily relamped from the poolside, incor-

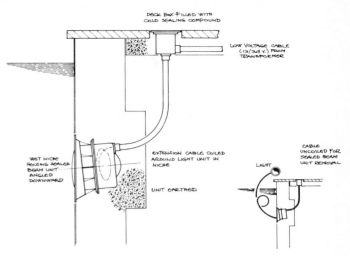

Underwater light and deck box

porate 300, 500 or 1000W sealed beam units with tough tempered glass facings, and operate at 12 to 24v. Wider ranges apply to the dry niche types which can be positioned at any depth, and do not need to operate at modified voltages for safety.

Underwater sound Sound travels five times faster and much farther in water than in air, but more power is needed to give adequate volume. Average private pools require at least 10W – the capacity of most modern hi-fi systems. Stereophonic effects cannot be achieved underwater as human hearing is insufficient: ears would have to be at least 1m apart to correlate the direction finding facility for high speed sound; furthermore, rapid reflections confuse.

As a guide, in pools 2 to 3m deep, sound units are audible over distances for:

	Clear speech	Background music
10W rating	10m	30m
50W rating	30m	80m

Units may be suspended over the edge temporarily, but mostly speakers are designed to fit into underwater lighting type niches with cables taken back to poolside deck boxes. In synchronised swimming, speakers and public address systems are linked: operating voltages will be 12 or 24v:

Stainless steel speaker unit designed to suit a standard type underwater light niche
Aquavox, Sussex

transducers in deeper pools require compensating for pressure: and inert materials are required, since speaker panels do suffer from caustic or acidic solutions. Reversed speakers can act as hydrophones for recording.

Underwater windows With an underwater sound link for coaching, these are useful in training pools; windows are best positioned along the sides where tumble turns can be seen. They usually start 0·25m below the water surface. Provide clear access to observation facilities behind the window; a basement bar or restaurant can be an unusual and popular feature (see chapter 9.4). Careful installation is essential to avoid potential leaks to seals.

Hydro massage and turbo units Plug-in massage extensions can be provided with wall mounted jet devices that create a strong current of water to swim again, or for fun. These units should be located in water 1·1 to 1·4m deep and arranged so that one swimmer does not monopolise the pool. The nozzle providing a variable stream of water up to 2m/s should be set about 0·25m below water, with suction inlet about 0·9m below that. A hydro alcove for massage equipment is suitable for private pools: a number of open bays will suit therapy pools. In shallow ends of public pools, children, disabled bathers and non-swimmers can be bowled over by the strong rush of water. All fitments must be non-corrosive and smooth faced; electrical isolation will be necessary for earth leakage, and 3-phase power for 3kW motors. There are portable deck models available, but the wall fitted offer longer term durability (see chapter 4.6).

Moving booms and moving floors Sales propaganda about equipment for temporary alterations of swimming activities describes the main pieces as offering 'movable bottoms, partial movable bottoms and pond dividers', the objective being to create two pools from one. Compromise can be expensive, but hydraulic moving floors and walls when installed, mainly in Germany, easily and quickly change a deep racing pool into a shallow leisure pool, eg Munich Olympic pool.

In the USA where aluminium adjustable flooring designs rather than concrete are promoted, facilities so dualised vary from teaching and paddling pools into dance floors and ice rinks. Movable bulkheads also safely separate swimmers from divers, or learners from racers, for 2 in 1 partitioned pools. The inflatable boom is less expensive, and less effective (see chapter 3.8).

Adjustable pools need inlets above and below the moving floor. They are raised right out of the water to clean underneath. Raising or lowering takes around two minutes per metre, with water flowing through slotted surrounds; inspection manholes are also required. Hydraulic rams raise the platform, gravity lowers it; steels are safeguarded by plastic coatings, and electronic controls or hand mechanisms move the floor.

All floor materials must be corrosion free and concrete slabs should be tiled in the raised position after 28 days curing (see chapter 11.2). The tank floor beneath is also best tiled. Full width or partial length designs with flap slopes or tilting arrangements are also available and particularly suitable when a wave machine is provided. Floors can be lowered right to the bottom to help circulation overnight; when in raised positions, special considerations must be given to potential dangers to divers and to clear warning signs.

High capital cost can still mean it is cheaper to have a separate smaller pool, but this will not necessarily provide the variety of facilities required nowadays. Neither is it practical to lower water levels for shallow pool activity as in the past, since circulation systems cannot operate properly.

Wave generators are now an essential component of the public leisure pool, but so far are less suitable for local 25m swimming tank designs. At least 33m lengths are considered necessary with beaching depths from 1·8m to 0, pump ratings at 2 × 60hp.

Wave pool designing has been taken up with gusto at Decatur, Ala, where 1m rollers break upon a 40m wide, carpeted beach – pump rating 4 × 75hp; also at Tempe, Ariz, where the giant surf pool is allied to a 100m, downhill water slide and the nearby Oceanside ice arena. Here 'Big Surf' has a 125 × 90m lagoon, shelving to 3m deep, offers 1 to 1·5m average breakers and guarantees 'a big one every minute' at 15 miles per hour, ideal for surfing. It takes a total of five pumps (3 × 250hp plus two circulating type) to feed a 15m high lift reservoir (of 2500m² recirculating basin capacity) at 160m³/min, from the huge main pool (18,000m³ capacity); the vast accumulation of energy is pneumatically released within one or two seconds.

Pneumatic systems need less power than paddle, piston or swing wing mechanics, but all systems working for long periods are expensive to operate and maintain. The less mechanical parts and out-of-water design for pneumatic systems encourage easy inspection, reduced maintenance,

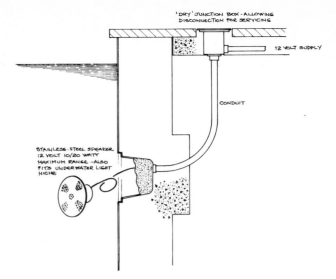

Underwater speaker and deck box

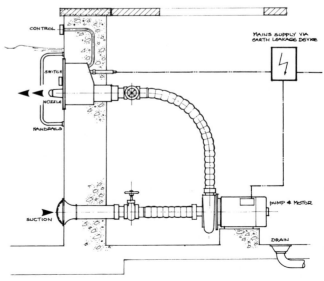

Deck mounted turbojet developing a fast flowing current of water in the pool
UWE Jetstream/New Haden Pumps

Turbojet

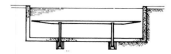
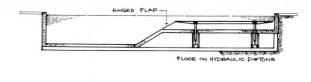

Adjustable floors

Both the pool floor and adjustable floor should be tiled
Anlagenbau für Wassertechnic, Robuc GmbH & Co KG, Hanover

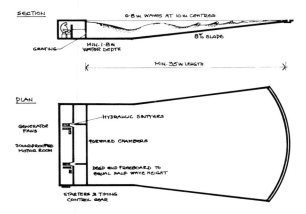

Pneumatic wave making by alternate pressuring and vacuuming centre to outer forward chambers at three-second intervals

less wear and tear. The pneumatic variety suck-out air from a caisson, which then allows poolwater to enter; when atmospheric air pressure is allowed back suddenly, the body of water is pushed down and out for the wave formation at an approximate cost of between 3 and 5kW/m width of pool wave. The regular rise and fall within the plenum chamber transmits energy to the poolwater as oscillation movement which is easier to maintain, than to start up. The waves must be fully absorbed before reaching the far end of the pool otherwise, choppy, reflected and disturbed wave patterns result – the beach being a practical necessity. The maximum wave height is determined by the still water depth at the wave generator outlet. Generally, the maximum wave amplitude is about 40 per cent of the still water depth, with waves starting to break when amplitude actually equals still water depth.

Large pools require more than one wave making machine, running synchronously for regular waves, or at different speeds for random, with 'rogue' waves occasionally. While only a few wave pools exist, the greatly increased revenue they attract from a widespread public easily pays the extra bills. Most pools restrict wave making to ten minutes in the hour, or half hour, not only to save costs, but to rest the bathers and staff (who have to be stationed specially and stay extra alert). On starting, power taken up can cause local voltage dips, noise levels can reach 105 decibels inside the fan room, 70 outside sealed doors. Therefore, the motor room and outer chamber should be constructed of about 200mm thick concrete, well insulated against sound transmission.

New pool shapes and designs make it worthwhile to conduct model tests for the best wave height, pool profile and surrounding freeboard. Rectangular shapes usually only require two-dimensional testing. As some guide, a useful wave of 0·7m amplitude, 12m wavelength, 2³/₄ second frequency, 4¹/₂m/s velocity on 1:14 beaching profile requires approximately 5kW of power per metre of pool width. In pneumatic systems, constant circulation of air keeps plant cool for continuously running generators.

Average waves are 0·8 to 1·2m high, 10 to 15m apart and made at two to three second cycles: 0·5m high waves are boring and 2m ones dangerous. Freeboard should be 0·7m higher than normal and reduce to zero at the beach end. The pool is best fan or wedge shaped with a broader, shelving beach area for young children. Wave outlet positions from the storage chamber (straight sides) require safety screens. A diamond wave pattern is thought by some to be better than single parallel wave processions. Extra duty staff should overlook bathers in turbulent aerated surf.

Public pool wave provisioning can incur around 10 per cent extra capital cost with a +3 per cent extra allowance for repairs and maintenance.

Warm floors and warm bench Heated flooring in changing areas is appreciated though encouraging to harbouring infections. Warm benches around a pool are always popular and help to counteract cold windows. Warm benches are especially beneficial for disabled bathers to regain body warmth and circulation: tiles can match surrounds, mosaics offer contrast and better grip, height required is 0·5m. Warm air ducts underneath should achieve around 32°C surface temperatures. One or two carefully positioned benches can offer indoor 'islands in the sun' for some indoor sunbathers (see chapter 5).

Ice rink As an example, for around 20 per cent extra capital outlay plus 2 per cent annual setting up cost, a 33¹/₃m New Jersey outdoor pool converts every autumn into a public ice rink, simply by lowering the water level, floating flexible polymer ice mats along the length and freezing the surface. Crash boards protect the perimeter walls. The mats circulate refrigerant to freeze the top 50mm of pool water; then a further 50mm depth of water is poured on top of this ice base to produce top quality ice; finally the base is extended down another 200mm for the winter season's skating. Underwater lighting is kept switched on all the time to stop deep freezing to eliminate undue expansion forces.

Sources: AAU/APHA/ASA/CNCA/IBM/NCAA/NSPI/SPATA/TUS.

12 Landscaping

Since landscaping is for people, and as people enjoy exploring, a pool-garden should arouse curiosity and invite discovery, but in a relaxed and friendly way. If it is difficult to decide where to start the landscape layout, try to follow Humphrey Repton's advice and 'first make an entrance'. Arrange that entrance clearly and safely and invitingly by the shallow end.

12.1 A concept

Landscaping, though visual, should appeal to *all* the senses. A glimpse into a sheltered, fragrant courtyard will invite interest and a wish to be there. On the other hand, a beautiful panoramic view over rolling countryside or open sea, while invigorating, can be bitterly exposed unless comfortable shelter is deliberately arranged. Shelter and security are the most basic needs of landscaping in every pool-garden. The pleasure garden is said to be a substitute for the countryside . . . the swimming pool for the seaside!

Another important point to keep in mind for such a flat subject as water is the dimension of height. Slopes and shapes, sculpture of the land, changes of level and contouring of spoil, will help. Topsoil can be retained and used for raised borders, hillocks and hollows can give shelter from breezes; rocky boulders can be built into the surround, and architectural structures, steps, sculpture and particularly plants will all emphasise height in producing a pleasant pool setting. By interacting colour, texture, line and form, the swimming pool will blend into the surroundings rather than blatantly stand out.

There is one most useful landscape device that arranges a covered pool to blend, yet loses height within the landscape – and that is a berm. An encircling embankment of soil round the pool can be shaped and used as the base for a translucent, low-domed roof enclosure. This smooth hill successfully supports, protects, insulates and blends a pool naturally into its surroundings (see photograph **4.18**).

Reinstatement should never be mistaken for landscaping. And decking surrounds or repairing garden damage is all part of *basic* poolwork. The two crafts of building and gardening are rarely provided by the same workforce (or even the same contracted company) as both skills require different specialists. It can be difficult, sometimes, to distinguish clearly where the pool design stops and the garden scheme begins, but there stands out clearly one firm idea to plant a place to enjoy.

12.2 Pool features

The personality, character, feeling, ambiance – call it what you will – of any pool-garden is there because of those features that people like to add.

Using water One favourite idea of the swimming pool landscaper is the horizon of water that disappears into the landscape – a kind of watery ha-ha. Another may seek to capture water reflections or fleeting images, and yet another the restful sound of splashing water. Or there is 'Sawara', the Japanese concept of borrowed scenery, to put the pool into another environment.

A pond beside a pool can be especially attractive. A pebbled rivulet feeding the pool, passing islets, across rapids and through deeper paddling sections, encourages youngsters to revel and play in water. Stepping stones into a pool create an accessible barrier between depths, and give confidence to timid bathers in shelving water. Occasionally on very lightly bathed pools, the water is pumped over and around a stream bed of sand and gravel to give some natural filtration.

An alternative to ordinary return flow inlets from the circulating pump might introduce water stairways, overflow curtains or wall cascades as part of the pool architecture. Filtered water returning to the pool across inverted and overlapping Spanish-style 'curly-tiled' capping on landscaped walls as a waterfall is also easily organised, and particularly effective. Fast moving waters, or cascading splashes, or fountain jets liberally release cooling chlorinated water into the air, becoming expensive on fuel and chemicals. But bear in mind also when linking any water display to the main filter pump circulation system that the flow-rate or water pressure will deteriorate as the filter becomes clogged and backwashing time approaches; or the backpressure from the water device will make the filter less effective. A separate circulating pump for fountains, cascades, sprays and jets is always preferable (see chapter 13.4 and 6). Evaporating water on paving surrounds will cool a swimming pool-garden. And dark paving containing water pipework can absorb solar energy to pump useful heat into the pool water temperature (see chapter 14.2).

Differing levels on a sloping site can offer pool-to-pool overflows, or linked water slides, or cascade saucers and spills, all emphasising exciting wet environment architecture. At his Chartwell home in Kent, Sir Winston Churchill took advantage of a local stream to design and build a series of natural and attractive ponds and pools all the way down

170

12.1

12.2

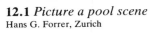

12.1 *Picture a pool scene*
Hans G. Forrer, Zurich

12.2 *'First make an entrance'*
Gilliam Continental, Paris

12.3 *Contouring – utilising the spoil*

12.4 *Contouring – arranging a cascade*
600 Group London (Jones Cranes)

12.3

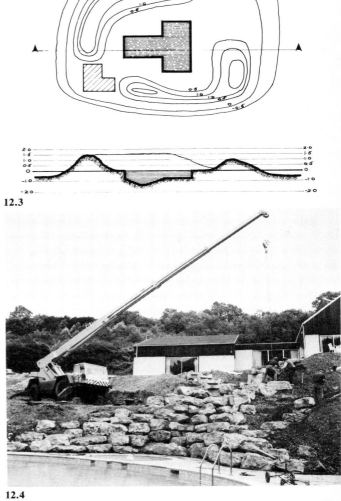

12.4

12.5

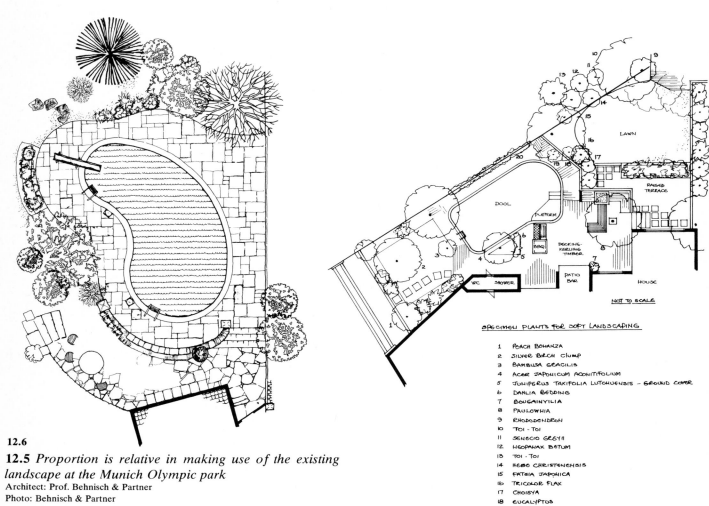

12.6

12.5 *Proportion is relative in making use of the existing
landscape at the Munich Olympic park*
Architect: Prof. Behnisch & Partner
Photo: Behnisch & Partner

12.6 *Paradiso: 10 × 5m on a sloping site*

12.7

12.7 *Pool garden for a tight site*
John Morton Landscape Design, Christchurch
Builder: Landmark Projects Ltd

SPECIMEN PLANTS FOR SOFT LANDSCAPING

1 PEACH BONANZA
2 SILVER BIRCH CLUMP
3 BAMBUSA GRACILIS
4 ACER JAPONICUM ACONITIFOLIUM
5 JUNIPERUS TAKIFOLIA LUTCHUENSIS – GROUND COVER
6 DAHLIA BEDDING
7 BOUGAINVILLA
8 PAULOWNIA
9 RHODODENDRON
10 TOI - TOI
11 SENECIO GREYII
12 NEOPANAX BETUM
13 TOI - TOI
14 HEBE CHRISTENENSIS
15 FATSIA JAPONICA
16 TRICOLOR FLAX
17 CHOISYA
18 EUCALYPTUS
19 CUPRESSUS MACROCARPA LAMB. AUREA
20 CLIMBERS

172

12.8

the hillside passing through a main freshwater reservoir – his own huge garden swimming pool – to finish up in a large lake on which glide his famous black swans. His garden contrasts sheltered arbors with open views, countryside against rolling lawns, running water with practical natural gravel and beach filtration.

Using form Land shape, slope and steps between levels, all contribute to a successful pool surround. Banks and rises are important for natural shelter and attractive display gardens. Freeform landscape suits rockeries; earth sculpture styles ziggurat structures; steps heighten an environment and add their own character, whether they are wide and comfortable, narrow and intimate, secret and winding, and so on.

Then there are the vertical facades, such as old stock walls; or new moulded panels in concrete reinforced with polyproplylene fibres, rather like horsehair plaster bas-reliefs; or safety barriers of rustic trellis and lattice, instead of functional wire fencing; or well-filled, pleasant shrubberies to form a background setting. For elaboration, try an individual piece of statuary, a central pool island, or an artificial mountain grotto. A swimming pool is a social feature that can improve with decoration – but not too much decoration.

12.3 Decking and coping

No pool is complete without a surround, or safe without definite demarcation. Pool surrounds require safe walkways with efficient drainage, and textured surfaces that always look attractive, either wet or dry. They may be made with materials that are light, heat reflective and cool, or dark, heat absorbent and warm. Sunbathers like permanent sun seats on the deck as much as children enjoy play sculpture in the pool. The sunbathing part of the surround must catch the afternoon sun, and be sufficient in area for the bathing load (see chapter 8.1). Terrace surrounds and patios help link the pool with a building: decking offers visual transition from water to wall, with coping acting as the pool frame between. This viewpoint is outstandingly apparent for the raised surround decking and coping to an above-ground pool.

12.9

12.10

12.8 *Joint entrance to pool and gymnasium blocks for Ambassador College, St Albans*
Architects: Denkers & Maddison in association with Daniel Mann, Johnson & Mendenhall
Architects' Journal
Photo: W. J. Toomey

12.9 *Small garden play pool in New Zealand*
John Morton Landscape Design Ltd, Christchurch
Photo: Euan Sarginson

12.10 *This attractive pool in the woods requires extra attention in dealing with leaves. NSPI Award winner 1972*
Midwest Pool and Court Co, Missouri

12.11 *South African Cape Dutch style house and pool. The large pebbles hiding the source of the fountain offer a focal* *point to the brick patio around this gunited pool*
Saphire Pools, Transvaal

12.12 *Vine clad stone columns as pool pergolas*
Senlac Stone Ltd, Sussex
Photo: John Dawes

12.13 *Brushed in-situ concrete decking bays are popular for curved or round pools in North America*
Aquarian Pools, Ontario
Photo: Preston Haskell

12.14 *Coping profile*

The sheltered peristylum of a colonnaded walk was very successful around Roman baths. Often stone ballustraded borders physically separated bathers from watchers, with interceding broad steps for safe access into the water. Plenty of space around a pool is always practical and definitely safer. The standard 1m perimeter surround for private pools can be improved vastly by including at least 2·5m wide and deeper spaces at intervals for social congregations. Deleting decking from some parts of the pool perimeter, with extra widths at other places, is interesting and breaks up possible regimentation around the pool. A jardinière interrupts large areas of paving, or some imbedded tufa rock cultivates blending greenery.

A coping band between pool and paving should be clearly seen on all public pools. And very distinct edges are necessary for decklevel schemes. A 0·5m parapet wall can reduce dangerous running dives, but no toe-stubbing steps must be located at the coping surround. The pool coping, or 'stone cushion' described by Vitruvius, separates walking from swimming. It also provides handholds and rapid drainage away from the pool, and should be textured or ribbed for grip as well as being comfortably attractive. Coping takes the brunt of wear and tear, especially on outdoor pools where it adds protection to perimeter decking, ring beams, pool shell edges or overlapped liners. When laid, using a weak mix mortar bed, single and spaced coping stones are set first, to act as levellers for the infilling straights and smooth curves. The weak mix bed should give under extreme stress – it is easier to relay coping than rebuild walling.

Wet and dry Surrounds inevitably are wet, and a layer of water standing on tiled decking is ideal for aquaplaning accidents. Continually wet surfaces greatly increase evaporation and humidity thereby affecting the scale of ventilation plant required (see chapter 14.6 to 9). Texturing, stippling, studding and so on, of all hard surfaced materials must be distinctive enough to be non-slip, but not so as to be coarse. In-situ concrete decking needs brush finishing, acid or water etching, or dressing with silicone carbide. Effective falls to drainage away from the pool and proper finishes to prevent cracks and crevices are necessary to stop any catchments of water, and breeding of bacteria.

The safest and most effective deck cleaning method is the washing away of water, dirt and germs, which means that surfaces must survive corrosive and abrasive treatments, high pressure steam cleaning and modern disinfectants. Some resistant organisms (such as Tycofytum mentagraphyes) can even survive doses of diluted sulphuric acid, making cleaning of all material away to waste most important (see chapters 15.2 and 16.2).

Surfaces and finishes An all-over plain deck surface finish can be as boring as a plain sheet of water. Contrast of materials will help, and perhaps a 'mix-it' policy for paving is necessary. Crazy and flags, wooden blocks and washed pebbles, hard engineering bricks and granite setts, earthenware and terracotta, granolithic and mosaic, all mix successfully. Bricks, cobbles or setts are ideal for uneven spaces, as boundary markers, and to distinguish sunbathing areas. Bear in mind that moss can accumulate on bricks, stains can develop on concrete, flags can darken, tiles chip, or wood attract algae, and so on.

Although it is easier to lay in-situ concrete decking

12.15 *Foundation walling for a perimeter decking around a freeform concrete block pool*
Photo: Arby Davis

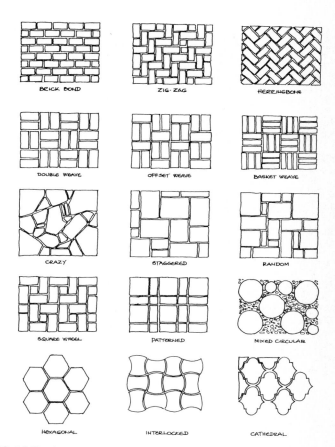

12.16 *Paving patterns*

175

around freeform pools, or to use the smaller pressed pavings, since they can cut to shape easily, formal flagstones arranged carefully in groups can look particularly attractive. Also moderate amounts of crazy paving beside a classical rectangular shape can be most effective.

Special deckings Timber decking which can be raised and lowered like a drawbridge will allow more swimming space for a cramped pool site. Fitted carpeting around a large leisure pool, patent Cooldeck mixtures for a hot climate, or solar collecting paving for temperate climates are some of the more interesting ideas for decking. The new, soft, synthetic surfaces are excellent for safety and comfort, but not always suitable for constant cleaning and hygiene. Rubber decking, as used around the Munich Olympic pool, demonstrates the warmth, colour and quietness of softer, safer finishes. In one school for the blind, where rubber tiles are laid around the pool, 'the flooring has so far proved very successful and shows no sign of deterioration in any shape or form. It has proved itself worthwhile in the effect that hard tiles surfaces have given difficulties through movement in the pool building, whilst the rubber tiles have been totally unaffected, to say nothing of the acoustic affects, lack of condensation and comfort underfoot'.[1]

Subflooring Whatever the top surface finish, a reliable subfloor is essential. Many private pool surrounds suffer winter eruptions or spring sinkages in decking. Very few pool shells get damaged in winter, but many of the paving surrounds suffer. Freezing, expansive soils, or poorly reinstated, high capillary backfills are the most troublesome. In bad cases, potentially heaving soils should be replaced with well-compacted backfill plus firm foundation below the decking. All pool paving is better fully bedded rather than set on pug spots of mortar, to infill with clean dry grouts, and no smudging. If splash or rainwater drains away rapidly and cannot get into or beneath the decking, the common cause of expensive damage is overcome.

12.4 Hard landscaping

Landscaping requires architectural body and horticultural dressing for the art of getting 'gardens to fade imperceptibly into the environment'. If decking helps blend a house with the pool, then walling helps keep a property in the grounds around.

Walls should try not to obstruct a scene. They are one of the most useful height formers, and nothing really beats an old mellow brick wall for visual appeal and practical shelter. Precise, functional walling is far too particular to be comfortable. The best walls should look natural in their surroundings, as though they grew there. They can stop wind across poolwater, provide a noise barrier, and be a place against which plants can grow. Walls will store and reflect heat from the sun and can be very useful sunbathing alcoves. Garden pools benefit from cosy arbors.

Dry crib walls of hollow bricks set on top of each other in ground banks and filled with earth, have been largely ignored in poolgarden surrounds. These earth-binding banks are perfect for pockets of plants. Walling that relies upon mass to withstand force often looks better in many landscapes than the slimmer, reinforced structural partition.

Stone seems better than concrete for walling, and timber better than metal for fencing. Maintenance is particularly

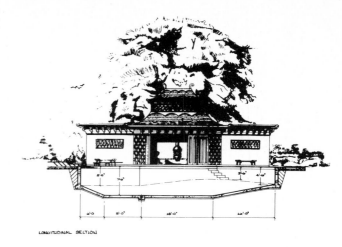

12.17 *Poolside pavilion – Chinois*
Seahorse Pools, Jersey

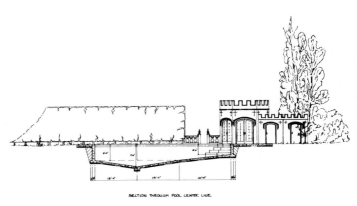

12.18 *Poolside pavilion – Norman*
Seahorse Pools, Jersey

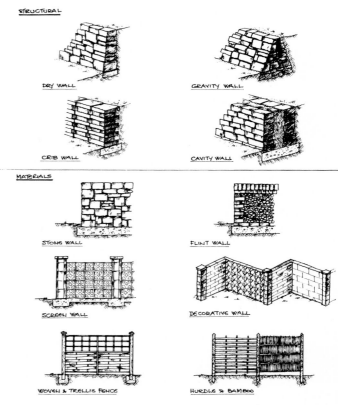

12.19 *Walling and fencing*

12.20 *Sculptured concrete relief around a cantilevered sun-bathing terrace set over an ornamental pool*
Architect: Sir Basil Spence
Cement & Concrete Association, London
Photo: Henk Snoek

important, since repair work can be costly. Some consider a self-repairing hedge is best of all! Other equally popular and attractive (with care) structures include translucent panels to show a tracery of trees and branches behind, or surrounding pergolas and trellises.

Concrete's analogy to natural foliage – the screen walling block – is best used in small amounts, mixed with other materials, interspersed with piers of brick, or alternated within a zigzag walling of supporting brick returns. Screen walling blocks show up poor workmanship if laid unevenly, or poorly pointed, or they can dominate if built in an exposed situation.

Walls or fences set too close to a pool or built too high become claustrophobic. If space is limited, and walling surrounds imperative, introduce windows, gaps or arches to stop any feeling of imprisonment.

Concrete also offers inumerable faces, soft colours, exposed aggregates, unusual architectural shapes and reliefs. Also, metal railings and wrought iron designs can make interesting arrangements for small sections, or GRP panels do offer high definition, distinctive finishes with small, or huge castings.

Decide early on the type of ground or structural hard landscaping required by the pool, and try to include 'remainders material' for cohesion of textures and colours, etc. And, of course, climbing plants will cover up any defects and smooth out any too rigid forms, while rock banks and ground cover help join up odd angles or levels.

12.5 Soft landscaping

Gertude Jekyll maintained 'planting ground is painting a landscape with living things'. The landscape architect creates a pool-garden with simple firm lines, the main plan for planting being to give height, add shape, soften edges, and create interest for all seasons.

Well-set plants help conserve pool heating and chemicals; but try to avoid any overhanging trees that drop bits and pieces all the time, even though it is claimed modern cleaning systems can cope. A small garden pool overlooked by trees will double or treble regular cleaning, making an automatic sweeping system basic specification (see chapter 16.2).

Medium, and even fairly large trees, can be transplanted, if carefully dug around and underneath, and then removed with sufficient root ball for replanting. They will need to be staked and wired, and then watered daily for at least six months. Trees are worth looking after: they give maturity and majesty to the environment. Try to protect them during building, especially from wounding the bark, or compacting the ground with machinery and blocking the fine spread of feed roots. These root systems equal the whole spread of the overhead crown of a tree. Pool surround walling foundations can be arched over large roots of established trees, and where necessary, pool walls must be protected with barrier renders and membranes against probing roots of close-by trees.

The pool indoors is as much in need of planting as any garden. Tropical and exotic specimen plants really add something extra to the environment of indoor leisure pools. Surprisingly, they seem to be able to cope with a chlorinated atmosphere, and can thrive in the hot, humid

12.21 *Luxuriant tropical plants in the Swindon Oasis Leisure Dome transform hard pool hall interior surfaces*
Architects: Gillinson Barnett & Partners
Photo: O. F. Clarke

environment. Arrangements must be made for watering and drainage; avoid too much toing and froing with fresh water which always makes a display of plants unpopular with pool attendants. Overhead mist sprays remove dust from leaves. But sometimes it is difficult to stop scale insect and mealy bug pests, or to control plant mildew with so much humidity near the pool. Watch out especially for those extra unusual insects sometimes imported with new plants. At one new leisure centre, where the amenities and recreation department first introduced tropical palms to British pools, one emergent, dead-looking locust stayed so until a spider happened by!

The immense variety of flowers and shrubs offer infinite form and colour. They are best arranged in orderly groups unless intended specifically as lone specimens. A raised, planted bed, positioned carefully beside a pool, suggests an ideal place to sit for the elderly. The bare and stark modern pool desperately needs converting to the clothed and friendly pool-garden, and plants provide that natural cover and wider variety.

In spite of all the scope for unusual and exotic plants, nearly all pool owners anywhere in the world still like an English-lawn landscaped setting beside their pool. A grassy bank is perfect for a poolside picnic, and a flat lawn ideal for the children's play park. Both sloping and level lawns make superb sunbathing lounges and the well-manicured grass that carpets the ground is a restful complement to any pool.

As one final thought; it is not unknown for old, retired pools to become working sunken gardens. And in self-sufficient times, these soon make admirable vegetable patches.

References
[1] D. J. Robson, Master of Works, Royal Blind Asylum and School, Edinburgh, 1976

INFORMATION SHEET 12.1

Principles of poolscapes

Landscaping

Water is a very strong influence in landscaping and should not compete for attention within a scene. Waterscapes look best where you expect to find them in nature, but most pools can still be partially raised out of the ground to advantage. Try to create individuality with personality and character. The following rules help with the art:

Theme Follow carefully the ideal in your mind's eye – the classical or contemporary layout for example. But do consider first the important features that already exist and then try to re-use them within the pool garden. Make sure there is good reason for your theme – elegant simplicity is best.

Proportion Aim for a pleasing relationship in shape and size, length and breadth, depth and height. Keep structures to a human scale, even small schemes in a tiny garden can visually borrow space from next door. There must be a close relationship between the pool or enclosure and its grounds. Work in three dimensions – and as water is only a level feature on one plane, create safe rises, heights, contours, structures, planting and verticals to avoid the overall flat look.

Composition Unify the swimming pool comfortably into the garden just like a room of a house. Suppress any 'look what I've got' expression which can creep in. Features and materials must balance, with not too much of one type, nor all cramped into one place.

Focal point   Clearly define the centre of interest, then draw the eye towards the focal point without obstruction on the way. This main feature might be a tree, arbor, statue, fountain, or whatever you please.

Style   There is ample opportunity with pools to include a personal stamp throughout the scene, but generally, individual expression should be subtle with only occasional highlighted trim for brilliance.

Mood   Consider how the five senses should be catered for. Develop contrast and harmony, pattern and texture, light and shade. Add or subtract colour for brightness, to give depth, for coolness and quietness. For example, an eye-catching idea playing upon brightness, colour and light would be an all-white pool-garden with appropriate plants, stonework and decor.

Cost   Take basic needs first putting priorities into economic order by all means, but always allow enjoyable surroundings even if they have to be created over several stages.

See information sheet 2.9.

INFORMATION SHEET 12.2

Pool garden planner

Sketch in existing features first, new ideas afterwards, within one complete garden room plan; include slopes, trees and structures, pool shape and setting, places for sitting and shelter; note down orientation, reinstatement, surcharge and drainage; measure out levels, mark in paths, steps and shrubs, show entrance and exit, especially note height, and depth, mark out surrounding fencing. Where is the view?

Decide usage as private or public, leisure or sporting, family or friends; resolve age groups, traffic pattern, poolside living needs or social customs. Does the design require active movement or still coolness?

Consider the microclimate of sun, shade, wind, rain and frost, including air and water drainage. Dark or light decking, bright or shaded colours, plain or patterned materials, plants or furnishings, sand or rock, all bring considerable bearing upon locality heating and cooling by varying natural reflection, reradiation, convection and conduction. Create a sun-trap rather than a wind-tunnel.
    How will the environment of the immediate surroundings be controlled?

See chapter 2.1 and 4.

INFORMATION SHEET 12.3

Checklist of suitable landscape features for pools
(To offer a wide range of design ideas for consideration at the planning stage)

Architectural	Sculptured	Groundwork	Aquatic	Horticultural	Leisure
Alcove	Ballustrading	Bank	Alcove pond	Arbor	Barbecue
Arch	Benches	Berm	Canal	Beds	Beach
Balcony	Column	Cave	Canal ride	Border	Chequer board patio
Bridge	Finial	Coping	Cascade	Bower	Chimney
Cloister	Furniture	Decking	Filler	Curtain foliage	Chute
Conservatory	Gargoyle	Dell	Flaming waters	Exotic plants	Firepit
Coping	In-situ shapes	Earth sculpture	Fountain	Glade	Fireplace
Courtyard	Jardiniere	Embankment	Jet	Ground cover	Fresco
Fencing	Mobile	Ha Ha	Mask	Hanging plants	Furniture
Folly	Obelisk	Hollow	Overflow	Hedging	Games area
Gateway	Ornament	Mound	Poolwater bar	Knot	Lighting
Gazebo	Pedestal	Path	Pond	Lawn	Maze
Grotto	Pillar	Patio	Pools	Parterre	Mirror facade
Inlet	Planter	Platform	Pneumatic rocks	Patio backdrop	Mural
Island	Plaque	Ramp	Rivulet	Pots	Paddling stream
Loggia	Play sculpture	Rockery	Spa	Raised bed	Picnic area
Orangery	Plinth	Rock outcrop	Spill	Shrubs	Play area
Pavilion	Pot	Scree	Spray	Specimen trees	Sandpit
Peninsula	Seat	Steps	Stepping stones	Tropical scene	Sunpocket
Pergola	Statuary	Terrace	Stream		Sunterrace
Peristyle	Sundais	Tufa Rock	Water curtain		Treewalk
Pool house	Sundial	Underground	Waterfall		Trompe l'oeil
Portico	Sun pallet	Ziggurat	Water parterre		
Rotunda	Trough		Water slide		
Ruins	Tub		Water stairway		
Screening	Urn		Water treadmill		
Sittery	Vase		Water wall		
Summer house	Wall box				
Temple	Wrought ironwork				
Walling					
Wellhead					
Verandah					

See information sheets 4.4, 7.8, 8.1, 12.6 to 9.

INFORMATION SHEET 12.4

Pool surround proportions

Deck area to water area – guide ratios

Pool type	Indoor pools	Outdoor pools (including sun terraces)
Swimming	0·5:1	1·5:1
Diving	1:1	1·5:1
Garden	1:1	2:1
Leisure	1·5:1	2·5:1 up to 4:1 for summer time peaks

Deck widths:

	Minimum	Preferred	
Private pools	1m	1·5m	widths best varied according to landscaping
Private pools including diving-board area	2m	3m	
Public pools	2m	3m – wider with temporary seating
Public pools shallow area	3m	4m – wider with fencing
Public pools including 1m spring-board area	4m	5m – wider with outdoor leisure area
Public pools competition	3m sides	5m ends for officials at least

Note: 3m bays are better than wide open terraces.

Steps guide:
(3:1 steps to riser ratio)

Risers	100 to 150mm
Goings	300 to 450mm
Tread width	1m minimum
Tread projection	20mm maximum
Gradients	1:2 to 1:7
Flights	10 step sections best between platforms 20 step sections maximum

See Pool profiles: information sheet 2.17.

INFORMATION SHEET 12.5

Landscape falls and slopes – guide ratios

Cater for constant cleaning and hosing.
Water is a lubricant and must be shed quickly.
Recommended wet coefficient of friction – 0·5

Ramps and pool coping profiles	1:10
Ramps for wheelchairs	1:12
Indoor decking – public	1:24 to 1:36 min
Footways	1:30 to 1:40 min
Outdoor decking – public and private	1:50 to 1:75 min
Lawns	1:60 max. mow slope 30°
Terraces	1:80
Subsoil drainage	1:100

Network in:	Depth	Spacing
clay	0·5m	5m
loam	1m	10m
sand	1·5m	15m

Sources: APHA/CNCA/DLF/IBM.
See Pool profiles: information sheet 2.17.

INFORMATION SHEET 12.6

Pool decks – specifications and materials

Range: carpet, raised-deck, lawn, path, patio, pavement, steps, stepping stones, terrace.
Overlay to be independent of pool and structurally sound:
● non-slip and non-fade
● none-too-coarse nor uneven
● resistant to acids, algae, bacteria, chemicals, flood, frost, fungus, moisture, thermal shock, UV and vandals
● attractive and cool, durable and well-drained, always easy to clean
● no asphalt, bitumen, gravel, hoggin, pitch nor tar paves
● no trowelled concrete, painted floors, smoothed materials
● no crazed, creviced, oiled, bright surfaces.

Subfloor: firm foundations over good drainage are essential. Since backfilling to fresh pool walls or trenches cannot always be completely consolidated, various forms of bridging, beams, rafts, reinforcements and X-braces usefully stop settlement that inevitably causes decking cracks and depressions. Good base dimensions are:

	Excavate (+ finish thickness)	Hard core	Concrete slab
Light soils	100mm+	50mm	50mm
Heavy soils	150mm+	75–100mm	50–75mm

	Decking materials		Coping materials
ah	Brick-hard burnt	aep	Aluminium
aehsv	Carpeting	as	Ballustrades
ahpv	Ceramic	ahp	Brick
h	Cobbles	ahpv	Ceramic
ehip	Concrete	ehip	Concrete
i	Earthenware	v	Epoxy mix
hp	Epoxy terrazzo	ev	GRP
aehp	Flagstones	eipv	Plastic
h	Granite setts	e	Polypropylene
h	Granolithic	ehs	Rubber textured
ev	GRP mouldings	ahp	Stone – natural
aei	Lawn surrounds	aehips	Stone – reconstituted
ahpv	Mosaic	ahpv	Tile
hip	Paving – crazy	eip	Vinyl
aehp	Paving – riven		
aehips	Paving – textured		
av	Plastic screeding		
ahpv	Polyester resin		
h	Quarry tiling		
aehps	Rubber texture tile	**Key:**	
ah	Stone	a = attractive blend	
aehps	Synthetic grass	e = easy to lay	
hi	Terracotta	h = hard wearing	
ahp	Terrazzo	i = inexpensive material	
ahpv	Vitreous tile	p = popular for pools	
ai	Wood – hardblock	s = safe and non-slip	
aeip	Wood – timber slat	v = versatile finishes/designs	

See information sheet 12.3.

INFORMATION SHEET 12.7

Pool decks – main types

SURROUNDS are required for: pool margins, safe walking, wet area drainage (no ponding), durability, comfort and relaxation.

Concreted
A convenient and rapid decking for freeform pools.
3 to 5m bay sections for large areas.
No seas of concrete.
Sound, even bases, reinforced over reinstated ground.
Ideal 75mm in-situ screed on 100mm base.
Textured, cool, non-glare reflective surface required.
Colour to blend with landscape or to create effect.
Never trowel smooth.

Paved
Suitable for rectangular pools and economical decking.
Popular sizes from 200mm square up to 1 × 0·6m, 40 to 50mm thick.
Never use standard, hydraulically pressed slabs.
Break up manufactured appearance with interesting patterns of shapes, or mixed border liners, with separating materials such as bricks, cobbles, etc.
Troublesome settlement is sometimes accepted for first year and slabs are bedded in 25mm of sand temporarily for lightly used pools.
No open joints, always firmly level finishes, otherwise toes get stubbed; 5mm joints almost dry infilled to avoid smudging.
Non-slip pavings should be set higher than garden surrounds.
Avoid foot traffic for 7 days after laying. Do not brush joints for 28 days.

Ensure waterproofed when suspended over ducting, and also provided with watertight jointing especially for concreted slabs abutting a steel tank.

Tiles

Specify *fully* vitrified for frost proofing bearing in mind some national standards permit water absorbtion up to 1 per cent maximum, while others allow a 4 per cent absorbtion causing frost resistance problems.

Indoor pool ceramics need not be so critically specified for moderated temperature variations.

Mosaic decks can be attractive and the grouting gives grip even if it harbours dirt: sharp edged glazed mosaics cut bare feet on decks when poorly laid.

Dimensions vary considerably, but generally thicknesses are:

- light duty – 10mm
- medium – 15mm
- heavy – 20–25mm

Expansion joints must coincide or abut other materials, and require 3 to 5m centres.

Always provide easily cleaned covings to walls.

Well defined channels in tiles to clear surface waters rapidly are vastly better than random rice grain patterns for pretty surfacing.

Never wax tiles, but degrease and cleanse regularly.

Carpeting New, synthetic materials ideally suited to the pool environment offer an all over protection. They are soft and safe, but must drain and dry quickly.

Flexible: synthetic, studded 5mm rubber reduces risk of injury; it must be colour fast and cigarette burn proof: it can cover both poolside and facility areas, adding insulating properties to general advantages. Surface drainage is as important as for all decking materials, particularly an even fall without any hollows.

Vinyl/rubber backed: glued down onto thoroughly cured (2 week minimum) concrete, and laid on warm days, since this carpeting retains stiffness below 5°C. All edges must be thoroughly sealed against water. Must be easy to clean and disinfect, rotproof and mothproof. Brushing and hosing 5 to 10mm pile keeps material clean, but difficult to guarantee total hygiene. Carpets help subdue sound when used on walls, and resist mildew or damp problems.

Loose laid: an alternative to fitted carpeting over pool decking is the polypropylene fibrous felt, which is also ideal for play areas and patios and general outdoor use. It is porous, fire-resistant and chlorine solution proof. Water drains right through and pressure hoses dislodge organisms that are resistant to disinfectants, washing them away. (On outdoor pools though, it is amazing how much 'wild-life' can collect beneath if regular cleaning is not carried out.) Such mats range from 10 to 20mm thick and are taped or clipped together for easy removal. Public pool carpeting for gallery decking surrounds to serve both bather and spectator are reasonably maintained with commercial vacuum cleaning once or twice daily, and steam cleaned once or twice weekly. See chapter 16.2 for safer, constant cleaning with amphoteric microbiocides, or spray disinfectants. The increasing range of soft carpeting and artificial turfs offers vastly improved safe surfaces to pool surrounds for the comfort of bathers.

EDGING is required for: pool perimeter, safe handgrip, rapid drain-off (1:10 slope), hard wear, demarcation and distinction.

Stone – natural

Expensive finish.

Continued from surround right to water's edge to create natural effect preferred by countryside purists.

Edging must be securely laid, and arrassed at water's edge.

Natural subdued tones of local materials are best.

Textured flagstones or random blocks generally vary from 50 to 75mm thick. Mix and match with contrasting materials or planted pockets.

Stone – reconstituted coping

Perimeter margin bands are made in 200 to 300mm widths, 500 to 1000mm long, 30 to 70mm thick, in straights, or as 1 to 10m internal and external radii.

Set evenly, level and gently curved, this elegantly distinctive framing completes the pool surround.

Dense whites and buffs are most popular: grime free, lightly textured stones recessed underneath in order to clip over and secure liners.

Bullnosing offers hardgrip and rapid drain-away facilities.

Perimeter joint between coping and decking requires a sealant strip well able to cope with summer heat and differential expansion of materials.

Lightweight materials, compacted mixes, hollowed undersides, frogged ends all contribute to more practical and economical moulded stones.

Aluminium

An ideal lightweight moulding for freestanding pools and prefabricated tanks.

Generally restricted to rectangular shapes and 100 to 200mm wide cappings.

Better inlayed with safe-grip material strips or textures for non-slip needs.

Plastics

Range from resilient covings to reinforced claddings.

Primarily for private pools supplied in kit form to finish rough or sharp edges of tank walls, or liner overlap.

Ceramics

Wide range for all designs of water overflow system – freeboard to decklevel. Essential for heavy duty pools, and where exact specification is critical. The most enduring finish for the pool environment, with units from simple mosaic tesserae to complex patent tiled mouldings.

A distinctive clear edging to the pool improves safety at the same time.

INFORMATION SHEET 12.8

Walling and fencing

Strive for an unobtrusive, maintenance-free boundary to be used as a support for plants, to screen the pool and sunbathing areas.

Consider environment and pollution:

- wind, rain and sun
- abrasive wear, chemical attack and frost action
- exposed concrete aggregate within graffiti range
- local safety fence byelaws.

Provide firm foundations upon stable subsoil:

Consolidate across infilled trenches with piers or beams.

Lay deep foundations in 200mm layers.

Set steps on 100mm concrete over 100mm hardcore.

Always include dpc and capping to freestanding walls.

Ensure structure can cope with expansion and contraction.

Use dowelled movement joints on concrete walling.

Include weepholes to retaining walls, otherwise only a dam is built.

Ensure there is adequate drainage near at hand, ie gravel backfill longitudinal drain and distance drainage run-off.

Maintain high standard finishes of workmanship to visual barriers, especially walling joints where no smudging should be allowed.

Specify ironed, rubbed, V-cut or sharp relief joints.

Access for repair is required now and for later.

Fences must be set with room to spare, and never like a cage around the pool.

	Types		Materials
ap	Atrium court	hv	Acrylic
aeh	Ballustrading	aei	Bamboo
aeipv	Banks	hpv	Brick – new
ep	Benches	ahpv	Brick – old
ap	Courtyard room	ap	Cedar
eipv	Embankment	ei	Chainlink
ei	Fence	ei	Chestnut paling
eiv	Ha-ha	ep	Close board timber
aeipv	Hedge	ehip	Concrete block
aeip	Lattice	aehipv	Concrete-faced block
apv	Mural	ehip	Concrete panel
ei	Paling	aehipv	Concrete split block
ep	Pallisade	ahv	GRP moulded
ep	Panel	aeip	Interwoven lathe
ehipv	Parapet pool	av	Ironwork
apv	Pergola	i	Larch
av	Railing rockery	ei	Mesh
eip	Russian shelter	av	Metal
ae	Rustic	ahv	Oak
ep	Screen	aip	Plaster stipple
ahpv	Screenwalling	aeipv	Plastic
ahv	Sculptured cladding	ei	Post and rail
ep	Seating	ei	Ranch rail
ep	Steps	e	Railway timbers
aei	Trees	ap	Redwood
ei	Trellis	aei	Reed

Types			Materials		Key:
ahpv	Wall				a = attractive
		ahpv	Screen blocks		e = easy to instal
		ahpv	Stone		h = hard wearing
		aip	Stucco		i = inexpensive
		ev	Synthetic fibres		p = popular for pools
		ei	Timber and wire		v = versatile
		p	Transluscent screen		
		aip	Tyrolean spatter		
		iv	Wattle		

INFORMATION SHEET 12.9

Guide to walling dimensions

	Thickness mm	Height m	Width mm	Founds X	Depth mm	Pier spacing m	Expansion joint spacing m
Freestanding							
Brick walls	100	1·2	300	×	150	4·0	9·0
	100	2·0	300	×	150	3·5	8·0
	100	2·5	300	×	200	2·5	7·0
	200	2·0	600	×	200	4·0	6·0
	300	3·0	900	×	300	5·0	6·0
Concrete walls	100	1·2	250	×	250	2·5	8·0
	150	1·5	350	×	250	3·0	7·0
	200	2·0	500	×	300	4·0	7·0
Screen walls	100	2·0	200	×	200	3·0	7·0

	Thickness Base	Thickness Top mm	Overall height (h) m	Width mm	Founds X	Depth mm	Walling batter	Note
Retaining								
Dry stone walls	1/3 h	200	1·0	600	×	250	45°	integral
	1/2 h	200	1·5 max	800	×	500	45°	wall/found
Unreinforced concrete gravity walls	1/3 h	200	1·5 max	800	×	300	20°	Weepholes 4m apart
Cantilever walls	1/2 h	300	3·5	1/2 h	×	1/10h	tapered	Weepholes 4m apart
Crib walls	2/3 h	1/3 h	2·5	1/3 h	×	600	5°	Leading edge takes footing

INFORMATION SHEET 12.10

Pool surround – planting and soils

Planting Consider shape before colour.

Frame the view and then make a place that is warm and secluded; surround the pool with patterns and textures, with plants in clumps or pockets within the deck, warmer colours to the front.

Select plants for effect. Use:
- dwarf varieties for precision
- ferns for odd corners and alcoves
- marginal plants at boundaries
- espaliers against walls and fences
- climbers to soften architecture
- specimen shrubs for their foliage
- trees to windward as screens and heat savers (if leaf-fall is no problem)
- and ornamental grasses for fun.

Avoid plants which:
- have soft, staining fruit
- bear needles and thorns
- exude resins, feed birds, or attract bees
- discharge seeds or drop hard, heavy fruit
- spread rampantly above or below ground
- grow fast near to the pool and deposit copious quantities of small leaves
- are toxic

Consider plants beside the pool that are chlorine resistant, such as: Acacia, Arbutus unedo, Tamarix, Washington Palm, etc.

Dimensions

Shrubs range from	Bush	½ standard	Standard	to Full standard
approx height	0·5m	1m	2m	3m
spacing apart	0·5m	0·75m	1·5m	2m

Trees are confined to:	Dwarf	Small	Medium
average height	1m	4m	10m

shapes: upright, horizontal, rounded, pyramid, weeping, decorative.

Soils

Well structured topsoil should be 200 to 300mm deep with most plants rooting to 0·5m depth.

Save all good topsoil from construction.

Revive stale soils with extra compost and leafmould dug to full topsoil depth.

Avoid soil spilling over onto deck.

Provide ample perimeter and ground drainage.

Chlorotic effect If soil is continuously saturated with chlorinated pool water, an anaemic effect can be induced in some plants that go straggly and spindly, through iron deficiency reducing their vitality. Plants such as azaleas and rhododendrons suffer badly, turn yellow-green, lose colour and hardiness. It is best to plant them clear of constant water splash, or replace them with hardy, broadleafed evergreens – though these can sometimes suffer leaf spot bleaching.

Conditions can be improved by spring and autumn applications of sequestrene, or with 1kg iron chelate in 10 litres of water treating the soil around the plants at maximum of 10 litre/m². Acid soils are best for most evergreens, shrubs and trees: flowers of sulphur reduces pH, otherwise lime neutralises too much sourness. Lawngrasses prefer soil pH at around 6.

Lawns require at least 100mm humus topsoil with sharp drainage and should be raised 25mm above decking and perimeter drainage. Lawns are best when absolutely flat and resilient, well drained and maintained.

Turfing provides lawns quickly at almost any time of year, but requires watering and careful protection from too much sun. Best type is sea-washed, where occasional tidal flooding allows only finest grasses to survive: downland is satisfactory with meadow grass suitable only as a standby. Coarse grasses succumb to close mowing – fine fescues and bents are the aristocrats of the grass world. Fast-growing, tufty, perennial rye grass suffers from constant close trimming; coarse annual meadow grass does not wear well; creeping bent displays well if wet feet can be kept off.

Seeding offers best all round turf grown from a good quality mixture (spread at around 40gm/m²), that mats slowly, densely and strongly, eg 70 per cent chewings fescue and 30 per cent browntop to include some meadow grass. Strictly limit dwarf perennial rye grass which can swamp finer grasses. Hardwearing seed-grassed areas can be stabilised with sand and bitumen, but kept clear of the pool.

Nitrogen fertilizer applications to lawns must not waft into poolwater where they provide rich feed for algae plants (see chapter 15.10). When cutting, a grass box should always be used to prevent mowings being carried into the pool on bathers' wet feet.

Alternative lawns of ornamental camomile, thyme or heather are most attractive.

A glimpse of a pool surrounded by conifers
E. Kobbler
Photo: John Dawes

INFORMATION SHEET 12.11

100 best pool plants
(some suggested plants for surrounds)

Cover and carpeters	Tubs and pots	Beds and banks	Climbers and clamberers	Shrubs and bushes
Ajuga (Bugle)	Agapanthus (African lily)	Alchemilla (Lady's mantle)	Ceanothus (Californian lilac)	Azalea
Alyssum (Madwort)	Bonsai	Alpines	Clematis	Buddleia (Butterfly bush)
Arabis (Rock cress)	Dwarf dahlia	Amaranthus (Love-lies-bleeding)	Hedera (Variegated ivy)	Camelia
Bergenia (Elephant's ear)	Fuchsia	Cotoneaster (Rockspray)	Hydrangea Petiolaris (Climbing hydrangea)	Choisya ternata (Mexican orange blossom)
Camomile lawn	Geranium (The Crane's bill)	Hypericum Calycinum (Rose of Sharon)	Jasminium (winter and summer Jasmine)	Elaeagnus (Silver berry)
Creeping Bents, chewings fescue and close-knit turf	Laurus nobilis (Bay)	Juniperus horizontalis	Lonicera (Honeysuckle)	Hibiscus (Tree hollyhock)
Erica (Heather)	Mahonia (Oregon grape)	Lavandula (Lavender)	Passiflora (Passion flower)	Hydrangea
Phlox subulata (Phlox cushions)	Nicotiana (Tobacco plant)	Ornamental grasses	Solanum crispum (Chilean potato tree)	Rhododendron
Thymus (Thyme)	Dwarf quince	Spring bulbs	Vitis vinifera purpurea (Virginia creeper)	Shrub rose
Vinca minor (Periwinkle)	Dwarf Veronica	Weeping forsythia (Golden bell)	Wisteria	Viburnum

Hedges and screens	Selected trees	Feature specimens	Water plants	Tropical effects
Berberis (Barberry)	Cedrus deodara pendula (Weeping cedar)	Acer palmatum dissectum and atropurpureum (Maple)	Butomus umbellatus (Flowering rush)	Arundinaria (Bamboo) Banana tree
Buxus (Box)	Chamaecyparis and Cypress	Betula pendula (Weeping birch)	Calla palustris (Bog arum)	Draceana draco (Dragon tree)
Cotoneaster (Rockspray)	Cornus florida (Flowering dogwood)	Cortaderia argentea (Pampas grass)	Eriophorum angustifolium (Cotton grass)	Ficus elastica (Rubber plant)
Cypressus	Eucalyptus gunnii (Cider gum)	Dierama pulcherrimum (Wand flower or Angels fishing rod)	Ferns	Monstera deliciosa (Mexican breadfruit)
Fagus sylvatica purpurea (Copper beach)	Juniperus	Gunnera manicata (Giant Brazilian water plant)	Glyceria maxima (Manna grass)	Palms
Lonicera nitida (Chinese honeysuckle)	Magnolia (Lily tree)	Hamamelis (Witch-hazel)	Iris laevigata (Japanese water iris)	Sanseveria trifasciata (Mother-in-law's tongue or Snake plant)
Potentilla (Primrose hedging)	Malus (Flowering crab apple)	Hosta undulata univittata (Plantain lily)	Nelumbiums album (Sacred lotus of the Nile)	Tradescantia (Wandering Jew)
Prunus laurocerasus (Laurel)	Mountain pine	Nerine Bowldenii (Guernsey lily)	Nymphaea (Water lily)	Vriesia Splendens (Zebra plant)
Floribunda rose	Rhus (Smoke tree)	Prunus amanogawa (Japanese cherry)	Scirpus albescens (Bulrush)	Yucca gloriosa (Adam's needle)
Thuya (American white cedar)	Syringa (Lilac)	Tetrapanax papyrifera (Rice paper plant)	Scirpus zebrinus (Zebra rush)	

13 Filtration and circulation

Water is mostly taken for granted. But in an arid country such as Syria where water is really precious, people respect and revere it. Indeed, Islam holds that water is holy.

13.1 Saving water

Water is the basis of every swimming pool, and even if it is considered to be freely available, once it is heated, disinfected, balanced, treated, monitored, recycled and rechecked to reach popular swimming pool standards, the enhanced value (or high control cost per cubic metre) makes it sensible to install holding tanks and energy recovery plant. And then it becomes necessary to avoid any equipment with wasteful washing cycles (see also chapter 14.10, Heat recovery). A modern swimming pool does not *need* to use water – or rather, to waste much of the initial stock.

Until quite recently, all pools were filled with fresh water and then emptied a few days later when the floor could no longer be seen. Nowadays, treatment plant can keep the first fill clear for 10 years. In practice, though, garden pools are regularly diluted with make-up water at the rate of 250 litres per m² throughout the year, or up to 100 times that amount for the average indoor public pool. Some countries recommend between 2 to 5 per cent of a heavily used pool's capacity should be run off daily for refilling with fresh top-up water as dilution to accumulating dissolved solids residual in the poolwater (see chapter 15.9). In most pools, however, the same litre of water is used over and over again, to such an extent that water use, or loss per bather, is far less than the average daily consumption required for each citizen of the western world; water 'consumption' even by the most reckless pool, is nothing like the 1 million litres of potable (or drinkable) water it takes to produce just one new automobile.

Expenditure upon quality control equipment in pools tends to vary from 10 to 50 per cent of the total contract value, though on average, about one third of the budget will be spent over all the pool services. And as purification and environmental systems have to work day and night to retain perfect standards, water is not really free.

The position was summed up appropriately by the Syrian delegate to a 1977 UN Conference in Argentina, when he represented that in the not too distant future, 'a drop of water will cost more than a drop of oil'.[1] As conservation of resources and energy grows in consequence, there is no reason why the pool's catchment potential cannot be tapped, with soft rainwater used for top-up and even a water surplus realised.

13.2 Plantroom

The plantroom houses an inter-related control system of water filtration, disinfection and heating that should follow the main direction of flow in order to present a logical sequence to the operator. A diagram of the circulation system with all pipes and valves colour coded, flow directions marked and equipment labelled, will be useful to the private pool owner, and essential to the professional pool operator; he also needs a mimic diagram display on view in the control room for easy monitoring and rapid fault-finding. Some plantrooms are set out for viewing through observation windows from the entrance area, an excellent way to encourage greater interest in the constant efficiency of machinery.

The amount of water flowing through a plantroom (usually well under control) makes it worthwhile to protect and waterproof the surroundings, yet still keep all the surfaces attractive, especially those in the main working areas. Salt water, particularly, wreaks havoc. The German practice of organising an equipment operations room to very high standard, with ceramic surfacing materials specified throughout, encourages greater personnel efficiency, as well as considerable saving on wear and tear. On the other hand, too much sophistication with elaborate equipment can mean less experienced operators being unable to cope with the whole complex system. This situation is rife in some Middle Eastern or African countries where there are insufficient numbers of trained personnel to deal with what has now become a highly skilled engineer's responsibility.

All plantrooms require good ventilation, 200 to 300 lux lighting, ample accommodation for equipment in clear floor space with sufficient headroom, non-slip flooring with rapid drainage, plus strict safety arrangements for all electrics (see chapter 13.8, Electrics and controls). Especially important for large plant is a 2 or 3 tonne overhead lifting gear and girder.

Checks at the planning stage (see chapter 2) concern the main services of water, electricity, gas, plus fire, health and licensing authorities, particularly for their bearing upon the building and central location of equipment. Try to utilise under-decking voids beside a large pool tank to shorten pipe runs and ducts, and to allow common returns for both air and water, heating and recovery (see chapter 11.4).

13.1 *Plantroom – 50m pool – pumping control, National Sports Centre, Crystal Palace*

Architects: Designed by the Greater London Council, Department of Architecture & Civic Design, Sir Hubert Bennett
Photo: GLC Photographic Unit

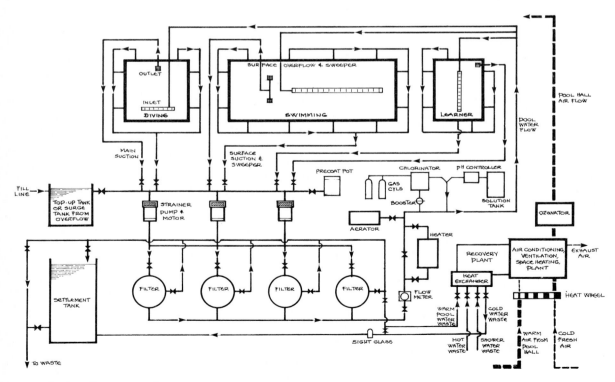

13.2 *Systems chart – diagrammatic*

The use of pre-packaged systems for smaller pool plant is on the increase. The module idea started with the above-ground pool scheme where filtration/chlorination/heating is assembled onto one skid set beside the pool. Units were then developed as practical and economical attachments to school pools – especially the playground type – and sometimes even came with their own transportation, or on mobile trolleys. Interchangeability between pools allows a spare unit to be wheeled in quickly, or means a portable suction sweeper/filter trolley can be brought in to clean a whole group of pools maintained by one local authority or education department (see chapter 16.2).

13.3 Filters

The filter deals with particulate matter. It strains out suspended solids down to sub-micron size in order to retain water clarity. It does not remove dissolved salts, nor does it deal with micro-organisms. Filtration combined with disinfection produces effective water purification treatment that keeps water:

- clear and non-toxic
- odourless and tasteless
- free of bacteria and algae
- balanced to prevent corrosion or scale formation.

It was simpler in the time of Vitruvius since 'water sprinkled over Corinthian Bronze (gold-silver-copper alloy) or any good bronze leaving no trace is pure'.[2]

The *working capacity* of a filter can be determined by the amount of dirt it is capable of holding without blocking, or passing more than, say, 10 micron sized particles, in a given time.

A pool's *recovery period* is the time it takes the filter to bring the whole body of water round to 99·9 per cent cleanliness after prolonged heavy bathing.

The *rate of filtration* is that flow of water through the filter designed to achieve a specified degree of clarification, say, down to 10 micron, or 0·01mm, within a certain period.

Filtration for pools is a continuing process of dilution and even a *100 per cent efficient* unit will require seven passes of the equivalent poolwater volume to remove 99·9 per cent of the original dirt. This means a private pool operating an 8-hour turnover of the whole pool volume, needs 56 hours to reach 99·9 per cent water clarity. Unfortunately, such simple circumstances do not take into account the common practice of operating a home filter for 8 hours only, every day. Therefore, the poolwater now takes 168 hours to reach equilibrium, providing there is no additional pollution whatsoever. And on top of this, since a filter's efficiency is always declining – it gradually gets blocked up until backwashing – a good 50 per cent average means the one-week period to reach equilibrium can extend into two weeks, in order to bring round a pool to perfect clarity, before trying to keep it in that state.

Filter flow rates The choice in filtration capability is critical. Since each kind of swimming pool suffers different pollution rates – shallow water has more bathers per cubic metre than deeper water, or an open air pool has greater surface pollution – the pace of the filter has to be sufficient to cope with the different loads. Each type of pool requires its own filtration pace to develop the specified turnover. Sometimes, central filter banks might be redeployed to support

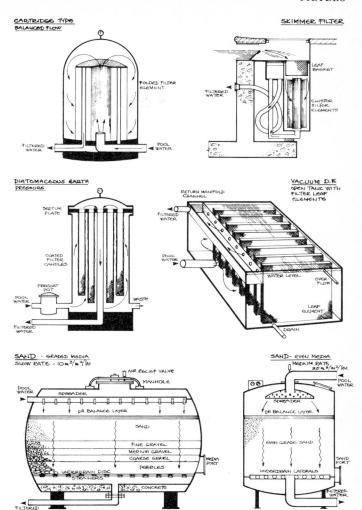

13.3 *Filtration systems*

the most polluted pool of a complex, but in practice, separate filtration for separate pools will give greater operating flexibility by arranging cleaning/washing cycles to suit the varied pollution rates.

Filter development – sand Water filtration has been known from antiquity and the principles of slow seepage to strain out deleterious material are well understood. Engineers nowadays are mainly concerned with speeding the whole process for greater re-use. Slow gravity filtration stayed with us right up to the 19th century. Then, with the Industrial Revolution providing ample power, flow rates through the surface area bed were forcibly increased to $5m^3/m^2/h$ to provide more cleaned water, faster. Unfortunately, such large, long-running filter designs too often required early pools to close during backwashing for total bed-reviving or digging-out of soiled media.

By the 20th century, flow rates had doubled or trebled, to give what has become known as the standard rate of water filtration through sand media beds. This rate for a graded bed of sand and gravel is still preferred by many designers of large pools, since it has been so well proven over almost 100 years. But the driving need to improve performance and to reduce capital cost has meant the doubling, and doubling again, of flow, for smaller and smaller filtration units. The medium rate ($25m^3/m^2/h$) filter with deeper even-grade sand bed has become more acceptable to public pools for cost effective reasons alone; but the

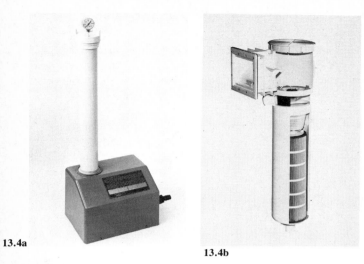

13.4a

13.4b

13.4c

13.4a *The simple filter: 3 m³/h throughput*
Certikin Ltd, Sussex

13.4b *Cartridge skimmer filter for in-ground pools draws in water at surface and returns water at bottom: 10 m³/h throughput*
Baker Hydro California

13.4c *High speed sand filter for semi-public pools: 30 m³/h throughput*
Rutherford Engineering Ltd, Sussex

13.4d *Medium rate sand filter for public pools: 110 m³/h throughput*
Rutherford Engineering Ltd., Sussex
Photo: MFS Photography

13.4e *Medium/slow-rate bank of filters for municipal baths at Southampton: 800 m³/h throughput*
Architects' Journal
Photo: W. J. Toomey

13.4f *Vacuum diatomaceous earth filter beds: 800 m³/h throughput*
Courtesy: Queen Elizabeth II Park Sports Centre, Christchurch
Photo: Green & Hahn

13.4d

13.4e

13.4f

188

most popular high rate ($50m^3/m^2/h$) compact unit, tends to be reserved for semi-public and private-type pools, where low capital cost is at absolute premium. These high speed units rely upon filtration through even grade sand in depth with increased cleaning frequency, but using little wash water in the process. Their dirt carrying capacity is limited, though, in the relatively small pressure tanks used.

Flow patterns within a pressure tank are super-critical, since even 4mm protected steel plate for heavy duty loads can be eroded rapidly by jet streams caused from blockages or bad design that chew away laterals and tank shells, just like an eroding sandblaster.

A tank, sized to suit a weekly cleaning cycle is acceptable, but the design tendency to underrate the filter to save on initial expense has developed distrust of the smaller high rate sand units by many professional pool people. Some manufacturers are retaining the original very slow water rates with very large filter area systems using modern regenerative precoats and replaceable cartridge units.

Superfine systems – septae and elements The huge market for pools in the private sector has promoted the introduction of many new low cost filtration systems. The successful ones – especially those that increase the filter surface area in favour of reducing the media volume in the filter – have stayed and grown in reliability and respectability to the extent they now compete actively with traditional sand systems for larger pools. They require a septum within the tank or filter element of specified porosity to support the media that traps the dirt – the larger the overall area the better.

The large surface area in pressure or vacuum filter units has been brought about mainly by the use of diatomaceous earth (DE) media – known on the Continent as Kieselguhr. This very fine powdered material of siliceous earth – fossilised external silica skeleton of plankton and looking rather like chalk – is found deposited in huge layers that were formed within prehistoric freshwater lakes, where the original diatoms or single cell plant life (numbering over 15,000 different species) lived and died 5 to 20 million years ago. Their varied shape and fine porosity enables the minute '3-D snowflake-like' particles to matt in evenly spread 'strawpiles', offering only 10 per cent solids and 90 per cent of voids (compared to 75 per cent sand with 25 per cent voids). The voids are so small that micron-sized dirt particles are easily trapped, under relatively fast flow rates for the tank volume involved. Unlike permanent, solid sand media bed particles, this finely porous material is used as rechargeable media – simple systems dispose of the blocked and used powder to add fresh coatings, whereas regenerative systems disturb and re-settle the existing cake many times for more economical and greater filtration.

Pressure DE units rated between 1 and $2m^2$ filter surface area can serve $10m^3$ poolwater, compared with the same size tank employed for the high speed sand unit which offers only about $0.1m^2$ filter surface area (plus in-depth sand bed interstices) for each $10m^3$ water in the pool.

A DE filter can offer low resistance, low running time, low media requirements and a low power consumption.

Alternative media of volcanic rock are also mined and crushed for use in appropriate precoat filter systems; or synthetic media, such as plastic granules some with floating properties for greater absorption, or interspersed with matted fibres, are introduced for longer-life materials and longer running cycles.

Precoating and recoating A precoat pot is usually included before the DE filter, in order to charge a slurry of earth in water over the withholding screens inside the filter tank. Non-corrosive internals of the filter's septum are made in vertical grids, or horizontal leaves, or cylindrical candles that must be coated thinly and evenly to trap dirt from the flow of water. When fully blocked and with water flow reduced, either the filter is sluiced out (in pool terminology – backwashed), or the media redistributed with a regenerative arrangement (perhaps as much as 50 to 200 times at 4 hour intervals, for the very long-run filter cycles).

Diatomite filtration is so 'sharp' it produces filtered water of brilliant clarity to a finer degree over all other systems; in fact, so fine that DE filters were introduced in the Far East after 1945 to collect chlorine-resistant cysts that were passing through sand beds and causing amoebic dysentry in the armed forces.

DE filter grades must not be so fine that they plug early, nor too open that they pass dirt straight through. Usually, medium-fast grades are better than the extreme ones, and they always improve in efficiency as the cake settles down. The accepted filter rate is similar to gravity sand systems (around $5m^3/m^2/h$) but with DE coating only 1 to 2mm deep. Coarser slow-rate sand has to use an alum coating (see chapter 15.10) to improve polish performance, while the large sand bed offers capacious volume for long-operating runs. Another improved sand filter performance in water treatment cultivates a biological bed – a Schmutz-decke – that forms in the first 100mm layer of sand for finer results.

Filter cleansing or backwashing As dirt trapped within the filter builds up, resistance to flow also increases, until rising pressure shows the filter to be below satisfactory operating efficiency. At this point, cleansing or purging is necessary. The greater the initial pressure differential, the longer the possible filter cycle. But, generally, an increase of $1kg/cm^2$ over clean running pressure is the normal maximum for most systems. When the filter is full, water flow is reversed through the septum or bed to expel captive dirt to waste. Low rate sand beds may be agitated or aerated at the time of backwash to loosen a soiled bed, but the whole process of reverse water flow must not disturb supporting media layers. High rate, deep sand beds at reverse flow are scoured or *boiled* to expel their dirt, but the design freeboard within the tank is greater than the distance that the sand particles can be lifted, allowing only lighter than sand dirt to be carried to waste.

Compact DE pressure vessel, precoat filter systems can be most efficient for long periods, scoring heavily in continuous quality of result. Recharging after cleansing is an extra duty that private pool operators do not like, while the disposal of soiled media is a problem local authorities find a nuisance. When drains are already taxed to overload (10 per cent considered so in USA), clogging waste media is increasingly barred from the sewers by building codes and health regulations (see chapter 9.3). However, if drains cannot cope with the sudden, short influx, holding or wash-out tanks, and garden sumps can provide for settlement of waste DE; a dry well soakaway drainage for private pools is ideal ground for a regularly watered and thriving

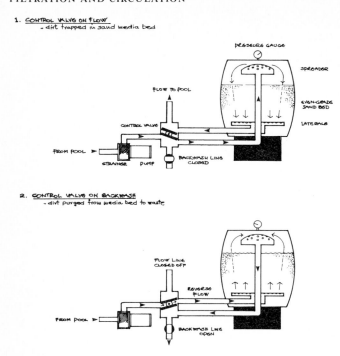

13.5 *High speed sand filter: flow-to-backwash circuits*

bog garden; or, very long-run vacuum type units or regenerative systems can reduce wastage to very reasonable proportions. Furthermore, body feeders that introduce DE continually also extend operating cycles; but variable flow filter designs that maintain optimum velocity per area rating for greater efficiency are usually far too elaborate for the smaller pools.

To help ensure thorough filter bed cleaning, a sight glass can be included in the backwash line, or pressure readings taken across the filter, or, best of all, an open tank vacuum type DE filter installed – then the actual state of the media can be seen at all times while the filter is working, and disposal is reduced to the minimum (information sheet 13.6).

There must be no resistance in the wash cycle to reversed flow, or by the waste outlet, to ensure that the filter is cleaned with minimum loss of water. Once again, the vacuum DE filter scores highly on conservation, since washwater will only equal the volume of the filter tank, which is finally cleaned out after runs of several months. This is similar in principle to the long-running cartridge filter unit which is washed or hosed down infrequently. Vacuum DE elements are easily cleaned and recoated for the filter to be constantly kept at a very high state of efficiency. Standard rate sand is washed weekly on average for five to ten minutes, at four times the normal flow rate, wasting large amounts of water and heat, unless a holding tank and recovery plant is installed. High rate sand units require only two to three minutes backwashing, also usually at weekly intervals (see chapter 9.3, Water and drainage).

Long-term performance The continuing theme of conservation, compactness and cheapness has encouraged development of diverse kinds of filter. Some designs are too elaborate, some too fragile and some are simply too small. But in the class of small, lightweight, variform units, the replaceable cartridge type element combines most of

the advantages. Just like the more common air filter element, the cartridge septae are most economical and easy to clean. Multi-folds within the cartridge enable very large surface areas to be presented to a wide range of flow rates, variable according to particular needs. Operating runs of at least 100 days mean private pool filter cycles can sometimes last a full summer season.

Space flight has shown that total recycling is possible, but expensive. Many potential total systems have been developed with all kinds of media, but the plain sand filter in its many forms is still the mainstay of the swimming pool water treatment system. Its rugged reliability is its greatest advantage. Modern nuclear power stations with their fuel cooling ponds in concrete, coated with chlorinated rubber paint, use pressure sand filters – double banked – to remove active and non-active nuclear waste from hot water with a 100 per cent reliability. Perhaps the need for higher technology in the water filtration of swimming pools is not really so demanding after all.

Filter choice When selecting a filter, consider the appropriate performance and categorise:
- flow rate per m² of bed
- size and location
- pump rating for the filter's working head
- backwash rate and time
- type of tank and components
- materials specification
- installation and operation cost
- degree of filtration
- serviceability of the system

(see also the information sheets at the end of this chapter).

All filters operate better with short pipe runs containing as few bends as possible, balanced flow and suction, and the pump working from a flooded condition. If there is any reservation on the expected design loading, it is better to uprate the filter.

13.4 Turnover

Pools become polluted at different rates. Generally, the shallower the water, the faster it becomes turbid, simply because more people wash off more dirt, occupying less water. An old and practical guide to sizing the filter used to call for 'the reduction of one hour to the pool's turnover rating for each foot depth of water'. Now variable formulae and balanced circulations are better with 10 hour turnovers for very light loadings in deep poolwater, right up to 10 minute turnovers for extreme loadings to beach shallows all within the same pool.

Formulae for turnover Turnover is the number of hours it takes the filter to pass one poolsworth volume of water. There are two fundamental ways of calculating turnover ratings for any pool. The first and most popular allocates commonly accepted ratings to each category of pool, even though contamination loadings vary from country to country, or according to personal hygiene standards. Information sheet 13.11 summarises the main types of pool according to their usual ratings, the more heavily used waters requiring more cleaning, and the faster turnround.

Such generalisations depend a lot upon whether that pool keeps the same bathing load per cubic metre throughout its whole working operation. Most leisure pools will deal with widely varying bathing loads between winter and summer, let alone from sunny to dull days; they can have different bathing load ranges as wide apart as 100 to 2000 bathers per square metre of surface water per year. So variable filter ratings in adjustable working arrangements do help considerably.

In order to deal better with variable bathing density, an alternative turnover formula can be used. Obviously, filtration plant has to be stepped up in size and rating to cope with heavier pollution, and this is already indicated by the improving turnover ratings allocated to the denser used pools from practical experience. The second formula works with varying bathing loads for varying pool capacities. Resulting bather density then indicates the necessary turnover rating, but once again suggested from experience (see information sheet 13.12).

As a contrast, a coal mining community's small leisure pool will tax the properly rated filtration system far more than a hospital's large therapy pool. Or more simply, the more dirt carried by each person into the pool, the higher the filtration performance required. As it is difficult to guess, let alone measure, the grubbiness factor of bathers, it can easily be argued that finer formulae are no real help. To illustrate this point, one very effective pool ruling ensuring full use of all precleanse arrangements (always stipulated in German pools) considerably affects water turbidity and hence the prescribed turnover; or rather, proper precleanse by bathers enables greatly improved filter performance at standard turnover.

Turnover and turbidity One further complicating factor to be taken into consideration through carefully organised circulation systems is the differing pollution rate for different parts of the same pool. Since straightforward bathing load still directly affects filter ratings, an average 3½ hour turnover public pool could well be arranged as:

- beach area – 1 hour turnover or less, up to 10 minutes
- shallow end – 2 hour turnover
- mid-way section – 3 hour turnover
- deep end – 5 hour turnover or more, down to 10 hours.

Turnover prescriptions are the practical working attempt to guarantee retaining safe water clarity at peak bathing loads. One clear measure of the clarity of water is taken in turbidity units, with reasonable standard being 0·5 JTUs. Low turbidity from improved filtration techniques actually enables disinfection levels to be reduced (see chapter 15.2) since fine organic material is extracted from poolwater. Water turbidity is accurately measured with a light absorbing photometer; but clarity, although critical, is easily seen with the eye – if not, then the pool is unsafe to swimmers.

13.5 Pumps and valves

The pump is the heart of a swimming pool system. It must operate economically and reliably, reasonably quietly and be compact. Pumping power must be greater than the total resistance for the *complete* circulation system – including that restriction from the filtration. This total head resistance comprises static head (vertical distance to be overcome from poolwater level to the point of delivery), plus dynamic head (friction resisting flow in suction and delivery lines, valves and equipment, but mainly from within the filter). The best rule is to keep static and frictional losses to the minimum, rather than having to upgrade the pump to overcome them.

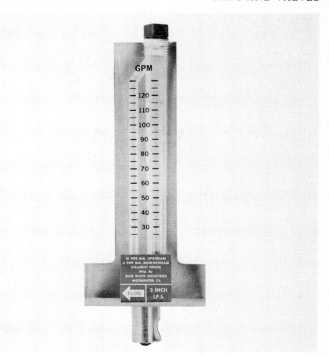

13.6 *Flowmeter 0–30 m³/h*
Blue White Industries, California

Standard home pool purification systems often provide pre-matched pump and filter for economy and convenience of installation. Abnormal systems, or the inclusion within the circuit of extra equipment, usually requires increased pipeline bores, or extra pumping capacity to cope with the greater resistance. For example, as a filter pump performance falls off, a solar heater or fountain water inlet also in the same circuit and relying upon the same main pump will deteriorate in operation as their additional resistance forces the filter circulation to become less effective much earlier.

As swimming pools increase in complexity and diversity, pump design performance is calculated to match the working head of the overall purification system: booster pumps and separate circuits become necessary to deal with disinfection units, pH control, heating and so on. Most automatic cleaning devices require a high duty head and therefore operate far better also on their own separately pumped circuit.

An inadequate main pump gives only short filter runs. An oversized pump drives or draws dirt down into the filter bed to clog the media. The filter pressure gauge with the system at rest will show static head, and at start-up, the clean running pressure shows the additional dynamic head. Increasing resistance from dirt load is shown by increased pressure on the gauge before backwashing. Each metre of head from the system reduces flow until the point when the filter is not working, and there is no flow at all, usually somewhere around 2kg/cm² and a 20m average working head.

The pool pump Most swimming pool pumps are the centrifugal type, powered by a close-coupled electric motor; they usually include an integral strainer basket before the impeller and volute; the impeller can be changed to uprate filtration flow by as much as a third. However, if the pump is starved of water when a more powerful impeller is fitted, cavitation will be caused by restricted suction. Most larger pumps also require a coarse strainer box set within the main supply suction pipework.

Even though most pool pumps are self-priming, they are still best situated just below poolwater level with a direct, flooded suction line rising evenly and slowly to the pump, and not surfacing before necessary. Most self-priming pumps can extract air from the circulation system even with a suction line full of air, providing there is some water in the pump chamber to lubricate the pump seal.

Non-self-priming pumps, particularly for freestanding pools, must be situated below water level, even if charged by hand with water to start working, since the smallest pinhole in the pipework can cause failure of prime.
The basic pump has:
- a large capacity strainer basket with quick release lid
- an impeller to create vacuum and pressure reaction through a single or double plate driving wheel alongside the chamber or volute
- a stainless steel shaft connecting to the sealed electric motor, which should include a thermal overload cut-out

13.7 *Self-priming swimming pool pump and strainer basket – cutaway*
Sta-Rite Industries, Wisconsin

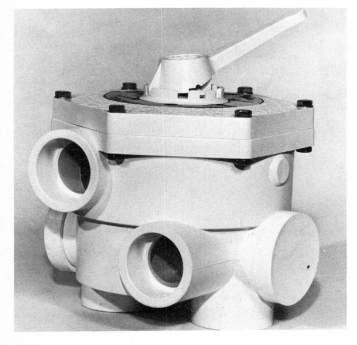

13.8 *Swimming pool filter multiport rotary control valve with six flow ways*
American Products Co, California

- low head for sand or vacuum filter units, and high head for high rate sand or pressure units.

The main suction line plays a critical part in the wear and efficiency of a pump. This pipeline should be short and straight and full-bored, allowing a water flow of around 1 m/s, the recommended optimum.

A spare pump is always useful. Next to out-of-condition water, it is the pump that gives most maintenance problems.

Normal poolwater can be capably handled by cast iron pump units, but salt or seawater require reinforced plastic, gunmetal or bronze. Strict specification applies to all fittings, control valves and equipment. If dissimilar metals are used within the same system and come into contact with each other through poolwater, corrosive electrolytic action will result. This can devastate the inside of a pump or filter, unless a sacrificial node is provided (see chapter 16.4).
Pool valves Each item of equipment within the plantroom, plus lines from pool circulation fittings, should be valved separately for servicing and for totally isolating the pool reservoir. Non-return foot valves of twice the suction pipe

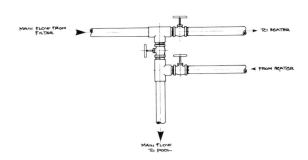

13.9 *Manifold. Example: heater by-pass tees and valves*

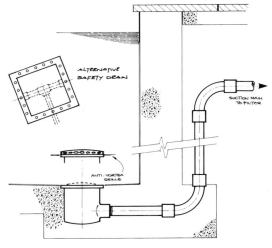

13.10 *Main drain and swanneck*

area, situated in the main suction line, will help the pump retain prime when standing idle.

The main control for the unit filter is preferably a five- or six-position multiport valve that is hydraulically efficient and totally corrosion resistant. Swimming pool main valve positions offer:

- Filter – normal filtration and suction sweeping
- Backwash – reversed flow purging dirt to waste
- Rinse – for resettling a filter bed after backwash
- Shut-off – pump outlet blocked, preventing all flow to filter and pool
- Waste – bypass filter for rapid pool drainage, or heavy suction sweeping
- Recirculate – bypass filter for rapid flow to spa pool, or hydrotherapy fittings.

These pool valves are now manufactured very economically. They are most efficient with few moving parts, positive sealing and no pressure impact when changing from one operation to another – an important point when lightweight fittings, filter tanks and pipework are involved.

Gate, butterfly, ball, diaphragm and motorised valves are part of larger filtration units and everyday pool circulation. Since all systems suffer hard wear and heavy handling, only long-term, reliable valves should be used. Increasingly popular are pressure triggered automatic backwash valves for filters, even though some can be heavy on waste water. The majority of small pool owners want simple mechanisms; and large pool operators also prefer straightforward practical systems. Elaborate automated overall flow control systems exist, at a price, but too often need sophisticated maintenance. Specialised equipment such as pH controllers, or water top-up valves, when individually automated, save on water treatment or inconvenience, but wholesale 'watermation' is not yet cost effective enough.

13.6 Circulation equipment

Simplicity of installation, resistance to corrosion and economy for labour and materials, are the dominating factors for all pool circulation installations. The Greeks used timber and terracotta, the Incas gold, the Romans silver and lead, and the Victorians copper and cast iron for their pool water circulation lines and fittings. Today's pool 'plumber' uses plastic pipe and sometimes cast iron or asbestos-cement when large-bore plastic fittings are difficult to get. Large-bore systems in plastic also provide strength and easy fixing plus excellent durability.

Pool pipework is a low pressure, low temperature recirculation system, but where extremes are involved – below freezing and above 40°C – special plastic grades will be required. Most pool systems try to standardise between 25 and 100mm lines with their relevant fittings, keeping larger diameter bores and their more costly fittings for main lines only.

For facings, panels, grilles, grids and drains, detailed specification is necessary. They must be tough and durable. They must not trap fingers nor toes, nor catch skin; they should not be adjustable by the swimmer, nor in anyway corrodible; main drain grilles especially must be designed never to allow excess suction, or to be removeable by swimmers. Maximum flow through a main drain grille can be 0.3m/s, but 0.2 or lower is better. There are still tragic accidents occurring with children drawn into the drain

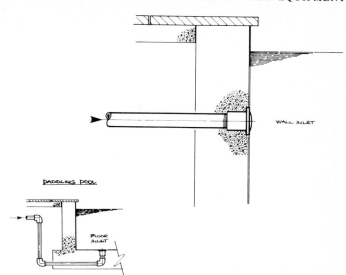

13.11 *Flow return inlet and pipetail*

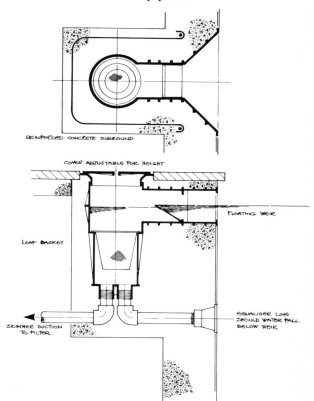

13.12 *Automatic skimmer weir with throat extension*

13.13 *Installing flexible deck level grating for a freeform pool*
Sorbo Leisure Surfaces Ltd, Manchester
Photo: Taylor Richardson Associates

193

pipeline, or sucked to the grille and drowned. Use only safety type drain grilles, or install a second drain (unvalved) to take the full flow should the first become blocked, or provide a large number of small outlets – vital for shallow pools.

Inlets and outlets, skimmers and overflows, offer diverse design arrangements to suit all circumstances and need to be professionally installed since most of the leaks occur around them.

13.7 Circulation systems

Many different circulation ideas have been with us for a long time – from direct to diffuse, high to low, fast to slow. Even the terra-cotta pipe sections in the palace of Knossos on Crete, between 1st and 2nd millennium BC, included their own patent shaping (reducing the diameter at short spaced intervals) to create a shooting movement to the flow of water to clear sediment from the joins. Ancient materials and pipes had to be carefully selected and laid, and a Roman conduit still serves the school pool at Sherborne Abbey; another example of early lead piping can be seen at the Roman Great Bath of Bath.

Channel Every pool system sets out to remove and return all poolwater efficiently, with the most polluted parts getting first priority. As 99 per cent of the pollution starts and stays for a while in the topmost millimetres of poolwater, very close attention must be directed that way. Early pools overflowed across a weir, or flooded over scum channels encouraged by the movement of bathers. In their recirculation systems, the main drain often carried 80 per cent water flow, but this gradually decreased to 50/50 share with surface draw-off. Today, the preference is to collect at least

13.14 *Surface water outlet for a stepped tiled gutter circulation system*
Villeroy & Boch, Saar

80 per cent from the water surface, and most of that from the shallows: some even prefer a 100 per cent water collection from surface overflow systems for their rapid water treatment.

Freeboard type public pools (those where you have to step down into the water) have been monopolised by perimeter gutters for a long time. These channels carry the dirtiest water away fast (providing outlets are not blocked), via a balance tank or surge channel to the filter; they also provide useful handholds all round the pool.

Skimmer Modern skimmer weirs, which monopolise private pool systems, are gradually making their way into the public sector for freeform shape pools. These suction units can be directional, draw-in surface water fast, and are not so critical on installation as with the perfect levelling necessary for gutters. The main advantage of skimmers is in their floating weir which adjusts to changing water level by as much as 100mm. And when it comes to saving costs, the skimmer weir positioned strategically in relation to inlet and outlet is favoured over all other systems. There are also portable skimmers, floating skimmers and special ladder skimmers for pools without pipework (see chapter 11.5).

Sufficient skimmers deal rapidly with surface pollution, but they fail to smooth out water turbulence or collect deck water, and can leave dead spots in the pool. In bad circulation, the same few litres are collected over and over again with corners and extremities ignored. Effective pool water circulation is three dimensional, requiring all round flow and suction.

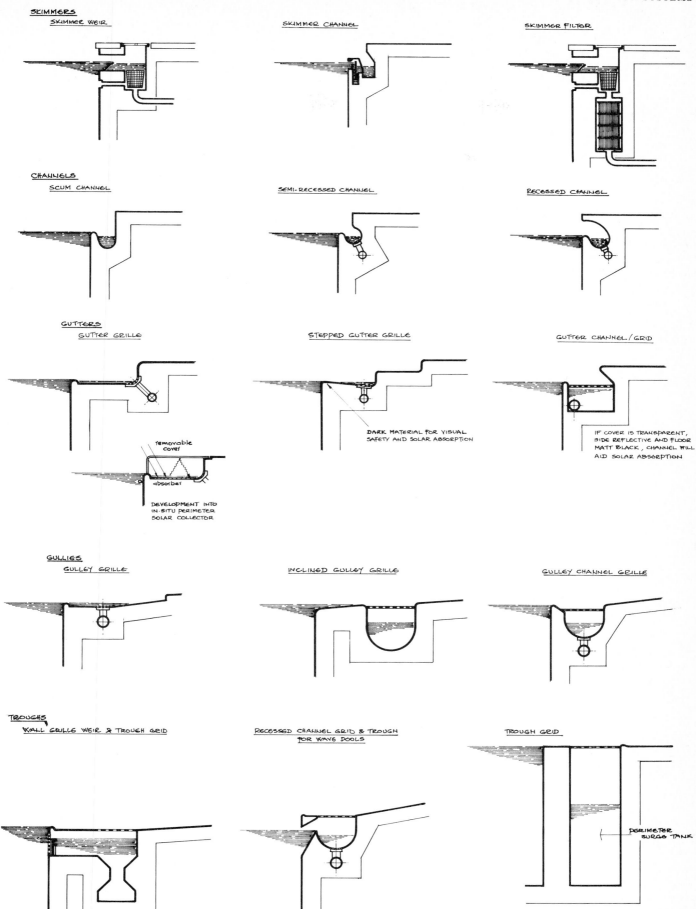

13.15 *Surface water outlet systems – freeboard and decklevel pools: skimmers, channels, gutters, gulleys and troughs*

A.) WALL INLETS

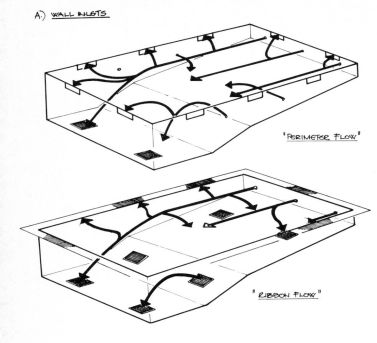

"PERIMETER FLOW"

"RIBBON FLOW"

B) FLOOR INLETS

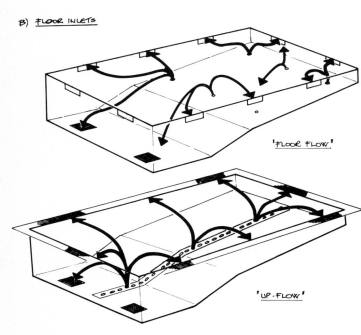

"FLOOR FLOW"

"UP-FLOW"

13.16 *Water circulation systems – wall and floor inlets: perimeter, ribbon, floor, up-flow*

A good circulation system must achieve effective mix of purified water and rapid removal of impure water – velocities, volumes and positioning require very careful design, which can still be varied to meet changing circumstances. *Deck level* Neither skimmers nor scum channels answer all the problems, but the deck level rimflow system that first originated in Canada can be most effective. There are many designs and shapes to receive and draw surface water fast, to collect deck water, and to provide hand holds. Deck level or flood level systems require less excavation for the pool, tank, and moreover, make it very much easier for swimmers to get into and out of the water. They have been instrumental in improving competitive swimming performances by helping to calm surface water turbulence, and

now they are frequently specified for international class pools throughout the world.

Deck level systems for public or semi-public pools have helped change the traditional image of the swimming tank into the leisure pool, for like skimmer weirs, this circulation system can cope with any shape of pool in skimming the entire surface.

Every level of system must offer total circulation (even above-ground pools need high and low suction), with flow returns arranged to drive water towards collection points. Some patent systems offer distinct advantages with adjustable flows, V-notch levellers in deck overflow tiling, or self-balancing surge channels. Only an all-round pool circulation with ample inlets/outlets provides the total guarantee for effective water turnover essential today.

13.8 Electrics and controls

Water and electricity do not mix. The current needed to light a 10 Watt Christmas bulb can easily kill a healthy adult in water.

The electrical network for a pool must be kept clear of water, and a suitable safety system provided. In the introduction to the 1973 American *Swimming Pool Wiring* code the analogy to the bird sitting safely upon a high voltage wire is made. The bird gets no shock while perching on the wire since it does not lead or ground the thousands of volts to earth. 'Shock occurs not from voltage, but from differences in voltage.'[3] Therefore, if every single item of metal, or electrical conductor, within the swimming pool is tied together, just like one wire, electrical shock through difference in voltage can be avoided. 'Anyone within the swimming pool environment will be at the same voltage as the pool.'[4]

The perimeter earthing method can balance electrical potential, but nevertheless every electrical device or outlet by the pool, or in the plantroom, must still be rapidly cut off from main supply should an electrical leak occur. Earth leakage breakers (ELB) or ground fault circuit interruptors (GFCI), to be safe, should operate within 75 millisecs, and cut out on currents leaking over 30 milliamps. Electrical supply sockets should be so protected and set at least 3m away from the pool.

Electrical devices such as water cooled underwater lights or electrically powered mobile underwater sweepers, whether on mains supply or transformed low voltage, must operate and fail safely. Providing well-established rules and regulations are all obeyed, protected electrical equipment can be used with complete safety around swimming pools. But always take into consideration the very nature of any safety line – the earth wire with the supply cable. It can actually introduce a hazard in the swimming pool situation because it might be at a small potential of a few volts above true earth. 'To ensure that the earthing circuit will be reliable it is connected to the "neutral" of the supply system at every installation,'[5] when zero impedance can be guaranteed.

Most filtration units require starter switch operation to take up the initial surge. The private pool time clock should only be installed with self-priming pumps, providing there is no interference to other essential equipment fed by the main pump. Standard control panels are generally available for the small pool with usual connections to filter,

13.17 *Automated control for a municipal pool in Hampstead*
Architect: Sir Basil Spence
Elliot Automation Ltd, London

chlorinator, heater and lighting. But the uniqueness of most large pool installations invariably requires a control console individually designed to suit each non-stop modern water filtration and circulation system.

References

[1] Saub Kaule, UN Conference on Water, Mar del Plata, March/1977
[2] Morris Hicky Morgan (trans), *Vitruvius: the ten books of architecture*, 1960
[3] NSPI, *Swimming Pool Wiring*, May/1973
[4] ibid.
[5] Scanalec, *Electrical Safety in Pools is No Accident*, CASPA, May/1976

INFORMATION SHEET 13.1

Water use
Per person per day

Litres	Location
1	average garden swimming pool per m²
30	average modern public swimming pool per m²
50	'consumption' western world at the turn of the century
250	London 1977
500	Paris 1977
600	Moscow 1977
1000	New York 1977
	and total demand is expected to be doubled by the end of the century
1500	Rome 52AD
	and delivered through 220 miles of aqueduct with only 30 miles built above ground.

INFORMATION SHEET 13.2

Plantroom sequence – closed circuit

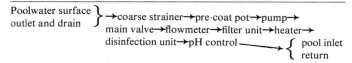

Poolwater surface outlet and drain } →coarse strainer→pre-coat pot→pump→ main valve→flowmeter→filter unit→heater→ disinfection unit→pH control ——— { pool inlet / return

INFORMATION SHEET 13.3

Progressive dirt dilution of poolwater

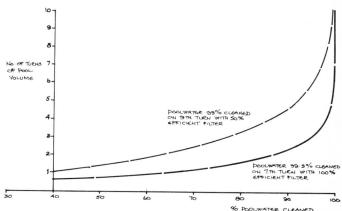

Progressive dilution of poolwater: throughput measured as number of times equivalent pool capacity handled by an efficient and semi-efficient filter, when there is no continual pollution (ie pool at rest overnight), and resulting in a satisfactory water clarity (0·5 JTU or mg/l turbidity)

INFORMATION SHEET 13.4

Filtration conversions and types

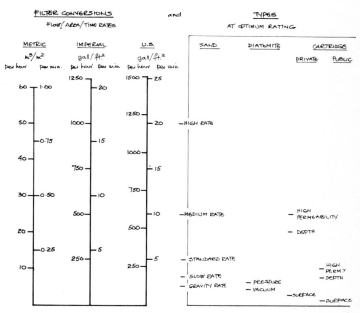

Filter conversions, (flow/area/time rates) and types at optimum rating

INFORMATION SHEET 13.5

Filter popularity
An indication of preference for pool filtration systems in USA

	Residential pools	Non-residential pools
Sand: standard rate	5%	5%
high rate	45%	50%
Diatomite: vacuum	—	15%
pressure	40%	25%
Cartridge	10%	5%
	100%	100%
Systems using skimmer weir overflow circulation	85%	70%

Source: SPW/A Swimming pool industry market reports.
See Guide to plantroom floor area: information sheet 13.8.

INFORMATION SHEET 13.6

Filtration systems

The main task of the filter is to remove inorganic particles from suspension: chemical treatment neutralises organic impurities and destroys soluble materials.

Fill and empty   **Rate: Weekly**
                                           Result: Fresh water

When water becomes turbid it is drained away, the pool flushed and refilled: this practice is unhygienic and wasteful, but very many small garden pools still survive summer months this way. Public pool authorities and swimmers no longer tolerate such deteriorating conditions, and the continuous closed circuit has almost universally replaced the weekly washdown.

Continuous flow   **Rate: Continual**
                                           Result: Natural water

Practical where clean and where warm water is abundantly available, ie with thermal waters in New Zealand, Iceland, Germany; but filtration is often still required for clarification, and continual disinfection for hygienic conditions. Natural waters from rivers and lakes are often used, though they are rarely satisfactory all the year for turbidity and warmth.

Gravity rate sand or Gravity flow   **Rate: 5m³/m²/h**
                                           Result: 40 micron

Early filters in the 19th century used 1m sand on gravel in brick basins – when slimy, top layers were dug out by hand. Sand filters developed into large, open vessels to deal with particulate matter visible to the eye; 1 to 2mm grade sand beds last 10 to 15 years with normal care.

Slow rate sand or Pressure sand and   **Result: 7·5m³/m²/h**
gravel or Anthracite   **Result: 20 micron or better**
                                           with alum

Large, horizontal open or pressure vessels designed to contain graded sands and gravels for long reliable filter runs. Sand bed free from clay and any soluble matter. Access to bed required and pressure vessels tested to twice working pressure at least. They offer simple operation and long term reliability, but are expensive on heated, disinfected wash water or fresh water unless holding tanks are provided. Backwashing is at 3 to 5 times flow velocity for up to 10 minute cleanse cycles, plus air scouring and/or mechanical agitation.

Standard rate sand or Rapid rate or   **Rate: 12·5m³/m²/h**
conventional Pressure sand   **Result: 5 to 10 micron or**
                                           sub-micron with alum

To reduce the size of sand units, the slow rate filter design was uprated by at least 50 per cent, and the bed deepened taking care to avoid channelling, excessive water pressure, uneven distribution or calcification.

Pressure tanks are 2 to 3m in diameter and range from 2m in height when termed vertical, to 10m in length when horizontal. Vertical tanks usually suit 500 to 2000m³ capacity pools, and horizontal tanks cover 2000 to 4000m³ schemes. Ideal for continuously operating public pools. Standard rate sand beds comprise:

layers of alum coagulant of pH control material

450mm 0·5–1·5mm	fine sand ⎫	filter media
150mm 1–3mm	coarse sand ⎭	
150mm 5–10mm	gravel ⎫	supporting media
150mm 10–20mm	pebble ⎭	

The wash water can be halved per m³ of filter media, but still requires storage at 2 to 200m³ capacity, since 5-minute cleanse cycles can dispose of large quantities of water. Backwashing is usual at 2 to 4 times flow velocity, plus air or mechanical scouring after 0·3 to 0·5kg/cm² increased pressure over clean running.

Medium rate sand or Deep bed sand   **Rate: 25m³/m²/h**
                                           Result: 5 to 10 micron

Filter rate is double the standard, and bed depth increased to 1·5m with finer fines of 0·5 to 1mm grains reducing overall volume of the tank and the waste water. Pool turnover ratings are often upgraded from 4 to 3, even 2¹/₂ hour on public pools as a safety factor on the question of efficiency, and reserve capacity of these units. Design ratings vary from 20 to 40m³/m²/h. This filtration improves in performance as the bed ripens, but it requires regular cleansing to prevent caking. The backwashing cycle might still involve some agitation, but time is reduced to 3 to 5 minutes at normal flow rate.

High rate sand or High speed sand   **Rate: 50m³/m²/h**
or Permanent media   **Result: 10 micron**

Ideally, smaller pools require smaller filters, hence this fast flow for a compact pressure vessel. Maximum rate of 60m³/m²/h is not acceptable by many standards authorities. Used mainly as single unit installations, but banks are suitable for larger pools providing multiples are not excessive. Tank diameters from 0·5 to 1·5m diameter for a 50 per cent deeper bed over standard, give in depth filtration without channelling, banking or mudballing. Small filters average 0·5m depth beds of even grade sand 0·3 to 0·5mm grain, uniformity coefficient 1·5, with 0·3m water freeboard above the sand: larger units reach 1m depth maximum. Tested to 2 or 3 times working pressure; higher for US semi-public pool standards at 4 times surge pressure. These popular filters save space, maintenance, installation and running costs, and are very versatile and easy to operate. They offer shorter working runs, and 2 to 3 minute backwashing cycles at normal flow rate reducing waste water to a minimum: backwashing pressure averages from 0·7 to 1·0kg/cm² increase on clean running. Their dirt-carrying capacity is limited by their size, but future filter media improvements, such as hydro-anthracite, will help considerably.

Pressure diatomite or pre-coat   **Rate: 5 to 10m³/m²/h**
                                           Result: 1 to 5 micron

This most efficient and effective system uses surface area filtration rate principles, with microscopically fine porous 1 to 2mm deep coatings of siliceous earth, or volcanic ash over septae or plates or candles. The large surface area within a very compact space offers filter sizes comparable to high rate sand – unit volume for volume. Single cell micro-marine diatoms, similar to algae, are mined from fossilised skeleton-form deposits, and enable the maximum possible finest filter area to be achieved, so that even moorland stains can be removed from water.

This system requires a dry media feed or slurry pot or skimmer feed of diatomaceous earth at 0·75kg/m² septum area: a continuous slurry feed allows a 50 per cent design flow rating increase to the filter, but there will be more media and energy consumed at increased pump pressure. Regenerative systems (popular in France, Netherlands and USA), or spin-type grids with water jets, or bump-down dislodgement, periodically break the cake to lengthen working cycles from 2 weeks to 2 months. Backwashing lasts 2 to 3 minutes, at normal filter flow rate after the operating pressure has increased approx 1·5kg/cm² maximum; on reverse flow the waste water can be reclaimed from a settlement tank with separating screen to trap the media. Pool disinfection is reduced by the filter's partial removal of bacteria and organic substances (see information sheet 15.6).

Vacuum diatomite   **Rate: 4m³/m²/h**
                                           Result: 1 to 5 micron

An open tank contains plates or leaves of septae to retain a diatomaceous earth coating under suction. 8 × 1·5 × 2m deep tanks for 300m² filter area need only to withstand the weight of water contained and a crushing pressure to 100mm of mercury – a 3 or 4 fold safety margin. These filters, made from simple, lightweight, corrosion-proof materials, are inexpensive to install, open to inspection all the time, easily cleaned and infrequently maintained, incurring low power costs for superb polish results. They are most practical for large international pool complexes. Low suction reduces DE cake compaction allowing long runs of up to 100 days. Claims are made that turnover can be lowered by 50 per cent, and the very high performance also reduces nitrogenous matter, most bacteria and algae, requiring only low residual chlorination for support purification. Backwashing is negligible, since it takes just 20 minutes to sluice out all the media for the loss of only 1 tankful of water.

Cartridge units

Rate:
surface type 1 to 2·5$m^3/m^2/h$
depth type 7·5 to 20$m^3/m^2/h$
high permeability 10 to
25$m^3/m^2/h$
Result: 5 to 25 micron

A porous surface membrane is used through which water passes and collects contaminents until completely clogged. Some filter cartridges or pads are disposable and expensive: others are easily cleaned and economical. They are made from high compact paper, or from synthetic porous membranes of cellulose acetate with a phenolic binder, giving filter runs of around 100 days. Thin cartridge material (up to 20mm) relies upon surface retention of dirt; thicker materials absorb particles into the cartridge; some recleanable systems use a mechanically interlocked, nonwoven fabric. Units must be easily accessible, and more often than not adopt the average maximum flow rate of 10$m^3/m^2/h$ to avoid special restructural design to resist collapse. This compact and very economical filter is preferred for above-ground pools, but too often is undersized on permanent schemes. No backwashing is necessary since cartridges are hosed down for cleaning.

Specials
(comprising osmotic, carbon, silver
candle, ion exchange, superconductive,
high biology, polygranular type filters)

Rate: variable
Result: 1 to 10 micron

For example, under osmotic pressure polluted water is exchanged for fresh water through a permeable membrane.
Carbon filtration removes colour and stain from water. Anthracite is half density of sand; angular grains to 2mm reduce backwashing times and save waste water.
Silver impregnated filter candles remove particles, and the water is disinfected at the same time.
Multilayer mixed media beds (eg anthracite, sand and garnet at 25$m^3/m^2/h$) offer long term quality filter runs with improvement to water clarity over plain sand.
A main long-term objective of development filtration systems is to carry out economical disinfection, or complete and balanced purification at the same time (see chapter 15.2 and 5).

INFORMATION SHEET 13.8

Guide to plantroom floor area
(Filter units requirement in m²)

Filter system only	Floor area m² Pool capacity (m³)				
	100	250	500	1000	2000
Reusable DE	5	10	15	20	30
High rate sand	7	12	20	30	45
Standard rate sand	20	30	45	60	90

See chapter 11.4.

INFORMATION SHEET 13.9

The filter

Contends with:
- particulate matter – suspended and colloidal
- debris and dirt
- street soil
- hair
- grease and oil
- air pollutants
- potions from bodies
- traces of faecal material and urine
- scaly skin
- sweat, saliva and mucus.

Effective pre-hygiene standards will save considerably on filtration stress.

Comprises:
The tank: which contains internals of filter media over a septum (separating frame), or the filter bed between spreader (delivering water and receiving backwash flow) and the underdrain (retaining media/dirt and returning water to pool). No galvanised vessels or dissimilar metals should be used avoiding electrolytic action – alternatively provide a sacrificial corrosion node. Also provide access to media, self-sealing lid or manhole; air release valve and pressure gauge/s.
The pump and motor: producing motive power provided with electrical safety cut-out or thermal overload switch; a pre-pump strainer. A rate of flow indicator is also useful.
The control valve: organising direction of water flow; arranging backwashing with a sight glass to assess the state of purged water.
All materials must be compatible, non-toxic and non-corrosive, such as plastic or GRP, stainless steel (types 304 or 316), bronze or coated steel.

INFORMATION SHEET 13.7

Relative filter sizes

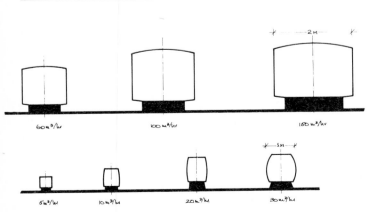

Filter sizes from 5 m³/h to 150 m³/h

INFORMATION SHEET 13.10

Relative prices – filtration units
(Approximate guide only)

Equipment is costed as a factor of 100, based upon spare pump
for 10m^3/h filter = 100 (cost factor)

m³/h ratings from information sheet 13.7 Filtration @	5	10	20	30	60	100	150m³/h
Installation		50		200		50–1500	
Spare pump		100		250		1000	
High rate sand	150	300	600	850	2500	5000	7000
Standard rate sand		–		3000		9000	
Cartridge		200		1000		4000	
DE: vacuum		350		700		3500	
pressure		500		1200		6000	
Suitable for:							
private pool of		75m³		250m³		–	
public pool of		10m³		100m³		400m³	

See information sheets 2.18, 7.6, 8.2, 14.19 and 15.12 for equipment relative prices.

INFORMATION SHEET 13.11

Basic turnover ratings for different pools

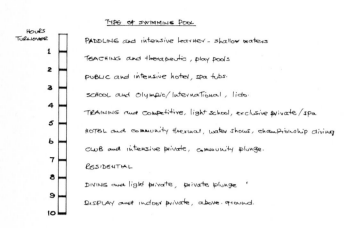

Basic turnover ratings: intensively used pools require a far higher turnover than rarely used or decorative pools

INFORMATION SHEET 13.12

Turnover formulae for pool filtration

Poolwater clarification at peak load conditions depends upon a filtration system meeting the rate of progressive pollution, which involves:

● the type of pool: its environment, indoor or outdoor, town or country;

● the water: area and volume, temperature and pH, soluble salts and chemical treatment; disinfection rates;

● the filter performance: its capacity and degree of filtration, flow rate and area, media and grade, the filter condition;

● the circulation efficiency: inlet and outlet positions, head loss in system and pump rating;

● the bathing load: the number of bathers and their distribution;

● personal hygiene standards: pre-cleanse facilities and even the wealth and the capability of the pool owner.

So many variables make calculations complex and unreal. Hence, turnover is best taken as a practical guide to optimum poolwater purification at different conditions, and it is based upon how often the whole water needs to be filtered: see information sheet 13.11.

1   Basic turnover with filter at clean running pressure and full working head:

$$\text{Turnover in hours} = \frac{\text{Pool capacity m}^3}{\text{Filter rating m}^3/\text{h}}$$

See information sheet 13.11 for applicable pool.

2   Density/turnover
(based upon NSPI formula)

$$\frac{\text{Total daily bathing load}}{\text{Pool capacity m}^3} = \text{Bathing density per m}^3 \text{ per day}$$

Bather density – number of people per volume in a given time

Turnover rating – number of hours to circulate the pool volume through filtration system

1	m³/day	requires an	8 hour turnover
2–3	m³/day	requires a	6 hour turnover
4–7	m³/day	requires a	4 hour turnover
8–11	m³/day	requires a	2 hour turnover
12–17	m³/day	requires a	1 hour turnover
18–25	m³/day	requires a	½ hour turnover

INFORMATION SHEET 13.13

Flow velocity formula for pool pipelines

$$\frac{\text{Water flow velocity m/sec}}{\text{in pool pipeline}} = \frac{\text{Pump flow m}^3/\text{min}}{50 \times \text{pipe diameter m}^2}$$

$$\frac{\text{Filter flow}}{\text{m}^3/\text{h}} = \frac{\text{Total water circulation rate}}{\text{m}^3/\text{h}} = \frac{\text{Poolwater volume m}^3}{\text{Pool turnover period h}}$$

INFORMATION SHEET 13.14

Turbidity — the scatter of light

Simple measurement of poolwater clarity used to be 'can you see the bottom', or perhaps, the placing of an extra attendant at the deep end to count the divers coming up when the water became too turbid, or too muddy.

Visual impression Common practice today requires that if a 50mm quartered red and white disc at the deepest point cannot be distinguished after 1 hour at full load conditions, then the filtration is inadequate and the pool no longer safe. Or, in a garden pool, if heads or tails of a small coin cannot be distinguished, the water is too murky. A more measurable alternative, requires a 150mm black target to be moved away gradually from an underwater 'viewing tube' periscope, until water turbidity makes the disc invisible to the viewer. The 'metres-seen-through' is the measure of pool water cloudiness: at 10m a tinge turbidity can just be recognised and the pool is suitable, or safe; but a 15m minimum clarity is preferred and safer.

Scientific measurement Poolwater containing finely dispersed solids (suspended or colloidal as small as 10 millimicrons) appears cloudy. A beam of light passing through is weakened by being scattered in all directions by the particles, which affect turbidity according to their size, shape, colour and refractive index.

Turbidity is the weakening measure of this light beam (absorption). A satisfactory turbidity level in a public pool should not exceed 1·0 Jackson Turbidity Units (JTUs), or the ppm SiO_2 equivalent (1ppm = 1JTU = 1mg SiO_2 per litre distilled water). Following peak bathing load conditions, it is considered the pool circulation system should be capable of returning the water to 0·5 JTUs within 8 hours (Swiss Standard 0·25ppm).

Turbidity and absorption photometer instruments are suitable for poolwater clarity measurement when scales range from 0 to 20ppm.

0·1 JTU is exceptional

0·3 JTU is good

0·5 JTU is acceptable

1·0 JTU is poor.

NB United States Public Health Service drinking water standard accepts 5 to 7 micron.

Sources: NSF, NSPI, Sigrist.

INFORMATION SHEET 13.15

Typical performance curves for pool pumps

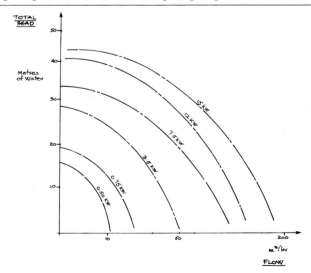

Performances of pool pumps

INFORMATION SHEET 13.16

Pump requirements

Maximum shut-off head:
residential pools 3·5kg/cm² approx
public pools 5·0kg/cm² approx

Performance design to consider:
● Matching flows to provide required filtration and backwashing flows.
● Effective suction head – suction lift is reduced by 1m approx for every 1000m altitude.
● Location to water level and proximity to pool: pump best situated just below water level, but isolated for flood conditions. Typical range for residential pools: +0·5m to −1·5m at 12m distance for 0·75kW pump, using 40mm pipelines with 25 bends and 10m³/h filter flow rate; outside these parameters expected performance loss will exceed the normal one-third.
Maximum lift: residential pools +2m, large pools +4m.
● Pipe sizes and flow rate velocities for total friction losses of the whole system: with direct lines and airtight joints: avoid backpressure by increasing the pipebore and inlet sizes (see information sheets 13.17 to 19).
● Optimum performance – pump is weakest on suction side, therefore ensure shortest possible suction run. Set on anti-vibration base, protect from splashes, keep cool for longer lasting motors, even though most pool pumps are designed to run hot.
Self-priming; easily removable motor and rotor assembly with easy attention to seal and impeller is important.

	Variable speed hi/low switch	100% high	25% low	
Power saving with				
Residential	for	summer	winter	use
Public	for	day	night (not after peak loads)	use

● Motor loadings and to include thermal overload switch: damp-proofing and good dry air circulation: 3-phase supply over 1kW: full voltage supply wire.
● Special conditions such as saltwater which requires gunmetal or bronze units, or unusual electrical supplies that call for, say 120V 60 cycle.
● Spare capacity with 2 × 60 per cent duty pumps being better than 1 at 100 per cent: test to 1½ times working pressure at least.
● Large coarse strainer – hole area 4 to 10 times larger than supply pipe.

INFORMATION SHEET 13.17

Pipework data

Use full flow valves and large inlets.
Bends are better than elbows; swept tees better than sharp junctions.
Valves in bronze, gunmetal, stainless steel and stressed plastics.
Fittings in chrome plated brass, stainless steel, aluminium alloy, GRP and stressed plastics.
● Provide flexible pipe connections at the pump, which is set on soundproof vibration pads to reduce the transmission of machinery hum. Pipe fitting couplings, or flanges, at equipment should be easily disconnected for servicing of plant.
● Consider expansion and contraction allowances up to 30°C, noting iron to plastic loosens at joints due to differential expansion, but with uPVC systems there are usually sufficient changes in pipe direction for small variations in length to be taken up by flexibility of the pipe. Softer plastics can give and take on freezing and thawing, but still need impact protection. Coefficient of linear expansion 0·08mm per m per °C. uPVC is thermoplastic and pool pipe grades at 40°C lose around ⅓ of their pressure rating.
● Solvent jointing and 24 hour setting is favoured for simplicity and savings. Solvent jointing, which is so often inadequately handled, requires only a simple procedure, but carried out with great care:
1 Lay up dry – cut pipe square-on.
2 Chamfer outer edge of cut pipe.
3 Roughen joint surfaces of pipe and fitting – test fit.
4 Degrease surfaces with cleaning fluid.
5 Brush apply adhesive cement to both surfaces – twice.

6 Push-fit immediately, twist quarter turn, hold ten seconds then wipe off surplus cement.
7 Handle carefully after 5 minutes.
Solvent cement/fluid is highly inflammable and should only be used in well ventilated conditions.
● Mechanical joints in plastic require tapered threads plus boss white and hemp, or the far easier PTFE (polytetrafluoroethylene) tape winding, or the use of expensive metal compression type fittings on flexible pipework.
● Pool plumbing involves a low pressure, low temperature system. After 24 hours, pipelines can be tested to 1½ times shut-off head of the pump, and held for 30 minutes usually around 3·5kg/cm² operating pressure.
● Do not lay pipes in made-up ground unless consolidated, or firmly secured in order to prevent sag in long horizontal runs.

Maximum flow rates

Copper and copper based alloys	— 2m/s	never use with saltwater
uPVC (class C or D unplasticised polyvinyl chloride), ABS (class T acrylonitrile butadiene styrene), polythene, polypropylene, alkathene, etc	— 3m/s	freshwater or saltwater (branded manufacture)
Black iron, galvanised steel	— 4m/s	not recommended for pool use
Nickel bearing alloys, stainless steel, naval bronze	— 5m/s	saltwater

INFORMATION SHEET 13.18

Flowrates – pipelines and grilles

Water to waste:

	Pipe diameter	Gradient	
Residential	50mm	1:50	allows for filter flow 5m³/h–20m³/h
Public	200mm	1:200	allows for filter flow 50m³/h–200m³/h

Recirculation:

Pipe diameter	Flowmeter measurement		Optimum pipeline flow deliveries		
	Minimum	Maximum	Sump suction @ 0·3m/s velocity	Suction @ 1·25m/s velocity	Return @ 2·5m/s velocity
mm	m³/h	m³/h	m³/h	m³/h	m³/h
25	1·5	6	0·5	2·2	4·4
40	4	16	1·3	5·5	11
50	6	25	2·1	9	18
75	15	60	4·7	20	40
100	30	120	8·5	36	72
150	60	250	19	80	160
200	110	450	34	140	280
250	200	800	53	220	440
300	300	1200	76	320	640

Rate of flow indicators should cover design range of filtration to include backwashing rate +10%

Grille velocities:		Sumps m/s	Inlets m/s
Public:	slow	0·1–0·2	0·5 –1·00
	fast	0·2–0·3	1·25–2·5
Private		0·2–0·5	0·3 –1·25

INFORMATION SHEET 13.19

Pipeflow characteristics
Plastic pipe to BS3505

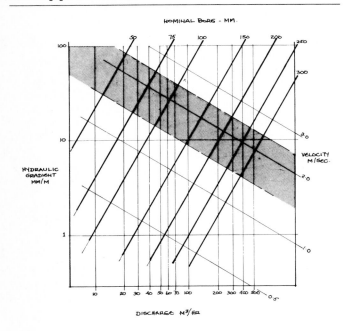

NOMINAL BORE - MM.

HYDRAULIC GRADIENT MM/M

VELOCITY M/SEC.

DISCHARGE M³/HR

INFORMATION SHEET 13.20

Circulation components

Pool filler must not project hazardously, nor permit cross contamination to mains water supply. Best situated with 50mm maximum spout beneath a diving board, and set 150mm above water line for a safe airgap to prevent reverse flow or back siphoning of poolwater into the mains. Automatic top-up arrangements are sometimes included with special skimmer weir systems. The German pool practice introduces a 5 per cent water make-up per day for improved water purity.

Inlet, spreader or return (flow) grille must have large enough aperture (4 times pipe area) to prevent backpressure onto filter: adjustable or eyeball or spa inlets are used for directional currents in freeform pools, but can place a heavy burden against filter flow. Hydrotherapy inlets introduce a 10 to 15mm diameter air line into their water stream for turbulent, bubbling spring-like appearance and spa massage. Public pool inlet diffusers spread return water to the side, up and down to mix with all shallow-end levels. Various dramatic effects can be used to return filtered water into the pool through gargoyles, spouts and cascades. High level inlets help push surface debris to skimming system, whilst low level inlets improve heat circulation: best arrangement is a mixture of floor, wall level and wall downward flow returns. Set wall grilles 0·4m below water surface though some designers prefer 0·2m above floor level.

Smaller pools require 1 inlet per 50m² area or 70m³ water.

Pools over 150m² or over 10m width, or 20m length, require 1 inlet per 5m perimeter equivalent.

Flow velocities: private pools 0·3–1·25m/s
public pools 0·5–1·0m/s slow, 1·25–2·5m/s fast.

Outlet, sump or drain (suction) The main drain is always situated at the lowest point in a pool: hydrostatic relief valves should be located separately, not within a drain sump. There must be no direct connections to sewers, and gravity drain or backwash lines require an air gap, or other means, to prevent possible backflow. Preferably organise 10 per cent of flow to filter through the main drain. Securely fixed cover grilles must not create dangerous suction for bathers. Aperture should be at least 4 times outlet pipework area. Maximum 10mm slots with maximum grille flow velocity 0·5m/s are much preferred on larger pools. Lower velocities are better with gratings at 6 to 10 times pipe area always recommended, eg:

0·3 × 0·3m grille for 45m³/h
0·6 × 0·3m grille for 90m³/h   } 0·2m/s flow rating
0·6 × 0·6m grille for 180m³/h

If only one main drain outlet is installed, an anti-vortex disc should be used, or the grille area should be big enough to prevent blocking by a bather; this is particularly important for spa pools where a high rate turn-over for a very small volume is involved. An alternative is the installation of vacuum sensing apparatus that cuts-out the pump when partial closing of the drain occurs: but, in practice, two drain outlets are better, or a suction equaliser as for spa pools. Average private pool drains are 150 to 200mm diameter outlets on 50mm diameter pipe. Pools over 10m width require more than one main drain located at maximum 5m intervals. Any pool without main drain outlets requires directional flow inlets set to overcome dead water areas.

Overflows: channels, gutters, gullies, troughs. Every system attempts to deal rapidly with surface pollution, when at least 50 per cent of the pool perimeter should be served by a continuous type overflow arrangement. In order to cope with changing bathing loads, a surge tank with satisfactory means of pool return flow, will be required for all fixed edge surface drainage. An average bather displaces 100 litres and suitable surge tank capacities are:

maximum 50 litres/m² pool area normal bathing,
maximum 100 litres/m² pool area heavy bathing.

Tough moulded ceramics offer wide selection, but profiles must not trap debris or bathers, and must be easily cleaned and inspected. Outlet grilles spaced every 3 or 4m must be tamper-proof, but still removable for cleaning and clearing blockages. Perimeter overflow systems are usually recommended, or required for pools over 150m² to deal with 60 to 80 per cent of the water to the filter. Conventional overflow channels offer only 10 per cent surface water collection and continental countries specify minimum surface draw-off of 30 per cent.

Surface skimmers: automatic floating weirs. This directional system is used almost exclusively for private pools, and increasingly for public schemes. Skimmers are individually adjustable for flow and level (up to 100mm) and matched to main drains for multiple installations. An 80 per cent skimmer flow is required to the filter, with shut-off valving for multiple skimmer unit suction sweeping arrangements. An equaliser line to the suction line is set 300mm beneath the floating weir to prevent the unit drawing in air should the surface water level fall below the main aperture. A coarse strainer basket in the main housing prevents leaves and debris being taken to the pump; the floating weir speeds the flow of water over a lip, increasing skimming action across a wider front (from 200mm throat); cover lid must be securely fitted for public pools.

Skimmers face the main drift from inlets, and prevailing wind outdoors. Multiple units should be spaced at no more than 10m intervals (not within 3m of corners) and each skimmer will deal with flows from between 6 to 10m³/h. Some authorities regulate against skimmers, especially for larger pools, but these rules are not always enforced.

Private pools require 1 skimmer per 50 to 70m² water area. Public pools over 150m² require 1 skimmer per 40m² water area.

Cycolac plastic, aluminium alloy or GRP materials are ideal for this continual overflow device. It has even been developed into a complete cartridge filtration system in the wall for smaller pools.

Suction points, vacuum sweeper point, an alternative to the skimmer suction line for underwater sweeper units. To avoid continually having to adjust multi-skimmer flow rates for suction sweeping on large pools, several 40 or 50mm diameter wall points are set 150mm below the surface, and away from corners. They allow floating flexible vacuum hose (10 to 20m lengths) to be plugged in for pool cleaning. Suction points are valved preferably at poolside, rather than in plantroom.

INFORMATION SHEET 13.21

Circulation systems

Removal of water pollutants must be rapid, even and continuous, leaving no dead-pockets. To ensure total and balanced circulation, inlets, overflows and outlets all require adjustable control valves.

As swimmers enter or leave the pool, the circulation system must cope with the displacement of water surge by one of two methods:
● lowering/raising overflow channels – floating weirs being most practical
● lowering/raising water levels – but wall grating overflows can carry surplus to and from holding tanks.

Recovery is important for conservation of water, chemicals and heat.

Overflows

Channel/gutter/trough to take 60 to 80 per cent of water to filter. Effective all round systems cream-off worst pollution such as grease which lies on the skin of surface tension. Channels are difficult to lay evenly and to great accuracy; just a 2mm error becomes problematical. Also, a too low water level will stop the surface flow working, unless the surge tank tops up the pool, or some transverse notches are cut into the overflow channelling at 0·5m intervals to allow a continued overflow. Integral channels/troughs can also act as a holding or balance tank, and to prevent overflow loss to waste. Grilles from channels sometimes easily become blocked, unhygienic and difficult to clean. However, the channel overflow lip reduces turbulence and offers a valuable handhold, and is still the most popular public pool circulation system installed today.

Surface skimmer weir – ideally throttled down to carry 80 per cent water to filter (50 per cent minimum). Fails to reduce turbulence, and floating weirs 'flip-flop' characteristically in waves. Introduced in USA 1950 to reduce pool construction costs, to offer simpler installation and to provide directional suction.

Consider poolshape, prevailing wind direction, circulation patterns and draw-off area when locating each unit: they cannot collect deck water, they can leave dead spots and they do foul up in bad conditions. Sometimes they are advantageously included with channelling, to cope with up to 100 to 150 mm changes in water level.

Usual pool freeboards are:

residential 100–150mm ⎫
public 150–200mm ⎬ in tropics, ensure extra provision for heavy rainfall
on board ship 300–400mm ⎭

A ladder skimmer or a floating mobile skimmer is useful for certain private schemes (see chapter 11.5).

Deck level/rimflow/gulley to carry minimum 50 per cent water flow to filter/100 per cent better. Overflow set in the deck can include a surge trough plus ducting for air/water heat reclaim. Main advantages for deck level pools include:

- reduction of surface water turbulence and rebound, particularly useful for racing
- easy entry into water for children, beginners and disabled
- less excavation, fewer steps and ladders, and less tiling
- continual all round surface overflow for hygiene and purity
- no grease lines and the deck is continually washed
- coping area grilles can collect deck waters.

Disadvantages mean:

- when there is a slow gully run-off, deck-level channel becomes insufficient for drainage, and there will be wet feet
- a wide, wet deck surface area greatly increases evaporation and humidity
- there is need for clear coloured distinction of edging and top tiles, plus some lipping to replace loss of channel handgrip
- detergents cannot be used for deck cleaning
- deck level diving is awkward, and ends of pool require raised walling above water level for competitive swimming.

Inlet returns

A   Wall inlet circulation systems

Side wall flow to main drain and skimmers, or perimeter overflow or opposite side wall outlet. High inlets help surface clearance, and low inlets help heat distribution. Inlets aim to sweep pool broadly or in streams, concentrating upon heavy load areas. Best for shallow pools, if short circuiting can be avoided.

Large inlets/low flow (laminar even distribution) sweep towards deep drain point. Small inlets/high flow (turbulent rapid distribution) increase mixing to avoid dead spots.

End wall ribbon flow to main drain/overflow or opposite end wall outlet. Clearing shallow end to deep ensuring a continual supply of treated water at maximum pollution load area. An even, wide flow requires careful inlet positioning for corners. Surface clearance at 25 to 50 per cent flow to filter. Ribbon circulation is boosted with secondary in-flow from grilles set in the transition slope towards main drains.

B   Floor inlet circulation systems

Floor flow grilles to main drain and/or skimmers/overflow. Effective circulation from pool floor with the number of inlets increased for shallow, polluted parts. The better distribution of heated water from this system is increasingly favoured in North America, plus a shallow to deep end drift arrangement.

Up-flow centre strip or low wall inlets (0·2m above floor), with or without floating weirs. 100 per cent surface clearance removing greatest pollution in shortest possible time. Treated water rises along whole pool floor centre line with maximum rate allocated to shallow end. Sometimes additional end wall inlets with deep end main drains are included to offer lengthwise circulation as well.

INFORMATION SHEET 13.22

Notes on electrical requirements

The main hazard of electricity in poolwater is from drowning through loss of muscular control. Faulty pump motors offer a prime source of power leakage into a pool, and require the inclusion of earth trip devices, as well as overload cut-outs plus standard starter switches. Smaller loading private pool pumps that are wired to domestic supply without starters, especially require leakage breaker protection.

mA levels for electrical safety

All electrical equipment for the swimming pool environment should be protected by the high sensitivity earth leakage circuit breaker that operates to provide substantial protection against the effects of electric shock. It should trip-out at leakage currents exceeding 30 milliamps, or very occasionally as low as 15mA. It must operate at ±15 per cent voltage, from $-35°C$ to $+60°C$, and within 75 millisecs. Effects on people range from:

1mA – noticeable sensation
2mA – tingling
5mA – first signs of cramp
10mA – let go level
20mA – US code B safety level
30mA – severe cramp

40mA – irregular heart beat and increased blood pressure ⎫
50mA – loss of consciousness ⎬ danger levels
60mA – heart fibrillation, when a current for 1 second kills. ⎭

All electrical sockets should be situated over 3m from the pool and waterproofed, hoseproofed, wired underground, and protected by an ELCB (ground fault interrupter). The most dangerous appliances for a pool are portable lights, electric tools and radios. Never sling overhead wiring across pools. Single phase outlets tapped from three-phase supply should be balanced to keep current in return neutral wire to a minimum, essentially for hazardous locations to retain zero impedance. Majority of private pools are served sufficiently by single phase supplies.

Bonding ground conductor or pool perimeter earthing (American system). All metal used in the pool's structure, ladders, inlets, outlets, diving-boards, handrailing, underwater lighting (but not low voltage since an ELCB operates on the primary side of the transformer), staging equipment, etc, is earthed to a common bonding conductor. Protected grounding leads can be efficiently connected to the pool steel reinforcement within the concrete shell or floor, and earth leads taken from diagonally opposite ends of the pool floor, led behind pool walls up above water level, and tied to the all enveloping bonding ground conductor. When *all parts of the pool* are at the same earth potential, there can be no different electric field in the water. This electrical network does not apply to UK systems, since each electrical unit is separately and directly earthed to the mains incoming supply, and relies upon zero impedance in the earth wiring circuit, with the ELCB increasingly used as an additional safety device.

Low voltage lighting

Common systems are 12 or 24v and they should be wired to provide balanced lighting intensity for multiple units: two-core (US) armoured cable size is selected according to the distance and load involved, with the maximum permitted voltage drop at $2\frac{1}{2}$ per cent. Transformers made in protective casing should be double-wound with grounded metal screen between primary and secondary windings: also they should include allowance for adjustment of low voltage tappings up to a 50 per cent variation. UK and other systems employ 3 core, low voltage cables, returning from the underwater light incorporating the extra earthing wire, to a centre tapped earth point on the secondary winding within the transformer, and optionally safeguarded by an ELCB. A flush deckbox is filled with cold sealing compound around electrical joint and situated outside the pool coping, or 1·5m from pool edge (US) behind light unit.

Also provide for separate 6 to 12v emergency lighting system for enclosed pools (see chapter 10.11).

In all circumstances, the safest possible situation is when each circuit is double protected by its own ELCB or GFCI.

INFORMATION SHEET 13.23

Swimming pool electrics – simplified outline

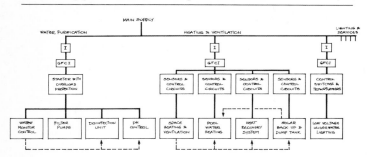

KEY
I — ISOLATOR
GFCI — GROUND FAULT CIRCUIT INTERRUPTOR
NB : ANY SOCKET OUTLET CLOSE TO THE POOL MUST
      BE PROTECTED BY A GFCI

INFORMATION SHEET 13.24

Outline electrics – component equipment

Water purification

main control panel comprising double pole main isolator and ELCB, indicator lamps and alarm plus ancillary equipment tappings, monitoring unit, filter pumps and starter/overload cut-out, disinfection system, pH control

Heating and ventilation

Poolwater heating
heater and pumping system
solar back-up
frost protection

Space heating
heater and pumping system
heat recovery units and heat pump
to dump tank back-up system

Ventilation and humidity
fans and humidifier
ozonator

Hot water services
heater and pumping system

Lighting and services

Water services
low voltage underwater lighting
underwater speaker units
moving booms ⎫
rising floors ⎬ specialised
wave machinery ⎭ industrial supply
mechanical pool covers

Ring main circuit
waterproofed socket outlets
vending machines
audio system
TV and sports requirements – 3-phase
sauna provision

Lighting circuit
main lighting system
emergency battery lighting
spot and flood lighting
impulse clocks
display console

Automatic control of chlorination and pH level by electro-chemistry reduces maintenance costs, saves chemicals and improves poolwater quality, sometimes by as much as 50 per cent on traditional techniques
Stranco, Illinois and Sussex

14 Heating and ventilation

A pool's environmental design for heat, light and sound, hygiene, humidity and fresh air must nowadays always relate to energy conservation.

14.1 The energy store

A swimming pool is a large energy store, where the least efficient system will leak heat like a radiator. The high specific heat of water (equivalent to 1·163 W/litre/°C) means that a small 25m public pool of 500m³ water volume raised in temperature by 20°C above winter ambient stores 11,630kWh of potential energy – enough to heat a well-insulated house for a whole winter. Such a mass of warm water, like a thermal flywheel, takes time and energy to overcome inertia in building up to working level. At full pace, it holds a huge amount of energy, and requires only small topping-up inputs to maintain momentum. Or the system can be run down, the hot house drained, and the store transferred elsewhere.

Skilfully designed swimming pools make ideal heat dumps, well able to store surplus energy for days and weeks at a time. Thermal engineering has now become a key technology in efficient pool design. To convert a bottomless heat sink into a useful energy warehouse takes about 20 per cent extra capital investment for better insulation, plus effective heat recovery to the pool environment, but with planned payback periods of between ten and twenty years.

Do not be lulled into overlooking the extent of the low temperature requirements for a pool; it is the quantity (amount) of heat that counts in costing, not the quality (temperature). Water temperature decays slowly, but a huge, low temperature heat bank can also take a long time to build up in the first place.

14.2 Temperature

Swimming pools are used far more when they are heated; approximately 10 per cent increased capital cost in heating equipment means the popularity and use of a pool can be doubled. Whether the heating system simply holds the daily temperature at a reasonable level, or extends the swimming season into winter, a basic heater must achieve the desired temperature in spite of the losses.

It is better to accumulate the whole store of heat in several stages, enabling heating units to be rated for topping-up, rather than grossed for the whole load, including that of the initial build-up. Obviously winter loading will be more than normal summer use, but less obviously, a fast heating rate can double the boiler rating required. As a guide, for every single degree rise in a pool's temperature, an extra 10 per cent heating energy output will be required.

Disabled bathers feel the cold more than active swimmers. Long immersion in cold water draws away six times more body heat than in air, and also reduces heart rates. Hyperthermia conditions can be dangerous, especially for small children who have a very limited store of body heat available: swimming in water under 20°C, they can lose 5°C body temperature in 45 minutes.

Consumption rates Pool heating loads depend upon many variables. For a very long time, the ideal rate to lift temperature has been quoted as *1°C rise per hour* ($\frac{1}{2}$°C is tolerable and even $\frac{1}{4}$°C is acceptable, if it can cope with initial build-up or extra top-up). When pool temperature losses exceed 2 or 3°C overnight, the faster make-up rates will be required. A heating rate of 15 BTU per gallon (now equalling 1kW/m³) is an ideal goal for cooler climates. Slow winter to summer natural heat build-up is practical for outdoor pools, providing sharp losses can be made up effectively and quickly.

14.1 *Training at 20° below in the open air pool in the grounds of the giant Luzhniki stadium in Moscow: the poolwater is heated*
Novosti Press Agency

205

14.2 *Geothermally heated poolwater shows that an outdoor pool is obviously best at Bad Harzburg, GFR*
Bad Harzburg Tourist Services
Photo: Herbert Ahrens

An uninsulated garden pool held at 25 °C for summer heating alone can consume 1000kWh/m² of energy; an average 25m public pool might get through at least 10,000kWh/m² for the whole year. Ordinary insulation and simple heat recovery methods can soon cut these colossal consumption rates. Super insulated energy recycling 25m community pools in Germany have already shown more reasonable prime energy use at 2500kWh/m²; similarly, well-protected private pools in Scandinavia also show as much as 75 per cent energy savings. Such figures mark only the beginning of changing the pool's *consumption* of energy into a potential *surplus*.

Cooling or extra heat A few fortunate places in the world are more concerned with cooling problems than with heating. With the sea temperature in the Persian Gulf reaching 33 °C in the summer, poolwater can become too hot for comfort. But it is easier to lose heat than to gain it: the traditional garden fountain playing or water sprayed onto paving cools the air and surroundings, losing heat *and* water by evaporation. A deep, shaded pool keeps cooler than a shallow one. A solar heater working at night will lower water temperature. A refrigeration pump can be designed to cool pools in summer, and to warm them in winter. Or the cooling circuit of a poolhall designed to daytime heat can be reversed to a heating phase at night.

14.3 Alternative technology and ambient energy
Half of all energy used in the western world is soaked up by existing buildings that gobble most of it on heating. A house (like a home pool) can easily exude a voluptuous 50,000kWh in a winter. But the average house can save 80 per cent of that heat with improved insulation and double glazing. Likewise with pools. It pays to insulate effectively first, and to install heating and recovery devices later.

Better insulation with energy recovery encourages the use of low grade heating – a tenet of alternative technology that points the way to converting natural ambient energy sources. Since the reservoir and distribution system already exist in a swimming pool, the only device needed is an economical and effective ambient energy convertor.

To reinforce the save-it philosophy, new restrictive trends are developing. States such as California (*the* place for pools) are banning pool gas heaters, following the 1974 fuel crisis, and have even refused pool building permits as a consequence of the drought of 1976/77.

Alternative means of heating, and of conserving heat, are being deeply researched, and at present it is in the swimming pool area where alternative ideas are the most productive. The solar convertor and the heat pump head the list, and although they have been used widely on pools since the 50s, it took the spiralling cost of fuel in the 70s to make them far more widely appreciated. So much so, American house owners are now offered tax concessions on new solar systems; in France, extra insulation and energy saving devices also already incur tax relief. Providing that storage and circulation is inexpensive, an 'alternative system' can pay for itself from fuel savings within a few years.

A large store of heat at low temperature is achieved and kept far more efficiently than a small store at high temperature; and losses are greatly reduced. By 2020 AD, it is suggested that prime energy can be shared equally in production between solar sources, atomic power and conventional fossil fuels.

On the spot production of heat from solar energy is a paying and direct proposition, but a plain and simple open air pool will naturally convert 80 per cent of the incident radiation it receives into heat without the aid of extra technology. If action is taken to *keep* this free low grade heat, and then to supplement it, a pool can become a more comfortable leisure area, as well as a most effective conversion and storage system.

Reviving old ideas Those who argue that sunlight is too weak to produce any dramatic effect should turn to their history books. Around 214 BC, according to ancient writers, Archimedes used solar power to set fire to Roman galleys besieging his home town of Syracuse. Modern historians argued this 'burning' story was a myth since ancient technology was not capable of concentrating enough power over distance. That was, until a modern Greek engineer Ioannis Sakkas proved otherwise in 1973. At that time, seventy sailors bearing man-size mirrors – like polished copper shields – were arranged to reflect and concentrate sunlight onto a boat 50m from shore. Within a few seconds the boat began smouldering.

All the solar energy imaginable for mankind falls on the Sahara. It is merely a matter of converting it into a transportable fuel; there lies the problem.

The first flat plate solar collector is credited to the 18th-century Swiss engineer Saussure. A 19th-century fuel crisis encouraged great activity in solar system design, as well as in heat pump development. The heat pump as an energy transformer was first suggested perhaps by Lord Kelvin in 1852 to heat buildings with air currents. Later solar energy devices were popularised in California in 1936 by F. A. Brooks and his DIY manual. But more lasting development did not really get under way until the 1970s when, again in California, fast flow low temperature rise, nonglazed solar units brought the price down and took the efficiency up.

Modern solar systems depend upon simplicity, imaginative application and practical economics, not expensively sophisticated techniques. In fact, straightforward solar heaters give up more heat when the pool water is cool; or, better still, they pick up more heat when they run cool. Swimming pool heating can be the most cost-effective application for solar energy.

Slow absorption of energy Constantly changing amounts of solar radiation for infinitely varying durations combine to make the sun a capricious if fundamental energy source, and one more suited to supplement conventional and more reliable heating than to replace it.

Solar collectors are often used successfully on pools to build-up slow rising temperature first and foremost for summer, then as an economical pre-warm in winter to a fossil-fuelled system. The large thermal water mass of a pool evens out temperature swings in the short term. Other useful sources, but this time more constant, are provided geothermally, and by sea or river temperature as cheap primary energy for the heat pump. In developing the heat store principle further, underground high temperature water tanks, heavily insulated, can absorb surplus electric heating when consumer loads are low overnight, or there is generating capacity to spare. One London leisure pool adopts this off-peak thermal store idea with 80m³ of water held at 150°C and stabilised with nitrogen pressure; the International pool at Coventry employs similar storage tanks to a total of 425m³ for superheated water, as well as employing air refrigeration circuitry absorbing high solar gains from a south-glazed wall to help with the heat load.

Low temperature, low cost The source temperature does not have to be high for useful heating:

• Translucent plastic pillows 200mm deep, filled with water and stood on metal that is covered with black plastic help make the Japanese evening bath so hot.

• American passive roof collectors covered one hour before sunset with insulated shutters contribute to night-time heating through the ceiling of houses in south-western states.

• The Thames River was used as the ambient mass for London's Festival Hall within a 2700kW heat pump system.

• A baker's oven principle of collecting and storing heat within large mass is adopted at the heavily insulated Wallasey School building in Cheshire; bright aluminium panels reflect sunlight in summer along the whole side facing the sun, and then they are reversed in winter to absorb radiation behind a 500m² area of double glazing. At this location the dry fabric evens out temperature to 18°C November-February, 19°C March-May, and 21°C June-October.

The ambient principle was clearly understood in ancient Arizona where a seven-storey structure known as Montezuma's castle was built into a cliff face between 700 and 1300 AD. Its massive structure is naturally heated and cooled by sunpower. More up to date, but on the same basis, is the sunwarmed 25m swimming pool designed by Dr Paolo Soleri for his ambient energy based community of Arcosanti, again in Arizona. This scheme has a solar chimney rising by a steep sunny slope, diverted beneath the pool floor to heat the water in similar fashion to an early Roman hypocaust for thermae, but using solar-warmed air instead.

It is really no longer worthwhile burning high grade fuel, just to produce low grade heat. All the time we can afford to waste heat, there will be no real reason to build the

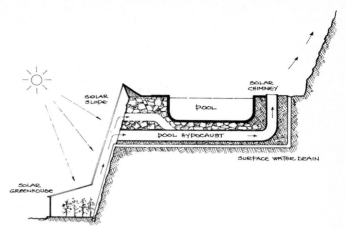

14.3 *Modern hypocaust heated pool – solar chimney at Arcosanti, Arizona*
Consanti Community Foundation
Architect: Paolo Soleri

thermal reservoir into a secure means of investing in the future. The policy of profligacy is like the Saracens' senseless method of heating – on entering Alexandria after ousting the Romans, they found some 4000 baths, huge and numerous, so they simply burned the 700,000 books from the extensive libraries to heat the waters!

14.4 Insolation and insulation

Radiation comes in streams of waves over a wide range of frequencies. The energy extends from the faster vibrating ultra violet end, down through blue to red and then infrared, which vibrates more slowly. Radiant energy or insolation, is absorbed by a matt black surface across the whole range of frequencies, but since a black surface is also highly emissive, a warmed body re-radiates and convects losses to passing air, unless protected by ordinary glass and insulation. Heat needs collecting and transferring through a transmitting medium such as water, to be carried away quickly. Therefore, an efficient collecting surface should always be cool. Similarly, solar gain with air as the collecting medium can either be troublesome behind double glazing of a poolhall by overheating the occupants, or useful with suitable distribution devices (see chapter 14.10). Heat-absorbing glass absorbs one third energy and retransmits away two thirds solar heat, but high temperature of the glass (similar to an aluminium panel in the sun) is hot to the touch, and requires provision for thermal movement (see chapter 10.11).

Since the angle of the sun varies throughout the year, for maximum effect the collection surface is better set perpendicular all the time to the rays. This means summer operating solar heaters are angled nearer to the horizontal for high sun; and winter, nearer to vertical for low sun. Higher latitudes have less overhead sun, greater cloud, but longer days. The overall solar energy available amounts to less than 50 per cent of that for tropical latitudes, but diffuse and reflected energy helps offset the loss of direct sunshine. To help gain the same amount of heat, a solar panel to pool area ratio should be made almost 1:1 for higher latitudes, reducing to ½:1 nearer the tropics.

To sum up, the intensity of solar radiation on a surface depends on:
• the sun's altitude

● the collector's surface angle to the sun and its materials absorptivity

● the increase of radiation by reflection and by surroundings, including local air temperature

● less the reduction of radiation by atmosphere, pollution, cloud, glass, covering dust, etc.

See information sheet 14.14.

Rapid collection The objective of any solar collecting system is to convert direct and indirect energy into heat, for fastest possible transfer to the thermal store. Maximum energy will be transferred when *the greatest water flow carries the greatest quantity of heat*, the optimum being the largest product of three main factors – total flow × time × temperature rise. Heat losses increase with rising operating temperature, therefore a small temperature rise of 1 or 2 °C in practice encourages an optimum situation providing there is fast water flow. There is no point in accumulating temperature (measurement of 'hotness'), but every point in accumulating the largest possible *quantity* of low grade heat.

Energy tends to arrive in packets or bursts, not evenly spread out, hence simple solar switches, or temperature differential controls, will be necessary to operate the ideal system.

Conservation is best alternative technology Slow poolwater temperature rise with solar collectors always requires the collateral of heat retaining covers to prevent losses outstripping gains. The fast fossil fuel heater masks these losses, although they are still there.

Floating covers that let radiation through, while retaining low frequency re-radiated and reflected energy, are ideal allies for the pool solar heater (see chapter 10.4). The keep-it-covered rule applies equally to indoor pools for reducing evaporation, and to saving heat overnight (see chapter 15.10).

Provident insulation A simple but telling insulation experiment in America showed clearly the effect of using a plain cover over a water surface (see information sheet 14.4). Two freestanding pools were stood together in the sun. They were exactly the same in every design detail, except that the water surface of one was covered in translucent, but thin, insulating polythene. After one day, the covered tank of water had increased in temperature by 6 °C more than the other. If these tanks had been installed in ground, they would have warmed more slowly, but ground insulated sides would have slowed heat loss as well. And then when water temperature drops, the surrounding ground store of heat outside the pool is drawn back again.

From open swimming pools, there are significant radiation losses to the sky at night, very significant convection losses to the wind, and most significant evaporation losses as latent heat of vaporisation. Between 80 and 90 per cent of a pool's heat loss arises from the water surface outdoors (and perversely, indoors also). Some Russian open air pools provide radiant heaters for the onlookers in the winter, while relying upon a natural enveloping steam pillow above the water to hold down heat losses.

An enclosure effectively insulates the water surface if the air contained is warm and moist. Then the pool building's thermal efficiency becomes extremely important. Common heat transmittance standards of between 1 and 2 W/m³/°C are not good enough for well-run pools. The overall standard should not exceed 0·5 W/m²/°C, wherever possible. Stop all draughts, and avoid thermal bridges through the fabric that waste heat or collect condensation. Reduce window area, where transmission coefficient ranges rise from between 2 and 5, to improve running costs and to save building costs. It is unnecessary to sacrifice light for insulation with the availability of suitable modern translucent sandwich GRP panels, or the heavier, wider-spaced, double glazing. Large glass expanses still add their own problems with cold-bridging, down draughts and condensation all needing counteraction of warm air curtains, or directional ventilation. Flame-retarding aluminium foil in the roof can also help reflect back pool radiated heat: a water surface cover considerably reduces evaporation and hence saves heat loss or air extraction needs.

14.5 Solar collectors and heat exchangers

There is at least 500 to 2000 kWh/m² of solar energy freely available every year between the 40° parallels, plus huge quantities of indirect energy from the surroundings.

The simple swimming pool solar collector offers the most efficient conversion of solar energy into useful heat that has yet been devised. Efficiency as high as 110 per cent can be obtained, with direct plus diffuse radiation, plus indirect warmth extracted from surrounding air sometimes exceeding the maximum available solar radiation per square metre. Pools need large quantities of low grade heat, which is the exact area where flat plate collectors are the most efficient.

Collection Even though the home swimming pool is usually situated in the sunniest position in the garden, extra heat collected and transferred from nearby warm spots will still need to be gathered economically. The simplest way of making the pool a more effective natural collector is to coat the floor with very dark paint, and paint pool walls brilliant white to reflect sunlight onto the heat absorbing floor.

Large water areas require large collector areas, which can be very space consuming in gathering such widespread, weak energy – a major disadvantage, greater than the everchanging intensity of sunlight.

Solar systems work extremely well in heat waves, but inadequately in cold spells. They are unattractively black, like funereal greenhouses. The search for sympathetic systems using natural surroundings to collect dilute energy has inspired development of ample collection pipes imbedded into dark paving around the pool, or into reproduction GRC tiling on the roof, or into the provision of wide sheets of water flowing across shallow black-bottomed moats to pour warmth into the water.

Copper panels and pipes are the most efficient, compact convertors, but if there is space to spare with heating time available consider a less expensive and more expansive solar transmitter material. Expensive, sophisticated devices or systems to gain a few extra Watts are most unsuitable for swimming pools.

Collectors need to be cheap and lightweight, made of durable and inert materials, easy to install and maintenance free. An economic plastic matrix panel can therefore be used to advantage. Their fixing or support (sometimes unnecessarily costly) must withstand high winds. Because the plastic solar system operates best at low temperature rise (+1° or 2 °C only), the extra, expensive glass covers are

14.4 *Aluminium flat plate solar convertor for a 33 m³ pool*
Photo: John Dawes

14.5 *The CDA Decade 80 Solar House at Tucson, Arizona integrates copper roofing with solar collection to provide about 75 per cent of cooling and nearly 100 per cent of heating needs*
Copper Development Association Inc, NY

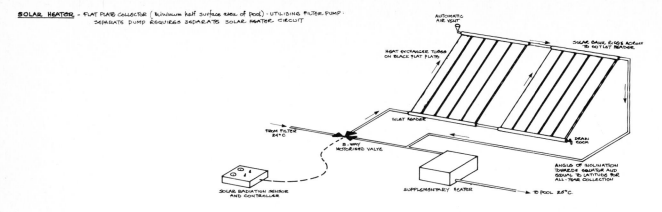

SOLAR HEATER - FLAT PLATE COLLECTOR (minimum half surface area of pool) - UTILISING FILTER PUMP: SEPARATE PUMP REQUIRES SEPARATE SOLAR HEATER CIRCUIT

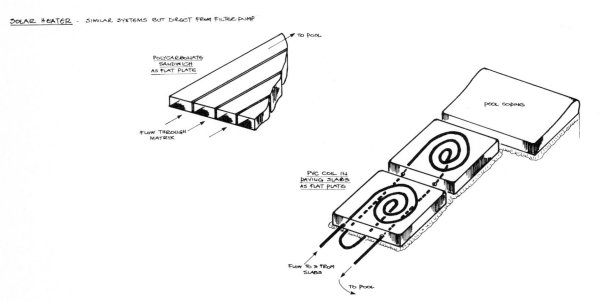

SOLAR HEATER - SIMILAR SYSTEMS BUT DIRECT FROM FILTER PUMP

14.6 *Pool heaters: (a) convertors; (b) solar heater and detail*

not usually required (in standing still conditions, a glazed panel can overheat and damage plastics). Covering glass reflects a significant proportion of solar radiation at low sun angles, but re-emitted radiation is small and the benefit due to the glass from the greenhouse effect is very limited.

However, metal plate collectors operating at higher temperatures, need backing insulation and the glass cover (sometimes double glazed for high temperature operation) to stop the panel re-radiating and losing too much higher heating efficiency.

As soon as the panel operating temperature exceeds ambient, diminishing returns set in. When a solar heater loses heat faster than it picks it up, it has reached the equilibrium temperature – this is higher on a warmer day than on an overcast one. Even then, there is often sufficient radiation around to operate the collector to positive advantage, and particularly so when the water transferring medium is relatively cold also.

Domestic hot water solar systems have to work up to 60°C, and continually recycle water to storage at increasing temperature, so rapidly reducing efficiency to around the 30 per cent figure. A pool solar system continually operates on one pool pass through principle: as the temperature difference between ambient and cool poolwater increases, the solar heater efficiency improves with tendency towards 100 per cent.

Exchange On the other hand, the opposite situation exists with the heat pump; efficiency is best when source and sink temperature are close together. The solar panel and heat pump are therefore complementary, with mutual advantage as widespread and narrowband ambient energy collectors. The solar-assisted heat pump therefore offers great promise for pool hall roofing to thermal control of the environment.

A heat pump arrangement for a pool system offers the very distinct advantage of producing between 3 and 7kW of heat for every 1kW of prime energy consumed, gas or electricity.

Even though the pool solar system has become more economic over the long run than the popular oil-fired boiler system, the heat pump installed as a complete package deal system is relatively more costly, mainly because there is still small demand plus extra maintenance care for adapted air-conditioning type design units. If the basic evaporator, condenser and pump units are organised into a simple primary circuit transferring heat from source to pool, and housed openly within the normal plantroom, the overall cost of this ambient heating system can become usefully competitive. And if a heating phase can be made complementary to a cooling phase (perhaps to warm poolwater from reclaimed exhaust air enthalpy – heat content) then in terms of value for money, the system is superb. In another version, the heat pump can refrigerate an icerink, and the rejected heat can be used to warm a swimming pool nearby! A modern leisure centre complex is ideal for such two-in-one energy partnerships.

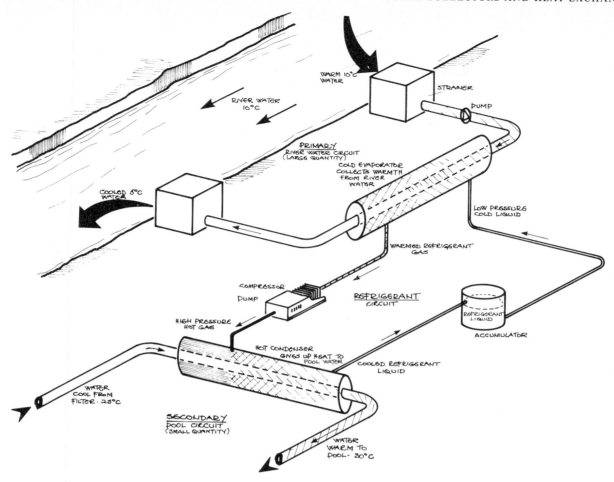

RIVER WATER 10°C

WARM 10°C WATER

STRAINER

PUMP

COOLED 5°C WATER

PRIMARY RIVER WATER CIRCUIT (LARGE QUANTITY)

COLD EVAPORATOR COLLECTS WARMTH FROM RIVER WATER

LOW PRESSURE COLD LIQUID

WARMED REFRIGERANT GAS

COMPRESSOR PUMP

REFRIGERANT CIRCUIT

HIGH PRESSURE HOT GAS

REFRIGERANT LIQUID

ACCUMULATOR

HOT CONDENSER GIVES UP HEAT TO POOL WATER

COOLED REFRIGERANT LIQUID

WATER COOL FROM FILTER · 25°C

SECONDARY POOL CIRCUIT (SMALL QUANTITY)

WATER WARM TO POOL · 30°C

Combination arrangements are not the only cost effective systems though, as has been demonstrated at Market Drayton in England since 1970. There a straightforward 80kW compressor plant with 3m long shell and tube type condenser and evaporator extracts low grade heat from nearby river water to pump energy into a 50m outdoor municipal pool. This most basic of heat pump systems has been operating successfully for five months of every year, with poolwater temperature maintained between 20 and 30°C by the unexpected and simple process of reverse refrigeration. Maintenance for the system is based upon two or three service calls a season with careful protection and constant checks against corrosion. The operating cost claimed is less than one quarter of that for an equivalent indoor heated swim. But when local weather conditions run a long bad spell, there is less chance to build up pool temperature with an ambient system, unless supplementary conventional back-up heating is included.

Another version in a Devon hotel employs solar panels to warm the pool in summer, but for the rest of the year collected energy is fed into the hotel's warm air system via a heat pump (see chapter 14.10 and 11).

Any heat source shared between home and pool, however, can cause a dilemma. For example, the main house boiler is usually insufficient to serve both central heating and swimming pool at the fringe seasons. Then one or the other only can be heated.

The provision of a calorifier heat exchanger means a

14.7 *Pool heaters – convertors: heat pump using low grade heat*

14.8 *This heat pump, driven by a 60 HP electric motor and working on refrigeration in reverse, upgrades river heat for the 50 m public pool at Market Drayton in Shropshire: the primary river circuit contributes 6 or 7 °C to the secondary pool circuit at 25 per cent normal fuel costs*
Prestcold, Berks

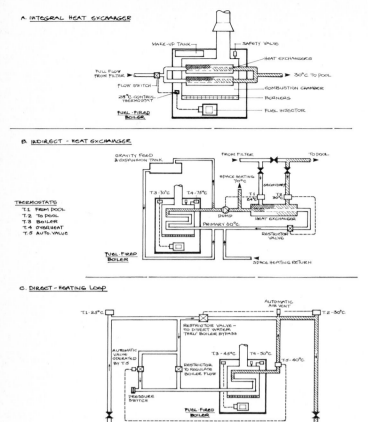

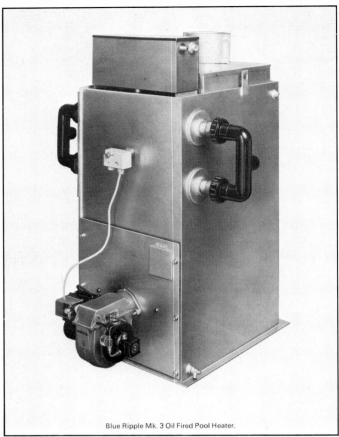

Blue Ripple Mk. 3 Oil Fired Pool Heater.

14.9 *Pool heaters – boilers: heat exchangers and heating loop*

14.10 *Oil-fired pool heater including integral heat exchanger suitable for a private swimming pool*
Blue Ripple Engineering, Chelmsford
Photo: Fidelity Creative Studios

boiler can be kept well clear of corrosive poolwater; this indirect system can easily serve multi-outlets also. However, a direct water flow system through the boiler requires a heating loop to control throughput and temperature. But heat exchangers are usually considered the better proposition, providing the higher temperature primary circuit does not have very far to go to serve the secondary circuit.

14.6 Heaters and boilers

The bypass manifold for the pool heater or exchanger, is situated after filtration and before chlorination. Pool heater controls should be electrically wired through the main pump to shut off directly main flow stops, or backwash starts, or low level controls operate. Dirty filters restrict flow, raise temperature and trigger the thermostat cut-out. The heater must not significantly increase resistance against the clean or dirty filter. Conversely, high velocity water entering the heater can wear interior components, unless baffles prevent direct impingement. Balanced flow design and higher temperature return cuts down possible condensation within the boiler, and reduces possible sooting-up, where 1mm can reduce working efficiency by 25 per cent.

Heating units are better situated safely below poolwater level, with bypass tees that include shut off valves for maintenance and flow control purposes. Pipelines and heater components often have to withstand high working temperature, vacuum and water hammer, as well as chemical attack and frost conditions. But high temperature and

fast flow increase precipitation and scaling, hence hard waters, especially for direct heating systems, really require softening, though excessively soft waters are corrosive.

The risk of flue condensation at low temperature can be overcome by forced ventilation (ensure fan always operates before boiler fires) and local air heating. Always consider boiler/burner noise which can be troublesome at night, since light timber sheds for private pools are often placed near the house. Flues and stacks should always be situated downwind from the pool. In winter shut-down, stop condensation to boilers and:

● arrange a low boiler setting to run at 5°C
● ensure air circulation is sufficient in the plantroom
● prevent chimney condensation which will rot the boiler fabric: keeping the flue fan running helps clear this problem
● keep plantroom and equipment warm, and frost protected.

See chapters 13.2 and 16.3.

Large pool heating systems best employ 2 × 60 per cent rated units, coupled and switched to suit priorities. Low pressure hot water boilers – 80°C flow/70°C return – can operate water-to-air exchangers for space heating, and water-to-water exchangers for the pool. A separate heat exchanger or heating system will be better for the higher temperature needs of therapeutic, paddling, or learner type pools.

High efficiency heater units pay back quickly, but not if constant maintenance is called for. The electrical heating system operates very successfully at nearly 100 per cent efficiency, for very little attention; an efficient, clean and convenient heating. In national terms, however, fuel conversion to electric power rates only a meagre 27 per cent efficiency, which means 'flick-of-a-switch' electricity is expensive and better employed for motive power, rather than for low grade heating, unless there is spare generating capacity requiring storage or redistribution, or continuing cheap off-peak rates, or efficient motive forms of heat production, eg heat pump.

Finally, following ever changing fuel policies, rising costs and troubled supplies, it is wiser to consider multi-fuelled systems or interchangeable arrangements whereby equipment can be reasonably converted from gas to oil, or from oil to coal-fired or even electric, as necessary in the future.

14.7 Space heating

Bathers at the poolside dislike cool air, which gives rise to the delusion that space heating is entirely for their benefit. But excess moisture in pool hall air accelerates deterioration, and the high capital investment in modern structures needs thorough protection. Not only is pool hall air too often underheated (the case for 50 per cent of UK enclosed pools), but in order to make further savings, the whole system is regularly switched off at night! Such malpractices rapidly increase condensation and deterioration inside roof

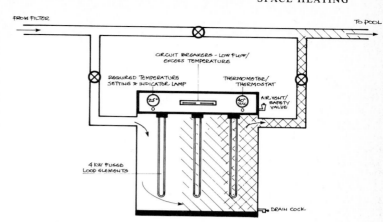

14.12 *Pool heaters – convertors: electric flow heater*

layers, between interleaved walls, within mechanical and electrical services, ensuring ultimate bills for early structural attention will greatly exceed any reduced running costs.

Indoor pools with air temperature set below water temperature can increase heat loss through evaporation. Pool-water warms the immediate air which rises, cools and condenses shedding latent heat; colder air then flows into contact across the warmer pool water to pick up more moisture, and so on. A good water surface insulating cover is essential, if heating *must* be switched off.

Heated floors must be well drained, roof spaces should

14.11 *Boilers for a public swimming pool at Bramcote, Nottingham*
Architect: Rex Savidge & F. Hayes

Architects' Journal
Photo: H. Tempest Industrial Ltd

14.13 *Warm air curtain for the pool hall heating which controls condensation to windows. Ambassador College, Herts*

Architect: Denkers & Maddison in association with Daniel Mann & Johnson, Mendenhall
Architects' Journal
Photo: W. J. Toomey

be preheated, large window areas reduced and double glazed or warmed, and space heating should be able to respond to several levels of operating changes. Without doubt, air temperature should always be kept at least 1 °C above water temperature, with air changes 4 to 6 per hour over the pool: 3m ceiling heights will bring considerable saving on the space to heat, as well as on the push to ventilate.

14.8 Ventilation

Adequate air changes are vital for the control of high humidity and excess condensation. Early system concepts cleared condensation with fresh air introduced through open gabled ends, and later with forced flow fans. Since fan failures can be overlooked, warning lights showing out-of-operation phase are particularly important. If installed, such indicators might have saved collapsed ceilings on more than one occasion.

In about 1950, half of all major public pools used only fixed rate ventilation, varying from 2 to 16 air changes an hour. Private pools simply opened their windows. From a swimming competitor's point of view, if lungs have to cope with condensation, carbon dioxide and chlorinated water vapour, so reducing the available oxygen, discomfort and poor performance is inevitable. Today, most pools strive for at least 3 to 4 air changes per hour, with 10 per cent achieving 5 to 6; the better rating of $60m^3/h/m^2$ average air replacement is now often suggested for public pools. Ventilation rates must vary to cope with changing patterns of demand, and the plant should be positioned centrally to increase efficiency.

Air smells can be eliminated by including an ozonator within the system, and by trapping air dust with a suitable filter. Deodorising arrangements are particularly important for dressing rooms and clothing stores, where air changes per hour should be trebled.

Extra heat is soon built up in a crowded spectators' gallery, but if a draught of cold fresh air could possibly chill poolside swimming competitors, a glazed, prewarming room is better provided.

Too many indoor pools still suffer 'that claustrophobic smell of chlorine'. This does not necessarily mean ventilation is inadequate or that pool water treatment is poor (see chapter 15). Worse than any unpleasant or corrosive by-product vapours is the real danger from raw chlorine gas escaping into the ducting. Even with stringent safety precautions surrounding every pool chlorine room, the risk of escaping poison gas being collected by a ventilation system and force fed into the pool hall is the nightmare of every chemical manufacturer and pool operator. Concerned suppliers and managers rigorously and regularly inspect systems, but bad pool designs are still being carried through, with basic faults such as the fresh air ventilation inlet set right alongside chlorine, or chemical stores. Unfortunately, liquid or dry chlorine is just as dangerous if operators mistakenly mix them with acids, producing dense, dangerous, acrid fumes. Even if restrictive rules are enforced, there must still be no chance whatsoever of ventilation collecting and circulating any fumes or gases. It is futile to prohibit one dangerous chemical (eg chlorine gas) when most others – bromine, ozone, etc (see chapter 15.3 and 4) – are just as dangerous.

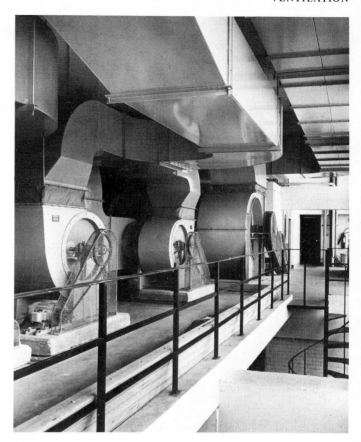

14.14 *Public pool air ventilation gallery: Whiteoaks Pool in Kent*
Architects' Journal
Photo: de Burgh Galwey

14.15 *Compact air heating and conditioning for a private pool in Germany*
Witte Haustechnik GmbH
Photo: H. Lohoff

14.9 Humidity control

Inadequate humidity control for enclosed pools can bring the roof down, as several semi-public pools in the UK and USA in recent years will testify (see chapter 10.3). The moisture laden environment affects structure and interior, fittings and maintenance, continuously, destructively and insidiously. Vapour barriers might stop bucketfuls of moisture being trapped in cool places, but concealed interstitial condensation from air leaks, transporting water vapour into walls and roofs is responsible for most building deterioration. Roof lights can make it difficult to achieve effective vapour barriers; even double glazing can accumulate water between the panes of glass. Manufacturers of suspended ceilings do not recommend placing reliance upon vapour barriers, since these are difficult to seal perfectly. Fixings must be corrosion proof and preferably protected by a positive air pressure in the void above. Ceiling material must not absorb moisture, but most insulation material is porous to vapour.

Although double glazing will reduce condensation, proper drainage gulleys must still be provided to all windows. Exposed softwoods and electrical fittings are especially prone to attack. Steel girders offer cold bridges for condensation, and encourage shrinkage cracks that open passages to vapour flow. All these problems are exceptionally critical in high temperature, high humidity places, such as the Sauna, Turkish, or Spa Bath. Effective control of humidity cuts evaporation by reducing the wet deck area, or by covering over the water area when not in use.

Swimming pool atmospheres can vary from 40 to 90 per cent relative humidity, but are best kept at around 60 per cent with 28°C air temperature for 27°C water, and a normal 60m³/h/m² ventilation rate with 25 per cent fresh air dilution, if a dehumidifer is not provided.

14.10 Heat recovery

The huge amounts of energy required to operate most swimming pools, private and public, make heat recovery extra worthwhile. A well insulated, and thermally balanced system will pay off, especially over the coldest months of operation. Since ventilation accounts for at least 50 per cent of a pool hall's heat loss, recovery systems were first developed to collect dry and wet heat from exhaust air.

The simple glass plate heat exchanger, and the refrigerated cooling circuit can recover large amounts of original energy being wastefully vented. Or a slowly revolving thermal wheel (a valuable device which has been almost overlooked for pools since its invention back in the 19th century), recovers energy very effectively to allow preheating of fresh air, or recycling of pool hall air especially when ozonation is used with marginal chlorination. 80 per cent of the total energy supply can be recovered and reused and in an everyday public pool, this can mean 7000 to 8000 kWh/m² per year.

Increasing attention is also directed towards heat recovery from backwash water, hot water services and showers to preheat fresh supplies. Even light fittings, or nearby 'water cooled' computers, contribute wealthily to heating stock.

14.16 *Total heat recovery system. 1 Moist warm air from pool hall. 2 Dry cool air – cooling coil primary heat recovery. 3 Secondary reclamation — thermal wheel heat recovery. 4 Cold exhaust air. 5 Incoming fresh air. 6 Filtered air plus thermal wheel heat recovery. 7 Supply air for preheat using other sources heat recovery (plus supplementary). 8 Warm supply air to pool hall. C.1 Refrigeration step controller. C.2 Supplementary heat input valve. T Thermostat*
The Electricity Council, London

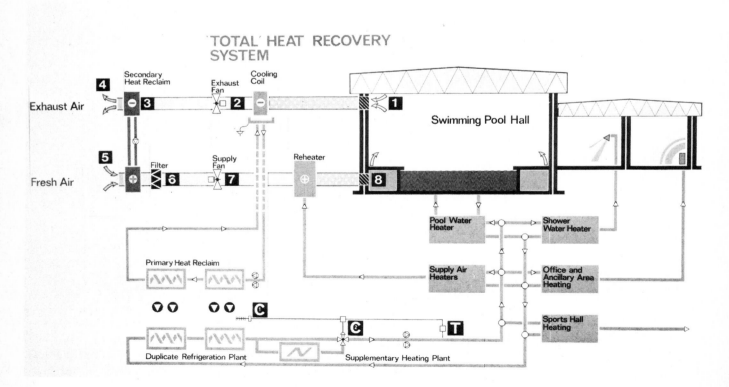

A recent device without any moving parts whatsoever like the heat pipe, recovers lost energy for the modern total heat reservoir. Invented by R. S. Gaugler of General Motors in 1944, it is a sealed recirculatory evaporation/condensation system, capable of transferring thermal energy at very high rate. Gas expansion change takes place at constant temperature in *vacuum* as an isothermal process, moving energy most efficiently from one end of the pipe to the other.

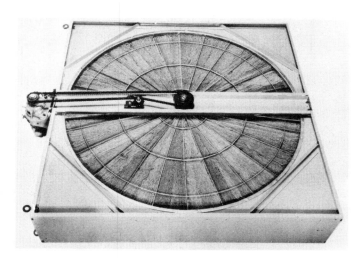

14.17 *Expelled warm air passes through the vanes of the thermal wheel which can collect almost 90 per cent of total heat in a ventilation system*
Curwen & Newbery Ltd, Westbury

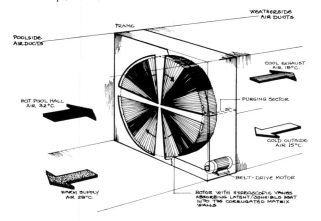

14.18 *Heat wheel*

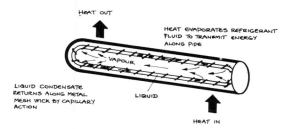

14.19 *Heat pipe*

14.11 Self-sufficiency

New headquarters buildings for electricity generating boards in the UK employ sophisticated designs of heat reclaim from light fittings, absorb solar gain, collect metabolic heat from the occupants (as much as 0·5 kWh production per sedentary person) and their electronic computers, and so on, to recycle or dump second-hand energy until required for re-use later.

Heat pumps then regenerate the heat when required, but meanwhile over 1100 staff have their own environmentally attractive pool, or heat dump, for a valuable social and health bonus. Further advantage of the storage tank facility is to provide ample water for fire fighting when needed. A swimming pool system buried deep within large commercial buildings can conveniently collect and regenerate heat most reliably, providing long term operational savings are required.

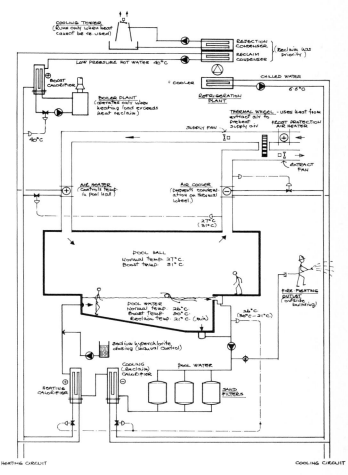

14.20 *Heat dump/leisure pool/fire-fighting tank*
Engineer: Steensen Varming Mulcahy
Architect: Gillinson Barnett & Partners

However, it does not require a large commercial enterprise to invest and make feasible 'a fair hump of heat' in the shape of a successful swimming pool heat dump. Solar houses under development throughout the world all need efficient and economic long-term heat storage to tide them over dull periods, in some cases, to store summer heat for winter use. One Australian idea, like nature's photosynthesis that converts radiant energy into a bound chemical form usable in combustion, now stores and transports energy. It is based upon a heat-absorbing chemical reaction – the decomposition of ammonia into nitrogen and hydrogen. The gases are transmitted to a central recovery plant, where they can be resynthesised to release energy in the form of heat.

Chemical conversion from liquid to crystal and back again might also be thermally interesting, but never so socially beneficial as a continually fluid pool of warmed water!

Solar architecture and pool engineering have reached the level where they can be thoroughly cost effective in energy conservation. Existing pools (never justified by any energy saving cost calculation) need only a solar collector or heat pump to start viable production. A new solar house to make its collector prove efficient, has to amortise the circulation system and the storage over the years ahead which the pool already has in existence. If relative pool costs continue to come down, the self-sufficient private house based around a swimming pool store for energy and exercise can contribute to conservation. Already, a private pool costs only half as much to build per square metre as a house or living-room extension – and if it can contribute to the economy of that house, then the extra room becomes a real asset as well. This point of view is similar to the idea to

dualise solar panels with roofing in copper; or, not so very long ago, to build a bathroom inside the house for hygiene and health reasons.

The optimum situation of linking solar heater and heat pump, to preheat and recycle stored energy from warmed poolwater, is explored in Ashville USA, in a concept that transfers heat collected by the house to the pool in summer, and from the pool or solar heater to the house in winter. The water gives a huge and practical buffer zone between the two. On another plane, one English public pool uses 1500m³/d of waste methane from the local sewage works to offer probably the highest temperature water in Britain.

Pools, like houses, do not depreciate quickly. They keep the same water year after year, bring conservation systems into the home, add enjoyment, and now can create a thermal reservoir as well. The hunt for the holy Energy Grail – the heat dump to tide us over till better times – need go no further than modern swimming pool technology.

14.21 *Zero energy house using a swimming pool as a heat store. A reasonably insulated (assuming 10 kWh heat loss) 150 m² house at 0°C ambient with solar energy collection, thermal stores and heat recovery, can retain in winter at least 14 days' energy stock in the swimming pool. Ground coil heat pump makes up excess deficits*

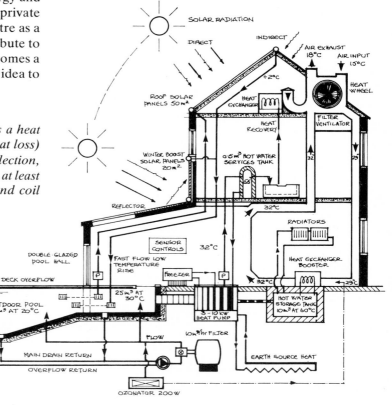

FLAT PLATE COLLECTOR PANELS CONVERT SOLAR ENERGY INTO LOW GRADE HEAT FOR DUMPING INTO A 75m³ INSULATED SWIMMING POOL IN SUMMER, AND INTO A 25m³ INDOOR SECTION OF THE POOL IN WINTER. A HEAT PUMP UPGRADES POOLWATER HEAT, OR SUBSOIL HEAT, FOR STORAGE IN INSULATED HOT WATER TANKS. HEAT IS ALSO RECOVERED FROM VENTILATION EXHAUST AIR, LOFT AIR AND WASTE WATER - TO BE RETURNED TO THE POOL HALL VIA A BOOSTER HEAT EXCHANGER. THIS AMBIENT ENERGY CONSERVATION SYSTEM IS SUPPLEMENTED BY CONVENTIONAL SWIMMING POOL PURIFICATION PLANT.

INFORMATION SHEET 14.1

Typical temperatures

Poolwater:

20°C	active swimming
25°C	competitive swimming
27°C	leisure and disabled swimmers (thermal waters at Buxton)
30°C	luxury swimming
35°C	thermal bathing
40°C	spa water bathing
50°C	thermal waters at Bath

Pool surroundings:

50°C	hot water services
40°C	poolside showers and maximum input temperature to pool
35°C	washbasins
28°C	natatorium when poolwater at 27°C
22°C	changing rooms
20°C	restaurant and staff room
18°C	entrance and spectators gallery
16°C	services area

INFORMATION SHEET 14.2

Water temperatures

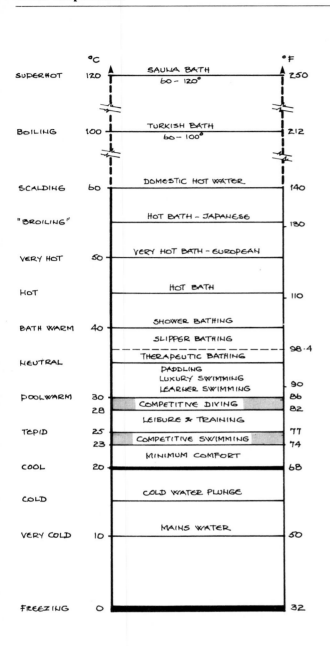

INFORMATION SHEET 14.4

Water temperature changes

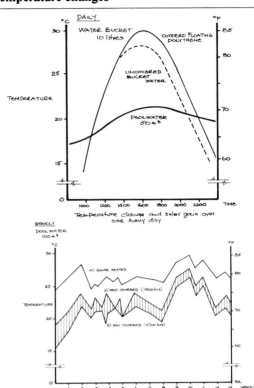

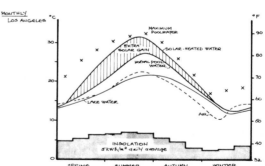

London swimming pool:
(a) maximum temperature: solar heated water with solar convertor equalling half water surface area
(b) maximum temperature poolwater using insulating
(c) minimum temperature only transparent floating cover

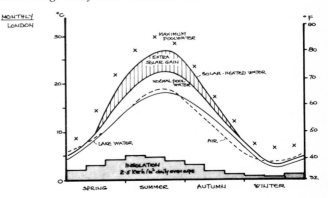

Temperature curves for a sheltered, insulating-covered, 50 m³ pool with solar converter equalling half water area; also average daily solar radiation received

INFORMATION SHEET 14.3

Outdoor swimming seasons
(Assuming low top-up heating when necessary)

Example range of locations	Climate	Coldest month °C	No of months for swimming: Out-doors	Convert-ibles	Indoors
St Johns/Oslo	Cold	−5	1	1	10
Vancouver/Paris	Cool	0	3	1	8
Canberra/Tokyo	Warm	5	5	2	5
Los Angeles/Perth	Hot	10	8	2	2
Miami/Brisbane	Tropical	15+	10	2	0

219

INFORMATION SHEET 14.5

Pool heater sizing guide
(To replace poolwater temperature losses)

Assuming:
a 3 day initial heat-up period,
a 100 per cent efficient heater source,
air movement does not exceed 1m/s across pool surface,
the pool tank is set into the ground:

and based upon	European practice (with minimum heat input)	rather than	American practice (with fast heat input)

Note:
Rule of thumb requirement:

	European practice	American practice
	0·45–0·65 kW/m³	0·8–1·0 kW/m³
	7–10 BTU/gal	12–15 BTU/gal

Saving capital costs with smaller equipment: but small pool heaters take time to recover losses, which requires higher pool temperatures to be maintained overnight, aggravating heat losses and raising running costs.

Saving operating costs with faster heat build-up: this in turn allows the pool temperature to drop overnight, for smaller losses with fast top-up offering cheaper running costs.

Heater sizing depends upon many variables such as:
- pool surface area to depth, and overall volume
- amount of losses and quantity of top-up water
- maximum temperature rise over ambient
- coldest months to be heated
- rate of heat-up and heater working hours
- the type and rate of water circulation
- location, exposure and enclosure
- insulation and air temperature
- sunshine hours and wind velocity
- relative humidity.

Sources: SPATA/NSPI.

kW table

Pool dimensions			Approximate		Pool heater requirement (kW) Minimum input to maintain the following poolwater temperature increases above mean air temperature for the coldest month of swimming use:			
Length	Breadth	Average depth	Pool Area	Pool Capacity				
m	m	m	m²	m³	5°C	10°C	15°C	20°C
10 ×	5 ×	1·0	50	50	12	25	40	50
		1·5		75	15	30	45	60
		2·5		125	20	40	60	80
15 ×	6⅔ ×	1·0	100	100	25	45	70	90
		1·5		150	30	55	85	110
		2·5		250	35	70	110	140
25 ×	10 ×	1·0	250	250	50	100	150	200
		1.5		375	60	125	190	250
		2.5		625	80	165	250	330
33⅓ ×	15 ×	1·0	500	500	100	200	300	400
		1·5		750	120	250	380	500
		2·5		1250	160	330	500	660
50 ×	20 ×	1·0	1000	1000	200	400	600	800
		1·5		1500	240	500	750	1000
		2·5		2500	320	650	1000	1300

Applicable to pools between latitudes: for example:	20-30°	30-40°	40-50°	50-60°
		Los		Edin-
	Miami	Angeles	London	burgh
	Rio de	Buenos	Christ-	Van-
	Janeiro	Aires	church	couver

Heater requirement adjustment factors Multiply each case by:
0·4 if pool enclosed and air temperature maintained 1°C above water.
0·6 when poolwater surface is protected with a heat retaining cover.
0·9 for each 1000m above sea level.
1·2 when wind across surface exceeds 2m/s.
1·4 when wind across surface exceeds 4m/s.

1·5 if pool is exposed and unprotected.
1·5 is shallow pool and depth is less than 1m.
2·0 to achieve swimming temperature within 24 hours.
See information sheets 14·13, 14·16 and 14·18

INFORMATION SHEET 14.6

Heating requirements

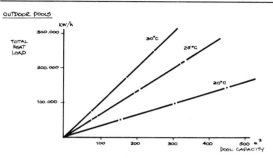

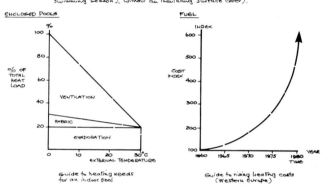

Guide to different heating needs for an outdoor pool of 1·5m average depth and operating within a temperate climate, over a 20 week swimming season, or a 'Mediterranean' climate over a 30 week swimming season.(without an insulating surface cover).

Guide to heating needs for an indoor pool

Guide to rising heating costs (Western Europe)

INFORMATION SHEET 14.7

Heat loads and consumption

Pool heat requirement, (to build up temperature over ambient)	= initial heat-up quantity plus losses less gains.

The swimming pool is a heat reservoir requiring a major outdoor boost in the spring, or for indoor schemes, spread 75 per cent for winter heating and 25 per cent for summer.
A private pool indoors generally requires as much heat as the whole house: between 25,000 to 50,000 kWh/per season (see information sheet 14.6).
An outdoor garden pool of 75³ requires for summer swimming in a temperate climate:
25,000 kWh for 20°C poolwater
45,000 kWh for 25°C poolwater
75,000 kWh for 30°C poolwater
or approx 10 per cent more heat for each degree rise.
(In ideal conditions, 1 tonne of water (1m³ or 1000 litres) increased by 1°C requires 1·163 kWh of energy or 1000 kilocalories of heat: therefore, a rule of thumb guide to achieve poolwater temperature rise requires a minimum 1kWh/m³/°C.) See information sheet 14.5

A typical indoor public pool for all year swimming in a temperate climate requires:

	Min	Average	Max	Per year
heating	1000	7000	15,000	kWh/m²
electricity	400	600	1000	kWh/m²
water	5	30	100	m³/m²

in providing for a swimmer density ranging from 200 to 1000 per m² per year, and assuming a typical 500m² surface area.
Note: An 80 per cent saving can be made with better insulation standards and heat recovery systems

Sources: EC/NSPI.

INFORMATION SHEET 14.8

Solar radiation – worldwide
Comparative daily average insolation (based upon Dr H. Heywood data)

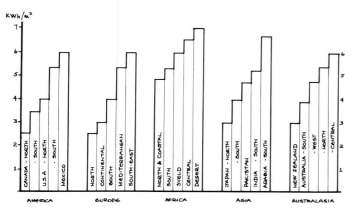

OPTIMUM SOLAR COLLECTOR
ANGLE AGAINST LATITUDE
(based upon CDA)

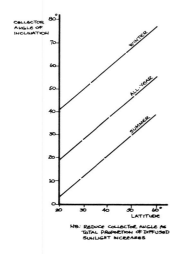

NB: REDUCE COLLECTOR ANGLE AS
TOTAL PROPORTION OF DIFFUSED
SUNLIGHT INCREASES

INFORMATION SHEET 14.9

Solar energy statistics

Solar constant or solar flux at the outer atmosphere = $1.395 \ kW/m^2$
Insolation or solar radiation maximum arriving on the earth's surface = $1.0 \ kW/m^2$ as direct or indirect energy (diffuse radiation ranges from 1–100 per cent of total and is non-directional).
Water reflects 5–10 per cent incident radiation back again.
Average radiation available for conversion = $0.5 \ kW/m^2$
(Garden pools are 80 per cent efficient solar collectors.)
Multiply by annual sunshine hours = solar energy available, eg UK 1600 hours × 0.5 = $800 \ kWh/m^2$
(ranging from 700 in Scotland to $1000 \ kWh/m^2$ SW England) which results in poolwater heated naturally to 20°C for 20 days only.
Total annual radiation available per day:
London $2.5 \ kWh/m^2$ . . . summer months average 4.5
Los Angeles $5.0 \ kWh/m^2$ . . . summer months average 7.0
Pyrenees $7.0 \ kWh/m^2$ . . . in view of pure air
(Winter share of average radiation can be as low as 5 to 10 per cent summer output.)

INFORMATION SHEET 14.10

Solar gains – fenestration

Thickness		Total radiation transmittance
Single glazing	3mm	86%
	4mm	84%
	5mm	82%
	6mm	80%
Double glazing	4 + 4mm	71%
	4 + 6mm	67%
	6 + 6mm	64%

Materials to reduce solar gain	Radiation transmitted		
	Visible	Direct solar	Total solar
	%	%	%
Clear float glass 4mm and	85	80	84
double glazing 6 + 6mm	78	74	64
Open weave curtain behind clear glass	40	70	82
Solar energy reflecting glass	42–58	47–59	52–62
Polyester film on glass	18–33	17–31	25–39
Tinted solar control glass:			
green*	62–76	30–52	51–66
grey	19–42	16–45	43–62
New corrugated aluminium	0	0	9
100mm concrete	0	0	15

Sources: Manufacturers/Specification/'Shading and glazing' section of AJ Information Library, Technical Study: Designing in the Tropics, 16.11.77.
*Unpalatable colour for pool waters; grey/blue, or amber perhaps, better.
See chapter 10.11 for Glazing and light.

INFORMATION SHEET 14.11

Low temperature rise/fast flow/high heat collected

Solar heaters for swimming pools best collect heat in quantity not quality. Summary of figures showing that: increasing water flow at small temperature rise on a large bore flat plate solar collector, increases the total quantity of heat collected (tested on outdoor garden pool water in Britain at 20°C for an even, bright, sunny summer's day, using $7m^2$ of panel and measuring temperature rise against increasing water flow through the collector).

Pool water through solar heater		=	Total (× 1·163)
Temperature rise ×	Water flow	=	Heat collected
°C	m^3/h		kWh
4	0·5		2·3
3	0·8		2·8
2	1·5		3·5
1	3·8		4·4
½	9·0		5·2
Falling quality	Rising flow		Optimum quantity

INFORMATION SHEET 14.12

Thermal efficiency
(Pool buildings can suffer high losses and be poor environmental modifiers)

Insulation
Insulate first then heat:
Thermal insulation must be impervious to water and water vapour. (It also improves sound insulation.) An inter-seasonal heat store of water at 50°C with 300mm of insulating expanded polystyrene will suffer only 5°C temperature drop in 1 month. Dry ground is an effective insulator for pool water: insulate pool-walls in wet ground, insulate above-ground pool-walls at night.
Rainwater on floating covers steals heat by evaporation (see chapters 9.4 and 10.4).

Thermal transmittance coefficient or U value

The amount of heat flowing through a structural material that separates an air temperature difference is measured in W/m²/°C.

Materials	W/m²/°C
Steel mullion: 100 mm wide	7·0
Single glazing: rooflight	6·0
window	5·0
Double glazing: 5mm space	3·0
20mm space	2·5
(100 to 200mm ideal for sound insulation)	
Dense concrete: 150mm	3·7
450mm	1·7
Brick walling: 125mm	3·5
250mm	2·5
Moderately dense cellular concrete: 150mm	1·7
450mm	0·5
Concrete block walling: 250mm	1·5
350mm	1·0
Glass fibre/polystyrene: 25mm	0·8
75mm	0·4

(Typical insulation thicknesses: roof 150mm; inter-floor 100mm; cavity walling 75mm; floor 50mm)

Construction	W/m²/°C	
Average house (containing 20 per cent area single glazing, or 45 per cent double glazing, and using 20,000 kWh per year)	1·7	
House (improved insulation – suitable for 22°C operation, but not 28°C)	1·0	
Pool enclosure: acceptable 1960	1·0	
UK 1970	0.85	
France 1975	0·60	
recommended	0·5	
		Current practice
Best for low heat transmittance: walls	0·4	(1·0)
roof	0·3	(0·6)
floor	0·3	(1·0)

Heat losses
(Outdoor pools without covers)

Mainly: kWh/m²	Evaporation	Radiation	Convection	Conduction	Dilution
	day	night	wind	wet	top-up
share:	2·5	0·25	0·25	0·10	0·05
Comments:	severe when 20% relative humidity	affected by cloud, dust and RH	shielding surround essential	small up to 25°C; double loss for above ground	for back-wash, splashout and evaporation

Conserve heat

Design a compact structure, limit glazing, increase thermal insulation, provide heat recirculation, reduce ventilation at night, always cover pool surface when not in use (especially hydrotherapy and spa pools) to prevent evaporation, lower amount of chemical treatment and save 50 to 80 per cent heat losses. Suitable surface covers include air mattresses and foamed quilts, bubble blankets and floating balls, solar circles and chemical heat sealants, insulating panels and suspended fabrics.

Large areas of glazing can increase pool hall heat losses by up to one-third.

INFORMATION SHEET 14.13

Poolwater heat collectors and exchangers

Calorifier or heat exchanger: 70–95 per cent efficiency.
Primary heated water counterflowing to secondary circuit of poolwater without mixing or corroding. Heat is carried across for small loss providing the hot water circuit is short and well insulated. Secondary lines may be longer, since water temperature is lower, and providing friction losses to flow over distance are satisfactorily met by the circulating pump. Separate exchangers effectively serve various heating needs from one boiler, providing it is rated to the appropriate loading. Even at the low temperatures required for poolwater, an exchanger unit can accumulate salt deposits and block-up. Non-corrosive equipment materials are preferable, with waterway tubes and plates designed for easy cleaning.

Concrete radiant systems: 80–95 per cent operating efficiency.
A complex circuit of 15mm copper tubeways is embedded into the tank floor and walls, to carry hot water transferring heat into the poolwater; alternatively, electric elements transmit heat. A very effective slow heat system for poolwater, but very expensive to build into the tank in the first place. If the system is installed and maintained correctly, long term savings by high efficiency conversion of primary or low grade energy can result.

Solar system or solar convertor: 70–110 per cent operating efficiency.
The flat plate collector converts direct *and* diffuse solar energy into heat, using cooler poolwater as the transfer medium, but raised in temperature by 1°C only between panel inlet and outlet. Copper convertors can replace roofs cooling the building beneath, aluminium panels can respond almost as quickly as copper, while less transmissible plastic will save installing costs. A spare sunny sheltered spot with reasonably reliable sun is essential, though pool solar systems can still donate heat in moderate cloud conditions from diffuse sunlight alone. Reflectors increase available radiation. Efficiency also increases with fast flow heat collection nearing ambient temperature – hence insulation becomes less important, unless systems are situated over 10m away. Solar systems are environmentally safe, producing no pollution. Fossil fuelled heaters rely upon fast temperature build-up, but the slow solar collector heat-up of 4 or 5 days (or even weeks) requires support with a water surface heat retaining cover. Fast heat-up though is practical with solar systems for the small water volume of a hot spa pool.

Solar banks in parallel, not series, should be unshaded, face the equator and slightly towards afternoon sun, with angle of inclination appropriate for the latitude to suit all year use, or set at lower angles to maximise summer sun effect, or towards vertical for winter optimum.

Slow feed tube and plate collector systems, can impose too great a resistance within the pool circulation, and therefore require their own pump, circuit and flow; however, fast feed matrix-panels can be looped from the pool's circulation, since they offer little resistance to the main pump, but they will deteriorate in effectiveness as filter pressure rises and slows water flow, and poolwater temperature increases over ambient causing increased heating dissipation at the exchanger panels.

Solar 'fuel' might be free, but the system and pumping is not. Savings in fuel costs enable an economic and unsophisticated solar system for pools to payback in 2 to 6 years.

Glazed: trickle flow, flat plate metal collectors requiring backing insulation, and relying upon the 'greenhouse effect' to trap re-radiated heat under glass, will raise water to domestic storage temperatures of 60°C, but only at 30 to 50 per cent efficiency.

Unglazed: Flood flow, honeycomb sandwich, plastic panels, without needing insulation or framework stands, and relying upon existing roof inclines for low fixing costs, will raise water to pool temperatures of 30°C twice as efficiently as trickle flow.

Structural: Solar heater banks are space consumers, hence systems that can become pool surround constructions without looking ugly gain in value, eg heat collecting concrete paving, or GRC roof tiles, that transfer warmth to poolwater flowing within the slab offering doubly cost effective 'area' solar systems.

Controls: All panels require control systems for maximum efficiency: a time switch being the simplest expedient. A simple solar triggered switching system is best of all.

Solar collectors operating 24 hours a day can cool a pool below ambient. At night, the collector becomes an efficient radiator and a useful cooler in hot climates.

Collector controls sensitive to ±1°C, should operate only when there is sufficient sun, and not when the poolwater demands heating as provided by standard differential thermostatic arrangements. An infra red detector can trigger such a system, but it is usually limited to direct radiation only and is expensive. Alternatively, temperature probes within the collector can measure that heat is being collected, if there is water circulation – which introduces problems if panels are self-draining. A valid sensor cell for solar systems is a matt 'black box', on which solar radiation is concentrated, and which also measures ambient air temperature. The solar heater can then be preset to operate according to prescribed levels of *direct and diffuse* energy – in other words, to sense the same state of affairs that works the panels.

INFORMATION SHEET 14.14

Designing solar heaters for pools
(As a direct heat exchanger of solar energy)

ISES, CDA and US National Bureau of Standards all publish design recommendations for flat plate collectors. Swimming pools already provide two essential components of a solar heating system – water circulation and storage reservoir: and require only the additional means of energy conversion.

Efficiency is the:
Maximum transmission of heat for the minimum loss.
Maximum absorption of energy for the minimum reradiation.
Maximum total heat gain for minimum temperature rise.
An efficient collector is cool to the touch.
Increased sunlight reflection, and a water surface cover will greatly improve the effectiveness of pool solar systems.

Rating increases with sunshine hours plus any additional diffuse radiation.
Annual sunshine
1000–1500 hours : UK/Scandinavia
1500–2000 hours : France/New Zealand
2500 hours : Canadian/US border
3000 hours : Florida/South Africa
4000 hours : Arizona/W Australia
4500 hours : Sahara and Great Sandy Desert

Collector types suited for pools in order of cost effectiveness:
1st unglazed, uninsulated, fast flow absorbers
2nd arrangements utilising pool surroundings
3rd glazed, insulated conventional flat plates
4th open, sheet-flood, shallow trickle cascades
. . . set out by weight:
5kg/m² – lightweight plastic sandwich
10kg/m² – medium-weight flat plates
20kg/m² – heavyweight, large volume pipe exchangers.

Materials compared in relative value for total thermal conductivity and durability:
● corrugated sheets of iron – cheap and useful for DIY systems.
● stone, reconstituted stone and GRC – practical for surroundings/landscaped solar collection.
● aluminium plus 5 per cent magnesium – economical for flat plate units but potential corrosion problems when other metals used within the pool circulation system, eg copper.
● copper – ideal for efficient high temperature collection if required: costly, also potentially corrosive, but transmits faster than any other material – even adopted to extent of heat transmitting copper-based epoxy adhesives replacing solder.
● polycarbonate – suitable for fast water flow, low temperature rise collection at low cost: must be protected from uv degradation and can craze by hydrolysis at 60°C.
● glass – excellent for increased efficiency at high working temperature and low radiation levels, but expensive for large quantity production low grae heat.
● GRP and heat stabilised polypropylene – potentially excellent low cost, low temperature, longlife, large area materials.

Manufacture – a low cost, easily installed, no maintenance system is essential for the long term feasibility of flat plate collectors.

Metal
extruded aluminium tube-in-strip
rolled copper tube-in-strip
roll-bonded channelled plates
ribbed sheet and close-fit tubes
flat plate and close-fit tubes

Glass
tubes in parallel collecting and condensing energy

Plastic
closed spaced black plastic pipes
honeycomb type waterways
plastic bag tanks
rigid plastic trays and flat metal cover
pipes in-situ surroundings

Note:
Never use copper for sea or saltwater pools.

Consider hazard of plastic melting in a fire to drip and start fresh outbreaks.
Plastic to metal connections offer expansion/contraction problems.
Plastic degrades in sun under glass if there is no water flow to carry heat away.
Best material should be thin walled for rapid heat transfer, and should not be affected by uv, chlorine, algae, bacteria, dust and dirt.
'Selective black' surfaces are anti-oxidants, matt blacks reduce longwave reradiation losses.
Reflection onto the plate increases output: simple materials such as foil glued onto surrounding laminate being most effective.

Glazing
Glass is transparent to high temperature solar radiation (short waves 0·3 to 4·8μm), but virtually opaque to longer reradiated infra-red wavelengths emitted by the plate at below 100°C. Glass covers stop wind taking away heat from across the plate, and block reradiation like a non-return valve; trapped air in the collector also acts as an insulator to the plate helping produce the 'greenhouse effect' – a basic requirement for hotter plate design.
Ordinary 4mm window float glass can be used but is best low in iron, ie blue not green.
Average solar radiation transmission for glass: (providing cleaned occasionally)
  7% reflected by cover
15% absorbed in glass
78% passes through
High temperature systems (above 65°C) are multiple glazed or use gas as an exchanger medium for improved efficiency (30 to 50 per cent), but unglazed, low temperature (below 35°C), uninsulated solar collectors offer a better performance per unit cost for swimming pool supplementary heating – especially if structural arrangements can be minimised or made DIY.
Low temperature rise solar heaters need no glass cover nor insulation – unless operated in winter.

Operational requirements
It is more effective to gain 50 per cent heating energy very cheaply than to aim for 100 per cent very expensively. Avoid unnecessary sophistication.
Area As a general guide for mid-latitude climates, solar collectors that are equal in area to one-half the surface of a pool are the most cost effective: eg the following allocations apply to California, the Balkans, South Africa, west and east Australia:

Solar collector panel area to poolwater area	Energy saving	Swimming pool use
¹/₂:1	75%	Summer
³/₄:1	50%	Summer and fringe months
1:1	35%	All year

(total water volume is less significant than pool surface area when considering sizing solar heating, or more correctly, replacing and exceeding heat loss).
Flow Collectors must offer as little resistance to water flow as possible. The pump is rated to overcome static head and maintain filter turnover. Separate pumps are essential for trickle flow systems, though heater collection units situated below pool water level can operate thermosyphonically. An effective surface to depth pool circulation system helps heating efficiency.
Water enters and leaves panels from diagonally opposite corners: best into bottom inlet manifold and along to final panel plumbed in parallel, for even rise or tilt across the whole bank to the top header manifold and outlet. A 50 to 100mm rise across the whole bank to one corner, or an air release valve, avoids air locks. Ideally, pool solar systems should drain down for winter nights.
Use 40 or 50mm heater circuitry pipework with 2m/s water velocity, though trickle flow systems satisfactorily use 25mm pipelines for small bore heater banks.
Flow rates might range from 1 to 10m³/h for private pool solar systems, when lagging is not required.
Too high flow into panels risks impingement attack on metal parts. Maximum distance of panels from pool should be 30m.
Supports Panel failures are most troublesome on roofs, especially flat roofs. Lightweight units stood at an incline require side skirts to prevent lifting in winds, or maybe even temporary removal before very high winds.
If special framework or housing can be avoided, maintenance and attention made insignificant, the system quickly becomes more cost effective.

Positioning Flat plate collectors require an optimum state between absorbent surface, glazing and insulation, rate of water flow, slope and orientation, and cost. The parameters in positioning solar collectors are summarised as follows:

Direct sun only	Theoretical solar energy maximum	Variation for peak solar energy collection	
Panel position	Ideal placing for all year	Optimum adjustment for:	
		summer	winter
Tilt	Geographic latitude	−10° to slope	+20° to slope
Orientation	Face equator	Set slightly towards afternoon sun to a maximum 20% from ideal	
When set at optimum for that time of year, increased solar energy	+25% over horizontal	+50%	+100%

Diffuse sun factor

Vary panel setting between 10 and 30 per cent nearer to the horizontal as non-directional to direct radiation proportion increases towards a 50/50 share.

Expected solar energy changes:

−20% in cities

+20% to collection sheltered positions

+25% with reflectors

Note: Facing solar panels for garden pools to the sun at existing roof angles is often more cost effective.

INFORMATION SHEET 14.15

Some special solar systems for water

Japan:	2 to 5m³ shallow pillow type polybags laid on roofs to collect heat for family evening bathing.
Holland:	re-use of unfrosted, redundant fluorescent tubes set on rows as 'solar energy windows' – with 75 per cent efficiency claims.
France:	1m wide decklevel overflow step, surrounding the entire pool and covered by translucent screen for a fast flow, in situ pool perimeter collector.
UK:	Concrete troughs and steps overflowing at level flood rates for high efficiency/low cost ratios on a 150m³ pool.
	Solar paving and solar tiling keep cool to the touch when used in pool surroundings solar architecture.
US (Los Angeles):	250m of pipe attached to the garden fence for low cost collection on a 12 × 6·5m pool.
US (Florida):	5000m of 40mm ABS thermoplastic pipe with carbon black colouration and 3 internal fins to maximise heat surface area, heats a 800m³ pool: solar manifold loads roof at 20kg/m² to a total of 22 tonnes of water.

INFORMATION SHEET 14.16

Heat pump or 'reverse refrigerator' (300 to 700 per cent production efficiency)

A heat pump is a device which transfers heat energy from a place where it is not needed to a place where it is needed, upgrading in temperature during transfer. It is the water chiller of the air conditioning scheme, but of heavy duty for almost continuous operation, since effort is concentrated upon production of heat rather than chilled water – in fact, the chilled water is now only a by-product of the heat production.

Heat pumps can be split to offer high, and then low grade heating of water, for space heating and thermal storage. They are at their most versatile when heat energy is collected, through a chilled water system, reclaiming heat from extracted air, waste shower water and pool filter backwash water; the secondary, warm water system serves air heater batteries, poolwater calorifiers, shower water, heating, wall and floor heating panels, indeed almost any heating function in a swimming pool.

The heat pump cooling cycle extracts heat for the pool by becoming a 'temperature amplifier'. By adding work to a large quantity of low temperature (low grade) heat, heat can be produced at a higher temperature. The ratio of production is termed the coefficient of performance, and is some measure of the system's quality.

$$\text{COP: coefficient of performance} = \frac{\text{heating coil output}}{\text{compressor input}}$$

The theoretical to actual COP value is measured by the performance/energy ratio (per). COP can vary from 1 to 20, but 3:1 in air is minimally efficient, and 5:1 or 7:1 reasonable for cool to warm waters. Claims are made that heat pumps can operate for one-third the cost of normal running costs, but this often excludes capital depreciation and maintenance, expected payback periods are 5 to 10 years at current fuel rates. The heat pump becomes less efficient as the temperature difference, or lift between source and sink, increases (a solar heater on the other hand becomes more efficient as temperature difference between cool poolwater and hot sun increases).

Liquid/gas circulation devices upgrading energy or concentrating heat, can operate from gas or electricity and only require sufficient energy to drive the fluid pump or compressor.

Large volume, low temperature heating sources can be taken from air, earth, water or geothermal sources, with the compressor using a refrigeration cycle transferring 3 to 7kW of energy for each 1kW expended: the main requirement being a large and continuously cheap energy supply of constant temperature, no matter if it is 10 or 15°C below pool.

Efficiency of device between heat source and sink:

heat pump is highest for small temperature differences,

solar panel is highest for large temperature differences.

INFORMATION SHEET 14.17

The pool boiler

Requires:

- to achieve between ¹/₂° and 1°C temperature rise per hour, with up to a 100kW rating for home pools, or up to a 1000kW rating for public pools
- a supply operating temperature to 40°C, with boiler circuit flow and return 80/70°C
- a fresh air supply ventilation of 3m³/h per kW rating, and combustion air to 6m³/h per kW rating, from a low level fresh air inlet near the boiler, and a high level outlet of at least half inlet area.

Includes:

boiler and waterways in cast iron, non-ferrous or coated steel

durable casing

flue and draught diverter (gas-fired) or induced draught fan and stack (oil-fired)

heat exchanger or control loop and 3-way blending valve

control tees and valves manifold to heater circuit

fuel injector pump and filter

pressurising vessel/expansion tank

oil tank, supply lines or gas pressure regulator

efficient burners and control box

temperature altitude gauge

pool stat/limit stat/flow valve and water pressure switch

pressure relief valve

air release cock

drain cock.

INFORMATION SHEET 14.18

Poolwater heaters and boilers

All public pools and half of all newly installed garden pools automatically include water heating arrangements.

Oil-fired boiler systems, or multi-fuelled. 70 to 80 per cent operating efficiency.

Highest capital cost of fossil fuelled heaters with supplementary exchangers or loops, but very competitive operating costs. Reliable, widely available components offer fast heat-flows, with an adaptable system that can be located anywhere, is well known and quickly installed. The most popular system if gas supplies are not available or are limited. Regular maintenance is important, since a dirty boiler can easily waste 25 per cent fuel. Cold water through the boiler induces condensation to corrode linings, but increased firing cuts cool operating condensation which otherwise can take 20 or 30 corroding minutes to dry out. Lower boiler operating temperatures will keep sludge and scale deposits down in certain waters.

There are environmental problems such as noise requiring effective separation from swimmers and neighbours; fumes can be blown over the pool area (but if induced draught fans are used to reduce the flue length which must have no sharp bends, they must operate before the boiler can fire; stack discolouration at the top indicates initial smutting); oil tanks need to be easily accessible for fuel deliveries and approved by fire authorities, especially for schools, hotel and municipal pools; fuel storage tanks, and bulky flue vent stacks are unsightly.

These are independent and flexible systems that are ideal for innumerable pools.

Gas-fired boiler systems or liquid gas. 80 to 95 per cent operating efficiency.

Less capital cost and lower fuel prices generally; though supplies are limited by production and policy. Moderate installation costs with lower maintenance. Often the lack of mains supply prohibits using natural/coal gas systems, which make bottled gas more practical. Gas-fired heaters can supply direct or indirect, to wall and floor coils, or even be immersed for highest efficiency with inlet/exhaust post provision.

The system is clean, efficient, automatic and requires no fuel store nor delivery schedules (except bottled gas).

Electric heaters or electrode boilers. 95 to 98 per cent operating efficiency.

Lowest capital cost, but most expensive of all fuel prices, unless abundant hydro-electricity or spare generating capacity available. Installation is very simple for flow-through heaters and maintenance very small. Mains supply will need to be 3-phase for 20kW units and over, and can be expensive to lay on for private pools. Electricity is an ideal motive power source. Politics and fuel prices affect supply costings – low off-peak rates are essential for viability. Systems operate simply, quickly and automatically; heat is available immediately required; units are compact, quiet, clean, highly efficient and require no operating labour or fuel storage. Small electric units are ideal supplementary heaters to solar systems, offering practical and environmentally safe alternative heating processes.

INFORMATION SHEET 14.19

Relative prices – heating systems

Indication initial cost for 75m³ garden pool
Equipment is costed as a factor of 100, based upon
heat exchanger = 100 cost factor

100	Heat exchanger
150	Electric poolheater
250	Gas-fired boiler

350	Oil-fired boiler
400	Heat pump
450	Coal-fired boiler
600	Solar convertor

See information sheets 2.8, 7.6, 8.2, 13.10 and 15.12.

INFORMATION SHEET 14.20

Space heating allocations

Ideally arranged as 60 per cent surface heat and 40 per cent air heat (0·20kW/m³ rating taken as rough estimating guidance for temperate climates).

Pool hall allocations: 4/6 airchanges per hour vented to waste without heat recovery arrangements can increase total heat load by as much as 100 per cent.

Heat load share based upon heat loss, ventilation and poolwater needs:

Air and fabric	Water	Pre-cleanse/showers	
50%	45%	5%	Private
60%	25%	15%	Public

Space heating must operate 1°C above water temperature to save evaporative heat losses; or a 'humidity blanket' should be provided over the pool: simple air-gap protective covers create this same insulating barrier for only 100mm enclosed water saturated space over the water.

Heat retaining or surface covers, are significantly useful for the natatorium, otherwise there can be continual dripping wet problems of condensation inside, especially on cold, damp days.

Heaters are best sized to replace losses from the fabric and structure, from the air ventilation and poolwater, involving:

Fan heaters or convectors: best before windows ensuring no draughts on poolside or water surface. Air heating coils designed for 40°C flow and 30°C return. Air or radiant heaters directed onto water or onto continually wetted surrounds, considerably aggravate evaporation, humidity and condensation.

Direct or indirect radiant heaters as warming panels or hot seats are preferred by swimmer spectators: warm floors are also favoured, especially in changing rooms, pool surrounds, pre-cleanse areas, etc.

Radiators must not be too hot – 50°C maximum (preferably 45°C maximum flow allowing a 10°C drop, also suitable for showers).

Solar radiation through large glazed walls facing the sun can overheat hall interiors unless control, conditioning or heat recovery systems are provided to re-employ the energy as a bonus: with total heat recovery, heat load can be reduced from 7500kWh/m² water area per annum to 2500 for an average 25m public pool.

Warm water technology for radiant heat emission through floor panels is a practical low temperature distribution system, ideally suited to the swimming pool environment, and to ambient energy devices. The system is uniform, efficient and above all, vandal-proof.

INFORMATION SHEET 14.21

Indication of space heating requirements

When water temperature = 27°C, air temperature = 28°C, relative humidity = 60 per cent, air changes per hour 4, and without introducing any heat recovery or additional insulation.

Pool	Dimensions	Area	Volume overall approx		Heater rating share (temperate climates) approx guide		Air allowance
			Water	Air	Pool water	Hall air	
	m	m²	m³	m³	kW	kW	kW/m³
Private	10 × 5	50	75	300	30	75	0·25
Local	25 × 13	325	500	3000	200	600	0·20
International	50 × 21	1050	3000	30,000	1000	4500	0·15

Note: Heat recovery design/high standard insulation will reduce annual heat load three- or four-fold.

INFORMATION SHEET 14.22

Ventilation – air changes

Airchange rates are greatly affected by the total volume and total wet area involved: eg diving stages greatly increase space to ventilate and adversely affect turnover situation. Higher airchange rates are more suitable for smaller rooms and halls, and recommended cubic ventilation rates are better for large schemes. Only small unheated enclosures depend entirely upon fresh air clearing the atmosphere without any circulation.

Facility	Average no airchanges per hour
General services areas	2 by natural circulation
Pool hall	4/6
Dressing room	6/8
Clothes storage and pre-cleanse	8/10
Steamy areas and roof	10/12 though 16 sometimes required

Air space ventilation: cubic rates are preferable. Systems should operate day and night, though two-speed fans of unequal size can be switched to reduce ventilation at low operating periods, or overnight: either operate at 30 to 50 per cent capacity for night-time economy, or install variable speed regulators controlled by humidity detectors. Always allow some margin to cover dirty heat exchangers or clogged filters slowing down specified air rates. Recirculation to be incorporated with modulation dampers for basic design at 100 per cent pool hall ventilation rate; override to be available whenever odour level requires fresh air dilution.

Pool hall air flow rate	Comment
25–50m³/h per swimmer	Private pools only
30–50m³/h per swimmer	France: maximum load one bather/m²
50–60m³/h/m² (or 0·015m³/s/m²)	UK: wetted surface area (old rate 0·005m³/s/m²)
60–75m³/h per person	US: generous provision and ideal for spectators

and heat recovery is vital

eg 0·005m³/s/m² approximates to 3 airchanges per hour, and 0·015m³/s/m² approximates to 9 airchanges per hour, which increases evaporation and heat loss from the pool by 50 per cent. Often, extra fresh air (cold usually) is required to 'mop-up' moisture.

Air velocity at 25°C to offer ventilation without draughts. Fresh air preferably should scour the surface water with main outside ventilation inlets set well clear of plantroom chemical stocks, and any other possible contamination. Pool hall supply air is best discharged vertically up all external window surfaces, and/or external wall surfaces.

Velocity at input grilles

0·10m/s	maximum preferred for swimmer spectators
0·15m/s	USA at 2·5m height
0·20m/s	UK
0·30m/s	FDR (and spectator areas USA)

Air pressure with pool hall extraction fans operating at 10 per cent higher capacity than input air supply:

allow −10 per cent air pressure, and always provide air flow to pool hall;
allow +10 per cent air pressure in suspended ceiling, as extra thermal/air flow aid to vapour barrier.

Sources: ASA/EC/IAKS/IBM/IHVE/NSPI/TUS.

INFORMATION SHEET 14.23

Ventilation – circulation systems

Recirculation: generally to avoid carryover of chlorine contamination, the pool hall air requires continual expensive change. When chlorine based water disinfection systems are used – with a 20 per cent fresh air dilution rate per hour for the pool's atmosphere – ventilation contamination usually indicates the water treatment is at fault. Breakpoint chlorination and by-product impurities defeat complete recirculation of air. Alternatively, ozonation of water with marginal chlorination only, will allow recovery and recirculation of air for heating economy, which is a high capital equipment cost system needing high voltages for on-the-spot ozone production in quantity (see chapter 15·5).

Circulation comparisons

Input	Extract	Comment
Low level	High level	Generally best results if counteraction is taken against down draughts: often unsatisfactory for spectator gallery.
High level	High level	Unusual arrangement: input is directed at water surface at high velocity and ceiling extraction provided. Careful design is necessary to avoid shortcircuiting.
High level	Low level	Most popular circulation: correctly sized and shaped inlets are important, and as extraction is non-directional the system draws air of least resistance. This arrangement poorly planned and operated, has provided some of the most spectacular H and V failures with smoke and fumes accumulating in the gallery or trapped areas, and condensation everywhere else.

Input	Extract	Comment
High and low	High and low	Ideal arrangement though more expensive on ducting. Low speed air currents directed at surface avoids evaporation and discomfort to swimmers but can raise relative humidity.

Sources: IAKS/IHVE/IBM.

INFORMATION SHEET 14.24

Relative humidity

Maintaining relative humidity at high levels reduces heat loss from poolwater, and lowers evaporation rates, but increases the quantity of heat wasted in ventilated air and promotes active corrosion; this is especially critical at over 70 per cent RH, with ample oxygen from continual fresh and colder air added into a pool's atmosphere, which might already contain corrosive salts, sulphur dioxide, nitrogen trichloride, etc. Smaller window space, double glazing, higher air temperature and air circulation, lowers condensation levels.

Variables: the pool's relative humidity, or dew point temperature, is related to:
- water temperature
- air temperature inside and out
- relative humidity outside
- water and wetted areas giving considerable influence
- air velocity over water surface and outside wind direction
- barometric pressure
- number of swimmers and spectators
- building insulation U value, and a solar facing glazing area, which is often the biggest single factor determining the ventilation rate of airchange, and can vary the relative humidity as a result from 40 to 90 per cent (at 100 per cent air is saturated).

The swimmer prefers a low range from 30 to 40 per cent relative humidity, the spectator from 30 to 70 per cent, (average office conditions range from 40 to 60 per cent). But an optimum relative humidity level is 60 per cent for pool halls with poolwater at 27°C, air at 28°C, and ventilation airflow at 60m³/h/m² wetted surface area (wetted area taken as 1·2 × pool area). Some countries recommend RH values of between:

60–80% – France
60–70% – Holland
50–75% – UK
50–60% – US

A pool hall atmosphere can hold large quantities of water – and consequently heat – in air ready to condense on any cool surface. A 25m natatorium with normal operating temperature and air of low RH at 40 per cent, can absorb over 3 tonnes of evaporated water in 24 hours.

Vapour pressure Water vapour as a gas exerts pressure and diffuses throughout the structure. The greater the difference between air and water vapour pressure, the greater the evaporation.

A natatorium atmosphere of high temperature and RH, against an external atmosphere of low temperature and RH, results in a considerable vapour pressure difference:

Inside   30°C at 70% RH = 27mb
Outside 10°C at 40% RH = 5mb

Producing a difference of   22mb or 17mm of mercury pressure exerted onto interior surfaces.

Interstitial condensation penetrating into porous materials and structures, greatly increases under pressure, unless a satisfactory vapour barrier is provided.

Vapour barrier All dead space should be vapour sealed on the warm side of the construction to stop condensation, especially inside the roof structure. Particularly avoid cold bridges between warm envelope and cold outside atmosphere, such as structural steel girders. Total sealing is expensive and difficult to achieve, and the hot air barrier overcomes having to rely upon a perfect seal. Private pool enclosures tend to rely upon inert non-porous bare materials and some dispersal of condensation, plus occasionally a stapled vapour membrane: but public pool detailing, and sealing needs to provide a total barrier as impermeable as the pool lining. This is so difficult to guarantee that positive hot air ventilation pressure above a suspended ceiling is the satisfactory compromise, providing it is maintained all the time the pool holds water.

Note: 'saturated vapour pressure' beneath suspended surface covers effectively stops any further evaporation, the major component of heat loss.

Dew point Condensation occurs on surfaces whose temperatures are below the dew point temperature of surrounding air. Pool air dew point relates to the evaporation rate from wet surfaces – hence dry surrounds, surface water covers, and variable ventilation save humidity which increases with poolwater temperature and dry air. As moisture content rises, so does dew-point temperature. Fresh air dilutes the internal atmosphere, reduces internal air dew point keeping condensation down. Heat recovery systems utilise to advantage the high heat content of warm moisture in the air.

Evaporation is continual to air above: space heating savings are made immediately by lowering air temperature, but only at the outweighing expense of increased condensation and long term ravages to a building.

Air conditioning is rarely required except for very hot and very humid climates – and then more for spectator comfort. But once again, the heat pump cooler can make good use of ambient energy by 'dumping' it in the poolwater.

INFORMATION SHEET 14.25

Heat recovery devices

Air, earth or water all have cheap, low grade heat available for extraction. But since chlorine in moist pool air is aggressively corrosive and vapour can be condensed in heat recovery, water ozonation with marginal chlorination (0·2 to 0·4ppm) helps reduce any contamination to safe levels. As a result, conservation further reduces pollution. The whole heat stock system should be like a 'thermal flywheel' not an 'energy drain', enabling thermal hardware to save at least 75 per cent primary energy requirements in pools.

Total heat reclaim (total enthalpy)	=	sensible heat (dry bulb thermometer) 'hot' heat easily recovered	+	latent heat (wet bulb thermometer) unseen heat difficult to detect

An ideal combination for 'save-it' leisure facilities is the 'in tandem' swimming pool/ice rink, where a heat pump can use interchangeable heat/freeze cycles for both parts of the duo-building at the same time, making full use of all hot and cold energy.

A varied range of devices are now available for the re-use or regeneration of heat:

Heat exchangers (static): payback period 2 to 4 years.

Air-to-air (50 to 80 per cent efficiency): counterflowing air streams recover sensible heat from exhaust air for transfer into return plenum using metal or glass plate exchangers. A luminaire device recovers heat from light fittings, which as a result improve in efficiency offering 10 per cent more light output.

Water-to-water (60 to 90 per cent efficiency): laminated counterflowing streams of water under pressure cross thin plates in alternate layers without mixing – turbulent flow stiffens these plates for good heat transfer at low cost. Keep water clean with dirt trap before plates.

Water/air and air/water: all heat exchangers aim to extend the area of contact between hot and cool media to maximise energy transfer.

Heat pipes: payback period 3 to 6 years (60 to 70 per cent efficiency). One end is set in a warm air stream to absorb and transfer heat (no moving parts – no maintenance) to the other end of the small diameter copper pipe in the cool air stream alongside. A working refrigerant vapour flows and condenses inside the sealed pipe, returning along a wick by capillary action to the warm end, where it evaporates to start the cycle again. These 'heat super-conductors' are 1000 times more effective than a solid copper bar, and are built into banks of warm expelled air collectors for maximum concentrated effect. (Range from 2 to 750kW units, or 'thermal transformers' acting as heat exchangers without pumps or electric motors for energy flow.)

Reverse refrigerant units: payback period 4 to 6 years at COP 5.

Heat pump (60 to 80 per cent efficiency) – upgrades temperature. Internal source device – recovers internal heat. External source device – provides primary heat. This thermal pump on heating cycle delivers more heat than the electrical/gas energy it consumes to drive the compressor. Heat pumps are versatile devices whose heat production can be used in many ways within pools: provision for 1kW cooling load per m^2 pool area without adjusting boiler ratings.

Refrigerant systems – run round coils (30 to 50 per cent efficiency). Two exchangers, one in inlet and one in outlet ducts, are connected by a pipe loop in which circulates a water and anti-freeze mixture. A simple and inexpensive system allowing separation of ducts yet offering reasonable heat transfer: low cost investment suitable for existing pool schemes. Rather than upgrade 0·005 to 0·015m^3/s/m^2 airchange systems, install a 1m^3/s dehumidifier for pool hall airheat recovery for a 2 to 3 year payback period.

Double bundle condensers (50 to 70 per cent efficiency). In addition to refrigeration plant and the condenser bundles of two entirely separate water coils carrying warm and cool water inside a shell cylinder, there is usually a water heat dump tank for storage – obviously this tank can be large for use at relatively low temperature . . . in fact a normal swimming pool facility.

Waste water tank capacity to cater for filter backwash volume, and full shower water usage over 5 hours, with provision for heat exchange to colder water.

Refrigerant systems can recover sensible and latent heat from shower and poolwater waste, air exhaust waste heat, and when acting as a dehumidifier the payback period can be halved. Ozonation improves efficiencies, and cooling tower dissipation of heat can be made unnecessary. Commonly, cooling coils are used to recover 65 per cent total heat with the thermal wheel recovering another 25 per cent enthalpy on top; this heat is used in the condenser coil to warm up and redeliver dry air back to the pool hall again.

Heat wheel: payback period 4 to 8 years (70 to 90 per cent efficiency). Slowly rotating air-to-air heat exchanger (10 RPM) recovers energy from expelled air and carries it round into the incoming cold air duct as preheat. The thick corrugated matrix wheel unimpeding to air flow, continuously absorbs both dry and wet heat achieving highly efficient transfer of total heat. A purge section cuts cross-contamination to a maximum of 0·1 per cent by volume of airborne materials and odours. A filter before the wheel is valuable and ozonation later in the system practical for all enclosed pools. Wheel diameters range from 0·5 to 5m with 0·7kW motors for 20m^3/h air handling. Efficiency improves as it gets colder outside.

Metallic units recovering sensible heat at 25 to 50 per cent efficiency have been in use since 1900. Fibrous asbestos laminate type impregnated with hygroscopic chemical (lithium chloride dessicant) recovering latent heat as originally designed by Carl Munter for 75 per cent average efficiency have been operating since 1960. If metallic non-hygroscopic material for the rotating matrix is used, there will be some transfer of moisture as condensate: hence dehumidify outgoing air with a cooling coil, as part of the heat pump recovery scheme.

The kind of savings from different heat recovery conservations

	Approximate share of	
	Total heat saving	Extra capital cost
Reduce water temperature 27–24°C	1%	–
Reduce air temperature 28–25°C	5%	–
Reduce heat transmittance with insulation to 0·5 U value standard	5%	8%
Reduce airchanges from 6 to 4 per hour	14%	–
Provide water cover reducing overnight evaporation	10%	10%
Provide ventilation shutdown to service and administration areas	5%	–
Install variable ventilation/humidistat	5%	2%
Install heat recovery plant (dehumidifier an inexpensive component for high heat recovery)	55%	80%

Energy requirements for swimming pools under continuous operation can be effectively *reduced by 80 per cent of conventional design systems,* which is sometimes worth in every year more than 10,000kWh per square metre of water surface.

INFORMATION SHEET 14.26

Energy saving procedures for pools

Structural	Mechanical	Air	Water
Insulate to 0·5U value at least	Provide heat recovery techniques	Always 1°C warmer than water	Cover when out of use
Insulate pool tank	Use alternative energy sources	Achieve 60m³/h/m², or at least 4/5 air changes	Reclaim
Design less airspace	Evaluate *all* heat pump possibilities	Reclaim and recirculate	Maintain filtration quality all time
Stop airleaks – especially around windows, doors, etc	Install multi-boiler systems	Consider an ozonator	Consider dual purification for extra clarity
Double glaze always	Ensure planned maintenance and effective boiler operation	Reduce fresh air dilution	Consider ozonation
Safely lag HW piping	Keep building fabric warm with time-clock cut-back 5–10°C when pool not in use	Slow airflow over water	Accurate automatic thermostatic controls only
Provide effective internal vapour barriers	Allow different lighting levels	Provide variable ventilation settings	1°C cut saves 10 per cent heating
Provide reflective insulation behind radiators	Use daylight, time switches, and maintain efficient relamping	Install humidity/dewpoint controllers	Recover waste water heat
Offer bright, light surface finishes		Maintain appropriate temperature according to facility	Collect and use rainwater

Note: Continually study pattern of energy usage to reduce wastage.
Sources: EC/IBM/IHVE/NAPO/NSPI/NZSPM.

INFORMATION SHEET 14.27

The energy warehouse
(Storing heat in quantity not quality)

12 solar houses, zero energy homes and minimum resource buildings incorporating pool size heat dumps – five operating as swimming pools and regenerating heat for potential energy autonomy.

Year	Location	Designer	Solar area m²	Water volume m³	Water temp °C	Heat capacity kWh	Remarks
			Approximate data				
1939	Cambridge, USA	MIT I	34	62	55–90	5000	Interseasonal storage of heat
1956	Albuquerque, USA	Solar Office: Bridges, Paxton & Haines	71	23	60	1000	Heat pump at 4·5 COP transfers heat from store or provides cooling
1958	Tokyo, Japan	Yangimachi	130 / 30	36 / 10	25 / 40	750 / 100	2·2kW heat pump upgrades energy from main to 'hot' tank: 0·75kW heat pump provides 70% house heating for year
1960	Toronto, Canada	Dept of Mechanical Engineering	57	225	60	9000	Surrounding ground holds energy also for interseasonal storage, and 100% annual heating requirements
1963	Washington, USA	Thomason	85	{ 6 / 45	55 / 30	200 / 300	Flat roof over secondary storage *swimming pool* assists solar collector with reflector: provides 95% house heating per year
1975	Aachen, FDR	Phillips	20	42 / 5 × 2	50 / 20/95	1200 / 300	Earth heat exchanger and hot water recovery heat pumps for annual heat storage dump tank
1975	Cheltenham, England	PSA–DOE Studies	– / Solar	15 / 27	53 / 53	600 / 1100	3kW heat pump transfers energy to house, and second study includes solar collector
1976	Avignon, France	Michaelis	35	150	30–80	9000	Wind generator supplement: *swimming pool* interseasonal storage, and 100% heating needs
1976	Lyngby, Denmark	NATO Study	42	30	60	1000	Low winter sun energy collection to 0·6m insulated storage tank
1976	Tucson, USA	Copper Development Association	100	{ 14 / 70	85 / 30	800 / 350	Linked swimming pool plus heat pump and air conditioners for 75% cooling and 100% heating
1976	Asheville, USA	Sheppard	34	136	30	1000	Linked swimming pool backed by 2 heat pumps for 60% cooling/heating needs
1978	CEGB HQ, Harrogate and Bristol, UK	Gillinson Barnett Steenson Varming Mulcahy/Arup	–	140	21–33	2000	Swimming pool buried in IED building, stores spent heat from computer cooling and 1100 staff: heat pump extracts from this pool dump for early morning warm-up to 20,000m² office floor area

15 Water treatment

Everybody knows water . . . and there lies the problem. It is easy to fill a pool with potable (or drinkable) water, but quite another matter to get it polished bright and to keep it perfectly clean. The chemistry of poolwater is complex, and can be a complete maze to non-chemical people.

15.1 Chemistry of waters

In designing pool hygiene systems, the main problems with water must be clearly understood since the equipment and the chemical dosing works ceaselessly, or the pool will be closed down. No matter which modern system is selected, hand worked or automatic, the purification process is often only as good as the ability of the operator. Every popular design must provide an ongoing system that can be tolerated by the unenthusiastic gardener, or understood by the handyman caretaker. Only when trained personnel professionally maintain swimming pool services can the subtleties of highly sophisticated waterworks supersystems be taken to full advantage: and then the unexpected still happens.

Soft waters lack calcium, and seek this element from plaster, Marblite and concrete in the pool. However, most waters are hard, with excessive salts that inevitably lime up the pool system. Even if the structure does not deteriorate, the equipment can, and the water will. Poolwater is a very slightly saline solution. It must be turned into a mild disinfectant that does not trouble swimmers.

15.2 Clarity and purity

The pool ideal is a sterile environment. Swimming pool water must be better than the water we drink, and remain so. It has to be clearer than drinking water, and *still* contain a palatable disinfectant. Unlike the waterworks practice, where there is a once and for all sterilising effort of untreated water, and which gets removed before it reaches the consumer, the swimming pool starts off fresh, and must stay fresh even though suffering continual contamination and bacterial pollution. Since each bather can introduce 600 million microbes at first plunge, the water sterilent must be continually present and very virile. At peak pollution times, material taken into the pool must not swamp filtration nor purification systems. The completely satisfactory treatment system stops the spread of infection, prevents algae formation, eliminates tastes and odours, improves the appearance and controls scaling and corrosion in water.

The ancient world used salt and lime compounds, and copper and silver vessels in purifying water. Mediaeval baths were generally emptied and cleaned at intervals (the bodies of dogs and cats, fowl and pigs being constantly found in Bath's murky mineral waters). The 19th-century floating baths on the Seine were luxurious and notorious: then the deck surrounding the piscine was well stocked with 'odoriferous plants' to mask the stench; an extra of two-horse hydraulics meant the whole bath could be emptied and refilled within the hour.

Sea, pond or river water made into a natural lido does not remain really attractive, nor warm enough, nor clean throughout the whole year. A modern recirculation and purification system, or even continuous flow pool for thermal and mineral waters, holds purity and clarity equally important for the complete safety of the swimmer. Accidents can go unnoticed in murky water – to the extent that even today in one disturbing case when a young person was drowned in a swimming pool, the body was not found until the tank was emptied a day or so later.

Hygeia Clear, pure poolwater sparkles because disinfection burns out all organic debris and filtration strains out inorganic material. Before total oxidation systems were developed, aeration was used to put back a sparkle into water that was uninviting, or lacked lustre. It released gases in poolwater from the decomposition of organic matter, but also dissipated any remaining chlorine. Since the 1950s, breakpoint chlorination (see information sheet 15.9) has been adopted by many public pools and aeration has almost completely disappeared. The much higher disinfection standard means bactericidal and virucidal efficiency is improved and chlorinous compound odours are totally burned away.

Over 80 per cent of the world's diseases are traceable to unclean water, fortunately not swimming pool water. 'When filtration is adequate and disinfection properly operated, coliform and E.coli will not normally be detectable in 100ml samples of water.'[1] To guarantee that no dangerous E.coli (which causes all kinds of nauseating troubles – it is a faecal bacteria and is equivalent to saying you are swimming in sewage or effluent) can appear in any samples, a very 'fast kill' residual disinfectant, such as free fast-acting chlorine, must exist in poolwater all the time. A high residual of fast-acting hypochlorous acid, resulting from superchlorination, acts rather like the white corpuscles that destroy bacteria within the blood stream. Ions of low molecular weight with absence of electrical charge make it relatively easy for the hypochlorous acid to

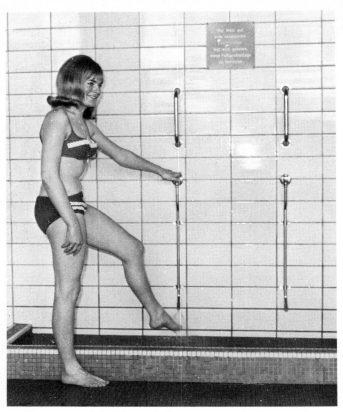

15.1 *Diatomaceous earth filter media is made up of the fossil remains from innumerable marine diatom such as Heliopel-teae family, and being so fine can help strain out some organisms: scanning electron micrograph magnification × 2200*
Johns-Manville Research and Development Dept, Denver

15.2 *Prophylactic footspray for better hygiene*
Th. Goldschmidt Ltd, Essen/London

penetrate cell walls of bacteria to burn them out. Invading bacteria is overwhelmed and absorbed, but in the process, some of the residual defence material also gets used up.

Fast and free chlorine (as hypochlorous acid) is easily dissipated by UV light and requires the support of a slower acting, more stable form of chlorine for back up. Ammonia used to be added into pools to produce a stable, combined chlorine residual. But such partially reduced materials, (chloramines) offer only relatively poor disinfection in kill-rate terms. It is well proved that natural donation of ammonia from perspiration and urine helps provide more than enough of this irritating combined form of chlorine.

To distinguish a subtle difference in purification terms, continual destruction of infection to pools is now termed disinfection, as opposed to the once-only, total and thorough dousing, implied by sterilisation. A pool in use never becomes that wishful sterile environment, but is a disinfected one repeatedly polluted. When bacteria combine with oxygen, they are made harmless. Chlorine speeds this oxidation process tremendously. In properly run pools, polluted water and infection is rare – almost impossible. But if treatment is below par, chlorine resistant organisms will develop. Superchlorination (beyond breakpoint) will therefore always be necessary to cope in heavier bathing loads, and higher water temperature.

The importance of pH There are many factors affecting the virility of a purification system and adding up to disinfection demand. A major aspect controlling the most efficient

kill-rate is the acidity or basicity (alkalinity) of water. The indicative pH factor must be balanced with addition of acids or bases to neutralise extreme conditions, not only for the comfort of bathers, but for optimum activity from the residual disinfectant (see information sheets 15.2, 15.20 and 15.24). Generally, it is accepted that pH is kept near neutral for more effective purification, but in New Zealand, for example, where one or two serious outbreaks of dangerous diseases occurred in thermal waters, a practice has been developed to use higher rates of disinfection, at higher pH levels to overcome any possible recurrences.

The most recommended pH position for the most active results from most disinfectants is 7·5 – also the pH of the tear duct and the most compatible level for the bather's skin. Whenever complaints are made about 'the chlorine', it is almost certain the pH is out, or there is insufficient free chlorine available in the poolwater to burn out all by-product compounds and all contaminants. An active swimmer can perspire one litre per hour. And when you think the average urine contribution per bather is in the region of 25 to 50ml, or almost 2 litres for every class full of children, the purifying method chosen for the water you swim in must work well.

Nowadays, most schools stress the value of hygiene, especially pre-hygiene before swimming. Reduced loading on the treatment system can halve disinfection dispensing rates. Continental European pre-cleanse standards and discipline, where soap and showers are practically obligatory, is very high – but not so high as in Japan where personal cleanliness is exceptional. Elsewhere, the traditional trip through a murky footbath just does not count as real pre-cleanse. In fact, the footbath offers only dubious protection against the more prevalent skin infections such as athlete's foot. It actually needs sulphuric acid to destroy the spores of this fungus.

The modern amphoteric microbiocide disinfectant footspray is excellent. But again, far better with strict supervision, soaping and washing away of contaminated skin flakes, plus pressurised footsprays delivering a potent 1 per cent disinfectant solution. Footspray units should also provide a footrest with well thought out rugged design to beat abuse (see chapter 11.4).

Attendance deteriorates with dirt The pool surround and changing area requires constant attention and thorough hygiene. Floors are often washed with 1 per cent chlorine solution, but the 1 per cent microbiocide solution that leaves a thin bactericidal film over the surface is becoming more popular. This wash treatment with spraylance does not affect poolwater, and is ideal for pool carpeting and rubber moulded surfaces. The same stock of disinfectant is available for portable dispensers, or piped around from a central source for use in changing room or footbath, channel or tunnel.

The search has been on for years for an all pervasive durable disinfectant, non-toxic, colourless and odourless, one that effectively treats water for the whole range of polluting conditions. Unfortunately, such an elixir is elusive and impractical. Disinfection, although the most critical of water treatment requirements, is only one aspect of effective control. Every chemical compound used in the pool brings some other side effect, or needs some counteractive pH control, or has insufficient staying power, and so on.

15.3 Chlorination, bromination and iodination

As with fuel, where there are different grades, so with chlorine, the main proven agent. There is gas for large scale use, liquid for practicality, and different concentrations of dry solids for convenience. Many other chemicals and compounds are efficient and available, but not with the economy and widescale use and acceptance of chlorine. The power of chlorine only requires one half litre residual for every one million litres of poolwater to ensure an immediate effect. But as with fuel, it gets used up as the pace hots up.

To illustrate the actual power of chlorine (at one part per million or ppm) in its control over dirt and bacteria, there is no one person in any city (of 1 million population) who alone can carry out all functions of emergency and police, hygiene and sanitation.

Residual In a swimming pool a rapid acting residual is required, since the period of contact is no more than the time it takes to pass an infection from one bather to the next. A disinfectant gets used up as it destroys organic matter, but some – the residual – must still be left over to work against new contamination. It is this residual with which we are most concerned for swimming pool disinfection.

Basically, there are two kinds of active residual – the fast, free uncombined kind that is ready for immediate action, and the slow, combined compound that follows the first process stage of breaking down organic matter. The free residual can act within a few seconds, but the combined

takes a few hours. Their ultimate rate of action depends upon the power of the disinfectant and the pH of the water (see information sheets 15.8 and 20). The most favourable level of pH varies also according to many factors, but as a rule just alkaline above neutral is preferred, though this need not necessarily be the optimum. Just acid will speed up disinfection processes and corrosion. Too alkaline will nullify a compound's properties, requiring greatly increased dosing rates (consequently increasing other reactions with their unattractive byproducts) just to deal with ordinary contamination.

When chlorine smell is strongly noticeable, there is *not enough* chlorine in the water to have oxidised all material and consequential combined chlorine. Uncombined or free chlorine in water is almost odourless. The best proportion for total available chlorine in pools amounts to three-quarters of the residual free, with the balance combined. Such levels mean there can be immediate action, plus long lasting action for safe water which also overcomes eye irritation, odours and algae. The practice of breakpoint or superchlorination enables this goal to be thoroughly achieved. But in view of the higher cost of the dry chemical compounds, only the more economical elemental gas chlorine, or liquid bromine, etc is usually preferred. Initial expense for metering equipment will be recovered quickly with less material used and more handling savings made for bigger pools and higher bathing loads.

Halogens for swimming pools The range of chemicals for swimming pool treatment most proven this century is the formidable halogen group of elements. All are dangerous in their raw state and require very careful control. Water supply works, and hygiene industrial processes, use very large amounts of the first favoured element, chlorine, which means there is an ample supply system available for reasonably priced raw materials, with trained labour and accurate equipment also widely available.

In handling chemicals, *all* materials are potentially hazardous and some suppliers of elemental disinfectants will not deliver to swimming pools they consider designed below certain safe standards. Unfortunately, most of the alternative dry, or liquid chemicals, that are widely available, are equally dangerous in inexpert hands, or with second rate systems.

A dosing system should be as foolproof and as elementary as possible. To the credit of the more elaborate control systems, the necessarily better trained personnel do reduce risks. It is in the semi-public, and private pool sector, where the greatest hazards of malpractice exist.

Chlorine currently dominates the disinfectant market. But bromine is equally effective, could probably be better and cheaper overall for swimming pool application, but is not so widely available. Different countries favour different processes ... with bromine in France, breakpoint chlorination in UK, hypochlorination in US, ozonation in Germany, and so on. Without any doubt, the halogen chemical group serves 90 per cent of all the pool market. Dry, liquid or gas chlorine control systems serve 80 per cent of all new US public pools, with bromine second at 5 per cent. A few operators still dispense chemicals by hand. Conversely, 60 per cent of US private pools hand-chlorinate (UK 75 per cent) with convenience chemicals ... 95 per cent are chlorines, of which over half are the longer lasting chloro-isos (see chapter 15.10 and information sheet 15.5).

Still the most satisfactory large scale disinfection treatment is breakpoint chlorination, which keeps water brighter longer, can turn bottle green water light blue, and also provides a pleasant feel. It ensures water is totally free of bacterial contamination, lengthens filter runs and provides a rapid acting free chlorine. On the other hand, chlorine requires greater care and better knowledge because of its side effects, enabling bromine to get ahead in new pool disinfection processes. Two pools in Paris, set side by side, and using chlorine and bromine respectively, reflect the practical difference. The brominated pool has greater polish over the chlorinated water – but this situation, really indicates how much easier it is to work a brominator and control the fewer side effects. Chlorination, when correctly carried out, will produce equally clear water equally fast.

Other effects of halogen chemicals Gas chlorine (and liquid bromine) is very acid in water. Neutralising alkaline dosing treatment is a necessary support. This means secondary-control equipment is always needed. Liquid chlorine is highly alkaline, requiring acid balancing alongside. Dry chlorine tends to be nearer neutral, but chlorine binders within the compound do affect pH – or fail to dissolve completely.

Increased bathing raises pH, and so do most dry chlorines. Whatever the treatment chemical selected, or the control unit, an automatic dosing system still does not replace a good manager. He anticipates heavy loads to step up disinfection beforehand. Necessary support equipment requires extra attention and maintenance, and preferably purer chemicals to dispense. For it is the impurities or the improper applications, that cause most trouble. There is no completely safe chemical system, but widespread usage of dangerous chlorine gas as poolwater hygiene, has become remarkably successful for both treatment and safety. Gas equipment has proved reliable, durable, effective, accurate and expensive. The search for an alternative has really been for a cheaper system, not a better one . . . and one which allows widescale production.

All pools require a good mix of disinfectant, and that means more inlets, better placed, with higher turnover ratings. But in open water lidos there can be difficulties. The popular London Serpentine lido originally employed a boat *Chlorine II* to cruise around and mix in disinfectant for the benefit of the bathers. Now the lido section is encircled with 300mm pipes bubbling chlorinated water into the bather polluted waters: and the rest of the lake's inhabitants don't seem to mind a bit.

Bromination and iodination In France, bromine was selected for the Concours des mille piscines. Basic equipment is inexpensive and very easily operated. Bromine acts immediately, is less irritating than chlorine since there are less byproducts, and is a particularly virile algicide. The secondary combined bromamine component, unlike chloramine, is very effective, faster acting, and additionally powerful. Control of pH is still necessary, but less critical with the dry form combination sticks of bromine/chlorine. These have even faster bacteriacidal effect at marginal rates, and mutually support each other; but their higher price tends to restrict sticks to private and to smaller pool applications at present.

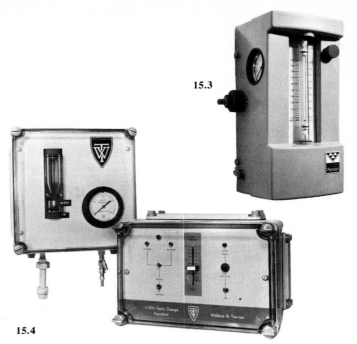

15.3

15.3 *Chlorinator (top right).*

15.4 *Control System (lower left). A Chlorine residual cell unit analyses a sample of poolwater to instruct the automatic chlorine dosage regulator, which in turn amplifies the signal for comparison with the original residual disinfection setting of the main chlorinator.*
Wallace & Tiernan Ltd, Kent and New Jersey

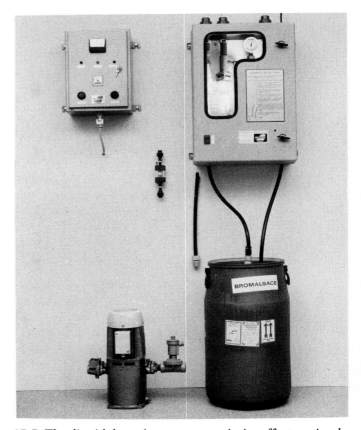

15.5 *The liquid brominator system is in effect a simple metering operation of a 'highly dangerous and corrosive' element: manually adjusted models suitable for 100m³, 1000m³ and automatic units for 3000m³ pool capacities*
Portacel Ltd, Kent/Bromalsace, Paris

Another particularly ideal combination, from the operator and swimmer point of view, with the total oxidation of organic matter organised within the plantroom, is ozonation or ultra violet treatment, supported in the pool with a small residual of bromine or chlorine (see information sheets 15.15 to 18). But at present these processes are still expensive, when compared with breakpoint chlorination.

The shift to an alternative to chlorination has been growing steadily for some years in the US, where another halogen, iodine, was proven active for pools in the 1950s, but in need of algicidal support. This element, donated from a safe crystalline form, is a potent disinfectant with very safe handling characteristics, and with even less irritating side effects. Initially it is expensive, but the iodine in the process is reusable many times over to bring overall costs down.

15.4 Chemo-disinfection techniques
Competitive chemicals succeed whenever the new dispensing method is easier, or the side effects in water less troublesome. They are not necessarily cheaper, nor more powerful oxidising agents – in fact, some only inactivate micro-organisms without burning out their remains. Such weaker compounds can make water safe, sometimes leaving it less than sparkling.

It is probably no exaggeration to say there are almost more redundant and discarded dispenser devices lying around in private pool plantrooms, than there are operational and worthwhile systems. Even the simplest idea – a floating container packed with chemicals – suffers snags, for if crammed too tight and tossed into the water, it can explode like a bomb. Or the uncomplicated metering pump so easily installed, so simple to operate, quickly gums up. A device to be effective must operate under almost total neglect, otherwise it soon becomes more convenient to drop in a sachet, or a tablet, or a jar full of chlorine, and so on.

There are a few excellent chemical metering devices that guarantee a constant liquid disinfection vigilance without

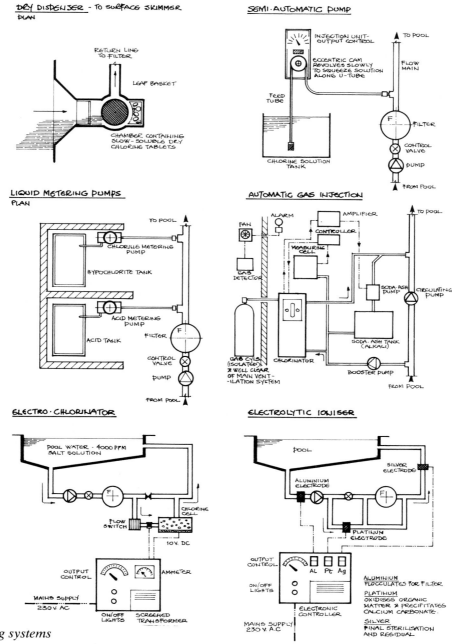

15.6 *Water sterilising systems*

15.7 *Manual controlled, mechanically or hydraulically operated, variable stroke metering pump for pH solution delivering up to 100 litres/h*
Wallace & Tiernan, Kent and New Jersey

15.8 *Chlorine dioxide systems are ideal for heavily contaminated waters with their reduction of side reactions: practical for public pools with efficient circulations offering odour and taste free quality water disinfection*
Esmil-Envirotech Ltd, Cambs/Interox, Brussels

15.9 *Disinfection system for 100 m³ pool creating chlorine from a dilute brine solution. Salt is dissolved in the poolwater to 3000 to 4000 ppm, about 10 per cent of seawater, to provide the electrolyte needed by the cell to manufacture nascent chlorine: installation; filter and unit; cell*
Chloromaker, Surrey

15.10 *Ionic sterilisation of poolwater (100 m³) using an aluminium cell to flocculate, a platinum cell to oxidize and a silver cell to add the disinfecting residual*
H. Einhell GmbH & Co. Kg Landau/Isar GFR

constant supervision by the operator. These units prove themselves for the medium load pools, but the heavier loads soon turn to more economical chlorine gas. Lighter loads only require a regular daily dose, and dry chemical dispensers suit these circumstances.

Of the alternative chemical systems, chlorine dioxide (used mostly in Europe) offers a 'purer chlorinous behaviour'. There are also new 'non-chlorine' synthetic biocides for lightly bathed pools, dosing at around 50 ppm residual for long-term active life, but not yet with short term cost savings.

Organic biocides are stable in poolwater and are very effective in destroying bacteria, but since they do not remove or burn out nitrogen compounds introduced with sweat and urine, as well as being less effective against algae, they require a supplementary oxidising agent to be added.

Probably the most intriguing idea to consider is the 'dog-eat-dog' biological principle, where saprophytic benevolent bacteria deal with their pathogenic malevolent cousins all within the filter, leaving only the need for a moderate marginal disinfection dosing to overcome fresh bather contamination.

15.5 Electro-disinfection techniques

A perfect way of putting electricity to work in disinfection is with the in situ breakdown of chemicals to act upon microbes in poolwater. Such processes stem from the principle of electrolytic corrosion, where dissimilar metals in poolwater conduct an electrical current between them. The pool is really a vast battery where dissimilar metals can actually be transferred back and forth in electrolysis. A lot though depends upon the amount of dirt in the water, the pH, the dissolved metals accelerating corrosion or staining electro-plating elsewhere (see chapter 16.4 and information sheet 16.7).

When a pool, or a brine tank, is charged with 4000 ppm common salt solution, electrolytic equipment can disassociate constituent elements. Nascent and fast acting chlorine is one of them. These electro-chemical systems work best with bathing loads not subject to sudden change and with balanced water, but can donate byproducts such as hydrogen, sodium, etc, which must be dealt with. Molecular chlorine is produced at the positive anode, with hydroxyl ions, plus water at the negative cathode.

By inserting other metallic plates to carry current, different water treatment actions can also be provided. Copper and aluminium plates will flocculate fine material for the filter to trap. Platinum and silver will purify and oxidise microbes (silver is highly bactericidal at levels ten times lower than marginal chlorination). Ion exchange systems can be very successful. They suit small pools admirably, but regrettably a little neglect goes a long way in limiting their very convenient advantages.

Ozonation The ideal oxidiser is that oxygen-free molecule which ozone contributes. But since ozone is hardly soluble and so short lived, it has to be produced on the spot and used straight away for five minutes of contact time – flow time through the plantroom system before water is returned to the pool. Higher voltages and purer air are necessary ingredients making large-scale production extra expensive. When ozone equipment, plus subsidiary disinfection metering units for necessary pool residuals are taken into full account, this technique can grow well clear of the price of ordinary breakpoint chlorination. But there are distinct advantages. Rapid and total oxidising of organic matter with purer agents cuts down the side effect problems, which in turn allows a far more comfortable swimming environment, plus the increased chance of operating very successful total heat recovery and recirculation systems. Approximately 2000 pools in continental Europe employ ozone, and many advertise the fact, which helps attract more people to an improved environment.

Ozonation really requires a constant residual from long-lasting marginal disinfection (bromine perhaps with five hours contact time) until the water can be dealt with totally back at the plantroom. A good example of another new combination or tandem disinfection system. In Germany, regulations require the extra, safeguarding residual halogen: in Switzerland there is no such insistence. Likewise, UV sterilisation of water carries no residual itself, but polluted material can be safely swamped with radiation in the first place. These methods rely upon concentrated electrical discharge, when such a blanketing one-time total kill takes away risk to bathers of overdosing of the water.

15.6 Water testing

Water testing is the measure of the practical disinfection levels that satisfy standards 99·9 per cent of the time.

The most important test in pool operation is the indication of disinfectant residual. Then comes pH comparison. Alkalinity, hardness and stabiliser levels also count, since they affect the ability of the disinfectant.

15.9

15.10

15.11 *Ozonation flow diagram (dual disinfection of poolwater) based upon Barr & Wray, Glasgow sequence*

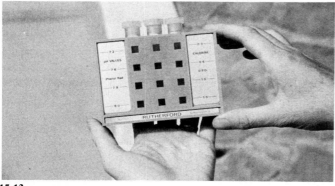

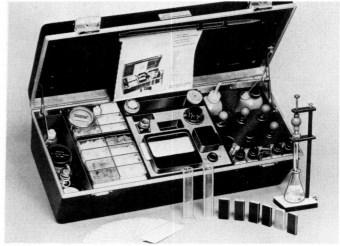

15.12 *Ozone generator for public pools producing up to 100 gm O_3/h at 1·5 kW*
Barr & Wray Ltd, Glasgow/Rheno AG. GFR

15.13 *Simple chlorine and pH water test set*
Tintometer, Salisbury
Photo: John Dawes

15.14 *Complete portable test laboratory for poolwater*
N. Jonas & Co. Pa

15.15 *Battery operated pH meter, with temperature compensator and mV Redox scale application*
Analytical Measurements Ltd, Middlesex

Water testing systems have improved over the years to make the processes very simple indeed. The Romans used wine drips to check the lime content of water; earlier this century titrative quantitative chemical analyses were used; now there is the pill, and a standard comparator to check the residual in two minutes, or solid state auto-testers growing more popular with their faster accuracy and closer control. All tests have to measure a poolwater solution to fractions of a part per million (1 ppm is similar to 1 hour in a lifetime). A consistent test unit provides the successful basis of all modern accurate purification control systems.

Contamination of water and the lack of adequate rapid disinfection is soon discovered by the presence of E.coli bacteria in the human intestinal tract, a potentially uncomfortable and dangerous situation.

There must be no coliform bacterial count in swimming pool water, though viral contamination is another and

more difficult problem. The virus is so small it can pass through a filter which ordinarily retains some bacteria. It requires far higher magnification microphotometry even to be seen. To date there is very little research on viral contamination in pools. Viruses are the main cause of most common illnesses, and they can survive for long periods at a time outside of host cells. Some viruses are not destroyed by normal chlorination (for example infectious hepatitis) and are not at all easy to detect in tests. When a rare infectious outbreak does occur, action is urgent for disinfection must be greatly increased. The cause has to be found quickly, as well as the cure.

15.7 pH control

pH indicates the active amount of acid or base in a swimming pool water; it is a measure of the strength or weakness of the solution. Another version says the hydrogen Potenz is the logarithm of the reciprocal of the hydrogen ion concentration. The amount of acidity or basicity of poolwater seems a little clearer!

The neutral point on the pH scale is 7, between extreme acid at 0 and extreme base (alkaline) at 14. As the number of hydrogen ions increase one place to the left along the scale, each new level indicates ten times greater acid strength: conversely, one place to the right for hydroxyl ions measures ten times the previous alkaline strength. When pH rises over 7, chlorine becomes less effective. At pH 8 and above though, monochloramines formed initially are oxidised to nitrogen without intermediate stages. This means higher amounts of free active chlorine (FAC) can be maintained for minimal taste, odours and eye irritations. This practice can reduce the troublesome di- and trichloramines and create a greater hygiene reservoir.

By far the most operators prefer pH controlled at around 7·5, with the finer the control, the more practical the process. There is a tendency to increase pH to 7·8 for breakpoint systems, to 8·4 for seawater treatment or to 8·8 for geothermal pools.

Alkalinity But pH the measure, is not the whole story. Other factors such as temperature and the amount of water hardness, total dissolved solids (TDS), trace elements and total alkalinity all affect the situation. To establish a clearer picture, Dr Langelier of University of California developed a water balancing equation in 1936. This formula is valuable today in assessing the corrosion, or scale forming tendency of swimming pool water. More than half today's pools in operation are out of balance, which means the activity of corrosion and scale exists wholesale. Consequently, in cases of low hardness or low total alkalinity, it can be better to operate a pool nearer to pH 8.

An acid will lower pH, but if there is a reserve of soluble alkalinity in poolwater, pH bounces back. This means dosing a little and often to keep average pH at 7·5, and maintaining hardness and alkalinity levels to around 150 ppm. Very few pools need to raise pH, and they exist mainly in softwater areas or operate gas chlorination.

At a given pH, alkalinity may be high or low. If low, pH tends to change more rapidly. Hence high alkalinity offers a stock that has a kind of stabilising effect. Most eye troubles occur at low pH, from chloramines, or from alum in the water. Highly corrosive nitrogen trichloride arises at low pH, when there is a sudden surge of nitrogenous matter entering the water in the presence of high chlorine levels.

The main lesson to be learned in effective water balancing is accurate and continual pH correction (see information sheets 15.25 and 26). Some excellent controllers exist, and can guarantee precise disinfection to prescribed pH levels, so paying for themselves in comfort, convenience and chemicals within a short space of time. An alternative, simple pH control method for sand filtration with gas chlorination, is the introduction of dolomitic limestone layering across the sand bed. This eliminates constant alkaline dosing to maintain pH equilibrium. As poolwater passes through this material, calcium ions are donated rather than sodium, to give lime-rust protective coating to steel, raised carbonate hardness and minimal chloride corrosion. Chloride levels need to be kept to 300 ppm, hence this control system is not suitable for sea or salt water, high

carbonate or sulphate waters, and most other forms of disinfection.

Breakpoint chlorination eventually forms hydrochloric acid from the continuous addition of chlorine in the pool. An equally continuous supply of alkaline solution proportional to the chlorine, neutralises the acid condition before the water enters the pool. Therefore, such dual chemical controls make a cost burden that other purification systems try to avoid. But bear in mind, bathing load and all chemicals will change pH from the norm – a fact consistently overlooked in nearly all private pools.

Deck or tile cleaners, lawn fertilisers and other potions that somehow get into pools all require regular oxidation with breakpoint or superchlorination.

15.8 Autometry

Electronic surveillance is definitely more accurate than other methods of achieving water balance. Several systems are available for public and private pools, to monitor free and combined chlorine, and to read pH through millivolt differences in potential.

Automatic control of water requires constant monitoring of redox (see information sheet 15.24), pH, salinity, temperature and turbidity for constant change. There is not one big chemical reaction, but millions of small ones. Electrodes and ultrasonic probes inserted into the pipework feed information to the controllers. Platinum electrodes read chlorine levels, and glass electrodes pH. Fine limit controls are linked closely to the oxidation reduction potential (redox) and to pH to save around 50 per cent chemical consumption, reduce labour overseeing the situation, and to stop all eye irritation complaints.

The potential of accumulated organic substances to be oxidised by a disinfectant at a given pH is shown by the redox-potential. This is a relationship between the chemical condition of poolwater, and the possibility of microbes surviving in it. It is not the concentration of disinfection, but the redox potential that determines efficiency.

The redox range necessary for pools, and sensitive to ± 0.1 ppm accuracy, operates throughout 0 to 1000 millivolts. A minimum of +700mV at pH 7 will achieve safe swimming pool water.

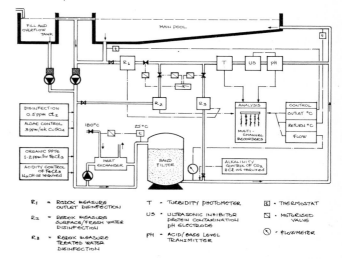

15.16 *Monitoring at Munich: Philips electronic automation control systems for each of the four pools at the 1972 Olympic complex*

Amperometric analysers for free and combined chlorine and pH, stop and start feeders, inform recorders, and keep effective checkpoints of all existing circumstances. They still cannot forecast problems though.

15.9 Soluble salts

Most poolwater is slightly hard (at around 150/200 ppm equivalent calcium carbonate), marginally alkaline (to 100/150 ppm) and reasonably vapid (TDS 1000 ppm). And it must be kept so.

At first fill of a Marblited pool, the pH rises to between 8 to 8·5, aggravated by cement dust or alkaline chlorine donators. It is essential to control pH from the start to avoid scaling of new plaster, or conversely, the etching of equipment in soft waters; to prevent precipitation when there are high carbonate levels, and to stop staining when there are unwanted mineral salts. A high pH liquid chlorine increases alkalinity and scaling; a low pH dry tri-chlorine aggravates soft water conditions and corrosion. Mineral salts can be brought out, or bleached with superchlorination, or flocculated out and swept away, or simply ion exchanged. The situation needs careful handling if the pool and equipment are to remain unharmed, and the swimmers to stay uncomplaining.

15.10 Special treatments

Some clarifying systems benefit from an alum pot through which is fed aluminium sulphate, to form a positive charge gelatinous sticky mass across the sand bed of the filter. This coagulation, or flocculation, only applies to sand and gravel type filters, and must be added slowly at distance from the filter to prevent suction through the bed and to the pool causing very sore eyes. By adding the hardly soluble compound before the pump, and over a 4 or 5 hour period at 7·4 to 7·6 pH range, a good stable coating can be obtained. If pH then changes outside of this range, the alum can get dissolved out of the bed to flow into the pool, deplete alkalinity, cause corrosion and much havoc generally.

Stains precipitate when there is a difference in electric charge. The softer metal is sacrificed to produce staining deposits. Sequestering agents change the form of metallic ions into an inactive compound giving a soft and soapy feeling to the water. They precipitate out salts which can be swept away. High velocity, high temperature and high alkalinity raise the chance of staining, especially at fast flow inlets, or in spa pool systems.

Stabilising In very strong sunlight conditions, it is impossible to hold free chlorine in poolwater for more than several hours. And as much as 2 ppm can be lost in 4 hours. A stabiliser additive of cyanuric acid up to 50 ppm at 7·5 pH, plus 50 per cent increase to chlorine levels will ensure a more durable residual. This pool conditioner filters the ultra violet and slows down the free available chlorine action: it is rather like radically increasing the combined chlorine share of the total residual. It means that although chlorine stays very much longer, and losses are drastically cut, the free chlorine reaction times are also considerably delayed.

In heavy bathing conditions, there can be an unsatisfactorily high occurrence of coliform bacteria in stabilised pools. Stabilising should be reserved for medium and lighter load pools. Reaction is further held up by ammonia in the water, when even at high chlorine levels, some organisms become resistant. Algae especially thrives upon the nitrogen base donated with pre-stabilised chlorine compounds – hence an alternative chlorine is required for superchlorination, and the oxidation of stabilising formed chloromides.

Too much cyanuric acid in the pool reverses the original stabilising process, and the level can only be reduced by dilution. Sulphamic acid and chlorinated chyantoins also offer chlorine stabilising facilities, but with less pronounced effect.

Cleaning Only safe cleansing compounds are suitable in pool circumstances: abrasive acids and potent chlorine solutions can be dangerous. There is always the thought 'if chlorine is good for cleaning and acetic cleaner good for toilets, then combined they must be doubly good'. Such thoughts result in hospital incidents. Instead of using a strong acid cleaner or chlorine, a detergent like sulphamic acid is not only more effective, but safe from obnoxious fumes and acid burning.

The algae A greenish or milky caste in poolwater invariably means there is a growing algae presence. Algae spores exist in the air all the time, and there are around 18,000 varieties. Complete chlorination will deal with *all* microorganisms, but a good algicide offers that second set of brakes, to operate when chlorine levels are low.

An algicide should complement marginal chlorination, for some compounds can deplete chlorine rapidly. A low pH is conducive to algae growth, and a rising pH indicates that algae is growing fast in the pool. They become visible when there are about one million spores per ml. At that point, frequent filter backwashing, green stains and blocked media all prove that algae is present. Algae bloom, intense in sunlight, warmth, and circulation dead spots, is well nourished by nitrogenous matter. A green phase can break out within two or three hours, especially after humid conditions and stormy weather. Around the pool, slimy surfaces of algae cause most accidents.

Algae needs nitrogen, carbon, hydrogen, oxygen and sunlight to grow and to reproduce in poolwater, for as a single cell plant, it contains chlorophyl and other pigments to make use of solar energy. A no-nutrient philosophy in the pool, denies ever present algae the opportunity to thrive. But there are some chlorines that donate, with their chemical compound binders, marvellous nutrients. However, if all traces of mineral molybdenum are removed, there can be no nitrogen fixing by algae. They become starved out of existence.

However, some more rife forms of algae learn to live in symbiosis with fungi for mutual support. Such black algae patches can send tendrils through pool walls, and into the earth 4 or 5m beyond in search of nutrient. And then there are yellow mustard algae which seem to survive all kinds of ingenious chemical attack. This all adds up to mean the poolman's motto must be 'contracept the teeming billions'.

Most algicidal preparations prevent growth; or they wet the surfaces, sinking and drowning the spores. Copper sulphate does destroy, but can stain black. Mercury compounds are active, but accumulate dangerously. The most popular backstop control, 'quats' at 20 ppm, offer no side effects of serious consequence. But if dosed in excess of 50 ppm, the poolwater can froth and foam when stirred up.

Down to 5 ppm gives no problems to dolphins – but best of all, normally balanced chlorine purification will not trouble any warm blooded animals while controlling the algae. By far the best algicide is sufficient chlorine or bromine in the first place.

Slow dissolving chlorine compounds in direct contact with algae deal with established colonies, unless there is a risk of bleaching spots and rotting liners. Shock chlorination to the water will deter quite a severe attack, but if the bridgehead is too strong, requiring huge quantities of chlorine, and causing continual blocking of the filter with dead organisms, the pool will be better emptied and cleaned out. And then the whole, proper purification process starts all over again with fresh, refilled water.

References
[1] DOE, *The Purification of the Water of Swimming Pools*, London, HMSO, 1976

Sodium bisulphate (dry acid): lowers pH and reduces alkalinity @ between 1 and 2kg/100m^3
Sodium carbonate (soda ash): raises pH @ 1kg/100m^3 or proportional rate, 1·5:1 with gas chlorine
Sodium hydroxide (caustic soda): raises pH, and a main component of liquid chlorine: proportional ratio 1·1:1 with gas chlorine
Sulphuric acid: lowers pH and serves as a cleanser.

INFORMATION SHEET 15.2

Average percentage kill
(of E.coli in water after 5 minutes @ 7·5pH)

Halogen level at:	0·15	0·25	0·5ppm	
Chlorine	0	10	60	% kill
Bromine	22	80	100	% kill
Bromine/Chlorine mix	76	100	100	% kill

Freshwater contains 1 million various micro-organisms per ml.

INFORMATION SHEET 15.1

Purification and pH chemicals checklist
(Necessarily non-toxic, colourless and odourless in use)

DISINFECTANTS OR STERILISERS maintain a pure and safe poolwater
Amphoteric-alkyl amino ethyl glycine: microbiocide dealing with resilient spores, fungus, bacteria colonies and surface disinfection
Bromochlorodimethyl-hydantoin: slowly soluble poolwater bromine/chlorine compound sticks
Bromine: fast acting oxidising element with less side effects than chlorine
Calcium hypochlorite: storable, powerful bleaching powder – a widely used pool disinfectant
Chlorine: low cost gas chlorine, a highly effective oxidiser and widely available
Chlorine dioxide: as a solution in water it is a powerful oxidiser with few chlorocompound problems
Hydantoins: mixed dimethyl compounds (Br + Cl$_2$) are generally expensive, but very effective bacteriacides
Iodine: crystalline concentrate, safe to handle with rapid bacteriacidal poolwater properties
Lithium hypochlorite: stable, granulated chlorine for rapid total solubility
Ozone: ideal oxidiser of organic matter without deleterious side effects
Polymeric biguanide: a liquid biocide pool sanitiser without chlorine
Potassium dichloroisocyanurate: almost neutral donator offering stabilised chlorine
Potassium iodide: releases free iodine by interaction with chlorine water: a reusable process
Potassium permanganate: slow oxidising agent, most effective at pH 6, but unsatisfactory for general pool application
Silver nitrate: unusual disinfectant, where minute traces of silver penetrate to destroy the cells of micro-organisms
Sodium dichloroisocyanurate: rapidly soluble, strong dry chlorine, with moderating stabiliser to reduce uv dissipation
Sodium hypochlorite: economical, widely available, liquid chlorine for rapid dispersal in poolwater
Sodium trichloroisocyanuric acid: slowly soluble, high availability chlorine, with moderating stabiliser to reduce dissipation

pH/ALKALINITY CONTROLLERS adjust the balance between acidity and basicity of poolwater
Calcium carbonate (dolomitic): replaces lost calcium in water to counteract pH depression automatically
Calcium chloride (flake): increases hardness and alkalinity @ 2kg/100m^3
Hydrochloric acid (muriatic): lowers pH and alkalinity @ 2 litres/100m^3, and serves as a cleanser
Sodium bicarbonate (dry alkali or baking powder): raises pH in soft water, but mainly increases alkalinity @ 2kg/100m^3/d

INFORMATION SHEET 15.3

Bather ailments
(From bacteria and virus, fungus, and poor conditioning)

Where epidemics occur, poolwater has been unsatisfactory and unhygienic. Some spores can be nourished for years in pools and filters. Water must be free from E.coli and streptococci in 100ml test samples. Samples must contain less than 100 bacteria per ml capable of growing in 2 days on Agar at 37°C.
Amoebic meningo-encephalitis: highly dangerous protozoa entering the brain via the nose – often fatal. Still occurs in modern pools in Europe, Australia and New Zealand, and there have been over 50 reported outbreaks around the world between 1965 and 1975. Amoebae can be retained in less effectively purged sand filters, a primary focus of pool infection, where they live on bacteria in the bed, thrive and migrate into the pool. Ensure no water 'spurt' return to pool after backwashing, and/or backwash twice weekly with hot (70°C) water.
Candida albicans (thrush): infections of mucous membranes from poorly disinfected and conditioned water.
Conjunctivitis: eye irritation from high or low pH, nitrogen trichloride, undissolved alum or soda; or plain water washing away the eye lubricant . . . and then a chlorine allergy.
Erythema: chlorine rashes, ear inflammations, etc.
Hepatitis: virus can display immunity to chlorine and collect in poorly maintained filter beds.
Infections: ranging from outbreaks of serious skin disorders to fatal illnesses are reported a dozen times a year in the western world.
Limax amoebae: in geothermal pools, control requires extra disinfection and caution.
Parasites: such as worms and flukes, mainly arise in faulty tropical pools.
Pharyngo conjunctival fever: the organism is readily destroyed by chlorine.
Poliomyelitis: first reaction is to shut down the pool, but a well run establishment is far more likely to improve hygiene, than to spread disease.
Scabies: the itch caused by a small parasite transmitted in clothing,
Septic spots and cuts: swimmers so affected should be prohibited from pool water to stop potential cross-infections.
Staphylococcus aureus: destroyed by well maintained chlorination.
Stinging eyes: caused by soaps, tile cleaners, suntan oils, suspended solids, algicides, alum, poor pH and sometimes incomplete disinfection.
Tinea pedis (athlete's foot): footbaths have little effect on foot mycosis, a form of ringworm, which is controlled by thorough washing, and antifungal powders or solutions – even special footsprays are too often inadequately used. Symptoms can last three or four years with inadequate washing – 25 per cent of swimmers might suffer symptoms of this fungus, and sometimes as high as 90 per cent males. Females respond better to treatment, indicating when informed, their greater awareness of personal hygiene.
Verrucae (foot warts): highly infectious to bare feet and atrophied skin,

and affects around 5 per cent of young swimmers. Virus grows in indoor pools, but seems to be destroyed outside by uv light. Emphasis at schools on personal hygiene, plus the discipline of foot inspections, rapidly controls both athlete's foot and foot warts.

Waterborne bacteria cause cholera, diarrhoea, dysentry, gastro-enteritis, typhoid, paratyphoid, etc. Major outbreaks occur every year mainly from contaminated drinking water. Chlorination destroys all bacteria, and one hour superchlorination destroys cysts.

INFORMATION SHEET 15.4

Disinfection demand

Factors affecting the amount of disinfection required in pool water

suspended solids	organic matter
hardness	bather load, grease and oil
iron, manganese, mineral salts	bacteria and fungus
alkalinity	algae
ammonia compounds	leaves
nitrates	pollen
hydrogen sulphide	faecal matter
pH	perspiration and urine
temperature	fertilisers
ultra violet	wind and rain
atmospheric pressure	sunlight
water flow and circulation	conditioning levels

Pre-hygiene can halve disinfection.
Disinfection of poolwater below 10°C can be lessened, since algae and bacteria no longer thrive.

INFORMATION SHEET 15.5

Chlorines available

Type	Advantages	Disadvantages
Gas chlorine Liquefied gas in cylinder. 100% available chlorine. pH 2–3	Lowest costs per kg. Failsafe vacuum equipment and piping employed. Highly effective system.	Special storage facilities required. Extremely acidic and corrosive in solution, requiring large dosing of soda ash to neutralise – HCl formed. Complex and expensive equipment with strict safety requirements, needing operators trained for responsible use.
Liquid chlorine Liquid bleach in drums. 10–15% available chlorine. 5% household bleach. pH 12–13	Reasonable cost. Rapid action and dispersal. No insolubles. Immediately ready for metering.	Decomposes fast, and must not be stored over 1 month. Drives pH up and requires continual acid dosing to pool for neutralising. Heavy and awkward to handle – bulk is a potential safety problem. Higher overall performance costs, and requires efficient supply services.
Dry chlorines Lithium hypochlorite Granulated bleaching powder prepacked. 35% available chlorine. pH 7–8	Totally soluble. Safer, less volatile chlorine bulk. Easily stored and handled. Purer compound form ideal for metering.	More expensive form per kg of chlorine. Adds 65% binder to pool TDS.
Calcium hypochlorite. Powder or tablet, powerful bleaching powder (chloride of lime) prepacked. 60–70% available chlorine. pH 11–12	Ideal for softer waters. Very effective disinfectant and widely used since 1928. Tablet form ideal for dispensers and continuous chlorination. Powder form is readily soluble and dry-fed into poolwater. Economical, easily handled and stored. Binder has no nitrogen significance.	Up to 5% insolubles can clog filter, or feeders, or cloud hard waters, or dissipate as fine powder. Strong oxidising agent, with potential safety hazard, highly combustible with oil, sawdust, organic material, solvents, etc.
Cyanurate chlorines Potassium dichloroisocyanurate Sodium dichloroisocyanurate Powder prepacked and stabilised. 60% available chlorine pH 6–7	Effective, self-stabilising disinfectant. Readily and completely soluble. Easy, long term storage, and conveniently handled. Ideal for bright sunlight and hard water areas – chlorine residual remains and remains.	More expensive initially. Slows down kill rate of chlorine action. Periodic superchlorination essential. Binder can help algae bloom and slow down destruction. Dosing continually raises cyanuric acid level, but perhaps balanced by top-up water. Compounds are incompatible with any contamination or any other chlorines.
Sodium trichloroisocyanuric acid powder or tablet, prepacked and stabilised. 90% available chlorine. pH 2–3	Powerful and ideal in bright sunlight. Effective, self-stabilising disinfectant – residual remains. Slowly soluble for long-term action and storage.	Initially expensive form. Slows down kill rate. Raises cyanuric level continuously. Periodic superchlorination required. Highly susceptible to hazardous contamination in store.
Cyanuric acid. Powder, prepacked. 25–100ppm max dosing. pH 3–5	Shields HOCl decomposition from UV. Stabiliser effect retained for all chlorines. Makes chlorine persist . . .	Induces a slow acting chloramine behaviour. CYA level reduced only by water loss. Only slowly soluble. but algae can persist also.

INFORMATION SHEET 15.6

Disinfection – before or after the filter

Pre-chlorination and longer contact

Uses more chlorine, but filter is kept cleaner with longer runs and greater backwashing efficiency: destroys bacteria and algae, taste and odour, aids sedimentation and oxidation in the bed.

Longer response time (2 or 3 minutes) unless monitor feed split before and after.

Ensures better mixing before pump into poolwater; less coagulant required.

Potential corrosion problems to equipment from harsher solutions.

Longer contact period with worst of pool water pollution can be checked by measure of residual downstream.

Post-chlorination and faster response

Saves chlorine, but filter bed left till last for exposure to remaining disinfectant residual.

Faster response to chlorine demand for poolwater.

Chlorine directly and fully available; depletion in effects to pool disinfection avoided.

Subsequent to all other treatment and corrosive action in heater reduced.

More suited to average bathing loads and expensive dry chlorine treatment materials.

Breakpoint chlorination: Higher chlorine levels (1 to 3ppm) entirely destroying all compounds and bacteria. Ensures total burn-out since it is not chlorine in water that smells and irritates, but its compounds. Produces higher standard of purity and greater clarity. Disinfection without doubt for heavy loads.

or Superchlorination: Periodic burn up at two or three times normal dose achieves a breakpoint to reduce all remaining nitrogenous materials or resistant organisms (or by *controlled* reduction of pH effectively increasing chlorine potency). Busy pools: weekly; private pools: monthly.

or Shockchlorination: Occasional extra strong treatment at five times normal dose to deal with algae attack, or smelly waters, following strong sunlight, rainstorm, high pollen fall or period of neglect.

Combined chlorine effects

Monochloramine (NH_2Cl): poor disinfectant, 100 times less effective than free chlorine.

Dichloramine ($NHCl_2$): better disinfectant, but less stable; with aeration produces unpleasant smell and eye irritation.

Trichloramine (tear gas): unwanted.

Nitrogen trichloride (NCl_3): nauseous odour and eye irritant formed when high available chlorine and high ammonia content exists at low pH: the product of sudden bathing surges in heavily used water carrying insufficient residual and partially reduced pollution.

INFORMATION SHEET 15.8

Chlorine levels

Quantities of chlorine suggested as guide levels for public pools:

1kg gas per 100m³ water per 8 hours (APHA)
1kg gas per 100 bathers (UK)
or 10 litres hypochlorite
or 2kg dry powder form
1kg gas dissolves in 300 litres water @ 20°C
1 per cent chlorine solution kills bacteria in 30 minutes.

Guide residuals at 7·5pH

Private pools	Semi-public pools	Public pools	Paddling pools	Neglected pools
0·2 to 0·5ppm	0·5 to 1·0ppm	1·0 to 2·0ppm	2·0 to 5·0ppm	5·0 to 10·0ppm
Marginal	Free residual including bromination	Breakpoint including iodination	Super-chlorination	Shock dose

Public pools operate mainly up to	1ppm – US/Europe
ideally . . .	2ppm – UK/NZ
satisfactorily	5ppm – heavy loads UK
tolerably . . .	30ppm – special waters Australia

Free chlorine is readily lost in sunlight, high temperature and by water agitation.

pH determines the amount of active HOCl, and slow acting OCl^- in total share:

level	pH	Molecular HOCl hypochlorous acid (per cent)	Ionised OCl^- chloramine (per cent)
Acid	6·5	90	10
Near acid	7·0	75	25
Safe ⎱	7·5	50	50
zone ⎰	8·0	25	75
Alkaline	8·5	10	90

Chlorine in air is:

detectable 1ppm – slight symptoms
disturbing 5ppm – breathing restrictions
coughing 25ppm – choking irritation
dangerous 50ppm – extreme irritation

INFORMATION SHEET 15.7

Chlorine equations and terms

Chlorine + water	→	Hypochlorous acid	+ Hydrochloric acid
$Cl_2 + H_2O$	→	HOCl	+ HCl
HOCl	→	HCl	+ O the oxidiser

Initial demand: chlorine dose needed to deal with existing pollution.

Residual demand: active chlorine remaining unused and expressed as parts per million (ppm).

Chlorine demand: difference between amounts of chlorine remaining after contact period.

Combined available chlorine (CAC): a long-term active chlorine working over 30 to 90 minutes (chloramines).
Residual chlorine existing in water in chemical combination with ammonium or nitrogen compounds.

Free available chlorine (FAC): a chlorine uncombined and ready for immediate action – within one or two minutes, but commonly 20 to 30 seconds effectiveness and 100 times more active than CAC.
Residual chlorine existing in water mainly as hypochlorous acid and less effective hypochlorite ion: OCl^-. FAC should be greater than CAC in breakpoint chlorination by at least 2:1.

Total residual chlorine (TRC): residual existing as free and combined chlorine.

	CAC	+ FAC	= TRC
	Longer contact chlorine with less loss in sunlight	Vital direct disinfectant but suffers UV losses	Chlorine reserve
Optimum proportion	25%	+ 75%	= 100%
ppm	0·5	+ 1·5	= 2

Marginal chlorination: Moderate chlorine levels (0·5 to 1ppm) requiring regular super boosts to oxidise accumulated organic matter, or when algae signs first noticed.

241

INFORMATION SHEET 15.9

Breakpoint graph

Chlorine added to water containing ammonium compounds reacts to form chloramines. As further chlorine is added to break down these compounds, the total residual of chlorine appears to drop to a minimum, the 'breakpoint' for that pH. Thereafter, all additional chlorine in the water exists in the free available state, a situation also termed 'superchlorination'.

Organic material + chlorine = ammonia → chloramines
+ chlorine = chloramines → breakpoint
+ chlorine = free available chlorine

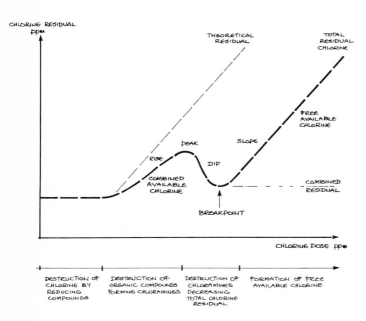

INFORMATION SHEET 15.10

The halogens
(The 'saltmakers' with similar properties)

Chemical equivalents

As oxidising agents Cl>Br>I

	Atomic number	Atomic weight	Salts in sea ppm
Fluorine – drinking water authorities use with dry feeders to reduce handling risks	9	19·0	1·4
Chlorine – universal pool acceptance	17	35·5	18,980
Bromine – less powerful oxidiser gaining greater acceptance	35	79·9	65
Iodine – less powerful still with reserved acceptance to date	53	126·9	0·05

INFORMATION SHEET 15.11

The halogens – properties

Chlorine

Forms		
(Heavy bathing)	**Gas:**	Inexpensive material requiring sophisticated control and stringent precautions. 2½ times heavier than air and highly dangerous. Conveniently stored in cylinders of 25 to 100kg capacities. Heavy, green, pungent gas, easily noticeable at 2ppm in air, or with reaction, white fumes from ammonium hydroxide. Burns eyes and skin; if added into poolwater at high concentration, will bleach costumes, pool liners, etc. Prohibited in some European countries and restrictions to use in UK and US.
(Medium bathing)	**Liquid:**	Relatively cheap solution requiring large amounts for disinfection. Weight and bulk inhibits economics – stored 50 to 5000 litre tanks. Ensure no backflow or siphon action when pumps off. Reacts with acids, generating heat and releasing chlorine, hence large spillages best absorbed in sand and removed to safe place, rather than neutralised. Simple dispensing equipment available. Requires careful handling and highly dangerous if cross-contaminated. Dilute supplies on receipt to slow down decomposition but not below pH 11. Widely used in US, Australasia, EEC, and medium/smaller pools everywhere.
(Light bathing)	**Dry:**	More expensive preparations, conveniently and easily handled. Mainly used for smaller pools and hand applications. Potentially hazardous if contaminated. Useful donating systems available either direct to poolwater from dispenser, or by metering pump when premixed in solution and residue removed. Long life forms – several years in good packaging against several weeks for liquid. Packs of 2 to 100kg capacity. Dangerous if mishandled. Extensively available as so easily distributed.

Action Free chlorine as hypochlorous acid is an excellent almost odourless microbiocide, but some virus can resist even marginal chlorination. Breakpoint chlorination supersaturates the water to achieve 100 per cent effective disinfection, but includes undesirable side effects in the process. These arise from trichlorides and chloramines, not from free chlorine in poolwater. Residual is lost quickly in sunlight requiring conditioning to retain some effect.

Other effects Gas chlorination is highly acidic, which coupled with oxidation of nitrogenous matter and acidity from alum treatment requires heavy soda ash neutralising. Strong solutions exist at points of application (100ppm) requiring care to corrosion of equipment, and bather. Twice plantroom floor area is required for gas systems against liquid.

Liquid chlorination is highly alkaline and together with oil and grease from bathers requires careful pH control with acid neutralising. Also, liquid 'hypo' and heat accelerates chemical decomposition in contact with metals, (especially iron and copper). Scaling problems exist in hard waters, and chloride accumulations need watching. Only 10 per cent chlorine in liquid reliably available – the remainder carrier is caustic. Hard water encourages studying.

Dry chlorines introduce a variety of carrier solutions into the pool invariably upsetting pH, alkalinity and eventually TDS. Impurer forms can cause havoc with equipment if counteraction is not taken.

Forms

Bromine

(Large pools)	**Liquid:**	Nasty to handle, and as obnoxious as chlorine but with more persistent effects. Requires stringent precautions with storage containers surrounded by treated vermiculate that changes colour, indicating leaks, and that can absorb all the red-brown liquid contained. Water is bubbled through bromine liquid for dosing, and equipment is relatively economical and simpler to operate than for chlorine. There are similar risks to operator and bather from dangerous fumes, and the whole process is currently more expensive: can become cheaper and longer lasting though than chlorine. Pioneered in US in the 1930s where gained a local acceptance and selected for French 'mille piscines'.
(Medium pools)	**Dry:**	Safer and more convenient form, but still more expensive and not yet widely available. Chlorine water passed over donating sticks of the compound produces an easily dispensed bromine solution. Simple operation, total solubility and fast action makes dry bromine a highly attractive disinfectant, suitable for variable bathing loads. Safe if handled considerately. A dual donation system from bromine/chlorine carrier blocks at 1:2·4 ratio. Increasingly accepted pool disinfection method in France and US, with rising interest in Germany and Israel.

Action Free bromine as hypobromous acid, including the combined forms as bromamines, are both effective bacteriacides, virricides and algicides, and oxidisers of organic matter. Breakpoint reaction with bromine at poolwater pH levels 'is reached almost instantaneously in the presence of even a slight excess of bromine'. Bromamines and free bromine cannot co-exist, other than momentarily (unlike chlorine and chloramines), hence only a small combined residual is necessary for a strong disinfectant property in pool water. By taking advantage of this facility, bromination becomes materially more economical than chlorine, as well as far less expensive in capital equipment terms. Bromination offers faster kill rates, plus less side effect problems. Residual remains longer and is dissipated slower by sunlight: cannot be cyanuric acid stabilised.

Other effects Bromination requires pH adjustment similar to chlorine, but to a less marked extent. Bromine attacks all metals, making glass, grp or plastic 'fail-safe' containers essential storage vessels. Bromamines are not irritating like chloramines, and at low pH, high disinfection/bathing loads, there is a reluctance to produce the corrosive equivalent to nitrogen trichloride. Absence of tribromides up to 5 or 10ppm, reduces irritation: even at 1 to 2ppm bromination (minimum 0·5ppm at pH 7·5) odours are not greatly noticeable. Dolomitic pH control is still viable. Seawater taken above breakpoint benefits by enhanced disinfection activity from bromides. For all the major benefits, there are still problems of green water pools, brown walls and brominous odours, from imbalance, other chemicals and contaminations. Generally, the side effects are not as great, nor as difficult to control, as for chlorine. Dispensing systems are not under pressure like gas chlorine – hence liquid bromination is less likely to be a ventilation hazard. Excellent algaecide and 3ppm superdoses invariably eliminate algae growth.

Forms

Iodine

Crystals: Very stable and safe to handle. Easily stored, converted to active solution and dispensed into poolwater, using practical and economical equipment, in raw state, iodine is as dangerous as any other halogen. Developed mainly in US in 1950s, but has gained little acceptance so far.

Action Chlorine activates iodine released from soluble potassium iodide into hypoiodous acid. No iodamines are formed and algicidal support treatment is necessary. Most modern algicides are incompatible with iodine, therefore intermittant superchlorination is necessary when free iodine has been dropped down to 0·3ppm. The iodine behaviour, being less irritating than chlorine, is an important advantage of this mutually supporting disinfection system. Iodination also requires less contact time. The iodide ion is not an effective bacteriacide, but can be reconverted into molecular iodine with chlorine, to be reused a dozen times and thereby halve material costs against straight chlorination.

Other effects Iodine attacks most metals, but other side reactions are less marked than with chlorine. A well-operated pool suffers no iodine taste nor odour, no eye irritation nor 'green hair' cases. Careful pH control prevents that dark green water appearance, though a greenish caste is always noticeable between 2 and 5ppm at 7·5pH: difficulty can be experienced in maintaining the required free and total concentrations.

INFORMATION SHEET 15.12

Relative prices – disinfection units (approximate only)
Equipment and materials are costed as a factor of 100
based upon semi-automatic liquid dosing units = 100

Equipment and installation		Operational and maintenance
25/50	floating dispensers	10
100	semi-automatic dosing units	100
200/300	metering pumps	80
400	activated silver dispensers	150
800	liquid bromination	100
1500	gas chlorination	75
2500+	automated control system	50
6000+	ozonation/hypochlorination	120

Chemical and energy supplies Cost factor: gas = 100	Inclusive disinfecting and balancing materials per m³
Chlorine – gas	100
liquid 15%	125
dry 35%	300
dry 65%	250
'Chloros-isos' – 60%	300
90%	350

Chemical and energy supplies Cost factor: gas = 100	Inclusive disinfecting and balancing materials per m³
Chlorine dioxide	150
Ozone/chlorine	150
Bromine – liquid	150
dry	350
Iodine – dry	300
Biocides	400

Since factors are constantly changing, *Purification Costs* for different pool systems require careful comparison for both:

Capital – Equipment and installation
    – Replacement
Recurring – Operational and maintenance
    – Chemical and energy supplies

throughout the projected life of the pool for the anticipated bathing load and the competitive trend of the products. A minimum 5 year projection study is essential for cost effective planning, a 25 year review is better, when other considerable and closely related factors such as heat recovery, superstructure renovation, filtration efficiency, bather appeal and attendance, etc can be taken into account.

See also information sheets 2.8, 7.6, 8.2, 13.10 and 14.19.

INFORMATION SHEET 15.13

Chemicals with care
They are hazardous and combustible

All chemicals must be non-toxic, non-irritant for the whole range
of levels required to operate in poolwater.

Never mix chemicals

Never

- store chemicals together: keep them clear of all other chemicals and
contamination, such as packaging materials, grease, oil, petroleum based
products, as well as other chlorine or disinfectant forms – especially
'chlorosisos'
- store in damp, dirty, hot and badly ventilated places
- heat chemicals or bring lighted cigarette near
- allow children to dispense or measure chemicals
- use unmarked containers
- dispose empty containers without first washing them
- interchange dispensers between different chemicals.

Always handle with care

Always

- add acid to water
- mix chemicals *only with water*
- wash hands after dispensing chemical
- wash away thoroughly any spillage
- keep chemicals clear of animals, clothing and skin: use safety face mask
where possible
- use clean dispensers and equipment
- provide proper storage, protection and safety from fire, explosion, gas or
corrosion. Even capped chemicals can emit corrosive fumes.

Emergency

- call service, giving full name of chemical involved

INFORMATION SHEET 15.14

Gas chlorination

Chlorinator: Units operate under vacuum and constant temperature 10°C
minimum for safety reasons. Any leaks involve an ingress of air with
pressure relief line. Flow is adjustable to 10 per cent accuracy with
automatic or manual control. Gas ratings for pool range 0·5 kg/d to 5
kg/h. Wall or floor mounted system, singly or in banks. Electricity supply
unnecessary except for pumps or solenoid valves. Install nearest to point of
application and on an outside wall.

Chlorine room: Separate room, dry, frostproof, fire resistant, well ventilated, above ground and with no interconnecting door to pool: secure,
safe and well clear of exits, main entrance and ventilation intakes. Doors to
open outwards. Air within room must be changeable within two minutes or
less by sparkproof fan connected to light switch: louvres set above floor
and below ceiling: provide ample working space around equipment.
Danger warning signs to be clearly posted (see chapter 11.4).

Gas cylinders: Ensure storage at temperature no higher than feed lines or
chlorinator, to prevent possible condensation; keep well clear of fire risk,
offer good access and ventilation. Carefully strap or cradle cylinders.
Weighing facilities will be required (to 150kg) to check chlorine remaining.
Move cylinders with care on trolleys if possible, and as a two-man operation: best rolled not lifted. Feed lines must not pass through areas of less
than 10°C. Always ensure valves well protected. Maximum withdrawal
rate, 15kg/24h. Changeover panel and header manifold required for new
cylinder.

Amplifier, residual recorder, measuring cell and controller: adjustable from
0 to 5ppm to 5 per cent accuracy with 1 minute process time.

Water test set, ammonium hydroxide bottle for leak tests: white fumes
given off in presence of chlorine traces.

Respirator required, rather than gas mask: if nearly all oxygen is depleted
in the room, then a gas mask offers no protection. Locate clearly for easy
availability – check operating efficiency constantly.

Chlorine gas and alarm: sensitive to 0·1ppm with low level indicator,
higher level alarm, chlorine source isolating valves and automatic boosted
extraction. Never immerse cylinder or pour water onto escaping chlorine
gas as hydrochloric acid mixture results: neutralise with strong alkali, ie
soda ash solution.

pH control: involving metering unit, booster pump, covered soda ash tanks
(in duplicate), with all crocks, lines and fittings inert to alkaline solution.

INFORMATION SHEET 15.15

Alternative disinfection chemicals

To be successful they must withstand environment and dangerous reaction
with other solutions.

Biocides A chlorine-free, synthetic organic microbiocide with algicidal
additive (hydrogen peroxide at 100ppm), mainly prepared for private pool
treatment. Safe and stable, offers long-term residual in sun, clear, tasteless
and non-odorous, non-corrosive, non-bleaching with neutral pH: incompatible with chlorine, which must be removed completely from poolwater
before using biocide at 25 to 50ppm, pH7·5, to be checked weekly. Does
not produce 'bright water', which can become definitely greenish when pH
off neutral; green caste also occurs with 'quats' algicides.

Chlorine dioxide Used mainly in continental Europe where it is proving
competitive to straight chlorination. It has no taste nor smell, offers no eye
or skin irritation, is simply, safely and easily used. Can induce a greenish
caste in poorly circulated waters. In Germany there is concern about undesirable chlorite in high alkaline waters causing irritation and stomach
upsets. A minimum 0·1ppm residual is required with 0·3 acceptable. Like
chlorine, it requires experience to operate sucessfully, therefore avoiding
any irritant side effects. Normal testing by DPD. Soluble chlorine dioxide
is produced by automatically drawing sodium chlorite solution and
hydrochloric acid solution from two containers for chlorine dioxide
production resulting from:

$$5NaClO_2 + 4HCl \rightarrow 4ClO_2 + 5NaCl + 2H_2O$$

though often some chlorine is produced as well. Mixed 3:1 with chlorine increases effectiveness.

Mildly acidic pH, and highly corrosive to copper; chlorine dioxide in air is
explosive; sodium chlorite supports combustion.

Combination systems Double treatments show the greatest potential in
avoiding the disadvantages of superchlorination to try and give more pleasing results.

Halogen plus ultra-violet: UV is a very effective steriliser but without
residual; requires support in pool from marginal Cl/Br.

Halogen plus ozonation: ozone is a very effective oxidiser with little lasting
residual, therefore needs marginal support.

Ultra-violet plus ozonation: UV total sterilisation by mercury vapour
lamps takes place with 100mm max flow water depth/fast filter turnover,
and ozone introduced as residual for lightly loaded pools.

Hydantoins: take best advantages of bromine and chlorine from a 90 per
cent active disinfectant donation.

Silver salts: silver nitrate is expensive and slow, and does not deal with
organic compounds. Silver ions purify actively, providing pH and con-
taminating compounds cannot interfere.

Silver/activated carbon: relatively stable residual washed from silver
deposited on charcoal, removes tastes and odours, destroys bacteria, inhibits algae, precipitates iron. Installed after the filter, the silver residual to
25 to 50 parts per *billion* is not affected by sunlight or temperature, does
not corrode pipes and can be cheaper to maintain than chlorine, when
reduced, neutralising and algicidal chemical costs are counted. No routine
maintenance necessary.

INFORMATION SHEET 15.16

Chemo-disinfection equipment

Hydraulically or electrically operated

All mechanical injection systems should stop when the main pump is off to
prevent feeding strong solutions directly into the pool.

All equipment must be easily serviced with wearing/corrodible parts simply
and economically replaced since most solutions become sticky, or
crystallise, or corrode, or leave deposits.

Floating dispensers: set into the skimmer weir, or freely floating around the
pool, they discharge consistently and increasingly according to water flow.
Very satisfactory provision for private pools.

Dry disinfectant eroders: soluble blocks or sticks, charged into a dispenser
or solution chamber, offer controlled dissolvement to patent chlorine type
disinfectants. Satisfactory for light and medium load pools.

Dry chemical feeders: variable rate dissolvement of powder/granulated disinfectant, reduces chemical bulk handling, and increases safety of operation. Most chemicals are hygroscopic and sometimes complex arrange-

ments are needed to stop dry chemicals gathering moisture. Best for medium loads.

Peristaltic drippers or squeeze pumps: regulated dosing without direct mechanical contact of corrosive solution. An eccentric cam squeezes a flexible tube at different rates to impress solutions into the water stream – injection difficulties exist against back pressures. Bends in lines tend to block, and some materials soften and react with solution. Suitable for private and smaller hotel pools.

Metering pumps: carefully controlled rates for all pool loadings. Ensure anti-siphon valves and flood protection arrangements incorporated: carefully segregate acid and alkali units, and their solution tanks.

Guide to ratings per 100m³ pool capacity:
light loading pools   0·5–1 litre/h
medium loading pools 1–5 litre/h
heavy loading pools   5–10 litre/h

Diaphragm type – simple and durable with few moving parts to gum up or corrode. Suitable for all solutions, acids and alum, alkalis and disinfectant. Piston type – very satisfactory in practice, though crystals tend to block non-return valves. Length of stroke is varied to alter dose.

Chlorine tanks should be covered, duplicated and non-corrodible and provide 24h capacity minimum public pools, weekly capacity optimum private pools.

Silver/activated carbon purifier: modular unit, regulated by water flow, requiring very little maintenance and annual recharging for light pool load applications. Larger cartridge units manufactured to suit up to 1 million m³ pools.

Brominator-liquid: apparatus is simple and relatively inexpensive, comprising a measuring cell, injection system, level indicator and control device, with a bromine container and spare. Containers must be handled with care; if changed colour to green, they indicate damage inside and must not be opened: bromine vapour is dangerous, and actively corrodes all metals. Average consumption for public pools between 5 and 10 g/m³ water per day.

INFORMATION SHEET 15.17

Electro-disinfection equipment
For easily regulated control

Electrolytic chlorination
Brine tank: sodium hypochlorite is produced by electrolysis of a saline solution, with molecular chlorine at the anode, and hydroxyl ions at the cathode, plus water: at 100W DC current, approx 150gm of chlorine can be produced per day to suit an average loading 100m³ pool. Ideal for stable bathing loads, but offers little sudden flexibility. Electrodes last 2 or 3 years.

Salt pool: common salt is dissolved in poolwater to a point just below the taste threshold – 3000 to 4000ppm. The salt is split by a DC electric cell into constituent elements. The pure, nascent chlorine is extremely effective and odourless, but dealing with sodium hydroxide and disposing of hydrogen gas, must be satisfactorily arranged. Suitable for pools up to approx 200m³.

Ionised metals
Dr Kause of Munich 1929 patented the Katadyn Silver Purifying process. The Swiss Vellos Casanovas process in the late 1940s included copper ions, as a sand filter fine material and algae flocculant. Subsequent re-introductions provided an aluminium plate for flocculation of colloids, and a platinum plate for oxidation of organic material, plus precipitation of calcium carbonate for filter removal. The silver residual is highly toxic to bacteria between 0·01 to 0·04ppm, which is far below limits for drinking water: it even destroys chlorine resistant micro-organisms. Poolwater ion systems require careful looking after, since they are sensitive to high pH, hardness or high chloride content. Not suitable for heavily loaded pools over 200m³ capacity. Use only recommended chemicals and ensure purifier unit stops when filter stops – minimum operation 16 hours out of 24.

Ultra-violet steriliser
Ultra-violet light is produced by a small, very high electric current, within an evacuated quartz tube, or by a heavy current to form a mercury arc: an UV generator can sterilise water in the plantroom within two minutes, producing no physical change in the water, or chemical constituents. There is no effect on pH, no possibility of overdosing and no residual. Therefore, marginal type disinfection support is necessary, with efficient filtration and fast circulation for lightly loaded pools. UV is the ideal system for medicinal and spa therapy baths, and since there can be no side-effects, on the mineral waters; it is admirable for aquaria. Results depend upon age of lamps, time of exposure and clarity of water: UV requires around 100W for 100m³ light load, high turnover pools; suitable up to 200m³.

INFORMATION SHEET 15.18

Ozonation – properties

Forms
Gas: Relatively expensive material because of sophisticated production system, the most powerful oxidisers known. It is between 10 and 20 times more powerful than chlorine to inactivate bacteria and viruses, cysts and spores, remove colour, taste and smell. A dangerous chemical in air, requiring that ventilation ozonation systems include safety alarms to operate at 0·1ppm: 1ppm induces headaches and tightness of the chest, 20ppm kills.

An unstable and allotropic form of oxygen, where the third atom readily detaches to become a powerful oxidising agent. Ozone dissipates so quickly it has to be made on the spot. A high electrical potential is silently discharged between two electrodes through glass or mica, using extremely dry, clean air, and generating spare heat.

Over 1000 operating systems exist in Austria, France, Germany, Switzerland: abundant cheap electricity helps improve high capital cost of equipment, and costs are spread further if heat recovery applications are developed.

Action
Poolwater saturation with this dissolved 'oxygen' reduces organic matter rapidly and totally, is both pleasant and healthy. Short life, low ozone residual (0·3ppm) retained in some systems, but in Germany 1ppm ozonation is introduced in the plantroom for total disinfection, then any residual removed by carbon filtration, with finally marginal chlorination (0·3ppm) provided as subsidiary disinfection, before the water returns to the pool. Ozone residual does not stay available for long, but can provide especially clear water, is ideal for chlorine sensitive swimmers, and those who stay in water for long periods. An ideal deodoriser in air allowing ventilation heat recovery systems to flourish. There are no harmful by-products, and it decomposes into pure oxygen; enclosure fabric maintenance should be lessened; ozonation control requires no special skills, outside of automatic equipment being well maintained and normal water checks carried out.

Ozone $O_3 \rightarrow O_2$ oxygen
$H_2O + O_3 \rightarrow H_2O_2 + O_2$
$H_2O_2 + organic \rightarrow H_2O + organic$ oxide
        matter

Oxygen free molecules combine with water to form hydrogen peroxide, a most powerful disinfectant and oxidiser of organic matter.

Other effects
Ozone is highly corrosive to metals. The addition of carbon filtration, plus a chlorine controller exaggerates the costing of an ozonator. Discharge tubes must be kept efficient to prevent runaway cost of ozone production – continuous dry air flow removes ozone quickly, and prevents any moisture build up in the pool's humid atmosphere. Short-life O_3 residual requires efficient water distribution and fast turnover. A slight excess of ozone in poolwater produces a redox-potential + 800mV @ pH 7·5 to destroy bacteria within a few seconds.

Ideal for aesthetic combination disinfection systems with halogen residual, (eg 0·2ppm Cl_2 – not marginal hypochlorination, but sufficient free residual since all oxidisable material has already been oxidised by ozone).

See also chapter 14.10.

INFORMATION SHEET 15.19

Test processes

Chloride and bromine

DPD tests developed by Dr A. T. Palin in England, single out different stages of chlorination in water samples by changing shades of pink to deep red.

Diethyl-p-phenylene diamine tablets:

Use for *free Chlorine* to *monochloramine* to *dichloramine*

Nos   1   →   +2   →   +3

Use for *free Chlorine* to   *combined chlorine*

Nos   1   →   +3

Use for *total residual chlorine*

No   →   4

	Test	
	public	private
No 1 for free chlorine, iodine,	2–4 hourly	daily
free and combined bromine,		
free chlorine plus stabilised chlorine,		
chlorine dioxide,		
No 3 for combined chlorine,	daily	weekly
No 4 for total available chlorine,	daily	weekly
ozone or total chlorine		
plus ozone		

Orthotolidine-benzidine: turns yellow in presence of free and combined chlorine. Deep orange in high concentrations, but does not distinguish forms. As this chemical incurs a potential cancer risk in small concentrations, it should only be used by trained personnel. Tests also for iodine when mercuric chloride first added to sample.

	Test	
Ortho-droplet additive for total residual	2–4	not
chlorine and pH	hourly	suitable

pH

High chlorine residual can bleach out the pH test colour: sodium thiosulphate first used to remove all chlorine from sample for accuracy.

	Test	
	public	private
Bromthymol Blue – pH 6·0–7·6 ⎫		
Phenol Red – pH 6·8–8·4 ⎪	daily	weekly
Diphenol Purple – pH 7·0–8·6 ⎬		
Thymol Blue – pH 8·0–9·6 ⎭		

or pH handmeter test in 5 seconds by electric potential.*

Alkalinity Calcium and Magnesium tablets

or by titration	weekly	monthly

Conditioner-cyanuric acid by turbidity of

sample with melamine, or colorimetric test.	monthly	seasonally
TDS by electrical conductivity for ppm count	monthly	seasonally

Colorimetric testing is inexpensive and generalised, whereas expensive electrometric testing offers greater accuracy of units. Colorimetric glass standard colours must be non-fade.

Total bacteria count zero on standard plate count (35°C) after incubation in nutrient for 24 hours to test for presence of Escherichia coli (E.coli)

*The Redox-pH meter (solid state circuitry) offers as a meter, or digital read off, measurement

pH 0–14

mV ± 1400 for Redox

INFORMATION SHEET 15.20

pH scale

7·07 pH is exactly neutral.

To minimise pH fluctuations, the alkalinity buffer level in poolwater should be:

  80–150ppm   private pools
100–250ppm   public pools

Balanced pH reduces the opportunity for nitrogen trichloride to form from ammonium compounds, urea, sweat and urine.

What lowers pH?	What raises pH?
gas chlorine	liquid chlorine
di- and tri-chlorines	calcium hypochlorites

What lowers pH?	What raises pH?
sodium bisulphate	caustic soda and bicarb
alum	algae and contamination
rainwater	most top-up waters
acid	alkali and base

Too acid water:
attacks and etches surfaces
irritates swimmers' eyes,
nose and throat.

Too alkaline water:
deposits, coats and corrodes;
inflames, reddens and softens
swimmers' skin.

Note: Operating at pH 8·5 rather than 7·5, requires a fivefold increase to HOCl free chlorine residual.

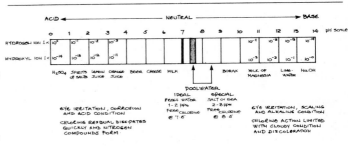

pH scale

INFORMATION SHEET 15.21

Chlorine/bromine disinfection dissociation

Chlorine activity shows a marked falling-off as pH increases; bromine much less so.

Activity		@ pH 7·0	@ pH 8·0
Powerful	**Weak**		
Free	**Combined**		
Chlorine			
Hypochlorous			
Acid HOCl		70%	20%
	Hypochlorite		
	ion OCl	30%	80%
Bromine			
Hypobromous			
Acid HOBr		99%	90%
	Hypobromite		
	ion OBr	1%	10%

Source: W. H. Humphrey: Public Swimming Pool Water Disinfection, *Baths Service* January 78.

INFORMATION SHEET 15.22

Langelier equation for water balancing

Acid corrodes: alkali scales.

Water balanced has no tendency to either.

The pH at which the water would be in equilibrium with calcium carbonate equivalent is termed pH at saturation, determined by applying the Langelier formula: — negative value is corrosive water, + positive value is scale forming water, and 0·0 is chemically balanced water; neutral can be practically considered between −0·5 to +0·5 poolwater condition.

Saturation index = pH + temperature + calcium + alkalinity −12·1
                          factor   hardness factor
                                     factor

SI   = pH +   TF   +   CF   +   AF   −12·1

This formula includes the four main significant factors for poolwater, though temperature variation over the swimming range is marginal, that is until spa pools are taken into consideration. Since TDS and trace elements in the normal range 50 to 1000ppm have little factor signification of 0 to 1, this pool equation does not include them.

Saturation index tables for Langelier equation

Temperature °C	15	20	25	30	35	40		
Temperature factor	0·4	0·5	0·6	0·7	0·8	0·9		

Calcium hardness ppm	25	50	75	100	150	200	400	1000	expressed as $CaCO_3$
Calcium factor	1·0	1·3	1·5	1·6	1·8	1·9	2·2	2·6	

Total alkalinity ppm	25	50	75	100	150	200	400	1000	expressed as $CaCO_3$
Alkalinity factor	1·4	1·7	1·9	2·0	2·2	2·3	2·6	3·0	

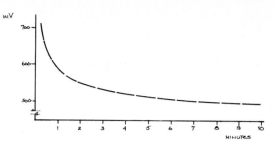

Redox potential measure for kill-rate at pH7

Source: DGfdB/Straner

INFORMATION SHEET 15.23

Water analyses

Possible	Mains water	Spa water	Sea water
	ppm	ppm	ppm
Total dissolved solids	500	32,000	40,000
Total hardness	200	4000	12,000
Mineral salts	Traces	500	200
Calcium salts	100	20,000	3000
Magnesium salts	20	4000	9000
Chlorides	25	8000	28,000

Perfect poolwater	level	
Free chlorine	1·5ppm	
Combined chlorine	0·5ppm	
Cyanurate acid	30ppm	
Calcium hardness	150ppm	higher for soft water supplies: 200 favoured UK
Total alkalinity	150ppm	lower for hard water supplies: 100 favoured US
Mineral salts	none	
Total dissolved solids	1000ppm	
pH	7·5	
Temperature	27°C	
Bacteria count	none	
Algae	controlled	
Turbidity	0·3 JTU	(maximum 0·5)

and applying Langelier equation:

Saturation index = pH + TF + CF + AF + − factor

$$SI = 7·5 + 0·6 + 1·8 + 2·2 − 12·1$$
$$= 0$$

INFORMATION SHEET 15.24

Redox-potential

Or oxidation-reduction potential (ORP)

The chemical condition of water electrically relates to the potential of a germicide's oxidising ability.

When chlorine or potential disinfectant present is combined forming ammonium compounds, its oxidation potential is low and slow in disinfecting the water (30 to 90 minutes).

When chlorine is in a free available form, it has a high oxidation potential, destroying bacteria and organic compounds in water very quickly (1 to 3 minutes).

Redox is very high, when there is abundant free chlorine whereas redox is low, when there is an excess of combined chlorine. A redox of 750mV = 0·8ppm free chlorine @ pH 7·7.

A greatly increased disinfectant effect is available from chlorine at pH 7·2, providing there is accurate pH control.

INFORMATION SHEET 15.25

Hardness

(A measure of the quantity of calcium and magnesium salts dissolved in water, expressed in terms of $CaCO_3$ ppm)

Scale of hardness	Aim for 100–150ppm levels (250ppm Marblite pools)	
Poolwaters are		
Soft	0– 50ppm	rainwater
Moderately soft	50–100ppm	
Slightly hard	100–150ppm	Ideal pool water
Moderately hard	150–200ppm	Ideal drinking water
Hard	200–300ppm	
Very hard	300–400ppm	

Hardness of water: the more soap needed to lather, the harder the water. Dissolved calcium and magnesium compounds tend to cake out and to corrode. Builds up scale.

Temporary hardness (alkaline): mainly the presence of calcium carbonate, followed by bicarbonate, magnesium carbonate and bicarbonate.

Permanent hardness (non-alkaline): the presence of chlorides, sulphates and nitrates of calcium and magnesium.

Scale: without excess calcium, scaling deposits on surfaces become unlikely. The factors involved are calcium hardness, total alkalinity, pH temperature and TDS.

Soft water: exists when dissolved matter is freely soluble and does not tend to come out of solution again. Easily lathered water.

Softening of water: by base exchange through zeolites, or ion exchange using resins: processes are regenerated when spent.

Total dissolved solids (TDS) – a measure of the total quantity of substances dissolved in water or the electrical conductivity.

Drinking water range	500–1500ppm	
Poolwater range	500–3000ppm	1500ppm preferred maximum
Salinity human body	8000–9000ppm	
Spa water mineral content	30,000	
Seawater saltiness	40,000	
Dead Sea	250,000	
Great Salt Lake	275,000	

'Tired water syndrome': Too high TDS reduces chlorine efficiency, increases scaling, adds a salty taste, dulls water and makes it difficult to maintain a balance. Empty and refill, or extensively dilute.

INFORMATION SHEET 15.26

Alkalinity

Alkalinity refers to the total quantity and types, of all the alkaline substances in the water, which help resist a change of pH: pH is closely related, and is the measure of the relationship of the temporary balance between acidity and basicity.

Alkalinity is the total amount in ppm, with pH being the distance from neutral.

To change the level, the amount and type of alkaline salt has to be changed. The pH can 'bounce' around, unless there is a total alkalinity reserve of 100ppm $CaCO_3$ equivalent. Alkaline salts include carbonates, bicarbonates, hydroxides, even phosphates and silicates contribute.

Levels of total alkalinity – Aim for 150 to 200ppm equivalent to act as a buffer and resist pH swing.

Poolwater alkalinity

Absolute minimum (APHA)	50ppm	private pools, but pH control is difficult
Ideal level (US)	100ppm	public pools using liquid chlorine
Hard water areas	150ppm	optimum
Ideal level (UK)	200ppm	public pools using gas chlorine
Soft water areas	250ppm	

Hard supply waters inviting scaling: total alkalinity from 200 to 500, pH 7·4 to 8·4.

Soft supply waters inviting etching: total alkalinity from 0 to 100, pH 6·8 to 7·2.

Most poolwater tends to be alkaline resulting from bather oils and disinfection donations.

Alkaline demand: the amount of base needed to raise pH and increase alkalinity.

Acid demand: the amount of acid needed to lower pH and reduce alkalinity.

INFORMATION SHEET 15.27

Some stains

Chlorine added to a bucket of warm water will darken in a short while if iron or manganese is present. Finely divided particles of metal in suspension, or in solution, are oxidised by chlorine, and precipitated out as insoluble staining compounds.

To achieve clear poolwater, which should have a blue tinge, bring pH to 7·5 and superchlorinate; add alum, crushed or hubbled, to sand filter to extract contaminents; or suction sweep away all material that has flocculated onto a diatomaceous earth coating previously set over the pool floor.

Minerals

Alum: coagulation not carried out properly can discolour the pool floor a greenish-brown.

Calcium: carbonate build-up discolours paint, tile or marblite, aggravated by residual bulk carrier from calcium hypochlorite: allow residue to settle out of dissolved powdered chlorine solution first.

Copper: black, or blue-green deposits on surfaces are removed by acid washing.

Iron: red or brown rust spots, or large patches of discolouration: always coat interior of boilers and heat exchangers to protect pool or ensure resistant materials used.

Manganese: poolwater turns grass green, to greenish-brown, and then deposits insoluble patches of purplish-black as pH raised.

Zinc: off-white deposits derived from plumbing.

Waters

Turbid: hazy water is either over-alkaline or under-filtered and under-chlorinated, or both.

Milky: faulty filtration, or over-acid condition, and low in alkalinity; sometimes a greenish hue; also a sign of an imminent algae phase.

Foaming: usually too much 'quats' algicide – dilute.

Greenish: algae attack phase in full swing – superchlorinate.

Surfaces

Slimy: milky water, and yellow, green or black walls, or spots indicate algae presence – shockchlorinate and scrub.

Scale: chalky grey or brownish coating indicates hard water – soften.

Etching: soft waters seeking calcium; tiling damage by sulphate from alum – harden.

Encrusted patches: mineral salts precipitated out – particularly in seawaters – acid treat.

Blacking of metals: pitting or discolouration of metals indicates electrolytic action – remove dissimilar metals or offer sacrificial metal (see chapters 11.2 and 16.4 for electrolytic action).

INFORMATION SHEET 15.28

Stabilising graphs

(Using Cyanuric acid – 'a suntan lotion for the pool')

At 30ppm CYA level, there are 30 molecules of cyanuric acid for every one of hypochlorous acid, helping protect the chlorine chemical disinfectant from destructive UV rays. Overstabilisation, or 'chlorine lock', above say a 100ppm level, and the protective shield becomes too thick and cumbersome, slowing down free chlorine effect until it is nullified. It is now more a conversion from a fast FAC to a slow CAC process. To revive chlorine effect, dilution of poolwater will be necessary, and absolutely vital when approaching the maximum 200ppm cyanurate level. CYA at this level and between pH 7 and 8 can in some instances almost double total alkalinity: the false alkalinity factor raises saturation index calculations which hides pool water corrosiveness causing plaster pitting. Consequently, it is better to raise free chlorine level, from, say, 2 to 3ppm, to support normal CYA progressive slowing down of disinfection treatment.

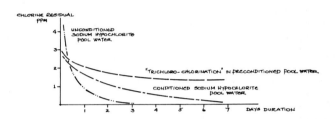

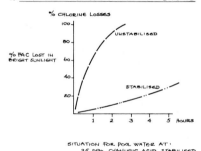

Stabilising graphs, using cynuric acid

INFORMATION SHEET 15.29

Conditioning and cleansing chemicals checklist
(Preferably non-toxic, colourless and odourless)

Stabilisers or conditioners: retard the depletion of poolwater chlorines.

Chlorinated chyantoins: long lasting disinfection compounds.

Cyanuric acid or isocyanurate chlorines: filter UV sunlight that dissipates chlorine; CYA dose @ 2 to 3kg/100m³ to 25 to 50ppm level, to slow down residual losses.

Sulphamic acid: less problematical chlorine stabiliser, with less dramatic saving effects.

In any conditioned pool:
- do not use sequestering agents or quats algicides
- do not allow combined chlorine to rise above 0·3ppm
- do not let CYA level exceed 100ppm
- do not neglect superchlorination especially when high bathing loads can overwhelm system.

Surface water sealant: a chemical cosmetic heat insulator (an alcohol derivation) a few molecules thick and lasting up to a week in calmer pools, saving ⅓ heating by reducing evaporation and indoor condensation.

Coagulant or flocculants: combine fine material for better filter collection, plus extra control of colour, taste and odour (not used with dolomitic filter layers).

Aluminium sulphate (alum): added slowly into suction line to avoid pressure build up and after backwashing, forms a sticky substance that traps fine particulate matter/colourations in sand filters: for an aluminium hydroxide floc to improve turbidity add @ 0·5kg/m² of filter area @ 7·6pH poolwater (¼ rate sometimes applied to private pools for overnight clearance of haze).

Ferric chloride: precipitates organic substances for filtration.

Organic polymer: an electrically-charged chain molecule causing oppositely charged micro-colloids in water to coalesce, forming large enough particles for filtration; also acts as scaling inhibitor by inducing dissolution of precipitating calcium molecules.

Potassium or sodium aluminium sulphate: sometimes used as alum charge.

Sodium silicate: helps line iron pipework with silica for soft waters to prevent corrosion @ 2kg/100m³

Chelating or sequestering agents: suspend or break-up metallic ions to prevent staining.

Calcium hydroxide (slaked lime): removes hardness to prevent pipe furring.

Calcium chloride: added to bring up calcium levels in pools: calcium deficiency reduces filter efficiency.

Ethyl endiamine tetra-acetic acid (edta): deals with very hard waters @ 0·5kg/100m³.

Sodium aluminate: water softening agent and flocculant.

Sodium hexametaphosphate: cuts down scale, keeps up polyphosphate count and prevents them changing to orthophosphate. Reduces hardness @ 2kg/100m³/d.

Zeolite: ion-exchange process for water softening.

Algicides: destroy or inhibit algae growth: a second front to disinfection.

Bromine: active algicide.

Chlorine: destroys algae, but even 'black' or 'mustard' plantcells can insulate themselves up to 2 or 3ppm free chlorine.

Copper chelates: short residual life, inhibits growth and can stain with prolonged use.

Copper sulphate (also silver or gold salts): selective toxic properties but attacks paints: does not really deal with black algae – generally more suitable for ponds not pools.

Hydrogen peroxide: supports non-chlorine biocides at 100ppm strength.

Mercurial salts (phenyl mercuric acetate): algicidal and algistatic properties, but mercury accumulation kills all forms of life.

Polymers: generally algicidal and available in different forms.

Quaternary ammonium compounds (quats): wets algae and 'drowns them': can be absorbed in filter media and deplete chlorine, or even stimulate some algae strains: a cationic substance toxic to fish at over 1ppm.

Quinones: specialised controls, without unhealthy side effects.

Silver compounds: selective and effective at very modest residual, but colloidal silver tends to turn water grey and can stain.

Cleansers: to treat floors and filters, walls and WCs.

Activated carbon: fine decolouriser.

Detergent: use only for removing oils and greases well away from pool water.

Hydrochloric acid (muriatic): for rust and scale, acid washing interiors and dissolving filter mudballs.

Sodium bisulphate: aids descaling filters.

Sodium dioxide: de-chlorinating compound.

Sodium metasilicate: an alkaline detergent.

Sodium sulphite: removes chlorine @ 2·5kg/100m³ per ppm residual.

Sodium thiosulphate: destroys free chlorine at 0·5kg/100m³ per ppm residual.

Sulphamic acid: descales filters, pipes; safely cleans surrounds and tiles, baths and toilets, etches concrete.

Problem	Mixture per 10 litres water	Cure
To remove discolourations from stainless steel and equipment	25gm	Sponge on, leave a while, wipe off
To clean surrounds, concrete floors and tiled surfaces	1kg	Swab on, leave for 10 minutes, wipe away
To cleanse toilets and remove bad stains	1½kg	Paint on, leave for 10 minutes, wash off
To descale baths, pipelines, heat exchangers and etch slippery concrete	2kg	Apply, leave standing overnight and wash away

Soft luxuriant landscaping for a pool in New Zealand
John Morton Landscape Design Ltd, Christchurch

16 Repair, renovation and maintenance

The upkeep of a modern swimming pool requires a balance between manpower and mechanical ingenuity. Most pools built today will last for at least 50 years. Most will operate at a loss, and all will become an increasing burden as time goes on.

Swimming pool after-care really counts. To optimise caretaking systems and set standards that survive, a much larger proportion of the capital expenditure budget must be allocated than for most other building projects. Once operating, this environment is wholly dependent upon good management and continual maintenance. Any method, procedure, or device that makes this continuous task more effective is a winner.

16.1 Safety

Swimming pool safety is a composite picture which is too frequently left until last, and then, economies mean cutting out any 'extras' (such as optional precautions with safety barriers, extra diving depth beyond the minimum, or even ample lifesaving gear). In the private pool sector, when negotiations arrive at the question of safety, risks are played down since it is an enjoyable environment that is being sold – optional safety items seem to overload the price and play up the danger.

Disaster: the Summerland example There is no short cut to safety; forethought and constant vigilance are key factors. In the panic following fire most people make for the door through which they entered, often apparently ignoring emergency exits on the way. This was the situation particularly in the Isle of Man Summerland Leisure Centre and Aquadrome disaster of 1973. Fifty people died when fire totally enveloped the whole translucent acrylic side of the main building within just four or five minutes. And the complex was gutted in only 30 minutes. Victims were trapped on fire-protected stairs, or within a few metres of emergency exits; and more confusingly, after hundreds of holidaymakers had managed to escape – through a congested main entrance – some immediately turned round and tried to fight their way back into the building, against the crowd still coming out, so as to try and save their children or relatives in other parts of the huge complex. Tragedy would have been further magnified if fire had started close to the main entrance.

On enquiry, errors were found to be very human, for this disaster like most others followed a series of muddles: different authoritative departments thought the plans had already been vetted by the other; planning regulations concerning two hour fire resistant materials were waived to suit the new kind of leisure structure; inflammable and asphyxiating properties of some new building materials were overlooked; insufficient and haphazard stairway arrangements were permitted, as were alternative escape routes into the basement; no compartmentation checks existed to slow down spread of fire; softwood structural flooring was used for upper terraces; the main entrance was severely constricted with barriers and payboxes; fire drill had not been practised by the management; and there was insufficient good quality and easily accessible fire fighting equipment.

Fortunately, the swimming pool area alongside was not badly damaged. It provided over 1000m³ of water in fighting the fire, and another major escape route for about 500 people.

Following the Isle of Man Summerland enquiry, valuable recommendations concerning modern structures were made in the investigating commission's report in 1974. On people and materials at risk, they suggested that 'any building roofed or clad with extensive areas of acrylic sheeting, and intended for occupation by a substantial density of population (say in excess of one person to every 3m² of the net area), should have a higher standard of means of escape than the normal provision for the same number of persons. For example, aggregate exit width, properly distributed, might be increased by half, and travel distances reduced by a third'.

They also recommended that acrylic cladding or roofing should be placed 3·5m out of normal reach; as well as 6m clear of any possible combustible material, or protected by a reliable and effective water-spray system.

With hindsight, it is said that no one person had stood back sufficiently to consider and to analyse the improbabilities, the risks, the stressed performance of new materials in new situations, the problems of handling separated families in crowded facilities, and tragically, the full implications of vandalism. For it was youngsters outside the Centre setting fire to rubbish by a storage hut that started the devastating blaze.

Safety enforcement National pool associations are concerned primarily with suggesting minimum standards, but they do not necessarily check they are carried out. For example, even if every American pool building company – which is not the case – agreed to adopt NSPI pool dimensions for diving, and always ensured their pools were clearly identified with the laid down categories, from a no diving possible situation to the 1m spring-board level, there would still be no authoritative guarantee, outside of each company's pledge, that the minimum requirements had actually been carried out.

Diving accidents still occur in swimming pools even when relevant statutory depth regulations have been strictly adopted. Multi-million dollar compensation law suits are filed and won, against pool operators who may have prohibited diving into shallow depth water, but then failed to provide proper supervision, or large enough warning signs, or clear and sufficient depth markings . . . and especially with drowning cases, it is impossible for lifeguards to see clearly into the middle of very large pools. Additionally, in the USA, if someone drowns in a cloudy water pool, the company who last checked and serviced the filter plant, regardless of the original manufacturer or installer, can be liable in law. With cases pending for $20 million claims, no wonder recreational dream facilities can be shattered.

Survival Hazards in pools can be electrical, chemical, physical, psychological or contagious. No infectious person – swimmer or pool attendant – should be permitted within the pool area. The debilitating effect of cold water upon young children is constantly underestimated. Given half a chance, most children will stay in water far too long, so lowering their ability to withstand infection. A physically fit person can suffer hyperthermia – dying of cold – at water temperature 15°C: survival time being just a few hours (see chapters 14.2 and 15.2).

16.1 *Structural designs are not always used in the way intended: Munich Olympic Pool*
Architect: Behnisch & Partner

16.2 *Pool under construction at Abingdon Old Gaol Sports Complex (conversion by the Royal College of Art, London)*
Photo: Thomas Photos

16.3 *Supervision control centre overseeing the children's pool and wave pool at Swindon Oasis Leisure Centre*
Architects: Gillinson Barnett & Partners
Photo: O. F. Clarke

16.3

Although there are perhaps three times as many above-ground pools to in-ground (the ratio in NSW, Australia is 4:1), five times as many children are drowned in the latter.

Another, not so obvious danger, is the teenagers' practice of hyperoxygenation – taking several deep breaths to swim great distances underwater; such efforts can cause sudden blackout and drowning at the point when all the spare energy within the body is used up. Although the world record for staying underwater is held by a doctor at almost 14 minutes, an average person can still drown within 2 minutes. Often people do not understand this – one manager in New Zealand, having rescued a small boy from drowning and then packed him off home to rest, got a strong complaint from the child's grandmother demanding return of admission money, for she claimed 'the boy had only been in the water a few minutes'.

Like the high numbers of people drowned every year, there are far too many paralysing accidents from diving and hitting the side, the floor, or another swimmer. Much more research into swimmer, diver and slider activities is still required, using standard pools, or special research tanks along the lines of the doughnut ring pool and its mobile monitoring bridge for technicians in the State University of New York at Buffalo, where research is carried out on the body's efficiency in water for many different kinds of work. In today's expanding world of water, outside of competitive swimming, there are widening commercial activities and new fields of knowledge that require special skills, training and supervision. After all, this planet is 70 per cent underwater.

16.2 Cleaning systems

Management controls cleanliness; the quality of management, or rather the lack of it, soon shows in any swimming pool. If pre-hygiene facilities are not properly used, additional dirt load on filtration and disinfection systems can soon double, and when an ordinary public pool expects around 600 or 700 bather/m^2/ annum on average, there is the cumulative effect of pollution to bear in mind.

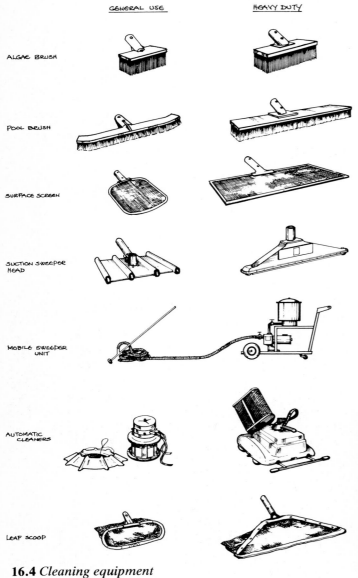

16.4 *Cleaning equipment*

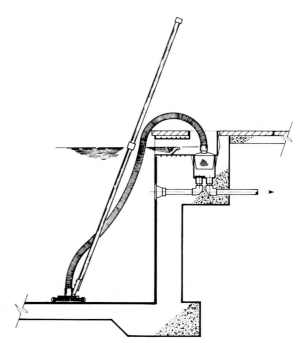

16.5 *Underwater vacuum cleaner: suction sweeper head, flexible hose and telescopic handle*

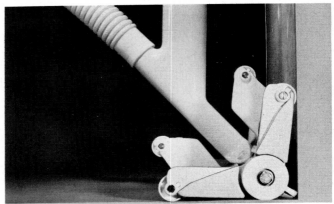

16.6 *Articulated poolwater suction sweeper head*
Fairlocks, Essex

One simple measure of a pool's efficiency can be seen immediately in dirty and neglected changing rooms, which invite vandalism and encourage down-at-heel care throughout the building. Most cause for complaint occurs within the changing area and the toilets. Repeated washing and hosing, scrubbing and disinfecting is critical.

Infectious materials do prove especially troublesome to the atrophied skin of some disabled bathers. Skin scales and fungi spores are persistent, unless all detritus is immediately washed away; and warm floor, wet or dry rooms, with non-slip texturing help hold and promote the incidence of verrucae.

Mechanical cleaners and sweepers soon make savings on pool care costs, providing building interior covings are rounded, partitions raised, and there are no crevices. Resilient rubber floors, synthetic carpeting, or polypropylene fibre grass make better and safer surfaces, but the cleaning system must be efficient – steam cleaning once a week is

definitely not sufficient. Daily 'hoovering', hosing-down, fast drainage and disinfecting are standard requirements (see chapters 2, 11.2 and 12.4/5).

For the poolwater, basic hand tools from the cleaning trade are suitably adapted to work at several arm's lengths distance. By far the most indispensable item in the collection is the underwater suction sweeper, either independently or directly connected to the filter, manually operated or automated, used regularly with as wide and as hydraulically efficient sweeping head as possible. The best is not always the cheapest, but for practicality, it is usually the simplest.

If an automatic device does not need undue maintenance, it can easily earn its keep in labour saving within the first year or two. Any pool not in operation, or without a recirculation system, can now use economic, self-contained filtering/cleaning/disinfecting units that are mobile and independent.

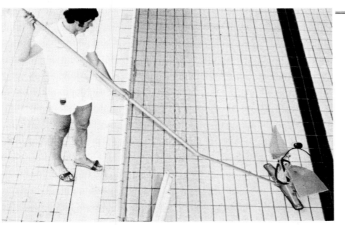

16.7 *Public pool suction sweeper and transport trolley*
Ospa, Middlesex and GFR

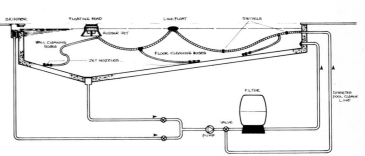

16.8 *Automatic pool cleaner*

16.9 *A Kreepy Krauly automatic pool sweeper that flaps across floor and walls collecting debris and dirt*
Unipools, Middlesex

16.10 *A mobile, underwater, pool floor robot sweeper for large pools*
Programmed Pool Cleaners, Sussex and Aqua-Vac Systems, Florida
Photo: Tim Farebrother

16.10

16.11 *Retractible, flexing, sweeper hoses automatically flailing clean the pool floor*
Poolmaid, Arizona

16.12 *Mobile poolside independent cartridge filter suction sweeper to 10 m³/h throughput*
Rutherford Group, Sussex
Photo: MFS Photography

16.3 Maintenance routines

Attendance improves when a pool is promoted by cleanliness. The real challenge is a pool that is inexpensive to run.

Routines should be developed for weekly, monthly and seasonal care, and be readily available when commissioning the plant. Working routines should plan for easy upkeep by as few staff as possible.

The total number of operational staff required is often underestimated, or cut to the bone, and then extra accommodation for subsequently increased manpower has to be squeezed in later. Labour saving arrangements, such as less, but efficient staff manning a combined clothing store, the effective use of closed circuit TV, are valuable. Cheerfulness and willingness in carrying out duties without prompting, minimal use of a public address system, ability to take an immediate firm stand against tomfoolery, are all good PR, and as valuable to a pool and its patrons as staff sharing in earned benefits from better attendance returns.

Most equipment well maintained, lasts for years, and the engineer's consideration for long-term availability of spares is usually far more important than a manufacturer's first year guarantee. Regularly inspecting the fabric of a swimming pool can catch deterioration before it becomes costly and dangerous.

16.4 Wear and tear

Vandalism Even though there is less vandalism in a good environment, every item in a swimming pool is still considered a challenge to the delinquent. Or is vandalism an expression of disapproval? Incidents can drop drastically when a few troublemakers are caught, but this is mainly because only a few produce nearly all the problems.

In public pools, every fixture and fitting, blank wall and painted surface within reach, receives hard use at the best of times, and if it cannot take continual wear and cleaning, then it is unsuitable.

Corrosion Plantroom equipment can meet hard use, long periods of operation or inactivity, sometimes with minimal attention. A surfeit of wetness and humidity promotes corrosion, and it is this type of continual deterioration that must be watched out for and avoided. Using the right materials might seem more expensive initially, but for example, it is no good whatsoever hoping a cast iron pump will survive seawater circulation. Salt water soon makes the metal spongy, high TDS promotes electrolytic action, the pump endures a year or two. A bronze or gunmetal pump, at twice the cost will continue to last without fail.

In fact, every single component, nut and bolt, screw and fitting, used in and around the humid pool, risks corrosion. More so, if softer less noble dissimilar metals are used, or meet, or galvanically unite through poolwater – the electrolyte – or suffer constant condensation and high humidity. Care and attention is necessary to every single detail to ensure that potentially different metals are never employed, and that passive and safe materials are coupled together to avoid the electrolytic corrosive problems.

Then there is oxidation to worry about. This means protection with tough coatings and film coverings, or repair and repainting regularly, unless inert and better materials are employed in the first place.

Leaks Probably the worst trouble a pool can suffer is a leak. Slow seepage is the most difficult to track down, and often becomes almost impossible to distinguish from surface evaporation. A test tank comparison can give a clue to the rate of evaporation (see chapter 9.5). Or a monomolecular surface chemical film over the pool will limit evaporation making it easier to determine if seepage is taking place.

If render is porous and pipework pressure tests prove the lines are sound, then the waterproofing emulsion coating taking only a few days to apply, usually is better than a whole new tank.

Pool tanks are only emptied when leaks are bad or there is extensive work to be carried out. In the event of a proven leaking concrete tank, cut out the crazed or porous plaster, cut back the crack, and repair the area using a two-part underwater hardening compound. Vinyl liners need underwater patching and appropriate solvents; a pool putty can harden underwater over an epoxy-resin bond (taking an hour at 30°C, or two hours at 20°C); damaged tiling can be removed and replaced with a suitable grouting cement that sets underwater – the maintenance diver usually taking around 10 minutes to chivvy out and replace each tile.

16.5 Conversion and refurbishing

One of the more interesting pool prospects is to convert or update old facilities. The more unusual the job, the better the prospect for an interesting result. Generally, most older establishments have the advantage of starting off with plenty of character to carry over into the new scene.

Alternative uses Successful conversions in pools have already been carried out from a wide range of different buildings (an old gaol, a corn exchange, redundant railway stations, a cattle market, and public laundries for example). But, primarily it is the dishevelled and antique bath houses, those plain old fashioned tanks designed to forgotten standards, or schemes built on far too large a scale, that really deserve original and more imaginative refurbishing (see chapters 5.5 and 11.3).

The 1934 international-sized pool built at Wembley was used for the 1948 London Olympics – but only just, for a major crack developed almost on the eve of the swimming events. As much as 250m³ of fresh water was needed every day just to keep the tank full. The pool survived the Olympics, but on investigation afterwards, the cost of repair and restructure was considered too much, so a temporary floor was laid across the tank to provide the basis of a rink for international ice shows. These interim arrangements lasted well until 1976, when a more permanent ice floor was installed within this multi-purpose sports complex. Undertaking the cost of converting, several times if necessary, can have very practical results.

Some places can be completely transformed to suit currently fashionable pastimes, such as the conversion of large pool tanks into skateparks where energetic enthusiasts race round some exciting Grand Prix-like hairpin courses on their skateboards – an idea actively encouraged by promotors and proving useful where the new sport is catching on faster than investment for new facilities. In fact, a profitable winter use for emptied outdoor pools.

Pools age slowly. It is the equipment that dates first. But when modernising the pool becomes necessary, plant is soon replaced. Sometimes new decking and surrounds need to be created, but more often it is the old tank that needs attention. Complete and overall refurbishing can be as expensive as the pool was originally, but bearing inflation in mind, it is still nowhere near as much as providing a new complex from scratch. Facelifts are growing more popular and often include replacement of waterline tiling with mosaics, extra inlets and outlets, skimmers instead of guttering that has been infilled and tiled over, the addition of in situ steps, or a new spa pool alcove. Other practical changes require removing of previous finishes, laying of resilient decking or adding contemporary bullnose coping, resurfacing or latexing Marblite render, new plastic pipework, and so on, all tasks in themselves that are not

16.13 *Pool liner repair kits for wet or dry patching*
Cranleigh Clark, Berks & NSW

16.14 *Converting the Empire pool in 1976 (originally opened at Wembley in 1936 for the Empire Games) into an ice skating rink: supporting structure and heat coil extractors*
J. M. Hill & Son, London
Photo: Sydney Newbery

16.15 *Re-lining a 19th-century 'bathing pond' with a glass-reinforced plastic membrane*
Sika Contracts Ltd, Surrey
Photo: Kingston Photographic Services

very costly, but do bring a new lease of life into a tired pool. Even outmoded spa town baths are now being revived for new treatments and old therapies.

Modernisation and refurbishing of pools and baths is practical and relatively inexpensive, and becoming the probable course of action for many authorities.

Renovating materials Vinyl sheet liners are ideal set inside old and cracked pools, approximately 2mm textured material at least being necessary for public projects (see chapter 9.5). Use PVC with fabric reinforcement and sanitised treatment to resist bacteria and fungus: these relinings on the spot are reliably installed and definitely heavy duty, requiring only cutting and careful fitting around inlets/outlets plus hot-air welding, hot-bar or high frequency welding, but even when there is no power source, a 'swell-agent solution weld' will be the answer. These overall surfacings make attractive finishes that will endure (but protect from materials like bitumen).

Occasionally, another tank can be built inside the original, but it is usually easier and cheaper to reline using one of the popular hard setting plastic overlays – such as reinforcement padding, resin laminate or plain painted coating. The most economical and practical treatment involves an epoxy-resin coating and admixture: the original tiling is cleaned, a bonding coat given, and finally the epoxy-resin emulsion applied to cure to a white, tough, waterproof finish. An even more durable and heavier lining will be the more skilfully hand-formed, GRP overlay (see chapter 11.2).

If the floor is suspect, a 6mm screed, 1:1:3 epoxy-resin cement and sand mix on a bonding tie-coat will often suffice. This offers tight bonding of chemically resistant new concrete on old, thin-set terrazzo flooring. Another version involves applying a bonding coat to old, but sound tiling, followed by a white cement Marblite render, based upon an epoxy binder which will also waterproof. This can even be applied to damp concrete, stone or brickwork. Then there is the all-purpose simple water-based two-part epoxy/polyamide chemically-curing emulsion – an effectively durable all round waterproofer. Two coats, brushed rollered or sprayed (not below 10°C or above 85 per cent relative humidity) offer a rapid tough surface that can be cleaned simply with warm water and detergent.

New shells of resin laminated glassfibre padding, hand-laid inside a cracked tank, or even monolithic polyester skins sprayed over all existing structures, help cut down on renovating costs.

16.6 From bathing and swimming to leisure

'For the last 200 years since the Industrial Revolution, economic activity – that is work – has been regarded as a principle focus of life.'[1] Water releases human inhibitions: 'there is a certain age-old relief to move into water and feel the pull vanish'.

Every recreational survey since 1950 has shown swimming in its broadest sense to be by far the most popular of all physical activities. But swimming is not the sole *bathing* activity in water. There is growing revival in tonal bathing for private and public pools, similar to the social therapy treatment with water offered in Continental municipal spas. And leisure bathing or playing about in water is the most popular form of active recreation ever.

16.16

16.17

16.18

16.16 *Prepare also for swimming pool events: 'Jeux sans frontières' festivities at Blackpool proving highly popular, locally and nationally on TV*
Blackpool Gazette and Herald

16.17 *Olympic swimming championships at Munich in 1972 prove worldwide popularity*
Münchner Olympiapark GmbH

16.18 *A Busby Berkeley film set style conversion of a 19th-century poor-school building. This above-ground pool structure built in the sanctuary of the Dance Centre, and designed by the dancing school owner, Gary Cockrell, is arranged on three levels beneath a conservatory roof to incorporate 100 arches and pillars, displaying tropical plants and water garden beside a 21m horseshoe-shaped bar, as well as providing swimming, or swinging from the 12m long trapeze.*
Consulting Engineers: Hurst, Peirce and Malcolm
Pool Systems: Peter Geekie Pools Ltd, Oxford
The Dance Centre Ltd, London
Photo: Percy Butler

Emphasis in design and demand is now changing the swimming pool into the leisure pool, rather like the coast has been turned into the beach. Admittedly, we have some technical advantage today, but it is still very debatable whether we yet have any social advantage. To make it clear, for all our modern technology, the art of sociability, particularly in baths, reached all those years ago at the peak of Roman influence has yet to be bettered.

Edward Bulwer-Lytton who wrote *The Last Days of Pompeii* (1834), drew a very clear picture in answer to the question, are the baths at Rome really so magnificent?

Imagine all Pompeii converted into Baths, and then you form some notion of the size of the Imperial Thermae of Rome, but a notion of the *size* only. Imagine every entertainment for the mind and body, enumerate all the gymnastic games our fathers have invented, repeat all the books that Italy and Greece have produced, suppose places for all these games, admirers for all these works, add to these, Baths of the vastest size, the most complicated construction, intersperse the whole with gardens, theatres, porticos and schools; suppose in one word a City of the Gods, composed but of palaces and public edifices, and you may form some faint idea of the Glories of the great Thermae of Imperial Rome.

Probably our greatest success in water so far this century is the mass teaching of swimming to youngsters – the future swimming pool public. Age-group swimming in USA, Australia and East Germany is the founding reason for success of these countries at international competitive events. Success for the swimming coach can be 'when a kid manages to swim a width, that's just like somebody winning an Olympic final . . . for the small person, the sense of achievement is exactly the same'.[2]

References
[1] Architects' Journal Technical Study, The Designing of Sports and Recreational Centres, 1976
[2] Chris Maloney, Getting in the Swim (about the Gloucester Leisure Centre), *Avon Life*, 1975

INFORMATION SHEET 16.1

Fire

A pool, besides being a useful static tank for firefighting, should additionally provide:
● an alarm bell operating on a fail-safe system
● obvious, clear, unlocked exits; safe, escape stairs; and an alternative route
● emergency lighting for continuous operation
● reliable sprinklers, accessible fire hydrants, all clearly marked and sited – especially near the plantroom, or close to areas at risk: fire extinguishers must be suitable to the possible fire . . . standard/chemical/electrical.
Consider carefully large open plan design, where the lack of compartmentation does not check the spread of fire; where cladding cavities can create 'chimney-risers' to spread fire rapidly upwards; the use of fire retardant facings and safe materials that are non-toxic, non-hazardous for fumes, and that do not melt or drip and spread fire.
Closed circuit TV is valuable for safety, anti-theft precautions and wider supervision.
Fire tests for air inflated structures (source Boyspan International Ltd/FROSI 9919/1 and 352/01).
Match test: 25mm² hole burnt in polythene, but was extinguished within 10 seconds by escaping air pressure.
Blow torch test: 200 × 100mm hole burnt after 30 seconds with flame drawn out of the hole by escaping air pressure.
Small fire: hole equal in size to fire area, and increased as wind around brought more polythene fabric into the flames. Airstructure increasingly flapped as hole increased, taking five minutes to collapse completely.
Medium fire: hole equal in size to fire, which was increased to 5 × 4m by wind around – but after 20 minutes structure still inflated though lacking pressure.
With these flame intensities, it was not possible to ignite polythene material when inflated, leaving people free to leave through exit doors and holes formed by fires. Cable supported air structures give better rigidity in wind, and do not flap as much as inflation deteriorates: cable networks also enable airdomes to survive even hurricane force winds.

See chapter 10.5.
Sources: Boyspan/SC.

INFORMATION SHEET 16.2

Safety items
See appendix IV for published pool safety codes

Provide:
● vigilant supervision
● good line-of-sight for the whole pool area
● alarm alert – tested daily
● poolwater alarms to operate when someone falls into a still pool: sonar sensor from pool floor (expensive); monitor tape at surface level (no adjustment to sensitivity); floating mercury switch, or aerosol unit (inexpensive)
● lifebuoys and lines to be in handy positions: centre pool life line/s left suspended when pool not in use
● rescue poles and hooks clearly visible
● resuscitator
● stretcher, and spine-board for diving accidents
● first aid kit/emergency room
● 'hot-line' telephone
● emergency display board for first-aid instruction posters, and telephone numbers of ambulance/fire/doctor
● accident book and liability insurance cover
● ample, large (100mm letters), clear warning signs
● depth markers and clear water
● lifeguard control point for each 200m² of water surface, or an attendant for every 100 bathers, plus duty attendant for diving/slide area
● recessed safety ledges (100 to 150mm) at 1·2m depth
● clearly distinguish any sudden change of water depth
● always protect low-level glazing
● non-slip, non-trip, resilient (rubberised) floors
● night lighting
● earth leakage contact breaker to electrical circuits.

Specialised needs:
- Full name list of chemicals in use, their neutralisers and antidotes
- Container facility for leaking gas cylinder absorption; eg 50kg chlorine is neutralised by 150kg of soda ash dissolved in 50kg water
- Respirator outside chlorine room.

See chapter 10.3 and 13.8 and information sheet 15.13.

INFORMATION SHEET 16.3

Common hazards and accidents

A swimming pool adds hazard, and attracts children.

Large pools are more difficult to supervise, and to maintain.

Constant vigilance is the main proven safeguard – especially beside diving boards.

US: Almost 8000 people are drowned every year: 600 in swimming pools, half at home
- a further 50,000 injured require hospital treatment
- and at least another 100,000 need the attention of a doctor
- three-quarters who suffer accidents are under 20 years old.

UK: Almost 1000 people are drowned every year: 50 in swimming pools
- most are under 5 years, half are under 15 years
- only 50 per cent of the population can swim and 10 per cent can life-save.

Accidents that result in:	occur mainly from:
Drowning:	swimming alone, lack of supervision, no safety fence (primarily to stop the toddler, and set at least 1·3m high, having no handholds and with self-locking gate)
Serious damage:	jumping or diving into shallow water, striking the diving board, hitting poolside or pool floor; loose board covering; increasingly similar numbers of accidents are occurring in US from slides, and almost as many people are paralysed, as are drowned in pools
Breaks and knocks:	poolside ladders, especially the up and over above-ground type
Falls and slips:	tripping over steps and raised kerbs, or skidding on greasy decking
Cuts and bruises:	sharp edges, collisions with fixtures and fittings, broken glass and windows.
Chemical burns:	mishandling of pool chemicals, or mixing them together, causing fumes or combustion
Most general casualties:	fooling around and damage from swimming aids, or pool leisure items.

INFORMATION SHEET 16.4

Pool cleaning equipment

Around the pool

Most contamination exists outside of the poolwater.

Main entrance mats, wipers, adherent surfaces considerably reduce street soil carried into the pool changing rooms – the more effective the shoe cleaning facility the better: two-way contra-moving matting systems are installed in FDR to great advantage.

Changing room flooring meets the worst contamination and requires repeated hosing clean, rather than just a daily dousing. Hose/power points should be ample and easily available, at 1m height, safe and close to hose reels. Regular 1 per cent chlorine washes help clear resilient organisms, but offer little residual effect. Biocides are better.

Wet area flooring can benefit from pressure steam cleaning, especially where poolside carpeting or crevices are involved. Again the effect is to wash out most material to sterilise daily rather then weekly, but the effect is non-lasting.

Disinfectant lances operating under pressure are best for spraying all wet area flooring, to provide a residual hygiene, similar to that of pool chlorination and to control any possibility of spreading infection.

Pre-cleanse hygiene should be compulsory to shower-wash, to visit toilets, to use footbaths. Electronic eye footbath tunnels ensure compulsory shower douses, but really offer totally insufficient personal hygiene. When routes involve sunken levels and steps, a disabled persons' bypass will be required.

See chapters 11.4, 5 and 15.10.

In the pool

Nearly all contamination starts at the surface of the poolwater.

Hand cleaning tools:

Leaf or skimmer screen (300 to 900mm) for surface debris collection.

Leaf scoop or rake (300 to 900mm) for floor debris collection.

Wall/floor brush (500 to 1000mm) to sweep to main drain.

Algae brush (100 to 250mm) with stainless steel bristles.

Equipment handles (2 to 6m), non-corrosive, telescopic (2 to 4m and 2·5 to 5m) and in lightweight material.

Floating pole or sweep (5 to 6m) to draw across the surface of water and rapidly remove scumming.

Pool magnet, carbon stone, pumice block, rim scouring pad and tile cleaner.

Manual suction sweepers: the most essential piece of pool cleaning equipment.

Simple 'vac' head (300mm) and collection bag with garden hosepipe induces suction by venturi effect (above-ground pools).

Generally flat, flexible head (300 to 500mm) with 40mm floating suction hose (10 to 15m) connected into a skimmer line, or separate suction line, both valved down as required at the time (private pools).

Brush disc-shaped head, rather than wheeled rectangular design: hoses over 10m long reduce power of small pump suction (liner pools).

Upright or articulated head (600mm) with floating hose (10 to 20m) and attachment for skimmer, or main drain suction line (private/hotel pools).

Various heavy duty head attachments (750 to 1000mm), with 40/50mm floating hose (15 to 20m) connected preferably to separate suction points (200mm below water level) set about 15m apart; the use of skimmer lines requires continual readjustment to valve settings, which becomes inconvenient and time wasting on large pools; the alternative is an independent submersible pump or trolley power source with tow line hauls and filter bag for debris collection (weight 20 to 40kg) to speed sweeping operation (public pools).

Mobile suction sweeper unit and poolside filter trolley entirely independent of recirculation system and suitable for a water throughput capacity range from 5m³/h to 25m³/h (public/hotel pools).

Automatic suction sweepers – labour saving, to operate whenever a pool is clear of swimmers.

Floating surface suction head and hose line plugged into a skimmer, sweeps debris towards a main drain collection pot: powered by suction of the filter pump (garden swimming pools).

Limpet flexible disc type working on suction from skimmer line, and which is modified by a piston, alternately creating and releasing a vacuum, that causes the unit to feel its way around from cleaned to uncleaned surfaces (private pools).

Random, roaming, water-driven floating head, carrying swivelling tile cleaning jets, honing flails and hose line feeder from a booster pipe on separate circuitry; flail hose lines whip around stirring up dust into suspension for more effective filtration, and sweep larger debris into a collection pot at the main drain deep point. This robot machinery is more costly, but maintains pools up to 15 × 7·5m in perfect condition with single units. A secondary effect of bringing cool bottom water to the top faster can improve heating efficiency by several degrees.

Peripatetic suction sweeper filter, crawling around the pool floor like a small half-track tank, collects debris within a 20 micron 2 to 5m² area cartridge, or collection unit; electrically powered, safely grounded, but operating from an ELCB protected socket; units range from 10 to 20m³/h rating, covering 250 to 500m²/h area; also ideal for mixing water dead spots, but unsuitable for steep inclines and hopper pools; used underwater only (public and private pools).

Retractable streaming hose lengths, flailing from pool walls move dirt into suspension, drive debris towards the deepest point, and polish all surfaces at the same time. When the flow control valve is closed diverting water into normal circulation, the hoses automatically retract into the walls. A less impressive, and less effective alternative, offers a series of directional inlet valves set strategically to drive material to the main drain, but, these restricted inlets can impose intolerable backpressure onto the filtration, which then fails to work efficiently (private/hotel pools).

INFORMATION SHEET 16.5

Typical pool services schedules

Commissioning list

Test supply water for possible special chemical treatment action.
Fill water supply to pass through strainer bag.
Check pipelines/valves/seals are properly installed.
Check pool fittings clear and ready to operate.
Inspect electrics, controls and switchgear, and check safety conditions.
Ensure heater, disinfection systems, etc can be isolated from main circulation.
Prime pump and filter, select backwash, operate filter.
Check and start up heater and adjust settings.
Check, charge and start up disinfection/pH units.
Set up, check and operate pool cleaner devices.
Induct pool owner.
Inspect system for correct operation after a few hours.
Re-check all safety equipment and devices.
Allow sufficient time for thorough commissioning.
Make out written report and provide written operating instructions.

General routines

Test and treat water daily, or hourly at peak bathing loads.
Check and clear baskets and traps and blockages.
Check operations, pressures, supplies and feeders.
Hose clean and disinfect decks and floors almost continuously.
Brush and sweep pools daily, but private pools weekly or even monthly if enclosed.
Backwash regularly, particularly after 'vaccing'.
Ensure electrics and motors remain dry.
Ensure pump seals do not dry out.
Top up/drain-off poolwater regularly.
Set heat-retaining/protection covers.
Frequently inspect services and equipment at low use and peak use times to determine operational problems. Shortcomings soon show up at heat waves.
Inspect outdoor pool fabric monthly; indoor pool fabric bi-monthly; all equipment annually.

Winterising

Keep pool filled to resist hydrostatic pressure and to offer protection to all pool surface finishes: check relief valves or drainage sumps.
Clean pool and backwash filter.
Adjust water, drain out pipes and superchlorinate pool.
Drain down filter, heater, etc.
Disconnect electrics, remove motors to dry store.
Grease metal valve stems, pump bearings, etc.
Frostproof, fit drain plugs.
Remove pool ladders, diving boards, and fittings – lift underwater lights onto deck if deep freezing expected.
Add ice-absorbers (timbers or capped and weighted polythene bottles creating weak spots in the ice to relieve stress).
Fit winter debris cover.
Arrange reconditioning needs.
Periodically test and chlorinate.
Alternatively: operate system at low-rate several hours daily with frost heater back-up: private pools increasingly adopt low-running upkeep, and clearance of obstructions throughout winter, to save closing and opening routines.

Spring opening

Remove cover and ice-absorbers.
Clear all baskets, leaftraps, remove plugs, check lining, remove stains and scale.
Inspect and clear relief valves and drainage lines.
Sweep pool floor, walls and surrounds.
Check water, condition and balance, and adjust level.
Check pool fittings are clear, and can function correctly.
Reconnect electric motors, fittings and equipment.
Check pipelines, valves and controls.
Fill up system, prime pumps, check for leaks.
Test all electrics, operate and check motors for signs of overheating (60°C normal running temperature).
Backwash filter thoroughly before putting on-stream, operate heater, disinfection units, etc and check after several hours.
'Vacuum' sweep pool.
Reinstall ladders, lights, diving board, etc.

Check, and clean, decking, coping, tiling for movement.
Recondition, repair and renovate.
Pack winter cover away dry.
Double check safety items and summer needs of chemical stocks.

INFORMATION SHEET 16.6

Vandal-proofing

Try to provide:

Heavy duty fittings throughout, and especially tough door furniture.
Doorkick plates to 0·75m height, and 0·5m long push plates.
Robust hinges.
Remove all removables – no exposed nuts, screws or bolts: even use non-return screws.
Short, extra strong coat hooks – without knobs.
Recess fitments and soap containers, inset mirrors and hidden supports.
No rails for gymnastics.
Non-removable grilles.
Exceptionally durable lockers and locker doors – after only a few months, sometimes as many as 50 per cent of inadequate lockers fail from the beating they meet.
Hard wall surfaces only – especially within reach of youths standing on seats.
Concealed plumbing – wash-basins with lever-operated plugs, or none at all; springloaded, unscrewable fitments.
Extra tough toilet seats or none; or anti-vandal WCs in stainless steel.
Limit the out-of-sight places.
Fit hot air hand dryers, hair dryers within supervision sight.
Push button showers on preselected timing.
Fit security cash safes into walls: free-standing units are as easily carried away as they were carried in.

See chapters 2.5, 11.2 to 5.

INFORMATION SHEET 16.7

Corrosion

In the main, it is still the same old troubles of deterioration that cause most of the routine new problems. Hazard analysis and preventative maintenance, when applied to the harsh swimming pool environment, will produce tangible results.

Equipment

Ladders, handrailing: stainless steel is best; chrome-plate brass if poorly plated blackens, peels and pits at the water line though this can be overcome with thicker nickel plate beneath the chrome (see chapter 11.5).
Underwater lighting: chrome-plated facings in certain conditions can be troubled with black discolouration: stainless steel offers less spoiling, and less sparkle (see chapters 10.11 and 11.5).
Grilles, facings: poorly chrome-plated items can pit badly.
Skimmers: generally high density, reinforced plastic is best; cast alloys stainless steel, even pre-cast concrete, offer suitable bodies for this unit that gathers the greatest amount of scum and pollutants (see chapter 13.6).
Pipework: plastic is mainly used nowadays with entirely satisfactory results: corrosion or etching of pipework, primarily occurs in poorly balanced waters – ie at least 10 per cent of all pools; maintaining the optimum flow velocity of 2m/s also avoids most impingement difficulties (see chapter 13.6 and 15.6 to 9).
Pumps: specially made for swimming pool application, these units with stainless steel shafts, and bronze or gunmetal or plastic bodies for sea or saltwater, stand up well against corrosion; standard pool pumps suffer out of balance water, when left standing, or from high chemical concentrations injected just before the pump (see chapter 13.5 and information sheet 15.6).
Filters: good GRP tanks suffer no corrosion problems other than usual liming snags in hard waters, stainless steel is very practical, coated steels are reasonable and their strength essential for heavy duty, commercial applications to take hard knocks. Troubles occur from oxidation and rusting of metals encouraged by disinfection oxidation, carbon dioxide, pitting from sodium bicarbonate in soft waters, chloride attack also in soft waters, and when there is no fresh water replenishment, and by electrolytic

action between dissimilar metals – a magnesium anode provides cathodic protection (see chapter 11.5, 13.3 and 15.6 to 9).

Corrosion resisting materials

Cast iron, galvanised iron and steel: bad to poor

Aluminium: best around pool, or when well protected in poolwater

Copper and copper based alloys: reasonable to good

Stainless steel: non-magnetic pool type 300 series quality: good to excellent

Plastics, PVC and ABS mainly: when thermally and UV protected, and if not subjected to punishing treatment, then they are excellent

Protective or isolating coatings are excellent when properly applied to totally cleaned surfaces (see chapter 11.2).

Anodised aluminium and aluminium pigment: excellent weathering facility

Enamel and asphalt: best in ground, and not exposed to sun

Vinyl/resins: fine hard, smooth tough, inert film, over well-prepared surface, and also suitable for exposure to sun

Paints: economical, practical range of durable coverings from chlorinated rubber based to epoxy-resin, zinc chromate to red lead

Polyurethane/latex: end grain sealing uses, and suitable for plaster, stone and concrete

Rate of corrosion relates to pool water humidity condition

Hardness and mineral salts: for sealing, etching and staining

Oxygenation, chlorides and sulphates: promoted by aeration and oxidising power of hypochlorous acid, ozone, etc

Total dissolved solids: conductivity increased from 2500ppm upwards

pH: especially outside of 7 to 8 pH range

Temperature: chemical reactions double their rate over a 30°C poolwater temperature rise

Flow: increased activity from erosion, impingement and cavitation breaks through surfaces continually to increase chemical reactions.

Galvanic and chemical action

In water Electricity flows between metallic areas in poolwater (the electrolyte); corrosion and pitting takes place where the current leaves the metal (the anode), and coats metals with corrosion products where it returns (the cathode). The rate of metal destruction within the 'pool battery' depends mainly upon the potential difference between the metals, their exposed surface area and the poolwater TDS. More reactive metals are galvanically high in corrosive potential and will displace any metal of lower potential voltage – more so in sea or saltwater. Current flows from least noble metal to most noble, the greater the gap in dissimilar metal in the series, the greater the current and the corrosion.

Least noble							Stain-less	Most noble
anode	Mg→	Zn→	Al→Fe→Pb→		Cu→	Ni→	steel	**cathode**
corrod-ed	(act-ive)	and galvanising	and tin-ning		and alloys	and bronze	(pas-sive)	protected

Galvanic corrosive effect can be controlled by cathodic protection with a least noble metal such as magnesium, kept as a sacrificial anode within a coated filter tank and bonded to the part to be protected; or controlled by an impressed reversed potential voltage; or with absorption inhibitors; or by protective coatings.

It is best always to use materials in humid areas that have no strong tendency to produce galvanic corrosion (most noble or inert), being especially safe when coupled together within the pool's circuit.

In ground Soils range from peaty acid pH3 to highly alkaline pH10, from highly oxidising to reducing conditions, with or without soluble salts present, as well as involving texture and temperature, moisture and permeability, oxygen and bacteria, all to affect corrosion.

Steel in galvanically corrosive soil (500 Ω/m³) deteriorates badly in 5 years, but in very slightly galvanically corrosive soil (10,000 Ω/m³), it is hardly damaged over 30 years.

Copper and alloys: unsuitable for acid or sulphate, in seawater soaked or

stagnant soils.

Galvanised iron: reasonable in tolerant and dry soils.

Aluminium: this metal protected is good in a wide variety of soil conditions.

Stainless steel: pool quality type series 300 suitable for all soils.

Plastics: a number are completely resistant to soil corrosion.

See chapters 9.4, 11.2 to 4, 13.3, 15.1, 15.9 and 16.4.

INFORMATION SHEET 16.8

Common pool design problems

Insufficient durability for hard and continuous heavy wear.

Too steep access inclines and too many steps for disabled.

Incoming bathers in outdoor shoes soiling pool area floors and wet and dry areas not properly segregated.

Tiles at water level cracking (where maximum pressure exists) and not always frost-resistant (outdoor), properly non-slip nor acid and abrasive proof.

Marblite crazing, hollow or coarse rendering, soft, scuffed or laminated liners.

Pool lining not coping with poor pH7 etching, and under 100ppm alkalinity.

Pipeline leaks at joints from settlement or vibration

Diving boards not in clear view and set against a too bright background.

Lightweight doors unable to meet heavy use, regular hosing or easily working loose from softwood surrounds – they should be flush for ease of cleaning, use no water soluble glues and provide toughened protection panels for the lower parts.

Window fitments failing.

Ducting corrosion, insulant condensation and roof deterioration.

Inadequate vapour barriers, ventilation or spaceheating.

Poor accessibility to clean or change light tubes, or ventilation outlets set out over pool.

Corrosion to structural uprights, cubicle stanchions, fitments, hinges, etc.

An unfinished and trammelled landscape surround that is left to fend for itself.

INFORMATION SHEET 16.9

Handicapped swimmers
Summary of essential needs
NB The disabled become mobile in water

Deeper water not shallow

Slopes not stairs

Wide handrailed pool: steps not vertical ladders

Deck level pools or 0·5m parapet not deep freeboard

Wheelchairs require ramps and easy parking near main entrance.

Notice to appear on new buildings indicating whether they are suitable for disabled persons, and whether providing accessible toilet (Chronically Sick and Disabled Persons Act 1970 UK).

Changes of level are the worst barriers in any swimming pool hall.

Short rise lifts when ramps are unsuitable at main level changes.

Larger, safer, securer lockers for disablement aids.

Pool hoist is only necessary for very few disabled bathers, and then at specialised treatment centres.

Changing facilities beside pool are best, and body dryers useful.

See chapters 5.3, 11.4, 11.5 and 12.4 and information sheet 2.19.

APPENDIX I

Acknowledgements

The author gratefully acknowledges the helpful information and data given by the following individuals and organisations:
AAHPER, Washington
ABBP, Charleroi
Acoustics & Environmetrics Ltd Surrey
AERE, Harwell
Anlagenbau für Wassertechnik, Hannover
Annexe Astrid, Spa
APHA, New York
Aquafun Alaska, Inc, Fairbanks
Aquamat Ltd, Stonehouse
Aquavox Ltd, Eastbourne
Aquaslide'n Dive Corp, California
Architectural Press Library, London
Arizona Highways, Arizona
ASA, Loughborough
Bader- und Kurverwaltung, Baden-Baden
Baker Filtration Co, California
Barr & Wray Ltd, Glasgow
Robert R. Barlett & Sons Ltd, Bristol
Bath Chamber of Commerce, Bath
Belgische Bond van Zweminrichtingen, Ghent
Big Surf, Arizona
Biwater Ltd, Dorking
John S. Bonnington Ptners, St Albans
Bouwcentrum, Rotterdam
Brighton Aquarium, Brighton
Bromine & Chemicals Ltd, London
BSAC, London
Buchtal GmbH, Schwarzenfeld
Alexander Budrevics & Assoc. Ontario
Building Research Establishment, Watford/East Kilbride
C & CA, Slough/London
California Cooperage, California
Hon Mrs Brenda Carter, Rogate
CASPA, NSW
CDA Inc, New York
Certikin Ltd, Horsham
Chester Products, Ohio
Chilstone Garden Ornaments, Horsmonden
CNCA, Maryland
Commission of the European Communities, Brussels
Cosanti Foundation, Arizona
H. et H. Dieken, St Paul-de-Vence
DGfdB, Essen/Düsseldorf
Electricity Council, London
Esmil/Envirotech Ltd, Sneek and St Neots
FINA, Illinois and Ontario
Fox Pool International, Berks and Pennsylvania
Dr H. T. Friermood, Connecticut
G. B. Sports & Leisure Surfaces, Yorks
Dr J. C. Gentles, University of Glasgow
David Gillespie Associates Ltd, Surrey
Gillinson Barnett & Partners, Leeds
GLC, London
Th. Goldschmidt, Essen and London
Francis Goodall, London
Graham Hill, Lusaka
Herringthorpe Leisure Centre, Rotherham
Hoffman Publications, Fort Lauderdale
IAB, Bremen
IAKS, Cologne
Impianti, Milan
Institute of Baths Management, Melton Mowbray
ISHOF, Fort Lauderdale
The Earl of Jersey
Landeshauptstadt, Hannover
Liftomatic Inc, California
LGTB, Luton
Maderna America Corp, Baltimore and Vienna
John Morton Landscape Design Ltd, Christchurch
Ministry of Works, Bulls, NZ
Münchner Olympiapark GmbH, Munich
NAPO, Needham
Novosti Press Agency, London
NSF, Michigan
NSPI, Washington
NSW Swimming Pools Association, NSW
NZ Association of Swimming Pool Managers, Bulls
Omega Electronic, Bienne
ÖN, Vienna
Papp's Constructeur de Piscines, Neuilly
PB Communications International, London
Penguin Swimming Pools, Chelmsford
Philips, GmbH, Kassel
Pilkington Bros, St Helens
Pilot Public Relations Ltd, Gravesend
Piscines, Paris
Playsafe Ltd, St Leonards
Portacel Ltd, Tonbridge
Powerlift Pool Cover Corp, Phoenix
Public Health Service, Center for Disease Control, Georgia
Queen Elizabeth II Park Stadium, Christchurch
RIBA Library, London
Robinsons of Winchester
Royal Blind Asylum and School, Edinburgh
Royal College of Art, London
Rutherford Group, Battle
St Christopher School, Letchworth
Schwimmbad und Sauna, GFR
Scoop Marketing, Sussex
Seahorse Pools, Jersey
SIA, Zurich
SPATA, Croydon
The Sports Council, London
Solar Energy Association, London
Stranco, Illinois and Eastbourne
Swimming Pool, London
Swimming Pool Weekly Reports, Florida
Swimming Pools (Filtration) Ltd, Staines
Swimming World Publications, Los Angles
Roger Taillibert, Paris
Technical Unit for Sport, London
The Thistle Foundation, Edinburgh
Tournesol International, Paris
Triconfort Ltd, Paris and Norwich
US Consumer Product Safety Commission, Washington
Peter Verdemato, Lisbon
Villeroy & Boch, Mettlach
VNG, The Hague
Wallace & Tiernan Ltd, Tonbridge

APPENDIX II

Swimming pool associations and swimming pool journals

Australia

CASPA — Council of Australasian Swimming Pool Associations, 530 Canterbury Road, Campsie, NSW 2194.
CASPA — Journal of the Australian Swimming Pool Industry, 4 Coppabella Road, Dural, NSW 2158

PSAA Pool Superintendents Association of Australia, 2A Frederick Street, Ashfield, NSW

SPA of NSW Swimming Pools Association of New South Wales Ltd, PO Box 42, Concord West, 2138, NSW

Austria

BBT Bundesministerium für Bauten und Technik, Stubenning, 1, A-1011 Vienna

FB Fachverband der Bäder, Hoher Markt 3, 1011 Vienna

Belgium
ABBP   Association Belge des Bains Publics, Rue Gendebien 1, 6000 Charleroi
THERMAE   Organe de l'Association Belge des Bains Publics, Houtenschoen 54, 2700 Sint-Niklaas-Waas

Canada
CSPF   Canadian Swimming Pool Federation, 3284 Keele Street, Downsview, Ontario
Home Swimming Pool (Magazine)   } Sound Publishing Ltd, 126, 14th Street West, Owen
Pools, Parks and Rinks (Magazine) } Sound, Ontario
OSPA   } Ontario Swimming Pool Association, 61 Alness Street, Downsview, Ontario M3J 2H2
OSPA   { Official Publication of the Ontario Swimming Pool Association, 61 Alness Street, Downsview, Ontario M3J 2H2

France
CSIP   Chambre Syndicale des Industries de la Piscine, 23 rue de Rome, 75008, Paris
Piscines   Editions Christian Ledoux, 9 rue Condorcet, 9, 94800 Villejuif
SGPB   Syndicat Général des Propriétaires de Bains, 163 rue Saint-Honoré, 75 Paris 1

Germany
BSI   Bundesverband Schwimmbad-Industrie, 6000 Frankfurt 17, Postfach 174038
{ DGfdB   Deutsche Gesellschaft für das Badewesen, ev, 43 Essen, Alfredistrasse 32, Postfach 369
{ *Archiv des Badewesens*   Verlag Arno Schrickel, 898 Oberdorf, Am First 9
{ IAB   International Board for Aquatic, Sports and Recreation Facilities, 874 Bad Neustadt/Saale, PO Box 1680
{ *Sport + Bäder Freizeit-Bauten*, 2800 Bremen, Waller Heerstrasse 154A
{ IAKS   International Working Group for the Construction of Sports and Leisure Facilities, D5000 Cologne 40 (Lövenich), Kölner Strasse 68
{ *Sportstättenbau + Bäderanlagen* D5000 Cologne 40 (Lövenich), Kölner Strasse 68
Pool   Technogram-Verlag GmbH, 8 Munich 2, Bavariaring 8-9
Schwimmbad und Sauna   Fachschriften-Verlag GmbH & Co Kg, 7012 Fellbach, Hohenstrasse 17, Postfach 1329
VDB   Verband Deutscher Badebetriebe ev, Spaldingstrasse 130-136, 2 Hamburg 1

Italy
Impianti   Attrezzature Sportive e Ricreative, 20148 Milan, 87 via Capecelatro
Piscine Oggi   SICAP spa, 40100 Modena, Piazza Roma, n4

Netherlands
NBBZ   Netherlands Union for Bath and Swimming Establishments and Buildings, PO Box 182, Bonifasiusstraat 3, Soest

New Zealand
{ NZ SPM   New Zealand Association of Swimming Pool Managers Inc, Lancewood, High Street, Bulls
{ *Pool Managers Newsletter* Lancewood, High Street, Bulls
NZ SPA   New Zealand Swimming Pool Association, Box 56028 PO, Dominion Road, Auckland

South Africa
SPISA   The Swimming Pool Institute of South Africa (Pty) Ltd, PO Box 39737 Bramley, Johannesburg 2018

Spain
Piscinas   Prensa XXI, SA, Valencia, 72 entio, la, Barcelona–15

UK
{ IBM   The Institute of Baths Management, Giffard House, 36/38 Sherrard Street, Melton Mowbray, Leics LE13 1XJ
{ *Baths Service*   Journal of the IBM, 83 Clinton Road, Redruth, Cornwall

SPATA   The Swimming Pool and Allied Trades Association, 74 London Road, Croydon, CRO 2TB
Splash   Peter Miers and Associates Ltd, Oast Cottage, Martins Farm, Boughton Monchelsea, Maidstone, Kent
Swimming Pool   Clarke and Hunter (London) Ltd, 61 London Road, Staines, Middx TW18 4BN

USA
{ NAPO   National Association of Pool Owners, PO Box 222, Needham, Mass 02194
{ *Swimming Pool Pleasure*   NAPO Newsletter, PO Box 222, Needham, Mass 02194
NSPI   National Swimming Pool Institute, 2000 K St, NW, Washington DC 20006
Poolscope   NSPI Magazine, 2000 K St, NW, Washington DC 20006
Poolife   Olin Chemicals Group, Olin Corporation, 120 Long Ridge Road, Stamford, Conn 06904
Pool News   } Leisure Publications, 3923 West 6th St, Los Angeles,
Pool 'n Patio } Cal 90020
Poolside Living   Monsanto Company, 800 N. Lindbergh Boulevard, St Louis, Miss 63166
SPCMA   Swimming Pool Chemical Manufacturers Association, 13966 Seal Beach Blvd, Seal Beach, Cal 90740
Swimming Pool Weekly and Swimming Pool Age   Hoffman Publications Inc, 3000 NE 30th Place, PO Box 11299, Fort Lauderdale, Flo 33306

APPENDIX III

Other organisations and journals publishing swimming pool information

Australia
ISES   International Solar Energy Society, National Science Centre, 191 Royal Parade, Parkville, PO Box 52, Melbourne, Victoria 3052
SAA   Standards Association of Australia, 447 Upper Edward Street, Brisbane, Queensland 4000

Austria
Der Aufbau
Bäder Journal
ÖN   Austrian Standards Institute, Postfach 130, A-1021 Vienna 2

Belgium
ABTP   Académie Belge des Techniques de la Piscine, Léopold II straat, 101, 9110 Sint Amandsberg
CEC   Commission of the European Communities, Rue de la Loi 200, B-1040 Brussels
IBN   Institut Belge de Normalisation, Avenue de la Brabanconne 29, 1040 Brussels

Brazil
Binario

Canada
BRI   Brace Research Institute, McGill University, Ste Anne de Bellevue 800, Montreal, Quebec
CASA   Canadian Amateur Swimming Association, ⎤
CFAA   Canadian Federation of Amateur Aquatics, |
ACUC   Association of Canadian Underwater ⎱ 333 River Road,
Councils, | Vanier City,
CAHPER   Canadian Association for Health, ⎰ Ottawa,
Physical Education and Recreation, | Ontario KIL 8B9
CIAU   Canadian Intercollegiate Athletic Union, |
CPRA   Canadian Parks and Recreation Association, |
SFC   Sports Federation of Canada, ⎦
CCCA   Canadian Council for Cooperation in Aquatics, 550 Church Street, Toronto, Ontario M4Y 2E1
CSA   Canadian Standards Association, 178 Rexdale Boulevard, Rexdale, Ontario, M9W 1R3

CUC   Canadian Underwater Councils, Box 1303, Winnipeg 1, Manitoba
FINA   Fédération Internationale de Natation Amateur, F 1908–N101, 508 Waterloo Street, London, Ontario N6B ZP7
NRC   Canadian National Research Council, Division of Building Research, Ottowa, Ontario
RLSSC   Royal Life Saving Society Canada, 550 Church Street, Toronto, Ontario M4Y 2EL
TURF   Technical Unit for Recreation Facilities, Ministry of Culture and Recreation, Ontario Sports Training Centre, 5 North Service Road, Oakville, Ontario L6H 1A1

Czechoslovakia
Architektura

Denmark
Arkitektur
DS-F   Dansk Svømme-Forbund, Brøndby Stadion 20, 2600 Glostrup

East Germany
Deutsche Architektur

Finland
Arkkitehti
FSS   Finish Sauna Society, Vaskiniemi, Helsinki 20
BII   Building Information Institute, Lönnrotinkatu 20, 00120 Helsinki 12

France
Acier, Stahl, Steel
L'Architecture d'aujourd'hui
L'Architecture française
Techniques et architecture
AFNOR   Association Française de Normalisation, Afnor Tour Europe, Cedex 7, 92080 Paris, La Défense
DJO   Direction des Journaux Officiels, 26 rue Desaix, Cedex 15, Paris
EDF   Electricité de France, Cedex 8, 92080 Paris, La Défense
IS   L'Institut des Sports, Avenue du Tremblay, Joinville, Paris XIV
ME   Ministère de l'Education, Académie de Nancy-Metz, Collège d'Enseignement Technique des Piscines, Le Chesnois, 88240 Bains-les-Bains, Vosges
MJS (SEJS)   Ministère de la Jeunesse, des Sports et des Loisirs, 34 rue de Chateaudun, Cedex 9, 75436 Paris
MTPB   Moniteur des Travaux Publics et du Bâtiment, 91 rue du Faubourg Saint-Honoré, 75008 Paris.

Germany
Architectur und Wohnwelt
Baden + Wohnen
Baumeister
Bauform
Bauwelt
Das Bad
Der Architekt
Deutsche Badebetrielb
Deutsche Bauzeitschrift
Deutsche Bauzeitung
Glasforum
BS   Bundesinstitut für Sportwissenschaft Fachbereich Sport-und Freizeitanlagen, 5 Cologne 40, Hertzstrasse 1, Postfach 400
DIN   German Standards Institution, Reichpietschufer 72–76, D-1000 Berlin 30
ISFA   International Swimming Federation Association

India
Indian Architect

Italy
L'Architettura
FIN   Federazione Italiana Nuoto, Viale Tiziano, 70, 00100 Rome

Iran
Art and Architecture

Japan
Japan Architect

Netherlands
Badcultur
Bouw
BC   Bouwcentrum, Weena 700, Postbus 299, Rotterdam 3003
RNSA   Royal Netherlands Swimming Association, Admiraal van Gent-straat 33–35, Utrecht
VNG   Union of Netherlands Municipalities, Nassaulaan 12, The Hague

New Zealand
Home and Building
MoW   Ministry of Works, Water Treatment Operators Training School, Taumaihi Street, PO Box 43, Bulls
NZWSC   New Zealand Water Safety Council, Department of Internal Affairs, Private Bag, Wellington
SANZ   Standards Association of New Zealand, World Trade Centre, 15–23 Sturdee Street, Wellington 1

Norway
Arkitektnytt
Byggekunst

South Africa
Architect & Builder
SABS   South African Bureau of Standards, Private Bag X191, Groenkloof, Pretoria 0001

Sweden
Arkitektur

Switzerland
Bauen & Wohnen
Industrielles Bauen
Schweizerische Bauzeitung
Schweizer Sport-Schwimmer
Werk
Archithese
IOC   International Olympic Committee, Château de Vidy, 1007 Lausanne
Sia   Société Suisse des Ingénieurs et des Architectes, Seinaustrasse 16, 8039 Zurich
SVG (ASTS)   Schweiz Vereinigung für Gesundheitstechnik, Postfach CH-8035 Zurich

United Kingdom
Architects' Journal
Architectural Review
Architectural Design
Building
Building Design
Building Services Engineer
Building Trades Journal
Design
Filtration & Separation
Heating & Ventilating Engineer
Homes & Gardens
House & Garden
Ideal Home
Municipal Journal
Recreation Management
Recreation Today
RIBA Journal
Sport and Recreation
Surveyor
Swimming Times
The Architect
AP   The Architectural Press Ltd, 9 Queen Anne's Gate, London SW1H 9BY
ASA   Amateur Swimming Association, Harold Fern House, Derby Square, Loughborough, LE11 0AL
AST   Association of Swimming Therapy, 24 Arnos Road, London N11 1AP
BCT   Building Centre Trust, 26 Store Street, London WC1E 7BT
BCTC   British Ceramic Tile Council, Federation House, Stoke-on-Trent, ST4 2RU

BGC   British Gas Corporation, 326 High Holborn, London WC1V 7PT

BOA   The British Olympic Association, 12 Buckingham Street, London WC2N 6DJ

BRE   Building Research Establishment, Department of Environment, Building Research Station, Garston, Watford WD2 7JR

BSAC   British Sub-Aqua Club, 70 Brompton Road, London SW3 1HA

BSI   British Standards Institute, 2 Park Street, London W1A 2BS

BSRIA   Building Services Research & Information Association, Old Bracknell Lane, Bracknell, Berks RG12 4AH

C & CA   Cement & Concrete Association, 52 Grosvenor Gardens, London SW1W 0AQ

CCPR   Central Council of Physical Recreation, 70 Brompton Road, London SW3 1HA

CIBS   Chartered Institute of Building Services (IHVE), 49 Cadogan Square, London SW1X 0JB

DOE   Department of Environment, Property Services Agency, Lambeth Bridge House, London SE1 7SB

DOE   Department of Environment Cttee on New Chemicals and Materials in Swimming Pools, 2 Marsham Street, London SW1P 3EB

DLF   Disabled Living Foundation, 346 Kensington High Street, London W14 8NS

EC   Electricity Council, 30 Millbank, London SW1P 4RD

ESSA   English Schools Swimming Association, 417 Tavistock Road, Roborough, Plymouth PL6 7HB

EHA   The Environmental Health Association (Formerly APHI), 19 Grosvenor Place, London SW1X 7HU

HMSO   Her Majesty's Stationery Office for DES   (Dept Education & Science), DOE   (Dept of the Environment), MHLG   (Ministry Housing & Local Government), MPBW   (Ministry Public Buildings & Works), MOH   (Ministry of Health), 49 High Holborn, London WC1V 6HB

IEE   Institution of Electrical Engineers, Savoy Place, London WC2R 0BL

IES   The Illuminating Engineering Society, York House, 199 Westminster Bridge Road, London SE1 7UN

IHVE   Institution of Heating and Ventilation Engineers (CIBS), 49 Cadogan Square, London SW1X 0JB

ISES   International Solar Energy Association – UK Section, c/o Royal Institution, 21 Albemarle Street, London W1X 4BS

IWES   Institution of Water Engineers and Scientists, 6/8 Sackville Street, London W1X 1DD

LGTB   Local Government Training Board, 8 The Arndale Centre, Luton LU1 2TS

MS & R   Minister for Sport and Recreation, Dept of Environment, 2 Marsham Street, London SW1P 3EB

NCB   National Coal Board, Hobart House, Grosvenor Place, London SW1

NPFA   National Playing Fields Association, Playfield House, 57b Catherine Place, London SW1E 6EY

RIBA   Royal Institute of British Architects, 66 Portland Place, London W1N 4AD

RLSS   Royal Life Saving Society, Desborough House, 14 Devonshire Street, London W1N 2AT

RoSPA   Royal Society for the Prevention of Accidents, Royal Oak Centre, Brighton Road, Purley, Surrey CR2 2UR

SC   The Sports Council, 70 Brompton Road, London SW3 1EX

STA   Solar Trade Association Ltd, The Building Centre, 26 Store Street, London WC1E 7BT

STA   The Swimming Teachers Association, 1 Birmingham Road, West Bromwich, West Midlands

TF   Thistle Foundation, 22 Charlotte Square, Edinburgh EH2 4DF

TUS   Technical Unit for Sport, Sports Council, 70 Brompton Road, London SW3 1EX

WRA   Water Research Association, Ferry Lane, Medmenham, Marlow, Bucks SL7 2HD

USA

American City	Inland Architect
Architectural Digest	Optimum
Architectural Record	Parks & Recreation
House & Garden	Progressive Architecture
House & Home	Swimming World

AAHPER   American Association for Health, Physical Education and Recreation, 1201, 16th Street, NW, Washington DC 20036

AAU   Amateur Athletic Union of the United States, 3400 West 86th Street, Indianapolis, Ind 46268

AIA   American Institute of Architects, 1735 New York Avenue, NW, Washington DC 20006

ANRC   American National Red Cross, 18th and E Streets, NW, Washington DC 20036

ANSI   American National Standards Institute, 1430 Broadway, New York, NY 10018

APHA   American Public Health Association Inc, 1015 18th Street, NW, Washington DC 20036

ASTM   American Society for Testing of Materials, 1916 Race Street, Philadelphia, Pa 19103

CNCA   Council for National Co-operation in Aquatics, 220 Ashton Road, Ashton, Maryland 20702, 1201 Sixteenth Street, NW, Washington DC 20036

CDA   Copper Development Association Inc, 405 Lexington Avenue, New York, NY 10017

FINA   Fédération Internationale de Natation Amateur, 555 N Washington Street, Naperville, Ill, and 601 Grand Avenue Des Maines, Iowa City, Iowa 50309

HP   Hoffman Publications, Inc, PO Box 11299, Sunrise Professional Building, 3000 NE 30th Place, Fort Lauderdale, Fla 33304

IES   Illuminating Engineering Society, 345 East 47th Street, New York, NY 10017

ISHOF   International Swimming Pool Hall of Fame, 1 Hall of Fame Drive, Fort Lauderdale, Fla 33316

NAUI   National Association of Underwater Instructors, 22809 Barton Road, Grand Terrace, Colton, Ca 92324

NCAA   National Collegiate Athletic Association, PO Box 1906, Shawnee Mission, Kansas 66222

NCMA   National Concrete Masonry Association, 2009 North 14th Street, Arlington, Va 22201

NRPA   National Recreation & Park Association, 1601 N Kent Street, Arlington, Va 22209

NSC   National Safety Council, 425 Michigan Avenue, Chicago, Ill 60611

NSF   National Sanitation Foundation, PO Box 1468, Ann Arbor, Mich 48106

NYOCA   National YMCA Operating Council on Aquatics, 291 Broadway, New York, NY 10007

SFOA   Swim Facility Operators Association, ISHOF, 1 Hall of Fame, Fort Lauderdale, Fla 33316

SWP   Swimming World Publications, 8622 Bellanca Avenue, Los Angeles, Cal 90045

USCPSC   United States Consumer Product Safety Commission, Washington DC 20207

USOC   United States Olympic Committee, Olympic House, 57 Park Avenue, New York, NY 10016

USPHS   United States Public Health Service, Department of Health, Education & Welfare, 330 Independence Avenue, SW Washington DC 20201

USPHS   United States Department of Health, Education and Welfare (HEW publications), Public Health Service, Bureau of State Services, Center for Disease Control, Atlanta, Ga 30333

USA   Underwater Society of America, 1701 Lake Avenue, Glenview, Ill 60025

USOE   United States Office of Education, OAC-BESE-Room 2010, Federal Building 6, 400 Maryland Avenue, SW Washington DC 20202

USSR

USSSO   The Swimming Federation of USSR, 4 Skatertny Pereulok, Moscow g69

APPENDIX IV

Codes, specifications and standards concerning swimming pools

Country and No	Title		Date
Australia			
AS CC1	Electrical equipment installation rules in buildings, structures and premises:		1973

Country and No	Title	Date	Country and No	Title	Date
	associated section concerns swimming pools wiring rules		India		
			IS 3328	Quality tolerances for waters for swimming pools	1965
AS 1838	Premoulded reinforced plastics swimming pools	1975			
AS 1839	Code of practice for in-ground installation of premoulded reinforced plastics swimming pools	1975	New Zealand		
			NZS 1900	Model building bylaw. Chapter 11.1 Concrete structures for the storage of liquids	1970
AS 1926	Fences and gates for swimming pools	1976	NZS 4441	Code of practice for swimming pools	1972
DR 76015	Safety covers for private swimming and wading pools	1976	NZS 9201	Model general bylaw, Chapter 16. Public swimming pools	1970
NSW	Advisory code on construction and use of swimming pools	1975			
			South Africa		
			DRAFT	Code of practice for safety fencing around domestic swimming pools	1977
Austria					
ÖNORM M 5800	Temperature control	1974			
ÖNORM M 5872	Ancillary control equipment for bathing water	1974	Sweden		
			REG	Safety fence protection for children using swimming pools	1973
ÖNORM M 5878	Ozone generator requirements for water treatment	1976			
ÖNORM M 5879	Chlorination and equipment requirements for water treatment	1975	Switzerland		
			SVG 16	Swimming pool overflows	1977
ÖNORM M 5886	pH control	1976	SIA Norm 173	Quality specifications for water and water treatment plant installations for public bathing schemes (open air, school and covered pools)	1968
ÖNORM M 6215	Water requirements for indoor and outdoor swimming pools	1976			
ÖNORM M 6216	Water treatment plant for indoor and outdoor swimming pools	1977			
ÖNORM M 6217	Supervision of water treatment plant for indoor and outdoor swimming pool waters	1976	Code of Practice	Ventilation plant in indoor swimming pools	1977
ÖNORM B 8110	Water heating				
			UK		
			BS 3505	uPVC Pipe for cold water services – pressure classes C & D	1968
Canada					
129/75 PH Act	Public swimming pools: Ontario regulation. DOH	1975	BS 5337 (replacing CP 2007)	The structural use of concrete for retaining aqueous liquids	1976
B140.12	Oil-fired service water heaters and swimming pool heaters	1976	CP 110	The structural use of concrete (unified code)	1972
C22.2 No 89	Swimming pool luminaires, submersible luminaires and accessories	1976	CP 111	Structural recommendations for load bearing walls	1970
			CP 112	Structural use of timber	1971
Finland			CP 114	The structural use of reinforced concrete	1969
RT 968.11	Swimming halls, general planning aspects	1968			
RT 968.21	Swimming pools, private	1971	CP 115	The structural use of prestressed concrete	1969
			CP 116	The structural use of precast concrete	1969
France			CP 117	Composite construction in structural steel and concrete	1965
NF C 15–100	Requirements for electrical installations in swimming baths	1976			
72–39B (MTPB)	Requirements for the use of bromine in poolwater sterilisation	1972	CP 118	The structural use of aluminium	1969
			CP 212	Ceramic wall tiling (also refer BS 5385 parts 1/2 (1978))	1972
8th Jul	Hygiene and safety requirements applicable to pools open to the public (Journal Officiel, DJO)	1969	CP 221	External rendered finishes	1960
			Part VIII Sections 221/4	Public Health Act applying to facilities and water purification	1936
Germany					
DIN Spec	Water treatment for swimming pool water	1972			
DIN 1946	Ventilation	1970	SPATA	Standards for swimming pools – design and construction, filtration and heating, saunas and accessories	1976
DIN 4701	Water heating	1970			
Safety regulations in pool halls			Tech Spec 5	BCTS – Ceramic tiling in indoor swimming pools: series 1–14	1972
DIN 7930	Pool tanks	1977			
DIN 7931	Swimming lanes	1977	HMSO	The Miscellaneous Provisions Act	1976
DIN 7932	Swimming boards	1977			
DIN 7933	Starting blocks	1977	USA		
DIN 7934	Touch pads	1977	ACI-302-66	Specifications for structural concrete for buildings	1967
DIN 7935	Springboard diving	1977			
DIN 0	Baths	1978	ACI-318-63	Building code requirements for reinforced concrete	
DIN 0	Non slip surfaces	1978			
DIN 19260	pH control	1976	334.1-18	Concrete shell structures, practice and commentary	
DIN 19605	Filters for water maintenance	1976			
DIN 19606	High rate filter flocculants	1975	ACI-506-66	Recommended practice for shotcreting	
DIN 19607	Chlorine for water maintenance	1975	ANSI Z21.56a/b	Standard for gas-fired swimming pool heaters	1974
DIN 19608	Sodium hypochlorite for water maintenance	1975	ANSI 108.2 & 5	Installation of ceramic tile	1967

Country and No	Title	Date
ANSI 137.1	Tile specification	1967
APHA	Suggested ordinance and regulations covering public swimming pools	1964
APHA	Suggested ordinance and regulations covering private residential swimming pools	1970
Article No 680	National electrical code. National Fire Protection Assoc.	©.1971
ASA A40.4	Air gap for potable water supplies used to fill pools	1942
16 CFR Part 1207	Consumer Product Safety Commission: swimming pool slides safety standard	1975
Dept of Health	California health and safety code: laws and regulations relating to swimming pools – public	1974
NSF	Swimming pool standards relating to: filters, pumps, multiport valves, skimmers, chemical feeding equipment, chemicals, test kits, artificial surfaces	1966–1975
NSPI	Swimming pool wiring. Article No 680, Code 1971	1973
NSPI	Suggested minimum standards for residential swimming pools	1974
NSPI	Suggested minimum standards for public swimming pools	1977
UL 1081	Swimming pool pumps, filters and chlorinators	1972

APPENDIX V

International bibliography

Definitive publications for a particular subject are in bold

The letter in brackets after each entry denotes the type of publication as follows

```
    KEY

    A  article          M  manual
    b  booklet          P  pamphlet
    B  book             R  report
    D  directory
```

Pools: General including their setting

Allsop, R. Owen (1894) *Public Baths and Wash-Houses,* Spon & Chamberlain, New York (B)

Architects' Journal (1964 to 1977) **Swimming Pool Building and Technical Studies,** Architectural Press, London (A)

Architects' Journal (1977/78) **The Designing of Sports and Recreational Centres,** Architectural Press, London (A)

Architectural Press (1977) *Specification: Building Methods and Products,* Architectural Press, London (D)

Bacon, W. (1960) *All About Swimming Pools,* Greenwich Press, Conn (B)

Birchall, R. H. (1976) *The Leisure Pool,* Vols I and II, Sports Council, London (R)

BRE (1973) **Symposium: Aspects of Swimming Pool Design,** BRE Publications, East Kilbride (R)

Britannica (1967) Baths, *Encyclopedia Britannica,* Chicago (A)

Brookes, John (1969) **Room Outside,** Thames & Hudson, London (b)

Chilstone (1976) *Garden Ornaments,* Chilstone, Kent (B)

Church, T. D. (1969) *Your Private World,* Chronicle Books, San Francisco (B)

Cobb, A. (1958) *Swimming Pool,* Friendship Press, New York (B)

Cross, Alfred W. S. (1906) *Public Baths and Wash-Houses,* Batsford, London (B)

Cross, A. W. S. and K. M. B. (1938) *Modern Public Baths and Wash-Houses,* Simpkin Marshall, London (B)

Cross, F. L. and Cameron, W. W. (1974) **Handbook of Swimming Pool Construction, Maintenance and Sanitation,** Technomic, Westport, USA (M)

Cunliffe, Barry (1969) *Roman Bath: Society of Antiquaries Report,* Oxford University Press, London (R)

—— (1971) *Aquae Sulis,* Ginn, London (b)

—— (1971) **Roman Bath Discovered,** Routledge & Kegan Paul, London (B)

Dawes, John (1975) **The Swimming Pool and the Garden,** Bartholomew, Edinburgh (B)

—— (10/75) Swimming Pools, *New Zealand Gardener,* Wellington (A)

—— (3/77) Swimming Pools (*Green Fingers*—series Encyclopedia), Orbis Publications, London (B)

Debaigts, Jacques (1973) **Swimming Pools,** Charles E. Tuttle, Rutland, USA (B)

Dervan, Ronald and Nichols, Carol (1976) *Book of Successful Swimming Pools,* Structures Publications, Farmington USA (B)

Dickmann, Helmut (1965) *Swimming Pools Bade – und Schwimmbecken im eigenen Garten,* Verlag Ullstein, Berlin (B)

DOE (1962) *Design Bulletin 4: Swimming Pools,* MHLG, London (b)

DOE (1975) *Sport and Recreation* (White Paper), HMSO, London (R)

Dowd, Merle (1968) **Pools in the Schools,** NSPI, Washington (b)

EC (1973) *Electrics* (swimming pools section), Electricity Council, London (M)

Eisinger, Larry (ed) (1960) *All About Swimming Pools,* Arco, New York (B)

Elgin-Refinite (1953) *Modern Swimming Pool Data and Design,* Refinite Corp, Illinois (b)

Elving, Phyllis (ed) (1970) **Sunset Swimming Pools,** Lane Books, Menlo Park, USA (B)

Fabian, Dietrich (1960 (I) 1971 (II)) **Bäder, Handbuch für Bäderbau und Badewesen,** Callwey, Munich (M)

—— (1966) *Moderne Schwimmstätten der Welt,* Shunemann, Bremen (B)

—— (1973) *Schwimmen im Haus,* Callwey, Munich (B)

Franck, Nicolette (1972) *Concrete in Garden-making,* C & CA Publications, London (b)

Gabrielsen, M. Alexander (ed) (1975) **Swimming Pools: a Guide to their Planning, Design and Operation** (a CNCA project), Hoffman Publications, Fort Lauderdale, USA (B)

Gage, Michael and Vandenberg, Maritz (1975) **Hard Landscape in Concrete,** Architectural Press, London (B)

Garland, Madge (1973) *The Small Garden in the City,* Architectural Press, London (B)

Gerhard, W. P. (1908) *Modern Baths and Baths Houses,* Stanhope Press, Boston (B)

Gillespie, John (1974) *Sunset Garden Pools, Fountains and Waterfalls,* Lane Books, Menlo Park, USA (B)

Glaus, Otto (1975) *Planen und Bauen moderner Heilbäder,* Verlag Karl Krämer, Zurich (B)

Granger, Frank (trans) (1931) *Vitruvius on Architecture* (Vol I, Book V), Heinemann, London (B)

Hale, John (1974) *Pools for Schools,* Home and School Council, Billericay (b)

Harris, H. A. (1972) *Sport in Rome and Greece,* Thames & Hudson, London (B)

Hawkins, R. R. and Abbe, C. H. (1951) *Garden Pools, Fountains, Swimming Pools, Sprinkling Systems, Recreation Areas,* Van Nostrand, New York (B)

Heathwood, Gail (1974) *House and Garden Guide to Pools and Terraces,* Collins, London (B)

Hogan, Elizabeth (1972) *Sunset Ideas for Landscaping,* Lane Books, Menlo Park, USA (B)

Howell, Sarah (1974) *The Seaside,* Studio Vista, London (B)

Hunt, Peter (1969) *Garden Shrubs,* Hamlyn, London (B)

Hyams, Edward (1971) **A History of Gardens and Gardening,** Dent, London (B)

James, P. Rowland (1938) *The Baths of Bath in the Sixteenth and Early Seventeenth Century,* Arrowsmith, London (B)

Jenkins, A. (1958) *Swimming Pools,* Heinemann, Toronto (B)

Joseph, J. (1963) *Poolside Living,* Doubleday, Toronto (B)

Kappler, Hans Peter (1974) *Das Private Schwimmbad,* Bauverlag GmbH, Weisbaden (B)

Konya, Allen and Burger, Alewyn (1973) **The International Handbook of Finnish Sauna,** Architectural Press, London (B)

Lee, Owen (1969) *The Skin Divers Bible*, Hale, London (B)
Loyd, Stephen (1976) *Bibliography: In the Swim – Literature on the Environmental Conditions and Services* (LB 105/76), BSRIA, Bracknell (D)
Midgley, Kenneth (1967) *Garden Design*, Penguin, Harmondsworth (B)
Morgan, Morris Hickey (trans) (1960) *Vitruvius: The Ten Books on Architecture*, Dover Publications, New York (B)
Moth, J. (1951) *The City of Birmingham Baths Department 1851–1951*, James Upton, Birmingham (R)
NAPO (1975) **Swimming Pool Manual**, NAPO, Needham, Mass (M)
NBA + Building (1976) *Swimming Pools and Sauna Baths*, NBA + Building Commodity File, London (D)
NCAA (1976) *1976 Swimming Guide*, NCAA, Kansas (b)
Neilson, D. W. and Nixon, J. E. (1954) **Swimming Pools for Schools**, Stanford University Press, Stanford (B)
NSPI (1978) *Symposia: Public Pools/Solar Heating*, NSPI, Washington (D)
Oppenheim, François (1970) *The History of Swimming*, Swimming World, North Hollywood (B)
Owen, A. H. (1971) *Swimming for Schools*, Pelham Books, London (B)
Perkins, Philip H. (1971) **Swimming Pools: a Treatise on the Planning, Layout, Design and Construction, Including Water Treatment and Other Services**, Applied Science, London (B)
Perrin, G. A. (1973) *Indoor Recreation Centres*, NPFA, London (b)
Peters, Paulhans and Rolmer, Ludwig (1971) *Garden Pools for Pleasure*, Callwey, Munich (B)
Piscines (ann) *Piscines Privées*, Chr. Ledoux, Paris (D)
—— (ann) *Piscines Publiques*, Chr. Ledoux, Paris (D)
Pool News (ann) *The Pool News Directory*, Leisure Publications, Los Angeles (D)
Pools and Parks Annual (ann) *Pool and Patio Show and Convention Directory and Buyers Guide*, OSPA/Sound Publishing, Owen Sound, Ontario (D)
Rinehart, M. R. (1958) *Swimming Pools*, Clarke, Irwin, Toronto (B)
Savidge, Rex (1970) *The Modern Swimming Pool*, Building Centre Trust, London (b)
Scharff, Robert (1958) *The Swimming Pool Book*, McLeod Barrows, New York (B)
Schools Council (1972) **Swimming Pools for Primary Schools**, Evans-Methuen, London (b)
Schuler, Stanley (1974) **How to Design, Build and Maintain your Swimming Pool**, Macmillan, New York (B)
Scott, Geo. Ripley (1939) **The Story of Baths and Bathing**, Werner Laurie, London (B)
SPATA (1976) *Planning your Swimming Pool*, SPATA, Croydon (b)
Sports Council (1972) *A Report on the Optimum Use of Existing Swimming Facilities*, Sports Council, London (P)
—— (1972) *Provision for Sport: DOE Report, Indoor Swimming Pools*, HMSO, London (b)
Sports Council (M. F. Collins) (1977) *Indoor Swimming Pools in Britain: National Survey of Attendance and Public Use*, Sports Council, London (R)
Stokes, H. G. (1947) *The English Seaside*, Sylvan Press, London (B)
Swiss Baths Conference Papers No. 43, SVG, Zurich (P)
Swimming Pool Directory (Ann), *Swimming Pool*, Guildford (D)
Swimming Pool Weekly (ann) *US Swimming Pool Industry Market Report*, Hoffman Publications, Fort Lauderdale, USA (R)
TUS (1973) **Public Indoor Swimming Pools Bulletin No 1** (Dept of Education and Science, Sports Council), HMSO, London (b)
VNG (1974) *Survey of Existing Pool Buildings in the Netherlands*, VNG, The Hague (B)
Wheeler, Mortimer (1973) *Roman Art and Culture*, Thames & Hudson, London (B)
Wollaston, Robert (1864) *Thermae Romano-Britannicae*, Robt Hardwicke, London (B)
Wright, Lawrence (1971) *Clean and Decent*, Routledge & Kegan Paul, London (B)

Design and planning

AAHPER and Athletic Institute (1968) *College and University Facilities Guide*, AAHPER Publications, Washington (B)
AAHPER and Athletic Institute (1974) *Planning Facilities for Athletics, Physical Education and Recreation* AAHPER Publications, Washington (M)

APHA (1975) *Recommended Practice for Design, Equipment and Operation of Swimming Pools and other Public Bathing Places*, APHA, New York (M)
Architects' Journal The Designing of Sports and Recreational Centres, op cit under General
Architects' Journal Swimming Pool Building and Technical Studies, op cit under General
Architects' Journal (29 May 1974) Summerland: the Reckoning, the Lessons, the Analysis, Architectural Press, London (A)
Architectural Review (5/67) Public Swimming Baths, Architectural Press, London (A)
ASA (1967) **Swimming Pools: Notes for the Guidance of Designers**, ASA Publications, Loughborough (b)
BRE, op cit under General
BSAC (1973) **Pools for Sub-Aqua Use**, BSAC Publications, London (b)
Dawes *The Swimming Pool and the Garden*, op cit under General
Dept of Education and Science (1968) *Building Bulletin No 26. Secondary School Design: Physical Education*, HMSO, London (L)
EC (1972) *Integrated Environmental Design*, Electricity Council, London (b)
EC (1976) *Buildings are for People*, Electricity Council, London (b)
Fabian, Dietrich (1970) **Aquatic Buildings Bäderbauten** II, Callwey, Munich (D)
—— (1975) **Aquatic Buildings Bäderbauten** I, Callwey, Munich (D)
—— *Bäder Handbuch für Bäderbau und Badenwesen*, op cit under General
Fairweather, Leslie and Sliwa, Jan A. (1973) *AJ Metric Handbook*, Architectural Press, London (B)
Gabrielsen, op cit under General
Huxley, Anthony (ed) (1975) *The Financial Times Book of Garden Design*, David & Charles, Newton Abbott (B)
IAB (1968) *Bäderbauten + Aquatic Buildings*, IAB, Bremen (M)
IAKS (1969 to 1976) *Congress Lecture Notes and Planners Swimming Pool Worksheets*, IAKS, Cologne (R)
IBM (1966 to 1976) **Institute of Baths Management Conference Reports**, IBM, Melton Mowbray (R)
—— (1971) **Swimming Pools Design Guide No 1**, IBM, Melton Mowbray (b)
IES (1972) *IES Lighting Handbook*, IES, New York (M)
—— (1974) *IES Lighting Guide: Sports No 7*, IES, London (M)
Konya and Burger, op cit under General
Lindley, Kenneth (1973) *Seaside Architecture*, Hugh Evelyn, London (B)
Mayo, A. P. (1975) *An Investigation of the Collapse of a Swimming Pool Roof Constructed with Plywood Box Beams*, BRE Publications, Garston (R)
Ministère de la Jeunesse et des Sports (1969) **Piscines couvertes et en plein air** No 269 DA, Institut Pédagogique National, Paris (R)
Ministry of the Environment (1973) *Recommended Swimming Pool Design and Operating Standards*, MOE, Edmonton (R)
NAPO, op cit under General
Perkins, op cit under General
Savidge, Rex (10/64) *The Local Authority Swimming Bath: Designs for the Present and Future, Architects' Journal*, London (A)
Silcock, H. and Hinkley, P. L. (1974) *Report on the Spread of Fire at Summerland in Douglas on the Isle of Man, 2 August 1973*, BRE Publications, Garston (b)
Sillitoe, K. K. (1972) *Planning for Leisure*, HMSO, London (R)
Terry, W. L. (1959) *Guide for Planning the School and College Swimming Pool and Natatorium*, Teachers College Press, New York (b)
TUS *Public Indoor Swimming Pools Bulletin No 1* op cit under General
TUS (1971) *TUS Design Note 1 (DOE) Plan for a Local Swimming Pool*, Sports Council, London (R)
—— (1972) **TUS Design Note 2 (DOE) Plan for a Swimming Pool at Ashton-under-Lyne**, Sports Council, London (R)
—— (1975) *TUS Design Note 3 Film and Broadcasting Requirements in Sports Facilities*, Sports Council, London (R)
—— (1975) *TUS Design Note 4 An Approach to Low-cost Sports Halls*, Sports Council, London (R)
—— (1975) *TUS Design Note 5 Swimming Pool Hall Roofs in Timber*, Sports Council, London (R)
Walter, Felix (1971) **Sports Centres and Swimming Pools for the Disabled**, Thistle Foundation, Edinburgh (b)
Wong, Henry (1977) *Facility Fundamentals: Swimming Pools*, MC & R, Sports and Fitness Division, Ontario (M)

KEY

A article   M manual
b booklet   P pamphlet
B book   R report
D directory

Construction including finishes

American Builder (1959) *How to Build Swimming Pools*, Simmons-Boardman, New York (b)

BCTC (1975) *Symposium on Swimming Pools*, British Ceramic Tile Council, Stoke-on-Trent (R)

Beadle, Dave (1972) *Concrete Round the House*, C &CA Publications, London (b)

BTJ (2/75) Swimming Pool Supplement, *Building Trades Journal*, London (A)

C & CA (1966) *Swimming Pool Construction: a Design for a Small Reinforced Concrete Pool*, C & CA Publications, London (b)

Collins, A. J. W. (8/72) Swimming Pools, Parts I and II, *RIBA Journal*, London (A)

David, Walter (ed) (1970) *Glass Fibre Swimming Pools and Ponds*, Isopon Chemicals, London (B)

Dampa (UK) Ltd (1971) *Dampa Suspended Ceilings in Swimming Pools*, Dampa (UK) Ltd, Oxford (P)

DGFdB (ed) (1977) *Guidelines for Swimming Pool Construction*, Tümmels Verlag, Nürnberg (B)

Dynamit Nobel (1971) *Installation Guide: Trocal Tank Lining*, Dynamit, Troisdorf, FDR (P)

Fletcher, K. E. (1974) *Admixtures for Concrete*, Building Research Establishment, Watford (R)

Gabrielsen, op cit under General

Gage, Michael (1970) *Guide to Exposed Concrete Finishes*, Architectural Press, London (B)

Gage and Vandenberg, op cit under General

Geekie, Peter (1972) *Practical Guide to Concrete Pool Construction*, Peter Geekie Pools Ltd, Oxford (b)

—— (1972) *Practical Guide to Liner Pool Construction*, Peter Geekie Pools Ltd, Oxford (b)

—— (1975) *Practical Guide to Liner Hopper Pool Construction*, Peter Geekie Pools Ltd, Oxford (b)

George Fischer Group (1973) **A Guide to the Installation of UPVC Pipework**, George Fischer Group, London (b)

Harris, John (1976) *How to Build your Own Patios, Paths and Walls*, Charcon Products, Derby (b)

IAKS, op cit under Design and planning

IBM *Institute of Baths Management Conference Reports*, op cit under Design and planning

NCMA (1975) *Plans for a Concrete Block Pool*, NCMA, Arlington, Va (M)

NSPI (1963) *Corrosion in Swimming Pools and General Guide to Materials Selection*, NSPI, Washington (b)

—— (1964) *The Role of Corrosion: Resistant Materials in Swimming Pools*, NSPI, Washington (b)

—— (1969) **Portable Pools**, NSPI, Washington (b)

Perkins, Philip H. (1972) *Building a Concrete Block Swimming Pool*, C & CA Publications, London (b)

Perkins, Philip H. (1977) *Concrete Structures: Repair, Water Proofing and Protection*, Applied Science, London (B)

Perkins, *Swimming Pools*, op cit under General

Pilkington (1966) *Swimming Pools: Glass and Windows Bulletin No 7*, Pilkington Glass, St Helens, UK (P)

Pittsburgh Corning (1971) *Foamglas Handbook 1: Insulation for Swimming Pools*, Pittsburgh Corning, Penn (P)

Rutherford Group (1974) **Swimming Pool Self-Build Dossier**, Rutherford Pools, Battle (M)

St Christopher School (1965) *Building a Swimming Pool*, St Christopher Press, Letchworth (b)

Trocal (1971) *Water Tank PVC Lining Guide*, Dynamit Nobel AG, Troisdorf, DFR (M)

TUS *Design Note 5*, op cit under Design and planning

—— (1975) *TUS Design Note 6 Air Supported Structures as Sports Buildings*, Sports Council, London (R)

VNG (1974) *Guidelines for the Establishment and Construction of Swimming Pool Buildings*, VNG, The Hague (B)

Weaver, Gabrielle (1975) *All You Need to Know about Designing your Garden* (Golden Homes), Marshall Cavendish, London (B)

Wills, Norman D. (1969) **Build your Own Swimming Pool**, John Gifford, London (B)

York, David (1976) *Landscape and Garden Contracting: Methods, Costing and Estimating*, Architectural Press, London (B)

Zanelli, Leo (ed) (1974) *All You Can Build in the Garden* (Golden Homes), Marshall Cavendish, London (B)

Heating and Ventilation

BGC (1973) *Gas Heated Domestic Swimming Pool: Installation Guide*, British Gas Council, London (b)

Biasin, K. and Krumme, W. (5/74) Evaporation in an Indoor Swimming Pool, *Elektrowärme International*, DFR (A)

Billington, N. S. (1973) *Radiant Heating of Small Swimming Pools* Technical Note 38/73, BSR IA (HVRA), Bracknell (P)

Braham, G. D. (1975) **Conservation and Management of Energy in Swimming Pools**, IBM/Electricity Council, Melton Mowbray (R)

—— (1975) *Heat Recovery as Applied to Public Swimming Pool Buildings*, Electricity Council, London (P)

Braham, G. D. and Hughes, L. (1971) *Fuels in the Seventies: the All-Electric Solution*, IBM Conference Paper/Electricity Council, Melton Mowbray (R)

—— (1977) *A Guide to Energy Cost Effectiveness in Swimming Pools*, Electricity Council IBM, London (R)

Brinkworth, B. J. (1972) *Solar Energy for Man*, Compton Press, Salisbury (B)

BSR IA (1972) *Thermal Environment for Indoor Swimming Pools* Technical Note 28/72, BSR IA (HVRA), Bracknell (P)

Carter, Brenda (8/1973) *Efficient and Inefficient Ways of Heating Pools by Solar Energy Collectors*, BSE, London (R)

Courtney, R. G. (1976) *Solar Energy Utilisation in the UK*, Building Research Establishment, Watford (R)

CTT (1976) *How to Use Natural Energy*, CTT, London (b)

—— (1976) *Solar Heating for Large Swimming Pools*, CTT, London (R)

Curtis, E. J. W. (1974) *Solar Energy Applications in Architecture*, North London Polytechnic, London (R)

Daniels, F. (1964) *Direct Use of the Sun's Energy*, Yale University Press, Yale, Conn (B)

Dept of Education and Science, op cit under Design and Planning

DGFdB (3/71) *Symposium Bad Nauheim 1970: Electric Heating and Air Conditioning of Indoor and Outdoor Swimming Pools*, Archiv des Badewesens, Düsseldorf (R)

DOE *Design Bulletin 4: Swimming Pools*, op cit under General

Doe, L. N. (1972) *Condensation and Swimming Pool Design*, Applied Science, London (R)

EC (1971) *Heat Recovery in Air Conditioned Buildings*, Electricity Council, London (b)

—— (1972) *Below the Surface: an In-Depth Study of the Advantages of Electric Swimming Pool Heating*, Electricity Council, London (b)

—— (1975) *Energy Effectiveness in Swimming Pools*, Electricity Council, London (b)

—— (1976) *An Appraisal of Solar Heating: Environmental Engineering Section*, Electricity Council, London (R)

—— (1976) **Heat Recovery**, Electricity Council, London (P)

—— (1977) *Understanding Swimming Pool Energy Use*, Electricity Council, London (P)

EDF (1976) *Le Chauffage électrique des piscines*, Electricité de France, Paris (b)

Erne-Erle-Drax RP (1962) *Solar Heated Swimming Pools*, J. Looker Ltd, Poole, UK (b)

Garden, G. K. (1966) **Indoor Swimming Pools – CBD 83**, National Research Canadian Council, Ottawa (R)

Gas Council (1971) *Swimming in the 70s: Gas Heating for the Modern Pool*, British Gas Council, London (P)

Geekie, Peter (1972) *Practical Guide to Swimming Pool Heating*, Peter Geekie Pools Ltd, Oxford (b)

Heywood, H. (6/71) *Operating Experiences with Solar Water Heating*, *JIHVE*, London (R)

Holt, J. S. C. (1962) *Some Aspects of Swimming Pool Design* Technical Note No 10, Heating and Ventilating Research Association (BSRIA), Bracknell (R)

IHVE (1970) *Guide Book*, IHVE, London (M)

—— (1977) *IHVE Energy Notes for Sports Centres*, IHVE (CIBS) London (b)

Information Canada (1972) *Points on Public Swimming Pools*, Information Canada, Ottowa (R)

ISES (UK) (1975) *Solar Water Heating*, UK Section ISES, London (R)

—— (1977) **Solar Energy for Heating Swimming Pools**, UK Section ISES, London (R)

—— (1978) *Practical Experiences with Solar Heated Swimming Pools*, UK Section ISES, London (R)

Loyd, Stephen and Starling, Colin (1975) *Bibliography: Heat and Power from the Sun (101/75)*, BSRIA, Bracknell (D)

McVeigh, J. C. (6/71) Some Experiments in Heating Swimming Pools by Solar Energy, *JIHVE*, London (A)

McVeigh, J. C. (1977) *Sun Power: an Introduction to the Practical Applications of Solar Energy*, Pergamon, Oxford (B)

Milbank, N. O. (1975) *Energy Consumption in Swimming Pool Halls*, BRE Publications, Garston (P)

NSPI (1976) *Solar Heating for Swimming Pools*, NSPI, Washington (P)

—— (1978) *Symposia-Public Pools/Solar Heating*, NSPI, Washington (D)

Pilkington (1976) *Glass in Solar Energy Collectors*, Pilkington Glass, St Helens, UK (R)

Potterton (1972) **Swim in comfort: Pool Heating by Potterton**, Potterton, London (b)

Senior, J. (1974) *Coal Utilisation in Industry*, NCB, London (b)

Sheridan, N. R. (1972) *The Heating of Swimming Pools: Solar Research Notes No 4*, University of Queensland, Brisbane (M)

SPATA (1973) **Enclosing your Swimming Pool**, SPATA, Croydon (b)

Summer, John (1976) *Domestic Heat Pumps*, Prism Press, Dorchester (B)

Szokolay, S. V. (1975) **Solar Energy and Building**, Architectural Press, London (B)

Vale, Brenda and Robert (1975) *The Autonomous House*, Thames & Hudson, London (B)

Whillier, A. (1973) *How to Heat your Swimming Pool Using Solar Energy*, Brace Research Institute, Montreal (P)

de Winter, Francis (1974) **Solar Energy and the Flat Plate Collector – Bibliography**, Copper Development Assoc Inc, New York (R)

—— (1975) **How to Design and Build a Solar Swimming Pool Heater**, Copper Development Assoc Inc, New York (b)

Water treatment

Briswim (1977) **Towards a Perfect Pool: the Briswim Guide to Swimming Pool Care**, Robt R. Bartlett, Bristol (b)

Cillichemie (nd) *The Private Swimming Pool*, Cillichemie Ernst Vogelmann, Heilbronn (b)

Commission of the European Communities (1975) *Proposal for a Council Directive Relating to Pollution of Sea Water and Fresh Water for Bathing*, Commission of the European Communities, Brussels (R)

Davis, H. S. (1978) *The Electrochemical Sodium Hypochlorite Generator*, NZ Water Treatment School, Bulls (R)

DOE (1958, 1976) **The Purification of the Water of Swimming Pools**, HMSO, London (b)

—— (1977) *New Chemicals and Materials for use in Swimming Pools*, Elphick, A. (1978) *The Treatment of Swimming Pool Water with Sodium Hypochlorite*, Wallace and Tiernan, Tonbridge (P)

DOE, London (R)

Faust, J. Philip and Waldvogel, R. L. (1972) **The HTH Water Book for Pool Professionals**, Olin Corp, Stamford, USA (b)

Gabrielsen, op cit under General

Griffiths, J. H. T. (nd) *Water and Water Treatment*, PCI Ltd, London (b)

Hartley, Dorothy (1964) **Water in England** (anthology), Macdonald, London (B)

Humphrey, W. H. (1972) *Purification of Swimming Pool Water*, Akdolit, London (b)

Humphrey, W. H. (1976) *The Use of Akdolit Filter Material for pH Correction*, Akdolit, London (b)

IBM *Institute of Baths Management Conference Reports*, op cit under Design and Planning

ICI (1975) *A Guide to the Breakpoint Chlorination of Swimming Bath Water* (TS/A/2333), ICI, London (b)

—— (1976) *Chlorination of Swimming Pools Using Sodium Hypochlorite* (TS/A/2386), ICI, London (b)

Illinois Dept of Public Health, (1970) *Sanitary Requirements for Swimming Pools*, Illinois Dept of PH, Springfield, USA (M)

Kroebet, Frederick V. (1976) *Public Swimming Pools: a Manual of Operation*, A. S. Barnes & Co, Cranbury, NJ (B)

LGTB (1973) **Operation of Small Swimming Pools Training Manual for School Caretakers**, Local Government Training Board, Luton (M)

Malpas, J. F. (1963) **The Chemical and Bacteriological Purification of Swimming Bath Water**, Wallace & Tiernan, Tonbridge (b)

Ministry of Works and Development (1975) **Swimming Pool Managers Lecture Notes**, Water Treatment Operators Training School, Bulls, NZ (M)

MTP et B (1972) Requirements for the Use of Bromine in Pool Water Sterilisation, *Moniteur des Travaux Publics et du Bâtiment*, Paris (A)

NSPI (1974) **Residential Pool Care Guide**, NSPI, Washington (P)

NZ Ass of SP Managers (1962 to 1976) **Annual Conference Reports of Swimming Pool Operations**, New Zealand Ass of Swimming Pool Managers, Bulls, NZ (R)

—— (1976) *Training Manual*, New Zealand Ass of Swimming Pool Managers, Bulls, NZ (M)

Oxford History (1958) *Oxford History of Technology*, Oxford University Press, London (B)

Palmer, Mervin C. (1959) *Algae in Water Supplies* Public Health Service Publication 657, US Dept of Health, Education and Welfare, Washington (M)

Reid, Field (1971) *Water Treatment for Industrial and Public Supply*, DTI, London (R)

Rutherford Group (1976) *Swimming Pool Technical Dossier*, Rutherford Pools, Battle (D)

SCPA (1972) *Pool Water Sterilization with Bromine*, SCPA, Paris (P)

Sigrist (1975) *Turbidity Units*, Sigrist-Photometer, Zurich (b)

Strand, Frank L. (1970) **Public Pool Care**, NSPI, Washington (M)

Summer, W. (1976) *Everything About the Water in your Swimming Pool*, USA (B)

Swimming Pool Ass of NSW (1975) *Seminar – Swimming Pool Report*, SPA of NSW, Concord (D)

Taylor, Charlie (1974) *Everything You Always Wanted to Know About POOL CARE – But Didn't Know Where to Ask*, Charlie Taylor Publications, Arlington, US (B)

Wallace & Tiernan (nd) *W & T Handbook of Pool Water Care*, Wallace & Tiernan, Belleville US/Tonbridge UK (b)

Wallis, A. P. L. (1963) *The Construction, Control and Maintenance of Small Swimming Pools*, EHA (PH I), London (P)

Waring, Brian D. (1971) *Handbook for Operation of Sand Filtration Plant for Swimming Pools*, Akwaplan Engineering, Leatherhead, UK (b)

White, G. C. (1972) *Handbook of Chlorination*, Van Nostrand, New York (B)

Operational and use

AAU (1976) **1976 Rules: Diving, Swimming, Water Polo and Synchronised Swimming**, AAU Publications, Indianapolis (b)

Action Committee for Bath Spa Preservation (1977) *Redevelopment of Bath as a Spa,* AC for Bath Spa, Bath (R)

Alderson, Fred (1973) *The Inland Resorts and Spas of Britain*, David & Charles, Newton Abbott (B)

APHA, op cit under Design and planning

Summerland, *Architects' Journal*, op cit under Design and planning

Archiv des Badewesens (8/71) 25 Indoor Swimming Pools, *Archiv*, Düsseldorf (R)

ASA (nd) *Synchronised Swimming Handbook*, ASA Publications, Loughborough (P)

—— (1977) **Swimming Pools: Requirements for Competition**, ASA Publications, Loughborough (b)

Ashe, Geoffrey (1950) **The Tale of the Tub: a Survey of the Art of Bathing**, Newman Neame, London (B)

Baden-Baden Spa (1966) *Baden-Baden: a Health Resort*, Ass of Spa Physicians, Baden-Baden (b)

Bate, S. C. C. (1974) *Report on the Failure of Roof Beams at Sir John*

```
KEY

A  article        M  manual
b  booklet        P  pamphlet
B  book           R  report
D  directory
```

Cass's Foundation and Red Coat C of E Secondary School Pool, Stepney, BRE Publications, Garston (R)

Baths Service (9/71) Golden Jubilee Year: Institute of Baths Management, *Baths Service*, Melton Mowbray (A)

Besford, Pat (1976) *Encyclopedia of Swimming*, Hale, London (B)

Briswim, op cit under Water treatment

Browne, Dr J. (1707) *An Account of the Wonderful Cures Perform'd by the Cold Baths, with advice to the water drinkers at Tunbridge Wells, etc.*, London (B)

BSAC, op cit under Design and planning

Buckley, J, (1888) *The Water Cure* (1973 reprint), Arkwright Society, Matlock (b)

Carey, Geo. Saville (1799) *The Balnea*, London (B)

Caskey, A. R. (1969) *Swimming Pool Operation*, ARC Ass, Illinois (M)

Consumer Product Safety Commission (US) (1973/4) *Staff Analysis of Swimming and Wading Pool Injuries*, Bureau of Epidemiology, Washington (R)

Council of Europe (1970) *Sport for All: Low-Cost Swimming Pools*, Council for Cultural Co-operation, Strasbourg (b)

CNCA (1965) *Water Fun for Everyone*, Association Press, New York (B)

—— (ann) **Aquatics: Conference Reports**, CNCA, New York (R)

Dawson, Rose Mary (1969) *Age-Group Swimming*, Pelham Books, London (B)

DGFdB (1959) *Deutsche Gesellschaft für das Badewesen*, A, Schrickel, Düsseldorf (M)

EH Depts (1976) *Advice on Safety, Health and Hygiene Standards in Swimming Pools*, Environmental Health Depts of Devon, Torbay (b)

ESSA (1975) *Teaching Swimming Bath Scheme*, ESSA, Plymouth (P)

FINA (1973/6) **FINA Rules and Laws: Olympics Handbook**, FINA Handbooks, Naperville, USA (M)

Geekie, Peter (1972) *Practical Guide to Swimming Pool Maintenance*, Peter Geekie Pools Ltd, Oxford (b)

Gemeindlichen, *Insurance Regulations: Preventing Swimming Accidents. (1954) Swimming Baths; (1962) Chlorination Plant; (1977) Ozone Plant*, Baguv, Munich (B)

Godfrey, J. A., Millbank, N. O. and Woodhouse, D. K. (1970) *Local Authority Covered Swimming Pools: Case Studies and Some Design Aspects*, BRE Publications, Garston (R)

Hess, Werner (1966) *Baden-Baden: Health Resort*, Blume, Velzen (b)

Hoyle, Julie (1977) *Swimming for the Family*, Lutterworth, Guildford (b)

IAB (1965 to 1976) *Protokoll Internationaler Kongress Bäder-, Sport- und Freizeitbauten*, IAB, Bremen (R)

—— (1972) *Aquatic, Sports and Recreation Facilities* (Munich Olympic Congress), IAB, Bremen (R)

IBM *Institute of Baths Management Conference Reports*, op cit under Design and planning

——*Swimming Pools Design Guide No 1*, op cit under Design and planning

—— (1977) *Students Manual for the Institute of Baths Management Examination*, IBM, Melton Mowbray (M)

Jowitt, R. L. P. and Dorothy (1971) *Discovering Spas*, Shire Publications, Tring, UK (b)

Kroelet, op cit under Water treatment

LGTB, op cit under Water treatment

Lightfoot, R. (ed) (1970) *Pool Service Technicians Handbook*, NSPI, Washington (M)

MacPherson, John (1888) *The Baths and Wells of Europe*, Stanford, London (B)

Mayo, op cit under Design and planning

Meslin, J. (1957) *Swimming Pool Operators Text*, Florida Swimming Pool, Miami (M)

Michigan Dept of Public Health (1974) *Swimming Pool Reference Handbook*, Michigan Dept of PH, Lansing, USA (M)

Ministry of Works and Development, op cit under water treatment

NABS (IBM) (1961) *Modern Baths and Laundries*, National Ass of Baths Superintendents, London (B)

NAPO, op cit under General

NSPI, op cit under Water treatment

NZ Ass of SP Managers *Annual Conference Reports*, op cit under water treatment

——*Training Manual*, op cit under Water treatment

Pederson, H. W. (1969) *Pool Owners Handbook*, Pederson, Miami (M)

Perkins, R. N. (1950) *Swimming Pool Operators Manual*, Perkins Laboratories, Omaha (M)

Sanderson, Ian (1974) *Building Swimming Pools for Profit*, Clark Pools, Melbourne (b)

Sarsfield, N. W. (1966) *Diving Instruction (ASA)*, Educational Productions, Wakefield, UK (B)

SEJS (1/77) *Équipments Sportifs et Socio-Éducatifs*, Le Moniteur, Paris (B)

SPATA (1970) *Winterising Guide for Swimming Pools*, SPATA, Croydon (P)

Sports Council (1974) *Leisure Pools, Adjustable Pool Floors, Gradients and Dividing Booms, Small Swimming Pools: Bulletin 1*, East Midlands Sports Council, Nottingham (b)

Stern, James F. and Hendry, Earl R. (1977) *Swimming Pools and the Law*, S & H Books, Milwaukee (B)

Thomas, D. G. (1972) *Swimming Pool Operators Training Manual*, NSPI, Washington (M)

Thomson, W. R. A. (1978) *Spas that Heal*, A. & C. Black, London (B)

Trussell, Elisabeth (1971) *Guide Lines for Teaching the Disabled to Swim*, STA, West Bromwich (b)

Turner, E. S. (1967) *Taking the Cure*, Michael Joseph, London (B)

US HEW (1976) **Swimming Pools – safety and disease control through proper design and operation**, US Dept of Health, Education and Welfare, EHS Div, Atlanta (M)

Wallis, op cit under Water treatment

Walter, op cit under Design and planning

Yates, Fern (ed) (1968) *Swimming and Diving: a Bibliography*, CNCA, New York (B)

Yeats, G. D. (1823) Some Hints on a Mode of Procuring Soft Water at Tunbridge Wells, *Journal of Science* Vol XIV, London (A)

YMCA (1958) *Your Swimming Pool*, YMCA of Canada National Council, Canada (b)

Yost, Charles Peter (1971) *Sports Safety – US Public Health Service*, AAHPER Publications, Washington (B)

APPENDIX VI

Sources of statistics and surveys concerning swimming pools

(see appendixes II and III for addresses)

ABBP	Charleroi	MJS	Paris
ASA	Loughborough	MOW	Bulls
BBT	Vienna	NAPO	Needham
CASPA	Campsie	NBBZ	Soest
CCPR	London	NSPI	Washington
CEC	Brussels	NZ SPM	Bulls
CNCA	Washington	SC	London
CSIP	Paris	SPATA	Croydon
CSPF	Downsview	SPISA	Johannesburg
DGfdB	Essen	SPW	Fort Lauderdale
D of E & S	London	US CPSC	Washington
EC	London	US PHS	Washington
IAB	Bremen	VDB	Hamburg
IAKS	Cologne	VNG	The Hague
IBM	Melton Mowbray		

APPENDIX VII

Conversions and equivalents

Number

10^{-6}	is	micron	μ	millionth
10^{-3}	is	milli	m	thousandth
10^{3}	is	kilo	k	thousand
10^{6}	is	Mega	M	million
10^{9}	is	Giga	G	billion – US
10^{12}	is	Tera	T	billion – European

Length

1 mm	=	0.0394 in	1 in	=	25.40 mm
1m	=	3.28 ft	1 ft	=	0.3048 m
	=	39.37 in		=	30.48 cm
1 km	=	0.62 mile	1 mile	=	1.61 m

Area

1mm²	=	0.00155 in²	1 in²	=	645.2 mm²
1 m²	=	10.76 ft²	1 ft²	=	0.093 m²
1 ha	=	2.47 acre	1 acre	=	4046.9 m²
	=	10.000 m²		=	0.405 ha

Volume

1 m³	=	35.31 ft³	1 ft³	=	0.0283 m³
	=	1000 litre		=	28.32 litre water
	=	1000 Kg water		=	62.4 lb water
	=	220 Imp gal water		=	6.24 Imp gal
	=	264 US gal water		=	7.48 US gal

Capacity

1 litre	= 0.220 Imp gal	1 Imp gal	= 4.546 litre
	= 0.264 US gal	1 US gal	= 3.785 litre
1 US gal	= 0.83 Imp gal	1 Imp gal	= 1.2 US gal
	= 8.35 lb water		= 10 lb water
1 cc	= 0.035 fl oz	1 fl oz	= 28.35 cc

Mass/weight

1 gm	= 0.035 oz	1 oz	= 28.35 g
1 kg	= 2.205 lb	1 lb	= 0.454 kg
1 tonne	= 0.984 ton	1 ton	= 1.016 tonne
	= 2204.6 lb		= 2240 lb
1 kg water	= 0.220 Imp gal	1 lb water	= 0.10 Imp gal
	= 0.264 US gal		= 0.12 US gal

Mass per unit measure

1 kg/m	= 0.672 lb/ft	1 lb/ft	= 1.488 kg/m
1 kg/m²	= 0.205 lb/ft²	1 lb/ft²	= 4.882 kg/m²
1 kg/m³	= 0.0624 lb/ft³	1 lb/ft³	= 16.019 kg/m³

Velocity acceleration

1 m/s	= 3.28 ft/s	1 ft/s	= 0.3048 m/s
1 km/h	= 0.62 mph	1 mph	= 1.61 km/h
	= 0.91 ft/s		= 0.447 m/s
g	= 9.81 m/s²	= 32.2 ft/s²
sound/air	= 335 m/s	= 1100 ft/s
1 Hz	= 1 c/s	= 1 cycle/sound

Flow

1 litre/s	= 2.12 ft³/min	1 ft³/min	= 0.472 litre/s
1 m³/min	= 35.314 ft³/min		= 0.028 m³/min
1 m³/h	= 35.314 ft³/sec	1 cusec	= 375 Imp g/min
	= 0.589 ft³/min	1 ft³/min	= 1.699 m³/h
	= 220 Imp gal/h	1 Imp gal/h	= 4.546 litre/h
	= 264 US gal/h	1 US gal/h	= 3.785 litre/h
1 m³/m²/min	= 20.45 I gal/ft²/min	= 24.54 US gal/ft²/min
	= 1226.77 I gal/ft²/h	= 1472.12 US gal/ft²/h
1 m³/m²/h	= 0.34 I gal/ft²/min	= 0.41 US gal/ft²/min
	= 20.45 I gal/ft²/h	= 24.54 US gal/ft²/h

Force

1 N	= 0.225 lbf	1 lbf	= 4.448 N
	= 1 kg m/s²		
1 kN	= 0.1004 tonf	1 tonf	= 9.964 kN

Pressure/stress

1 N/mm²	= 0.0647 tonf/in²		
	= 145.04 lbf/in²	1 tonf/in²	= 15.44 N/mm²
1 kN/m²	= 0.145 lbf/in²		= 15.44 MN/m²
1 bar or atmosphere	= 14.5 lbf/in² = 199 kN/m²	1 lbf/in²	= 0.0689 bar = 68.948 mb
1 atmosphere	= 760 mm of mercury		= 29.9 in/Hg = 33.5 ft of water
1 m head	= 1.42 lb/in²	1 lb/in²	= 2.3 ft head

Power

1 W	= 1 J/s	1 hp	= 745.7 W
1 hp metric	= 735 W		= 0.746 kW
1 kW	= 3412 Btu	1 Btu	= 0.293 W
	= 1.341 hp	1 hp	= 2545 Btu
1 kW/m²	= 317 Btu/ft²	1 Btu/ft²	= 3.15 W/m²
1 kW/m³	= 15.5 Btu/Imp gal	Btu/Imp gal	= 64.5 W/m³

Temperature

1 °C	= 1.8 °F	1 °F	= 0.55 °C
1 °K	= 1 °C on absolute scale from −273 °C		
°C	= 5/9 (°F−32)	°F	= (°C × 9/5) + 32

Heat

1 cal	= 4.187 J	1 Btu	= 252 cal
1 k cal	= 1.164 W		= 1.055 kJ or kW-secs
	= 3.968 Btu		= 0.252 kcal
1 W	= 3.412 Btu		= 0.293 W
1 kWh	= 3412 Btu/h	1 Therm/h	= 100 000 Btu/h
	= 859.6 kcal/h		= 29.3 kW/h
	= 3.6 MJ		= 25.2 Mcal/h
1 GJ	= 10⁹ joules	= 1 ton Refrigeration	= 12000 Btu/h
	= 275 kW	= 9·5 Therms	= 75 ton Refrigeration

Heat per unit area

1 kW/m²	= 317 Btu/ft²	1 Btu/ft²	= 3.155 W/m²
	= 0.27 cal/cm²		= 0.27 cal/cm² or Langley
	= 3.6 kJ/m²		= 2.7 kcal/m²

Thermal coefficient – value

1 W/m²/°C	= 0.176 Btu/ft²/°F	1 Btu/ft²/°F = 5.678 W/m²/°C

Illumination

1 lux	= 0.093 ft candle	1 lumen/ft²	= 10.76 lux
	or lumen/ft²	= lumen/m²	

Clarity or turbidity

1 JTU	= 1 ppm	= 1mg SiO₂/litre distilled water
1 ppm	= 1 mg/litre	

1 μm	= 1 millionth m	micron
1 nanometer	= 1 millionth mm	micro-mm
1 nm	= 10^{-9}m	
1 Ångstrom	= 10^{-10}m	
1 $\mu\mu$	= 10^{-12}m	micro-micron
25 μm	= 0.025 mm	= 1 thousandth of an inch

Index